NORMATIVITY AND NORMS

Normativity and Norms

Critical Perspectives on
Kelsenian Themes

Edited by
STANLEY L. PAULSON
BONNIE LITSCHEWSKI PAULSON

Translations by
BONNIE LITSCHEWSKI PAULSON
STANLEY L. PAULSON
MICHAEL SHERBERG

With an Introduction by
STANLEY L. PAULSON

CLARENDON PRESS · OXFORD
1998

Oxford University Press, Great Clarendon Street, Oxford OX2 6DP
Oxford New York
Athens Auckland Bangkok Bogotá Buenos Aires Calcutta
Cape Town Chennai Dar es Salaam Delhi Florence Hong Kong Istanbul
Karachi Kuala Lumpur Madrid Melbourne Mexico City Mumbai
Nairobi Paris São Paulo Singapore Taipei Tokyo Toronto Warsaw
and associated companies in
Berlin Ibadan

Oxford is a registered trade mark of Oxford University Press

Published in the United States
by Oxford University Press Inc., New York

The preparation of this volume was made possible in part
by a grant from the National Endowment for the Humanities,
Washington, D.C., an independent federal agency.

British Library Cataloguing in Publication Data
Data available

Library of Congress Cataloging in Publication Data
Normativity and norms: critical perspectives on Kelsenian themes /
edited by Stanley L. Paulson, Bonnie Litschewski Paulson;
translations by Bonnie Litschewski Paulson, Stanley L. Paulson,
Michael Sherberg; with an introduction by Stanley L. Paulson.
p. cm.
Includes bibliographical references.
1. Law—Philosophy. 2. Kelsen, Hans, 1881–1973. I. Paulson,
Stanley L. II. Paulson, Bonnie Litschewski.
K339.N67 1998 340'.1—dc21 98–49338
ISBN 0–19–876315–8

Typeset by Hope Services (Abingdon) Ltd.
Printed in Great Britain
on acid-free paper by
Biddles Ltd., Guildford and King's Lynn

IN MEMORY OF

Carlos E. Alchourrón (28 June 1931 – 13 January 1996) and
Carlos Santiago Nino (3 November 1943 – 29 August 1993)

Editors' Preface

Hans Kelsen (1881–1973) published his first major treatise, *Main Problems in the Theory of Public Law*, in 1911. His last major work, the *General Theory of Norms*, appeared six years after his death. While the earlier work sets the stage for what emerged in the 1920s as the Pure Theory of Law, the later work marks Kelsen's own rejection of large parts of that theory. Along with sustained work on the Pure Theory of Law through the early 1930s, Kelsen wrote on a variety of other topics in legal theory during his long, intellectually active life. His contributions in constitutional law, public international law, and political theory were substantial, in some areas fundamental. And there were forays into anthropological speculation, important studies of classical philosophers, most notably Plato, and a good deal more along the way.

Kelsen's influence in legal philosophy and legal theory is unrivalled in this century. It is seen not only in the extraordinary juridico-philosophical controversies surrounding the Pure Theory of Law, but also in the Kelsenian concepts and doctrines—ranging from legal power to centralized constitutional review—that have profoundly affected the way jurists look at the law.

Three papers in the present volume stem from Kelsen himself. Two are statements in which he takes stock—one looking back, from 1923, to the beginnings of the Pure Theory of Law, and a second, ten years later, assessing the role of neo-Kantianism, and of Hermann Cohen's philosophy in particular, in the Pure Theory; the third of Kelsen's own papers is his last major statement in defence of monism in public international law. The other papers in the volume reflect, fairly clearly we think, Kelsen's remarkable influence. It is equally clear that none of these authors slavishly follows Kelsen. Rather, through their rigorous judgments on Kelsen's work and their own development of concepts and doctrines that stem in part from that work, they pay Kelsen the high compliment of a serious and critical reception.

In selecting material for the volume, always with an eye to the various rubrics we had established, we have chosen papers by established writers in the field as well as by promising younger writers. Several papers were written especially for the volume, and in this connection we should like to acknowledge José Juan Moreso (Barcelona) and Pablo E. Navarro (Buenos Aires), Geert Edel (Bonn), Neil MacCormick (Edinburgh), Dick W.P. Ruiter (Enschede, Holland), and Deryck Beyleveld and Roger Brownsword (Sheffield). Other pieces are reworked versions of earlier papers, and here we wish to mention Ernesto Garzón Valdés (Bonn), Riccardo Guastini (Genoa), Agostino Carrino (Naples and Rome), Bruno Celano (Palermo), and Stefan Hammer (Vienna).

A 'publication history' is included in the asterisk footnote on the first page of each paper; credits for reprinting are found in a consolidated list of acknowledgements following this preface. Following the table of contents, there is a table of abbreviations providing full bibliographical data on selected books and papers of Kelsen's, as well as English approximations of their titles; other frequently cited titles and journals are also found here. Finally, it is worth mentioning that when a footnote invites the reader to 'see' a particular place in a given work, that particular information is preceded by 'at'; thus, 'at § 13 (pp. 67–9)' refers to all of § 13, which spans pp. 67–9, while '§ 13 (at pp. 67–8)' refers to particular pages within § 13.

Michael Sherberg has been our indefatigable partner in the translation effort, and we are grateful for the signal collaboration of the authors in helping us get the translations right.

Along with many of the contributors to the volume, other friends and colleagues have advised and supported us, and we wish to thank them here: Günter Schilling (Aalen), Alida Wilson (Aberdeen), Albert Calsamiglia and María Cristina Redondo (Barcelona), Carla Faralli, Enrico Pattaro, and Gianfrancesco Zanetti (Bologna), Lukas H. Meyer (Bremen), Roberto J. Vernengo (Buenos Aires), Henrik Palmer Olsen (Copenhagen), Ruth Zimmerling (Darmstadt), Martin Schulte (Dresden), Letizia Gianformaggio (Ferrara), Massimo La Torre (Florence), Pierluigi Chiassoni and Paolo Comanducci (Genoa), Okko Behrends, Malte Dießelhorst, and Ralf Dreier (Göttingen), Peter Koller (Graz), Joachim Schwietzke (Heidelberg), Izhak Englard (Jerusalem), Robert Alexy and Alexander Molter (Kiel), Bernard S. Jackson (Liverpool), William Twining (London), Uta Bindreiter and Aleksander Peczenik (Lund), Ulises Schmill and Rodolfo Vásquez (Mexico City), Werner Krawietz (Münster), J.W. Harris and Richard Tur (Oxford), Mirella Urso (Palermo), Michel Troper (Paris), Tecla Mazzarese (Pavia), Giuliana Stella (Rome), Eric C. Mueller (St. Louis), Tercio Sampaio Ferraz Jr. and Ari Marcelo Solon (São Paulo), Iain Stewart and Alex Ziegert (Sydney), Theo Öhlinger, Wolfgang Pircher, Alexander Somek, Ewald Wiederin, and Günther Winkler (Vienna). We remain grateful to Peggy McDermott, formerly of the Washington University Law Library, who gave us untold hours of help on bibliographical details. And we should like also to extend our special thanks to Marcia Denenholz and Andrea D. Powell for their exacting work at the computer, as well as to our cheerfully stalwart collaborators at the Oxford University Press, in particular Michaela Coulthard and Myfanwy Milton.

Speaking in his capacity as editor and translator, Stanley L. Paulson wishes to acknowledge three institutional debts: first, to the Research Division of the National Endowment for the Humanities (Washington, D.C.) for a generous grant that made the project possible; second, to the Alexander von Humboldt Foundation (Bonn) for research support at a number of different points over the years; third, to the School of Law, Washington University in St. Louis, for research support, and to the School's Dean, Dorsey D. Ellis, Jr., for his unstinting interest and encouragement.

The volume is dedicated to the memory of Carlos E. Alchourrón and Carlos Santiago Nino.[1] Both were widely admired as gifted philosophers and as generous, compassionate human beings. They enriched our lives.

Stanley L. Paulson and Bonnie Litschewski Paulson
31 December 1997
St. Louis, Missouri

---

[1] On Alchourrón, see David Makinson, 'Carlos Eduardo Alchourrón—A Memorial Note', *Rechtstheorie*, 27 (1996), 125–31; on Nino, see Owen Fiss, 'The Death of a Public Intellectual', *Yale Law Journal*, 104 (1994–5), 1186–200.

Acknowledgements

Ch. 1. Printed in translation with the kind permission of the J.C.B. Mohr Verlag, Tübingen, and the Hans Kelsen Institute, Vienna.

Ch. 2. Reprinted with the kind permission of Blackwell Publishers, Oxford.

Ch. 3. Reprinted with the kind permission of the author and the Oxford University Press.

Ch. 4. Reprinted with the kind permission of Mrs. Jenifer Hart, Oxford, and the Oxford University Press.

Ch. 5. Reprinted with the kind permission of the author and the Oxford University Press.

Ch. 6. Original contribution.

Ch. 7. Reprinted with the kind permission of Héctor Sandler, Buenos Aires, and Strange Ross, Allerød, Denmark.

Ch. 8. Printed in translation with the kind permission of Jacques Commaille, Paris.

Ch. 9. Printed in translation with the kind permission of the author, and the Manz Verlag, Vienna.

Ch. 10. Original contribution, in translation.

Ch. 11. Printed in translation with the kind permission of the author, and Duncker & Humblot, Berlin.

Ch. 12. Reprinted with the kind permission of the author and the Oxford University Press.

Ch. 13. Reprinted with the kind permission of Mrs. Susana Nino, Buenos Aires.

Ch. 14. Printed in translation with the kind permission of Ernesto Garzón Valdés, Bonn.

Ch. 15. Original contribution.

Ch. 16. Reprinted with the kind permission of the author, and Blackwell Publishers, Oxford.

Ch. 17. Printed, in a new version, with the kind permission of the author, G. Giappichelli Editore, Turin, and Blackwell Publishers, Oxford.

Ch. 18. Printed in translation with the kind permission of Amedeo G. Conte, Pavia.

Ch. 19. Printed in translation with the kind permission of the author, and G. Giappichelli Editore, Turin.

Ch. 20. Reprinted with the kind permission of the author, and Kluwer Academic Publishers, Dordrecht: © 1985.

Ch. 21. Reprinted with the kind permission of Mrs. Martha Alchourrón and Eugenio Bulygin, Buenos Aires, and Kluwer Academic Publishers, Dordrecht: © 1980.

Ch. 22. Reprinted with the kind permission of the author, and Kluwer Academic Publishers, Dordrecht: © 1985.

Ch. 23. Printed in translation with the kind permission of the author, and the Edizioni Scientifiche Italiane, Naples.

Ch. 24. Reprinted with the kind permission of the author, and by courtesy of the Editor of the Aristotelian Society, London: © 1972.

Ch. 25. Original contribution.

Ch. 26. Original contribution.

Ch. 27. Printed in translation with the kind permission of the author, and the Edizioni Scientifiche Italiane, Naples.

Ch. 28. Printed in translation with the kind permission of the de Gruyter Verlag, Berlin.

Ch. 29. Reprinted with the kind permission of the author and the Oxford University Press.

Ch. 30. Reprinted with the kind permission of Mrs. Jenifer Hart, Oxford, and the Oxford University Press.

Contents

Abbreviations

The abbreviations are divided into three groups. First, an alphabetical list of abbreviations of Kelsen's works, including collections, that are frequently cited; these abbreviations appear in the footnotes without Kelsen's name. Second, an alphabetical list of works by other authors; here the abbreviations appearing in the footnotes include the author's name. Third, an alphabetical list of abbreviated titles of frequently cited journals.

Where possible, Kelsen's works are cited not only by page number, but also by section number; the latter facilitates reference to other editions of the same work (say, the German original, or a translation into Italian or Spanish).

I. KELSEN'S WORKS

AI	Kelsen, *Aufsätze zur Ideologiekritik*, ed. Ernst Topitsch (Neuwied am Rhein and Berlin: Luchterhand, 1964), repr. under the title *Staat und Naturrecht. Aufsätze zur Ideologiekritik* (Munich: Wilhelm Fink, 1989). English equivalent of title: 'Essays on the Criticism of Ideology'.
ASL	Kelsen, *Allgemeine Staatslehre* (Berlin: Julius Springer, 1925, repr. Bad Homburg v.d. Höhe: Max Gehlen, 1966). English equivalent of title: 'General Constitutional Theory'.[1] Cited by section and page number.
'Derogation'	Kelsen's paper 'Derogation' first appeared in 1962, and is cited from the reprinting in *Essays* (see below), 261–75. The paper was first published in *Essays in Jurisprudence in Honor of Roscoe Pound*, ed. Ralph A. Newman (Indianapolis and New York: Bobbs-Merrill, 1962), 339–55; in addition to the reprinting in *Essays*, it was reprinted in *WS II* (see below), 1429–43.
Essays	Kelsen, *Essays in Legal and Moral Philosophy*, ed. Ota Weinberger, trans. Peter Heath (Dordrecht and

---

[1] In this case, the English equivalent is not a literal translation but rather one that reflects something of the import of these expressions in Kelsen's treatise.

Boston: Reidel, 1973). (Save for 'Derogation' and 'Norm and Value', which Kelsen published in English, all of the essays in the volume were translated by Peter Heath.)

'Foreword' to *HP* (See, for details, at '*HP*' below.) Translated in this volume, chapter 1.

GTLS Kelsen, *General Theory of Law and State*, trans. Anders Wedberg (from an unpublished manuscript) (Cambridge, Mass.: Harvard UP, 1945, repr. New York: Russell & Russell, 1961).

GTN Kelsen, *General Theory of Norms*, trans. Michael Hartney (Oxford: Clarendon Press, 1991). The treatise was first published as *Allgemeine Theorie der Normen*, ed. Kurt Ringhofer and Robert Walter (Vienna: Manz, 1979). Cited by chapter and section, and by page number.

HP Kelsen, *Hauptprobleme der Staatsrechtslehre* (Tübingen: J.C.B. Mohr, 1911), reprinted in 1923 with a new 'Foreword', which is translated in this volume, chapter 1. The 1923 edition was then reprinted in 1960 (Aalen: Scientia). English equivalent of title: 'Main Problems in the Theory of Public Law'. In footnote references, *HP* itself and the 'Foreword' to its 2nd printing are treated as separate works (see above at 'Foreword').

'Letter to Treves' Kelsen's 1933 letter to Renato Treves, translated into French by Michel Troper, was first published in *Droit et Société*, 7 (1987), 333–5; the German original, along with an Italian translation by Agostino Carrino, appeared in Hans Kelsen and Renato Treves, *Formalismo giuridico e realtà sociale*, ed. Stanley L. Paulson (Naples: Edizioni Scientifiche Italiane, 1992), 55–8. Translated in this volume, chapter 8.

'LL' Kelsen's 'Law and Logic' first appeared in 1965, and is cited from Peter Heath's translation in *Essays* (see above), 228–53. The paper was first published as 'Recht und Logik', *Forum* (Vienna), 12 (1965), 421–5, 495–500, 579, repr. *WS II* (see below), 1469–97.

LT Kelsen, *Introduction to the Problems of Legal Theory*, trans. Bonnie Litschewski Paulson and Stanley L. Paulson (Oxford: Clarendon Press, 1992). The book was first published as *Reine Rechtslehre*, 1st edn. (Leipzig and Vienna: Franz Deuticke, 1934, repr. Aalen: Scientia, 1986). Cited by section and page number.

Phil. Fds.   Kelsen, *Philosophical Foundations of Natural Law Theory and Legal Positivism*, trans. Wolfgang H. Kraus as an appendix to Kelsen, *GTLS*, 389–446. This monograph, *Die Philosophischen Grundlagen der Naturrechtslehre und des Rechtspositivismus* (Charlottenburg: Pan-Verlag Rolf Heise, 1928), was originally published under the auspices of the Kant-Gesellschaft or Kant Society (as lecture no. 31 in its series), repr. *WS I* (see below), 281–350. Cited by section and page number.

PS   Kelsen, *Das Problem der Souveränität und die Theorie des Völkerrechts* (Tübingen: J.C.B. Mohr, 1920, repr. Aalen: Scientia, 1960). English equivalent of title: 'The Problem of Sovereignty and the Theory of International Law'. Cited by section and page number.

PTL   Kelsen, *Pure Theory of Law*, trans. Max Knight (Berkeley and Los Angeles: University of California Press, 1967). The book was first published as *Reine Rechtslehre*, 2nd edn. (see '*RR 2*' below). Cited by section and page number.

RNK   Fritz Sander and Hans Kelsen, *Die Rolle des Neukantianismus in der Reinen Rechtslehre*, ed. Stanley L. Paulson (Aalen: Scientia, 1988). A collection of papers by Sander and Kelsen on the role of neo-Kantianism in legal theory generally and in the Pure Theory of Law.

RR 2   Kelsen, *Reine Rechtslehre*, 2nd edn. (Vienna: Franz Deuticke, 1960). Kelsen's original, German-language text includes two lengthy appendices, 'Die Normen der Gerechtigkeit' and 'Die Naturrechtslehre', which—along with certain passages and footnotes— were regrettably omitted in *PTL* (see above). Thus, where cited material does not appear in *PTL*, reference is made to *RR 2*. Cited by section and page number.

'RWNKW'   Kelsen's enquiry into the theories of Heinrich Rickert and Emil Lask, 'Die Rechtswissenschaft als Norm-

oder als Kulturwissenschaft. Eine methodenkritische Untersuchung', first appeared in *Schmollers Jahrbuch für Gesetzgebung, Verwaltung und Volkswirtschaft im Deutschen Reich*, 40 (1916), 1181–239, repr. *WS I* (see below), 37–93. English equivalent of title: 'Legal Science as a Science of Norms or of Culture. A Methodologico-critical Enquiry'.

'RWR'   Kelsen's lengthy paper 'Rechtswissenschaft und Recht. Erledigung eines Versuchs zur Überwindung der "Rechtsdogmatik"' first appeared in *ZöR* (see below), vol. 3 (1922), 103–235, repr. *RNK* (see above), 279–411. English equivalent of title: 'Legal Science and the Law. Foiling an Attempt to Surmount "Legal Dogmatics"'.

SJSB   Kelsen, *Der soziologische und der juristische Staatsbegriff* (Tübingen: J.C.B. Mohr, 1922, repr. Aalen: Scientia, 1962). English equivalent of title: 'The Sociological and the Legal Concept of the State'. Cited by section and page number.

WJ   Kelsen, *What is Justice?* (Berkeley and Los Angeles: University of California Press, 1957). A collection of papers (all but two of which had appeared previously).

WS I, WS II   *Die Wiener rechtstheoretische Schule. Schriften von Hans Kelsen, Adolf Merkl, Alfred Verdross*, ed. Hans Klecatsky et al., 2 vols. (Vienna: Europa Verlag, 1968). A major collection of representative papers. English equivalent of title: 'The Vienna School of Legal Theory. Writings of . . .'.

II. OTHER AUTHORS' WORKS

33 Beiträge   *33 Beiträge zur Reinen Rechtslehre*, ed. Rudolf Aladár Métall (Vienna: Europa Verlag, 1974). A collection of papers by writers who were, in many instances, closely associated with the Vienna School of Legal Theory. English equivalent of title: '33 Contributions on the Pure Theory of Law'.

Cohen, *ErW*   Hermann Cohen, *Ethik des reinen Willens*, 2nd edn. (Berlin: Bruno Cassirer, 1907), repr. as vol. 7 in Cohen, *Werke*, ed. Helmut Holzhey (Hildesheim: Georg Olms, 1981). English equivalent of title: 'Ethics of Pure Will'.

Cohen, *LrE*   Hermann Cohen, *Logik der reinen Erkenntnis*, 2nd edn. (Berlin: Bruno Cassirer, 1914), repr. as vol. 6 in Cohen, *Werke*, ed. Helmut Holzhey (Hildesheim: Georg Olms, 1977). English equivalent of title: 'Logic of Pure Cognition'.

Hart, *CL*, [and   H.L.A. Hart, *The Concept of Law* (Oxford: Clarendon
CL] 2nd edn.   Press, 1961), and 2nd edn., with a Postscript edited by Penelope Bulloch and Joseph Raz (Oxford: Clarendon Press, 1994). Because the pagination of the two editions differs, both are cited.

Kant, *CPR*   Immanuel Kant, *Critique of Pure Reason*, trans. Norman Kemp Smith (London: Macmillan, 1929), trans. Werner S. Pluhar (Indianapolis: Hackett, 1996), and trans. Paul Guyer and Allen W. Wood (Cambridge: Cambridge UP, 1998). Cited with the standard pagination for the A and B editions.

Kant, *Pro.*   Immanuel Kant, *Prolegomena to any Future Metaphysics*, trans. Peter G. Lucas (Manchester: Manchester UP, 1953), and trans. Gary Hatfield (Cambridge: Cambridge UP, 1997). Cited by section and page number.

Raz, *AL*   Joseph Raz, *The Authority of Law* (Oxford: Clarendon Press, 1979).

Raz, *CLS*   Joseph Raz, *The Concept of a Legal System*, 2nd edn. (Oxford: Clarendon Press, 1980).

Ross, *LJ*   Alf Ross, *On Law and Justice*, trans. Margaret Dutton (London: Stevens & Sons, 1958).

von Wright, *NA*   Georg Henrik von Wright, *Norm and Action* (London: Routledge & Kegan Paul, 1963).

WS I, WS II   These volumes, listed above under Kelsen's works, also contain papers by Adolf Julius Merkl and Alfred Verdross, the other leading figures in the Vienna School of Legal Theory.

III. JOURNALS

AöR   *Archiv des öffentlichen Rechts.* Beginning in 1921 (vol. 40), a new numbering of volumes, a new series (N.F.), ran alongside the continuing, original numbering; after 1963, the new series was discontinued. Since writers may cite *AöR* volume numbers from either the original or the new series, citations in the footnotes include both; thus, the first volume of the new series is cited as '*AöR*, 40, N.F. 1 (1921)'.

ARSP   *Archiv für Rechts- und Sozialphilosophie.*

ARWP   *Archiv für Rechts- und Wirtschaftsphilosophie.*

ÖZöR   *Österreichische Zeitschrift für öffentliches Recht,* first series, 1914–18, 3 vols., predecessor of the *ZöR* (see below); second series ('neue Reihe'), 1947 to date, successor to the *ZöR* (see below).

RIFD   *Revista internazionale di filosofia del diritto.*

ZöR   *Zeitschrift für öffentliches Recht.* Kelsen founded the journal in 1919, and served first as editor-in-chief and then (until his resignation in 1934) as a member of the editorial board.

Introduction

STANLEY L. PAULSON

Normativity and Norms consists of six parts, and divides in a fairly straightforward way into two halves. The first half, parts I–III, is devoted to Kelsen's greater project in legal theory. Part I includes the 'Foreword' to the Second Printing (1923) of *Main Problems in the Theory of Public Law* (*Hauptprobleme der Staatsrechtslehre*). The 'Foreword', Kelsen's sketch of the development of his legal theory in the early years, adumbrates the normativity problematic, a theme that has both fascinated and exasperated writers in the field for nearly three generations. The normativity problematic is the focus of much that follows in parts II and III of the volume. Specifically, part II contains general statements on Kelsen's normativity project, some of them highly critical, while part III is devoted to arguments and counterarguments, both neo-Kantian and *sans* Kant, that either address the normativity problematic directly or presuppose it in the course of examining other doctrines.

In the second half of the volume, parts IV–VI, the foci are more specific. Part IV is devoted to developments of Kelsen's late, sceptical phase, with special attention to the theory of norms, part V focuses on the concept of legal power or empowerment, and part VI brings together central writings on legal monism, Kelsen's unity of law thesis.

A good number of the contributors to the volume explore doctrines and themes that are tied only indirectly to Kelsen's own work. In these introductory remarks, by contrast, I concentrate on Kelsen's own views and their connection to the leitmotifs represented in the volume. Part I of the volume, entitled 'Kelsen's Shift to the Classical Phase', presupposes the general outlines of a periodization, a sketch of the phases of development in Kelsen's legal theory. I begin there.

PART I. KELSEN'S SHIFT TO THE CLASSICAL PHASE

A Brief Periodization. Three phases of development in Kelsen's theory can be distinguished:[1] an early phase, *critical constructivism* (1911–21),

---

[1] For a range of opinion on 'periodization questions', see e.g. Eugenio Bulygin, 'An Antinomy in Kelsen's Pure Theory of Law', in this volume, ch. 16; Vladimír Kubeš, 'Das

then the long, *classical phase* (1921–60), and, finally, the late, *sceptical phase* (1960–73). The early phase is seen most clearly in Kelsen's *Habilitationsschrift*,[2] the treatise entitled *Main Problems in the Theory of Public Law*, which first appeared in 1911.[3] In 'critical constructivism', my name for the early phase, 'constructivism' stems from 'construction', which in traditional German legal science means concept formation. One of Kelsen's central aims in the early phase—but not just there—is to establish legal science as a 'normative' discipline, by which he understands a discipline that is addressed to normative material and whose statements are formulated in normative language.[4] And this aim makes sense of his effort to 'construct' the fundamental concepts of the law, for, as he argues, to understand these correctly is to understand them as peculiarly normative concepts, and not as concepts that lend themselves to restatement in factual terms. The adjective 'critical' in 'critical constructivism' marks a Kantian influence that is already evident at some points in Kelsen's early work—in his effort, above all, to 'purify' key

neueste Werk Hans Kelsens über die allgemeine Theorie der Normen und die Zukunft der Reinen Rechtslehre', *ÖZöR*, 31 (1980), 155–99, at 158–65; Mario G. Losano, 'Saggio introduttivo', in Kelsen, *La dottrina pura del diritto*, trans. Losano (Turin: Giulio Einaudi, 1966), pp. xiii–lvii, repr. (1990), xxi–lxv; Stanley L. Paulson, 'Toward a Periodization of the Pure Theory of Law', in *Hans Kelsen's Legal Theory. A Diachronic Point of View*, ed. Letizia Gianformaggio (Turin: G. Giappichelli Editore, 1990), 11–47; Günther Winkler, *Rechtstheorie und Erkenntnislehre* (Vienna: Springer, 1990), at 59–65 *et passim*. The most recent effort in this genre is Carsten Heidemann, *Die Norm als Tatsache. Zur Normentheorie Hans Kelsens* (Baden-Baden: Nomos, 1997); on this ambitious and in many ways impressive periodization, see Stanley L. Paulson, 'Four Phases in Hans Kelsen's Legal Theory? Reflections on a Periodization', *Oxford Journal of Legal Studies*, 18 (1998), 153–66.

   [2] The *Habilitationsschrift* is the post-doctoral thesis submitted by the candidate in support of an application for admission to the *venia legendi* (literally, 'permission to lecture', thus, a licence to lecture); the *Habilitation* itself is the procedure by means of which lecturers at central European universities are licensed.

   [3] For bibliographical data on *Main Problems*, see the Table of Abbreviations, at *HP*.

   [4] On legal science qua 'normative' discipline, see e.g. Hans Kelsen, 'The Pure Theory of Law and Analytical Jurisprudence', *Harvard Law Review*, 55 (1941–2), 44–70, at 51–2, repr. *WJ* 266–87, 390 (notes), at 268–9; see also Bulygin, 'An Antinomy' (n.1 above); Riccardo Guastini, 'Normativism or the Normative Theory of Legal Science: Some Epistemological Problems', in this volume, ch. 17; Joseph Raz, 'The Purity of the Pure Theory', in this volume, ch. 12. Rewarding discussions of other aspects of legal science include Eugenio Bulygin, 'Legal Dogmatics and the Systematization of Law', in *Vernunft und Erfahrung im Rechtsdenken der Gegenwart* (*Rechtstheorie* Beiheft 10), ed. Torstein Eckhoff et al. (Berlin: Duncker & Humblot, 1986), 193–210; J.W. Harris, *Law and Legal Science* (Oxford: Clarendon Press, 1979); Neil MacCormick, 'Powers and Power-Conferring Norms', in this volume, ch. 26; Nigel Simmonds, *The Decline of Juridical Reason* (Manchester: Manchester UP, 1984), at 1–36, 82–98; Richard Susskind, *Expert Systems in Law* (Oxford: Clarendon Press, 1987), at 75–80 *et passim*; Vittorio Villa, 'Legal Science between Natural and Human Sciences', *Legal Studies*, 4 (1984), 243–70. On the history of European legal science, see generally Franz Wieacker, *A History of Private Law in Europe*, trans. Tony Weir (Oxford: Clarendon Press, 1995), the *locus classicus* in the field. In an illuminating study, Manfred Baldus shows how German legal science (and legal theory) in the nineteenth and the earlier twentieth century struggled to establish the idea of legal unity; see Baldus, *Die Einheit der Rechtsordnung* (Berlin: Duncker & Humblot, 1995).

constructions of traditional German legal science, especially (but by no means exclusively) in the German *Staatsrechtslehre* or theory of public law.[5]

A period of transition runs from 1913 up to the beginnings of the classical phase in the early 1920s. In an important paper of 1913, Kelsen adduces fundamental arguments on the question of material unity, that is to say, on the question of the 'consistency' of legal norms, maintaining that material unity is a presupposition of legal knowledge or cognition.[6] In a major paper of 1914, Kelsen introduces the basic norm, albeit without the 'transcendental' garb of the classical phase.[7] In *The Problem of Sovereignty*, published in 1920 but largely completed in 1916, Kelsen anticipates themes of the classical phase, offers a reading[8] of the normativity problematic (to which I return in my discussion, below, of part II of the volume), and develops at length his theory of legal monism, that is, the unity of public international law and state law (to which I return in my discussion, below, of part VI of the volume).

The early 1920s mark the beginnings of the Pure Theory of Law,[9] Kelsen's theory in the form in which it is generally known. Following the received opinion, I shall term this long phase (*circa* 1921–60) the 'classical phase'. It is ushered in by two major developments in Kelsen's work, both of which he addresses in the 'Foreword' to the Second Printing (1923) of *Main Problems*. First, going well beyond the work of his early phase, Kelsen now attempts to adduce a neo-Kantian argument not only for some of the constructions he worked up in *Main Problems* and other early writings, but also, and more fundamentally, as a means of resolving the normativity problematic. In this connection, the Kantian doctrines Kelsen introduces in the classical phase are fundamental. Second, no later than 1923,[10] Kelsen adopts lock, stock, and barrel Adolf Julius

---

[5] See Stanley L. Paulson, 'Hans Kelsen's Earliest Legal Theory: Critical Constructivism', in this volume, ch. 2, at § II.

[6] See Hans Kelsen, 'Zur Lehre vom öffentlichen Rechtsgeschäft', *AöR*, 31 (1913), 53–98, 190–249, at 200–2; and see generally Stanley L. Paulson, 'Kelsen's Early Work on Material and Formal Unity', in *Justice, Morality and Society. A Tribute to Aleksander Peczenik*, ed. Aulis Aarnio et al. (Lund: Juristförlaget, 1997), 331–45. On the distinction between material and formal unity, see generally Baldus (n.4 above), at 29, 124–5, 137–54, 160–1, *et passim*; Raz, *AL*, at 79.

[7] See Hans Kelsen, 'Reichsgesetz und Landesgesetz nach österreichischer Verfassung', *AöR*, 32 (1914), 202–45, 390–438, at 215–20; and see generally Stanley L. Paulson, 'On the Early Development of the Grundnorm', in *Law, Life and the Images of the Law. Festschrift for Jan M. Broekman*, ed. Frank Fleerackers et al. (Berlin: Duncker & Humblot, 1997), 217–30.

[8] See text at nn.44–5 below.

[9] The adjective 'pure' modifying 'theory' first appears in Kelsen's 'Foreword' to *PS*, at the title page and at p. v, and also in the text proper at 275; on 'purity', see ibid., at pp. vi–vii, and at 105. The most accessible statement of the Pure Theory of Law in its mature form is found in *LT*.

[10] See n.25 below.

Merkl's[11] doctrine of hierarchical structure (*Stufenbaulehre*). The doctrine offers a dynamic characterization of the law, a view of the law 'in motion, in the constantly regenerating process of its self-creation'.[12] Like the first development, this development, too, had a profound effect on Kelsen's legal theory, marking the beginnings of his interest in questions of lawmaking (as distinct from questions about the validity of law already made). This interest of Kelsen's is reflected, *inter alia*, in his increasing attention to questions about the nature of the legal system generally and the role of empowerment in particular. (I return to the latter in my discussion, below, of part V of the volume.)

Beginning in the later 1930s, Kelsen introduces certain empiricist and analytical doctrines that are either new or at any rate a good bit more evident here than in earlier work, for example, his flirtation with Hume's doctrine of causality,[13] his introduction and defence of the doctrine of the legal proposition (*Rechtssatz*),[14] and his growing interest in and increasingly explicit attention to the role of formal logic in the law.[15] These and other doctrines and interests do not, however, supplant the earlier Kantian doctrines. Rather, the new stands alongside the old. For example, in several of his writings in the history and philosophy of science, Kelsen endorses Hume's doctrine of causality, an endorsement that stands alongside his continuing defence, in his writings in legal theory, of the doctrine of imputation, inspired by the Kantian doctrine of causality. In order to take account of these post-1935 developments, it is useful to think of the classical phase as breaking down into two periods, a neo-Kantian period (1921–35) followed by a hybrid period that reflects both neo-Kantian and analytical elements (1935–60). Still, these periods are parts of a single whole, the classical phase, whose neo-Kantian dimension remains predominant from beginning to end.[16]

[11] Kelsen aside, Adolf Julius Merkl (1890–1970) was far and away the most gifted and original thinker in the Vienna School of Legal Theory. Early work of Merkl's on the *Stufenbaulehre* and other juridico-conceptual questions proved to be very influential in Austria (likewise for his work in administrative law), but attracted relatively little attention beyond its borders. See references at nn.24, 26 below.   [12] *LT* § 43 (p. 91).

[13] See e.g. Hans Kelsen, 'Die Entstehung des Kausalgesetzes aus dem Vergeltungs-prinzip', *Erkenntnis*, 8 (1939), 69–130, at 125–6 *et passim*, trans. by Peter Heath as 'The Emergence of the Causal Law from the Principle of Retribution', in *Essays*, 165–215, at 199–200 *et passim*.

[14] See Kelsen (n.4 above); Hans Kelsen, 'Value Judgments in the Science of Law', *Journal of Social Philosophy and Jurisprudence*, 7 (1942), 313–33, at 312–16 *et passim*, repr. *WJ* 209–30, 389 (notes), at 209–13 *et passim*; *GTLS*, at 45–6, 50, 163–4. Compare, for Kelsen's earlier view, 'Foreword' to *HP*, in this volume, ch. 1, at nn.1, 5; and see generally *LT*, Appendix I, at Supplementary Note 5 (pp. 132–4).

[15] See, in particular, Hans Kelsen, 'Was ist die Reine Rechtslehre?', in *Demokratie und Rechtsstaat. Festgabe zum 60. Geburtstag von Zaccaria Giacometti* [no editor] (Zurich: Polygraphischer Verlag, 1953), 143–62, repr. *WS I* 611–29. See also Georg Henrik von Wright's remarks on this development in 'Is and Ought', in this volume, ch. 20, at §§ 2, 4, 7.

[16] See generally Paulson, 'Four Phases' (n.1 above).

Finally, there is Kelsen's late, 'sceptical phase', marked initially by certain doctrines in the Second Edition of the *Pure Theory of Law* (1960) and by ideas that are given expression in the Kelsen-Klug correspondence.[17] Although there is no consensus on just how far Kelsen departs from the motifs of the classical phase, let alone a consensus on the reasons for the departure, one thing is clear: Kelsen now abandons all of the Kantian doctrines familiar from the classical phase. And it seems equally clear that he is defending, in this late, sceptical phase, a voluntaristic or 'will' theory of law, the very type of theory he criticized so vehemently in both earlier phases. The sceptical phase begins around 1960 and persists to Kelsen's death in 1973. Its most complete expression is found in the posthumously published *General Theory of Norms* (1979). (I return to this last phase in my discussion, below, of part IV of the volume.)

In summary, the periodization of Kelsen's work looks like this:

Critical Constructivism (*circa* 1911–21)
— Transition (*circa* 1913–21)
Classical Phase (*circa* 1921–60)
— Neo-Kantian Period (*circa* 1921–35)
— Hybrid Period, with both neo-Kantian and analytical elements (*circa* 1935–60)
Sceptical Phase (*circa* 1960 to Kelsen's death in 1973)

Kelsen's 'Foreword'. Translated as the opening chapter of the present volume, Kelsen's 'Foreword' to the Second Printing (1923) of *Main Problems in the Theory of Public Law* is a remarkably candid and wide-ranging statement on the development of his views, written when his shift to what has come to be known as the classical phase was a *fait accompli*. In the 'Foreword', Kelsen touches on such themes as the imperative theory of law, the reconstructed legal norm, the dualism of objective law and subjective right and of public and private law, the specifically legal will, central and peripheral imputation,[18] the identity of law and state, the analogy between the problems of theology and those of jurisprudence, the concept of legal person, Georg Jellinek's[19]

---

[17] See Hans Kelsen and Ulrich Klug, *Rechtsnormen und logische Analyse. Ein Briefwechsel 1959 bis 1965* (Vienna: Franz Deuticke, 1981). See generally Eugenio Bulygin, 'Zum Problem der Anwendbarkeit der Logik auf das Recht', in *Festschrift für Ulrich Klug zum 70. Geburtstag*, ed. Günter Kohlmann, 2 vols. (Cologne: Peter Deubner, 1983), vol. I, 19–31, also in Spanish under the title 'Sobre el problema de la aplicabilidad de la lógica al derecho', trans. Jerónimo Betegón, in Hans Kelsen and Ulrich Klug, *Normas jurídicas y análisis lógico* (Madrid: Centro de Estudios Constitucionales, 1988), 9–26.

[18] See my discussion, below, of part III of the present volume, with further references at n.66 below.

[19] Born in Leipzig, Georg Jellinek (1851–1911) spent the formative years of his life in Vienna. In 1890, after studying law and philosophy (in Vienna, Heidelberg, and Leipzig), Jellinek was appointed professor of law in Heidelberg, a position he held until his death.

self-obligating theory of the state, Jellinek's 'two-sides' theory of law, the problem of law and power, and, finally, monism and public international law. If, however, the theme at hand is Kelsen's shift to the classical phase, then three foci in the 'Foreword' merit special attention. First, there is the introduction in the early 1920s of a 'pure' theory of law as the solution to the antinomy stemming from the notion that although traditional, fact-based legal positivism and natural law theory are not, either of them, defensible,[20] they appear nevertheless to be exhaustive of the possibilities in legal theory. Second, there is the role played by the leading figure in the Marburg School of Neo-Kantianism, Hermann Cohen, in providing Kelsen with 'the definitive epistemological point of view' for his legal theory,[21] a claim of Kelsen's that is carefully examined by Geert Edel in the present volume.[22] And, third, there is Merkl's doctrine of hierarchical structure, along with the steps that lead Kelsen to abandon the 'static' view of the law evident in *Main Problems* in favour of Merkl's doctrine, which promises a 'dynamic' view of the law. I return to aspects of the first of these foci in my discussion, below, of part II of the volume, and I leave the details of the Kelsen-Cohen problematic to Edel.[23] I should like to take up the third focus here.

Having shown his colours in *The Problem of Sovereignty* (1920), identifying himself closely with Merkl's *Stufenbaulehre* or doctrine of hierarchical structure,[24] it is a short step for Kelsen to incorporate the whole of

Already recognized internationally at the turn of the century for his theoretical work in fields within public law as well as for his work on human rights, Jellinek, both positively and negatively, was the single most important intellectual influence on Kelsen.

[20] See Raz, 'Purity' (n.4 above), and Horst Dreier, *Rechtslehre, Staatssoziologie und Demokratietheorie bei Hans Kelsen* (Baden-Baden: Nomos, 1986), at 27–9; both Raz and Dreier provide exemplary statements of the 'two fronts' on which Kelsen wages battle, pitting himself against the tradition. Much earlier, Alf Ross offered a comparable interpretation of Kelsen's position, along with a stinging rejoinder; see Ross, *Theorie der Rechtsquellen* (Leipzig and Vienna: Franz Deuticke, 1929, repr. Aalen: Scientia, 1989), at 229–32, 258–69.

[21] See 'Foreword' to *HP* (n.14 above), at § VI.

[22] See Geert Edel, 'The *Hypothesis* of the Basic Norm: Hans Kelsen and Hermann Cohen', in this volume, ch. 10, at § I.

[23] See ibid.

[24] Merkl's most complete statement of the doctrine appears under the title 'Prolegomena einer Theorie des rechtlichen Stufenbaues', in *Gesellschaft, Staat und Recht. Untersuchungen zur Reinen Rechtslehre*, ed. Alfred Verdross (Vienna: Springer, 1931, repr. Vaduz, Liechtenstein: Topos, 1983), 252–94, repr. *WS II* 1311–61, and repr. in Adolf Julius Merkl, *Gesammelte Schriften*, ed. Dorothea Mayer-Maly et al., 3 vols. projected, each vol. in 2 pts. (Berlin: Duncker & Humblot, 1993–), vol. I.1 (1993), pp. 437–92. A much earlier statement, to which Kelsen invites attention in *PS* (published in 1920), § 29 (at pp. 118–19n.), is Merkl, *Das Recht im Lichte seiner Anwendung* (Hanover: Helwing, 1917), repr. *WS I* 1167–201; a longer version, whose initial installments ran under the title 'Das Recht im Spiegel seiner Auslegung', appeared in journal format in *Deutsche Richterzeitung*, 8 (1916), 584–92, ibid. vol. 9 (1917), 162–76, 394–8, 443–50, ibid. vol. 11 (1919), 290–8, repr. in Merkl, *Gesammelte Schriften* (this note, above), vol. I.1, pp. 84–146.

the doctrine into his own theory. The first more or less complete statement of the *Stufenbaulehre* in Kelsen's own hand is found in a lengthy paper of 1923, where he devotes roughly 30 pages to the doctrine; two years later, the same text appears *verbatim* in the *Allgemeine Staatslehre*.[25] Merkl's general idea[26] is that the law governs its own creation. In particular, it is a legal norm that governs the procedure by means of which other legal norms are issued.

Just how far Kelsen has come, having adopted Merkl's doctrine, can be appreciated by comparing his repertoire of legal norms before and after the adoption. In *Main Problems* (1911), Kelsen considers only general legal norms, arguing that individual legal acts require no special attention since they have already been determined *in abstracto* in general norms.[27] In the period 1916–23, however, he comes to recognize that confining his attention to general legal norms is to ignore not only individual legal acts but, indeed, an entire spectrum of legal norms between the general statutory provision and the concrete legal act. The only way to set things straight, Kelsen now argues (following Merkl's lead), is to introduce a graduated scheme that exhibits all the levels of legal norm in the legal system, from the most general constitutional and legislative norms to the most concrete legal acts. This scheme can be visualized in terms of '[t]he relation between the norm determining the creation of another norm, and the norm created in accordance with this determination', a scheme depicting, then, 'a higher- and lower-level ordering of norms'.[28] A higher-level norm is the 'conditioning' norm in relation to the lower-level norm it 'conditions', which is, then, the 'conditioned' norm. The figure of conditionality, a bit strained in English, is nevertheless useful in capturing a fundamental idea of Merkl's doctrine of hierarchical structure, namely, that the reconstructed legal norms of the hierarchy are empowering norms.

---

[25] Hans Kelsen, 'Die Lehre von den drei Gewalten oder Funktionen des Staates', *ARWP*, 17 (1923–4), 374–408, repr. *WS II* 1625–60; *ASL* §§ 32–6 (pp. 229–55).

[26] For a range of opinion on Merkl's work and significance, see e.g. Robert Walter, *Der Aufbau der Rechtsordnung* (Graz: Leykam, 1964), 2nd printing (Vienna: Manz, 1974); Theo Öhlinger, 'Zum rechtstheoretischen und rechtspolitischen Gehalt der Lehre vom Stufenbau der Rechtsordnung', in *Rechtsphilosophie und Gesetzgebung*, ed. Johann Mokre and Ota Weinberger (Vienna: Springer, 1976), 79–96; Jürgen Behrend, *Untersuchungen zur Stufenbaulehre Adolf Merkls und Hans Kelsens* (Berlin: Duncker & Humblot, 1977); Werner Krawietz, *Recht als Regelsystem* (Wiesbaden: Franz Steiner, 1984), at 133–43; Peter Koller, *Theorie des Rechts*, 2nd edn. (Vienna: Böhlau, 1997), at 118–27; Wolf-Dietrich Grussmann, *Adolf Julius Merkl. Leben und Werk* (Vienna: Manz, 1989), which also contains a full bibliography; Stanley L. Paulson, 'On the Implications of Kelsen's Doctrine of Hierarchical Structure', *Liverpool Law Review*, 18 (1996), 49–62.

[27] See 'Foreword' to *HP* (n.14 above), at § V.

[28] *LT* § 31(a) (p. 64); compare Merkl, 'Prolegomena' (n.24 above), at 272–3, repr. *WS II*, at 1335–6, and repr. *Gesammelte Schriften*, vol. I.1 (n.24 above), at 464–5.

Kelsen's adoption of Merkl's doctrine, as I noted above, is one of the developments marking the beginnings of his classical phase. It is, however, the other development—Kelsen's effort to resolve the normativity problematic—that receives special attention in the present volume. It is the leitmotif of part II of the volume, and the underlying concern of part III.[29]

PART II. THE NORMATIVITY PROBLEMATIC

When Kant, in a well-known passage in the *Rechtslehre*, poses the classical philosophical question, 'What is law?',[30] he is following a juridico-philosophical tradition that extends over two millennia. Couched in terms of *reason*, or alternatively in terms of *will*, the leading answers are familiar from the tradition—natural law theory on the one hand, and legal positivism or legal voluntarism on the other.[31] Indeed, it is often claimed that the tradition in legal philosophy consists of the various solutions developed in response to the problems posed by these two types of legal theory.[32] To be sure, 'legal positivism' is modern parlance, but the argument of legal positivism—law as convention, law as institutionalized power—is traceable back to Hellenic Greece.[33]

Taking this estimate of legal philosophy a step further, many writers assume that natural law theory and traditional, fact-based legal positivism are together exhaustive of the possibilities on the 'nature of law' problematic:[34] *tertium non datur*, there is no third possibility. Pretenders—that is to say, theories that purport to be distinct from both traditional types of theory—turn out to be disguised versions of one or

[29] It is no doubt an exaggeration to say, with Brian Bix, that 'the normative nature of law is the *sole* purpose of Kelsen's theory', but it is an instructive form of exaggeration. For, as I remark at the outset, it is Kelsen's normativity problematic more than anything else in his work that has both fascinated and exasperated writers in the field. Brian Bix, *Jurisprudence: Theory and Context* (London: Sweet & Maxwell, 1996), 56 (Bix's emphasis).

[30] Immanuel Kant, *The Metaphysics of Morals*, trans. Mary Gregor (Cambridge: Cambridge UP, 1991), 'Introduction to the Doctrine of Right', § B, 55 (Akademie edn., 229–30) (trans. altered). (The first part of Kant's *Metaphysik der Sitten*, namely the *Rechtslehre*, was first published in 1797.)

[31] See e.g. Otto von Gierke, *Johannes Althusius und die Entwicklung der naturrechtlichen Staatstheorien* (Breslau: Wilhelm Koebner, 1880), at 73–4.

[32] For a recent example of work in this genre, see Robert Alexy, *Begriff und Geltung des Rechts* (Freiburg and Munich: Karl Alber, 1992).

[33] See e.g. the characterization of the law defended by Pericles in Xenophon's dialogue on the nature of law, *Memorabilia*, I.ii., at 40–6, repr. *LT*, at pp. xxii–xxiii. On medieval sources of the concepts of positivity and positive law, see John Finnis, 'The Truth in Legal Positivism', in *The Autonomy of Law*, ed. Robert P. George (Oxford: Clarendon Press, 1996), 195–214.

[34] See e.g. the papers in *Naturrecht oder Rechtspositivismus?*, ed. Werner Maihofer (Darmstadt: Wissenschaftliche Buchgesellschaft, 1962).

the other. The argument on behalf of *tertium non datur* is straight-forward: Since natural law theory is characterized in terms of the *morality thesis*, namely, the idea that there is a conceptually necessary connection between the law and morality at some juncture or another, and since legal positivism is characterized in terms of the *separation thesis*, the contradictory of the morality thesis, the theories inevitably and unavoidably exhaust the possibilities; their respective theses are contradictories.

This view of the tradition is Kelsen's point of departure. But far from endorsing the idea that natural law theory and traditional, fact-based legal positivism together exhaust the possibilities, Kelsen challenges it. What is more, he challenges it in precisely the right way, adducing arguments at the level of abstraction at which the dictum *tertium non datur* is pitched.[35] So long as representatives of the tradition characterize the competing types of theory in terms of a single pair of theses, the separation and morality theses, it will indeed appear as though the traditional types of theory were together exhaustive of the possibilities. There is, however, a *second* pair of theses, the facticity and normativity theses. Where the 'nature of law' problematic is concerned, these theses, Kelsen insists, play every bit as fundamental a role as the separation and morality theses. According to the *facticity thesis*, the law is ultimately explicable in terms of a concatenation of fact, and precisely this position is denied by the *normativity thesis*, the contradictory of the facticity thesis.

The two pairs of theses can also be introduced in terms of the 'is'/'ought' distinction. As Kelsen argues, the distinction is systematically ambiguous; on one reading, 'is' and 'ought' take their values from the first pair of theses, on another reading, from the second pair. Thus, from the standpoint of the separation and morality theses, norms of the law belong to 'is', and norms of morality, to 'ought',[36] while, from the standpoint of the normativity and facticity theses, legal norms belong to 'ought', and concatenations of fact, which are contrasted with legal norms, to 'is'.

Kelsen draws the second pair of theses, facticity and normativity, from the fact/value distinction of the South-West or Heidelberg neo-Kantians, who introduced and defended the distinction in the name of 'methodological dualism'.[37] Having drawn on both pairs of theses in order to show that the traditional types of theory are not exhaustive of the possibilities after all, Kelsen follows through on his strategy, placing his own

---

[35] The argument I attribute to Kelsen here is, to be sure, a reconstruction; for details, see Stanley L. Paulson, 'The Neo-Kantian Dimension of Kelsen's Pure Theory of Law', *Oxford Journal of Legal Studies*, 12 (1992), 311–32, at 313–22, or *LT*, at pp. xix–xxix.

[36] I have adopted Kelsen's nomenclature here; see *Phil. Fds.* § 3 (at p. 394).

[37] See Paulson, 'Kelsen's Earliest Theory' (n.5 above), at § II.

theory within this framework as a new type of theory representing a 'middle way' between the theories of the tradition.[38] His theory is new in bringing together the separation and normativity theses, and it counts as a middle way between the old theories in taking from each of them what is defensible—the separation thesis from legal positivism and the normativity thesis from natural law theory[39]—while leaving behind what is not defensible—the facticity thesis from legal positivism and the morality thesis from natural law theory.

In defending a version of the separation thesis, which, in later formulations at any rate, resembles its British counterpart,[40] Kelsen is speaking as the legal positivist. In replying, however, to a host of European predecessors and colleagues in the field,[41] he takes a tack that distinguishes him sharply from the positivist tradition. Whereas proponents of traditional legal positivism defend the facticity thesis, Kelsen, defending the normativity thesis, calls for an explication of the law, and of legal obligation in particular, altogether independently of fact. Kelsen's endorsement of the normativity thesis represents his rejection of every fact-based legal theory, his rejection of every appeal to fact.[42] As one might expect, the ensuing theory—Kelsen's Pure Theory of Law, as developed in his classical phase—has given rise to a great variety of interpretations. Those found in part II of the present volume underscore the point.[43]

There is more to be said on the normativity problematic and on how Kelsen's normativity thesis serves to distinguish his theory from traditional, fact-based legal positivism. If one follows an early statement of Kelsen's in this genre, in *The Problem of Sovereignty* (1920), it appears

[38] Kelsen expressly characterizes the Pure Theory of Law as a 'middle way' ('*Mittelweg*'); see *PTL* § 34(g) (at p. 211).

[39] In *HP*, at 7, Kelsen tacitly acknowledges a tie between the normativity thesis and traditional natural law theory. See also Joseph Raz, 'Kelsen's Theory of the Basic Norm', in this volume, ch. 3: Kelsen, though rejecting natural law theories, 'consistently uses the natural law concept of normativity, that is, the concept of justified normativity.' Ibid. § VIII.

[40] Formulations of the separation thesis as such are clear in Kelsen's post-World War II work; see e.g. *PTL*, at §§ 7–13 (pp. 59–69). Positions defended by Kelsen in his earlier work that suggest a separation thesis take a variety of different forms.

[41] See Paulson, 'Neo-Kantian Dimension' (n.35 above).

[42] Not surprisingly, critics have taken Kelsen to task here. See e.g. Bulygin, 'An Antinomy' (n.1 above), at § II; Paulson, 'Kelsen's Earliest Theory' (n.5 above), at §§ V–VI.

[43] Joseph Raz, 'Kelsen's Theory of the Basic Norm', ch. 3, and H.L.A. Hart, 'Kelsen Visited', ch. 4, are basically sympathetic interpretations (and I take up one aspect of Raz's view in my discussion, below, of part III, B, of the volume). Whereas Raz focuses specifically on Kelsen's idea of the basic norm, Tony Honoré, in 'The Basic Norm of a Society', ch. 5, examines the basic norm idea generally. Deryck Beyleveld and Roger Brownsword, in 'Methodological Syncretism in Kelsen's Pure Theory of Law', ch. 6, and Alf Ross, in 'Validity and the Conflict between Legal Positivism and Natural Law', ch. 7, engage in hard-hitting criticism. In a broad-ranging enquiry, Beyleveld and Brownsword argue that Kelsen's middle-course between 'idealism' and 'realism' must fail; Ross, in § VI of his paper, contends that Kelsen's 'normative notion of validity' represents an ill-fated effort to retain an ostensibly 'moral, *a priori* quality' familiar from natural law theory.

that he is posing a justificatory question. The query is familiar to readers of legal and political philosophy: Why ought I to obey the law? Kelsen looks to schemata that purport to offer reasons, of normative import, for the obligation to obey in legal, moral, and religious contexts. Why, for example, ought I to obey the legal command *C*? 'Because', the standard answer runs, 'the legal authority has issued *C*.' Similarly, *mutatis mutandis*, for imperatives stemming from morality and from God. The moral imperative ought to be obeyed '[b]ecause reason would have it be so, or because conscience dictates that it be so'; and God's directive ought to be obeyed '[b]ecause God has commanded it.'[44] Kelsen objects that the normative import of the command is not clear in any of these cases. On the contrary, the 'because'-clauses simply reiterate facts, and facts cannot answer the justificatory question. As Kelsen puts it, turning the traditional scheme upside down: The command is valid 'not because God, conscience, or reason commands that I ought to conduct myself in a particular way'; rather, it is valid 'because I ought to comply with the command of God, of reason, or of conscience.'[45] Even if Kelsen, in *The Problem of Sovereignty*, leaves unanswered the justificatory question of why one ought to comply with the command, he makes abundantly clear his rejection of every factual answer to it.

Again, this is an early statement of the normativity problematic, stemming from a work that antedates Kelsen's classical phase. In the classical phase itself, the justificatory question yields to a different but closely related motif, the irreducibly normative character of legal concepts, what Alf Ross in discussions of Kelsen's normativity problematic terms their *sui generis* character.[46] The most instructive statement in this vein is found in Kelsen's *Introduction to the Problems of Legal Theory* (1934):

If one deprives the norm or the 'ought' of meaning, then there will be no meaning in the assertions that something is legally allowed, something is legally proscribed, this belongs to me, that belongs to you, *X* has a right to do this, *Y* is obligated to do that, and so on. In short, all the thousands of statements in which the life of the law is manifest daily will have lost their significance. For it is one thing to say that *A* is legally obligated to turn over 1,000 talers to *B*, and quite another to say that there is a certain chance that *A* will in fact turn over 1,000 talers to *B*.[47]

---

[44] *PS* § 24 (p. 95); on this early statement of the normativity problematic, see also ibid. § 5 (at p. 25), § 26 (at p. 107).

[45] *PS* § 24 (p. 95).

[46] Ross (n.20 above), 229; Alf Ross, 'Recht und Wirklichkeit', *Juristische Blätter*, 59 (1930), 245–51, at 245; Ross, *Towards a Realistic Jurisprudence*, trans. Annie I. Fausbøll (Copenhagen: Einar Munksgaard, 1946, repr. Aalen: Scientia, 1989), 39–40.

[47] *LT* § 16 (p. 33).

One can appreciate the force of these lines by reading them as a criticism of a 'predictive theory of law', a view familiar from Oliver Wendell Holmes.[48] The 'chance' that *A* will turn over 1,000 talers to *B* does not capture *A*'s having a legal obligation to do so. Still, Kelsen's text is not merely one critical statement among many. What sets Kelsen's position apart is the normativity thesis, the idea that the import of such concepts as legal norm, 'ought', and obligation has to be explicated, at every juncture, independently of any appeal to fact—in contrast, say, to H.L.A. Hart's appeal to social facts.[49]

More than anything else in his work, the normativity thesis distinguishes Kelsen's theory from other legal theories. The normativity thesis cannot be fully appreciated, however, apart from the separation thesis, which Kelsen is of course also defending. In the tradition, versions of the normativity thesis are found in theories of natural law, where the normativity thesis is a corollary of the morality thesis. But in Kelsen's theory—a point no less important than it is obvious—the defence of the separation thesis precludes any appeal to the morality thesis as a means of shoring up the normativity thesis. Kelsen has set himself the task of making a case for the normativity thesis without any appeal to the morality thesis. (Since the tie between the normativity and separation theses in Kelsen's theory is an intimate one, it is convenient to use the expression 'normativity problematic' to refer to Kelsen's defence of both theses. The usage is close to the familiar Continental nomenclature of 'normativism', in whose terms Kelsen's legal theory has often been distinguished from the fact-based legal positivism of the Continental tradition.[50])

Having ruled out both traditional avenues of appeal, morality and fact, how then does Kelsen proceed? What does his resolution of the normativity problematic look like? The answer, during Kelsen's long, classical phase, is found in his appeal to Kantian doctrines. For example, Kelsen formulates a juridical version of the Kantian transcendental question, a version that may be read as a plea for an argument in support of the constitutive function of cognitive legal science. He contends that legal science renders 'objective' the raw data of the law, its legislative enactments, judicial decisions, and the like, by subjecting them to systematic constraints, thereby constituting them anew. As objects of cognition, the

---

[48] Oliver Wendell Holmes, 'The Path of the Law', *Harvard Law Review*, 10 (1896–7), 457–78, repr. in Holmes, *Collected Legal Papers* (New York: Harcourt, Brace and Howe, 1920, repr. New York: Peter Smith, 1952), 167–202. See generally William Twining, 'The Bad Man Revisited', *Cornell Law Review*, 58 (1972–3), 275–303; Patrick J. Kelley, 'Was Holmes a Pragmatist? Reflections on a New Twist to an Old Argument', *Southern Illinois University Law Journal*, 14 (1989–90), 427–67.

[49] See Hart, *CL*, at 54–7, 84–8, 244, *et passim*, 2nd edn., at 55–8, 86–91, 291, *et passim*.

[50] See e.g. Guastini, 'Normativism' (n.4 above).

data of the law, like the data of sense perception in Kant's theory of knowledge, must conform to the conditions under which alone they can become objects for us. On one reading, the cognized, objectively rendered data take the form of reconstructed legal norms[51] (the hypothetically formulated sanction-norms addressed to the legal official, and their correlates, the hypothetically formulated imputation-norms addressed to the legal subject), which are, at any rate in Kelsen's earlier work, the proper objects of legal cognition. These and other Kantian doctrines, ostensibly giving Kelsen the wherewithal to forge a 'middle way' between traditional, fact-based legal positivism and natural law theory, are the initial concern in part III of the present volume.

PART III. THE NORMATIVITY PROBLEMATIC, CONTINUED: KANTIAN DOCTRINES VERSUS KELSEN WITHOUT KANT

A. A Neo-Kantian[52] Dimension in the Pure Theory of Law?

There are two closely related reasons for taking seriously the neo-Kantian dimension of Kelsen's Pure Theory of Law. The first speaks to Kelsen's effort to resolve the normativity problematic in the terms of a Kantian 'middle way'. The second reason is a textual one. A number of doctrinal themes of Kantian import are evident in Kelsen's texts, among them—sketched below—the juridico-transcendental question, the constitutive function of legal science, and peripheral imputation as intellectual category. Finally, I briefly address the inevitable question of how the basic norm is to be understood.

The Juridico-Transcendental Question. In a well-known line in the *Critique of Pure Reason*, Kant writes that he is using 'transcendental' to speak of cognition or knowledge that is concerned 'not so much with the objects of cognition as with how we cognize objects, in so far as this may be possible *a priori*.'[53] This distinctively Kantian reading of 'transcendental' flags the conditions for the possibility of *Erkenntnis* or cognition. Kelsen, following the lead of other *fin de siècle* neo-Kantians who sought

---

[51] See generally *LT*, Appendix I, at Supplementary Note 5 (pp. 132–4).

[52] On first glance the nomenclature may seem confusing—sometimes 'Kantian', other times 'neo-Kantian'. In 'A Neo-Kantian Theory of Legal Knowledge in Kelsen's Pure Theory of Law?', in this volume, ch. 9, Stefan Hammer writes: 'The common approach taken by the various philosophers falling under the rubric of neo-Kantianism is perhaps best clarified— as already suggested by the label "neo-Kantian"—in terms of their particular understanding of Kant, that is, the particular orientation reflected in their reception of Kant.' Ibid. § I. Thus, some of Kelsen's doctrines are properly labeled 'Kantian', whereas the persuasion is 'neo-Kantian'.

[53] Kant, *CPR* B25 (trans. altered).

to apply elements of Kant's transcendental philosophy to the standing disciplines, looks to the conditions for the possibility of *Rechtserkenntnis* or legal cognition. He alludes, in 'Legal Science and the Law' (1922),[54] to a formulation of the juridico-transcendental question proffered by his younger colleague Fritz Sander,[55] and then, in *Philosophical Foundations* (1928), he poses the juridico-transcendental question himself: 'How is positive law qua object of cognition, qua object of cognitive legal science, possible?'[56] Much later, in the Second Edition of the *Pure Theory of Law* (1960), he provides a more fully elaborated formulation of the same transcendental question, this time expressly drawing out the analogy to Kant:

Kant asks, 'How, without appealing to metaphysics, can the facts perceived by our senses be interpreted in the laws of nature, as these are formulated by natural science?' In the same way, the Pure Theory of Law asks, 'How, without appealing to meta-legal authorities like God or nature, can the subjective sense of certain material facts be interpreted as a system of objectively valid legal norms that are describable in legal propositions?'[57]

In effect, Kelsen is asking for an argument in support of the constitutive function of cognitive legal science.

  The Constitutive Function of Cognitive Legal Science. Kelsen introduces the idea of the constitutive function of cognitive legal science no later than 1922, and it remains prominent throughout his classical phase.[58] Cognitive legal science has the task of creating a 'unified legal system'[59] from the 'chaotic material' of the law, from its 'statutes, regulations, judicial decisions, administrative acts, and the like'.[60] Just as natural science 'creates' its object, namely, nature qua system of synthetic *a priori* judgments, so likewise cognitive legal science 'creates' its object, the law qua materially unified system of legal norms.[61]

  The idea, in Ernst Cassirer's words, of transforming 'chaos' into a 'cosmos',[62] into a materially unified legal system, recurs in Kelsen's most complete statement on the constitutive role of legal science.

It is . . . true, in terms of Kant's theory of knowledge, that legal science qua cognition of the law is like all cognition: It is constitutive in character, 'creating' its

---

  [54] 'RWR' 128, repr. *RNK* 304.
  [55] On Fritz Sander, see n.70 below, and see Kelsen's 'Letter to Treves', in this volume, ch. 8, at p. 171 n.9.   [56] *Phil. Fds.* § 36 (p. 437) (trans. altered).
  [57] *PTL* § 34(d) (p. 202) (trans. altered).
  [58] 'RWR' 181, repr. *RNK* 357; see also *PTL* § 16 (at p. 72), quoted in text at n.63 below.
  [59] 'RWR' 107, repr. *RNK* 283.   [60] 'RWR' 181, repr. *RNK* 357.
  [61] See 'RWR', at 181–2, repr. *RNK*, at 357–8. See also Hans Kelsen, 'Aussprache über die vorstehenden Berichte', *Veröffentlichungen der Vereinigung der Deutschen Staatsrechtslehrer*, 4 (1928), 168–80, at 174.
  [62] Ernst Cassirer, *Das Erkenntnisproblem in der Philosophie und Wissenschaft der neueren Zeit*, 3 vols. (Berlin: Bruno Cassirer, 1911–20), vol. II (1911), 667.

object in so far as it comprehends its object as a meaningful whole. Just as natural science, by means of its ordering cognition, turns the chaos of sensory impressions into a cosmos, that is, into nature as a unified system, so likewise legal science, by means of cognition, turns the multitude of general and individual legal norms issued by legal organs—the material given to legal science—into a unified system free of contradiction, that is, into a legal system.[63]

That which is constituted by cognitive legal science manifests the structure of the hypothetically formulated or 'reconstructed' legal norm.[64] The key to its distinctive structure lies with the intellectual category applicable in cognitive legal science.

Peripheral Imputation as Intellectual Category. Imputation qua category of cognitive legal science, Kelsen argues, can be compared directly to causality qua category in the natural sciences.

Just as the law of nature links a certain material fact as cause with another as effect, so the law of normativity links legal condition with legal consequence (the consequence of a so-called unlawful act). If the mode of linking material facts is causality in the one case, it is imputation in the other.[65]

Kelsen's category is peripheral imputation,[66] understood as the attribution of a material fact (say, a delict) to a legal person qua legal subject, whereby the subject's legal liability is established. Kelsen sees peripheral imputation as the peculiarly normative link between a material fact as condition (delict) and another material fact as consequence (sanction). When he says that the legal 'ought' designates a 'relative *a priori* category for comprehending empirical legal data', he has this category of imputation in mind.

This category of the law has a purely formal character . . . and remains applicable whatever the content of the material facts so linked . . . No social reality can be excluded, on the basis of its content, from this legal category, which is cognitively and theoretically transcendental in terms of the Kantian philosophy, not metaphysically transcendent.[67]

So far, so good. These and other doctrines in Kelsen's texts are unmistakably Kantian. As soon as one goes beyond these doctrines, however, and presses Kelsen for the neo-Kantian argument he adduces in their name, little is clear, and this lack of clarity shows up in the absence of any

---

[63] *PTL* § 16 (p. 72) (trans. altered). See also Hans Kelsen, 'Reine Rechtslehre und Egologische Rechtslehre', *ÖZöR*, 5 (1953), 449–82, at 473.

[64] See *ASL*, at § 10(e) (pp. 54–5); and see generally *LT*, Appendix I, at Supplementary Note 5 (pp. 132–4).

[65] *LT* § 11(b) (p. 23) (trans. altered).

[66] See 'Foreword' to *HP* (n.14 above), at § III. See also *ASL*, at § 13(d) (pp. 65–6); *LT*, at § 11(b) (pp. 23–5), § 25(d) (pp. 50–1); and see generally *LT*, Appendix I, at Supplementary Note 6 (pp. 134–5).

[67] *LT* § 11(b) (p. 25).

consensus on the details of Kelsen's neo-Kantian argument. The general predicament one faces here is reflected in the quagmire surrounding Kelsen's basic norm.

The Basic Norm. The basic norm, too, is a concept profoundly informed by Kantian doctrines. As Kelsen writes:

In formulating the basic norm, the Pure Theory of Law is not aiming to inaugurate a new method for jurisprudence. The Pure Theory aims simply to raise to the level of consciousness what all jurists are doing (for the most part unwittingly) when, in conceptualizing their object of enquiry, they . . . understand the positive law as a valid system, that is, as norm, and not merely as factual contingencies of motivation. With the doctrine of the basic norm, the Pure Theory analyses the actual process of the long-standing method of cognizing positive law, in an attempt simply to reveal the transcendental logical conditions of that method.[68]

Over and above this single point, namely, that Kelsen's basic norm is Kantian in character, a more exacting description of the basic norm and its role in Kelsen's theory presupposes a reconstruction of the theory from within the framework of this or that neo-Kantian persuasion.[69] There are many possibilities here. Some writers contend that it was Kelsen's aim to work up a 'transcendental argument' to the effect, roughly, that legal cognition is not possible without an *a priori* category.[70] Others argue, with impressive textual support, that Kelsen took

[68] *LT* § 29 (p. 58), and compare *PTL* § 34(d),(i) (at pp. 204–5, 218) for virtually the same text a quarter of a century later. It is well known that Kelsen formulated the basic norm in a great variety of different ways, and some of the distinctions in formulation are of theoretical interest; see generally Stanley L. Paulson, 'Die unterschiedlichen Formulierungen der "Grundnorm"', in *Rechtsnorm und Rechtswirklichkeit. Festschrift für Werner Krawietz zum 60. Geburtstag*, ed. Aulis Aarnio et al. (Berlin: Duncker & Humblot, 1993), 53–74.

[69] To be sure, beyond the various possibilities within a neo-Kantian framework, adumbrated in the text below, there is a panoply of still other basic norm doctrines, ranging from Alfred Schutz's notion of the basic norm qua principle for the construction of ideal-typical interpretative schemes to J.W. Harris's construction of a 'basic legal science *fiat*'. See Alfred Schutz, *The Phenomenology of the Social World*, trans. George Walsh and Frederick Lehnert (Evanston, Ill.: Northwestern UP, 1967), at 246–8 (Schutz's work was first published in 1932); Harris (n.4 above), at 70–92. In an altogether different genre, writers in the late 1960s and early 1970s invoked Kelsen's basic norm on the question of the legitimacy of the revolutionary regime in Rhodesia; see e.g. R.W.M. Dias, 'Legal Politics: Norms behind the *Grundnorm*', *Cambridge Law Journal*, 26 (1968), 233–59; J.M. Eekelaar, 'Principles of Revolutionary Legality', in *Oxford Essays in Jurisprudence*, 2nd ser., ed. A.W.B. Simpson (Oxford: Clarendon Press, 1973), 22–43; and, in the same volume, J.M. Finnis, 'Revolutions and Continuity of Law', 44–76. The most recent paper in this vein, addressed to the status of Hong Kong after June 1997, is Raymond Wacks, 'One Country, Two *Grundnormen*? The Basic Law and the Basic Norm', in *Hong Kong, China and 1997. Essays in Legal Theory*, ed. Wacks (Hong Kong: Hong Kong UP, 1993), 151–83.

[70] Here the leading commentator is William Ebenstein, *The Pure Theory of Law* (Madison, Wis.: University of Wisconsin Press, 1945, repr. New York: Rothman, 1969); Ebenstein, 'The Pure Theory of Law: Demythologizing Legal Thought', *California Law Review*, 59 (1971), 617–52. See also Hans Köchler, 'Zur transzendentalen Struktur der "Grundnorm"', in *Auf dem Weg zur Menschenwürde und Gerechtigkeit. Festschrift für Hans R. Klecatsky*, ed. Ludwig Adamovich and Peter Pernthaler, 1 vol. in 2 pts. (Vienna:

some of his cues from the South-West or Heidelberg neo-Kantians, and these writers proceed to reconstruct aspects of Kelsen's argument from this vantage point.[71] Still others, pointing to Kelsen's express references to Hermann Cohen, take the Marburg School as a point of departure.[72] And, finally, some argue that whatever the details of Kelsen's appeal to a *fin de siècle* neo-Kantian theory, the appeal is wrongheaded, that, for Kelsen, the only sensible appeal to Kant would be an appeal to Kant's moral philosophy (leading, of course, to an utterly different legal theory).[73] The papers in part III, A, of the present volume, including Kelsen's own paper, offer the reader a full range of opinion on these difficult and unresolved problems.

Other writers, taking seriously the idea that Kelsen sought to forge a 'middle way' between traditional, fact-based legal positivism and natural law theory, adumbrate arguments on Kelsen's behalf without appealing to Kant or the neo-Kantians at all. I should like now to turn to this work, the focus of part III, B, of the volume.

B. Kelsen without Kant, and 'Validity qua Bindingness'.

A point of departure for work on some problems in legal philosophy is a second characterization of legal validity found in Kelsen's writings. It is sometimes termed 'validity qua bindingness' (by Kelsen himself and by some who have developed the notion), sometimes 'applicability' (by some who have developed the notion, but not by Kelsen himself).[74]

Braumüller, 1980), vol. I.1, pp. 505–17, repr. (in part) in Köchler, *Philosophie, Recht, Politik* (Vienna and New York: Springer, 1985), 15–24. Within the Vienna School of Legal Theory itself, the most ambitious, albeit short-lived, Kantian theory of legal knowledge stems not from Kelsen but from the *enfant terrible* of the School, Fritz Sander. Breathtaking in its audacity is Sander's wholesale transfer of the entire 'transcendental analytic' in the *Critique of Pure Reason* to the legal sphere. See Sander, 'Die transzendentale Methode der Rechtsphilosophie und der Begriff der Rechtserfahrung', *ZöR*, 1 (1919–20), 468–507, repr. *RNK* 75–114. For both a reconstruction and a criticism of 'neo-Kantian' arguments in Kelsen's theory, see Hammer, 'Neo-Kantian Theory of Legal Knowledge?' (n.52 above); Paulson, 'Neo-Kantian Dimension' (n.35 above), at 322–32, or *LT*, at pp. xxix–xlii.

[71] See e.g. Rosemarie Pohlmann, 'Zurechnung und Kausalität', in *Rechtssystem und gesellschaftliche Basis bei Hans Kelsen* (*Rechtstheorie* Beiheft 5), ed. Werner Krawietz and Helmut Schelsky (Berlin: Duncker & Humblot, 1984), 83–112.

[72] On the Kelsen-Cohen problematic, see generally Edel, '*Hypothesis* of the Basic Norm' (n.22 above). See also Helmut Holzhey, 'Die Transformation neukantianischer Theoreme in die Reine Rechtslehre Kelsens', in *Hermeneutik und Strukturtheorie des Rechts* (*ARSP* Beiheft 20), ed. Michael W. Fischer et al. (Stuttgart: Franz Steiner, 1984), 99–110. On Cohen generally, see the references in Kelsen's 'Letter to Treves' (n.55 above).

[73] See Gerhard Luf, 'On the Transcendental Import of Kelsen's Basic Norm', in this volume, ch.11, who clearly and forcefully defends this position; see also Ralf Dreier, 'Bemerkungen zur Theorie der Grundnorm', in *Die Reine Rechtslehre in wissenschaftlicher Diskussion* [no editor] (Vienna: Manz, 1982), 38–46.

[74] All of the papers in part III, B, of the present volume turn on interpretations of legal validity in Kelsen's work and, in particular, on 'validity qua bindingness' or 'applicability'.

Understood as a criterion of legal validity, this second characterization is distinct from the more familiar criterion, that of membership,[75] although the distinction between the two is not appreciated, much less taken up, by Kelsen himself.[76] In keeping with the second characterization, Kelsen writes, '[t]o say that a norm is valid is to say that . . . it has "binding force" for those whose behaviour it regulates.'[77] Similarly, '[t]hat a norm referring to the behaviour of a human being is "valid" means that it is binding (*verbindlich*), that the human being ought to behave in the way the norm specifies.'[78] Understood in these terms, the normativity problematic represents a challenge to the legal theorist to explicate 'binding force', the legal obligation of the subject, without falling prey to the purported solutions of either the traditional, fact-based legal positivist or the natural lawyer—that is, to provide a Kelsenian 'middle way', but without Kant. This is a part of Joseph Raz's programme in 'The Purity of the Pure Theory', which appears in the present volume as chapter 12.[79] His enquiry turns not least of all on the introduction of the 'legal man' as a means of capturing what he terms the 'legal point of view'. Raz's effort is of interest for the light it sheds on the normativity problematic.

For two kinds of problem that may be addressed with this second reading of validity, see the papers to which I refer in n.76 below. A third problem, a non-Kantian approach to Kelsen's normativity problematic, is introduced in the text. For a wide-ranging exploration of Kelsen on validity, see Ernesto Garzón Valdés, 'Two Models of Legal Validity: Hans Kelsen and Francisco Suárez', in this volume, ch. 14. Garzón Valdés, too, defends a reading of 'validity qua bindingness' or 'validity qua duty to obey' in Kelsen's work, and in a comparison with the model of validity defended by Suárez, he is able to point to remarkable similarities.

[75] See e.g. Bulygin, 'An Antinomy' (n.1 above), § IV, at B; Pablo E. Navarro and José Juan Moreso, 'Applicability and Effectiveness of Legal Norms', *Law and Philosophy*, 16 (1997), 201–19, at 209–10 *et passim*.

[76] Arguably, one can use the second criterion to identify valid norms that do not qualify as valid according to the criterion of membership. One context in which the second criterion makes a difference is that of the 'tacit alternative clause'. See generally Eugenio Bulygin, 'Cognition and Interpretation of Law', in *Cognition and Interpretation of Law*, ed. Letizia Gianformaggio and Stanley L. Paulson (Turin: G. Giappichelli Editore, 1995), 11–35; Juan Ruiz Manero, 'The Tacit Alternative Clause', ibid. 247–55. Another context is the reception of pre-revolutionary legal norms in the post-revolutionary legal system; see generally José Juan Moreso and Pablo E. Navarro, 'The Reception of Norms, and Open Legal Systems', in this volume, ch. 15.

[77] *GTLS* 30. See also Carlos Santiago Nino, 'Some Confusions surrounding Kelsen's Concept of Validity', in this volume, ch.13; Raz, 'Basic Norm' (n.39 above), at § V.

[78] *PTL* § 34(a) (p. 193) (trans. altered). See also Hans Kelsen, 'Why Should the Law be Obeyed?', *WJ* 257–65, at 257 (the first appearance of the essay is in *WJ*).

[79] For criticism, see Eugenio Bulygin, 'Enunciados jurídicos y positivismo: respuesta a Raz', *Análisis Filosófico*, 1 (1981), 49–59; Roberto J. Vernengo, 'Kelsen's *Rechtssätze* as Detached Statements', in *Essays on Kelsen*, ed. Richard Tur and William Twining (Oxford: Clarendon Press, 1986), 99–108.

Raz begins by introducing Kelsen's 'purity' thesis, namely, that a legal theory is 'pure' only if the legal propositions[80] formulated within legal science do not state either moral or empirical facts. Drawing on this characterization of 'purity', Raz proceeds to construct a dilemma. First, legal propositions flag Kelsen's cognitivist approach to normative discourse. As Raz puts it,

Kelsen advances a cognitivist interpretation of all normative discourse. . . . For him a normative [proposition], be it legal, moral, or other, expresses . . . a belief in the existence of a valid norm, and a norm constitutes a value.[81]

If, however, the normative import of Kelsenian legal propositions lies in their stating the existence of a binding norm qua value, then, Raz argues, it is hard to escape the conclusion that legal propositions are 'moral statements'. Thus, 'the law and its existence and content, which is what legal [propositions] state, seem to be essentially moral facts.'[82] And legal propositions, understood as statements of moral facts, cannot be squared with Kelsen's 'purity' thesis.

Herein lies the dilemma. If Kelsenian legal propositions have normative import, they state moral facts, in violation of the 'purity' thesis. Or, lacking normative import, they state empirical facts, once again in violation of the 'purity' thesis.

Raz does not leave the matter there. On the contrary, the whole point of his paper is to work up an interpretation of the Pure Theory of Law that provides Kelsen with an escape from the dilemma, and in several steps.[83] In the first step, Raz introduces the all-important normative component in a way that sets the stage for an escape from the dilemma. People have moral beliefs, and for every one of us it is likely that some of our moral beliefs coincide with the law, while others do not. Imagine, now, an individual 'whose moral beliefs are identical with the law',[84] so that they can be mapped isomorphically onto corresponding legal norms. What is more, the isomorphism of moral belief and legal norm is no accident, for the moral beliefs of this individual 'all derive from his belief in the moral

---

[80] The topic of the normative or legal proposition is of course an issue of considerable interest in its own right. See e.g. Eugenio Bulygin, 'Norms, Normative Propositions, and Legal Statements', in *Contemporary Philosophy. A New Survey*, ed. Guttorm Fløistad, 4 vols. (The Hague: Nijhoff, 1981–3), vol. III (1982), 127–52; Guastini, 'Normativism' (n.4 above); Tecla Mazzarese, '"Norm Proposition": Epistemic and Semantic Queries', *Rechtstheorie*, 22 (1991), 39–70; von Wright, *NA*, at 104–6, 131–2, 165, *et passim*. See also the papers by Bulygin and Vernengo cited in n.79 above. For Kelsen's own views on the doctrine of the legal proposition, see the references at n.14 above.

[81] Raz, 'Purity' (n.4 above), § IV.   [82] Ibid. § V.

[83] My compressed statement does not contain all of the steps in the argument Raz develops, and the reader will want to consult Raz's text, ibid.

[84] The quotations, here and below, are all drawn from Raz's text, ibid.

authority of the ultimate law-making processes.' Raz calls this individual the *legal man*.

Introducing the legal man counts as the first step in providing Kelsen with an escape from the dilemma. Drawing on the idea of the legal man, Raz turns next to the role of the legal scientist. Although legal scientists study the law as a normative system, they do not thereby commit themselves to its normativity. Rather, the legal propositions that legal scientists formulate are conditional:

If the legal man is right, then one ought to do thus-and-so.

Or, using the doctrine of the basic norm to mark the same conditional formulation of legal propositions:

If the basic norm is valid, then one ought to do thus-and-so.

As Raz puts it: By means of these conditional formulations of legal propositions, 'legal science can both be pure and describe the law as a normative system.'

A second step, Raz continues, is required to take into account legal practitioners. For although legal scientists are merely stating what the law is *if* it is valid, practising lawyers go further. 'They do not merely talk about the law. They use it to advise clients and to present arguments before courts.' In a word, they are stating *that* the law is valid. They 'actually presuppose the basic norm themselves.'[85] Their presupposition of the basic norm is, however, a presupposition with a difference. That is, unlike categorical legal propositions, which reflect one's belief in the existence of a norm qua value, the practising lawyer's presupposition of the basic norm marks the assumption of the point of view of the legal man, but without any commitment to it. The statements corresponding to this second step are, in Raz's terminology, 'detached' statements. He writes:

Detached statements state the law as a valid normative system [rather than merely describing what is] valid *if* the basic norm is valid. But they do so from a point of view, that of the legal man, to which they are not committed.[86]

Thus, from both vantage points, that of the legal scientist and that of the practitioner, legal science is free of moral commitment 'despite its use of normative language'.[87]

It might be said that the legal man's repertoire of reasons for action[88] is impoverished, owing to the isomorphic mapping of his moral beliefs

---

[85] Ibid. As Kelsen puts it: 'The basic norm really exists in the juristic consciousness.' *GTLS* 116, quoted by Raz, 'Purity' (n.4 above), § V. See also *LT*, at § 29 (p. 58).

[86] Raz, 'Purity' (n. 4 above), § V (my emphasis).   [87] Ibid.

[88] For Raz's theory of reasons for action, see Raz, *Practical Reason and Norms*, 2nd edn. (Princeton: Princeton UP, 1990); see also the illuminating sketch of Raz's theory in J.E. Penner, *The Idea of Property in Law* (Oxford: Clarendon Press, 1997), at 7–13.

onto the law. But this observation counts not at all against Raz's point, namely, that there is a way for Kelsen to escape the dilemma. In a word, Raz provides a showing that Kelsen's normativity problematic can be resolved.[89]

PART IV. TOWARD A THEORY OF LEGAL NORMS

Kelsen's Late, Sceptical Phase. As I noted above, there is no consensus on the reasons for Kelsen's departure, *circa* 1960, from the theses of his long, classical phase. That there was a major shift, however, is clear.[90] One way to conceptualize the shift is to think in terms of a clash between the Kantian and the juridico-positivist motifs in Kelsen's work, with the latter in the end prevailing over the former; in this connection, I invite attention to Eugenio Bulygin's statement in 'An Antinomy in Kelsen's Pure Theory of Law', appearing in the present volume as chapter 16.

The changes marked by Kelsen's shift to a sceptical view are in some instances dramatic. I mention just three. First, Kelsen abandons his earlier view to the effect that legal norms are subject to constraints imposed by logic. Second, he gives up the idea that legal science has a 'normative' dimension. Third, he defends an utterly emaciated version of the basic norm thesis, namely, the basic norm qua fiction. The present volume offers thorough examinations of the first theme—in part IV, A, with an eye to Kelsen's own views,[91] and in part IV, B, with attention both to the fact/value distinction and to competing conceptions of norms.[92] Similarly,

[89] It goes without saying that the claim is controversial. For a radically different view of Kelsen's project, see e.g. Beyleveld and Brownsword, 'Methodological Syncretism' (n.43 above).

[90] For the nature and implications of Kelsen's shift, see the well-known paper by Amedeo G. Conte, 'In margine all'ultimo Kelsen' (1967), translated as 'Hans Kelsen's Deontics', in this volume, ch. 18, and equally the examination by Bruno Celano, 'Norm Conflicts: Kelsen's View in the Late Period and a Rejoinder', in this volume, ch. 19. See also Kazimierz Opałek, *Überlegungen zu Hans Kelsens "Allgemeiner Theorie der Normen"* (Vienna: Manz, 1980); Ota Weinberger, *Normentheorie als Grundlage der Jurisprudenz und der Ethik. Eine Auseinandersetzung mit Hans Kelsens Theorie der Normen* (Berlin: Duncker & Humblot, 1981); Bruno Celano, *Dover essere e intenzionalità. Una critica all'ultimo Kelsen* (Turin: G. Giappichelli Editore, 1990); Heidemann (n.1 above), at 159–213, 245–9, *et passim.* See also the references in Paulson, 'Kelsen's Earliest Theory' (n.5 above), at n.6.

[91] See Conte, 'Hans Kelsen's Deontics' (n.90 above); Celano, 'Norm Conflicts' (n.90 above).

[92] See von Wright, 'Is and Ought' (n.15 above); Carlos E. Alchourrón and Eugenio Bulygin, 'The Expressive Conception of Norms', in this volume, ch. 21; Ota Weinberger, 'The Expressive Conception of Norms: An Impasse for the Logic of Norms', in this volume, ch. 22. On related problems, including the question of the possibility of a logic of norms (as distinct from a logic of normative sentences or propositions), see Eugenio Bulygin, 'Das Problem der Normenlogik', in *Institution und Recht* (*Rechtstheorie* Beiheft 14), ed. Peter Koller et al., with an introduction by Werner Krawietz (Berlin: Duncker & Humblot, 1994),

the second theme is examined in the volume carefully and at length.[93] The last theme—the basic norm qua fiction—is not, however, addressed explicitly in the volume,[94] and I therefore provide a brief sketch here.

More conspicuously than anything else in his shift to the sceptical phase, the basic norm qua fiction bespeaks Kelsen's complete abandonment of the Kantian doctrines that figured so prominently in the classical phase. During Kelsen's classical phase, the basic norm is itself a reflection of Kantian doctrines;[95] then, in his late, sceptical phase, everything on this front changes. Writing toward the end of his life, Kelsen underscores the point:

According to Vaihinger, a fiction is a cognitive device used when one is unable to attain one's cognitive goal with the material at hand. The cognitive goal of the basic norm is to ground the validity of the norms forming a positive moral or legal system, that is, to interpret the subjective meaning of the norm-issuing acts as their objective meaning, that is, as valid norms, and to interpret the acts in question as norm-issuing acts. This goal can be attained only by means of a fiction.[96]

Hans Vaihinger, in a well-known treatise, described a legal fiction as 'the subsumption of a case under a conceptual construct that does not properly include it.'[97] Whereas *hypotheses* set out assumptions whose truth might well be established by verification, *fictions* are never verifiable, for they are known to be false.[98] Instead, fictions are employed because of their 'utility'.[99] Wherever one's cognitive material 'resists a direct procedure', the fiction makes it possible to accomplish one's cognitive purpose 'indirectly'.[100]

Again, this is Vaihinger's position, and Kelsen follows it to the letter. He writes:

35–50; Carlos E. Alchourrón and Antonio A. Martino, 'Logic without Truth', *Ratio Juris*, 3 (1990), 46–67; Georg Henrik von Wright, 'Is there a Logic of Norms?', *Ratio Juris*, 4 (1991), 265–83; Hajime Yoshino, 'Zur Anwendbarkeit der Regeln der Logik auf Rechtsnormen', in *Die Reine Rechtslehre in wissenschaftlicher Diskussion* (n.73 above), 142–64.

[93] See Bulygin, 'An Antinomy' (n.1 above), at § III; and see generally Guastini, 'Normativism' (n.4 above).

[94] To be sure, there is a very interesting discussion of the basic norm in Bulygin, 'An Antinomy' (n.1 above), at § VI, but that discussion is not directed primarily to Kelsen's defence, in the late, sceptical period, of the basic norm qua fiction.

[95] See e.g. text quoted at n.68 above.

[96] *GTN* ch. 59, § I, D (p. 256) (trans. altered). See also Hans Kelsen, 'Die Grundlage der Naturrechtslehre' and (with others) 'Diskussionen', *ÖZöR*, 13 (1963), 1–37, 117–62, at 119–20, repr. under the title *Das Naturrecht in der politischen Theorie*, ed. Franz-Martin Schmölz (Vienna: Springer, 1963) (same pagination).

[97] Hans Vaihinger, *Die Philosophie des Als-Ob*, 9th and 10th printing (Leipzig: F. Meiner, 1927, repr. Aalen: Scientia, 1986), 46 (Part One, ch. 5); 2nd Engl. edn., *The Philosophy of 'As If'*, trans. C.K. Ogden (London: Kegan Paul, Trench, Trubner & Co., 1935), 33.

[98] See Vaihinger (n.97 above), at 143–54 (Part One, ch. 21), Engl. edn., at 85–90.

[99] Vaihinger (n.97 above), 152, Engl. edn. 90.

[100] Vaihinger (n.97 above), 19 (General Introduction, ch. 4), Engl. edn. 13.

[T]he basic norm is not a hypothesis in terms of Vaihinger's philosophy of 'as if'—as I myself have sometimes characterized the basic norm—but is, rather, a fiction. A fiction differs from a hypothesis in that it is, or ought to be, accompanied by the awareness that reality does not agree with it.[101]

To say, with Vaihinger, that the concept in question is a fiction for failing to 'agree with' reality is to say that the concept 'contradicts' reality. Kelsen takes this first step with Vaihinger, arguing that the basic norm is 'contradictory' for failing to correspond to a real act of will. Then Vaihinger raises the ante. Constructions in the *strict* sense are fictions only if they 'contradict' reality and, in addition, are 'self-contradictory'.[102] Kelsen takes this second step, too.

[T]he basic norm of a positive moral or legal system is not a positive norm, but a norm merely thought or imagined—which is a fictitious norm; it is the meaning not of a real act of will, but of a merely fictitious act of will. And as such, the basic norm is a genuine or 'proper' fiction in terms of Vaihinger's philosophy of 'as if', a fiction characterized not only in that it contradicts reality, but also in that it is self-contradictory.[103]

Granting that the basic norm is 'contradictory' owing to its failure to agree with reality, does it make sense to say that it is also 'self-contradictory'? The basic norm is self-contradictory, Kelsen argues, for (1) it 'represents the empowering of an ultimate moral or legal authority', and therefore (2) 'emanates from an authority . . . even higher' than the ultimate authority.[104] The 'ultimate authority' is both ultimate and not ultimate.

Kelsen's talk of the 'self-contradictory' character of the basic norm may be a contrivance, but the general significance of his use of Vaihinger is unmistakable. By means of the basic norm, now a fictitious construct, one proceeds *as though* the material of the law were irreducibly normative. And this, it scarcely need be added, amounts to a fundamental concession on Kelsen's part: The normativity thesis, claiming the irreducibly normative character of the law, is not defensible.

---

[101] *GTN* ch. 59, § I, D (p. 256) (trans. altered).
[102] See Vaihinger (n.97 above), at 24 (Part One, General Introductory Remarks), Engl. edn., at 16, and compare *Die Philosophie des Als-Ob*, at 143–54 (Part One, ch. 21), Engl. edn., at 85–90.
[103] *GTN* ch. 59, § I, D (p. 256) (trans. altered).   [104] Ibid.

PART V. POWER, LEGAL POWERS, AND EMPOWERMENT

Legal power or empowerment is everyday fare in the law and indispensable, but the concept of legal power has not enjoyed a great deal of attention in general legal theory.[105] To be sure, squares of opposition depicting the logical juxtaposition of the so-called deontic modes—prescription, permission, proscription, and indifference[106]—had already been developed in the eighteenth century. One thinks, for example, of Bentham's extraordinary work in this genre.[107] It is only in this century, however, that Wesley Newcomb Hohfeld (1879–1918) developed something roughly comparable for the so-called empowerment modes—power, disability, liability, and immunity.[108]

[105] The writers represented in part V of the present volume are exceptions to the rule: Norberto Bobbio, 'Kelsen and Legal Power', ch. 23; Joseph Raz, ' Voluntary Obligations and Normative Powers', ch. 24; Dick W.P. Ruiter, 'Legal Powers', ch. 25; Neil MacCormick, 'Powers and Power-Conferring Norms', ch. 26; and Agostino Carrino, 'Reflections on Legal Science, Law, and Power', ch. 27. Bobbio, Raz, Ruiter, and MacCormick have all written extensively on legal powers and empowerment, and readers may find a summary useful.

Bobbio's papers in the field are now collected, thanks to the initiative of Agostino Carrino, in Bobbio, *Diritto e potere* (Naples: Edizioni Scientifiche Italiane, 1992).

Raz's work on legal powers includes *CLS*, at 105–9, 112, 116–18, 138, 156–67, 224–30, *et passim*; *Practical Reason and Norms*, 2d edn. (n.88 above), at 97–106, 111–12, 114–17, 129–30, 207–8 (notes); *AL*, at 13–20 *et passim*; *Ethics in the Public Domain* (Oxford: Clarendon Press, 1994), at chs. 10–12.

Ruiter's paper, written especially for this volume, reflects the argument developed in his book, *Institutional Legal Facts. Legal Powers and their Effects* (Dordrecht: Kluwer, 1993).

MacCormick's work in the field includes 'Law as Institutional Fact', *Law Quarterly Review*, 90 (1974), 102–29, repr. in MacCormick and Ota Weinberger, *An Institutional Theory of Law* (Dordrecht: Reidel, 1986), 49–76; *H.L.A. Hart* (London: Edward Arnold, 1981), at 71–87, 103–6; 'Jurisprudence and the Constitution', *Current Legal Problems*, 36 (1983), 13–30, repr. in *An Institutional Theory of Law* (this note, above), 171–88; 'Speech Acts, Legal Institutions, and Real Laws', with Zenon Bankowski, in *The Legal Mind. Essays for Tony Honoré*, ed. MacCormick and Peter Birks (Oxford: Clarendon Press, 1986), 121–33; 'General Legal Concepts', in *The Laws of Scotland: Stair Memorial Encyclopaedia*, ed. Thomas B. Smith and Robert Black, 25 vols. (Edinburgh: The Law Society of Scotland, London and Edinburgh: Butterworths, 1987–96), vol. XI (1990), paras. 1001–136 (pp. 359–419), at 1059–66 (pp. 384–7), 1083–90 (pp. 395–8).

[106] With the expression 'deontic modes' I have in mind what von Wright terms 'the deontic modes or modes of obligation', nothing more; see Georg Henrik von Wright, 'Deontic Logic', *Mind*, 60 (1951), 1–15, at 1, repr. in von Wright, *Logical Studies* (London: Routledge & Kegan Paul, 1957), 58–74, at 58.

[107] See Jeremy Bentham, *Of Laws in General*, ed. H.L.A. Hart (London: Athlone Press, 1970), 15n. (at h), and at ch. X (93–132); see generally H.L.A. Hart, 'Bentham's *Of Laws in General*', *Rechtstheorie*, 2 (1971), 55–66, repr. (in expanded form) in Hart, *Essays on Bentham* (Oxford: Clarendon Press, 1982), 105–26. For work in this vein by another eighteenth-century giant, see Gottfried Wilhelm Leibniz, *Elementa Juris naturalis*, in *Sämtliche Schriften und Briefe*, ed. Deutsche Akademie der Wissenschaften zu Berlin, 6th ser., vol. I (Berlin: Akademie, 1971), at 465–85; see generally Gerhard Otte, 'Leibniz und die juristische Methode', *Zeitschrift für Neuere Rechtsgeschichte*, 5 (1983), 1–21.

[108] Wesley Newcomb Hohfeld, *Fundamental Legal Conceptions*, ed. Walter Wheeler Cook (New Haven: Yale UP, 1919). See Manfred Moritz, *Über Hohfelds System der*

Hohfeld was not alone in inviting attention to the sharp distinctions that exist between the empowerment modalities and their deontic counterparts. Other theorists had made the same point, but without Hohfeld's ambitious schematization. August Thon, Alois Brinz, and Ernst Rudolf Bierling[109] come to mind, as does Georg Jellinek, who wrote in his *System der subjektiven öffentlichen Rechte* that '[a]ll provisions on the validity of legal acts and legal transactions establish a *legal "can"* expressly conferred by the legal system. And this "can" stands in sharp contrast to "may".'[110] Beyond this point of general agreement,[111] however, there is little that could count as a consensus, even today, on the concept of empowerment or legal power.[112]

Kelsen's own case is something of an oddity. On the one hand, no fewer than three central doctrines of his classical phase point clearly to an absolutely fundamental role for empowerment or legal power. First, the doctrine of hierarchical structure (*Stufenbaulehre*),[113] providing— with an eye to lawmaking—a dynamic characterization of the law, turns

---

juridischen Grundbegriffe (Lund: C.W.K. Gleerup, and Copenhagen: Ejnar Munksgaard, 1960); Alf Ross, *Directives and Norms* (London: Routledge & Kegan Paul, 1968), at 118–35; Robert Alexy, *Theorie der Grundrechte* (Baden-Baden: Nomos, 1985), at 185–94, 211–19; R.W.M. Dias, *Jurisprudence*, 5th edn. (London: Butterworths, 1985), at 23–46; Peter Jones, *Rights* (New York: St. Martin's, 1994), at 12–25 *et passim*.

[109] See Alois Brinz, *Lehrbuch der Pandekten*, 2d edn., 4 vols. (Erlangen: Andreas Deichert, 1873), vol. I, at § 65 (pp. 211–13); August Thon, *Rechtsnorm und subjektives Recht* (Weimar: Böhlau, 1878, repr. Aalen: Scientia, 1964), at ch. VII (325–74); Ernst Rudolf Bierling, *Zur Kritik der juristischen Grundbegriffe*, 1 vol. in 2 pts. (Gotha: F.A. Perthes, 1883, repr. Aalen: Scientia, 1965), pt. 2, at §§ 147–9 (pp. 49–57). Although I have not examined the matter at length, I have the impression that the older analytical jurists in Britain, those writing before Hohfeld, gave a good bit less attention to powers than did their Continental counterparts. For example, neither William Markby, *Elements of Law*, 5th edn. (Oxford: Clarendon Press, 1896), nor Thomas Erskine Holland, *Jurisprudence*, 11th edn. (Oxford: Clarendon Press, 1910), contains anything of note. Bentham, of course, is the great exception. See *Of Laws in General* (n.107 above), at 22–6, 61, 68n. (68–9), 77–92, 136n., 137n. (137–9), 251–72, 275–6, 283n., 287–8, 290–7, *et passim*; see generally H.L.A. Hart, 'Bentham on Legal Powers', *Yale Law Journal*, 81 (1971–2), 799–822, repr. under the title 'Legal Powers', in Hart, *Essays on Bentham* (n.107 above), 194–219.

[110] Georg Jellinek, *System der subjektiven öffentlichen Rechte*, 2nd edn. (Tübingen: J.C.B. Mohr, 1905, repr. Aalen: Scientia, 1979), 47 (Jellinek's emphasis), and see generally at 45–53, 227–45, *et passim*.

[111] Even here it would be misleading to speak as if there were a widespread consensus. For discussion, see Eugenio Bulygin, 'On Norms of Competence', *Law and Philosophy*, 11 (1992), 201–16, at 205–7, and Torben Spaak, *The Concept of Legal Competence*, trans. Robert Carroll (Aldershot: Dartmouth, 1994), at 80–7; both writers criticize modern theorists' attempts to explicate power in terms of permission, 'can' in terms of 'may'.

[112] See Spaak, ibid., who offers, *inter alia*, a helpful overview of the present state of the art. See also the rich perspectives in Lars Lindahl, *Position and Change* (Dordrecht: Reidel, 1977); Andrew J.I. Jones and Marek Sergot, 'A Formal Characterization of Institutionalized Power', in *Normative Systems in Legal and Moral Theory. Festschrift for Carlos E. Alchourrón and Eugenio Bulygin*, ed. Ernesto Garzón Valdés et al. (Berlin: Duncker & Humblot, 1997), 349–67.

[113] For some details, see § I above.

on the idea of empowerment as the typical means of issuing legal norms, that is, of creating law. Second, Kelsen's 'narrower' (and in his view more basic) concept of the constitution, a concept reflecting the greater *Stufenbaulehre*, is tantamount to a set of rules for the formation of law[114]—in a word, a set of empowering norms. And, third, Kelsen's 'logical constitution'[115]—the basic norm—is properly understood in some contexts as having the form of an empowering norm.[116]

On the other hand, Kelsen gives empowerment surprisingly little attention in his earlier work. Indeed, he does not turn to anything even approximating a close analysis of empowerment before the late 1930s, twenty years, then, after the beginnings of the classical phase. In his later work, empowerment fares a bit better, and Norberto Bobbio, in his paper 'Kelsen and Legal Power', appearing in the present volume as chapter 23, traces some of these developments.

Considering briefly Kelsen's initial analysis of empowerment in the late 1930s, I begin by backing up a step or two in order to take into account the character of the operator in Kelsen's hypothetically formulated sanction-norm. Is it, as many writers have assumed, a deontic operator?[117] Is it, in other words, a conditional *command* addressed to the official to impose a sanction? Or is the operator a mere empowerment? In the earlier writings, Kelsen does not spell out his position on this issue in any detail, but he seems pretty clearly to be saying that the norm addressed to the official is a conditional command. In the late 1930s, however, in the course of a close examination of Georges Scelle's theory of public international law,[118] Kelsen offers a precise statement: The hypothetically formulated sanction-norm is an empowerment to officials to impose sanctions.

Here Kelsen defines the empowerment as 'the capacity to bring about certain legal changes by means of one's behaviour', he confirms the wide scope of empowerment, from public and private law to public international law, and he juxtaposes the notion of being obligated with that of

---

[114] See Hans Kelsen, 'Wesen und Entwicklung der Staatsgerichtsbarkeit', *Veröffentlichungen der Vereinigung der Deutschen Staatsrechtslehrer*, 5 (1929), 30–88, at 36, repr. *WS II* 1813–71, at 1819.

[115] See *ASL* § 36 (at p. 249).

[116] Joseph Raz has emphasized this reading of the basic norm in his work; see e.g. Raz, 'Basic Norm' (n.39 above), at § I. Alf Ross offers the same reading; see Ross, *Towards a Realistic Jurisprudence* (n.46 above), at 47. For several distinguishable 'empowerment' readings of the basic norm (directed to norm issuance and to the imposition of sanctions), see Paulson (n.68 above).

[117] See e.g. Hart, *CL*, at 35, 2nd edn., at 35–6.

[118] Hans Kelsen, 'Recht und Kompetenz. Kritische Bemerkungen zur Völkerrechtstheorie Georges Scelles', in Kelsen, *Auseinandersetzungen zur Reinen Rechtslehre*, ed. Kurt Ringhofer and Robert Walter (Vienna: Springer, 1987), 1–108. (Reproduced from Kelsen's manuscript, the study dates from the late 1930s.)

being empowered, explicating the related modality of immunity as that modality according to which, say, an individual's freedom of expression corresponds to the state's inability (or 'disability'), legally speaking, to restrict that freedom. In particular, in introducing the hypothetically formulated sanction-norm as an empowerment, Kelsen characterizes obligation in terms of the competence to impose sanctions. There is the possibility, he writes,

of basing . . . the concept of legal obligation on that of competence, of tracing the former to the latter. If, namely, the legal obligation of an individual to behave in a certain way is acknowledged as given only if another individual is empowered by the legal system to impose a sanction on the first individual in the event that the opposite behaviour is forthcoming, and if the empowerment to impose a sanction counts as a 'competence', then the legal obligation of one individual is based on the 'sanction-competence' of the other.[119]

To be sure, this early sketch of empowerment hardly counts as a full statement, but Kelsen returns to the theme in *General Theory of Law and State* (1945) and in other works. Noteworthy is his later argument to the effect that 'ought' need not coincide with the concept of legal obligation. Rather, 'ought' in the hypothetically formulated sanction-norm is simply a placeholder[120] indicating that an official can impose a sanction under certain conditions, while leaving open the question of whether the official is obligated to impose the sanction. If official A is obligated to impose a sanction on a subject, that is simply to say that a higher official B is empowered to impose a sanction on A if, under the designated conditions, A fails to impose the sanction on the subject. Thus understood, empowerment is fundamental, and the idea of an 'obligation' imposed on official A is simply a construction drawn from the norm empowering A along with the norm empowering B. Kelsen adds that since this chain of hypothetically formulated sanction-norms, addressed to officials, 'cannot be extended indefinitely',[121] there must be a final hypothetically formulated sanction-norm, a terminating norm that empowers an official. Since this norm is terminating, it cannot then be complemented by a still higher-level empowering norm in virtue of which this official could be said to be obligated to impose a sanction; in other words, not even the peculiarly Kelsenian notion of constructed obligation, turning on paired empowerments, is possible at this highest level. Here all that remains is

---

[119] Ibid. 75.

[120] See *GTLS*, at 59–62. For Kelsen's later, express statement of the same thing, namely, that 'ought' is akin to a variable expression and ranges over the various modal verbs, including 'may' and 'can', see *PTL* § 4(b) (at p. 5), § 4(c) (at p. 10), § 28(b) (at pp. 118–19); *GTN*, at ch. 25, § II (p. 97). See also H.L.A. Hart, 'Kelsen's Doctrine of the Unity of Law', in this volume, ch. 30, at § II, B(1); Raz, *CLS*, at 47.

[121] *GTLS* 60.

the terminating norm, the empowerment as hypothetically formulated sanction-norm, *sans* obligation.[122]

In still later works, namely, the Second Edition of the *Pure Theory of Law* (1960) and the posthumously published *General Theory of Norms* (1979), Kelsen introduces empowerment in the guise of a 'dependent legal norm' or 'normative function'.[123] When spelled out, however, this guise is simply a variation on the theme Kelsen introduced earlier: the empowerment as hypothetically formulated sanction-norm.[124]

PART VI. MONISM AND PUBLIC INTERNATIONAL LAW

Writing in 1914, Alfred Verdross, Kelsen's younger colleague in what would become the Vienna School of Legal Theory, sets out the possibilities for resolving the problem of the relation between public international law and state law: In a dualistic construction, the systems of international law and state law are understood to be altogether separate and independent of one another, while, in a monistic construction, either state law is brought within the system of international law or international law is brought within the system of state law.[125]

Kelsen, addressing the same issue[126] in the same year, gives the impression that he would like to leave open the question of whether the dualistic solution is defensible,[127] but the argument that he would develop a short time later against the very possibility of dualism is already discernible here. Would it be warranted, he asks, to characterize as 'law'—on a univocal reading—two fully independent normative systems? And in the case of a conflict of duties, where each of the conflicting norms belongs to a different, fully independent normative system, would

---

[122] Although this position is already evident in *GTLS*, at 59–60, Kelsen develops it further in response to Alf Ross's regress argument. See Ross, *Towards a Realistic Jurisprudence* (n.46 above), at 45, 75, 110–11; *RR 2* § 28(b) (at pp. 124–5 n.) [this material in *RR 2* is not reproduced in *PTL*].

[123] See e.g. *PTL*, at § 6(e) (pp. 54–8) *et passim*; *GTN*, at chs. 25–7 (pp. 96–105) *et passim*.

[124] See e.g. *PTL* § 5(a) (at p. 25), § 18 (at p. 78); *GTN* ch. 14 (at p. 52).

[125] Alfred Verdross, 'Zur Konstruktion des Völkerrechts', *Zeitschrift für Völkerrecht*, 8 (1914), 329–59, at 336, repr. *WS II* 1995–2022, at 2002. Compare *PS* § 25 (at p. 104); Hans Kelsen, 'Les rapports de système. Entre le droit interne et le droit international public', *Recueil des cours*, 14 (1926), 227–331, at 275–6.

[126] For general background on the issue, see Joseph G. Starke, 'Monism and Dualism in the Theory of International Law', in this volume, ch. 29; and for a close examination of some of Kelsen's arguments, see Hart, 'Unity of Law' (n.120 above). For recent attention to Kelsen's theory vis-à-vis the law of the European Union, see Catherine Richmond, 'Preserving the Identity Crisis: Autonomy, System and Sovereignty in European Law', *Law and Philosophy*, 16 (1997), 377–420.

[127] See Hans Kelsen, 'Über Staatsunrecht', *Grünhutsche Zeitschrift für das Privat- und öffentliche Recht der Gegenwart*, 40 (1914), 1–114, at 100–1 *et passim*, repr. *WS I* 957–1057, at 1045–6 *et passim*.

it be proper to treat both norms as legal norms?[128] Kelsen has grave doubts. In his first mature work on legal monism, *The Problem of Sovereignty* (1920), these doubts carry the day, and, aside from some details,[129] the positions Kelsen developed here—his arguments against dualism, along with a tenacious defence of monism—are the very positions he is defending forty years later in the paper 'Sovereignty', appearing in the present volume as chapter 28.

As Kelsen sees it, the proponents of dualism, by hermetically sealing the respective legal systems, international and state, close the door to all juridico-normative ties between them. And this view of dualism is no straw man of Kelsen's making. Heinrich Triepel, whose defence of dualism at the turn of the century set the stage for the modern European debate on the unity of law, writes that international law and state law are, at best, 'two spheres that impinge upon one another but do not intersect'.[130] Dionisio Anzilotti, a distinguished proponent of dualism, defends that view as 'the concept of the absolute and complete separation of the two legal systems', international and state.[131] Verdross writes that dualism, representing a 'doubling of the normative base', means that the systems of international law and state law are 'complexes of norms that cannot be squared with each other'.[132] More colourful is Kelsen's own characterization: The proponent of dualism envisages the two legal systems as standing 'alongside each other, unconnected, like windowless monads'.[133]

Why, beginning in *The Problem of Sovereignty*, does Kelsen argue so doggedly against dualism? Two doctrines prepared the way: first, stemming from dualism, the doctrine of a complete separation of the two

---

[128] See ibid.

[129] For example, in *PS* Kelsen expressly defends the view that a state legal norm conflicting with a higher-level norm of international law is 'null and void'; it is not, in other words, 'to be regarded as a valid norm . . . at all.' *PS* § 28 (p. 113), and see § 35 (at p. 146). By 1932, however, he has changed his mind, arguing that a state legal norm conflicting with a norm of international law, while invalidatable, is not null and void. See Hans Kelsen, 'Unrecht und Unrechtsfolge im Völkerrecht', *ZöR*, 12 (1932), 481–608, at 507–10, 516–17; *LT*, at § 31(h) (pp. 71–5), and at § 50(f) (pp. 117–19); Kelsen, *Principles of International Law* (New York: Rinehart, 1952), at 446, 2nd edn., ed. Robert W. Tucker (New York: Holt, Rinehart and Winston, 1967), at 587. See also Georg Dahm, Jost Delbrück, and Rüdiger Wolfrum, *Völkerrecht*, 2nd edn., 2 vols. projected, with vol. I in 2 pts. (Berlin: de Gruyter, 1989–), vol. I.1 (1989), at p. 106.

[130] See Heinrich Triepel, *Völkerrecht und Landesrecht* (Leipzig: C.L. Hirschfeld, 1899, repr. Aalen: Scientia, 1958), at 111.

[131] Dionisio Anzilotti, *Corso di diritto internazionale*, 3rd edn. (Rome: Athenaeum, 1928), 48; 4th edn. (Padua: CEDAM, 1964), 51 (first published in 1912). Despite their fundamental disagreement, Kelsen had a high opinion of Anzilotti's work. See Kelsen, 'Unrecht und Unrechtsfolge im Völkerrecht' (n.129 above), at 525n., 555–9; 'Letter to Treves' (n.55 above), at 171.

[132] Verdross (n.125 above), 334, repr. *WS II* 2000.

[133] *PS* § 36 (p. 152).

normative systems, international and state, and, second, Kelsen's own doctrine of the unity of law, which presupposes material unity, that is, the 'consistency' of legal norms,[134] and which is defended by Kelsen as a presupposition of legal cognition. At the same time, there are practical considerations of great magnitude, arising from the need to be able to resolve norm conflicts.[135]

How do these doctrines bear on the problem of inter-systemic norm conflicts? The dualist doctrine, in ruling out the possibility of any juridico-normative tie between the norms of the respective systems, rules out the very possibility of a juridico-normative resolution of inter-systemic norm conflicts as they are ordinarily understood. Kelsen, like the rest of us, regards this conclusion as absurd, and he therefore sees himself justified in rejecting the premiss that he believes gives rise to it— the dualist doctrine of a complete separation of, *inter alia*, the normative systems of international and state law. His own doctrine of the unity of law presupposes both material and formal unity,[136] limiting the scope of 'the juridico-normative'—more precisely, limiting the range of legal norms—to whatever can be brought within the framework of a single, materially and formally unified scheme, and thereby pointing the way to a juridico-normative resolution of inter-systemic norm conflicts. In short, Kelsen defends monism.

Kelsen's argument on behalf of monism is a straightforward reflection of his neo-Kantian theory of knowledge. Just as the unity of cognition is presupposed in the sciences, so likewise,

[t]he postulate of the *unity* of cognition . . . applies without qualification in the normative field, and finds its expression here in the unity and exclusivity of the normative system . . . It must be emphasized again and again: The unity of the system is the fundamental axiom of all normative cognition.[137]

The argument against dualism and the argument for monism are pieces of a single puzzle. One will have the wherewithal to resolve, in legal terms, what were heretofore described as 'inter-systemic' norm conflicts only if normative cognition does indeed reach to the norms of both systems, and it will reach to them only if both 'systems' are properly understood as parts of a single, unified juridico-normative whole. To be sure, this is to say that the conflicts, properly understood, are '*intra-systemic*' norm conflicts. Whether the starting point is international

---

[134] See n.6 above.

[135] Kelsen had expressed concern on this issue earlier, albeit in a different context; see, in particular, Kelsen, 'Reichsgesetz und Landesgesetz' (n.7 above). There, addressing norm conflicts, he writes that if an individual, subject to the norms of a legal system, is not 'able to comply with each of them in turn without thereby violating some other norm of the same system', the legal system will not be 'reasonable'. Ibid. 207.

[136] See n.6 above.   [137] *PS* § 25 (p. 105), and § 27 (p. 111) (Kelsen's emphasis).

law—the first of the monistic options set out by Verdross—or whether the starting point is state law—the second option—makes no difference, Kelsen insists. The monistic construction can proceed in either direction, and each direction represents a distinct world view, 'subjectivistic' (primacy of state law) or 'objectivistic' (primacy of international law).[138] Since the choice between monistic starting points is made on extra-legal grounds, it will not affect the content of the positive law at all:

The choice of one or the other of the two constructions of the relation between international law and state law . . . has no influence on the content of international law. The content of state law, too, remains untouched by the construction of [this] relation . . .[139]

In his voluminous writings on public international law, Kelsen never takes his argument on behalf of monism significantly beyond the programmatic statement of *The Problem of Sovereignty*.[140] It is clear, however, that the task of adducing a fully adequate argument here is part and parcel of Kelsen's greater project in the classical phase, namely, the reconstruction of legal science from the standpoint of a neo-Kantian theory of knowledge.[141] Often regarded as extravagant and dispensable,[142] Kelsen's legal monism in fact brings us full circle, back to the issues surrounding the normativity problematic.

[138] See Kelsen, 'Sovereignty', in this volume, ch. 28, at § III. See also Kelsen, *Principles* (n.129 above), at 444–7, 2nd edn., at 585–8. In *PS*, to be sure, Kelsen makes a great deal more of the *political* consequences of the choice than he does elsewhere, arguing that 'the subjectivistic view of the *law* must lead in the end to a denial of the law generally and, therefore, to a denial of legal cognition and legal science, too.' Ibid. § 63 (p. 317) (Kelsen's emphasis).

[139] Kelsen, 'Sovereignty' (n.138 above), § III. See also Kelsen, *Principles* (n.129 above), at 445–6, 2nd edn., at 586–7.

[140] Compare Kelsen, *Principles* (n.129 above), at ch. V (399–447), 2nd edn., at ch. V (549–88).

[141] See Starke, 'Monism and Dualism' (n. 126 above).

[142] As Izhak Englard points out, many of those who dismiss Kelsen's monism out of hand confuse his distinctly normative point of view with a factual standpoint. If one proceeds from a factual standpoint, dualism (or, indeed, pluralism) is of course obvious. See Englard, *Religious Law in the Israel Legal System* (Jerusalem: Harry Sacher Institute for Legislative Research and Comparative Law, 1975), at 37–40.

PART I

Kelsen's Shift to the Classical Phase

1

'Foreword' to the Second Printing of
*Main Problems in the Theory of Public Law**

HANS KELSEN

Main Problems in the Theory of Public Law, originally published twelve years ago, was my first book in legal theory. It marked the earliest stages in a revision of the methodological foundations of the theory of public law, a revision I have pursued since then in other works. As my understanding has grown, I have had occasion to alter my earlier formulations, but the epistemic direction determined then has remained constant. The groundwork laid in *Main Problems* has stood the test of time, notwithstanding substantial changes on important individual issues. Because a reworking of the book, however, would indeed have resulted in a different book, I am submitting it unaltered for reprinting, but not without at least inviting attention, in these prefatory remarks, to the most important of the subsequent developments in my insight into the problems it addresses.

I.

In common with all of my later work, *Main Problems* has as its goal a *pure theory of law qua theory of positive law*. From the outset, in this first book, the purity of the theory or—amounting to the same thing—the independence of the law as an object of scientific cognition is what I am striving to secure, specifically in two directions. The purity of the theory is to be secured against the claims of a so-called '*sociological*' point of view, which employs causal, scientific methods to appropriate the law as a part

---

* *Editors' note*: Kelsen added this new 'Foreword' to the Second Printing (1923) of *Hauptprobleme der Staatsrechtslehre*, pp. v–xxiii. (For bibliographical data, see the Table of Abbreviations, at *HP*.) The 'Foreword' was translated by the editors, who wish to thank Stefan Hammer (Vienna) for helpful suggestions. Kelsen's profuse use of italics has generally been preserved, and, except where otherwise noted (in brackets), the footnotes are based on Kelsen's shorthand references in the text.

of natural reality. And it is to be secured against the *natural law theory*, which, by ignoring the fundamental referent found exclusively in the positive law, takes legal theory out of the realm of positive legal norms and into that of ethico-political postulates. Opposition to natural law is unequivocally expressed in *Main Problems*, which emphatically supports the view that legal science can construct legal norms (*Rechtssätze*)[1] only from the material of the positive law, in particular from statutes.[2] At the forefront of my enquiry, however, is the former tendency, that against a causal, scientific sociology. In general, it is taken for granted that legal theory can only be a theory of positive law, and the many dangers threatening legal science through the often unconscious insinuation of ethico-political points of view are simply mentioned in passing.[3] I did not give this latter element its due until my subsequent writings, for example, an article of 1913.[4] In *Main Problems*, what matters above all is securing the *autonomy of the law* as against nature or a social reality patterned after nature.

Main Problems takes as its point of departure the fundamental dichotomy between *Sollen* and *Sein*, *ought* and *is*, first discovered by Kant, so to speak, in his effort to establish the independence of theoretical reason as against practical reason, value as against reality, morality as against nature. Following Wilhelm Windelband's and Georg Simmel's interpretation of Kant, I take the 'ought' as the expression for the autonomy of the law—with the law to be determined by legal science—in contradistinction to a social 'is' that can be comprehended 'sociologically'. The *norm* qua *ought*-judgment, then, is contrasted with the law of nature, and the reconstructed legal norm (*Rechtssatz*),[5] understood as a norm qua *ought*-judgment, is contrasted with the law of causality that is

---

[1] [Kelsen is speaking here of the legal norms (*Rechtssätze*) that are, qua norms, the subject-matter of legal science; see text at n.5 below. Beginning in the 1940s, he introduces in the name of the '*Rechtssatz*' the legal statement or legal proposition, which he uses to 'describe' legal norms; thus, the subject-matter of legal science now becomes the propositional counterpart of the legal norm. See e.g. Hans Kelsen, 'The Pure Theory of Law and Analytical Jurisprudence', *Harvard Law Review*, 55 (1941–2), 44–70, at 51–3, repr. (with the omission of 45–9) in *WJ* 266–87, 390 (notes), at 268–70; see also *GTLS*, at 45–6, and *PTL*, at § 16 (pp. 71–5). (The English-language terminology for '*Rechtssatz*' employed by the translators of *GTLS* and *PTL*, namely 'rule of law', is misleading.)]

[2] See *HP*, at 510–14.   [3] See e.g. *HP*, at 367, 416.

[4] See Hans Kelsen, 'Zur Lehre vom öffentlichen Rechtsgeschäft', *AöR*, 31 (1913), 53–98, 109–249, at 247–9.

[5] ['Reconstructed legal norm' ('*Rechtssatz*') is Eugenio Bulygin's terminology for Kelsen's hypothetically formulated legal norm, a construction of legal science. See Bulygin, 'Zur Problem der Anwendbarkeit der Logik auf das Recht', in *Festschrift für Ulrich Klug zum 70. Geburtstag*, ed. Günter Kohlmann, 2 vols. (Cologne: Peter Deubner, 1983), vol. I, 19–31, at 20, also in Spanish under the title 'Sobre el problema de la aplicabilidad de la lógica al derecho', trans. Jerónimo Betegón, in Hans Kelsen and Ulrich Klug, *Normas jurídicas y análisis lógico* (Madrid: Centro de Estudios Constitucionales, 1988), 9–26, at 11. See also n.1 above, and *LT*, Appendix I, at Supplementary Note 5, pp. 132–4.]

specific to sociology. For me, therefore, the core problem becomes the *reconstructed legal norm*, understood as the expression of the specific lawfulness, the autonomy, of the law, as the legal counterpart to the law of nature (*Naturgesetz*)—the 'law of the law', so to speak, the *law of normativity* (*Rechtsgesetz*). And from this point of view, the law that is the subject-matter of legal science emerges as a system of reconstructed legal norms, that is to say, as a series of judgments. In the same way, nature—the subject-matter of natural science—represents for transcendental philosophy a system of judgments, but these judgments express the causal lawfulness specific to the context of nature, whereas it is the specific lawfulness, the autonomy, of the law that is manifest in the reconstructed legal norm. Just as in the judgment specific to the law of nature, so likewise in the reconstructed legal norm, a certain consequence is linked to a certain condition; in the latter case, however, a different linking principle replaces the causal nexus that links consequence to condition in the law of nature. The sense in which the reconstructed legal norm unites one material fact as condition with another as legal consequence is expressed in the 'ought'. If there is the necessity of an absolute 'must' when the law of nature links cause and effect, so there is the equally rigorous 'ought' when the law of normativity sets out the synthesis of conditioning and conditioned material facts. In the sphere of the law, which in a later essay I termed 'legal reality',[6] delict is linked to punishment with the same necessity as, in the sphere of nature or in 'natural reality', cause is linked to effect. And the judgment, 'If someone steals, he ought to be punished', has no less a claim to validity in the domain of a positive legal system than the principle, 'If a substance is heated, it expands', has in nature's domain.

This is the point—perhaps not yet recognized by me with complete clarity at the outset—of my concerted effort to formulate the reconstructed legal norm as a *hypothetical judgment*. This is why, from the very beginning, I emphatically reject the received opinion that the law is a collection of *imperatives*, which are in essence directed to addressees qua subjects and which therefore must be both received and recognized by these addressees. What is obviously of importance in *Main Problems* is securing the *objectivity of validity*, without which there can be no lawfulness whatever, let alone the specific lawfulness, the autonomy, of the law. But without the expression of that autonomy, without the law of normativity, there can be no legal knowledge, no legal science. Therefore: objective judgment, not subjective imperative.

---

[6] See Hans Kelsen, 'Zur Theorie der juristischen Fiktionen', *Annalen der Philosophie*, 1 (1919), 630–58, at 639, repr. *WS II* 1215–41, at 1223.

The law of normativity is—outwardly—like the law of nature, in that it is directed to no one and valid without regard to whether it is known or recognized.[7]

If the analogy between the law of normativity and the law of nature is still fairly limited here, this is in order to prevent the confusion of the two, indeed not to lose sight—because of the analogy—of the specific lawful-ness, the autonomy, of the law as against the causal lawfulness of nature. I am perfectly willing to grant that, in original usage, the concept of *Sollen*, of *ought*, which serves to express the objective lawfulness of the law, still carries with it some elements of the subjective imperative, and that the characterization set out in *Main Problems* sometimes lapses into this sphere of imperative theory. My concern here is to uncover the basic tendency that I continue to pursue in my later writings, a tendency man-ifestly aimed at securing in all directions the objectivity of the law, along with its positivity.

II.

This aim is manifest in particular in the treatment of the problem of the *subjective right*, that is, in the rejection of the subjective right as essen-tially different from objective law, outside, so to speak, the system of objectively valid reconstructed legal norms, indeed the opposite of this legal system qua objective law. While talk of 'deriving' the subjective right from objective law is still somewhat tentative in *Main Problems*, my effort there to trace the subjective right to objective law amounts to both giving up dualism, inadmissible within a unified system of cognition, and bringing legal theory back from a sphere of natural law to the sphere of positive law. Of greatest significance is the emphasis on the concept of *legal obligation*. For in destroying the familiar notion of the subjective right as existing exclusively in the entitlement, which is directed—qua claim—to the state or the objective legal system, legal theory not only frees itself from one of the most questionable instruments of natural law speculation, but, in eliminating the elements of will and interest reflected in the subjective right, it eliminates, too, a principal occasion for muddling the legal point of view with reasoning from psychology and sociology. Legal theory thereby frees itself from a questionable heritage, taken over from the theory of Roman advocacy jurisprudence, which considers the law only from the standpoint of the subjectively interested party, only from the perspective of whether and to what extent this law is 'my' law. From this standpoint of a subjective right, however, it is impos-

---

[7] *HP* 395. [In *HP*, but not in Kelsen's 'Foreword', 'outwardly' appears in italics.]

sible to construct a system or a science of law, for the law in its very essence is valid objectively, independently of the subject.[8]

Like the dualism of objective law and subjective right, so likewise the opposition between *public and private law* threatens to break apart the unified legal system propounded in *Main Problems*. This opposition, which dominates our whole juridico-scientific systematic, also stems from Roman law theory. And—again, just like the opposition between objective law and subjective right, to which it occasionally bears a 'family resemblance'—it is the mask worn by certain political or natural law elements as they creep into the characterization of the positive law. Thus, in *Main Problems*, I completely reject this distinction in so far as it is meant to express differences reaching to the *essence* of the law. I established this point in greater detail in an article of 1913.[9] Before that, however, in 1908, Franz Weyr had already laid the foundation in an article stating the basic idea.[10] And in a number of papers since then, he has contributed substantially to a pure theory of law.[11]

III.

In *Main Problems*, I introduced *imputation* as the specific lawfulness, the autonomy, of the law, corresponding to the causal lawfulness of nature. As I did then,[12] I must still characterize imputation as the connection that exists between the elements brought together within the reconstructed legal norm, the connection that is created grammatically by the 'ought'. The account I offered in *Main Problems* suffers, however, from the fact that I did not distinguish the case of linking two *material facts* within the reconstructed legal norm from another case, also characterized as imputation, that of linking a material fact to a *person*. It is precisely this latter reading of imputation that is of greatest significance for *Main Problems*. For it is as a problem of this reading of imputation that the question as to the essence of the state arises, in so far as the state is considered, as it usually is, to be a legal person, a subject of human will, or simply will *per se*—because, in the realm of legal thought, personality

---

[8] See 'RWR'.

[9] See Kelsen (n.4 above), at 53–98, 109–249.

[10] See Franz Weyr, 'Zum Problem eines einheitlichen Rechtssystems', *AöR*, 23 (1908), 529–80.

[11] See Franz Weyr, 'Über zwei Hauptpunkte der Kelsenschen Staatsrechtslehre', *Grünhuts Zeitschrift für das Privat- und öffentliche Recht der Gegenwart*, 40 (1914), 175–88, repr. *33 Beiträge*, 455–66; Weyr, 'Zum Unterschiede zwischen öffentlichem und privatem Recht', *ÖZöR*, 1 (1914), 439–41; Weyr, 'Zur Lehre von den konstitutiven und deklaratorischen Akten', *ÖZöR*, 3 (1918), 490–549, repr. *33 Beiträge*, 467–519; Weyr, 'Rechtsphilosophie und Rechtswissenschaft', *ZöR*, 2 (1921), 671–82, repr. *33 Beiträge*, 521–31.

[12] See *HP*, at 71.

exists only in the 'will', and legal person and legal will are identical. And in that the state is revealed as will, or the will of the state is revealed as a point of imputation, as the 'unity referent' of specifically legal cognition, then the *specifically legal 'will'*, altogether different from psychological will, is revealed for the other fields of law, too. It does not represent a real psychical material fact that is the *subject-matter* of causal, scientific cognition, as one is tempted by ambiguity to assume again and again; rather, it represents simply a *means* of juridico-normative cognition. In that the concept of legal will is only an expression for the legal *ought*—more accurately, for the unity of the legal *ought*—its sharp separation from the psychological concept of will becomes an especially efficacious means of securing the purity of legal theory against the inroads of psychology and sociology. Clearly separated from the *psychical act* of willing, in particular even from the willing of a norm, is the *ought* of the norm qua specific *meaning-content* (*Sinngehalt*).[13] Thus, already in *Main Problems*, the opposition between a pure theory of law and psychologico-sociological speculation runs parallel to the general opposition between logicism and psychologism, expressed in classical terms in Edmund Husserl's *Logical Investigations*.[14] This direction is pursued in later writings of mine,[15] and especially in the writings of Felix Kaufmann and Fritz Schreier, oriented as they are to Husserl's logic and phenomenology.[16]

IV.

In *Main Problems*, following a broadly disseminated idea, I characterize the law as the will of the state, and hence the reconstructed legal norm as a hypothetical judgment about the will of the state with regard to its own behaviour. This can only mean that the reconstructed legal norm, in the logical form of condition and consequence, links two material facts to one another, and to claim that the consequent material fact is willed by the state is simply to express an *imputation to the state qua unity of the aggregate of all reconstructed legal norms*; it is simply to express the reference to the unity of the legal system. The reconstructed legal norm

---

[13] See *HP*, at 9.

[14] Edmund Husserl, *Logische Untersuchungen*, in two parts (Halle: M. Niemeyer, 1900), 2nd edn. (1913, 1920). [*Logical Investigations*, 2 vols. (London: Routledge & Kegan Paul, 1970), is a translation, by J.N. Findlay, of the 2nd edition.]

[15] See especially my 'RWNKW', appearing in 1916.

[16] See Felix Kaufmann, *Logik und Rechtswissenschaft* (Tübingen: J.C.B. Mohr, 1922, repr. Aalen: Scientia, 1966); Fritz Schreier, 'Die Wiener rechtsphilosophische Schule', *Logos*, 11 (1923), 309–28, repr. *33 Beiträge*, 419–36; Schreier, *Grundbegriffe und Grundformen des Rechts* (Vienna: Franz Deuticke, 1924). See also the essay by Ernst Seidler, 'Die Theorie des Rechts und ihre Grenzen', *Philosophie und Recht*, 1 (1920–2), 50–5, 118–22.

means above all simply that a certain material fact is set, *on the basis of the law*, as *consequence* of a certain material fact as condition. To say that the state 'wills' the legal consequence means simply that this material fact is included in the unity of a system of reconstructed legal norms or legally qualified material facts. This is the actual sense of reducing the concepts 'state' or 'state will' to mean 'unity of the system', 'point of imputation', or 'point of reference'—a sense not given sufficiently clear and univocal expression in *Main Problems*. In the characterization of the state and the state will as points of imputation, what is expressly recognized is that a point of imputation is in essence simply a conceptual device. Nevertheless, it does sometimes appear—as in the received opinion—as if implicit in the assertion that the law is the will of the state there were some sort of conceptual determination of the law, as if 'being willed by the state' served as some sort of objective criterion of the law, an essential mark of the collective material fact, law. That is an impossible view, however, once the concepts of state and state will are resolved into mere means of legal cognition. If my statement in *Main Problems* contributes to this misunderstanding, it is because the relation of law and state finds no fully satisfactory resolution there, appropriate to the methodological presuppositions provided in *Main Problems* itself. I return to this theme below.[17]

The discrepancy arises from the fact that, in *Main Problems*, I am not yet in complete command of the consequences of the concept of state will that I set out there. This is especially evident in the distinction between the reconstructed legal norm in the narrower sense and the *reconstructed legal norm in the wider sense*. A conceptual analysis of the legal norm, highlighting the specific difference between it and the moral norm, seems to be impossible without the help of the element of coercion. The law is in essence a coercive norm, that is, a norm that regulates the application of coercion to human beings, thus, a norm qua coercive directive. In *Main Problems*, the reconstructed legal norm is formulated in such a way that the material fact specified in the 'then'-clause of the hypothetical judgment is a coercive act, namely punishment or the execution of judgments. Alongside this reconstructed legal norm in the narrower sense, one can distinguish a reconstructed legal norm in the wider sense, which in its 'then'-clause imputes to the state other material facts in addition to coercive acts, and represents them as 'willed' by the state. This is meant to express the undeniable fact that the state is able not only to punish and to execute judgments, but also to care for the poor, to operate the railroads, to deliver the mail, and so on. The case of the state coercive act appears simply as one special case of the great variety of possible state acts, and the

---

[17] [See, in particular, § VI.]

coercive act appears simply as one of many material facts that can be imputed to the state. However obvious it is that there may be state acts other than coercive acts, it is no less certain that they are imputed to the state in an altogether different sense than the coercive act is, which is always the conditioned material fact in the reconstructed legal norm formulated essentially as a coercive norm. This imputation to the state is simply the reference to the unity of all coercive norms. The legal act in this narrower sense refers to a concept of state that is altogether different from the concept of state underlying the reconstructed legal norm in the wider sense. The former concept of state is the formal concept of the essence of the law, which means nothing other than the unity of the comprehensive legal system as a system of norms qua coercive directives, and which constitutional theory has in mind in speaking of the state as the 'bearer' of the law. The latter concept of state, the concept underlying the reconstructed legal norm in the wider sense, is a material concept of the content of the law, thus, the state as a concrete legal institution, as an institute of the law existing alongside other institutes, a component legal system characterized and individualized by its specific content. The difference in question is illuminated most straightforwardly in that the conditioned material fact of the reconstructed legal norm in the narrower sense is specified as willed by the state and, qua state act, is specified solely as a coercive act, in so far as state system qua legal system is tantamount to a coercive system, and state acts are tantamount to a reaction of the law. State acts that appear in the 'then'-clause of the reconstructed legal norm in the wider sense are actions that must be taken by human beings who are legally qualified in a very precise way, and who for the sake of simplicity shall be designated here as 'officials'—this is an outline, however, of a highly complicated material fact of the positive law. The concept of the reconstructed legal norm in the wider sense, as employed in *Main Problems*, tacitly presupposes—without warrant—this material fact, this legal content, whereas it should presuppose nothing other than the concept of law *per se*. With this latter presupposition, however, one does not get beyond what is characterized as the reconstructed legal norm in the narrower sense. A further point: Whether and how legal norms establishing coercion-avoiding behaviour can be constituted—alongside reconstructed legal norms qua coercive directives—is something I have attempted to suggest in a theory of primary and secondary legal norms.[18] An intensive further development of the theory of the reconstructed legal norm—in part taking a direction different from the one I have taken—may be found in the works mentioned above of Felix Kaufmann and Fritz Schreier.[19]

[18] See *PS* § 29 (at p. 118).
[19] See n.16 above. See also Rudolf Löbl, 'Zum Problem der reinen Rechtslehre', *ZöR*, 3 (1922), 402–48.

V.

A *dynamic point of view*, emerging as a complement to the static legal cognition that, in *Main Problems*, is still held to be in principle the exclusive method, marks a significant change in the system of the Pure Theory of Law as against the original conception of the system in *Main Problems*. To be sure, the presuppositions arrived at in *Main Problems* already threaten to explode the notion of the legal system as a static system of general norms. In that the entirely state-like character of the law and the entirely law-like or legal character of the state is recognized,[20] and in that it is maintained that the same state will appears in the legal system qua aggregate of general legal norms and in the individual enforcement acts of the 'acting state',[21] then all state acts—not only the abstract norms, but also the concrete acts of so-called enforcement, acts of state administration and jurisdiction—must be understood as acts of state will and thus as acts of law, as legal acts, that is, as the content of reconstructed legal norms. In *Main Problems*, this last requirement is indeed expressly set,[22] but it appears to be regarded as already fulfilled in that the concrete enforcement acts of the state are determined in the general legal norms, thus, *in abstracto*. Nonetheless, I am thoroughly aware in *Main Problems* that the abstract legal norm is significantly different in content from the concrete state act enforcing it, that the latter contains not only the elements established in the abstract norm, but also many others, an abundance of contentual elements that the abstract norm does not determine and cannot completely determine, and that therefore cannot be *logically* deduced from the abstract norm—a position mistakenly attributed to me. The necessity, for the act of enforcement, of a legal determination by the general norm is tied to the unavoidability of discretion. The relation between the general legal norm and the individual act of enforcement is comparable to the relation between abstract concept and concrete representation.

An actual tree has innumerably more qualities than the concept of tree, but is, nevertheless, in its *totality*, with all its innumerable qualities, a tree precisely because of those few qualities that are essential to the concept. So likewise, the concrete act of the organ [what is meant is the state executory organ] is, in its individual variety and its special presuppositions, a state act, to be imputed to the state, even though the rule of imputation—the reconstructed legal norm expressing the will of the state with regard to the concrete act [what is meant is the general norm]—by no means exhibits all elements of the act that is to be imputed and its presuppositions, and even though imputation occurs only in so far as the elements expressed in the reconstructed legal norm are present in the

---

[20] See *HP*, at 253.   [21] See *HP*, at 513.   [22] See *HP*, at 511.

organ's act and its presuppositions. The will of the state is always more or less *abstract* in the legal system, while the acts of the state, by contrast, are always entirely *concrete*.[23]

Enforcement appears initially as the concretization of abstract norms, which alone are characterized as a legal system. The concrete enforcement acts of the state, however, must—according to the very premises set out in *Main Problems*—be legal acts, since it is the same state will that appears in them as in abstract norms. Just as the actual tree is a tree because of those few features that correspond to the abstract concept but, nevertheless, is in its totality, with all its features, a tree, so likewise the concrete act of the state must be law because of, but not only with regard to, its correspondence to general norms; it is, in its totality, law. The individual enforcement acts of the state must be understood as legal norms, and their content, in so far as it overlaps the content of the general norm, must be understood as the content of reconstructed legal norms if it is to be understood legally at all. Thus, the legal system must encompass not only general legal norms but also individual legal norms. The reason this obvious consequence of the presuppositions of *Main Problems* is not yet drawn there is, once again, that I still shrank from taking the last step in this direction, I still believed I must somehow differentiate between law and state.

If the general legal norm, like the individual state act, must be comprehended in terms of unity within the legal system, then this postulated unity between general and individual legal norm within the system cannot be established in such a way that one thinks—statically—that the individual norm is essentially contained, so to speak, in the general norm. For it is indeed presupposed that the content of the individual norm goes far beyond the content of the general norm. Here, clearly, a dynamic point of view must assert that the sought-after unity can only be the *unity of a rule of creation*; law creation itself, as a legally relevant material fact, must be understood as the content of a reconstructed legal norm. While it is occasionally said in *Main Problems* that general norms are 'actualized' in being carried out,[24] it is essentially the static point of view that prevails, thus precluding any appreciation of the *problem of law creation as a legal problem*. So too, in *Main Problems*, there is the doctrine of the metajuridical—because nonstate—character of legislation qua creation of general legal norms, a view supported in *Main Problems* by appeal to older theories, albeit theories reflecting certain political biases.

This notion of the metajuridical character of law creation is not entirely mistaken. The error in *Main Problems* is simply that the notion is

---

[23] *HP* 505–6 (Kelsen's emphasis, and his insertions in brackets).   [24] *HP* 511.

introduced too soon. If the law has even the possibility of regulating its own creation in terms of its own development, and even if one would like to see a characteristic feature of the law in this self-regulation of the process of law creation, it must nevertheless not be overlooked that the logically first legal norm cannot itself be beneath a higher legal rule that determines its creation. The *basic norm*, as the highest rule of law creation, establishing the unity of the entire system, is indeed on hand for the issuance of other legal norms, but it must itself be assumed to be *presupposed* as a legal norm and not *issued* in accordance with other legal norms. Its creation must therefore be seen as a material fact outside the legal system. In an article of 1913, referred to above,[25] it is evident that I was already aware of the necessity of a dynamic view of the law, aware of the legal problem of juxtaposing the becoming (creation) of the norm with the being (existence) of the norm. And in an article of 1914,[26] I clearly presented the concept of the *basic norm* qua presupposition establishing the unity of the legal [system][27]—albeit without the distinction, developed only later, between the basic norm qua constitution in the juridico-logical sense and the basic norm qua constitution in terms of the positive law. Alfred Verdross, in an article of 1916,[28] developed substantially further the idea of the basic norm qua constitution in the juridico-logical sense, seeing it—by analogy to the hypothesis in the natural sciences—as a hypothesis referring to the material of the positive law. On the question of characterizing the basic norm as the presupposition of legal cognition, Leonidas Pitamic made a valuable contribution in an article of 1918.[29] And it is Adolf Julius Merkl who deserves the credit for recognizing and then characterizing the legal system as a *genetic* system of legal norms that proceed from one level of concretization to another, from the constitution to the statute to the administrative regulation and to other intermediate levels, right down to the individual legal act of enforcement. In a number of writings,[30] Merkl energetically put

[25] At n.4.
[26] Hans Kelsen, 'Reichsgesetz und Landesgesetz nach österreichischer Verfassung', *AöR*, 32 (1914), 202–45, 390–438, at 215–20.
[27] [Reading 'system' for 'norm'.]
[28] Alfred Verdross, 'Zum Problem der Rechtsunterworfenheit des Gesetzgebers', *Juristische Blätter*, 45 (1916), 471–3, 483–6, repr. *WS II* 1545–57.
[29] Leonidas Pitamic, 'Denkökonomische Voraussetzungen der Rechtswissenschaft', *ÖZöR*, 3 (1918), 339–67, repr. *33 Beiträge*, 297–322. See also Pitamic, 'Eine juristische Grundlehre', *ÖZöR*, 3 (1918), at 734–57; Pitamic, 'Plato, Aristoteles und die reine Rechtslehre', *ZöR*, 2 (1921), 683–700, repr. *33 Beiträge*, 323–38; Pitamic, 'Kritische Bemerkungen zum Gesellschafts-, Staats- und Gottesbegriff bei Kelsen', *ZöR*, 3 (1923), 531–54, repr. *33 Beiträge*, 339–59.
[30] Adolf Julius Merkl, 'Das doppelte Rechtsantlitz', *Juristische Blätter*, 57 (1918), 425–7, 444–7, 463–5, repr. *WS I* 1091–113; Merkl, *Das Recht im Lichte seiner Anwendung* (Hanover: Helwing, 1917), repr. *WS I* 1167–201; Merkl, 'Die Rechtseinheit des österreichischen Staates', *AöR*, 37 (1918), 56–121, repr. *WS I* 1115–65; Merkl, 'Hans Kelsens System einer

forward this *theory of hierarchical levels of the law* qua theory of *legal dynamics*, combatting the prejudice—still firmly held in my *Main Problems*—that the law is found only in the general statute. Merkl also *relativized* what had ossified into the absolute: the opposition between statute and enforcement, between law creation and law application, between general and individual norm, between abstract and concrete norm. Drawing support from the work of Merkl and Verdross, I took up the theory of hierarchical levels in my own later writings, adopting it as an essential component in the system of the Pure Theory of Law.

VI.

The most important development in the Pure Theory of Law to date—with, to be sure, virtually all the presuppositions already arrived at in *Main Problems*—is cognition of the *unity of the state and the legal system*. As the relatively highest coercive system of human behaviour, the state is identical with the legal system; as the 'creator' or 'bearer' of the legal system, and also as the subject of obligations and of the system, subordinate to the legal system, the state is simply the personification, the expression for the unity of this system. In *Main Problems*, I emphatically reject a metajuridical concept of state, and stress the 'entirely law-like or legal character of the state'.[31] In particular, however, I rule out a basic notion that is a central pillar of the prevailing dualistic theory of law and state: the view that the state, as a fact historically preceding the law, creates the law.[32] In the context of public law theory, I do not recognize the state as a natural reality, part of the chain of cause and effect; I presuppose—though, once again, perhaps not yet with complete clarity—the methodological requirement that the state qua legal essence is to be constructed in terms of the law, that is to say, it is to be specified purely legally. In *Main Problems*, the state qua person is seen simply as the end point of a legal imputation, as a conceptual tool of specifically legal cognition. That the state is simply an expression for the unity of the legal system, simply the personification of that legal system, is declared again and again in *Main Problems* and in my immediately subsequent writings.[33] I lacked full insight, however, into the essence of the personification, and this

reinen Rechtstheorie', *AöR*, 41, N.F.2 (1921), 171–201, repr. *WS II* 1243–65; Merkl, *Die Lehre von der Rechtskraft* (Leipzig and Vienna: Franz Deuticke, 1923).

[31] *HP* 253.   [32] See *HP*, at 406.

[33] See Hans Kelsen, 'Über Staatsunrecht', *Grünhuts Zeitschrift für das Privat- und öffentliche Recht der Gegenwart*, 40 (1914), 1–114, repr. *WS I* 957–1057. [The paper also appeared, under the same title, as a self-contained work (Vienna: Alfred Hölder), dated 1913; Kelsen refers to the work, with this date, in the text at n.40 below.] See also Kelsen, at nn.4, 26 above.

kept me from realizing that the personified object and its personification are not two different objects of cognition, but *one* object and a means of cognition. Nevertheless, the correct result is already very close at hand in *Main Problems*:

The state-like character of the law and the law-like or legal character of the state do not differ materially in meaning; they are simply the two sides of a single coin whose core or content is formed by the substantial, not formal, identity of law and state.[34]

Clearly, the distinction here between form and content is simply the clumsy expression of a relation that is in essence correctly understood. Still, in *Main Problems*, my final characterization of this relation does not yet go beyond the formula: 'Law and state must certainly be seen as two sides of the same fact.'[35] Here, that which is in essence already comprehended as identical is claimed again as different, and the insight already won into the identity is nervously taken back. This, too, is based on the prejudice referred to above of a narrow concept of the legal system, an overly narrow concept restricted to general legal norms alone. The state cannot be identical with a legal system thus conceived, for it is precisely in individual legal acts that the state is most clearly manifest. In addition to all of this is the fact that the word 'state' has many meanings, usually in a narrower or a wider sense than the concept of legal system, and I could not yet decide on one of them in *Main Problems*—although the book does indeed aim principally at the state as conceived by general constitutional theory, that is, the state identical with the legal system.

It was by way of Hermann Cohen's interpretation of Kant, in particular Cohen's *Ethics of Pure Will*,[36] that I arrived at the definitive epistemological point of view from which alone the correct employment of the concepts of law and of state was possible. In 1912 in the *Kantstudien*,[37] a review of *Main Problems* appeared in which my book was recognized as an attempt to apply the transcendental method to legal science, and this brought to my attention the wide-ranging parallels that existed between my concept of legal will and Cohen's views, which at that time were not known to me. I came to appreciate as the consequence of Cohen's basic epistemological position—according to which the epistemic orientation determines its object, and the epistemic object is generated logically from an origin (*Ursprung*)—that the state, in so far as it is the object of legal cognition, can only be law, for to cognize something legally or to

---

[34] *HP* 253.   [35] *HP* 406.   [36] Cohen, *ErW*.
[37] Oscar Ewald, 'Die deutsche Philosophie im Jahre 1911', *Kantstudien*, 17 (1912), 382–433, at 397, and see generally at 396–8. [The English translation of Ewald's review, appearing in *The Philosophical Review*, 21 (1912), 499–526, with discussion of Kelsen's *Hauptprobleme* at 507–8, contains a number of errors and omissions, and has not been used here.]

understand something juridically means nothing other than to understand it as law. Hans Vaihinger's analysis of personifying fictions (his
'philosophy of the *as if*')[38] was also illuminating, inviting my attention to
analogous situations in other fields of scientific enquiry. My new perspective reached even to the analogy I occasionally drew in *Main
Problems*, that between the personification of the universe in *God* and
the personification of the law in the *state*.[39] And there is the parallel
between problems of *theology* and problems of *jurisprudence* (theodicy,
and unlawful acts committed by the state), which I had begun to investigate in a study of 1913.[40] This epistemological enrichment is reflected in
a study [on the Heidelberg neo-Kantians] that appeared in 1916,[41] in an
essay of 1919 on legal fictions,[42] and especially in my book, *The Problem
of Sovereignty and the Theory of International Law*, published in 1920.[43]

It is in this last work in particular that the problem of a *unified concept
of person* is resolved, a resolution that is of central importance for the
relation of law and state. In *Main Problems*, express emphasis is already
placed on the opposition between *person* and *human being*, and, at the
same time, on the fact that there can be no difference between the so-
called 'physical' person and the so-called legal person, that there can be,
from the legal point of view, only legal persons, and that in particular the
state qua legal person must be the same as all other legal persons. This
concept of person is only postulated in *Main Problems*, however, and not
fully realized. The difficulty found there is first resolved in *Problem of
Sovereignty*, and, following its resolution, the way is clear to the unity of
law and state. What is already plain in *Main Problems* is that the state qua
'bearer' of the legal system is simply the expression for the unity of the
legal system. But in that the state qua person—that is, qua subject of
rights and obligations—is subject to the legal system, it seems to be different from, and not amenable to identification with, the legal system.
This is all the more so since the state qua legal subject must be coordi-
nate with other persons, in particular with physical persons, while the
state qua legal system, in so far as it is the authority imposing obligations
on subjects, appears to be supraordinate to these subjects.[44] This 'supra-
ordination' of the legal system, however, in which the legally binding

---

[38] Hans Vaihinger, *Die Philosophie des Als-Ob* (Berlin: Reuther & Reichard, 1911), 2nd
edn. (1913), 5th and 6th edn. (1920). [*The Philosophy of 'As If'* (London: Kegan Paul,
Trench, Trubner & Co., 1924) is a translation, by C.K. Ogden, of the 5th and 6th edn.]
[39] [See *HP*, at 40–1, 246–9, 405–7, 433–4, 448, 526, and 684–7, where, to be sure, Kelsen
develops only the latter side of the analogy. His full development of the analogy comes
later; see Hans Kelsen, 'Staat und Recht im Lichte der Erkenntniskritik', *ZöR*, 2 (1921),
453–510, at 472–510, repr. *SJSB* §§ 33–45, at §§ 36–45 (pp. 205–53, at 219–53), and repr.
WS 1 95–148, at 112–48.]
[40] See Kelsen, at n.33 above.   [41] See 'RWNKW'.
[42] See Kelsen, at n.6 above.   [43] *PS*.   [44] See *HP*, at 648.

obligation is given expression, refers not to 'persons' but to human beings. In this sense, the legal system imposes obligations only on human beings. In this sense, only human beings 'have' rights or obligations, since it is precisely 'human' behaviour that is the content of legal norms. The 'person'—physical as well as legal—is nothing other than the personification of a complex of norms establishing human behaviour; specifically, the physical person is the personification of the legal norms imposing obligations on a particular human being. Thus, the person 'has' rights and obligations in an altogether different sense than does the human being. That the *human being* has legal obligations means that the behaviour of this human being is, in a specific way, the content of legal norms. That a *person* has obligations means that human behaviour established as a legal obligation is linked to the unity of a system of norms, is within the unity of a system alongside other reconstructed legal norms regulating human behaviour. There actually cannot be any talk at all of the legal system imposing obligations on persons, for persons are merely component legal systems, related to the comprehensive legal system not as subordinate to supraordinate, but as part to whole. The exception is the state qua person, which is simply the expression of the whole itself, and which, precisely because and in so far as it is a legal system, 'has' rights and obligations in the sense of 'containing' them. A replacement is needed for the dualism of a human being confronting— and thus outside, so to speak—the legal system, who is to be understood legally but, precisely because outside the legal system, cannot be understood legally. This dualism is replaced by human acts and forbearances *as the content of legal norms*; and these legal norms, combined and personalized according to various points of view, yield the legal person. Thus it is apparent that only with the attainment of the unified concept of person—the personification of norms—is it possible to understand the identity of the state and the legal system, even the state as legal subject, that is, as having rights and obligations.

From now on, too, the so-called *self-obligating theory of the state*[45] is completely unmasked and shown for what it really is: the pseudo-solution to a pseudo-problem. Already rejected in *Main Problems*,[46] this theory aims to explain the existence of legal obligations of the state by having the state first set up a legal system and then subject itself to this very legal system. As I argue in *Main Problems*, the setting up of a legal system by the state, qua creation of the law by the state, is conceptually wrongheaded and therefore impossible. If one recognizes the legal

---

[45] See Georg Jellinek, *Die rechtliche Natur der Staatenverträge* (Vienna: Alfred Hölder, 1880), 6–45; Jellinek, *Allgemeine Staatslehre*, 3rd edn. (Berlin: O. Häring, 1914 [many reprints]), 367–75.
[46] See *HP*, at 317–20, 354, 397, 400–6, 430–5, 447–50.

person as the personification of a complex of norms and thereby comes to understand the sense in which a person can 'have' obligations, then one sees the self-obligating theory—which has a metajuridical state imposing obligations on itself as on a human being—as an unwarranted hypostatization of a personification, one of those misleading 'doublings' [of the object of cognition] that Vaihinger's theory of fictions has so effectively exposed.[47]

Only from the epistemological position leading to insight into the unity of law and state[48] does one also manage to surmount Georg Jellinek's so-called 'two-sides theory', according to which the state is not only a socio-natural reality existing in the causally determined world of being, but also a legal entity, a legal person.[49] It is, therefore, the object of two methodologically disparate points of view: a causal, scientific theory of society, and a normative theory of law. The 'entirely law-like or legal character of the state', already set out in *Main Problems*, first acquires its logical foundation in the principle that one and the same epistemic object cannot be determined by way of two epistemic orientations that are, according to their respective presuppositions, fully distinct from each other—as the causal *Sein*/*is*-view and the normative *Sollen*/*ought*-view are. Cohen's claim that a theory of state can only be a theory of state law[50] must prove itself in entirely positivistic terms, not in the ethical terms of natural law that Cohen himself had in mind. In *Main Problems* and in a shorter work also appearing in 1911,[51] I raise questions about a concept of the state qua causally, scientifically determined reality. I rule out from the beginning the possibility that the state in normative legal theory—a state that has its specific existence in the realm of the legal *ought*—could at the same time be the state in a causally, scientifically oriented sociology, whose subject-matter is found only in natural reality. There are in *Main Problems* itself occasional lapses into an entirely similar 'two-sides theory', when law and state are claimed as two sides of one and the same thing (which thing?), or when the law is characterized as the normal *ought*-form of a phenomenon whose contents are the naturally real, causally determined *is*-processes of social life.[52] This view is altogether indefensible, alone on the ground that it cannot be reconciled with the presupposed opposition between *is* and *ought*. And I had already abandoned it in my essay of 1916.[53] Having completely separated

[47] See *PS* § 4 (at p. 18), and at § 44 (pp. 190–6).
[48] [See text at beginning of § VI above.]
[49] See Jellinek, *Allgemeine Staatslehre* (n.45 above), at 9–12, 136–9, 174–83. [For Kelsen's unusually vigorous criticism of the 'two-sides theory', see *SJSB*, at § 20 (pp. 114–20).]
[50] See Cohen, *ErW*, at 63 *et passim*.
[51] See *HP*, at 162–88; see also Hans Kelsen, *Über Grenzen zwischen juristischer und soziologischer Methode* (Tübingen: J.C.B. Mohr, 1911), 24–30 *et passim*.
[52] See *HP*, at 42, 92.
[53] See 'RWNKW'.

normative cognition from causal cognition, I proceed in later works—on sovereignty and international law,[54] and in particular in a 1922 work dedicated to the relation of law and state, *The Sociological and Legal Concepts of State*[55]—to provide the solution to the problem I had posed in *Main Problems* in 1911, a solution reached by proving that the concept of state is not possible except as a concept of law, and that even sociology has in principle only this concept of law in mind.

In the traditional theory of state (or constitutional theory), the human being *en masse*, qua 'state's people', is, alongside the state's territory and the state's power, a so-called *element of the state*. But the Pure Theory of Law—which is at the same time the pure theory of state—cannot take the 'human being' into consideration as the human being of biologico-psychological cognition, as an object confronting the legal system, standing outside the system of law and therefore within a system alien to the law. Rather, this 'human being' must be replaced by human behaviour as the *content of legal norms*. Similarly, another element of the state—its territory—must be transposed into the sphere of the law from its position as a natural, geographic reality, its usual position in the theory of state. It must be reduced to a common denominator, so to speak, with the state's people. It must be understood as the *spatial sphere of validity* of the legal norms forming the state system. It is obvious that the state's 'power', considered from this unified point of view, can only be the binding validity of the legal system, or this legal system itself, or a particular content of this legal system, say, the coercive acts the system establishes—but that it cannot be any kind of natural reality.[56] In a recent work, Walter Henrich made a valuable contribution to the reform of the doctrine of the elements of the state.[57]

That the state, as a normative legal system, as an *ideal system* of valid norms, is assigned its position in the realm of the ideal should in no way obscure the problem that arises from the fact that there is something in the system of cause and effect, in the system of nature, that somehow corresponds to this ideal validity. However different the legal norm qua specific meaning-content is from the psychical act that 'carries' the norm, so to speak, the fact nevertheless remains that only efficacious norms, that is, norms sustained by motivating ideas or desires, are presupposed as valid. Here lie the roots of the ancient question as to the relation of law and power, which inherently exclude one another and are

---

[54] *PS.*   [55] *SJSB.*

[56] See *PS* § 18 (at pp. 72–6), and *SJSB* §§ 14–15 (at pp. 84–8).

[57] See Walter Henrich, *Theorie des Staatsgebietes entwickelt aus der Lehre von den lokalen Kompetenzen der Staatsperson* (Vienna: Hölder-Pichler-Tempsky, 1922); see also Henrich's paper, 'Das Sollen als Grundlage der Rechtswissenschaft. Eine Auseinandersetzung mit Gegnern der normativen Jurisprudenz', *ZöR*, 2 (1920–1), 131–75, repr. *33 Beiträge*, 75–112.

nevertheless somehow linked. And here, too, the difficult *problem of the positivity of law* reaches its zenith. My monograph on the sociological and legal concepts of state, to which I referred above,[58] represents an effort toward a solution—in so far as there is any prospect at all of a solution to such a problem.

The ultimate insight into the relation of law and state—this core problem of our science, whether of the theory of law or the theory of state—could be achieved only by means of an epistemic critique. In a number of writings, Fritz Sander made a notable contribution in precisely this direction.[59] His discovery, in particular, of the analogy between the *concept of substance* in natural science and the *concept of state*, as well as his attempt to explore in general the parallels between law and natural science, have been enlightening. In acknowledging this, I am inhibited by neither the material opposition nor the personal animosity that Sander arrayed against me in his later writings, where he parts ways with the Pure Theory of Law.[60]

VII.

The investigations of *Main Problems* refer only to the single-state legal system, omitting from consideration the *relation of individual states to each other as well as to the international legal system*. In my paper on unlawful acts of the state,[61] my account of this relation is not yet in any way distinct from the conventional view that international law and the single-state legal system are two different systems, with no unifying relation between them. In the subsequent essay, on the relation between a federation and its member states, I do investigate in a fundamental way the problem of the relation between two complexes of legal norms, arriving by way of juridico-logical reflection at the dictates of their unity,

---

[58] At n.55.

[59] See Fritz Sander, 'Rechtswissenschaft und Materialismus', *Juristische Blätter*, 47 (1918), at 333–5, 350–2, repr. *RNK* 27–39; Sander, 'Das Faktum der Revolution und die Kontinuität der Rechtsordnung', *ZöR*, 1 (1919–20), 132–64, repr. *RNK* 41–73; Sander, 'Die transzendentale Methode der Rechtsphilosophie und der Begriff des Rechtsverfahrens', *ZöR*, 1 (1919–20), 468–507, repr. *RNK* 75–114; Sander, 'Alte und neue Staatsrechtslehre', *ZöR*, 2 (1921), 176–230.

[60] See Fritz Sander, 'Rechtsdogmatik oder Theorie der Rechtserfahrung', *ZöR*, 2 (1921), at 511–670, repr. *RNK* 115–278; and see my 'RWR' for reply. See also Sander, *Staat und Recht. Prolegomena zu einer Theorie der Rechtserfahrung*, 2 vols. (Leipzig and Vienna: Franz Deuticke, 1922, repr. Aalen: Scientia, 1969), vol. I; Sander, *Kelsens Rechtslehre* (Vienna: Franz Deuticke, 1923). Replies to Sander include Felix Kaufmann, 'Theorie der Rechtserfahrung oder reine Rechtslehre', *ZöR*, 3 (1922), 236–63, repr. *RNK* 425–52; Emanuel Winternitz, 'Zum Streit um Kelsens Rechtslehre', *Juristische Blätter*, 52 (1923), 120–2; Winternitz, 'Zum Gegenstandsproblem der Rechtstheorie', *ZöR*, 3 (1922), 684–98.

[61] See Kelsen, at n.33 above.

namely, that unity is established when one complex of norms is supra-ordinate (or subordinate) to the other.[62] A practical application is provided, however, only for the relation of federal and member-state law, in other words, only within the single-state (federal) legal system. It was Alfred Verdross who set out for the first time the problem of the relation between state law and international law from the standpoint of the Pure Theory of Law. In an essay of 1914,[63] Verdross distinguishes two possibilities: either to conceive of international law from the standpoint of the single-state legal system, as a component of that system, or—the reverse—to subordinate the single-state legal systems under (or to incorporate them into) international law. While Verdross, in this essay, does not yet rule out the dualistic construction whereby international law and the single-state legal systems are juxtaposed but unrelated, he expressly sets out, in his monograph of 1920, the requirement 'that international law and state law must be contained in a unified legal system.'[64] Supported by Verdross's investigations, I then developed these ideas further in my book on sovereignty and international law[65]—specifically, the notion that international law, in order to be *law*, can only be conceived of within a common system with the single-state legal systems, and, furthermore, the notion that the unity of the collective system comprehending both international law and the single-state legal systems is the necessary consequence of the unity of the juridico-cognitive point of view, and, finally, the notion of the consequences for the *concept of sovereignty*. I assume the theoretical legitimacy of both the primacy of the international legal system and the primacy of the single-state legal system, as two equally possible but mutually exclusive legal hypotheses for establishing, in accordance with cognition, the unity of the collective legal system. Verdross, for his part, would derive the unity of the law exclusively from international law.[66]

---

[62] See Kelsen (n.26 above), at 206–8, 213–16.

[63] Alfred Verdross, 'Zur Konstruktion des Völkerrechtes', *Zeitschrift für Völkerrecht*, 8 (1914), 329–59, repr. *WS II* 1995–2022.

[64] Alfred Verdross, *Die völkerrechtswidrige Kriegshandlung und der Strafanspruch der Staaten* (Berlin: H.R. Engelmann, 1920), 41, repr. (in part) *WS II* 2063–72, at 2069. [In the monograph by Verdross, but not in Kelsen's 'Foreword', 'unified legal system' appears in italics.]

[65] *PS.*

[66] See Alfred Verdross, 'Grundlagen und Grundlegungen des Völkerrechts. Ein Beitrag zu den Hypothesen des Völkerrechtspositivismus', *Niemeyers Zeitschrift für Internationales Recht*, 29 (1921), 65–91; Verdross, *Die Einheit des rechtlichen Weltbildes auf Grundlage der Völkerrechtsverfassung* (Tübingen: J.C.B. Mohr, 1923). See also Josef L. Kunz, *Völkerrechtswissenschaft und reine Völkerrechtslehre* (Leipzig and Vienna: Franz Deuticke, 1922).

* * *

The Pure Theory of Law, whose foundation was laid in part in *Main Problems*, is the concerted work of a continually growing circle of theoretically like-minded men. Today, interest in the Pure Theory goes well beyond the boundaries of German scientific enquiry. Perhaps I may therefore entertain the hope that even our opponents will appreciate our effort to go deeper philosophically into the problems of legal and constitutional theory and to connect them with analogous problems in other scientific fields, to free our own science thereby from its unhealthy isolation and to establish it as a member in good standing of the greater system of scientific enquiry.

Vienna, September 1923.　　　　　　　　　　　　　　　Hans Kelsen

2

Hans Kelsen's Earliest Legal Theory: Critical Constructivism*

STANLEY L. PAULSON

INTRODUCTION

Legal positivism in the juridico-scientific tradition of the European Continent is characterized by what might be called the facticity thesis: The constructions of the law are ultimately 'reducible to', or explicable in terms of, a concatenation of fact—for example, the will of the sovereign.[1] Shifting the idiom to a semantic counterpart of the facticity thesis, the legal theorist of a reductive persuasion 'provide[s] eliminative definitions of normative terms',[2] introducing instead non-normative, descriptive terms, in what Joseph Raz has called the reductive semantic thesis.[3] Kelsen's conviction that the facticity thesis is wrongheaded drives his theory, particularly in the very early work. In place of the legal positivist's

* *Editors' note*: This paper first appeared in the *Modern Law Review*, 59 (1996), 797–812; the present version contains minor changes. The author would like to thank Okko Behrends, Malte Dießelhorst, Ralf Dreier, and Cosima Möller (Göttingen), Bonnie Litschewski Paulson (St. Louis), and Stefan Hammer and Alexander Somek (Vienna) for very helpful criticism. Much earlier, the author turned to the nineteenth-century background of Kelsen's theory for a presentation at the first Siena Kelsen Symposium; he remains grateful to Letizia Gianformaggio (Ferrara) for the Symposium and, indeed, for four more that followed.

[1] By legal positivism, thus characterized, I have in mind an ideal type, not a particular historical view. And it is this ideal type that Kelsen uses as a part of his strategy in forging a 'middle way' between legal positivism and natural law theory; see Stanley L. Paulson, 'The Neo-Kantian Dimension in Kelsen's Pure Theory of Law', *Oxford Journal of Legal Studies*, 12 (1992), 311–32, at 313–22. On the 'middle way' generally, see Joseph Raz, 'The Purity of the Pure Theory', in this volume, ch. 12; Deryck Beyleveld and Roger Brownsword, 'Normative Positivism: The Mirage of the Middle-Way', *Oxford Journal of Legal Studies*, 9 (1989), 463–512.

[2] Raz, 'Purity' (n.1 above), § I.

[3] Ibid. § II. I do not mean to suggest that the differences between the facticity thesis and the reductive semantic thesis amount to a mere shift in idiom. For example, H.L.A. Hart's theory reflects the facticity thesis but not the reductive semantic thesis; see generally Stanley L. Paulson, 'Continental Normativism and its British Counterpart: How Different are they?', *Ratio Juris*, 6 (1993), 227–44, at 236–41. Both theses apply, however, to the many theorists relegated by Kelsen to the legal positivist camp.

facticity thesis, Kelsen introduces a normativity thesis, which calls for an explication of the law—and of legal obligation in particular—altogether independently of fact. Shifting the idiom to a semantic counterpart of the normativity thesis, the legal theorist of a non-reductive persuasion argues that juridico-normative terms cannot be eliminated in favour of non-normative, descriptive terms, or explicated by means of them. Kelsen's endorsement of the normativity thesis represents, *inter alia*, his rejection of every fact-based legal theory. At its core, Kelsen's legal theory does not consort with facts at all.

These developments—Kelsen's early case against the facticity thesis and his introduction of the normativity thesis— are a part of his earliest phase, critical constructivism,[4] which has received almost no attention at all in the post-War English-language literature on Kelsen.[5] The early post-War reception focused, understandably enough, on the *General Theory of Law and State*, which appeared in 1945, while a good part of the recent reception has focused on Kelsen's late, sceptical phase.[6] In other languages, too, there is little recent work on Kelsen's earliest, constructivist phase.[7]

The neglect of Kelsen's critical constructivism is regrettable. His efforts at the beginning of his middle, classical phase and, in particular, the factors that led him to adumbrate a neo-Kantian argument on behalf of the normativity thesis are hard to appreciate without some general sense of their roots in his early, constructivist phase.

Three doctrines are fundamental to this early phase. First, there is *constructivism* itself, the aspect of the 'juridico-scientific' tradition—specifically, Pandectism in nineteenth-century German legal science—that survives in Kelsen's own work. Also fundamental, representing the philosophical dimension of Kelsen's theory, is *methodological dualism*, a hard and fast 'is'/'ought' or *Sein/Sollen* distinction as defended by the

---

[4] For a brief sketch of the phases of development in Kelsen's legal theory, see my 'Introduction' to this volume, at § I.

[5] For an overview, see my 'Short Annotated Bibliography of Secondary Literature in English', in *LT*, at Appendix III (145–53).

[6] See *Essays* and *GTN*. On the *Essays*, see e.g. Joseph Raz, 'Critical Study: Kelsen's General Theory of Norms', *Philosophia*, 6 (1976), 495–504; Bernard S. Jackson, 'Kelsen between Formalism and Realism', *Liverpool Law Review*, 8 (1985), 79–93. On *GTN*, see e.g. Deryck Beyleveld, 'From the "Middle-Way" to Normative Irrationalism: Hans Kelsen's *General Theory of Norms*', *Modern Law Review*, 56 (1993), 104–19. A recent examination and reconstruction of legal validity in Kelsen's late, sceptical phase is Dick W.P. Ruiter, 'Legal Validity qua Specific Mode of Existence', *Law and Philosophy*, 16 (1997), 479–505.

[7] Welcome exceptions to the rule stem from Italy; see Agostino Carrino, *Kelsen e il problema della scienza giuridica* (Naples: Edizioni Scientifiche Italiane, 1987); Giuliana Stella, *Stato e scienza. I fondamenti epistemologici della dottrina pura del diritto* (Naples: Edizioni Scientifiche Italiane, 1997); Mirella Urso, 'Hans Kelsen: Coerenza dell'ordinamento e teoria della scienza giuridica', in *Studi in memoria di Giovanni Tarello* [no editor], 2 vols. (Milan: A. Giuffrè Editore, 1990), vol. II, 579–615, at 583–91.

Heidelberg neo-Kantians and developed in a more expansive way by Kelsen. Finally, there is *central imputation*, which Kelsen introduces as an alternative to the traditional concept of the legal person. If Kelsen's adoption of methodological dualism shows his theory, in its initial form, to be a radical departure from will theories of law, it is central imputation that shows both how Kelsen implements this radical change and what kinds of difficulties he faces in doing so.

Among these difficulties two are of special interest. I examine the first of them under the rubric of *avoiding fictions*. As part of his juridico-normative theory, Kelsen develops various legal constructions aimed, *inter alia*, at avoiding fictions, but he provides, in this earliest work, no foundation for the normativity thesis and therefore no defence of the claimed normative status of his legal constructions either. On the contrary, their normative status is simply assumed. Later, in work that marks the beginnings of his long, classical phase, Kelsen returns to this problem, and his effort to defend the normativity thesis is reflected, above all, in the Kantian or neo-Kantian argument that he hints at in the name of the basic norm.

The second of the difficulties arising in Kelsen's earliest theory falls under the rubric of *avoiding anthropomorphization*. Kelsen avoids anthropomorphization, he contends, by means of a rigorous and pervasive application of his expansive *Sein/Sollen* distinction, drawn from methodological dualism. This, however, proves to be too much of a good thing, for, as he himself argues, the *Sein/Sollen* distinction commits him to a denial of the very possibility of any theoretical connection between facticity and normativity, between human being and 'imputative' legal relation. The ensuing 'antinomy', as Kelsen terms it, is the price to be paid for a 'pure' theory of law.

I begin by introducing, in section I, constructivism and, in section II, methodological dualism. I then turn, in section III, to Kelsen's notion of central imputation and to its counterpart in nineteenth-century German legal science, the fictitious legal person; in comparing these doctrines, I take up aspects of the nineteenth-century debate on the legal person and Kelsen's reasons for replacing the doctrine of the tradition with his own new doctrine, central imputation. All of this sets the stage for a closer look at the two difficulties to which I allude above, difficulties generated by Kelsen's need to avoid fictions on the one hand and anthropomorphization on the other. These difficulties are the topics of sections IV and V respectively, and, in section VI, I try to put them into perspective, examining their disposition in the early years of Kelsen's middle, classical phase.

I. CONSTRUCTIVISM IN GERMAN LEGAL SCIENCE

In German legal science, 'construction' stands for concept formation. Kelsen's work in *Main Problems in the Theory of Public Law* (1911) as well as in other early writings is a case in point.[8] He speaks of the subject of criminal liability as 'clearly [a] construction from a specifically *normative* point of view',[9] and in the course of his important discussion of central imputation, he suggests that the 'end point' or ultimate reference point of imputation 'serves as a construction'.[10] In the same vein, he notes that 'a "constructed" concept' in which a normative point of view supplants the wrongheaded 'psychical' notion of will is a conceptual tool, not a fiction.[11]

The mechanics of Kelsen's constructivism bear witness not only to the work of Carl Friedrich von Gerber, Paul Laband, and Georg Jellinek, his nineteenth-century predecessors in the *Staatsrechtslehre* or theory of public law in Germany, but also to their ancestry in earlier nineteenth-century Pandectism, whose method Gerber transferred over to public law. Though Gerber was not a Romanist, his treatise on German private law reflected the method of Pandectism.[12] Then, with the publication of a short monograph in 1852, he shifted his attention—and his conceptual scheme—to public law. What is it, specifically, that public law takes over from private law? It is, Gerber answers, 'something wholly *formal*, the legal construction'.[13]

In the private law, it was Rudolf von Jhering who provided in his earlier period the most trenchant statement of legal constructivism. The

---

[8] (For bibliographical data on *Main Problems*, see the Table of Abbreviations, at *HP*.) On construction, see *HP*, at 142, 145, 181–4, 226, 237, 249, 253, 335, 341, 343, 497–8; although these are especially instructive passages, *Main Problems* is in fact chock full of constructions and allusions to the idea of construction. On concept formation, see also Hans Kelsen, *Über Grenzen zwischen juristischer und soziologischer Methode* (Tübingen: J.C.B. Mohr, 1911), at 5, repr. *WS I* 3–36, at 5 (English equivalent of Kelsen's title: 'On the Boundaries between Legal and Sociological Method'); *SJSB* § 20 (at p. 114).

[9] *HP* 142 (Kelsen's emphasis).　　　　　　　　[10] *HP* 145.　　　　　　[11] *HP* 181.

[12] See Carl Friedrich von Gerber, *System des Deutschen Privatrechts*, 2nd edn. (Jena: F. Mauke, 1850). 'In the eyes of his more dogmatic fellow *Germanisten*', Gerber had become 'a "romanizing *Germanist*"', Peter von Oertzen, *Die soziale Funktion des staatsrechtlichen Positivismus* (Frankfurt: Suhrkamp, 1974), 217, drawing on Roderich von Stintzing and Ernst Landsberg, *Geschichte der Deutschen Rechtswissenschaft*, 3 vols., vol. III in 2 pts. (Munich and Berlin: Oldenbourg, 1880–1910, repr. Aalen: Scientia, 1957), vol. III.2 (1910), p. 781.

[13] Carl Friedrich von Gerber, *Ueber öffentliche Rechte* (Tübingen: Laupp & Siebeck, 1852), 36 (Gerber's emphasis), see also at 28. On Gerber generally, see Mario G. Losano, *Studien zu Jhering und Gerber*, 2 vols. (Ebelsbach: Rolf Gremer, 1984), vol. II, at 90–113, 130–49; Michael Stolleis, *Geschichte des öffentlichen Rechts in Deutschland*, 3 vols. projected (Munich: C.H. Beck, 1988–), vol. II (1992), at 330–8; Walter Pauly, *Der Methodenwandel im deutschen Spätkonstitutionalismus* (Tübingen: J.C.B. Mohr, 1993), at 92–167.

law appears in two different forms, namely, 'as the legal *institute*, the legal *concept*, and as legal *norms*, legal *principles*'.[14] The latter is 'the *imperatival*, the *directly practical* form of the command or prohibition';[15] it provides the raw material of the law.[16] This material is then re-formed, that is to say, *constructed* as the elements and qualities of legal institutes, which are not mere collections of individual legal norms but are, rather, 'juridical bodies' with their own distinct properties.[17] For this ambitious constructivist programme, Jhering goes so far as to set out 'laws of construction'.[18]

Gerber writes that the 'dissection and analysis' familiar from private law, which reveal its 'simplicity and pristine purity', are needed in public law, too.[19] And his transfer of the conceptual apparatus of Pandectism to public law marks the beginnings of what came to be seen, in German public law theory, as a new school, associated most closely with Gerber, Laband, and Jellinek.

II. METHODOLOGICAL DUALISM: THE SOUTH-WEST OR HEIDELBERG NEO-KANTIANS AND KELSEN

Kelsen is properly considered, for some purposes, the fourth and last major figure in the Gerber-Laband-Jellinek School.[20] He sees in their

[14] Rudolf von Jhering, *Geist des römischen Rechts*, 4th edn., 3 vols., vol. II in 2 pts. (Leipzig: Breitkopf & Härtel, 1878–88, repr. Aalen: Scientia, 1993), vol. II.2, § 41 (at p. 359) (Jhering's emphasis). On von Jhering's constructivism, see e.g. Walter Wilhelm, *Zur juristischen Methodenlehre im 19. Jahrhundert* (Frankfurt: Klostermann, 1958), at 88–128 *et passim*; Maximilian Herberger, *Dogmatik* (Frankfurt: Klostermann, 1981), at 403–10; Alexander Somek, *Rechtssystem und Republik* (Vienna: Springer, 1992), at 112, 128–48, *et passim*; Annette Brockmöller, *Die Entstehung der Rechtstheorie im 19. Jahrhundert in Deutschland* (Baden-Baden: Nomos, 1997), at 191–215. On von Jhering generally, see Okko Behrends, 'Rudolf von Jhering (1818–1892). Der Durchbruch zum Zweck des Rechts', in *Rechtswissenschaft in Göttingen*, ed. Fritz Loos (Göttingen: Vandenhoeck & Ruprecht, 1987), 229–69; Athanasios Gromitsaris, *Theorie der Rechtsnormen bei Rudolph von Ihering* (Berlin: Duncker & Humblot, 1989).

[15] Jhering, *Geist*, 4th edn. (n.14 above), vol. II.2, § 41 (at p. 358) (Jhering's emphasis).

[16] See ibid., at 358–60.   [17] Ibid. 360, and see at 362–9.

[18] See ibid., at 370–82. In his later period, Jhering dismantles his constructivist programme and takes to twitting his former allies, the constructivists. See Jhering, 'Über die civilistische Konstruktion', *Preußische Gerichts-Zeitung*, III, no. 41 (26 June 1861), repr. in Jhering, *Scherz und Ernst in der Jurisprudenz* (Leipzig: Breitkopf & Härtel, 1891, repr. Darmstadt: Wissenschaftliche Buchgesellschaft, 1980), 3–17, at 6, trans. in *LT*, Appendix I, at Supplementary Note 7 (pp. 136–7).

[19] Gerber (n.13 above), 36, see also at 28.

[20] For other purposes, it is of course necessary to distinguish Kelsen sharply from his predecessors in the Gerber-Laband-Jellinek School—for example, with respect to the Austrian provenance of Kelsen's work. On this topic, see generally Günther Winkler, *Rechtstheorie und Erkenntnislehre* (Vienna: Springer, 1990), at 30–69 *et passim*; Peter Goller, *Naturrecht, Rechtsphilosophie oder Rechtstheorie? Zur Geschichte der Rechtsphilosophie an Österreichs Universitäten (1848–1945)* (Frankfurt: Peter Lang, 1997), at 146–355.

theories, however, elements of naturalism and psychologism, despite their best efforts to 'purify' legal science, and he carries the constructivist programme a great deal further than his predecessors had. This effort of Kelsen's, in its scope and its appeal to Kantian and neo-Kantian sources, is marked by the phrase 'critical constructivism' in my title.

The notion of 'purity', ultimately traceable to Kant's characterization of knowledge that is free of any 'empirical admixture',[21] meant freedom from an illegitimate combining or fusion of different methods of cognition. The effort to avoid this 'vice' is familiar, above all, from Jellinek, who writes:

If one has comprehended the general difference between the jurist's conceptual sphere and the objective sphere of natural processes and events, one will appreciate the inadmissibility of transferring the cognitive method of the latter over to the former. Among the vices of the scientific enterprise of our day is the vice of methodological syncretism.[22]

The same language reappears in Kelsen,[23] but with a difference. Gerber, Jellinek, and others, concerned with promoting the purity of method, are at the same time perfectly content with the idea that the same object may well be the focus or subject-matter of different methods.[24] Indeed, this becomes a central tenet in Jellinek's 'two-sides' theory of law, whereby one side is examined juridically or legally, the other sociologically.[25] Kelsen, like his predecessors, is committed to the purity of method but, unlike them, he has no truck with the idea that one and the same object might be the focus or subject-matter of different methods. And his critique of Jellinek's 'two-sides' theory of law is scathing. A substratum holding the two sides together, Kelsen argues, is required by Jellinek's theory, but no explication of the notion is possible within the confines of the theory.[26]

Kelsen draws support for his position from his unwavering commitment to an expansive interpretation of methodological dualism, which is defended, most prominently, by the philosophers Wilhelm

---

[21] See Kant, *CPR*, at B3.

[22] Georg Jellinek, *System der subjektiven öffentlichen Rechte*, 2nd edn. (Tübingen: J.C.B. Mohr, 1905, repr. Aalen: Scientia, 1979), 17.

[23] See e.g. *SJSB* § 19 (at p. 110), § 20 (at p. 116).

[24] See Jellinek (n.22 above), at 13; Carl Friedrich von Gerber, *Grundzüge eines Systems des Deutschen Staatsrechts*, 2nd edn. (Leipzig: Bernhard Tauchnitz, 1869), at 1–3.

[25] See Georg Jellinek, *Allgemeine Staatslehre*, 3rd edn. (Berlin: Springer, 1914), at 11–12, 74, 137–9, 174–83, *et passim*; see also Theodor Kistiakowski, *Gesellschaft und Einzelwesen. Eine methodologische Studie* (Berlin: Otto Liebmann, 1899).

[26] See *SJSB*, at §§ 20–3 (pp. 114–40), anticipated in *HP*, at 253 n.1. See generally Oliver Lepsius, *Die gegensatzaufhebende Begriffsbildung* (Munich: C.H. Beck, 1994), at 156–62.

Windelband,[27] Heinrich Rickert,[28] and Emil Lask,[29] by the philosopher and sociologist Georg Simmel as Kelsen reads him,[30] by the legal philosopher Gustav Radbruch,[31] and by Max Weber.[32] Simmel's formulation, reflecting the precept that an 'ought'-statement cannot be derived from an 'is'-statement, is straightforward:

That we ought to do this or that—*if it is supposed to be logically demonstrated*—can be shown only by means of the appeal to another 'ought', presupposed as certain.[33]

Setting out methodological dualism in the opening pages of *Main Problems*, Kelsen refers to both Windelband and Simmel as sources:[34]

Logically speaking, enquiring into the 'why' of a concrete *Sollen* can only lead to another *Sollen*, just as the answer to the 'why' of a *Sein* can only be another *Sein*.[35]

The 'insuperable abyss' between the world of facticity and that of normativity follows straightaway from the opposition of *Sein* and *Sollen*, which are, for their part, 'ultimate categories'. Fundamental to the explication of everything else, they cannot themselves be explicated. '[J]ust as

[27] See Wilhelm Windelband, 'Normen und Naturgesetze', in Windelband, *Präludien* (Tübingen: J.C.B. Mohr, 1884), 211–46, at 212 *et passim*.

[28] See Heinrich Rickert, *Die Grenzen der naturwissenschaftlichen Begriffsbildung*, 1st edn. (Tübingen and Leipzig: J.C.B. Mohr, 1902), at ch. III, § 2 (esp. pp. 255–6), 5th edn. (1929), at 227–8; abridged trans. (of the 5th edn.) by Guy Oakes, *The Limits of Concept Formation in Natural Science* (Cambridge: Cambridge UP, 1986), at 53–4.

[29] See Emil Lask, 'Legal Philosophy' (first published in 1905), in *The Legal Philosophies of Lask, Radbruch, and Dabin*, trans. Kurt Wilk (Cambridge, Mass.: Harvard UP, 1950), 1–42. On Lask, see generally Stephan Nachtsheim, *Emil Lasks Grundlehre* (Tübingen: J.C.B. Mohr, 1992); Alexander Somek, 'The Concept of Value and the Transformation of Legal Philosophy into Legal Theory: Lask's Silent Revolution', *Diritto e cultura*, 2 (1992), 161–92.

[30] See Georg Simmel, *Einleitung in die Moralwissenschaft*, 2 vols. (Berlin: W. Hertz, 1892–3, repr. Aalen: Scientia, 1964), vol. I, at 1–84. Arguably, Simmel's own reading of *Sein* and *Sollen*, 'is' and 'ought', is psychological in nature; see ibid., at 5, 8, 11, 12, 20, 30, 55, 58–61, 65, 68, *et passim*, and see Alf Ross, 'Recht und Wirklichkeit', *Juristische Blätter*, 59 (1930), 245–51, at 249–50.

[31] See Gustav Radbruch, *Grundzüge der Rechtsphilosophie* (Leipzig: Quelle & Meyer, 1914), at 1–28, 82–96, *et passim*. On Radbruch's methodological dualism, see Stanley L. Paulson, 'Radbruch on Unjust Laws: Competing Earlier and Later Views?', *Oxford Journal of Legal Studies*, 15 (1995), 489–500, at 490.

[32] See generally Max Weber, *Gesammelte Aufsätze zur Wissenschaft* (Tübingen: J.C.B. Mohr, 1922). Weber was influenced by Rickert on questions of methodology. See generally Peter-Ulrich Merz, *Max Weber und Heinrich Rickert* (Würzburg: Königshausen & Neumann, 1990); Thomas Burger, *Max Weber's Theory of Concept Formation* (Durham: Duke UP, 1976).

[33] Simmel (n.30 above), vol. I, 12, quoted in *HP*, at 8 (Kelsen's emphasis).

[34] See *HP*, at 4, 8.

[35] *HP* 8; see also Kelsen, *Über Grenzen* (n.8 above), at 6–7, repr. *WS I*, at 6–7.

one cannot describe what . . . *Sein* is, so likewise, there is no definition of *Sollen*.'[36]

Methodological dualism represents more for Kelsen, however, than simply the 'is' / 'ought' or *Sein / Sollen* distinction employed by others as a defence against the illegitimate fusion of different methods of cognition. Rather, for Kelsen, *Sein* and *Sollen* also mark two completely independent spheres that are epistemologically unbridgeable—the external, physical world and a normative or ideal sphere.

The opposition between *Sein* and *Sollen*, between 'is' and 'ought', is a logico-formal opposition, and in so far as the boundaries of logico-formal enquiry are observed, no path leads from one to the other; the two worlds are separated by an insuperable abyss.[37]

Armed with this expansive version of methodological dualism and determined to 'purify' a legal science infested with elements of naturalism and psychologism, Kelsen turns first to civil law, taking aim at the traditional 'dogma of will'.[38] Bernhard Windscheid, the last great representative of Pandectism, resorts to metaphor in an effort to flesh out his notion of the will as something psychological or 'psychical', speaking of the will in terms of 'motion that, contained within, is inchoate, a wave that is engulfed by the next wave.'[39] While Windscheid's metaphor is indeed grist for Kelsen's mill, elsewhere Windscheid speaks of the will without a hint of metaphor covering for something putatively psychological or psychical. He writes, for example: 'If someone says that he intends [to do something], it will be presumed that he does intend [to do this], until objectively cognizable facts establish the contrary.'[40] Kelsen responds that Windscheid, as a psychical-will theorist, has no business mixing categories of legal presumption with psychical will[41]—but whether Windscheid's concept of will is juridico-normative rather than psychical is precisely what is at issue.

Be that as it may, Kelsen, with an eye to his own programme, exploits Windscheid's text at the point where the psychologistic reading is inescapable. He argues that Windscheid has equated 'the quality of legal validity [in a legal transaction] with the property of being willed', and that

[36] *HP* 7.

[37] *HP* 8. See generally Carsten Heidemann, *Die Norm als Tatsache* (Baden-Baden: Nomos, 1997), at 24–6.

[38] See generally *HP*, at 122–33.

[39] Bernhard Windscheid, 'Wille und Willenserklärung' (June 1878 lecture in Leipzig), *Archiv für Civilistische Praxis*, 63 (1880), 72–112, at 76–7, repr. in Windscheid, *Gesammelte Reden und Abhandlungen*, ed. Paul Oertmann (Leipzig: Duncker & Humblot, 1904), 337–74, at 341.

[40] Bernhard Windscheid, *Lehrbuch des Pandektenrechts*, 9th edn., 3 vols. (Frankfurt: Rütten & Loening, 1906, repr. Aalen: Scientia, 1984), vol. I, para. 75, at p. 376 n.1.

[41] *HP* 125.

the equation counts as a fundamental mistake.[42] Lending an element of hyperbole to his quest for 'purification', Kelsen stands the received opinion on its head: Far from concluding that a 'legal transaction is valid because and in so far as it is (psychologically) willed',[43] Kelsen endorses

the opposite conclusion: A transaction is willed in so far as or because it is valid, with the property of validity serving as the cognitive basis for the property of being willed. 'Will' in this relation is seen at a glance to be something other than a so-called psychical fact. It is no more the case that a real psychical or physical fact is claimed with the property of being willed than with the property of being valid. . . . [And] it is in this inversion—indeed, precisely in this inversion—that the dogma of will in the civil law [acquires] its actual legal sense.[44]

Thus, whereas the traditional view is that *if willed, then legally valid*, Kelsen's view is that *if legally valid, then willed*. 'Will', the *explicans* of the law in traditional legal voluntarism or positivism, survives in Kelsen's work only as a derived notion.

Kelsen makes comparable 'inversions', as he terms them, in criminal law and in public law,[45] each marking a complete departure from the tradition. His arguments in public law, addressed primarily to Jellinek's work, are of special interest. Jellinek, like his near-contemporary Otto von Gierke, strives toward a 'unified state will',[46] taking as his point of departure a psychological or psychical interpretation of will. Beginning with what he describes as the 'content' of individual psychical wills, Jellinek aims for a normative construct, the unified state will, familiarly expressed in the statute as 'legislative will' or purpose. He argues that a common purposive element is abstracted from the content of the psychical wills of individual state organs, making possible the state's representation of itself 'as a teleological unity, despite its changing constituency of persons.'[47]

Kelsen's reply is in two parts. He argues, first, that a psychological or psychical interpretation of will has nothing whatever to do with the

---

[42] *HP* 133.   [43] Ibid.

[44] Ibid. Ronald Dworkin defends the same sort of inversion, addressed to the same theme: '[I]t would be a mistake . . . to say that our theory about the proper reach of a statute follows from our independent theory of intention. The argument goes the other way around.' Dworkin, 'The Forum of Principle', *New York University Law Review*, 56 (1981), 469–518, at 480, repr. in Dworkin, *A Matter of Principle* (Cambridge, Mass.: Harvard UP, 1985), 33–71, 399–403 (notes), at 42.

[45] See *HP*, at 133–44 (criticism of Alexander Löffler in criminal law), and at 162–88 (criticism of Otto von Gierke and Georg Jellinek in public law). Kelsen's inversions, in a variety of contexts, were prominent in later work, too. See e.g. Hans Kelsen, 'Wer soll der Hüter der Verfassung sein?', *Kritische Justiz*, 6 (1930–1), 576–628, at 589, repr. *WS II* 1873–922, at 1885 (English equivalent of Kelsen's title: 'Who Ought to be the Guardian of the Constitution?'); *GTLS*, at 51.

[46] See Georg Jellinek, *Gesetz und Verordnung* (Tübingen: J.C.B. Mohr, 1887, repr. Aalen: Scientia, 1964), at 189–225, esp. 192–3.

[47] Jellinek (n.22 above), 26.

notion of 'legislative will'. The legislator's intention to enact a bill into law—in traditional parlance, the will of an individual state organ—is essentially different from the expression of 'legislative will' found in the bill. For it is well known that 'in many cases, indeed in most cases, the members of parliament voting for a legislative bill will not be familiar with the provisions of the bill', that, in most cases, only those who have actually worked on the bill in the parliamentary committee will know its provisions.[48] Typically, then, there is no basis for abstracting a common element of purpose, the 'legislative will', from the content of the individual psychical wills of those voting for a bill in the legislature.

Second, Kelsen argues, even if there were a basis for speaking of a 'legislative will' as the common element abstracted from individual expressions of psychical will, there would be no basis for claiming that the abstraction yields anything normative or ethico-legal; Jellinek's own express policy proscribes this fusion of empirical and normative methods of cognition. As Kelsen points out, Jellinek's view is that what is abstracted is drawn from an aggregate of acts, expressions of psychical will, and if

the abstraction, as Jellinek carries it out, is based . . . on something existing in fact, then it is hard to understand how it could lead to a concept other than a concept in the explicative disciplines [the empirical sciences]; and if the abstraction proceeds solely from psychical 'facts', it is hard to see how one could arrive at something other than a purely psychological concept, at, for example, a specifically ethico-legal concept, as Jellinek contends.[49]

Thus, Kelsen interprets Jellinek, too, as a 'will theorist'.

Having taken up Jellinek's effort to avoid the illegitimate fusion of different methods of cognition, Kelsen turns the underlying doctrine against him. Jellinek's assumption that psychological or psychical data will yield normative results is precisely the kind of mistake that Kelsen identifies as a flagrant violation of the *Sein/Sollen* distinction. In place of Jellinek's factual point of departure, Kelsen adopts a thoroughgoing normative framework—indeed, as we shall see, so thoroughgoing that no systemic relation is possible between the factual and the normative, between human being and fictitious legal person. The fundamental notion in this normative framework is 'central imputation'.

---

[48] *HP* 170, and see generally at 169–70, 173–4.
[49] *HP* 178–9, see also *SJSB* § 20 (at p. 120).

III. CENTRAL IMPUTATION AND THE LEGAL PERSON: THE NINETEENTH-CENTURY 'DUALITY PROBLEM' AND KELSEN'S PURPORTED RESOLUTION

Imputation—later termed 'central imputation' by Kelsen in order to distinguish it from a second species, 'peripheral imputation'[50]—is the attribution of an act to a legal person, to a complex of legal norms, or, in Kelsenian parlance, the attribution of an act to a 'point of imputation' in the legal system. By means of central imputation, the legal character of the act is established. To impute, then, is to attribute, and that to which the act is attributed is a point of imputation. Roughly speaking, a point of imputation, like the fictitious legal person of the tradition, is shorthand for a *cluster of legal relations*.

Kelsen's constructions—'imputation', 'points of imputation', and the like—represent his response to a set of striking developments in nineteenth-century German legal science.[51] What had begun, in Friedrich Carl von Savigny's *System des heutigen römischen Rechts*,[52] as an enquiry about the legal subject qua natural person, whereby the construction of the legal person as *persona ficta* represented something anomalous, is transformed by later nineteenth-century public lawyers and ultimately by Kelsen into a scheme whereby it is the natural person that turns up as a *contradictio in adjecto*.[53] In its place, the fictitious legal person—or, in Kelsen's theory, the point of imputation—emerges as the only possible concept of legal personality. And the state qua fictitious legal person—or, in Kelsen's theory, the legal system as the ultimate reference point of all constructions in the law—has the same personality as that of other legal subjects,[54] but it personifies the whole of the legal system, whereas other legal subjects personify subsystems, parts of the whole. As Kelsen himself

---

[50] For some details of the shift and for the meaning of 'peripheral imputation', see § VI below. On imputation generally, see the stimulating paper by Neil MacCormick, 'Persons as Institutional Facts', in *Reine Rechtslehre im Spiegel ihrer Fortsetzer und Kritiker*, ed. Ota Weinberger and Werner Krawietz (Vienna: Springer, 1988), 371–93.

[51] See generally Julius Binder, *Das Problem der juristischen Persönlichkeit* (Leipzig: A. Deichert, 1907, repr. Aalen: Scientia, 1970); Franz Wieacker, 'Zur Theorie der Juristischen Person des Privatrechts', in *Festschrift für Ernst Rudolf Huber zum 70. Geburtstag*, ed. Ernst Forsthoff et al. (Göttingen: Otto Schwartz, 1973), 339–83.

[52] Friedrich Carl von Savigny, *System des heutigen römischen Rechts*, 8 vols. [hereafter cited as '*System I*', '*System II*', with section and page numbers] (Berlin: Veit, 1840–9, repr. Aalen: Scientia, 1981). On Savigny's concept of the legal person, see Malte Dießelhorst, 'Zur Theorie der juristischen Person bei Carl Friedrich von Savigny', *Quaderni Fiorentini*, 11–12 [pt. 1] (1982–3), 319–37. On Savigny generally, see Joachim Rückert, *Idealismus, Jurisprudenz und Politik bei Friedrich Carl von Savigny* (Edelsbach: Rolf Gremer, 1984).

[53] See generally Eggert Winter, *Ethik und Rechtswissenschaft* (Berlin: Duncker & Humblot, 1980), at 294–310; Binder (n.51 above).

[54] *HP* 185.

would put it in later work, the construction amounts to nothing less than 'reducing the concepts "state" or "state will" to mean "unity of the system", "point of imputation", or "point of reference".'[55]

In order to get a bit closer to what Kelsen understands by central imputation, it is well to ask first of all why he is convinced that his own constructions in the name of central imputation count as an improvement over the fictitious legal person of nineteenth-century German legal science. The modern debate on the legal person began with Savigny, who answers the question of the identity of the legal subject in terms of the human being and then modifies his answer to include 'artificial subjects'. Savigny's 'duality'—the legal subject as human being and as artificial legal person—generates the anomalies that launched the greater nineteenth-century debate on the legal person, first in private law and later in public law.[56]

A. Savigny and the Emergence of the Duality Problem.

Savigny developed his civil law system from the idea of private autonomy, a development that marked a new beginning. In *System*, he puts the question that would serve as a leitmotif throughout much of the nineteenth century: Who is the legal subject?[57] The paradigm shift wrought by Savigny's deliberations on this question is underscored by Gierke: 'Departing from the merely collective "moral person"' of the past, Savigny moves 'a self-contained artificial individual, under the rubric of "legal person"', to the forefront of the private law.[58]

Savigny's initial answer to the question of the identity of the legal subject stems from outside the legal system. The legal subject, in a word, is the human being. And this point of departure is no accident, for Savigny has an argument of moral import that underscores the central significance of the human being in his theory.[59]

All law exists for the sake of the moral freedom inherent in every individual human being. Therefore, the original concept of the person or legal subject must coincide with the concept of the human being.[60]

---

[55] 'Foreword' to *HP*, in this volume, ch. 1, § IV.

[56] See generally Binder (n.51 above); Wieacker (n.51 above); Winter (n.53 above).

[57] Savigny, *System II* (n.52 above), § 60 (p. 1).

[58] Otto von Gierke, *Deutsches Privatrecht*, 3 vols. (Leipzig: Duncker & Humblot, 1895–1917), vol. I (1895), 464. On the earlier concept, that of 'moral person', see Horst Denzer, 'Die Ursprünge der Lehre von der juristischen Person (persona moralis) in Deutschland und ihre Bedeutung für die Vorstellung von der Staatspersönlichkeit', in *La formazione storica del diritto moderno in Europa* [no editor] (Florence: Leo S. Olschki Editore, 1977), 1189–202.

[59] See Binder (n.51 above), at 10.

[60] Savigny, *System II* (n.52 above), § 60 (p. 2); see also *System I* (n.52 above), § 52 (at pp. 331–2).

Thus, Savigny continues, there is an 'original identity' of the concept of the legal subject and the concept of the human being. 'Every individual human being, and only the individual human being, has legal capacity.'[61]

Savigny then goes on to alter this pattern of identity, increasing the size of the class of legal subjects by extending it beyond human beings. Legal capacity, initially established as 'coinciding with the notion of the individual human being', is now 'extended to artificial subjects admitted by means of a pure fiction'.

We designate such a subject a *legal person*, that is to say, a person who is assumed to be so for purely legal reasons. Thus, just as the individual human being is a bearer of legal relations, so likewise for the legal person.[62]

The next step in tracing the doctrine of the fictitious legal person leads to anomalies, which Savigny himself develops. Granted that the legal person is fictitious, there can be no question of attributing human will or human acts to it. What, then, of property rights? These are acquired by means of acts, but acts 'presuppose a thinking and willing being, an individual human being, precisely what legal persons qua pure fictions are not.' The result is an anomaly, the 'internal contradiction', as Savigny puts it, of a subject's having 'the capacity to hold property rights but being unable to satisfy the requisite conditions for acquiring them.'[63] Savigny purports to resolve the anomaly by appealing to the idea of representation:[64] Standing in for the fictitious person, a natural person must perform the acts that are required.

This solution, however, merely gives rise to another anomaly, namely, that the acts performed by the representative are attributed to the fictitious legal person as its own acts. In Savigny's words, the 'real existence' of the legal person 'rests on the representative will of certain individual human beings, and, thanks to a fiction, this will counts as the legal person's own will'.[65] In this way, the legal person acquires an 'artificial will'.[66]

It was these and other anomalies, stemming from Savigny's doctrine, that set the stage in nineteenth-century German legal science for a long and protracted debate on the status and role of the legal person generally. Following Savigny for the most part, Georg Friedrich Puchta defined legal personality as 'the possibility of legal will'. At the same time,

---

[61] Savigny, *System II* (n.52 above), § 60 (p. 2).
[62] Ibid. § 85 (p. 236) (Savigny's emphasis).
[63] Ibid. § 90 (p. 282).
[64] Likewise, *mutatis mutandis*, in public law. See quotation in text at n.75 below.
[65] Savigny, *System II* (n.52 above), § 94 (p. 312).
[66] Ibid. § 94 (p. 316).

however, he offered what appears to be a second definition of legal personality—quite simply, 'the capacity to have subjective rights'.[67] And this
second definition, read independently of the first, marks Puchta's anticipation of things to come. For rather than beginning, as Savigny did, with
a characterization from outside the legal system, namely, the legal subject qua human being, Puchta—in keeping with this second definition—
characterized the legal subject entirely from within the legal system:[68]
Where 'X' stands for an unspecified reference point, then, if subjective
rights can be attributed to X, it follows that X is a legal subject.

Other theorists developed altogether different doctrines. Alois Brinz,
for example, argued that the legal person was not a legal subject at all
('subjectless'), but rather a conceptualization of property earmarked for
a particular purpose.[69] And Gierke argued that the legal person was a living being, an organism: 'The corporation qua real collective person not
only has legal capacity but is also *capable of willing and acting.*'[70]
Gierke's position in particular became notorious. He builds into the collective person precisely those attributes that are conspicuous by their
absence in Savigny's fictitious legal person—the capacity to will and to
act. He would have us believe that the legal subject is neither a human
being nor an invented subject, but nevertheless a living person, albeit a
'collective' living person.

My concern, however, is not with the details of the general debate on
the legal person. Rather, I have sketched the debate with an eye to
Kelsen's response to a specific aspect of it, namely, that part of Savigny's
doctrine that might be termed the duality problem, generated by a pair
of radically distinct candidates for the title 'legal subject'.

B. Kelsen on the Duality Problem.

Kelsen's response to the duality problem is two-fold. His first step is to
reject the natural person as a possible candidate for the legal subject,
leaving only the fictitious legal person, a single concept rather than a
duality of concepts. To couch Kelsen's resolution in the parlance of the
tradition, however, is not *stricto sensu* correct. For, having eliminated

---

[67] Georg Friedrich Puchta, *Pandekten*, 9th edn., ed. Adolph August Friedrich Rudorff
(Leipzig: Johann Ambrosius Barth, 1863), § 22 (p. 37).

[68] See Uwe John, *Die organisierte Rechtsperson* (Berlin: Duncker & Humblot, 1977), at
26–34; Wieacker (n.51 above), at 363.

[69] See Alois Brinz, *Lehrbuch der Pandekten*, 2nd edn., 4 vols. (Erlangen: Andreas
Deichert, 1873–95), vol. I (1873), § 61 (at p. 202).

[70] Otto von Gierke, *Die Genossenschaftstheorie und die Deutsche Rechtsprechung* (Berlin:
Weidmann, 1887, repr. Hildesheim: Georg Olms, 1983), 603 (Gierke's emphasis), and see at
607 *et passim*. On Gierke, see Wieacker (n.51 above), at 368–70; Stolleis (n.13 above), vol. II,
at 359–63 *et passim*.

the natural person as legal subject, he takes a second step, eliminating the fictitious legal person, too, and replacing it with 'points of imputation', 'conceptually constructed points of normative reference', and the like.[71]

Kelsen's first step, his rejection of the natural person as a candidate for the legal subject, has ample precedent.[72] And, more importantly, it is dictated by the doctrine of methodological dualism.

His second step, however, is less clear-cut. Kelsen contends that his rejection of the fictitious legal person is warranted on two grounds. On the one hand, he thereby avoids the charge that he, too, has introduced a fictitious notion into his legal theory. On the other, he avoids the dangers of anthropomorphization, dangers that loom all too large for the public lawyers, inclined as they are to adapt the legal person to the role of 'state personality'. As we shall see, both of these grounds for Kelsen's rejection of the fictitious legal person give rise to difficulties.

IV. AVOIDING FICTIONS, AND KELSEN'S *PETITIO PRINCIPII*

Kelsen believes that substituting the 'reference point of imputation' for the fictitious legal person of the tradition protects him against the objection that a fundamental concept in his own legal theory amounts to nothing more than a fiction. Kelsen's reply to the objection, in a word, is that it fails to take account of the import of normative cognition. That is, like other basic concepts in the reconstruction of the fundamental concepts of the law, the idea of a 'reference point of imputation', characterized from within the legal system and therefore accessible only by means of normative cognition, is to be sharply contrasted with the legal fiction. Far from being fictions, points of imputation are the proper objects of normative cognition, as 'real' as anything in the legal system can be.

Kelsen's position gives rise to a vexing question. These points of imputation, representing legal subsystems, make reference to other points of imputation, also representing legal subsystems albeit at a more fundamental level. And ultimately, points of imputation representing legal subsystems make reference to the legal system itself, which is the end point of imputative reference. And what is its basis? The legal system, as the ultimate reference point of imputation, must presuppose itself. Or so

---

[71] See *HP*, at 71–8, 121–46, 183–7, 517–20, 707–9, *et passim*; *ASL* § 10(c) (at pp. 48–51), § 13(d) (at pp. 65–6), § 15(a)(b) (at pp. 71–2), § 38(c) (at pp. 267–8), § 43(a) (at pp. 310–11).

[72] See e.g. Paul Laband, *Das Staatsrecht des Deutschen Reiches*, 2nd edn., 2 vols., vol. II in 2 pts. (Freiburg: J.C.B. Mohr, 1888–91), vol. I (1888), at § 10 (pp. 86–93), 5th edn., 4 vols. (Tübingen: J.C.B. Mohr, 1911, repr. Goldbach: Keip, 1997), vol. I, at § 10 (pp. 94–102).

one might surmise in light of Edmund Bernatzik's argument from self-
presupposition, a possible source of Kelsen's own adumbration of an
argument along these lines in *Main Problems*.[73]

If this is Kelsen's early answer to the question of the foundation of his
pure constructions, it may be a heroic gesture, but as an argument it is a
blatant *petitio principii*. If the notion of the legal system as the ultimate
imputation point means that the legal system must presuppose itself,
then far from providing an independent ground for assessing Kelsen's
scheme of pure constructions, the notion simply poses anew the question as to the basis of these constructions. To be sure, Kelsen returns to
the question in the early 1920s, and his efforts there mark his search for
a foundation in Kantian or neo-Kantian terms.

It remains to consider Kelsen on the anthropomorphizing tendencies
of nineteenth-century German public law theory, which are part and
parcel of its concept of legal person. Despite its value as a heuristic device
in some contexts, Kelsen decries as a source of confusion the anthropomorphizing tendency of his predecessors, not least of all Gerber.

V. AVOIDING ANTHROPOMORPHIZATION:
KELSEN'S ANTINOMY

Gerber's transfer of the constructivist method of private law Pandectism
to public law (the remarkable development of the 1850s and 1860s
referred to above) is reflected, too, in his doctrine of the state qua legal
person. Legal science invests the state (commonwealth) 'with the property of *personality*'. And just as this legal construction is available to private law, so also 'it is available to public law for shaping the legal form of
the powers of the state.'[74]

In applying the concept of the legal person to public law, it may appear
as if Gerber were following to the letter Savigny's notion of the fictitious
legal person. In particular, like Savigny before him, Gerber appeals to the

---

[73] See Edmund Bernatzik, 'Kritische Studien über den Begriff der juristischen Person
und über die juristische Persönlichkeit der Behörden insbesondere', *AöR*, 5 (1890),
169–318, at 244–5, repr. in Bernatzik, *Über den Begriff der juristischen Person*, with a foreword by Günther Winkler (Vienna: Springer, 1996), at 57. Kelsen was well acquainted with
Bernatzik's work, including the 'Kritische Studien'. For Kelsen's own language along these
lines, see *HP*, at 91–2, 143–6, *et passim*. For an early critical statement directed to the argument from self-presupposition, see Carl Schmitt, *Politische Theologie*, 1st edn. (Munich
and Leipzig: Duncker & Humblot, 1922), at 53, and see at 28; trans. (of the 2nd edn.) by
George Schwab, *Political Theology* (Cambridge, Mass.: MIT Press, 1985), at 40, and see at
18–19. See also Carl Schmitt, *Verfassungslehre* (Munich and Leipzig: Duncker & Humblot,
1928), at 9, 22, *et passim*.
[74] Gerber (n.24 above), 219 (Beilage II) (Gerber's emphasis).

notion of representation, introducing state organs to act on behalf of the state and thereby to represent it. 'As with every legal person, the state, too, requires a representative through which the abstract power of will ascribed to the state becomes concrete act.'[75]

In Gerber's scheme, however, the state qua legal person is not the fictitious legal person of Savigny's doctrine. Rather, Gerber draws on 'juridical' and 'natural' points of view in order to provide a twofold characterization of the state—seen juridically, the state is a legal person, seen naturally, it is an organism.[76] And Gerber rejects the notion that 'the personality of the state' might fall within 'the category of the legal person of private law'. Rather, 'the personality of the state is unique', bearing no relation whatever to other concepts in the law.[77]

Kelsen is reacting to anthropomorphizing tendencies like these—the state qua legal person and, in Gierke's work, the legal person qua organism—when, at the high point of his long, classical phase, he writes:

The assumption that the legal person is a reality different from individual human beings, a reality curiously imperceptible to the senses or a supra-individual social organism made up of individual human beings—this is the naive hypostatization of a thought, of a heuristic legal notion.[78]

He believes that by replacing the legal person with a cluster of imputative concepts, he avoids the danger of anthropomorphization.

As with his effort to avoid fictions in resolving the duality problem, Kelsen's effort here, too, gives rise to fundamental difficulties. Referring to the distinct mode of normative cognition, Kelsen readily concedes that 'the human being of biology and psychology . . . cannot be comprehended by legal science at all'.[79] An 'unavoidable antinomy' emerges, which Kelsen himself sketches with remarkable candor in a major work of his long, classical phase. On the one hand, the jurist must recognize 'a connection, in content, between the two orders', the order of reality and that of value.[80] In particular, the contentual connection is marked by legal obligation, for 'the content of a legal obligation . . . can only be human behaviour'.[81] On the other hand, the jurist, 'necessarily presupposing' the methodological dualism of 'is' and 'ought', must grant that there cannot be any connection at all between these two orders.[82] The

---

[75] Ibid. 225 (Beilage II).

[76] See ibid., at 1–3, 211–19 (Beilage I); see also Pauly (n.13 above), at 137–40, 149–51.

[77] Carl Friedrich von Gerber, 'Ueber die Theilbarkeit deutscher Staatsgebiete', [*Aegidis*] *Zeitschrift für Deutsches Staatsrecht und Deutsche Verfassungsgeschichte*, 1 (1867), 5–24, at 9–10, repr. in Gerber, *Gesammelte juristische Abhandlungen*, 2 vols. (Jena: Mauke, 1872), vol. II, 441–69, at 448; see also Gerber (n.24 above), at 2 n.2.

[78] *LT* § 25(b) (p. 49) (trans. altered).

[79] *ASL* § 13(b) (p. 62).

[80] *ASL* § 5(c) (p. 19).

[81] *LT* § 49(c) (p. 109).

[82] See *ASL* § 13(b) (at p. 62).

denial of any such connection follows straightaway from methodological dualism—with the result, in Kelsen's legal theory, that there is no connection whatever between human being and legal person.

VI. CONCLUDING REMARK: THE STATUS, IN KELSEN'S CLASSICAL PHASE, OF THESE DIFFICULTIES

In Kelsen's earliest phase, critical constructivism, both of his grounds for rejecting the fictitious legal person and substituting reference points of imputation give rise to difficulties. The difficulty with the first ground, avoiding fictions, is that Kelsen, in his effort to provide a foundation for the ultimate imputation point, is arguably driven to the idea that the legal system must presuppose itself. The difficulty with the second ground, avoiding the anthropomorphization illustrated by Gerber's 'invest[ing] the commonwealth with personality',[83] is Kelsen's 'unavoidable antinomy', a separation of the order of reality and the order of value so uncompromising that no point of interaction between them is possible.

In Kelsen's classical phase, these two grounds and the difficulties arising from them fare very differently. As for avoiding anthropomorphization, Kelsen continues to stand by his claim that the concomitant antinomy is unavoidable. The Pure Theory of Law of Kelsen's classical phase, like the critical constructivism of his earliest phase, rejects any and every connection between human being and legal person, between *Sein* and *Sollen*, between the factual and the normative.

The consequences of the 'antinomy'—Kelsen's own expression in the present connection[84]—appear to be disastrous. Kelsen relegates certain legally relevant matters to the world of fact, thus—given the *Sein/Sollen* distinction—rendering them unintelligible from a legal standpoint. An example is Kelsen's notion of efficacy as a condition for legal validity.[85] Kelsen rightly argues that legal validity and factual efficacy cannot be identified;[86] rather, he continues, the validity of the legal system as a whole 'depends on the efficacy of the system'.[87] Factual efficacy is not,

---

[83] See n.74 above.

[84] See text at n.80 above.

[85] See e.g. *LT*, at § 30(b)(d) (pp. 60–1, 62–3).

[86] See *LT*, at § 30(b) (pp. 60–1).

[87] *LT* § 30(d) (p. 62), see also *GTLS*, at 41–2. Compare, however, *PTL* § 4(c) (at p. 10), § 34(g) (at pp. 211–13), *GTN*, at ch. 34, § II (pp. 139–40), where Kelsen also defends the view that individual legal norms require efficacy as a necessary condition of their validity. This view is effectively criticized in Rudolf Thienel, 'Geltung und Wirksamkeit', in *Untersuchungen zur Reinen Rechtslehre*, ed. Stanley L. Paulson and Robert Walter (Vienna: Manz,

however, a possible object of legal cognition, and, with perhaps one exception,[88] Kelsen makes no sustained effort to come to terms with the implications of factual efficacy, this necessary but 'alien' factor, indiscernible from a legal standpoint.[89] In short, factual efficacy is a reflection of Kelsen's 'unavoidable antinomy'.

If one sought to render Kelsen's 'unavoidable antinomy' innocuous, the task would be to show that legally relevant matters relegated to the world of fact can be given a full account within Kelsen's legal theory. Perhaps the most obvious example requiring attention—the very example of the antinomy—is the 'human behaviour that is governed by norms', which has, in sharp contrast to the so-called legal person, a 'natural, real existence'.[90] Apart from his statement of the 'unavoidable antinomy', Kelsen gives the issue very little attention, and I am not sanguine about the prospects of saving, within the framework of his legal theory, legally relevant matters relegated to the world of fact.

By contrast, Kelsen pays a great deal of attention to the first of the two grounds and the difficulty arising from it, namely, his effort to avoid fictions by means of reference points of imputation, and the resulting difficulty, that the legal system qua ultimate imputation point must presuppose itself. A development of special interest here is the fate of central imputation. Fundamental in *Main Problems*, central imputation loses much of its lustre in the wake of Kelsen's adoption of Adolf Julius Merkl's doctrine of hierarchical structure (*Stufenbaulehre*), often termed Kelsen's 'dynamic' turn.[91] In order to bring his own theory into line with what he takes over from Merkl, Kelsen moves away from central imputation[92] and introduces 'peripheral imputation', that is, a scheme by means of which a material fact (for example, a delict) is attributed to a legal subject, thereby establishing the legal liability of the subject.[93] The

1986), 20–50, at 33–7. On the 'efficacy' motif generally, see also Mario G. Losano, 'Das Verhältnis von Geltung und Wirksamkeit in der Reinen Rechtslehre', in *Die Reine Rechtslehre in wissenschaftlicher Diskussion* [no editor] (Vienna: Manz, 1982), 82–96.

[88] See the statement in *PS*, at § 24 (pp. 94–101), where Kelsen attempts to harness Mach's principle of cognitive economy for service on this front. For further references, see Hans Kelsen, 'Letter to Treves', in this volume, ch. 8, at n.14.

[89] For another statement of this criticism, see Eugenio Bulygin, 'An Antinomy in Kelsen's Pure Theory of Law', in this volume, ch. 16, at § II.

[90] *LT* § 25(b) (p. 49), see also § 49(c) (at pp. 109–10), from which I have quoted at n.81 above.

[91] For the 'dynamic' turn in the context of the phases of development in Kelsen's legal theory, see my 'Introduction' to this volume, at § I.

[92] This is not to say, however, that Kelsen in his classical phase moves away from central imputation altogether; when, for example, he explores questions of international law apart from the *Stufenbaulehre*, the role of central imputation is conspicuous. See Hans Kelsen, 'Unrecht und Unrechtsfolge im Völkerrecht', *ZöR*, 12 (1932), 481–608, at § 2 (pp. 495–504) *et passim*.

[93] See e.g. *LT*, at § 11(b) (pp. 23–5), § 25(d) (pp. 50–1); see also *LT*, Appendix I, at Supplementary Note 6 (pp. 134–5).

result is a new, twofold scheme—peripheral imputation and the hierarchical structure itself. In a conceptualization of this new scheme, peripheral imputation would be represented on a horizontal axis, the doctrine
of hierarchical structure on a vertical axis. The doctrine of hierarchical
structure makes sense of the idea of empowerment[94] as stemming from
higher-level norms. Thus, particular applications of the scheme for
peripheral imputation are valid if the attributions of material fact to legal
subject have been made in accordance with the appropriate higher-level
empowering norms.

Another development of special interest here stems from Kelsen's
determination to get past the question-begging character of his early
effort, in *Main Problems*, to provide support for the doctrine of imputation, which he now recasts as peripheral imputation and couples with
empowerment. This development, nothing less than Kelsen's search for
a foundation for his constructions, is already evident in the years leading
up to the classical phase; as early as 1914, Kelsen had embarked on the
search for an 'ultimate' or 'basic norm'.[95] And in the early years of the
long, classical phase itself, he hints at details of a neo-Kantian argument,
with an eye to demonstrating imputation as the fundamental legal category[96] underlying and making possible the particular applications of the
scheme for peripheral imputation.

The neo-Kantian argument on behalf of the fundamental legal category, however it is formulated or interpreted, remains problematic.[97] But
this does not diminish the significance of the fact that constructivism,
methodological dualism, and central imputation, the leitmotifs of

[94] Kelsen does not, however, offer a close analysis of empowerment in the early years of
the middle, classical phase. His first effort in this direction comes in the late 1930s, in a
paper that was published posthumously. See Hans Kelsen, 'Recht und Kompetenz. Kritische
Bemerkungen zur Völkerrechtstheorie Georges Scelles', in Kelsen, *Auseinandersetzungen
zur Reinen Rechtslehre. Kritische Bemerkungen zu Georges Scelle und Michel Virally*, ed.
Kurt Ringhofer and Robert Walter (Vienna: Springer, 1987), 1–108, at 61–91 (English equivalent of Kelsen's title: 'Legal Rights and Competences. Critical Remarks on Georges Scelle's
Theory of International Law'). For a brief sketch of Kelsen's position as found in the study
of Scelle and, as developed therefrom, also in later writings, see my 'Introduction' to the
present volume, at § V.

[95] See Hans Kelsen, 'Reichsgesetz und Landesgesetz nach österreichischer Verfassung',
AöR, 32 (1914), 202–45, 390–438, at 215–20 (English equivalent of Kelsen's title: 'Laws of the
Reich or Federation and of the *Land* or State according to the Austrian Constitution'). See
also 'Foreword' to *HP* (n.55 above), ch. 1, at § V. On this theme generally, see Stanley L.
Paulson, 'On the Early Development of the Grundnorm', in *Law, Life and the Images of
Man. Festschrift for Jan M. Broekman*, ed. Frank Fleerackers et al. (Berlin: Duncker &
Humblot, 1996), 217–30.

[96] See generally 'RWR'; see also *LT* at §11(b) (pp. 23–5).

[97] See e.g. Stefan Hammer, 'A Neo-Kantian Theory of Legal Knowledge in Kelsen's Pure
Theory of Law?', in this volume, ch. 9; Geert Edel, 'The *Hypothesis* of the Basic Norm: Hans
Kelsen and Hermann Cohen', in this volume, ch. 10; Gerhard Luf, 'On the Transcendental
Import of Kelsen's Basic Norm', in this volume, ch. 11; Paulson (n.1 above), at 322–32, or
LT, at pp. xxix–xlii.

Kelsen's early phase, led him to his effort to provide a neo-Kantian foundation for his legal theory—foundational work that counts as one of the most provocative efforts in our century to come to terms with the perennial problems of legal philosophy.

PART II

The Normativity Problematic

3

Kelsen's Theory of the Basic Norm*

JOSEPH RAZ

Of all the various doctrines of Kelsen's legal philosophy it is his theory of the basic norm that has attracted most attention and captured the imagination. It has acquired enthusiastic devotees as well as confirmed opponents. Both admirers and critics owe much to the obscure way in which Kelsen explains his theory. The obscurity was criticized and led people to suspect that the whole theory is a myth; but it also provided admirers trading on ambiguities with an easy escape from criticism. In the following pages yet another attempt to demythologize the theory will be made. An explanation of the concept of the basic norm as Kelsen's attempt to provide an answer to some well-known jurisprudential problems will be offered. It will be further claimed that the attempt has not been altogether successful, but that its failure is illuminating. It sheds light on the intricacies of the problems involved and on their possible solutions.

Criticism will follow the exposition. The exposition, however, cannot be faithful to all the relevant texts. Some ambiguities and even contradictions cannot be eradicated by interpretation, however ingenious. Not wishing to trace the development of the theory or to present an exhaustive discussion of all the texts, the strategy I adopt will be always to prefer the more interesting of two conflicting interpretations, and to disregard the rest. The theory will be examined in relation to the problems it was designed to solve. It stands or falls according to its success in dealing with them. Kelsen regards the concept of the basic norm as essential to the explanation of all normative systems, moral as well as legal. Only his use of the concept in legal theory will be examined here.

* *Editors' note*: First published in *The American Journal of Jurisprudence*, 19 (1974), 94–111, and reprinted, with revisions, in Joseph Raz, *The Authority of Law* (Oxford: Clarendon Press, 1979), 122–45.

I. EXPLAINING THE DOCTRINE

According to Kelsen's theory it is logically necessary that in every legal system there exist one basic norm. The basic norm can be said to exist, for Kelsen says that it is valid,[1] and validity is the mode of existence of norms.[2] This does not mean that all basic norms are identical in content. Indeed, no two basic norms can have the same content. They are all called basic norms not because of their content but because they all share the same structure, the same unique position each in its own system, and because they all perform the same functions.

Kelsen postulates the existence of basic norms because he regards them as necessary for the explanation of the unity and normativity of legal systems. A legal system is not a haphazard collection of norms. It is a system because its norms, as it were, belong together. They are interrelated in a special way. Kelsen accepts two propositions which he considers too self-evident to require any detailed justification. They can be regarded as axioms of his theory. The first says that two laws, one of which directly or indirectly authorizes the creation of the other, necessarily belong to the same legal system.[3] For example, a criminal law enacted by Parliament and a constitutional law authorizing Parliament to enact criminal laws belong to one legal system just because one of them authorizes the creation of the other. The second axiom says that all the laws of a legal system are authorized, directly or indirectly, by one law.

It follows from the second axiom that two laws, neither of which authorizes the creation of the other, do not belong to the same system if there is no law authorizing the creation of both. It follows from the first axiom that if one law authorizes the creation of another or if both are authorized by a third law then both belong to the same legal system. Thus the two axioms provide a criterion for the identity of legal systems and make it possible to determine with regard to any law whether it belongs to a certain legal system or not.[4]

Assuming, as I think one should, that Kelsen is trying to elucidate the common concept of the legal system and is not simply using the term to introduce a completely different concept, the second axiom looks on the

---

[1] See e.g. *GTLS* at 111, *PTL* § 34(a) (at p. 94).

[2] *GTLS* 30; see Hans Kelsen, 'Value Judgments in the Science of Law', *Journal of Social Philosophy and Jurisprudence*, 7 (1942), 312–33, at 317, repr. *WJ* 209–30, at 214; Kelsen, 'The Pure Theory of Law and Analytical Jurisprudence', *Harvard Law Review*, 55 (1941–2), 44–70, at 50, repr. *WJ* 266–87, 390 (notes), at 267.

[3] A law authorizes indirectly the creation of another if and only if there is a third law authorized, directly or indirectly, by the first and authorizing the second.

[4] For Kelsen's criterion of identity of legal systems see *GTLS*, at 111; *PTL* § 34(a) (at p. 195).

face of it like an empirical generalization. To ascertain its truth one will have to examine all legal systems and determine whether there is in each one a law authorizing the creation of the rest. Is there, for example, a law in Britain authorizing both Parliament and the common law? This problem is implicitly recognized by Kelsen in the following passage:

If a legal order has a written constitution which does not institute custom as a form of law creation, and if nevertheless the legal order contains customary law besides statutory law, then, in addition to the norms of the written constitution, there must exist unwritten norms of constitution, a customarily created norm according to which the general norms binding the law-applying organs can be created by custom.[5]

In such a legal system there will be no positive law authorizing all the rest. Some laws will be authorized by the customary constitution, whereas others will be authorized by the enacted constitution, and there will be no positive law authorizing both constitutional laws. Kelsen, therefore, is aware that as an empirical generalization his second axiom is false. He overcomes this problem by postulating that there is in every system one non-positive law—a law which authorizes all the fundamental constitutional laws and the existence of which does not depend on the chance action of any law-creating organ, but is a logical necessity. These laws are the basic norms of legal systems and their existence is necessary for the truth of the second axiom; they make it a logical truth. Since Kelsen's criterion of identity of legal systems depends on the truth of the second axiom, it also depends on the theory of the basic norm.

This is one line of argument which Kelsen implicitly uses to prove the necessary existence of a basic norm in every legal system. Kelsen has a different and independent argument which he employs to reach the same conclusion. It aims to show that only the basic norm can explain the normativity of the law.

All laws are created by human actions, but human actions are facts and they belong to the realm of the 'is', whereas laws are norms and belong to the realm of the 'ought'. It is another of Kelsen's unquestioned beliefs that there is an unbridgeable gap between the 'is' and the 'ought'; that norms cannot derive their existence from facts. This can be regarded as a third axiom of his theory. He says: 'Nobody can assert that from the statement that something is, follows a statement that something ought to be.'[6] Therefore, he concludes: '. . . the objective validity of a norm . . . does not follow from the factual act, that is to say, from an *is*, but again from a norm authorizing this act, that is to say, from an *ought*.'[7]

---

[5] *GTLS* 126.   [6] *PTL* § 4(b) (p. 6).
[7] *PTL* § 4(b) (pp. 8–9) (Kelsen's emphasis). This principle is often repeated by Kelsen; see his paper 'Value Judgments' (n.2 above), at 321, repr. *WJ*, at 218.

The principle of dichotomy, of the unbridgeable gap between the 'ought' and the 'is', entails the principle of the autonomy of norms. Norms exist only if authorized or entailed by other norms. In the law the autonomy of the legal norms is secured by the fact that they are all links in what may be called chains of validity. The term is not used by Kelsen, but the idea is essential to his philosophy. He explains it as follows:

To the question why this individual norm is valid as part of a definite legal order, the answer is: because it has been created in conformity with a criminal statute. This statute, finally, receives its validity from the constitution, since it has been established by the competent organ in the way the constitution prescribes. If we ask why the constitution is valid, perhaps we come upon an older constitution. Ultimately we reach some constitution that is the first historically and that was laid down by an individual usurper or by some kind of assembly. . . . It is postulated that one ought to behave as the individual, or the individuals, who laid down the first constitution have ordained. This is the basic norm of the legal order under consideration.[8]

Thus, though every law is created by human action, it derives its validity not from the act, but from another law authorizing its creation. Ultimately all positive laws owe their validity to a non-positive law, a law not created by human action. Only a non-positive law can be the ultimate law of a legal system; only it does not presuppose another norm from which it derives its normativity. This non-positive law is the basic norm.

The idea of a chain of validity is central to Kelsen's solutions of the problems of the normativity and the unity of the legal system. Two laws belong to one chain of validity if one authorizes the other or if there is a third law authorizing both. The unity of the legal system consists in the fact that all its laws belong to one chain of validity and all the laws of a chain of validity are part of the same system. The normativity of laws is assured by the fact that each of the laws in a chain derives its validity from the one before it. The basic norm is essential to the solution of both problems. It provides the non-factual starting-point essential to the explanation of normativity, and it guarantees that all the laws of one system belong to the same chain of validity.

The functions assigned to the basic norm explain its content and its special status. It must be a non-positive norm. Basic norms are not enacted, nor are they created in any other way. It is presupposed by legal consciousness, but Kelsen makes it clear that it is not created by being presupposed.[9] Nor is it created by the acts of enacting other laws,[10] or by the recognition by the population of a duty to obey the law,[11] as some commentators have assumed. It does not make sense with regard to any

---

[8] *GTLS* 115; see also *PTL* § 34(c) (at pp. 199–200). On Kelsen's concept of chains of validity see Raz, *CLS*, at 97–9. Two chains of validity linked together by a common link are regarded as parts of one chain.

[9] *PTL* § 34(d) (p. 204).   [10] *RR 2*, 207n.   [11] *PTL* § 34(i) (p. 218 n.83).

basic norm to ask when it was created, by whom, or how. These categories simply do not apply to it. Nevertheless, they can be said to exist, for they are valid, and despite their uniqueness basic norms are part of the law, for they perform legally relevant functions.[12]

For them to explain the normativity and unity of a legal system, basic norms must authorize the creation of the laws of the various legal systems. Thus the functions of the basic norm account for its structure. It is an authorizing norm. It 'qualifies a certain event as the initial event in the creation of the various legal norms. It is the starting point of a norm-creating process.'[13] 'The basic norm of any positive legal order confers legal authority only upon facts by which an order is created and applied which is on the whole effective.'[14] The basic norm is a power-conferring law. Kelsen, however, formulates it as duty-imposing: '. . . the basic norm . . . must be formulated as follows: Coercive acts ought to be performed under the conditions and in the manner which the historically first constitution, and the norms created according to it, prescribe. (In short: One ought to behave as the constitution prescribes.)'[15] It is always possible to describe every law conferring legislative powers by saying that it imposes a duty to obey the laws made by the authorized organ.[16] This possibility should not obscure the nature of the law as power-conferring. The basic norm will, therefore, be regarded as conferring legislative power on the authors of the first constitution.

The formulation given by Kelsen in the quoted passage is not of any particular basic norm of any legal system. It merely exhibits the structure common to all basic norms. The content of basic norms varies according to the facts of the systems to which they belong. Kelsen explains that the content of a basic norm 'is determined by the facts through which an order is created and applied'.[17]

II. THE BASIC NORM AND THE UNITY OF LEGAL SYSTEMS

Kelsen's doctrine of the unity of legal systems fails for two independent reasons. As I have discussed them rather extensively elsewhere,[18] the following discussion will be brief. His doctrine depends on the first two axioms explained above. It is not difficult to see that both axioms must be rejected.

The first axiom asserts that all the laws belonging to one chain of

---

[12] See Hans Kelsen, 'Professor Stone and the Pure Theory of Law', *Stanford Law Review*, 17 (1964–5), 1128–57, at 1141.

[13] *GTLS* 114. [14] *GTLS* 120. [15] *PTL* § 34(c) (pp. 200–1).

[16] See further on this subject Raz, *CLS*, at 21, 23, 166–7.

[17] *GTLS* 120. [18] See Raz, *CLS*, at 100–9.

validity are part of one and the same legal system. If this axiom were correct, certain ways of peacefully granting independence to new states would become impossible. Suppose that country *A* had a colony *B*, and that both countries were governed by the same legal system. Suppose further that *A* has granted independence to *B* by a law conferring exclusive and unlimited legislative powers over *B* to a representative assembly elected by the inhabitants of *B*. Finally, let it be assumed that this representative assembly has adopted a constitution which is generally recognized by the inhabitants of *B*, and according to which elections were held and further laws were made. The government, courts, and the population of *B* regard themselves as an independent state with an independent legal system. They are recognized by all other nations including *A*. The courts of *A* regard the constitution and laws of *B* as a separate legal system distinct from their own. Despite all these facts it follows from Kelsen's first axiom that the constitution and laws of *B* are part of the legal system of *A*. For *B*'s constitution and consequently all the laws made on its basis were authorized by the independence-granting law of *A* and consequently belong to the same chain of validity and to the same system.

Kelsen's mistake is in disregarding the facts and considering only the content of the laws. For his theory the only important feature is that the legal system of *A* has a law authorizing all the laws of *B*. That the courts and population of *B* do not consider this law as part of their own legal system is irrelevant. But the attitude of the population and the courts is of the utmost importance in deciding the identity and unity of a legal system in the sense in which this concept is commonly used.[19]

This criticism does not directly affect Kelsen's theory of the basic norm. However, if the doctrine of the unity of legal systems is rejected, one of the reasons for accepting the theory of the basic norm disappears. Kelsen's theory of the unity and identity of legal systems is vitiated by a second flaw which directly concerns the role of the basic norm.

The second axiom on which his theory of the identity and unity of the legal system depends says that all the laws of one system belong to one chain of validity. When discussing this axiom we saw that Kelsen admits, at least by implication, that disregarding the basic norm, all the positive laws of a system may belong to more than one validity chain. Some may owe their validity to a customary constitution while others derive their validity from an enacted constitution. It is only the basic norm that unites them in such a case in one chain of validity by authorizing both constitutions.[20]

---

[19] The same point is made in H.L.A. Hart, 'Kelsen's Doctrine of the Unity of Law' [in this volume, ch. 30].

[20] It should be noted that the basic norm in such cases is said to authorize several constitutional laws created by several norm-creating acts. It is not clear in which sense a basic norm doing this is itself one norm rather than a conjunction of several norms.

A legally minded observer coming to such a country and wondering whether the enacted and the customary constitutions belong to the same legal system will be referred by a Kelsenite to the basic norm. It all depends, he will be told, on whether or not there is one basic norm authorizing both constitutions or whether each constitution is authorized by a different basic norm. Being told in answer to further questions that to know the content of the basic norm he should find out 'the facts through which an order is created and applied',[21] for they determine it, he may very well be driven to despair. It seems that he can only identify the legal system with the help of the basic norm whereas the basic norm can be identified only after the identity of the legal system has been established. Even if our diligent observer succeeds in establishing that at least two sets of norms are effective in the society, one, a set of customary norms, the other, of enacted norms, there will be nothing a Kelsenite can say to help him decide whether or not they form one system or two. There is nothing in the theory to prevent two legal systems from applying to the same territory. Everything depends on the ability to identify the basic norm, but it cannot be identified before the identity of the legal system is known. Therefore, the basic norm cannot solve the problem of the identity and unity of legal systems, and Kelsen has no other solution.

III. KELSEN ON NATURAL LAW THEORIES

If the previous criticism is correct the case for the basic norm must rest on its function in explaining the normativity of the law. It is with this problem that the rest of the essay will be concerned.

The role of the basic norm in explaining the normativity of law, and indeed Kelsen's explanation of that normativity, is closely connected with his critique of natural law theories. He conceived his own theory as an alternative, the only possible alternative to natural law. Kelsen even refers to the basic norm as a natural law.[22] This is not the place to examine in detail Kelsen's criticism of natural law theories, but a few remarks on some of the key ideas are essential to the understanding of his theory of the basic norm.

According to Kelsen's account, natural law theories claim that there is a set of norms, discoverable by reason, which have absolute and objective validity. They are completely and objectively just and good. Positive law, in so far as it is valid, derives its validity from natural law. It is valid

---

[21] *GTLS* 120.
[22] 'If one wishes to regard it [the basic norm] as an element of a natural law doctrine . . . very little objection can be raised. . . . What is involved is simply the minimum . . . of natural law, without which . . . a cognition . . . of law is [im]possible.' *Phil. Fds.* § 36 (p. 437).

to the extent that the natural law pronounces it just and good. Statutes, court decisions, etc. which are contrary to natural law are not valid and hence not laws at all. Kelsen correctly points out that according to natural law theories there is no specific notion of legal validity. The only concept of validity is validity according to natural law, that is, moral validity. Natural lawyers can only judge a law as morally valid, that is, just, or morally invalid, that is, wrong. They cannot say of a law that it is legally valid but morally wrong. If it is wrong and unjust, it is also invalid in the only sense of validity they recognize.[23]

Kelsen has four major reasons for rejecting all natural law theories. They are burdened with objectionable metaphysics, they are conceptually confused, they thrive on moral illusion, and they are unscientific.

(1) Natural law theories presuppose the dualistic metaphysics which has bedevilled the Western world since Plato.[24] They presuppose an ideal reality of completely just and good laws enjoying some form of objective existence independent of human acts or will which is contrasted with the imperfect social reality of man-made statutes, regulations, and decisions. The latter are imperfect and less real than the former, and whatever reality they have is due to the ideal reality. Only by imitating the ideal laws do human laws acquire validity. Kelsen is very much opposed to this kind of metaphysics and rejects it in favour of the anti-metaphysical flavour of Kant's critical philosophy. Rejecting this metaphysical dualism deprives natural law theories of their metaphysical foundation.

(2) Natural law theories are conceptually confused. They are of two varieties, one secular, and the other religious. The secular theories regard natural laws as rationally binding and self-evident in themselves. The religious theories regard them as the commands of God revealed to man through rational speculation about nature.[25] Both varieties commit the naturalistic fallacy of deriving an 'is' from an 'ought'. Whatever is natural can only be a fact, and God's commands are also facts, even if divine facts, and from facts no norm is entailed. To avoid the naturalistic fallacy both types of natural law theory must be assumed to postulate a basic

[23] See e.g. Hans Kelsen, 'The Natural-Law Doctrine before the Tribunal of Science', *Western Political Quarterly*, 2 (1949), 481–513, at 488, repr. *WJ* 137–73, 384–8 (notes), at 144; Kelsen, 'Why Should the Law be Obeyed?', in *WJ* 257–65 (the first appearance of the essay is in *WJ*); Kelsen, 'Law, State, and Justice in the Pure Theory of Law', *Yale Law Journal*, 57 (1947–8), 377–90, at 383–4, repr. *WJ* 288–302, 390–3 (notes), at 295.

[24] See *Phil. Fds.* §§ 22–32 (pp. 419–33); Hans Kelsen, 'Absolutism and Relativism in Philosophy and Politics', *American Political Science Review*, 42 (1948), 906–14, repr. *WJ* 198–208, 388 (notes). Kelsen is not rejecting the possibility of regarding laws as abstract entities provided they are given adequate interpretation relating them to human behaviour. Such a doctrine does not have the metaphysical implications of Platonism.

[25] For the explanation of the two types of natural law theories see e.g. Kelsen, 'Analytical Jurisprudence' (n.2 above), at 68–70, repr. *WJ*, at 285–7.

norm investing the facts with normative character.[26] The secular basic norm is that nature be obeyed, the religious basic norm dictates that God be obeyed.[27] The basic norms must be considered self-evident. They cannot be derived from any other norm, yet they are said to be objectively valid and binding. In this way Kelsen attempts to rectify the confusions committed by the proponents of the natural law.

(3) 'The doctrine is a typical illusion, due to an objectivation of subjective interests.'[28] On Kelsen's analysis the natural law's claim to objective validity rests on the assumption that its basic norms are self-evident. Kelsen rejects all such claims as illusions. He is a moral relativist.[29] No moral position can be objectively proved and defended. There are no intuitively true moral beliefs.[30] Moral opinions are matters of personal preferences. By claiming objective validity, natural lawyers breed illusions and use them for various ideological purposes. Most commonly the natural law illusion has been used by conservative optimists to justify existing legal and political institutions. Occasionally the same illusion has been turned into a tool for promoting reform or revolution.[31]

Kelsen's relativism does not preclude the possibility or necessity of assessing the law by moral standards. He simply insists that every evaluation is valid only relative to the particular moral norm used, which in itself has no objective validity. Consequently moral criticism or justification of the law is a matter of personal or political judgment. It is not an objective scientific matter and does not concern the science of law.[32]

(4) By condemning natural law theories as unscientific Kelsen means that they cannot be objectively confirmed. Therefore, Kelsen's desire to construct a scientific theory of law leads him to renounce the morality of the law as a subject of the theory. 'The problem of law, as a scientific problem, is the problem of social technique, not a problem of morals.'[33] Legal theory is and should be concerned with a special type of social technique for controlling human behaviour. Natural law theories, by distinguishing between just statutes which are law, and unjust ones which are not law, obscure the issue. For they thereby exclude some normative

---

[26] Kelsen, 'The Natural-Law Doctrine' (n.23 above), 485, repr. *WJ* 141.

[27] Kelsen, 'Why Should the Law be Obeyed?' (n.23 above), *WJ* 258, 260–1.

[28] Kelsen, 'Value Judgments' (n.2 above), 331, repr. *WJ* 228.

[29] See Kelsen, 'The Natural-Law Doctrine' (n.23 above), at 484, repr. *WJ*, at 141; Hans Kelsen, 'A "Dynamic" Theory of Natural Law', *Louisiana Law Review*, 16 (1955–6), 597–620, at 602–3, repr. *WJ* 174–97, 388 (notes), at 179–80; Kelsen, 'Value Judgments' (n.2 above), at 330–2, repr. *WJ*, at 228–9; Kelsen, 'Why Should the Law be Obeyed?' (n.23 above), *WJ*, at 259; Kelsen, 'Law, State, and Justice' (n.23 above), at 383–4, repr. *WJ*, at 295; *PTL* § 11 (at p. 64).

[30] *PTL* §34(j) (p. 221).

[31] See Kelsen, 'Law, State, and Justice' (n.23 above), at 385–6, repr. *WJ*, at 297.

[32] See Kelsen, 'Law, State, and Justice' (n.23 above), at 383, 390, repr. *WJ*, at 295, 302; *Phil. Fds.* § 35 (at p. 436); *PTL* § 13 (at pp. 68–9).   [33] *GTLS* 5.

systems from being classified as legal, even though they are instances of the use of the same social technique.

IV. THE BASIC NORM AND A VALUE-FREE
STUDY OF LAW

To perform its task legal theory must be value-free. Consequently its explanation of the normativity of law must be independent of the moral value of the law. How is the notion of legal validity and normativity to be explained? Kelsen resorts to the conceptual framework of Kantian critical philosophy. Kant himself adopted a version of natural law theory only because he did not remain true to his own premises.[34] His philosophy, however, provides the intellectual tools which Kelsen wishes to use.

A legal concept of validity and normativity is made possible only through the concept of the basic norm:

To interpret these acts of human beings as legal acts and their products as binding norms, and that means to interpret the empirical material which presents itself as law as such, is possible only on the condition that the basic norm is presupposed as a valid norm. The basic norm is only the necessary presupposition of any positivistic interpretation of the legal material.[35]

The basic norm is necessarily presupposed when people regard the law as normative, irrespective of its moral worth:

... the basic norm as represented by the science of law may be characterized as the transcendental-logical condition of this interpretation, if it is permissible to use by analogy a concept of Kant's epistemology. Kant asks: 'How is it possible to interpret without a metaphysical hypothesis, the facts perceived by our senses, in the laws of nature formulated by natural science?' In the same way, the Pure Theory of Law asks: 'How is it possible to interpret without recourse to meta-legal authorities, like God or nature, the subjective meaning of certain facts as a system of objectively valid legal norms . . . ?' The epistemological answer of the Pure Theory of Law is: 'By presupposing the basic norm that one ought to behave as the constitution prescribes. . . .' The function of this basic norm is to found the objective validity of a positive legal order.[36]

The concept of the basic norm provides legal theory with an objective and value-free concept of legal normativity. 'The presupposition of the basic norm does not approve any value transcending positive law.'[37] '[I]t does not perform an ethical-political but only an epistemological function.'[38]

---

[34] See *Phil. Fds.* § 40 (at pp. 444–5). Kelsen's interpretation of Kant can be disputed, but this need not concern us here.

[35] *GTLS* 116.

[37] *PTL* § 34(d) (p. 201).

[36] *PTL* § 34(d) (p. 202).

[38] *PTL* § 34(i) (p. 218).

Not performing a moral or political function the basic norm is objective:

To the norms of positive law there corresponds a certain social reality, but not so to the norms of justice. . . . Juristic value judgments are judgments that can be tested objectively by facts. Therefore they are admissible within a science of law.[39]

The basic norm, therefore, is not the product of free invention. It is not presupposed arbitrarily in the sense that there is a choice between different basic norms when the subjective meaning of a constitution-creating act and the acts created according to this constitution are interpreted as their objective meaning.[40]

With the aid of the concept of a basic norm Kelsen claims he has established a value-free legal theory using a specific legal concept of normativity:

The postulate to differentiate law and morals, jurisprudence and ethics, means this: from the standpoint of scientific cognition of positive law, its justification by a moral order different from the legal order, is irrelevant, because the task of the science of law is not to approve or disapprove its subject, but to know and describe it. . . . [T]he postulate to separate law and morals, science of law and ethics, means that the validity of positive legal norms does not depend on their conformity with the moral order; it means that from the standpoint of a cognition directed toward positive law a legal norm may be considered valid, even if it is at variance with the moral order.[41]

V. KELSEN ON THE NATURE OF THE NORMATIVITY OF LAW

Thus far it has been established that Kelsen regards the concept of a basic norm as necessary to the understanding of law as a normative system, and that he thinks that only by using this concept can legal theory be value-free and objective and avoid the blunders of natural law theories. Nothing has been said so far about the nature of the normativity accruing to the law by virtue of the basic norm. To this problem we must now turn.

Two conceptions of the normativity of law are current. I will call them justified and social normativity. According to the one view legal standards of behaviour are norms only if and in so far as they are justified. They may be justified by some objective and universally valid reasons. They may be intuitively perceived as binding or they may be accepted as justified by personal commitment. On the other view standards of

---

[39] Kelsen, 'Value Judgments' (n.2 above), 332, repr. *WJ* 229.
[40] *PTL* § 34(d) (p. 201).   [41] *PTL* § 13 (p. 68).

behaviour can be considered as norms regardless of their merit. They are social norms in so far as they are socially upheld as binding standards and in so far as the society involved exerts pressure on people to whom the standards apply to conform to them. Natural law theorists characteristically endorse the first view, positivists usually maintain the second view. The most successful explanation of the normativity of law in terms of the concept of social normativity is Hart's analysis in *The Concept of Law*. Theorists using the concepts of justified normativity claim that a legal system can be regarded as normative only by people considering it as just and endorsing its norms by accepting them as part of their own moral views. Theorists using the concepts of social normativity maintain that everyone should regard legal systems as normative regardless of his judgment about their merits.

Much of the obscurity of Kelsen's theory stems from the difficulty in deciding which concept of normativity he is using. It will be claimed that:

(1) Kelsen uses only the concept of justified normativity.
(2) According to him an individual can consider a legal system as normative only if he endorses it as morally just and good.
(3) Legal theory considers legal systems as normative in the same sense of 'normative' but in a different sense of 'consider' which does not commit it to accepting the laws as just.

Let us consider the first statement first. Quite often Kelsen considers a concept of social normativity only to reject it as not being really a concept of normativity or at any rate as not being appropriate for legal theory. Thus he distinguishes between a subjective and an objective 'ought',[42] claiming that legal norms are objective norms, explained by the concept of an objective 'ought'. His subjective 'ought' is a variety of social normativity. Connected with this distinction is his comparison between objective and subjective value judgments. The latter are an explanation of one type of social normativity and are judged by him to be factual rather than normative judgments:

The value constituted by an objectively valid norm must be distinguished from the value that consists (not in the relation to a norm, but) in the relation of an object to the wish or will of an individual directed at this object. If the object is in accordance or not in accordance with the wish or will, it has a positive or negative value. . . . If the judgment describing the relation of an object to the wish or will of an individual is designated as a value judgment . . . then this value judgment is not different from a judgment about reality. For it describes only the relation between two facts, not the relation between a fact and an objectively valid

---

[42] E.g. *PTL* § 4(b) (p. 7). Here as elsewhere when Kelsen examines and rejects the concept of social normativity he considers only crude explanations of it. Social normativity cannot be explained in terms of efficacious commands.

norm. . . . The value that consists in the relation of an object . . . to the wish or will of an individual can be designated as subjective value.[43]

Describing laws as commands of a sovereign is, on this theory, describing them as subjective 'ought'. If one does not presuppose the basic norm, then judgments about the lawfulness of action, understood as judgments about their conformity to the commands of a sovereign, are merely subjective value judgments. Kelsen acknowledges that the law can consistently be interpreted in this way, but in this case it is not regarded as normative:

The fact that the basic norm of a positive legal order *may* but *need not* be pre-supposed means: the relevant interhuman relationships may be, but need not be, interpreted as 'normative', that is, as obligations, authorizations, rights, etc. constituted by objectively valid norms. It means further: they can be interpreted without such presupposition (that is, without the basic norm) as power relations (that is, relations between commanding and obeying or disobeying human beings)—in other words, they can be interpreted sociologically, not juristically.[44]

This is a key passage. Kelsen claims in effect that the concept of social normativity is not a concept of normativity at all. It does not allow the interpretation of law as imposing obligations, granting powers, rights, etc. It makes the law indistinguishable from the commands of a group of gangsters terrorizing the population of a certain area.[45] Only by using the concept of justified normativity can one understand the true character of legal systems as normative systems.

Because Kelsen regards the concept of justified normativity as the only concept of normativity, he considers law as an ideology. For law is nor-mative, that is, justified and good for everyone who regards it as norma-tive: 'This is the reason why it is possible to maintain that the idea of a norm, an "ought", is merely ideological. . . . In this sense the law may be considered as the specific ideology of a certain historically given power.'[46]

One should be careful to distinguish between the two senses in which legal norms are said by Kelsen to be objective. In the first sense they are objective for they reflect a social reality, that is, because they are norma-tive in the sense of social normativity. In the second sense they are objec-tive for they are normative in the sense of justified normativity; they are an ideology. The two senses are manifested in the following passage: 'If we conceive of the law as a complex of norms and therefore as an ideology, this ideology differs from other, especially from metaphysical,

[43] *PTL* § 4(e) (pp. 19–20) (Kelsen's emphasis omitted).
[44] *PTL* § 34(i) (p. 218).
[45] Kelsen uses this example for a different purpose in *PTL* § 6(e) (p. 47).
[46] Kelsen, 'Value Judgments' (n.2 above), 329–30, repr. *WJ* 227.

ideologies so far as the former corresponds to certain facts of reality. . . .
If the system of legal norms is an ideology, it is an ideology that is parallel to a definite reality.'[47]

In other words, it is normative in the sense of justified normativity
(that is, it is an objective 'ought') but also normative in the sense of social
normativity (that is, corresponding to objectively ascertainable facts the
meaning of which is the subjective 'ought'). This constant shift from one
sense of objective to the other has not helped scholars to understand
what concept of normativity Kelsen is using.

To anyone regarding the law as socially normative, the question 'why
should the law be obeyed?' cannot be answered by pointing out that it is
normative. The law is normative because of certain social facts. It should
be obeyed, if at all, for moral reasons. The normativity of the law and the
obligation to obey it are distinct notions. Not so to people who admit
only the concept of justified normativity. For them to judge the law as
normative is to judge it to be just and to admit that it ought to be obeyed.
The concepts of the normativity of the law and of the obligation to obey
it are analytically tied together. Kelsen, therefore, regards the law as
valid, that is, normative, only if one ought to obey it. 'By "validity", the
binding force of the law—the idea that it ought to be obeyed by the
people whose behavior it regulates—is understood.'[48] '[That a] norm
referring to the behavior of a human being is "valid" means that it is
binding—that an individual ought to behave in the manner determined
by the norm.'[49] These statements are unavoidable for a theorist working
with the concept of justified normativity. They are misleading if the normativity of the law is explained as social normativity only.

VI. AN INDIVIDUAL'S 'POINT OF VIEW'

The normativity of the law is justified normativity; its reason is the basic
norm which is, therefore, a justified norm. But it is not justified in any
absolute sense. Kelsen believes in moral relativism. For him moral opinions are matters of personal preference which cannot be rationally confirmed or refuted. Hence he claims that the basic norm is presupposed,
that is, accepted, and the law is regarded as normative only by people
who consider it to be just:

But there is no necessity to presuppose the basic norm. . . . The system of norms
that we call 'legal order' is a possible but not a necessary scheme of interpretation.
An anarchist will decline to speak of 'lawful' and 'unlawful' behavior, of 'legal

[47] Kelsen, 'Value Judgments' (n.2 above), 330, repr. *WJ* 227.
[48] Kelsen, 'Why Should the Law be Obeyed?' (n.23 above), *WJ* 257.
[49] *PTL* § 34(a) (p. 193).

duties' and 'legal rights', or 'delicts'. He will understand social behavior merely as a process whereby one forces the other to behave in conformity with his wishes or interests. . . . He will, in short, refuse to presuppose the basic norm.[50]

. . . an anarchist, for instance, who denied the validity of the hypothetical basic norm of positive law . . . will view its positive regulation of human relationships . . . as mere power relations.[51]

A communist may, indeed, not admit that there is an essential difference between an organization of gangsters and a capitalistic legal order. . . . For he does not presuppose—as do those who interpret the coercive order as an objectively valid normative order—the basic norm.[52]

For an individual to presuppose the basic norm is to interpret the legal system as normative, that is, as just. For Kelsen all the values endorsed by one individual, all his moral opinions, form necessarily one normative system based on one basic norm. One can speak of an individual's normative system, or of the normative system from the point of view of a certain individual. Regarded from one point of view every set of norms necessarily forms one consistent and unified normative order. The individual may think that some of the norms to which he subscribes conflict. But this is a psychological not a normative fact. He may feel torn between two opposing modes of action.[53] But it makes no sense to say that his normative system contains conflicting norms. It is of the essence of the concept of a normative system that it guides behaviour; it guides the behaviour of those persons who adopt the relevant point of view. But if conflicting norms are assumed to be valid from one point of view, then they do not guide behaviour for they point in opposing directions at the same time. Therefore all the norms held valid from one point of view necessarily form one consistent system:

It is logically not possible to assume that simultaneously valid norms belong to different, mutually independent systems.[54]

If two different systems of norms are given, only one of them can be assumed to be valid from the point of view of a cognition which is concerned with the validity of norms.[55]

---

[50] Kelsen, 'Value Judgments' (n.2 above), 329, repr. *WJ* 226–7.
[51] *Phil. Fds.* § 18 (p. 413).　　　　　　　　[52] Kelsen (n.12 above), 1144.
[53] See *GTLS*, at 375. In 'Derogation' [see the Table of Abbreviations] and in 'Law and Logic', [the version] published in *Philosophy and Christianity. Philosophical Essays Dedicated to Professor Dr. Herman Dooyeweerd* (Amsterdam: North-Holland Publ. Co., 1965), 231–6, Kelsen retracted his claim that valid norms are necessarily consistent. Unfortunately he did not discuss there the reasons that led him to accept this doctrine in the first place, nor did he modify those parts of his theory that depend on his previous doctrine, such as the relation of law and morality, municipal and international law, etc. Consequently his theory of the normativity of law is intelligible and consistent only on the assumption that valid norms are necessarily consistent.
[54] *GTLS* 363.　　　　　　　　　　[55] *Phil. Fds.* § 13 (p. 407).

If one assumes that two systems of norms are considered as valid simultaneously from the same point of view, one must also assume a normative relation between them; one must assume the existence of a norm or order that regulates their mutual relations. Otherwise insoluble contradictions between the norms of each system are unavoidable.[56]

All this is incomprehensible if it is assumed that Kelsen uses the concept of social normativity. It gains some plausibility if it is recognized that Kelsen is operating throughout with a concept of justified normativity. Then it is possible to appreciate Kelsen's reasons for maintaining that (1) for an individual to acknowledge that something is a norm is to accept it as just; (2) from an individual's point of view all his moral beliefs form one normative system; (3) all the norms held valid from one point of view must be consistent. For the normative interpretation of a person's belief is not a psychological but a rational enterprise intended to elucidate the direction in which his views guide him.

One rather surprising consequence of this analysis is that the concept of normative systems loses much of its importance. The most important concept is that of a point of view. It is logically true that from every point of view there is just one normative system, and therefore just one basic norm. An individual accepting the justice of his country's laws, but subscribing to further values not incorporated in the law, accepts not two normative systems but one. His country's laws are part of this system, though they can be viewed as a subsystem of his total normative system. To assert that all the norms held valid from one viewpoint constitute one system with one basic norm is, of course, to assert more than that they do not conflict. It is to claim that they all derive their validity from one basic norm. This is tacitly assumed rather than argued by Kelsen. Granting, however, that the basic norm can confer validity on more than one norm renders this a rather technical matter of no great importance.[57]

VII. 'THE LEGAL POINT OF VIEW'

So far the notion of a point of view has been considered only as applying to particular individuals; only points of view adopted by individuals have been discussed. But there are also more complex points of view. One can ascribe a point of view to a group of individuals, to a population, provided the population shares the same values. It is possible to consider hypothetical points of view, for example, to discuss what norms are adopted by individuals who accept all and only the laws of their country

---

[56] Kelsen, 'Analytical Jurisprudence' (n.2 above), 67, repr. *WJ* 284.
[57] See n.20 above.

as valid, without assuming that such individuals exist. One may call this particular example of a hypothetical point of view the point of view of *the legal man*. Throughout his work Kelsen uses the concept of a point of view of legal science. He talks about 'the basic norm of a positive legal order, the ultimate reason for its validity, seen from the point of view of a science of positive law'.[58] He also says that the science of law presupposes the basic norm, but nevertheless is not committed to regarding it as just.

There is, for Kelsen, a great difference between a personal point of view and the scientific point of view. Norms judged as valid from a personal point of view are those adopted as just. But legal theory is value-free and norms judged to be valid from its point of view are not thereby adopted as just. Any individual can discuss the law sometimes from his personal viewpoint, sometimes from the point of view of legal science. Adopting the latter, '[e]ven an anarchist, if he were a professor of law, could describe positive law as a system of valid norms, without having to approve of this law.'[59] At the same time the anarchist will reject the validity of the law when considering it from his personal point of view. What is the nature of the point of view of legal science? How can it be value-free, and at the same time regard the law as normative in the only sense admitted by Kelsen, that is, that of justified normativity? One tempting explanation is that legal theory asserts that a legal system exists only if adopted, from the personal viewpoint, by the population to which it applies, and describes the law as seen from this point of view. Kelsen, however, rejects this interpretation:

[T]he doctrine of the basic norm is not a doctrine of recognition as is sometimes erroneously understood. According to the doctrine of recognition positive law is valid only if it is recognized by the individuals subject to it, which means: if these individuals agree that one ought to behave according to the norms of the positive law. This recognition, it is said, actually takes place, and if this cannot be proved, it is assumed, fictitiously, as a tacit recognition.[60]

The Pure Theory of Law does not assert or assume any attitude of the population to the law. A legal system exists if it is effective and this does not entail acceptance as morally just.

An alternative interpretation would be that legal science describes not the population's point of view but the point of view of the hypothetical legal man, that is, of a person accepting from a personal viewpoint all and only the legal norms, without assuming that such a person actually exists. Such an interpretation is supported by various passages like the following:

---

[58] Kelsen, 'Why Should the Law be Obeyed?' (n.23 above), *WJ* 262.
[59] *PTL* § 34(i) (p. 218 n.82).   [60] *PTL* § 34(i) (p. 218 n.83).

The Pure Theory describes the positive law as an objectively valid normative order and states that this interpretation is possible only under the condition that a basic norm is presupposed. . . . The Pure Theory thereby characterizes this interpretation as possible, not necessary, and presents the objective validity of positive law only as conditional—namely conditioned by the presupposed basic norm.[61]

This interpretation comes very near the core of Kelsen's doctrine but it is not free from difficulties. On this interpretation the Pure Theory itself does not adopt any point of view; it does not presuppose any basic norm. It merely describes the point of view of the legal man and the basic norm he adopts. Is Kelsen mistaken in regarding legal science as having a point of view and presupposing a basic norm? Does he use these terms in a completely different sense when applied to legal science? Kelsen himself is unsure of his position on this crucial point, for occasionally he can be seen to waver.[62] The difficulty results from the fact that Kelsen does not distinguish between the science of law dealt with by jurists talking *about* the law, and the activities of lawyers and judges *using* the law. He considers both under the one title of juristic cognition. He wants to claim that:

By offering this theory of the basic norm, the Pure Theory of Law does not inaugurate a new method of legal cognition. It merely makes conscious what most *legal scientists* do, at least unconsciously, when they understand the mentioned facts not as causally determined, but instead interpret their subjective meaning as objectively valid norms. . . . The theory of the basic norm is merely the result of an analysis of the procedure which a positivistic *science* of law has always applied.[63]

Kelsen, however, makes a similar claim not only about legal scientists, but also about legal practitioners. The following passage applies to lawyers as well as law professors:

That the basic norm really exists in the juristic consciousness is the result of a simple analysis of actual juristic statements. The basic norm is the answer to the question: how—and that means under what condition—are all these juristic statements concerning legal norms, legal duties, legal rights, and so on, possible?[64]

It can perhaps be claimed that legal scientists do not adopt a point of view; they do not regard the law as valid but simply describe what is con-

---

[61] *PTL* § 34(i) (pp. 217–18).

[62] Compare his treatment of the anarchist in *PTL* § 34(i) (at p. 218 n.82) with his discussion of the same problem in previous and subsequent publications. See also his explicit discussion of the question whether the Pure Theory presupposes the basic norm, *PTL* § 34(d) (at p. 204 n.72).

[63] *PTL* § 34(d) (pp. 204–5) (emphasis added).   [64] *GTLS* 116–17.

sidered valid from the point of view of some other person, that is, the legal man. But legal practitioners do not describe what somebody else regards as valid; rather, they themselves consider the law as valid, refer to it as valid, and apply it to particular cases. They cannot be said merely to describe a point of view; they actually adopt one. Yet when acting professionally they need not express their personal point of view. An anarchist can be not only a law teacher, but also a lawyer. As a lawyer he adopts and expresses a professional point of view, the point of view of legal science, as Kelsen calls it, which does not commit him, and is understood not to commit him, to the view that the law is just.

For Kelsen the legal scientist, as well as the legal practitioner, not only describes a point of view, but actually adopts one. Legal science regards the laws as valid and hence presupposes the basic norm. The point of view of legal science is that of the legal man. It is not merely described but actually adopted, and it is adopted in a special sense.

If a man were actually to adopt the point of view of the legal man he would adopt the law as his personal morality, and as exhausting all the norms he accepts as just. Legal science does not accept the point of view of the legal man in this sense. Legal science is not committed to regarding the law as just. It adopts this point of view in a special sense of 'adopt'. It is professional and uncommitted adoption. Legal science presupposes the basic norm not as individuals do—that is, by accepting it as just—but in this special professional and uncommitted sense.

VIII. CONCLUSION

The analysis of Kelsen's theory of normativity and of the basic norm clarifies some of Kelsen's fundamental theses. It explains his insistence that the basic norm presupposed by legal science authorizes the first constitution and does not refer to any non-legal authority like God or nature. Individuals from their personal point of view are indeed unlikely to adopt this norm as their basic norm. They are likely to appeal to God or to nature or some other moral norm as their basic norm. But this is irrelevant to legal science, which has a special point of view, that of the legal man, which it adopts in the special professional sense of adopting. Legal science, therefore, presupposes, in the special sense, this particular basic norm, for it is concerned as a science only with positive law.

On the present analysis Kelsen's position on the relation of law and morality is seen as entailed by the rest of his theory:

When positive law and morality are asserted to be two distinct mutually independent systems of norms, this means only that the jurist, in determining what is legal, does not take into consideration morality, and the moralist, in determining what is moral, pays no heed to the prescriptions of positive law. Positive law and morality can be regarded as two distinct and mutually independent systems of norms, because and to the extent that they are not conceived to be simultaneously valid from the same point of view.[65]

Kelsen is discussing here the professional points of view of the legal and moral scholar. He is not denying that a legal order can incorporate moral rules or that morality can incorporate the law and regard it as morally valid. Nor is he denying that an individual from his personal viewpoint can regard both legal and non-legal norms as valid. To the individual they will all form part of his personal normative system, based on his personal point of view. From the point of view of legal science, however, only the law is valid, just as from the point of view of ethical theories only moral norms are valid.

Kelsen's insistence that from a single point of view there can be just one normative system and just one basic norm explains why his theory of normativity in itself entails that there is just one basic norm to every legal system. In so far as basic norms are necessary only to enable us to consider the law as normative, there is nothing to prevent one from postulating several basic norms relating to one system. One basic norm can make the criminal law normative, another will relate to the law of property, etc. However, on Kelsen's theory this will mean that there is no one point of view from which the legal system is considered but several, each corresponding to every one of the basic norms.

Furthermore, since there is one general science of law, it follows, on the Kelsenian premiss of the unity of a point of view, that all the laws form but one legal system. The ultimate reason for Kelsen's theory of the unity of national and international law is his theory of normativity. Since all the norms held valid from one point of view form one normative system, it follows without further argument that since both national and international law are considered valid from the point of view of one legal science, they are parts of one system. All that remains to be done is to explain how they should be thus understood. 'The unity of national and international law is an epistemological postulate. A jurist who *accepts both* as sets of valid norms must try to comprehend them as parts of one harmonious system.'[66] '[O]nce it is conceded that national and international law are both positive law, it is obvious that both must be considered as valid *simultaneously from the same juristic point of view*. For this reason, they must belong to the same system.'[67] '[I]f both systems

---

[65] Kelsen, 'Analytical Jurisprudence' (n.2 above), 67, repr. *WJ* 284. See also *GTLS*, at 374; *Phil. Fds.*, at § 15 (p. 410).

[66] *GTLS* 373 (emphasis added).

[67] Kelsen, 'Analytical Jurisprudence' (n.2 above), 67, repr. *WJ* 284 (emphasis added).

are considered to be *simultaneously* valid orders of binding norms, it is inevitable to comprehend both as *one* system.'[68]

This analysis of Kelsen's doctrine of the basic norm in its function in establishing the normativity of law is based on the claim that though Kelsen rejects natural law theories, he consistently uses the natural law concept of normativity, that is, the concept of justified normativity. He is able to maintain that the science of law is value-free by claiming for it a special point of view, that of the legal man, and contending that legal science adopts this point of view; that it presupposes its basic norm in a special, professional, and uncommitted sense of presupposing. There is, after all, no legal sense of normativity, but there is a specifically legal way in which normativity can be considered.

This is the core of Kelsen's theory. To it he adds the further claim that all the norms held valid from one point of view must be considered as one consistent system. This further thesis can and should be criticized and rejected. It leads to a distorted view of the relations between the various values subscribed to by an individual. It also leads to a distortion of the common concept of a legal system. This is not the place to examine the inadequacies of Kelsen's view of personal morality. Kelsen's failure to account for the concept of a legal system is treated elsewhere.[69] It is, however, important to remember that it is possible to reject Kelsen's identification of the concepts of a normative system and a normative point of view while retaining the other basic tenets of Kelsen's theory of normativity and the basic norm.

It seems to me that Kelsen's theory is the best existing theory of positive law based on the concept of justified normativity. It is deficient in being bound up with other essentially independent as well as wrong doctrines and it is incomplete in not being supported by any semantic doctrine or doctrine of discourse capable of explaining the nature of discourse from the point of view of the legal man.

---

[68] *PTL* § 43(c) (p. 332) (in first case of italics, emphasis added).
[69] See § II above, and see Hart, 'Unity of Law' (n.19 above).

4

Kelsen Visited*

H.L.A. HART

In November 1961, I had the enjoyable and instructive experience of meeting Hans Kelsen and debating with him at the Law School of the University of California in Berkeley some topics which I had previously selected for discussion from his *General Theory of Law and State*. The meeting was arranged by Professor Albert Ehrenzweig,[1] who introduced us. We warned our very large audience that they might be disappointed or bored or both disappointed and bored: for the questions we proposed to discuss might excusably appear to them to be dry and technical, and our differences to be mere disputes over detail within the 'positivist' camp of jurisprudence, of no great interest to those outside it. I explained that my view was that Kelsen's great work deserved the compliment of detailed scrutiny, and that it had too often been used as an excuse for the debate of vast and vaguely defined issues, such as the hoary perennial known as 'Natural Law versus Legal Positivism'. In spite of the technical nature of our discussion it was I think enjoyed by our audience, which included, as well as lawyers, a sprinkling of philosophers, political theorists, and students of other disciplines. Certainly it proved most instructive to me: it made me understand better the point of certain Kelsenian doctrines which had long perplexed me, even if it did not finally dispel my perplexities. I am reluctant to believe that I am alone in finding these difficulties in Kelsen's work; so some account of our discussion may be of use to others. In what follows I shall try both to explain why the points I raised seem to me important as well as to delineate our respective positions.

* *Editors' note*: Hart's essay first appeared in the *UCLA Law Review*, 10 (1962–3), 709–28, and was reprinted in H.L.A. Hart, *Essays in Jurisprudence and Philosophy* (Oxford: Clarendon Press, 1983), 286–308.

1 [Albert A. Ehrenzweig (1906–74) was Kelsen's colleague and friend at the University of California, Berkeley. Like Kelsen, Ehrenzweig spent his early years in Vienna and settled in Berkeley, California. Ehrenzweig's major field was conflicts of law; he also wrote *Psychoanalytic Jurisprudence* (Leiden: A.W. Sijthoff, 1971).]

The points which I chose for discussion were these:

I. Kelsen's expression: 'rules of law in a descriptive sense'.[2]
II. The definition of delict.[3]
III. The relationship between positive law and morality.[4]

Besides these three issues there were others which we agreed to discuss if there was time. In fact there was no time for any of these others at our public discussion.

Before concluding this brief introduction I should like to record the fact that our discussion had its entertaining moments. The first was when Kelsen remarked that the dispute between us was of a wholly novel kind because though he agreed with me I did not agree with him. The second was towards the end of our debate, when upon Kelsen emphasizing in stentorian tones, so remarkable in an octogenarian (or in any one), that 'Norm is Norm' and not something else, I was so startled that I (literally) fell over backwards in my chair.

I. RULES OF LAW IN A DESCRIPTIVE SENSE

In the following passages taken from *General Theory* I have italicized the particular expressions which I found difficult to understand.

It is the task of the science of law to represent the law of a community, i.e. the material produced by the legal authority in the law-making procedure, in the form of statements to the effect that 'if such and such conditions are fulfilled, then such and such a sanction shall follow.' These statements, by means of which the science of law represents law, must not be confused with the norms created by the law-making authorities. It is preferable not to call these statements norms, but legal rules. The legal norms enacted by the law-creating authorities are prescriptive; *the rules of law formulated by the science of law are descriptive*. It is of importance that the term *'legal rule' or 'rule of law' be employed here in a descriptive sense.*[5]

The rule of law, *the term used in a descriptive sense*, is a hypothetical judgment attaching certain consequences to certain conditions. . . . The rule of law says: If *A* is, *B* ought to be. *The rule of law is a norm (in the descriptive sense of that term).*[6]

The ought-statements in which the theorist of law represents the norms have a merely descriptive import; they, as it were, descriptively reproduce the 'ought' of the norms.[7]

---

[2] See *GTLS*, at 45–6, 50, 163–4.   [3] See *GTLS*, at 54–6.
[4] See *GTLS*, at 373–6; *Phil. Fds.*, at §§ 13–15 (pp. 407–10).
[5] *GTLS* 45 (emphasis added).   [6] *GTLS* 45–6 (emphasis added).
[7] *GTLS* 163 (emphasis added).

The general drift of these passages is of course tolerably clear. Kelsen has told us, in his introduction to *General Theory* and elsewhere, that the 'general orientation' of his Pure Theory of Law and of analytical jurisprudence are the same. Neither of these disciplines is concerned with the moral or political evaluation of law, nor with the sociological description or explanation of law or legal phenomena. Instead both are concerned with the analysis or elucidation of the meaning of positive law. They differ according to Kelsen because the Pure Theory is more consistent and so avoids certain errors made, for example by Austin, in the analysis of rights and duties and of the relationship between law and state.

This characterization of the Pure Theory of Law as a stricter, more consistent, and more systematic version of analytical jurisprudence, together with Kelsen's frequent references to the task of juristic theory as being that of 'grasp[ing] the specific meaning of the legal rules',[8] naturally leads one to expect that the main product of this form of jurisprudence will be statements giving or explaining the meaning of expressions such as 'law', 'legal system', 'legal rule', 'right', 'duty', 'ownership', and 'possession'. Austin certainly was much occupied with such analysis, and indeed conceived the elucidation of the law's fundamental notions to be the special task of the analytical science which he styled 'General Jurisprudence'.[9] Of course the ideas of 'analysis', 'elucidation', and even 'definition' are vague, and can take many forms. It is not to be expected that the analytical jurist should always, or even usually, provide definitions *per genus et differentiam* of single words in which the definition provided is a synonym for the word to be defined. If the distinctive feature of analytical jurisprudence is its concern, in Kelsen's words, to grasp the 'specific meaning of legal rules', there are many different ways in which this may be done. The analytical jurist may give not definitions of single words, but synonyms or 'translations' of whole sentences ('definitions in use'); or he may even forgo altogether the provision of synonyms and instead set out to describe the standard use of certain expressions.

Now, undoubtedly, in Kelsen's *General Theory* there are *some* statements which seem to be definitions or analyses. They are statements which directly or indirectly explain the meaning of certain expressions distinctive of the law in terms of other more familiar or better understood expressions. One example of these (about which I say more later) is what Kelsen himself terms the 'juristic definition' of delict as 'the behavior of the individual against whom the sanction as the consequence of this

---

[8] *GTLS* 164.
[9] John Austin, 'The Uses of the Study of Jurisprudence', in *The Province of Jurisprudence Determined*, ed. H.L.A. Hart (London: Weidenfeld and Nicolson, 1954), 363–93, at 367. [Austin's 'Uses' was first published in 1863.]

behavior is directed'.[10] Another related example is Kelsen's statement
that to be legally obligated to a certain behaviour 'means that the contrary behavior is a delict and as such is the condition of a sanction stipulated by a legal norm.'[11] But though these and numerous other instances
could be found in Kelsen's book of what might be construed as definitions or analyses of expressions, it is plain that the main concern of the
Pure Theory of Law is not to provide these, but to do something rather
different. More often than not Kelsen seems concerned to introduce new
expressions and with them new ideas rather than to define old ones.
Such definitions as there are of current legal expressions are incidental to
the task which Kelsen at the outset says is the main task of the Pure
Theory of Law: to enable the jurist concerned with a particular legal system to understand and to describe as exactly as possible that system of
positive law. For this purpose the Pure Theory 'furnishes the fundamental concepts by which the positive law of a definite legal community can
be described.'[12]

It is important to observe that such a description of a particular system
of law is not the task of the Pure Theory of Law; it is the task of 'the normative science of law' or 'normative jurisprudence'. It is very easy especially for an Englishman trained in Austin's jurisprudence to think that
all these three quoted expressions mean the same thing and can be simply identified with 'analytical jurisprudence'. It is indeed true that all
these forms of jurisprudence have some important features in common:
they are all sciences whose subject-matter is positive law; they are not
concerned to evaluate or criticize that subject-matter in moral, ideological, or in any other ways; they are not concerned to provide factual
descriptions or explanations of the actual operations of the law. They are
thus all 'pure' or free of ideology and sociology. But in spite of these similarities it is vital to distinguish the Pure Theory of Law from the normative science of law or normative jurisprudence, which last two are I think
synonymous for Kelsen. The Pure Theory is a general theory which in
effect tells the jurist concerned with some particular legal system how to
'represent' or describe that system; what sorts of 'concepts' he should
use and what he should not use; and generally what form his description
or 'representation' of the legal system is to take if it is to be fit to rank as
the normative science of that system. Now it is at this point that Kelsen
introduces the notions that I and others have found so puzzling.
Speaking in the character of the Pure Theorist, Kelsen tells the jurist
engaged in the normative science of a particular legal system that his
description or representation of it must take the form of 'rules' or 'ought-
statements', but 'in a descriptive sense'. This is such a surprise because

[10] *GTLS* 55.   [11] *GTLS* 59.   [12] *GTLS* p. xiii.

what we should naturally expect from a lawyer who tells us that he is engaged in the description or representation of English or California law would not be a set of rules or 'ought-statements', but a set of statements explaining what the rules of English or California law as found in, for example, statutes mean. So we would expect the general form of the statements of the normative science of English or California law, if its task is simply that of describing or representing the law of those systems, to be of the kind indicated by the following blank schemata:

Section 2 of the Homicide Act 1957 which provides . . . means that . . .

or

Section 18, subsection 2, of the California Penal Code means the same as . . .

Statements of the form of these two schemata are of course *about* the rules of English or California law in the sense that they tell us what these rules mean, but they are not themselves to be identified with the rules whose meaning they explain. They are jurist's statements *about* law, not legislative pronouncements *of* law. To add to the puzzle, Kelsen himself, as can be seen from the quotations set out above, warns against identifying these two diverse things. Yet he insists on calling the statements of the normative science of law 'rules of law' or 'ought-statements' in a 'descriptive sense'. Why?

Two admirable writers on jurisprudence have been concerned with this question before me, and it is a diverting, if also, in a way, a discouraging, fact that whereas one of them condemns Kelsen's talk of rules in a descriptive sense as both confused and confusing the other does not find much difficulty with it. Thus Professor Alf Ross thinks that Kelsen in using this terminology is perpetuating a very bad continental tradition that it is possible to conduct a science of law or a science of 'norms' *in norms*.[13] This would be to use the expression 'normative science' not in the innocuous sense of a science that had norms or legal rules for its subject-matter but in a sense, laden with the theory of natural law, of a science whose *conclusions* are laws. On the other hand Professor Martin Golding, in his important article 'Kelsen and the Concept of a "Legal System" ',[14] plainly thinks that no such charges are warranted. He concedes that the expression 'normative jurisprudence' is an unhappy name for the jurist's task of representing or describing the law of a particular system in the forms prescribed by the Pure Theory; and he notes that some passages in Kelsen's work may suggest that in order to carry out his task the jurist must exercise a mysterious faculty of 'norm cognition'

---

[13] See Ross, *LJ*, at 9–10 n.4.
[14] Martin P. Golding, 'Kelsen and the Concept of "Legal System" ', *ARSP*, 47 (1961), 355–86, at 364, repr. in *More Essays in Legal Philosophy*, ed. Robert S. Summers (Oxford: Blackwell, 1971), 69–100, at 78.

instead of an ordinary ability to say what the laws of some legal system are and what they mean. But it is manifestly Professor Golding's view that all that is needed to dissipate confusion and to do justice to Kelsen's meaning is to bring in at this point a distinction familiar to modern logicians between the *use* and the *mention* of words.

The force of this distinction may be sufficiently conveyed (to the uninitiated and for my present limited purposes) by a single example. Consider the statement: 'The word "puppy" means in English the same as the expression "young dog".' In this statement certain words are mentioned or referred to as words and we are told that these mentioned words are equivalent in meaning. So the statement is in a pretty obvious sense about the meaning of the words which are enclosed in internal inverted commas. Contrast with this the statements 'Fido is a puppy' and 'Fido is a young dog'. These latter two statements are not about words but about the animal Fido, and in them the words 'puppy' and 'young dog' are *used*, not mentioned, and not enclosed in internal inverted commas. In these latter statements the meaning of words is not discussed but taken as known.

If we apply this distinction to the law we can say that the legislature in enacting a law *uses* certain words and the jurist who undertakes to tell us what the law means *mentions* both the words of the law and the words which he gives by way of paraphrase or explanation of meaning. So the schemata set out above will be filled out with words that are mentioned, not used. On this footing we might say that all Kelsen meant by the puzzling assertion that the statements of the normative science of law are themselves 'rules' and 'ought-statements' though 'in a descriptive sense' is that his statements explaining the meaning of a legislative enactment will mention certain ought-statements or rules as the equivalent in meaning of the enactment. They will have the form of 'Section 2 of the Homicide Act 1957 means the same as the rule "If *B* . . . then *A* . . . ought to be".'

On this view therefore we could regard Kelsen as having most acutely anticipated the important distinction between the use and mention of words, but as having expressed it unhappily as a distinction between a prescriptive and descriptive sense of words like 'ought'. Now in our debate I pressed this point of view on Kelsen, though as I had not then seen Professor Golding's article, I, no doubt, did not put the point with his clarity. I thought this was the way in which Kelsen might reply to Professor Alf Ross's strictures, which I also quoted. To my surprise Kelsen would have none of it. He insisted that the statements of the normative science of law representing the law of a given system were *not* paraphrases at all: he said they were not 'second-order' statements about the law in which words were mentioned, not used. He stood by his terminology of rules and ought-statements 'in a descriptive sense' and he urged me to read the works of the nineteenth-century logician, Christoph Sigwart, who also spoke of a descriptive sense of 'ought'. I teased Kelsen a little with the suggestion that perhaps since Sigwart (whom I had not and have not read), logic had made some progress. *Vixere fortes post Agamemnona*.[15] But here our argument on this point came to a stop.

At the time I thought Kelsen was wrong in not accepting the solution in terms of the distinction between the use and mention of words. Since our debate however I have come to think that he was perhaps right, and that that distinction is too crude to characterize precisely the relationship between the statements of the normative science of law as Kelsen conceives of them and the law of the system which they represent. To understand that relationship we should consider that between a speaker of a foreign language and his English interpreter. Suppose a German commandant in a prisoner-of-war camp barks out to his English or American prisoners the order '*Stehen Sie auf*!' The interpreter, doing his duty, shouts out 'Stand up!' No doubt, without consciously mimicking the tone or mien or gesture of the commandant, the interpreter will reproduce enough to make clear to the men that the original was an order, and not, for example, a plea or a request. How shall we classify in relation to its German original the interpreter's speech-act in uttering the English sentence 'Stand up'? Shall we say that it was the giving of an order? But plainly the interpreter had no authority to give orders: he had a duty to interpret the commandant's orders and if the men obeyed or disobeyed it was not he but the commandant who was obeyed or disobeyed. Does the use-and-mention distinction fit the situation? Does the interpreter make a second-order statement mentioning the German words and say that they mean the same as the English words 'Stand up'? This seems very far from a literal description of the situation. It would be like saying that when one man imitates another's words, conversation, or gestures, he is *talking about* them. Of course between the interpreter's words in the situation I have envisaged and the explicit second-order statement that the commandant's German words meant the same as the interpreter's English words there is an important relationship. If asked why he said 'Stand up' when he did, he would have to include in any full explanation his belief that the second-order statement was true; just as the mimic of another's gestures would have to include in any full *explanation* of his activities his belief that his own gestures resembled his victim's. But (to use Kelsen's language) the interpreter and the mimic manage to 'represent' their originals without *mentioning* them, though of course without doing or being exactly the same kind of thing as the

---

[15] ['Gallant heroes lived after Agamemnon.']

originals. Theirs is a special use of language, not a mention of it. From this we *might* go further with Kelsen and say of the interpreter that he represented the original order by 'an order in the descriptive sense' and his use of the grammatical imperative mood was 'descriptive' not prescriptive. At least we can see the reasons for inventing such terms even if we can also see the danger of using them.

All this can be transferred back to the law to justify Kelsen's terminology in characterizing as he does the statements of normative science which represent the law. Moreover I think Kelsen's whole picture of the jurist's activity may be misunderstood if we do not stress the points made in the last paragraph. For, as Professor Golding points out,[16] Kelsen does not conceive of the jurist's statements as having a simple one-to-one correspondence with the laws of the system in question. His finished representation of the system will have a clarity, consistency, and order not present in the original: indeed it will include for example a basic norm 'postulated' by the jurist which may not ever have been explicitly formulated within the system but will explain the validity and the systematic interrelation of the subordinate norms. Even this aspect of the jurist's 'representation' of the system we might reproduce, and so come to understand a little better, in a further use of the analogue of the interpreter. Suppose the commandant to be a somewhat stupid man and very much afraid of fire. Whenever he sees anything inflammable lying around he orders the prisoners to pick it up. Day in and day out he stomps round the camp shouting in German 'Pick up that box', 'Pick up that paper', 'Pick up that bundle of straw'. The interpreter dutifully barks out the English equivalents, and then one day, being a man of superior intelligence, adds on his own motion 'and pick up all inflammable material'. The commandant on being told of what he has said says 'Good: that's exactly what I would have said, only I couldn't think of the right words. What a fine interpreter you are! In fact you do more than interpret my orders: you do what Professor Golding says the normative science of law does for the law of a particular system: you *rationally reconstruct*[17] my orders.'

Now it seems to me that this feature of the jurist's activity explains further why Kelsen would be reluctant to identify his representation of the law with mere statements about the meaning of laws or paraphrases in which rules and 'oughts' are mentioned but not used. I do not think his terminology of rule and ought 'in a descriptive sense' happy, but I do think he was wise to reject the alternative I proffered; for, again like the interpreter's words, the statements of the jurist representing the law are a specific kind of use of language and not a mention of it.

[16] See Golding (n.14 above), at 365, repr. at 79.
[17] See Golding (n.14 above), at 357–61, repr. at 71–5.

II. THE DEFINITION OF DELICT

Kelsen offers in his book what he terms a 'juristic definition' of delict or, as English and American lawyers would say, of civil and criminal wrongs. In our debate I discussed this definition only as far as it related to crime, and I was mainly concerned with the following quotations from *General Theory*. These seem to me important because they show that Kelsen's Pure Theory differs from the usual conception of analytical jurisprudence in certain further respects beyond those already discussed above. They also seem to me to suggest certain limitations on the capacity of the Pure Theory to further the aim which Kelsen attributes to it of promoting the understanding of a system of positive law.

From a purely juristic point of view, the delict is characterized as a condition of the sanction. But the delict is not the only condition. . . . What then is the distinctive characteristic of that condition which is called the 'delict'? Could no other criterion be found than the supposed fact that the legislator desires conduct contrary to that which is characterized as 'delict', then the concept of delict would be incapable of a juristic definition. The concept of delict defined simply as socially undesired behavior is a moral or a political, in short, no juristic but a metajuristic, concept.[18]

A juristic definition of delict must be based entirely upon the legal norm. And such a definition can in fact be given. Normally, the delict is the behavior of that individual against whom the sanction as a consequence of his behavior is directed. . . . The criterion of the concept of 'delict' is an element which constitutes the content of the legal norm. . . . It is an element of the norm by which the legislator expresses his intention in an objectively cognizable way; it is an element which can be found by an analysis . . . of the legal norm. . . .

The definition of delict as the behavior of the individual against whom the sanction, as a consequence of this behavior, is directed presupposes—although it does not refer to the fact—that the sanction is directed against the individual whose behavior the legislator considers to be detrimental to society . . .[19]

. . . The legal concept of delict presupposes in principle that the individual whose behavior has from a political point of view a socially detrimental character, and the individual against whom the sanction is directly or indirectly executed, coincide. Only on this condition is the juristic definition of the delict, as the behavior of the individual against whom the sanction as a consequence of this behavior is directed, correct.[20]

The general outline of this definition of delict is clear: a delict, for example, a crime, is simply the behaviour upon which according to law a sanction becomes applicable to the person whose behaviour it is. What is not clear is what Kelsen means by, on the one hand, insisting that this is all that a juristic definition of delict can and should say and, on the other hand, acknowledging that this definition presupposes, though it

[18] *GTLS* 53.   [19] *GTLS* 54.   [20] *GTLS* 56.

does not refer to, the socially detrimental character of the delict and is only correct if the condition thus presupposed is satisfied.

It is of course plain from many passages in Kelsen's book (and it is an important fact) that the Pure Theory imposes certain very severe restrictive conditions on the permissible forms of definition. It also seems clear that a science of positive law which disregarded these would not for Kelsen be a 'normative' science. These restrictions indeed constitute one reason why no simple identification between analytical jurisprudence and either the Pure Theory or a 'normative science' of law can be made in spite of their similarity in spirit and general orientation. For though Austin and his followers distinguish as sharply as Kelsen does between the analysis of law and moral, political, or ideological evaluations of it, there is no counterpart in their work to Kelsen's distinctive insistence that in defining or analysing, only certain restricted elements may be used. In general the Pure Theory insists that the clarificatory task of a normative science of law be performed with elements drawn from the law itself, and care must be taken in defining or analysing legal concepts to avoid using moral, political, or psychological elements which are not, in Kelsen's words, 'part of the legal material'.

It is not very easy to make out precisely what elements these restrictions allow, but there are clear examples in Kelsen's book of what they exclude. Thus in criticizing Austin's analysis or definition of legal obligation Kelsen considers the definition that to be obliged is to fear the sanction, but he does not simply treat this, as a modern analytical jurist might, as an example of a mistaken definition. So he does not, for example, criticize it on the footing that a person may very well be under a legal obligation and yet not fear a sanction. What he does say is that such a definition is 'incompatible with the principles of analytical jurisprudence'[21] because 'no analysis of the contents of commands can establish the psychological fact of fear'.[22] His point is that it is wrong in principle to bring into the juristic definition of a concept psychological elements such as fear, or other elements which are not part of the content of the law. Kelsen's own juristic definition of obligation states that legal duty is 'the behavior by the observa[tion] of which the delict is avoided, thus the opposite of the behavior which forms a condition for the sanction'.[23] No doubt Kelsen thinks that this definition is correct as complying with the restrictive condition that a juristic definition may use only elements which form part of the content of the law. It is worth noting, however, in order to prevent a common misunderstanding that though Kelsen rejects Austin's 'psychological' conception of duty or obligation, he does not mean that a juristic definition can never use any psychological ele-

---

[21] *GTLS* 72.   [22] *GTLS* 72–3.   [23] *GTLS* 60.

ment. For Kelsen expressly says that in a case where the law itself makes such elements relevant, for example, where *mens rea* is a condition of criminal responsibility, then the sanction is directed to a psychologically qualified delict. The idea of responsibility based on fault is thus defined by Kelsen, and no doubt he would claim that it is a sound juristic definition because though it uses psychological terms these are elements found in the relevant law.[24]

Though these examples throw some light on Kelsen's restricted form of juristic definition, it is not easy to understand why, given the aims of the Pure Theory, the restrictions it imposes should be observed; nor precisely how we are to determine what elements are to count as 'found by an analysis of the content of the legal norm'[25] or 'are expressed in the content of the norm'[26] or 'are expressed in the material produced in the law-creating procedure'[27] or 'are manifested in the contents of the legal order'.[28] Kelsen certainly does insist that we must not bring into the definition of delict such elements as the supposed desire of the legislator, or the fact that the delictual conduct is socially harmful or against the purpose of the law: the juristic definition of delict must be 'based entirely upon the legal norm',[29] and he considers his own definition of it to be so based. But this leaves much unexplained. Suppose that in fact the laws of a given system always contained (as Bentham wished) an explanatory statement that the actions to which the law attached criminal sanctions were regarded as social evils and that was why they were punished. Would the juristic definition of delict then rightly include a reference to such social facts? I am fairly sure that Kelsen's answer would be 'No', though I much regret not having raised this point with him. He would, I think, in consistency with his general doctrine, have to say that the laws of an actual system, before they have passed through the clarifying filter of the normative science of law, contain much that is irrelevant to that science. For the representation or description of the law which is the concern of that science is concerned only with its strictly normative elements; that indeed is why it is, in spite of Professor Alf Ross's protests, properly called a 'normative science' and not merely a science *of* norms. I think this means that the permitted elements which may be used in juristic definition are those contained in the canonical form for the representation of the law which Kelsen lays down: statements that if such and such conditions are fulfilled then such and such a sanction shall follow. These are the statements by which the normative science of law is said by Kelsen to describe or represent law. They are 'hypothetical judgment[s] attaching certain consequences to certain conditions':[30] If *A* is, *B* ought to be. So the explanatory statement of the law's purpose which

---

[24] See *GTLS*, at 55, 66.   [25] *GTLS* 54.   [26] Ibid.   [27] *GTLS* 51.
[28] Ibid.   [29] *GTLS* 54.   [30] *GTLS* 45.

would have pleased Bentham would, even if it were contained in the text of a statute, be quite irrelevant to normative science.

At this point Kelsen's restrictive conception of juristic definition can be seen to have points of contact with some themes of American Legal Realism. We must compare the restrictions insisted on by Kelsen to Holmes's 'bad man' theory[31] that we should include in our definition, for example, of duty, only those elements which the 'bad man' would want to know. Of course the permitted elements are quite different in the case of the two theories. The Realist permits only elements relevant to the *prediction* of the sanction, whereas Kelsen permits only elements which according to the legal rule are conditions under which the sanction 'ought' to be applied. But notwithstanding these differences the comparison does suggest a criticism of Kelsen's definition of delict and indeed of the whole programme of his severely restricted juristic definition.

Briefly, the criticism is that such definitions will not serve any useful purpose, theoretical or practical, and may introduce at points a confusion. That confusion may be generated is perhaps evident from the following simple case. Sanctions may take the form of compulsory money payments, for example, fines; but taxes also take this form. In both cases alike, to use Kelsen's terminology, certain behaviour of the subject is a condition under which an official or organ of the system ought to demand a money payment from the subject. So if we confine our attention to the content of the law as represented in the canonical form 'If *A*, then *B* ought to be', it is impossible to distinguish a criminal law punishing behaviour with a fine from a revenue law taxing certain activities. Both when the individual is taxed and when he is fined, the law's provisions when cast into the Kelsenian canonical form are identical. Both cases are therefore cases of delict unless we distinguish between them by reference to something that escapes the net of the canonical form, that is, that the fine is a punishment for an activity officially condemned and the tax is not. It may perhaps be objected that a tax, though it consists of a compulsory money payment as some sanctions also do, is not a 'sanction' and that Kelsen's juristic definition of delict refers to a 'sanction'. But this does not really avoid the difficulty; it only defers it, for we shall have to step outside the limits of juristic definition in order to determine when a compulsory money payment is a sanction and when it is not. Presumably it is a sanction when it is intended as or assumed to be a punishment to discourage 'socially undesired behavior'[32] to which it is

---

[31] See Oliver Wendell Holmes, 'The Path of the Law', *Harvard Law Review*, 10 (1896–7), 457–78, repr. in Holmes, *Collected Legal Papers* (New York: Harcourt, Brace and Howe, 1920, repr. New York: Peter Smith, 1952), 167–202.

[32] *GTLS* 53. The difficulty of distinguishing a penalty from a tax for the purpose of art. I, sec. 8, of the United States Constitution is well known. See e.g. Steward Machine Co. v. Davis, *United States Reports*, 301 (1937), 548–618.

attached; but this is precisely the element which Kelsen considers to be excluded from the juristic definition of delict.

It is plain that Kelsen himself is aware of these difficulties, because he concedes that the juristic definition only holds good on the presupposition that the behaviour which is a condition for the sanction is considered detrimental to society. But does not this concession show that the severely restricted juristic definition is useless as well as confusing? Here it is important to stress that many of the illuminating definitions of the Pure Theory are not and could not be *juristic* definitions in the severely restricted sense that Kelsen intends. Plainly for the reasons given above the definition of a sanction is not.[33] It is even possible to doubt whether the definition of a legal norm (quite apart from its dependence on the definition of a sanction) conforms to the strict requirements of juristic definition. For Kelsen tells us that the norm 'is the expression of the idea that something ought to occur, especially that an individual ought to behave in a certain way'.[34] But though a norm may *be* an expression of an idea it is not clear that 'an expression' or 'an idea' or 'an expression of an idea' are *contents* or *elements* of the norm or fit any other of the descriptions given by Kelsen of what may be used in a strictly juristic definition. So we should perhaps distinguish the most fundamental definitions of the Pure Theory to which the jurist conducting the normative science of law will *conform* in representing the law of a particular system as 'metajuristic' definitions, to mark the distinction between them and the juristic definitions which the jurist will actually *use* in representing the law of some particular system. He will not use in his representation of the system, but will take for granted, definitions of 'sanction' or of 'legal rule', but he will use definitions of delict. Perhaps indeed some such distinction between definitions which are metajuristic and those which are juristic is needed for any analytical account of law.

I pressed these points on Kelsen in our debate, but I cannot say that he retreated or was moved by my claim that he had in fact given his case away by saying that his definition of delict held good on the 'presupposition in principle that the behavior against which the sanction is directed has or is considered to have a socially detrimental character'. I did however learn from our discussion two important things. The first is that Kelsen had an interesting and possibly a good reason for talking not merely of a science of norms but of a 'normative' science of law, and this is not open to Professor Ross's criticism, though it may be to others'. The second is that any one who, like myself, would wish to bring into the definition of crime or delict the idea that the behaviour to which sanctions

---

[33] See the discussion of coercion and the distinction between civil and criminal sanctions in *GTLS*, at 18–19, 50–1.
[34] *GTLS* 36.

are attached is unlike behaviour which is simply taxed, and differs from it because it is in some way condemned, must be careful to state how in the case of any given law the presence of this factor of condemnation is ascertained.

III. THE RELATIONSHIP BETWEEN LAW AND MORALITY

Let us consider the case of a conflict between a norm of positive law and a norm of morality. Positive law can, for instance, stipulate an obligation to render military service, which implies the duty to kill in war, while morality, or a certain moral order, unconditionally forbids killing. Under such circumstances, the jurist would say that 'morally, it may be forbidden to kill, but that is irrelevant legally.' From the point of view of positive law as a system of valid norms, morality does not exist as such; or, in other words, morality does not count at all as a system of valid norms if positive law is considered as such a system. From this point of view, there exists a duty to perform military service, no contrary duty. In the same way, the moralist would say that 'legally, one may be under the obligation to render military service and kill in war, but that is morally irrelevant.' That is to say, law does not appear at all as a system of valid norms if we base our normative considerations on morality. From this point of view, there exists a duty to refuse military service, no contrary duty. Neither the jurist nor the moralist asserts that both normative systems are valid. The jurist ignores morality as a system of valid norms, just as the moralist ignores positive law as such a system. Neither from the one nor from the other point of view do there exist two duties simultaneously which contradict one another. And there is no third point of view.[35]

Against our thesis that two contradictory norms cannot both be valid, one might argue that, after all, there are such things as collisions of duties. Our answer is that terms like 'norm' and 'duty' are equivocal. On the one hand, they have a significance that can be expressed only by means of an ought-statement (the primary sense). On the other hand, they also are used to designate a fact which can be described by an is-statement (the secondary sense), the psychological fact that an individual has the idea of a norm, that he believes himself to be bound by a duty (in the primary sense) and that this idea or this belief (norm or duty in the secondary sense) disposes him to follow a certain line of conduct. It is possible that the same individual at the same time has the idea of two norms, that he believes himself bound by two duties which contradict and hence logically exclude one another; for instance, the idea of a norm of positive law which obligates him to render military service, and the idea of a norm of morality which obligates him to refuse to render military service. The statement describing this psychological fact, however, is no more contradictory than, for instance, the

[35] *GTLS* 374.

statement that two opposite forces work at the same point. A logical contradiction is always a relation between the meaning of judgments or statements, never a relation between facts. The concept of a so-called conflict of norms or duties means the psychological fact of an individual's being under the influence of two ideas which push him in opposite directions; it does not mean the simultaneous validity of two norms which contradict one another.[36]

These passages from *General Theory* concerning the relationship between law and morals are to my mind among the most difficult of that difficult book. They are also to many people very alarming, because statements like 'the jurist ignores morality as a system of valid norms just as the moralist ignores positive law as such a system' seem to exclude the possibility of a moral criticism of law, and this has of course always been among the errors or even sins imputed, if somewhat indiscriminately, to legal 'positivists' by their opponents.

Involved in these passages are some complex issues which stem from Kelsen's highly idiosyncratic views concerning the possible relations between sets of valid norms and concerning the very idea of validity. I cannot deal with all these views here, and at our debate I did little more than scratch the surface of Kelsen's approach to these problems, which I thought instructive but mistaken. I shall proceed here as I did there by noting that we have in these passages two main tenets. There is first a destructive doctrine, namely, that contrary to common beliefs, there *cannot* be a relationship between law and morals such that a valid rule of law conflicts with or, as Kelsen puts it, is 'contradicted' by a valid moral rule; secondly, there is a constructive account of the idea of 'a collision of duties' designed to reconcile it with this destructive doctrine. For ease of exposition I shall consider the constructive account first.

Kelsen notes, as a possible objection to his theory that two contradictory norms cannot be valid, that there are such things as 'collisions' of duties. People indeed think and speak of these (usually calling them 'conflicts of duties') as an important feature of life. But he does not mention another case, equally important, where law and morals are thought of as conflicting: namely, the case of the moral criticism of law. This, as much as the conflict of duties, calls for explanation from any one who asserts, as Kelsen does, that 'two contradictory norms cannot both be valid'.[37] The difference between these two cases is as follows. We speak of a collision, or more usually of a conflict, of duties when a person recognizes that he is required by a valid rule of the law of his country to do something, for example, kill another human being, and also recognizes that he is required not to do this by a moral rule or principle which he accepts. But in the case of the moral criticism of law the conflict between

[36] *GTLS* 375.   [37] Ibid.

law and morals need not thus bear on a particular person or his actions. Thus an Englishman (whom we will call 'the critic') who is not himself liable to military service may morally condemn, on the ground that no one should kill, not only the law of England in regard to military service, but contemporary American law and the law of ancient Rome. In each case he considers the law in question valid but to be in conflict with morality. There is, however, in this case no conflict of duties for the critic himself or for any Englishman, American, or ancient Roman except those who were *both* liable to military service *and* had moral objections to it. Plainly the two cases are so different that separate consideration is needed of the bearing of Kelsen's destructive doctrine upon them.

Kelsen's account of the conflict of duties is that though we may naïvely think that in such cases a valid legal norm is in conflict with a valid moral norm, this is not so and cannot be so. But there is an ambiguity in words like 'norm' or 'duty' which suggests that it is so. Sometimes these words stand for what can be expressed by an ought-statement such as 'I ought to do military service'. This is their primary normative sense; but there is a secondary sense in which they refer to psychological facts such as that a person believes himself to be bound to do something and is therefore disposed to do it. We can therefore (and according to Kelsen we must) interpret the statement that a given person has a conflict of duties as simply a reference to the psychological fact that he is 'under the influence of two ideas which push him in opposite directions'.[38] This does not mean, according to Kelsen, that two valid norms are simultaneously valid; this, according to his destructive doctrine, is logically impossible. Interpreted in Kelsen's way, the statement that a person has a conflict of duties is a mere statement of fact like the statement that two opposite forces work at the same point, and does not state a relation between the meanings of norms or ought-statements. It is therefore, so interpreted, admissible, and is indeed the kind of statement that a psychologist or sociologist makes. But they are not concerned with the normative aspect of law. They, according to Kelsen, do not conceive of law or morality as valid norms. Their standpoint is that of 'factuality', not of 'normativity'.[39]

This account seems to me to be wrong, for the following among other reasons. If a man says that he has a conflict of legal and moral duties and we ask him to say why or how this is so, it plainly would be no adequate answer if he replied that he felt disposed to do and also not to do something; or, to use Kelsen's phrase, that he felt pushed in opposite directions. More is required if we are to count him as having a conflict of legal and moral duties. It must be the case that a valid rule of law actually requires him to do something and that a moral principle or rule requires

---

[38] *GTLS* 375.   [39] *GTLS* 376.

him to abstain from doing it; it must also be the case that he believes all this to be the case and that it is impossible for him to fulfil the requirements of both the legal and the moral rule. It is very important to notice that if it turned out that he was mistaken in believing that a valid rule of law required him to do what the moral rule forbids (as he might be if he did not know that the law in question had been repealed) then he would not in fact have a conflict of duties. We would tell him that though he *believed* his duties conflicted, in fact they did not really do so, for he was mistaken about the law.

It is plain, I hope, from the foregoing that it is an essential element in what we call a conflict of duties that the requirements of a valid law should conflict with those of a moral rule or principle. To discover therefore whether or not there is such a conflict in a given case we must consider the meaning of the legal rule and the moral rule, treating them for this purpose (to use Kelsen's terminology) as ought-statements. Only if they are inconsistent in the sense that they cannot be simultaneously fulfilled can we truthfully say that there is a conflict of duties. An assertion that a person has a conflict of duties is, contrary to Kelsen's view, made 'from the point of view of normativity'. It is not a mere statement of psychological fact, like 'He feels disposed to act in contrary ways' or 'He fancies that he has a conflict of duties.'

Kelsen's psychological analysis of the conflict of law and morals must also, and perhaps more obviously, fail as an account of the case of the moral criticism of law. For a moral critic who condemns the law of his own or some other system because it requires behaviour contrary to that required by some moral principle is not committed to any statement of psychological fact about individuals being under the 'influence of ideas that push [them] in opposite directions'. The critic plainly considers the meaning of what Kelsen calls ought-statements, viewing them as norms, and finds that they conflict.

Consider now Kelsen's destructive doctrine. Why does he insist that valid norms *cannot* exist side-by-side and conflict? He has I think two principal reasons. The first may be summarized in his own words:

The jurist ignores morality as a system of valid norms, just as the moralist ignores positive law as such a system. Neither from the one nor from the other point of view do there exist two duties simultaneously which contradict one another.[40]

Now in one sense these words seem to me to be quite true, but irrelevant to our question, which is whether valid norms can conflict. For if by a 'jurist' Kelsen means, as he often does, a student of the law setting out to describe or 'represent' a particular system of law, it is quite true that he would disregard nonlegal norms whether they were in conflict with the

---

[40] *GTLS* 374.

law or not; for they would simply be outside the scope of his task. The same is true *mutatis mutandis* of the moralist if he is a person engaged exclusively in describing a moral code. It is therefore true that neither *moralist* nor *jurist* would make statements about conflicts between law and morals. But this does not show that such statements cannot be made both meaningfully and truthfully. Kelsen denies this when he adds, 'And there is no third point of view.'[41] But this seems just a blank assertion which I see no reason to accept. No human being is *just* a lawyer or *just* a moralist. Some at least think about both legal and moral norms and consider their meaning as norms and find that they conflict. No doubt Kelsen would say that this is possible only if he abandons the point of view of 'normativity' for that of 'factuality' and looks upon law not as valid norms but as facts, as a psychologist or a sociologist would. But this for the reason already stated seems untrue.

Kelsen's second destructive argument is that a statement that a valid legal rule and a moral principle conflict is itself a logical impossibility. For him, it is tantamount to the assertion of both '*A* ought to be' and '*A* ought not to be' (where *A* is some human action); and this, he says, is like asserting both '*A* is' and '*A* is not', a contradiction in terms and hence logically impossible.[42] To this argument there are many objections, and I shall conclude by briefly outlining the main ones. First, the argument assumes that a statement that a legal rule is valid simply means that the actions it refers to ought to be done ('*A* ought to be'). But this, it seems to me, is to confuse a statement about a law either with the pronouncement of the law by the legislator, or with the jurist's statement of its meaning or, as Kelsen would say, with his 'representation' of the law. For it is a tolerable (though I think not wholly acceptable) theory that the law as enunciated by the legislator or 'represented' by the jurist is an ought-statement. But the statement *that* the law is valid surely does not merely repeat the law: it refers to the place of the law within the legal system. I will not elaborate on this point here, partly because I have discussed the meaning of validity at length elsewhere,[43] but also because even if we waived this objection Kelsen's conclusion would still not follow. For even on Kelsen's interpretation of validity the statement that a valid legal rule *conflicted* with a valid moral rule would not be equivalent to the joint assertion of '*A* ought to be' and '*A* ought not to be' which he considers a contradiction; it would be equivalent to the statement *about* '*A* ought to be' and '*A* ought not to be' to the effect that they conflict. This certainly is not a contradiction or logically impossible, though Kelsen would be entitled to argue that it was false.

---

[41] *GTLS* 374.   [42] Ibid.
[43] See Hart, *CL*, at 100–7, 245–7, 2nd edn., at 103–10, 292–5.

Let us however waive, for the sake of argument, both these points, and concede that the statement that a valid rule of law conflicts with a valid moral rule does mean the same as '*A* ought to be and *A* ought not to be'. Is this a contradiction? Technically the contradictory of (1) '*A* ought to be' is not (2) '*A* ought not to be', but (3) 'It is not the case that *A* ought to be'; and of course the joint assertion of (1) and (3) does sound pretty meaningless. But if, which has been doubted, any of the usual logical terms are applicable to ought-statements, '*A* ought to be' and '*A* ought not to be' are contraries, not contradictories. This however is not a serious objection because Kelsen might well say that the joint assertion of contraries is a logical impossibility. What is serious is the point that there are many interpretations which we could reasonably give to ought-statements which would explain why '*A* ought to be done and *A* ought not to be done' expresses a conflict between law and morals and yet does not amount to an attempt to state a logical impossibility. Here I will suggest only one possible interpretation. An intuitively acceptable meaning for '*A* ought to be done' is that 'there are good reasons for doing *A*'. If we give 'ought' this meaning then '*A* ought legally to be done and *A* ought morally not to be done' is equivalent to 'There are good legal reasons for doing *A* and good moral reasons for not doing *A*'. This expresses a conflict because it is logically impossible for one person at the same time to *do* both *A* and not *A*. But it does not, as far as I can see, assert anything contradictory or logically impossible.

Finally I should say that in our debate we did not get far into these rather complex matters concerning the logical relations of law and morals. Kelsen did however say that he was considering afresh the question of the possible logical relations between norms, and particularly the possibility that one norm might logically conflict with another. I do not record this to show that Kelsen was impressed by my arguments, for I think he had in mind quite different considerations. But it is very much to be hoped that on this most difficult of subjects we shall have more from the most stimulating writer on analytical jurisprudence of our day.

POSTSCRIPT

For criticism and comments, see Joseph Raz, 'The Purity of the Pure Theory'.[44]

---

[44] [Postscript added by Hart to the reprinting of this paper in Hart, *Essays in Jurisprudence and Philosophy*. Raz's paper appears in the present volume as ch. 12.]

5

The Basic Norm of a Society*

TONY HONORÉ

Hans Kelsen[1] made lawyers familiar with the controversial notion of a basic norm. He resorts to it in order to explain how laws can be interpreted as objectively valid norms which ought[2] to be obeyed. He sets out to show how laws can create obligations which the individual can, if he chooses, rationally regard as binding.[3] As a lawyer and legal theorist, he wants to find out whether laws in themselves, irrespective of the moral or political ideology they reflect, can have a value such that they bind those to whom they apply. Can law be taken seriously?

Given this perspective, it would be pointless to rely, as an argument for the binding character of laws, on a particular moral or political ideology, say utilitarianism or democracy. That would merely show why there was an obligation to obey certain laws in certain conditions or certain societies. The idea Kelsen is looking for, and which steers him towards the hypothesis of the basic norm, though it must be normative, has also to be neutral between competing moral and political ideologies. It must aim, as it were, to be a non-ideological ideology. But can such a creature exist?

---

* *Editors' note*: This paper first appeared in Tony Honoré, *Making Law Bind* (Oxford: Clarendon Press, 1987), 89–114.

[1] This interpretation of Kelsen builds on Joseph Raz, 'Kelsen's Theory of the Basic Norm' [in this volume, ch. 3], to whose exegesis I am much indebted. My reflections on Kelsen's theory develop his ideas in terms which he would doubtless have resisted, but which seek to preserve the spirit of his undertaking. His ideas were foreshadowed in *HP* (1911) and expounded in *LT* (1934), *GTLS* (1945), *WJ* (1957), and *PTL* (1960). [For full references to these works, see the Table of Abbreviations.]

[2] In Kelsen's use, 'ought' includes, besides 'has an obligation (or duty) to', 'may' and 'has the power to'. For purposes of this chapter, however, 'ought' means 'has an obligation (or duty) to'. Any distinction there may be between duty and obligation is not relevant to the argument here presented; see Ronald Dworkin, *Taking Rights Seriously* (London: Duckworth, and Cambridge, Mass.: Harvard UP, 1977), at 48–9.

[3] That is, morally binding, if morality is taken in a broad sense which comprises all obligations whether or not created by morality in the narrow sense; see Tony Honoré, 'Nécessité oblige', in Honoré, *Making Law Bind* (Oxford: Clarendon Press, 1987), 115–38, at 136–8. To Kelsen, who did not believe in objective values, 'binding' meant binding from the point of view of some norm postulated as binding.

I believe that Kelsen was right in thinking that, if the law of any society imposes obligations on its members,[4] this must be by virtue of a basic norm which is in an important respect neutral between competing moral and political ideologies.[5] But, rejecting his way of identifying the basic norm of a municipal legal system,[6] I propose a different method. This leads to a basic norm which is more than just the norm of a particular social system, such as the legal system. It is the basic norm of a society.

Kelsen's legal philosophy was haunted by a perennial problem. Law involves organized coercion. It is, in his terminology, a coercive order. But banditry or terrorism also involve coercion and are, or from the terrorist point of view should be, properly organized. In what way is law different from banditry or terrorism? The difference, Kelsen thinks, resides in the fact that a legal system can be interpreted as a system of norms which impose obligations.

Norms prescribe how people ought to behave. They consist of rules or principles of behaviour and also of particular instructions (keep off that land, pay this tax) derived from such rules or principles. For a human being to prescribe how another ought to behave is to express his will, or at least attitude, towards that other person's conduct. That is, for example, what legislators do when they legislate. But that a legislator, or anyone else, has expressed his will about someone else's conduct is simply a fact. Why should it have normative consequences? Why should the enactment of a law by the legislator be regarded as anything more than a presumptuous or threatening piece of behaviour? How can legislative behaviour be interpreted as creating an objectively valid[7] norm? How can it justify the conclusion that the ordinary citizen or official has an obligation to conform to it?

Suppose the legislator imposes a poll-tax. Can one jump from the premiss that the legislator has imposed the tax to the conclusion that

---

[4] The legal relations *between* societies are not within the scope of this essay.

[5] It is not necessary for each law to be a norm. Individual laws impose obligations (in so far as they do) in conjunction with the basic norm or with other norms; see Tony Honoré, 'Real Laws', in Honoré, *Making Law Bind* (n.3 above), 69–88.

[6] For the basic norm of international law see Tony Honoré, 'How is Law Possible?', in Honoré, *Making Law Bind* (n.3 above), 1–31, at 15.

[7] A legal norm is 'objectively valid' in Kelsen's terminology if (i) it belongs to a system which is by and large effective, and (ii) it is validated by a higher norm which serves as a justification (see n.11 below) for holding that those to whom it applies have an obligation to conform to it.

Kelsen uses 'objective' differently in different contexts; see Raz, 'Basic Norm' (n.1 above), at § V. An expression of attitude is objective when it is not merely that of one person, for example, the legislator, but is shared generally. A discipline such as legal theory is objective when it studies a social reality, for example, power relationships between human beings. A norm is objective when it can be interpreted as creating an obligation.

'Valid' is used in such a way that only a valid norm can be said to exist. It exists when it imposes an obligation on those to whom it applies.

citizens to whom the law applies ought[8] (have an obligation) to pay it or, as Kelsen has it, that the tax officials and judges ought to coerce those who do not pay?[9] Is not the gap between fact and valid norm unbridgeable?

At first sight, perhaps, there is a way of bridging it. The lawmaker, besides wanting people to behave in a certain way, intends them to believe that they have an obligation to behave in that way. For example, he wants them to think that they have a duty to pay the poll-tax. Suppose the authorities succeed in persuading the populace that they have a duty to pay the tax. The poll-tax law is accepted as a standard of behaviour. Those who pay are treated as fulfilling their obligation. Those who evade the tax are criticized as failing in their duty. The tax law possesses what Joseph Raz calls social normativity.[10] Has it now become an 'objectively valid' norm?

It might seem that it had. The status of the law is now objective in at least one respect. It is not just officials but members of society as a whole, or at any rate the bulk of them, who treat it as creating a duty. The attitude they adopt towards the potential taxpayer's behaviour is like that of the legislator and the government. But that they adopt this attitude is no more than a social fact. Their behaviour differs from that of the legislator who has enacted the statute mainly in its complexity. The disorganized conduct of a great many people is involved, rather than the regular procedure of a legislature. The fact that citizens behave in this way does not show that they, any more than legislators, are justified[11] in treating the law as imposing an obligation. The mere fact that a legal norm is generally regarded as binding does not make it objectively valid.

Perhaps there is, after all, a way round the difficulty. Suppose those who treat the tax law as valid reached that conclusion not because they were persuaded by the government of its merits, but because they had studied the constitution. Suppose further that, according to the accepted

---

[8] See n.2 above.

[9] This feature of Kelsen's theory makes it psychologically easier to accept the idea that laws are obligatory whatever their content. Officials would generally be regarded as having a duty by virtue of their office to apply the laws of their society whatever these might be. But the substance of the argument for the basic norm remains unaffected whether laws are taken to be directed both to ordinary citizens and to officials, as most people would suppose, or solely to officials.

[10] Raz, 'Basic Norm' (n.1 above), § V.

[11] I use 'justified' advisedly, despite Kelsen's denial that he is seeking to show how legal norms might be justified (see e.g. *PTL* § 34(i), at pp. 217–18), and the fact that in his theory all justification depends on assuming the validity of some basic norm and is therefore conditional. All he means, in my opinion, by his disclaimer is that he is interested not in a political or ethical but rather in some other (neutral, specifically legal) justification of the binding character of legal norms. As Raz has plausibly argued, 'Kelsen uses only the concept of justified normativity', in 'Basic Norm' (n.1 above), § V. How could one norm derive its validity from another unless the latter justified the assertion that the former was binding? See n.20 below.

constitutional view, a tax imposed by the Queen in Parliament is valid. The poll-tax was imposed by Parliament. It therefore possesses what may be termed conventional validity.[12] Does that not show conclusively that those who treat the tax law as imposing a duty to comply are justified in doing so?

Not according to Kelsen. The tax law is indeed valid by conventional legal criteria, but conventional validity is not enough. It has to be shown that a law framed according to conventional criteria justifies the use of coercion against those who break it; that it imposes on those to whom it applies a duty to conform. So far, no argument to this effect has been adduced. Laws are in Kelsen's thinking acts of will. But why should anyone be bound to respect the will of another, and so obey him? What difference can it make that the person who expresses his will is a legislator? Why should I not, if I think it prudent, disregard even the unanimous view of others as to my proper behaviour? Even if their opinion conforms to constitutional doctrines, why should I respect the constitution?

Kelsen's answer to this question would have been that no reason can be adduced which will convince a sceptic that he should respect the constitution or conform his behaviour to the general view. There are no absolute values, and so there can be no absolute duty to conform to, say, the will of God or the state or the dictates of utility or nature. Nothing is good or just except from the point of view of this or that person. So there can be no demonstrably good or just laws. Even if it is conceded that we should obey good laws, the concession is an empty one. No particular law can be shown to be good. All that can be shown is that from the point of view of this or that person or group—*X* or *Y* or lawyers or Christians or utilitarians—it ought to be obeyed. But this is enough to make the norm, in Kelsen's terms, objectively valid: that is, binding and justified *from the chosen point of view*.

Since there is no way of proving which point of view is the correct one, we have to abandon all hope of showing that laws really impose obligations. The most that is possible is a more modest project. We can study the implications of the assumption, which this or that person or group may entertain, that laws create obligations. We can try to find out if there is a point of view from which laws which are effective can also be held to impose binding obligations.

A person who, instead of taking for granted that laws create obligations, asks on what assumptions it could be true that they do so, adopts a distinctive point of view. It is not the point of view of any particular per-

---

[12] Not the same as social normativity. The difference is between conventional acceptance of a prescription as a valid law (conventional validity) and as setting a standard of conduct (social normativity). It will usually, but not always, be the case that what is conventionally treated as valid will also be socially normative.

son who may think laws binding. The appropriate point of view is rather that of legal science or theory, that is, of the theorist[13] who has a professional concern with the whole legal system and, indeed, with legal systems in general. This is the point of view that Kelsen, himself a legal theorist, adopts. Though as a private citizen he might not think this or that law or system of laws objectively valid and so binding, as a theorist he is committed to examining the implications of the view that they are. He is committed to taking law seriously. Otherwise, as he sees it, the study of law will be reduced to nothing more exalted than a sociological discipline. It will be an empirical enterprise, exclusively concerned with how laws affect behaviour. But, unlike natural science, legal science, if it is to be worth while, cannot be purely empirical. It is indeed objective, because the object of its study—laws which are by and large effective—is real, not imaginary. But it studies this reality from a normative, not an empirical point of view.[14] The legal theorist, short of throwing up his hands in despair, must at least explore the idea that laws succeed in doing what they purport to do: that besides influencing people's conduct they actually create obligations.

I. THE BASIC NORM:
MORAL AND POLITICAL PRINCIPLES

Exploring this idea, Kelsen puts forward the following hypothesis. Legal norms are objectively valid if they are derived from a basic norm which is itself valid. The same is true of moral or ethical norms. Anyone who supposes that laws create obligations is therefore committed to supposing that a certain basic norm is valid, and that the other norms of the legal system are valid by derivation from it.

The basic norm is something we discover. We do not invent it. Whatever norm could validate the other norms of the system is the basic norm. Its identity is a question of fact. But though we may be able to discover what the basic norm is, we cannot know that it is valid. We can at most suppose that it is, and that, in consequence, the laws of the system which it validates create obligations.

How can we identify the basic norm of a system of municipal law? No mere fact can make a norm objectively valid. The validating feature, if there is one, must take the form of another valid norm. The poll-tax norm, for example, if it is to be regarded as valid, must be validated by another norm.

---

[13] In practice, legal practitioners and government officials often adopt, for professional purposes, the point of view which Kelsen allots to legal theory.

[14] This does not exclude a separate, sociological discipline concerned with law. But the sociological discipline is not to be confused with the normative one.

What might this be? The obvious strategy would be to look for some moral or political principle that could be regarded as justifying the poll-tax. One principle that might be appealed to is fairness. Is the tax a fair one? If so, the poll-tax law should be obeyed; if not, perhaps not. Democracy is another. Was the tax imposed by a democratically elected legislature? If so, it will be binding; if not, perhaps not. It is certainly possible to couch these principles (fairness, democracy) in the form of norms which, if valid, would then justify or fail to justify the poll-tax law. The relevant norm might be put in the form that people should behave as fairness requires, or as democratically elected institutions prescribe. Given that the poll-tax law is fair, or imposed by a democratic body, it follows that it should be obeyed.

Kelsen is not however prepared to adopt this line of argument. He declines to look for an ethical or political justification for the binding character of legal norms. Why so? His refusal to entertain the idea that moral or political principles make laws binding is dictated, I think, by an aspiration which is at the core of his concern. He wants to show that, given that it is impossible to secure agreement on moral and political principles, law can be regarded as an autonomous system of social control, independent of morals and politics. If it is to be so regarded, it must possess its own justification, based on its own ideology.[15] It cannot parade in borrowed finery.

If this aim is borne in mind—and it is an aim which must be close to the heart of any partisan of the rule of law—any political principle, or set of principles, to which appeal is made in order to validate laws will in some way fail to perform the required task. The principles selected will turn out to be too indeterminate, selective, or internally inconsistent; and even if they are none of these, they will distort the distinctive ideology of law.

Many moral and political principles are indeterminate. If adopted to test the validity of laws, they fail to settle beyond dispute whether a legal norm is valid. Fairness is an example. People differ in their conception of what constitutes fairness. They are unlikely to agree whether a poll-tax is fair. To some it will seem so, to others not, and the division of opinion will in all probability follow political lines. The same will be true if the criterion chosen is not fairness but utility, nature, or true religion. Nearly all moral and political ideas of the sort which might plausibly be adduced to

---

[15] The theory must be 'conscious, so to speak, of the autonomy of the object of its enquiry and thereby conscious of its own unique character', *LT* Preface (1). That is, the theory must take account of its specific character as a theory of law—its ideology—as well as of the specific mode of creation of its object of study, that is, of laws. See also Dworkin (n.2 above), at 105, who speaks of the 'autonomy' of the law 'provided by its distinct constitutive and regulative rules'.

justify laws are objectionably vague or disputable. In the upshot it will not be possible, by applying them, to say which of the legal norms that are conventionally treated as valid impose obligations.

The indeterminacy of these notions is not, however, a knock-out objection. Kelsen holds that systems of morals and ethics must, like legal systems, be justified by reference to a basic norm; and the basic norm of an ethical system is certain to be indeterminate, perhaps to the point of vagueness. It will be something like 'behave in the way which will maximize utility', or 'behave on the basis that you should love your neighbour as yourself'. These basic norms of an ethical system will leave a great deal of leeway when it comes to deciding whether a particular course of behaviour is obligatory: for example, whether a person called up for military service ought to obey the summons. That does not rule out the possibility of a viable morality based on utility or loving one's neighbour. It merely shows that most, perhaps all, systems of morality are indeterminate. If an indeterminate principle will serve as the basic norm of a system of morals, why should it not serve equally for a system of law?

The indeterminacy of moral and political criteria is not Kelsen's only objection to the use of these notions to justify legal norms. Suppose that those criteria were far more precise than in practice they are. Imagine that utility is the principle of justification chosen to test laws, and that everyone can calculate the utility of a course of conduct with a pocket calculator. One could then sharply divide what are conventionally called laws into those justified by utility and those not so justified. There would be little room for dispute.

Some effective laws would not be justified by this test. They would not possess sufficient utility. Would these laws have to be treated as invalid? Not necessarily. The laws which are not justified by the utility test might be justified by another principle, for example that of conformity to nature. In the upshot all the effective laws of the system which were conventionally treated as valid might be shown to be justified, some by the utility test and some by the test of conformity to nature. There would then be two principles of justification. The basic norm would be split.

This possibility Kelsen rejects. If some laws are justified by utility and others by conformity to nature or something else, what is to happen when these criteria conflict? What about laws which possess utility but are unnatural, or conform to nature but lack utility? Suppose that in a given society there is a law, valid by conventional criteria, which permits abortion, and another which bans contraception. Both abortion and contraception may be taken for present purposes to be contrary to nature but to possess utility. When the two laws are tested for validity, one of the two principles will prevail. Either utility prevails over nature, or nature over utility. Hence if the abortion law is valid, the contraception law must be invalid, and vice versa. Surely there must ultimately be a single basic norm which requires utility or conformity to nature but not both together. Whichever principle prevails in case of conflict will constitute the basic norm to the exclusion of the other principle.[16]

Let us suppose that conformity to nature prevails. Conformity to nature is therefore the basic norm of the coercive order in question. It must follow that all those norms that fail to conform to nature are invalid. So whichever moral or political principle forms the basic norm, whether utility, nature, or something else, there will be some coercive norms which are conventionally regarded as valid but are not in fact so. Any single moral or legal principle or combination of principles which is put forward to justify coercive norms will therefore be, at least potentially, selective. Some such norms will turn out, when the principle is applied, to be valid, while others, which belong to the same coercive order and are equally effective, will be invalid. The coercive order as a whole will not have been validated.

If on the other hand two or more principles of justification, say utility and conformity to nature, are relied on and neither has priority over the other, the result will be either indeterminate or inconsistent. It will be indeterminate if we cannot discover which of the principles to apply in a given case, say that of contraception. In that case, the contraception law remains in limbo. We do not know whether it is valid. On the other hand, there will be an inconsistency if we apply one principle in one case and another in another:[17] for example if utility prevails in the case of abortion, and conformity to nature in the case of contraception.

Why should this inconsistency not just be accepted? It is obvious that in fact different laws belonging to the same system often give effect to different principles, depending, for example, on when and by whom they were enacted. Conservative housing laws are different from socialist housing laws. Laws enacted in the nineteenth century which remain in force display a different moral outlook from those enacted in the twentieth. It is, however, one thing to accept that for historical and political reasons laws are sometimes based on inconsistent principles, and another to tolerate an inconsistent justification of those laws.[18] The justifying norms are meant to warrant the conclusion that the laws validated by them impose obligations. Those to whom they apply, whether officials or ordinary citizens, are surely entitled to demand that their duty

---

[16] The basic norm might contain more complex combinations of principles, but all would be potentially selective.

[17] Unless some further conflict-resolving principle determined which was to apply in a given case of conflict: but then there would be a single basic norm, embodied in the further principle.

[18] See Dworkin (n.2 above), at 119, 126.

to obey should be governed by a consistent set of principles. There cannot be a duty to act inconsistently. A person who is required to act inconsistently is not treated as a rational person.

If, then, law is a system of social control which is meant to appeal to the reason of those who are expected to conform, it cannot be validated by an appeal to inconsistent principles. It is surely right to insist that anyone who is trying to establish the conditions in which laws could be interpreted as imposing obligations should respect the requirement of consistency. Unless he does this, he is treating law as no more than a technique of manipulation. An inconsistent set of principles will therefore not do as the basic, justifying norm of a legal system.

The upshot is that any set of two or more moral or political principles which is put forward to justify the norms of a legal system will prove to be either indeterminate, inconsistent, or reducible to a single (perhaps complex) principle. If appeal is made, for example, to both utility and conformity to nature, either one principle consistently prevails over the other; or some more ultimate principle resolves the conflicts between them in such a way that neither prevails consistently over the other; or the conflict between them is left undecided; or each arbitrarily prevails over the other in different contexts. In the first two cases there is a single basic norm; in the third the result is indeterminate; in the fourth it is inconsistent.

From the point of view of legal theory the only acceptable justification for a system of norms is therefore a single basic norm. The norm may be complex; it may specify that different principles prevail in different circumstances. But consistency requires that there should only be one. Only if there is a single basic norm can all those coercive norms which are, in practice, effective be treated as valid laws which create obligations. Though one cannot argue from fact to norm, the two must correspond if law is to be taken at face value and a genuine legal science—one which both respects the facts and satisfies the normative claims of the law—is to be possible.

The moral and political principles so far adduced fail to ensure a correspondence of fact and norm. Notions such as utility and conformity to nature invalidate some legal norms which are both valid by conventional criteria and effective. It is possible to overcome this deficiency by choosing a moral or political principle which, instead of picking and choosing between effective laws, justifies them all. There are principles, or combinations of principles, which will achieve this. In a democratic society the principle of democracy may suffice. Suppose that all the effective laws of a given society have been enacted by a democratically chosen legislature. The basic norm of the system in question will be that one should behave in accordance with norms prescribed by democratic institutions. This basic norm will validate the laws of the democratic society in question.

That should satisfy the citizens and officials of the society who wish to interpret the laws as valid.

But it will not be enough to satisfy those who wish to take municipal legal systems in general seriously. Legal theory has to be able to deal not merely with the law of democratic societies, but with dictatorships and one-party states. Many of the societies whose laws form the subject-matter of legal theory and so, if law is to be shown to possess an independent value, require justifying are non-democratic. Of course different legal systems are bound to have different basic norms; at the very least they must be different in that they refer to the history or circumstances of different societies. But if the point of view of legal theory is itself to be a coherent one—which it clearly must be if the discipline is to have any value—these basic norms must be consistent with one another. Legal theory cannot simultaneously entertain the hypothesis, in relation to one system, that only laws proceeding from democratic institutions are valid and, in relation to another, that only laws proceeding from Marxist institutions are valid. To do so would make it impossible to entertain the hypothesis that both systems were valid. As in the case of utility and conformity to nature, it is not a coherent point of view to entertain the hypothesis that both democracy alone and Marxism alone justify laws. The hypothesis must, at a minimum, be amended so as to provide that neither democracy nor Marxism is an exclusive justification. Each is capable in different conditions of justifying laws; and the hypothesis must go on to specify the conditions in which the one or the other can be held to do so.

If, then, both democratic and Marxist institutions are to be treated as validating the laws of different societies, this must be by virtue of a wider or more complex principle, such as the principle that behaviour should conform to whatever is prescribed by the powers that be. Might is Right. Whoever possesses political power is entitled to exercise it.

The obverse of this is the principle of conformism. Conformism is indeed the most plausible candidate for a moral or political principle on which to base the validity of municipal legal systems in general. According to conformism, citizens should defer to authority. They should accept the conventional tests of constitutional validity in the society in which they live. If the principle of conformism is adopted, the effective norms of a legal system will all be justified. The correlation between fact and norm will be guaranteed. We do not have to eliminate any norm which is conventionally regarded as a legal norm. No matter what the political complexion of the society, the statute-book and law reports need not be mutilated by the normative censor. The laws of countries with different political ideologies can be treated as equally valid. Legal theory can proceed.

Kelsen does not however adopt conformism as the basic norm of a municipal system of law. Why not? The reason, I think, is that it fails to capture the specific ideology of law. Only if the basic norm expresses this distinctive ideology can legal theory be an independent discipline. Otherwise, it will be no more than a branch of moral or political philosophy.

Obviously, no one is bound to agree with Kelsen that legal theory is an autonomous discipline. But his view is not just a piece of special pleading on behalf of law professors. It expresses an important claim: that there can be normative principles which create obligations independent of moral and political ideologies. Whether this is the case is certainly worth investigating, since upholders of the rule of law are committed to holding either this view, or something not far removed from it.

There is an argument which seems to tell in favour of Kelsen's view that, if anything justifies the assertion that legal norms are binding, what justifies them must be a principle specifically concerned with the legal system.[19] In laying down what citizens and officials ought to do, legislators purport to exercise certain powers. They are not satisfied just to present their citizens with demands, and then claim that in meeting these demands citizens ought to be animated by a spirit of conformism. The legislators claim rather that citizens and officials should conform to the norms they set because they are entitled to legislate. Conformism, or 'Might is Right', is not a principle that can capture this point of view. Legal discourse, with its talk of rights, duties, and obligations, does not reflect the ideology of conformism.

The point may be made in another way. One reason why no moral or political principle will serve by itself to validate a legal norm is this. No one regards utility or fairness, without more, as justifying a demand by the state, backed by coercion, for £200. Take the example of a tax. A tax is a contribution to the expenses of government; and moral and political principles are certainly relevant to fixing the contribution which it is proper for each of us to make to these expenses. Yet no one thinks that I ought to pay the government a particular sum of money merely because that is the amount required by utility, fairness, or the law of nature. Even the most fanatical devotee of Bentham, when presented with a tax bill for £200, does not pay the Inland Revenue £400 on the ground that the latter sum, rather than the former, represents the contribution which the principle of utility requires. Nor is this simply because of the indeterminacy of the principle of utility. Our attitude would hardly change if we all had the pocket calculators previously mentioned with which to perform the utilitarian calculus, and if these showed that £400 was the utile amount.

---

[19] See n.11 above.

It is at least a condition of being bound by a legal norm that it should conform to the conventionally accepted criteria for the validity of such
norms, for example that it should be prescribed by or under an Act of
Parliament. It must satisfy institutional tests. The basic norm must therefore justify these institutional criteria. Moral and political principles can
of course justify institutions, as they can norms. But, once again, the justification will be selective. Some institutions in some societies will pass
muster, others not. Not even conformism will serve as a general justification of institutional criteria, since conformism presupposes the existence of these criteria, and goes on to hold that subjects have an
obligation to conform to them. It offers no argument to show that the
conventional criteria are justified. In short, no moral or political principle will meet the case.

II. THE PEDIGREE THEORY

It is for these reasons, I believe, that Kelsen looks elsewhere. He appeals
to a specifically legal notion,[20] that of a chain of entitlements which constitutes the pedigree of a valid legal norm. According to this notion a person or body which has the right to prescribe how others shall behave can
transmit this right to another person or body by way of succession or delegation. Thus a norm which validates the law-making power of a particular person or body and justifies the assertion that it possesses that
power also justifies the law-making power of a successor chosen according to norms laid down by the predecessor. Again a norm which justifies
the exercise of law-making power by a given person or body also justifies
the exercise of such power by a person or body to whom the first has delegated a part of that law-making power. If this notion is accepted, the
right of an official to demand a poll-tax from X can be justified if his
demand is backed by a proper pedigree. The demand is justified by the
poll-tax law. The poll-tax law is justified by the principle that Parliament
has legislative power. But by virtue of what principle does Parliament
have the power to legislate? What is Parliament's pedigree? In the general
understanding of lawyers and laymen its legislative power is not derived
from any superior body which was itself entitled to confer such power.
There is no prior link in the chain of entitlements. The validity of
Parliamentary legislation rests squarely on convention. Its status can no

---

[20] It is specifically legal in that its point is to validate legal norms and nothing else. But
since in doing so it justifies the conclusion that those subject to the legal norms are bound
to obey them, it is in a broad sense (not that of conventional morality) 'moral'. Indeed, it
can be regarded as 'the minimum . . . of natural law without which a cognition of law is
impossible'. *Phil. Fds.* § 36 (p. 437).

doubt be explained historically, but to explain is not to validate or justify. Parliamentary legislation happens, no matter for what reason or combination of reasons, currently to be regarded by citizen and official alike as valid. It possesses social normativity.

For Kelsen's purposes, of course, social normativity is not enough. For Parliamentary legislation to be objectively valid there must in addition be some valid norm by virtue of which Parliament has the competence to legislate. There must be some justification for the assertion that we ought to behave as Parliament prescribes beyond the current widespread acceptance of the view that this is the case.

Such a justification can be found, Kelsen thinks, if we are prepared to assume that the original constitution, from which the present constitution is derived, was validly made. Let us assume that the framers of the original constitution had the power validly to prescribe how members of the society in question should behave. They ought, on this assumption, to behave as the framers of the original constitution and their successors and delegates prescribe. By a chain of succession Parliament today has legislative powers indirectly derived from the original constitution, and the tax official has a delegated power to make a tax demand. The tax demand is valid and creates an obligation to pay the tax.

The phrase 'original constitution' may mislead. What is meant by this phrase is the last constitution to which the present constitution is linked by a chain of entitlement. No revolution must therefore intervene between the original constitution and the present one. If there has been a revolution, the original constitution will be the one which has emerged from the last revolution. So far as the present constitution of Britain is concerned, we can perhaps go back no further than the Glorious Revolution of 1688. The settlement which arose from that revolution will count as the original constitution. Only if we suppose that William III and those who brought about that revolution were entitled to make a new constitutional settlement can we conclude, via a chain of entitlements, that the recently enacted poll-tax law is valid.

What is true of the law of Britain is true *mutatis mutandis* of the law of any other country. Though the original constitutions of different countries naturally differ, the currently effective system of legal norms in each can be validated by appeal to the assumed validity of its original constitution. The validity of the original constitution is in no case demonstrable. It is, to all intents and purposes, an article of faith embraced by those who wish to take law at face value and can find no other way of doing so.

In one respect the validity of the first constitution is like the occurrence of the Big Bang. The Big Bang is a singularity which some cosmologists postulate as having occurred at a remote period in the past. They adopt the hypothesis of the Big Bang in order to explain how the universe is as it now is. They infer that there must have been such an event, but they cannot carry causal explanation further back. They cannot explain the occurrence of the Big Bang in terms of pre-existing physical laws. It was with the Big Bang that the physical laws originated. In much the same way, the supposedly valid original constitution originated a system of valid norms. We cannot discover, or even sensibly enquire, how its framers came to have the right to frame it. We bump our heads against an un-normed norm.

In another respect, however, the basic norm is unlike the Big Bang. Its function is not to explain why the present norms of the legal system are what they are. It is intended rather to show how the present laws of the system, whose identity can be determined independently of the basic norm[21] since they are valid by conventional criteria, could be interpreted as binding. But no one is compelled to interpret them as binding. Anyone who prefers may regard them instead as constituting a network of threats. Since there is, in the last resort, no way of showing that one interpretation is better than the other, we do not know that there is anything for the basic norm to explain; whereas we do know that there is something for the Big Bang to explain, namely the existing state of the universe. The gap between fact and valid norm remains unbridgeable; but if it were to be bridged, the bridge would have to pass via the basic norm.

It is generally agreed that Kelsen's pedigree theory, with its reliance on the validity of the original constitution, is unsuccessful. In the first place, no intelligent and candid person will suppose the Kelsenian basic norm to be valid. Everyone knows that, if validity is to be tested by a chain of entitlements, the original constitution of virtually every country was invalid. It was made by people who were not entitled to rule. They seized power by conquest, usurpation, or revolution. In Britain, for example, the 'original constitution' was made by William of Orange, who did not have a good claim to the throne and whose Parliament was not a lawful Parliament. It is only if Might is invariably Right that it can appear plausible to suppose that the framers of the original constitution were entitled to engage in constitution-making. But, as we saw, if law is to be taken seriously this dubious political principle cannot serve as the basic norm of a legal system. Those who wish to interpret legal norms as objectively valid do not seek to justify their view on the basis that Might is Right. If they did, they would see no distinction between a robber band or a group of terrorists and a valid coercive order. It is because they do see a difference between law and terrorism that they wish to know on what terms legal norms can be interpreted as objectively valid. They will therefore

---

[21] Kelsen thought the contrary. He is corrected on this point by Raz, *CLS*, at 100–5.

reject Kelsen's appeal to the validity of the original constitution as a justification of the norms of a municipal legal system. Kelsen is trying to have it both ways. His basic norm claims to be independent of moral and political values. At the same time it can only validate laws as imposing obligations on the implausible assumption that the authors of the original constitution were morally and politically entitled to lay it down. Partisans of the rule of law will look for something which has a more plausible claim on our allegiance. Whatever their respect for Kelsen, they can neither suppose, nor pretend to suppose, the validity of the Kelsenian basic norm.

But does it matter that individuals are unlikely to presuppose the basic norm? Legal science can be left to do so; and legal science, being abstract, need not be committed to the validity of the basic norm. It need only presuppose the basic norm in a detached, uncommitted way.[22] It can adopt an attitude towards the basic norm like that of the expert in the Mosaic law, who, though not himself a strict believer, expounds the law to an orthodox Jew: something like 'On the assumption that God should be obeyed and that he laid all this down, you must abstain from eating so-and-so.'

It is, however, of no interest to attribute to legal science the point of view that laws are justified and obligatory unless there are a fair number of people who actually share or are likely to share this point of view. The basic norm ought to have some plausibility.

Apart from its implausibility, Kelsen's basic norm encounters another obstacle. Even if individuals, or legal science in the abstract, could be got to presuppose the norm, that would not do the trick. The fact that the framers of the original constitution had the right to prescribe how people should behave does not entail that their successors at the present day have the right to make law. To suppose that present title can be deduced from historical entitlement is to make the mistake that Robert Nozick makes when he argues that because my predecessor in title rightfully acquired property I am currently entitled to keep it.[23] Of course, as a matter of convenience, systems of property law make use of the notion of the unsullied transmission of title. But acceptance of this notion does not guarantee that what is transmitted is a justified title. It may be that circumstances have so changed that, although the original holding could be justified, the present property holding cannot be. So in the case of constitutional entitlement. Even if the original constitution-makers were entitled to lay down what they did, it does not follow that their present successors are entitled to exercise the powers which they derive indi-

---

[22] On detached as opposed to committed normative statements see Raz, *AL*, at 153–7.
[23] See Tony Honoré, 'Property, Title and Redistribution', in Honoré, *Making Law Bind* (n.3 above), 215–26.

rectly from the original constitution. Circumstances may have changed. What was justified in conditions prevailing long ago may by now have given place, albeit by a gradual and peaceful process, to a distribution of power which is to be condemned as oppressive or tyrannical.

One cannot therefore argue from the validity of the basic norm to the validity of the present constitution. The system by which title to property, or title to legislate, is transmitted from one holder to another stands in need of justification. Except as a technical device, the justification for it is not self-evident. The fact that the pedigree principle is independent of moral and political ideology does not exempt it from critical scrutiny. Kelsen's basic norm is only valid if the principle of transmission of title is valid, and this principle stands in need of a normative justification, which Kelsen does not provide.

Kelsen's attempt to find a plausible basic norm for municipal systems of law therefore fails. Does it follow that the search should be abandoned? I do not think so. Many people in many societies take law seriously. They are minded to interpret most laws as imposing obligations on them and on others. Obviously not everyone is so minded, and few will want to interpret all laws in this way. A sensible person will interpret a law which forbids parking in a convenient area simply as a threat that, if he is caught parking there, a fine will be imposed. He will not think that he has a duty to refrain from parking in the forbidden spot. So, if the convenience of parking outweighs the threat of the fine, he will run a small risk, but violate no duty,[24] by disregarding the law.

In other instances some people will look on a law as imposing a duty but others will regard it merely as constituting a threat. A law which calls up citizens for military service in a war may be regarded by those who favour the war as having a claim on their allegiance but by opponents of the war as a threat to be evaded.

It is true that in these cases, though the ordinary citizen may treat the parking or conscription law as a mere threat, the official who is charged with law enforcement is likely to see it as imposing on him a duty to exact the fine or to punish the draft evader. That may be a reason why Kelsen treats legal norms as directed to officials. It is plausible to think that an official, such as a judge or policeman, has a duty to enforce the norms of the system as a whole and that they are consequently all binding on him. The official has—though, from Kelsen's point of view, this is strictly irrelevant—undertaken an office which involves law enforcement. But even officials may be disaffected. They may have been

---

[24] Other than a legal duty. The expression 'legal duty/obligation' is ambiguous, since it can mean either a duty justifiably created by law or a purported duty, as in the parking case, which is, however, treated as normative according to the language of the legal system or the attitude of lawyers and officials who operate the system.

pressed into taking office. The character of the laws may have changed since they did so. In some societies nearly everyone, including the highest functionaries, regards the laws as tyrannical, and the state as a robber band. The laws of that tyrannical state may nevertheless be effective. It may be, as in Stalinist Russia, that even top people are so cowed by an interlocking system of threats that they see no possibility of escape. Officials go on enforcing and citizens go on obeying laws which they abhor.

In that case hardly anyone in the society will interpret the laws as creating objectively valid norms. But the fact that not everybody interprets laws as imposing obligations, and that in some societies few people do so, does not rob the search for the conditions of justification of its interest. The language of right and obligation in which legal argument is carried on positively invites such a search. Perhaps it will, if successful, enable us to understand and improve legal systems so that they more often deserve, and more often win, respect than they do at present.

III. THE BASIC NORM OF A SOCIETY

In his search for the basic norm Kelsen attempts both too much and too little. He attempts too much because the stringent conditions he imposes lead to overkill. That all the norms of a given legal system are objectively valid and impose obligations is not something that a sensible person will even want to believe. Only if he has adopted an exclusively law-oriented ethical system, by which obedience to law prevails over all else, will he wish to maintain that all laws without exception bind those to whom they apply. A rational person will want to adopt a more selective point of view. He will not be attracted by hard-line positivism. His point of view will be that there can be valid laws which, though treated as binding by the legal system, are not really binding: laws which it is justifiable to disobey. There are plenty of oppressive and tyrannical laws. Even a legal system which is in general well designed will inevitably comprise some laws which are pointless, out of date, or inept. It would be strange to think that these dysfunctional laws deserved obedience, even from officials. On the contrary officials, including judges, will be praised if they can find ways of evading them. These laws at least can properly be treated as mere threats or nuisances.

Nor need legal theory adopt a different, more pedantic standpoint. The task of legal theory is to draw together in a theoretical focus the points of view of ordinary people and officials who think that by and large laws impose obligations.

Kelsen imposes too restrictive a condition, therefore, when he requires that the basic norm should justify dysfunctional or oppressive laws. On the other hand it ought surely to do more than to validate the pedigree of the remainder. There are two reasons why in this respect Kelsen's aims are under-ambitious.

Conventional criteria often fail to settle the correct interpretation of the laws which the basic norm is supposed to justify. Yet without knowing how a law is to be interpreted, we may not be able to judge whether it creates an obligation. The interpretation of a law and its duty-imposing character are often interdependent. The interpretation of the norm, and so its content, may be influenced by the claim, implicit in the ideology of law, that it imposes an obligation. A law providing that 'the airport authority shall destroy the contents of any unclaimed crate' may be judged valid if it requires no more than that the inanimate contents of an unclaimed crate be destroyed. If, on the other hand, it required the airport authority to kill a human being who had unfortunately been kidnapped and packed in a crate, it could not be said to impose an obligation but, at most, to threaten a fine or some other penalty. The fact that one of the two possible interpretations does not yield a duty-imposing law clearly has a bearing on the correct interpretation of the statute. Yet Kelsen's basic norm does not allow for any distinction between the validity of rival interpretations. It validates all laws with a proper pedigree, irrespective of how they are interpreted. It can never be said that one interpretation fits the basic norm better than another.

Kelsen's refusal to distinguish between the status of different interpretations of a norm is, of course, true to his rigorous version of positivism. On this rigorous view, positivism admits no exception to the principle that laws which possess a proper pedigree create obligations. It leaves no place for valid but unjust laws. Once it is accepted that this theory involves an overkill, at least in the case of dysfunctional and oppressive laws, the basic norm can be given a wider scope. Why should it not influence the choice between alternative interpretations?

Indeed, it might serve a still more ambitious end. A legal system is not exhausted by the norms it contains. It reaches further than that. It purports to deal with the whole of human conduct and to classify it as lawful or unlawful, according to whether the conduct violates a duty. This is true even as regards conduct which has not yet been the subject of legislation or adjudication. When a court classifies conduct of this sort as unlawful, the classification is by definition retrospective, in the sense that at the time the conduct occurred, no institutional test settled that it was unlawful.

Is it, for example, a legal wrong to render someone *pro tanto* a non-person by eliminating his name from a computer data base? The question has not, I think, been determined, at least not in this abstract form, by legislation or judicial decision. Nevertheless one cannot rule out the possibility that it is a legal wrong to depersonify another in this way. But how could one justify the conclusion that this form of data-base manipulation was a wrong despite the fact that this had not been settled, or even mooted, in any prior statute or judicial decision? How could one show, despite the lack of authority, that the person who manipulated the data base was violating an obligation? There seems to be no way of doing this except by pointing to a basic norm whose justifying force goes beyond the norms that have so far received institutional endorsement. This basic norm may be capable of justifying norms which no court or legislature has so far endorsed.

Of course it may be objected that these 'retrospective' wrongs are not genuine wrongs. The term 'wrong' misdescribes cases in which the court for reasons of policy inflicts a penalty. The possibility of a retrospectively imposed penalty should have been foreseen by the person held responsible and treated by him as a threat. Either the person who manipulated the data base took a chance and was unlucky or, perhaps, he is simply penalized *pour encourager les autres*.

Though sometimes plausible, this cool interpretation of the instances where conduct is retrospectively assessed as a wrong is not always convincing. As Ronald Dworkin points out,[25] legal discourse assumes that in such situations one can meaningfully talk of rights and duties. Intuitively that assumption often seems well founded. The 'wrong-doer' had no business to manipulate the data base as he did, though one cannot subsume what he did under any recognized legal prohibition. The decision which the court ultimately reaches is seen in retrospect to draw on elements of the legal system which were immanent in it but which had not previously been fully deployed.[26]

It is not necessary, I think, to maintain that all hard cases or cases of first impression are of this sort. Sometimes a case of first impression, though within the jurisdiction of a court, calls simply for a considered decision. There is no justice about it. To which of the testator's three heirs should a striking family portrait be awarded? None is more entitled to it than another. A choice must be made, and while there may be reasons pointing one way or another, they are not reasons of justice. In this sort of case the decision imposed by a (presumptively) wise and experienced judge is both acceptable and the best we can do. But in other situations, of which data-base manipulation may be one, a decision is expected which will genuinely set forth the rights and duties of the

---

[25] See Dworkin (n.2 above), at 81–130.
[26] Dworkin (n.2 above), 105. Joseph Raz, in 'The Inner Logic of the Law', in Raz, *Ethics in the Public Domain* (Oxford: Clarendon Press, 1994), 238–53, shows how material internal to a system can suggest developments which in retrospect seem implicit in it. But this type of creative development itself needs, in my view, to be justified by reference to a basic norm.

parties, though it is only in retrospect that these can be specified. Even though in a case of this sort the judge makes new law, an essential part of the justification for his doing so resides in the fact that the new law specifies the content of an existing obligation.

This is an area in which legal and moral argument run parallel. We feel justified in describing conduct as morally wrong, even when we cannot subsume what has been done under some settled rubric like breaking a promise. We can sensibly discuss whether it was wrong for X to reveal what Y said on his deathbed, even if Y made no request and X no promise to keep it secret. It is possible to do what is morally wrong without breaking any item in the moral code. The moral code, so far as convention provides one, may leave the point open; but that code does not embrace every moral demand which can justifiably be made. Morality and law share an open-ended character. Each comprises a combination of specific and unspecific demands. Of course, since legal norms are coercive, it is only fair to make them as specific, and to give as much notice of their specific terms, as possible. But this principle cannot, at least in civil law, be treated as a charter of immunity for those who evade their duties to others.

The basic norm ought therefore to justify a wide spectrum of legal obligations. It ought to endorse, by and large, those legal norms which are valid by conventional criteria, for example the convention that Parliament has legislative power. It should be of service in choosing between different interpretations of these norms. It ought to point towards the solution of hard cases to which there is no settled institutional answer. That is a tall order, but nothing less is called for if legal discourse is to be taken at face value.

In the face of such far-reaching demands some may be inclined to retreat from Kelsen's position and opt not for a single justifying norm but for a number of different ones tailored to justify different parts of the legal system. For example, a particular branch of the law, such as the law of succession, reflects a limited number of principles, such as respect for the wishes of the dead and caution in ascertaining what those wishes were. Different principles, again, underlie the law of torts, or the structure of the court system. But at a more abstract level, we should resist the splitting of the basic norm into a number of separate norms. All the demands which the state can properly make on us must be consistent with one another.[27] If the state requires us to act inconsistently, it fails to treat us as rational beings. In that case it fails to reflect the specific ideology of both law and morals as forms of social control which operate by appealing to our reason. All the principles which properly command our

[27] See Dworkin (n.2 above), at 88, 116, 119, 126.

obedience must be capable of reconciliation and hence of reduction to a single, even if complex, principle.

Kelsen is not the only prominent jurist to reach this, at first sight, surprising conclusion. Dworkin approaches the problem from a different point of view. He asks on what theory a judge is to decide hard cases. Faced with a hard case, he argues, a judge must look for the political theory which best justifies the legal material which, in the exercise of his jurisdiction, he has to apply.[28] In attempting to solve the hard case he must take as his basic norm this 'best political justification', in conjunction of course with the institutionally endorsed rules and principles which it justifies. Whatever the merits in detail of Dworkin's rights-oriented theory, it is hardly a coincidence that both he and Kelsen embrace a form of holism. It is true that Dworkin's form of holism is more restricted than that of Kelsen. In this view, the fact that the underlying theory of the system requires a certain decision in a hard case does not necessarily entail that a citizen should conform to that solution, or even, if the system is a corrupt one, that the judge should declare the law to be what the underlying theory requires it to be. Still, they are both at least partly holists, since they both take seriously, or want to take seriously, the language of oughts, rights, and duties in which laws are couched and in which legal argument is generally conducted. This cannot be done without an overall justification by virtue of which laws, by and large, impose obligations.

Kelsen's basic norm—the validity of the original constitution—provides a pedigree which is similar for all municipal legal systems. They all go back to an original constitution, though naturally the content of that first constitution varies from system to system. Dworkin's basic norm—the validity of the best justifying theory—has a similar structure. Every legal system rests on some political theory, but the content of the theory will vary from one society to another. The form of holism which I favour is in one way closer to Dworkin's, in another to Kelsen's. It is surely clear, for reasons given earlier, that the basic norm cannot consist in a specifically legal principle such as the notion of a chain of entitlements.[29] But, if law is to be taken seriously, it must, as Kelsen asserts, be neutral between competing moral and political doctrines. Those doctrines, varying from one legal system to another, may feature at a subordinate level as principles of a given system, but they cannot constitute its ultimate justification. The ultimate justification, and so the basic norm, must be a normative principle of a more platitudinous sort, which will appear plausible to a variety of people living in societies with different social and political structures. Whatever may be said of Kelsen's and Dworkin's

---

[28] See Dworkin (n.2 above), at 81, 87, 116–17, 340.   [29] See at § II above.

norms, they cannot truthfully be called platitudinous. They are unlikely to have a wide appeal. To believe in Kelsen's basic norm one must be able to assert: *credo quia incredibile*. Everyone knows that the original constitution to which he appeals was invalid. Dworkin's norm is not so much incredible as unattainable. Since it requires the powers of a Hercules to discover the correct theory, it leaves us at the mercy of Herculean pretensions.[30]

A more plausible basic norm with which to test and, in a proper case, justify the law, morality, and political institutions of a society is the norm which prescribes that *the members of a society have a duty to co-operate with one another*. This platitudinous norm is bland enough to appeal to almost everyone, but it is not on that account empty. If it is accepted as binding, it, or some more ultimate norm from which it can be derived, becomes a necessary element in the justification of every law. The duty to co-operate is not itself a principle of either law or, in the narrow sense, morality. It is in a broad sense a moral principle, which constitutes a necessary presupposition of both social morality and law so far as these are interpreted as systems of obligation. Only if such a duty is presupposed can the members of a society have a duty to conform to any particular mode of co-operation. Only on the basis of this fundamental duty can they be bound to keep promises, tell the truth, refrain from harm to others, and conform to rules, including rules of law.

If the members of a society have a duty to co-operate, they have also prima facie a duty to observe (i) social conventions which restrict their freedom in the interests of others, if these are thought by members of the society to be important, and (ii) duties specified in appropriate cases by institutions of the society such as legislatures and courts. The platitudinous basic norm engenders equally platitudinous sub-norms such as 'Respect customs', 'Pay debts', 'Perform contracts', 'Abstain from wrongs'.[31] The legal institutions give body to these sub-norms by specifying the wrongs to be avoided, the debts to be paid, and so on.

Obviously there can only prima facie be a duty to comply with what is thus specified. The modes of co-operation which conventions require or which institutions impose may be pointless or oppressive. But if the members of a society have a duty to co-operate with one another at all they must as a corollary have a duty to comply with conventional and institutional requirements, unless there is a strong reason to the contrary. It is only by way of such compliance that co-operation is in practice possible. Necessity, therefore, born of the need for consistency, grounds this obligation of compliance, rather than consent or custom. Those who

---

[30] Hercules' struggles are described in Dworkin (n.2 above), at 105–23.
[31] See Tony Honoré, 'Real Laws', in Honoré, *Making Law Bind* (n.3 above), 69–88, at 87–8.

purport to accept the basic norm cannot consistently reject the only viable modes of operation of the principle they purport to accept.

The principle of co-operation extends to situations not covered by any convention or institutional ruling. For this reason it can be relied on in disputes about interpretation. It can also be appealed to in situations, like that of the data base, where conventional and institutional sources do not compel an answer. The co-operative principle will of course often fail to provide a determinate answer. Different people will have different conceptions of what co-operation requires. In any particular society it will need to be filled out with notions of justice or utility entrenched or current in that society and its legal system. The principle of co-operation is a framework rather than a brooding omnipresence in the sky. Its relation to the subordinate principles, rules, and institutions of a legal system is a complex topic which demands further attention.

Despite the fact that this essay provides no more than a sketch of the theory of co-operation as the basic norm of a society, the sketch provided is perhaps enough to establish an important point. We are not confronted with a bleak choice between two implausible views of laws and legal systems. We are not bound to choose between the view that laws are mere threats which have as such no claim on the allegiance of those to whom they apply and the view that any claim they may have rests on their conformity to some preferred ideology such as utilitarianism, Marxism, or natural law. There is a middle ground between these alternatives. This middle way respects the ideology of law as an enterprise which by and large creates obligations and yet is not committed to flying the banner of any particular moral or political party.

How does the view advanced in this essay stand in relation to the traditional battle lines between positivists and anti-positivists? Perhaps the old battles should no longer be fought on the same lines or even by the same contestants. Positivism has undoubtedly stood in the past, and may still need to stand, for a healthy idea. Nothing is law simply because it is good or just. A rule or principle becomes law only when it is adopted as such by a given society. If the institutions of the society reject a supposed rule or principle of law then, however unwise they may be to do so, the rule or principle in question is not part of the law of that society.

It is useful to be reminded of this elementary point. One of the uncertainties from which law rescues us is the uncertainty that competing conceptions of justice and the common good otherwise engender. Law has a specific technique for doing this. It does it by adopting verbal formulae, in the form of authoritative texts which acquire a certain independence of the reasons, moral or political, that have led to their adoption.

But, beyond this, we need a more discriminating terminology in which to formulate the great debates of legal theory. Kelsen is in his own eyes an arch-positivist; Dworkin, a declared enemy of positivism. Yet they have much in common. Each presents a holistic theory of law as a system of obligations or rights—two sides of the same coin. This type of interpretation seems to me viable for most societies and most laws, to the extent that they seriously attempt to give effect to the duty to co-operate. But if anyone shies at the notion that a particular law or legal system binds him, and thinks of it rather as a network of menaces, he need not be wrong. The law or system in question may fail dismally to reflect the co-operative principle; it may be plainly oppressive or tyrannical. The correct interpretation of a legal system is, in the last resort, the interpretation that seems persuasive to those rational creatures who feel its impact. It is hard work to make laws bind.

6

Methodological Syncretism in Kelsen's Pure Theory of Law*

DERYCK BEYLEVELD AND ROGER BROWNSWORD

INTRODUCTION

In *Pure Theory of Law*, first published in 1960, Kelsen makes two claims that might be taken to imply an espousal of Legal Idealism. These are

(1) a 'doctrine of presupposition', the view that the characterization of a norm as a legal norm, and the characterization of an order of norms as a legal order,[1] presupposes a 'basic norm', which specifies that the constitution of the positive, effective, coercive order ought to be applied and obeyed; and

(2) the contention that the presupposition of a basic norm is the transcendental-logical foundation of legal science, that which makes possible the designation of laws as rules that ought to be applied and obeyed.

Kelsen is, however, a moral relativist. By itself, this may merely prompt the thought that Kelsen advocates a relativized version of Legal Idealism.[2] However, Kelsen advances the Pure Theory in the service of Legal Positivism.

If Kelsen is to be understood as a legal positivist, he must assent to the Separation Thesis. He must hold that legal validity does not hinge upon the satisfaction of some necessary material moral condition, but simply

---

* *Editors' note*: This paper, written for the present volume, is based on ch. 6 of Deryck Beyleveld and Roger Brownsword, *Law as a Moral Judgment* (n.1 below).

[1] Stanley L. Paulson has pointed out to us that the translator's rendering of '*Rechtsordnung*' in *PTL* as 'legal order' would have been better as 'legal system'. We have decided to stick with 'legal order' not just because this is what we did in *Law as a Moral Judgment* (London: Sweet & Maxwell, 1986, repr. Sheffield: Sheffield Academic Press, 1994), but because we prefer not to change the translation we employ, and, although there are some places where 'system' appears instead of 'order' in the translation, to use 'system' in the text with 'order', for the most part, in the quotations tends to jar. There are also parallel difficulties with 'moral order' and 'moral system'.

[2] In *Law as a Moral Judgment* (n.1 above), we did not use the term 'Legal Idealism'. We used the term 'Natural-Law Theory' to cover both 'Relativized' and 'Objectivistic Legal Idealism' (referring to 'Relativistic' and 'Objectivistic Natural-Law Theory'). In this paper, when we use 'Natural Law Theory', this is to be taken as meaning 'Objectivistic Legal Idealism'.

upon the *de facto* (positivist) tests for legality operative within the polity. Apparently, this is Kelsen's position. For Kelsen, the only condition that a rule must satisfy if it is to be legally valid is that it be part of a coercive normative order that is positive and by and large effective. Given that the coercive normative order associated with a robber gang is to be interpreted as not legal, on the grounds that it is less effective than the surrounding 'legal' order,[3] the relevant positive, by and large effective, order for the purposes of judging legality is simply the most effective coercive normative order within the polity. The condition for a rule being legally valid is simply that the rule be a rule within the positive, effective, coercive order.

The apparent paradox in Kelsen is that we have what may be construed as a thoroughly moral account of the concept of law, presented in terms of the basic norm and the doctrine of presupposition, running alongside a textbook legal positivist account of legal validity, presented in terms of positivity and effectiveness. If we act on the moral side of this presentation we must see the basic norm as a moral condition for legal validity. We must hold that the basic norm sets a material moral test for legal validity and that failure to conform with the moral condition is fatal to legality. Even if Kelsen's moral relativism is fed into this, conformity with some moral requirement (understood relativistically) will be a prerequisite for legality. Of course, the relativistic idealist must concede that his particular criteria for legality have no privileged status epistemologically but, within the framework of his own moral commitments and concomitant conceptual scheme, the relativist must hold that legal validity/invalidity hinges upon conformity with his relativistic basic norm. In Kelsen's case, however, this moral account and its implications are turned on their heads once we focus upon the presentation of legal validity in terms of positivity and effectiveness. In this presentation the basic norm figures not as a condition of validity, but as a 'reason' for validity. Whatever moral gloss the basic norm casts upon the rules that compose the positive, by and large effective order, it is clear that legal validity no longer depends upon the satisfaction of some material moral requirement.

The general structure of this paper is as follows: first, we consider the doctrine of presupposition and argue that it should be interpreted as a doctrine of moral presupposition (in section I), thus creating the apparent paradox we have outlined. We then consider (in section II) Kelsen's arguments for the compatibility of such a doctrine with Legal Positivism under three headings that are persistent themes in *Pure Theory of Law*: 'Positivity, Effectiveness, and Legal Validity'; 'Kelsen's Moral Relativism';

---

[3] See *PTL* § 6(c) (at pp. 47–8).

and 'The Non-Prescriptive Nature of Legal Interpretation'.[4] We argue that none of Kelsen's arguments for Legal Positivism are compelling in the context of the doctrine of moral presupposition. We contend (in section III), that the doctrine of presupposition is inconsistent with Legal Positivism and that Kelsen's arguments for these two doctrines derive from inconsistent methodological bases.

I. KELSEN'S DOCTRINE OF PRESUPPOSITION: INTRODUCTION AND PRELIMINARY INTERPRETATION

One of the most distinctive features of the Pure Theory is that legal validity is not a property that an object, or more generally an act, possesses in itself. It is a property imputed in an act of interpretation. Characterization of an act as legally valid depends upon a specific act of interpretation. To understand the nature of this act of interpretation we need first of all to attend to two distinctions that Kelsen draws. The first is between a *causal* and a *normative* interpretation, the second is between a *subjective* normative interpretation and an *objective* normative interpretation. The interpretation required to characterize an act as a legally valid act is an objective normative interpretation.

According to Kelsen, to view an act in terms of those of its properties that can be perceived by the senses is to view the act as a natural phenomenon that exists in space and time and is governed by causal laws.[5] Kelsen tells us nothing about the specific nature of this interpretation, although his claim does have a distinctive Kantian 'ring' to it, and a Kantian reading (which should not, however, be pressed too far)[6] is also prompted by Kelsen's suggestion that his doctrine of normative interpretation may be understood on an analogy with Kant's theory of the transcendental-logical categories that make it possible for us to have empirical knowledge.[7]

It is, however, clear that viewing an act as a natural event is not the same as viewing it in terms of its legal meaning, that is, the meaning conferred upon it by the law.

For if you analyze any body of facts interpreted as 'legal' or somehow tied up with law, such as a parliamentary decision, an administrative act, a judgment, a contract, or a crime, two elements are distinguishable: one, an act or series of acts—

---

[4] In the relevant chapter of *Law as a Moral Judgment* (n.1 above), we considered a fourth heading, 'Kelsen's View that there are No *A Priori* Limits on Norm-Creation'.

[5] See *PTL* § 4(a) (at p. 4).

[6] For reasons that have to do with Kelsen's view that there are no *a priori* limits on norm-creation.

[7] See *PTL* § 34(d) (at p. 202).

a happening occurring at a certain time and in a certain place, perceived by our senses: an external manifestation of human conduct; two, the legal meaning of this act, that is, the meaning conferred upon the act by the law. For example: People assemble in a large room, make speeches, some raise their hands, others do not—this is the external happening. Its meaning is that a statute is being passed, that law is created. . . . To give other illustrations: A man in a robe and speaking from a dais says some words to a man standing before him; legally this external happening means: a judicial decision was passed. A merchant writes a letter of a certain content to another merchant, who, in turn, answers with a letter; this means they have concluded a legally binding contract. Somebody causes the death of somebody else; legally, this means murder.[8]

An act may be viewed either normatively or as a natural phenomenon. To view an act normatively is to view it as something that is commanded, permitted, or authorized (or the converse or reverse of these); to view it normatively is to view it as 'good' or 'bad'. To interpret an act normatively is to view it in relation to a norm that prescribes something. To interpret an act in terms of its legal meaning is to view the act in relation to a norm that is viewed as a legally valid norm.

How does Kelsen define 'norm'? 'By "norm" we mean that something *ought* to be or *ought* to happen, especially that a human being ought to behave in a specific way'.[9]

However, in this statement, and very generally, Kelsen attaches a special meaning to his use of the term 'ought'. 'Ought'

is the meaning of certain human acts [of will] directed toward the behavior of others. They are so directed, if they, according to their content, command such behavior, but also if they permit it, and—particularly—if they authorize it. . . . According to customary usage, 'ought' corresponds only to a command, while 'may' corresponds to a permission, and 'can' to an authorization. But in the present work the word 'ought' is used to express the normative meaning of an act [of will] directed toward the behavior of others; this 'ought' includes 'may' and 'can'.[10]

If what the norm prescribes is that a specific action is prohibited, not permitted, or unauthorized, then its meaning should (strictly speaking) be expressed by 'ought not'. Kelsen, however, generally uses 'ought' to cover 'ought not' as well. This seems reasonable enough, since to command something is necessarily to prohibit something else (if only its negative).

If an object is in accordance with a norm then Kelsen says it has a positive value and is 'good' (in relation to the norm). If the object is not in accordance with a norm then it is 'bad' (in relation to the norm).[11]

---

[8] *PTL* § 2 (p. 2).   [9] *PTL* § 4(b)(p. 4).   [10] *PTL* § 4(b)(pp. 4–5).
[11] See *PTL* § 4(e) (at p. 19).

A normative interpretation attaches a value ('good' or 'bad', 'it ought' or 'it ought not' to be done) to an object or behaviour. The value attached depends on the specific relation of the object or behaviour to a norm. The 'ought' that is the meaning of the norm is, however, also open to interpretation. It may be interpreted as a subjective meaning or as an objective meaning.[12] An 'ought' is regarded as a subjective meaning when it is treated as what someone wishes to be or not to be, or as what someone approves or disapproves. An 'ought' is regarded as an objective meaning when this meaning is treated as independent of what anyone wishes to be or not to be, approves or disapproves.

There are two levels of normative interpretation in Kelsen. The first level is interpretation that invests an 'ought' with objective or subjective meaning. The second is interpretation by which an object (which may be a norm) is valued by its relation to an 'ought'.[13] At the second level of interpretation, an objective value judgment is made when an object *is described* as being in conformity or not in conformity with an 'ought' interpreted objectively (first level of interpretation).[14] A subjective 'value judgment'[15] is made when an object is regarded as something wished or not wished, approved or not approved;[16] or when an object is described as being in conformity or not in conformity with an 'ought' interpreted at the first level of interpretation as a subjective meaning. Kelsen appears to

---

[12] Having defined a norm as a prescription (see *PTL* § 4(b) (at p. 4)), Kelsen restricts norms to occurrences of 'ought' interpreted objectively. ' "Ought" is the subjective meaning of every act of will directed at the behavior of another. But not every such act has also objectively this meaning; and only if the act of will has also the objective meaning of an "ought", is this "ought" called a "norm" ' (*PTL* § 4(b) (p. 7)). As will shortly be seen, given the way Kelsen defines 'objective meaning', this makes it redundant to refer to *objectively valid* norms; but Kelsen often continues to refer to objectively valid norms, see e.g. *PTL*, at § 4(e) (pp. 17–23). Which of the two definitions we work with is a matter of significance in relation to Kelsen's definition of a legal order. We take it that, at least in the latter context, a legal order as an order of norms refers to objectively valid 'oughts' in relation to a basic norm. But, in general, this contradiction creates problems that could only be dealt with satisfactorily in a line by line annotation of *PTL*.

[13] See *PTL* § 4(e) (at pp. 17–19).

[14] Kelsen (see *PTL* § 4(e) (at p. 22)) refers to a value judgment as ' "objective" if the judging individual pronounces it without regard of whether he himself approves or disapproves of the behavior, but simply ascertains the fact that one individual or many individuals wish or will an object (or its opposite), particularly that they approve or disapprove a specific behavior.' This is not quite the same as the definition given ibid., at pp. 17–19. The latter is a 'hypothetical ascription'. The definition on p. 22 is a 'transferred ascription'. Hypothetical ascriptions have to be logically sound inferences of what follows from a norm. Transferred ascriptions do not presuppose that logically sound inferences from an objective meaning are being made—and to confuse matters more, the transferred ascriptions referred to by Kelsen on p. 22 operate with subjective meanings, not objective meanings.

[15] See *PTL* § 4(e) (at pp. 20–1), where Kelsen reveals that 'subjective value judgments' are not properly speaking judgments at all.

[16] See *PTL* § 4(e) (at p. 18).

treat these two formulations as the same.[17] An objective value judgment states an objective value; a subjective value judgment states a subjective value.[18]

What, more precisely, is involved in interpreting an 'ought' as an objective meaning of an act of will? We will divide Kelsen's first elaboration into two, for reasons that will soon be obvious.

(1) If the 'ought' is also the objective meaning of the act [of will], the behavior at which the act is directed is regarded as something that *ought* to be not only from the point of view of the individual who has performed the act, but also from the point of view of the individual at whose behavior the act is directed, and of a third individual not involved in the relation between the two. That the 'ought' is the objective meaning of the act manifests itself in the fact that it is supposed to exist (that the 'ought' is valid) even if the will ceases to exist whose subjective meaning it is—if we assume that an individual ought to behave in a certain way even if he does not know of the act whose meaning is that he ought to behave in this way. Then the 'ought', as the objective meaning of an act, is a valid *norm* binding upon the addressee, that is, the individual at whom it is directed.

(2) The ought which is the subjective meaning of an act of will is also the objective meaning of this act, if this act has been invested with this meaning, if it has been authorized by a norm, which therefore has the character of a 'higher' norm.[19]

As we understand Kelsen, he is not saying, in (1), that a norm is objectively valid (that an 'ought' has an objective meaning) on condition that everyone agrees that the behaviour prescribed ought to be done. It is not a consensus of wills that converts a subjective 'ought' into an objective 'ought'. He is saying that to regard a norm as being objectively valid is (that is, means) to regard what the norm prescribes as binding upon all whose behaviour (actual or potential) is being addressed by the norm regardless of whether anyone (including the person who is doing this objective regarding) wishes this behaviour or not (that is, regardless of whether anyone wills this 'ought' in the subjective sense).

How are we to regard the relationship between (1) and (2)? This is a very difficult question, which we consider to be one of the most important issues in the interpretation of the Pure Theory. We think that, if Kelsen means what he says in (1), then there is only one plausible inter-

[17] They are not the same. Whereas the first is a 'direct' ascription, the second may be a 'hypothetical' ascription. The latter could be 'objective' in one of the ways Kelsen uses 'objective'—'If the judgment pronounces the relationship of an object (especially of human behavior) to the wish or will of an individual (that is, a subjective value), then this value judgment is "objective" if the judging individual pronounces it without regard of whether he himself approves or disapproves of the behavior . . .', *PTL* § 4(e) (pp. 21–2). All in all, these definitions present tremendous problems of interpretation and (at least seem to) contradict almost sentence by sentence.

[18] See *PTL* § 4(e) (at pp. 19–22).   [19] *PTL* § 4(b) (pp. 7–8).

pretation. We will present this interpretation in this section. Kelsen's legal positivist aims will, however, necessitate that we consider another possible view. We will pay particular attention to this alternative in the section devoted to Kelsen's view that the interpretation provided by the science of law is non-prescriptive (section II, C, below).

According to our preliminary interpretation, (1) states the meaning of 'objective validity' and (2) is a statement to the effect that a norm is objectively valid on condition that it is authorized by a higher norm, and that a norm may only be regarded as objectively valid if it is so authorized. Furthermore, (1) states that to view an 'ought' as objectively valid is to view the 'ought' as an 'ought' of a moral discourse, as an 'ought' that expresses a moral obligation, moral prohibition, moral permission, etc. It is, after all, a characteristic of regarding prescriptions as made from a moral point of view that they are proffered as 'exclusionary reasons' for action, as norms with a prescriptive force that remains intact in the face of any subjective sentiments or wishes to the contrary.

If any reader, aware of Kelsen's legal positivist intentions, jibs at this then it may be pointed out that such a reading is encouraged—to put it mildly—not only by Kelsen's willingness to concede that legal norms have moral meaning,[20] but most specifically by the following statement that is made almost immediately after the presentation of (1) and (2) above *as part of their elucidation*.

If a man in need asks another man for help, the *subjective* meaning of this request is that the other ought to help him. But in an objective sense he ought to help (*that is to say*, he is morally obliged to help) only if a general [that is, 'higher'] norm—established, for instance, by the founder of a religion—is valid that commands, 'Love your neighbor'. And this latter norm is objectively valid only if it is presupposed that one ought to behave as the religious founder has commanded. Such a presupposition, establishing the objective validity of the norms of a moral or legal order, will here be called a *basic norm* (*Grundnorm*).[21]

Not only does this suggest that an objective 'ought' has the meaning of a moral obligation, it also suggests that authorization by a higher norm (and ultimately by the basic norm) offers a reason for accepting that there is a moral obligation, that the function of authorization is to offer such a reason.

What distinguishes a legal order of norms from a purely moral order of norms is, according to Kelsen, that a legal order is a positive, by and large effective, coercive order, whereas a purely moral order is not a coercive order. In a legal order, coercive sanctions are threatened as penalties for disobedience, whereas in a purely moral order, disobedience is

---

[20] See esp. *PTL* §§ 11–13 (at pp. 65–7).
[21] *PTL* § 4(b) (p. 8) (emphasis added in line 3).

countered merely by disapproval.[22] The question of objective validity is not one that distinguishes norms of a moral order from norms of a legal order,[23] for both the norms of a moral order and the norms of a legal order may be regarded as objectively valid. The bearing of Kelsen's discussion of objective validity is not upon the legal (versus the non-legal, for example, the moral), but upon the meaning of legal *validity* (and moral *validity*).

When an act is interpreted as a legally valid act there are two components to this interpretation (not always clearly distinguished by Kelsen's terminology). The first component is the context in which we place the act so as to bring the significance of 'legal' to bear on it: the second component is the interpretation that enables us to characterize it as a valid act within this context. The context in which we place the act is that the act is viewed in relation to a norm backed by coercive sanctions as an act that 'ought' or 'ought not' to be performed. This norm is regarded as an enactment, as the product of an act of will of some individual or group, that conforms to specified procedures (in the form of a constitution). That the act is legally valid rather than illegal, however, is not determined by the fact that the act conforms or does not conform with such a norm, nor by the fact that the enactment of the norm conforms to constitutional norms. The act may only be characterized as legally valid or invalid if the norm is regarded as objectively valid, and it can only be so regarded if the constitutional norms according to which it is enacted are regarded as objectively valid.

On the interpretation we are considering, a norm is only objectively valid *if it is* authorized (that is, legitimate),[24] and *it may only be regarded* as objectively valid *if it is regarded* as legitimate. For Kelsen, a norm has the meaning of an 'ought', and (as he constantly reminds us) like Hume, he holds that an 'ought' can only be authorized by another 'ought'.[25] This is why authorization of a norm must be by another, 'higher' norm.[26]

According to Kelsen, 'authorization' may be effected in one of two ways.

---

[22] See *PTL*, at § 6(b) (pp. 33–44, esp. 33–5). The distinction between moral orders and legal orders is not that the former operate according to the 'static' principle, the latter according to the 'dynamic' principle. In general, it seems to us, that Kelsen holds all normative orders, as human orders, to be dynamic, see *PTL* § 23 (at p. 95). Legal orders may combine the static and dynamic principles, see *PTL* § 34(b) (at pp. 197–9).

[23] This is notwithstanding Kelsen's identification of objective validity with legal validity (see *PTL* §3 (at p. 3)), for this is cancelled by Kelsen's reference to the objective validity of norms of a purely moral order, see e.g. *PTL* §4(b) (at p. 7).

[24] See *PTL* § 34(d) (at p. 203).

[25] See *PTL* § 4(b) (at p. 9), § 34(a) (at pp. 193–4), § 34(d) (at pp. 202–3).

[26] Unless the norm is 'self-evident'. But Kelsen holds that there are no self-evident norms.

(a) By deducing a norm from another norm, as an instance of the particular from the general.
(b) By the norm being enacted in a particular way which, according to another norm, is the way that norms 'ought' to be enacted.

Kelsen calls authorization according to (a) authorization according to a 'static principle' and authorization according to (b) authorization according to a 'dynamic principle'.[27] According to the static principle, a norm such as 'Thou shalt not kill' may be deduced from a norm such as 'One ought not to harm one's fellow man' (in conjunction with the minor premiss that killing causes harm). According to the dynamic principle, 'Thou shalt not kill' may be authorized by a norm such as 'Norms that are inscribed on tablets of stone by the hand of God ought to be obeyed'. Thus, if 'Thou shalt not kill' was inscribed on a tablet of stone by the hand of God, then 'Thou shalt not kill' is authorized by 'Norms that are inscribed on tablets of stone by the hand of God ought to be obeyed', because it was 'created' ('posited', 'enacted') according to the required procedure, namely, being inscribed on a tablet of stone by the hand of God.

Now, whether authorization is viewed according to the static or the dynamic principle, no one need regard a norm addressed at their behaviour as objectively valid in the exclusionary sense, binding them to behave according to the norm, simply because in a *logical or formal sense* this norm is authorized by another norm. After all, from 'You ought to cause as much pain as possible' it may be held to follow that 'You ought to burn people alive', but we cannot see why from the fact that the latter may be deduced validly[28] (in the logical sense) from the former it follows that we ought to burn people alive in the exclusionary sense of 'ought'. Logico-formal authorization does not *simpliciter* provide anyone with a reason for doing anything, apart from assenting to the fact that a premiss formally compels a conclusion. Certainly, authorization or validation may be regarded, in a formal sense, as a relationship between a premiss and a conclusion quite independently of either the truth or the acceptance of the premiss. For example, from 'Napoleon was a Greek' and 'All Greeks are six foot tall' it follows validly, according to laws of logic, that 'Napoleon was six foot tall', even though all these statements are false, and even if no one accepts (believes) any of these statements (assuming we are speaking of the Napoleon who was defeated by Wellington at Waterloo). But, precisely because logico-formal authorization is independent of the truth-value and belief-value of what it connects[29] it does not provide a reason for accepting the conclusion.

---

[27] *PTL* § 34(b) (pp. 195–8).
[28] The derivation, of course, requires certain facts of physiology to be given.
[29] This is subject to one absolute qualification: false conclusions can never be validly inferred from true premisses.

What is required for a reason for accepting the conclusion to be provided by logico-formal authorization is that the premises must be either true or accepted. If, for the sake of argument, it were true that Napoleon was a Greek, and all Greeks are six foot tall, then there is what we may call an 'objective reason' for accepting 'Napoleon was six foot tall'. If, though these are false beliefs, we believe that Napoleon was a Greek and that all Greeks are six foot tall, then we have a reason (which we may call a 'subjective reason') for accepting 'Napoleon was six foot tall'.

We see no reason why this reasoning should not apply to the authorization by norms. Although an 'authorizing' norm formally provides a reason for regarding an 'authorized' norm as binding, no one is thereby provided with a 'material' reason (either objective or subjective) for accepting (regarding) the 'authorized' norm as binding. Logico-formal authorization does not amount to material authorization, and material authorization is necessary for an 'ought' to be regarded as objectively valid in the exclusionary sense. For a norm to be materially authorized, the formally authorizing norm must be either true or accepted, or formally authorized by a still higher norm that is either true or accepted, or formally authorized by a still higher norm. But, if there is to be a material reason for accepting a norm as binding, then this chain must end, and it can only end with a formally authorizing norm that is either true or accepted.

Consider, then, the following.

The command of a gangster to turn over to him a certain amount of money has the same subjective meaning as the command of an income-tax official, namely that the individual at whom the command is directed ought to pay something. But only the command of the official, not that of the gangster, has the meaning of a valid norm, binding upon the addressed individual. Only the one order, not the other, is a norm-positing act [one that posits a binding norm], because the official's act is authorized by a tax-law, whereas the gangster's act is not based on such an authorizing norm. The legislative act [positing the tax norm], which subjectively has the meaning of *ought*, also has [this] objective meaning—that is, the meaning of a valid norm—because the constitution has conferred this objective meaning upon the legislative act. The act whose meaning is the constitution has not only the subjective but also the objective meaning of 'ought', that is to say, the character of a binding norm, if—in case it is the historically first constitution—we presuppose in our juristic thinking that we ought to behave as the constitution prescribes.[30]

And, we may just add, to round off the picture, *only if* we presuppose that we ought to behave as the constitution prescribes can we characterize the constitution as objectively valid.

[30] *PTL* § 4(b) (p. 8).

In this chain of authorization each norm is authorized by an authorizing norm ending with a norm whose specific character is that it must be presupposed, not *simpliciter*, but if we are to be able to characterize the tax official's command and all the intermediate authorizing norms down the chain as 'objectively valid' (which, if we are speaking within the context of an order backed by coercive sanctions, means 'legally valid').

Kelsen denies that norms can have a truth-value.[31] The basic norm that ends the chain cannot be true. So, if we are to interpret 'objective validity' by 'exclusionary reason', then the burden of Kelsen's account of authorization must fall squarely on the notion of acceptance in some sense. Undoubtedly a basic norm is, for Kelsen, one that is accepted in a sense, for a specific characteristic of a basic norm is that it is a norm that is not questioned.[32] This would seem to be equivalent to saying that a basic norm is one that, though it cannot be true, is treated as though it were true without permitting any questioning of this attitude. To say that the basic norm is not questioned is to say that it is accepted without question.

A second characteristic of a basic norm is that it is a presupposed norm. According to Kelsen, this implies that a basic norm is not posited by the order that it validates. A basic norm is not a norm of a legal order or moral order.[33] Instead, a basic norm refers to the order it validates in a particular way.

The way in which it refers, its relation, to the order it validates has two components. The basic norm relates to the order it validates (1) presuppositionally, and (2) definitionally.

The presuppositional component is expressed in the formula 'The possibility of regarding an order and the norms it validates as objectively valid entails that the basic norm is accepted.' As we understand Kelsen, this means that we can never *assert categorically* that an order or norm *is* objectively valid. Such an assertion can only be made if the basic norm can have a status independent of its acceptance. This can only be the case if the basic norm is either objectively valid or true. According to Kelsen, the basic norm cannot be true, because no norm can be true. And, if the basic norm is objectively valid, then this requires that it be validated by a higher norm, in which case the 'basic' norm is no longer basic. In order to be basic, a basic norm must be the 'highest' norm, the end of the chain of authorization.[34]

---

[31] See e.g. *PTL* § 4(e) (at pp. 19–21), § 16 (at p. 74).   [32] See *PTL* § 34(d) (at p. 203).

[33] See *PTL* § 34(c) (at pp. 199–200).

[34] See *PTL* § 34(a) (at pp. 194–5). But see also *PTL* § 34(d) (at p. 203), where Kelsen states: 'The norm whose validity is asserted in the major premise is a basic norm if its *objective validity* is not questioned' (emphasis added).

This means that the presuppositional relation is (a) essentially hypo-thetical, and (b) essentially dialectical. To say that the relation is essen-tially hypothetical means that we can never say, 'Order *X* is objectively valid.' We can only say, '*Only if* the basic norm is accepted can we char-acterize the validated order as objectively valid.' We cannot say, '*Because* the basic norm is accepted the validated order is objectively valid.' To say that the relation is essentially dialectical means that we can only say, 'Only if the basic norm *is accepted* (*regarded as if true*) can we *character-ize* (*regard*) the validated order as objectively valid.' Essential hypotheti-cality means that the conditionality of the presuppositional formula can never be deleted, thereby transforming the formula into a categorical one. The essentially dialectical nature of the formula means that the regarding or claim context of the formula cannot be removed, thereby transforming the formula into an assertoric one.[35]

Although the hypothetical and dialectical nature of the relationship cannot be stressed too strongly, the idea that the basic norm is a presup-posed norm means that this does not affect the essentially logical char-acter of the relationship. In formal logic, to assert (where '*p*' and '*q*' are any propositions) that *p* entails (or implies) *q* is to assert that *p* presup-poses *q*, and this means exactly the same thing as asserting that *q* is a necessary condition for *p* and that *p* is a sufficient condition for *q*. And, in logic, if *p* entails *q*, then not-*q* entails not-*p*. Thus we find that, from 'An order can only be regarded as objectively valid if the basic norm is presupposed (regarded as if true, claimed as if true)', it follows, for Kelsen, that if the basic norm is not presupposed then the order that it would validate if it were presupposed cannot be regarded as objectively valid.[36]

The definitional component of the reference of the basic norm to the order it validates resides in the property of defining the order validated as the order it is rather than as another order of the same kind: as one legal order versus another legal order (or one moral order versus another moral order). In effect, Kelsen distinguishes one legal order from another by its structure of delegation. The basic norm states that an order having a particular structure of delegation ought to be applied and obeyed. If, and only if, the order has a particular structure of delegation ought it to be applied and obeyed. The basic norm does not validate the delegation structure (constitution) of any order other than that which it prescribes. This is the basis of Kelsen's view that norms are unified as norms of the same order by sharing the same basic norm and explains the sense in

---

[35] Kelsen does not always adhere rigidly to this. He constantly employs categorical, assertoric formulations. If our reading is correct, and it is most strongly supported by *PTL* § 26 (pp. 101–7, esp. 103–4), then such formulations must be regarded as elliptical.

[36] See *PTL* § 34(d) (at p. 201), § 34(i) (at p. 218).

which he regards a basic norm as, in a logical sense, the constitution of the order that it validates.

All norms whose validity can be traced back to one and the same basic norm constitute a system of norms, a normative order. The basic norm is the common source for the validity of all norms that belong to the same order—it is their common reason of validity. The fact that a certain norm belongs to a certain order is based on the circumstance that its last reason of validity is the basic norm of this order. It is the basic norm that constitutes the unity in the multitude of norms by representing the reason for the validity of all norms that belong to this order.[37]

If by the constitution of a legal community is understood the norm or norms that determine how (that is, by what organs and by what procedure—through legislation or custom)[38] the general norms of the legal order that constitute the community are to be created, then . . . the basic norm determines the basic fact of law creation and may in this respect be described as the constitution in a logical sense of the word . . . in contradistinction to the constitution in the meaning of positive law.[39]

At this point it would not be unreasonable for the reader to presume that Kelsen presents a relativized version of Legal Idealism. This means that if the orthodox view of the Pure Theory as a version of Legal Positivism is correct, then either the interpretation of the doctrine of the basic norm we have given is incorrect or there is a radical inconsistency in the Pure Theory.

II. KELSEN'S LEGAL POSITIVISM

Kelsen's Legal Positivism, his denial of Legal Idealism, reveals itself most importantly in the following propositions.

(a) The basic norm performs only an epistemological function, not an ethical or a political one.
(b) The presupposition of the basic norm does not entail an attitude of approval towards the order of norms that it validates.
(c) Neither the basic norm nor the norms validated by it have any required content. Inasmuch as they are moral norms, they are only formally moral. They are not substantively (materially) moral.
(d) A positive, effective, coercive order can never be described as legally invalid though, by failing to refer to it in terms of a basic norm, it may be given a description in non-legal terms.

---

[37] *PTL* § 34(a) (p. 195).
[38] This reference to legislation and custom is illustrative only as Kelsen envisages highly complex possibilities for constitutional arrangements.
[39] *PTL* § 34(c) (pp. 198–9).

These are closely related propositions, and each implies that moral illegitimacy does not entail legal invalidity. It is convenient to distinguish them, however, for the reasons that Kelsen gives for his Legal Positivism impinge more directly on some of these propositions than on others. For convenience, we will term (a) and/or (b) 'moral-neutrality', we will call (c) 'moral formalism', and (d) 'exclusion of positive invalidity'.

With the exception of his view that Legal Idealism (in the form of Natural Law Theory) involves various undesirable practical attitudes, usually reactionary ones, all of Kelsen's arguments for Legal Positivism are directed at establishing one or more of (a)–(d). These propositions may be regarded as qualifications of the doctrine of the basic norm through which this doctrine is made compatible with, or is made to entail, Legal Positivism. For convenience, we will consider Kelsen's arguments for Legal Positivism in conjunction with three themes that pervade his discussion. To a considerable extent these themes inform each other and their separation can only be justified as an exegetical device. These themes are

(A) the view that positivity and effectiveness are conditions of legal validity;
(B) Kelsen's moral relativism;[40]
(C) Kelsen's distinction between the descriptive function of interpretation by the legal scientist and the prescriptive function of interpretation by legal organs.[41]

A. Positivity, Effectiveness, and Legal Validity.

According to Kelsen, the correct determination of the relationship between the validity and the effectiveness of law

is one of the most important and at the same time most difficult problems of a positivistic legal theory. . . . A positivistic legal theory is faced by the task to find the correct middle road between two extremes which are both untenable. The one extreme is the thesis that there is no connection between validity as something that ought to be and effectiveness as something that is; that the validity of the law is entirely independent of its effectiveness. The other extreme is the thesis that validity and effectiveness are identical. An idealistic theory of law tends to the first solution of this problem, a realistic theory to the second.[42]

The 'correct middle road', Kelsen's compromise solution, is that validity is not identical to effectiveness; nor is effectiveness the reason for

---

[40] Moral relativism is a thesis that, in particular, features in the other themes as well, particularly in (C), and our discussion of it cannot be wholly self-contained.

[41] In *Law as a Moral Judgment* (n.1 above), we consider a fourth theme, Kelsen's view that there are no *a priori* limits on norm-creation.

[42] *PTL* § 34(g) (p. 211).

legal validity (a presupposed basic norm is this reason); but effectiveness is a *condition* of validity (together with the positive existence of a coercive order).[43]

This is also offered as a solution to a problem about the relationship between right and might.

If we replace the concept of reality (as effectiveness of the legal order) by the concept of power, then the problem of the relation between validity and effectiveness of the legal order coincides with the more familiar problem of the relationship between law and power or right and might. And then, the solution attempted here is merely the scientifically exact formulation of the old truism that right cannot exist without might and yet is not identical with might.[44]

Why is validity not identical to effectiveness? Because

Effectiveness is an 'is-fact'—the fact that the norm is actually applied and obeyed, the fact that people actually behave according to the norm. To say that a norm is 'valid', however, means something else than that it is actually applied and obeyed; it means that it *ought* to be obeyed and applied . . .[45]

Because it is an 'ought'

[a] legal norm becomes valid before it becomes effective, that is, before it is applied and obeyed; a law court that applies a statute immediately after promulgation—therefore before the statute had a chance to become 'effective'—applies a valid legal norm.[46]

A legal norm is valid even if it is not wholly effective—it suffices if it is effective 'by and large', that is, if it is applied and obeyed to some degree. The possibility of the norm being ineffective—that in individual cases it may not be applied or obeyed—must always be present.[47]

'Validity' of a legal norm presupposes . . .that it is possible to behave in a way contrary to it: a norm [prescribing] that something ought to be done of which everyone knows beforehand that it must happen necessarily according to the laws of nature always and everywhere would be as senseless as a norm [prescribing] that something ought to be done of which one knows beforehand that it is impossible according to the laws of nature.[48]

---

[43] See *PTL* § 34(g) (pp. 211–12).   [44] *PTL* § 34(g) (p. 214).
[45] *PTL* § 4(c) (pp. 10–11).   [46] *PTL* § 4(c) (p. 11).
[47] *PTL* § 21 (pp. 87–8). It is worth noting that the notion of partial effectiveness is not one that seems to give legal positivists any problems. If so then they really should have no difficulty with the idea of partial legality, which is central to Fuller's view (see Lon L. Fuller, *The Morality of Law*, rev. edn. (New Haven: Yale UP, 1969)), and which we are prepared to countenance, with qualifications. If a norm is effective when it is applied and obeyed, then, strictly, it is not partially effective if it sometimes is not applied or obeyed, it is, rather, not effective at all. But, no doubt, saying that a norm is by and large effective means that it is applied and obeyed more often than not—or something like that. Similar constructions can, however, be made for 'partial legality'. But Dworkin does object to 'partial effectiveness', see Ronald Dworkin, 'Philosophy, Morality, and Law—Observations Prompted by Professor Fuller's Novel Claim', *University of Pennsylvania Law Review*, 113 (1964–5), 668–90.
[48] *PTL* § 4(c) (p. 11).

If the validity, that is, the specific existence of the law, is considered to be part of natural reality, one is unable to grasp the specific meaning in which the law addresses itself to reality and thereby juxtaposes itself to reality, which can be in conformity or in conflict with the law only if reality is not identical with the validity of the law.[49]

Why then is effectiveness a condition of validity? The only explicit reason that Kelsen gives is that

[a] general legal norm is regarded as valid only if the human behavior that is regulated by it actually conforms with it, at least to some degree. A norm that is not obeyed by anybody anywhere, in other words a norm that is not effective at least to some degree, is not regarded as a valid legal norm.[50]

Kelsen also asserts that positivity is a condition of validity, that 'a relation exists between the *ought* of the legal norm and the *is* of physical reality also in so far as the positive legal norm, to be valid, must be created by an act which exists in the reality of being.'[51]

Before we attempt to evaluate this we must ask, 'What role does this thesis of the conditioning of validity by positivity and effectiveness play in the Pure Theory?' Kelsen tells us that

[t]o understand the nature of the basic norm it must be kept in mind that it refers directly to a specific constitution, actually established by custom or statutory creation, by and large effective, and indirectly to the coercive order created according to this constitution and by and large effective; the basic norm thereby furnishes the reason for the validity of this constitution and of the coercive order created in accordance with it.[52]

As we understand Kelsen, what he wishes to do is to restrict the application of 'a basic norm', of a rule to the effect that '*X* constitution ought to be applied and obeyed', to the constitution of a positive, by and large

---

[49] *PTL* § 34(g) (p. 213).

[50] *PTL* § 4(c) (p. 11). The following example illustrates Kelsen's thinking. According to Kelsen, one reason why Natural Law Theory is unacceptable is that it is 'idealist', holding that effective coercive orders may not be legally valid.

A concept of law with such consequences is unacceptable by a positivist legal science. A legal order may be judged to be unjust from the point of view of a certain norm of justice. But the fact that the content of an effective coercive order may be judged unjust is no reason to refuse to acknowledge this coercive order as a legal order. After the victory of the French Revolution in the 18th century and after the victory of the Russian Revolution in the 20th, the other states showed the distinct inclination not to interpret the coercive orders established by the revolution[s] as legal orders and the acts of the revolutionary governments as legal acts, because the one government had violated the monarchic principle of legitimacy and the other had abolished private property of the means of production. For the last-named reason, even American courts refused to acknowledge acts of the revolutionary Russian government as legal acts; the courts declared that these were not acts of a state but of a robber gang. However, as soon as the revolution-born coercive orders turned out to be effective, they were recognized as legal orders, the governments as state governments, and their acts as state acts, that is, legal acts.

PTL § 6(c) (pp. 49–50). We comment on this in n.53 below.

[51] *PTL* § 34(g) (p. 211).

[52] *PTL* § 34(d) (p. 201).

effective, coercive order. Furthermore, this restriction categorically pre-cludes the permissibility of predicating legal validity of anything other than such a constitution and the norms created in accordance with it. Apart from anything else, this interpretation of Kelsen's intentions pro-vides us with a clear meaning for the term 'condition' that is neither a reason for validity nor a semantic condition. What Kelsen means when he says that positivity and effectiveness are conditions of legal validity is that 'legal validity' may only be predicated of a positive, by and large effective, coercive order, and of (by and large effective) norms created according to its constitution.

The point of this restriction is that it excludes applying '*X* constitution ought to be applied and obeyed' to an imaginary ideal constitution that may be compared with the constitution of a positive, by and large effec-tive, coercive order, the latter being declared invalid if it does not match the imaginary ideal constitution. Thus interpreted, the thesis of the con-ditioning of validity by positivity and effectiveness ('the conditioning thesis', henceforth) is, first, intended to support the thesis of the exclu-sion of positive invalidity that is a keystone of Kelsen's Legal Positivism. Secondly, the conditioning thesis may be seen to support the moral for-malism thesis as well. For, under the conditioning thesis, the basic norm does not operate as a blueprint for a legal order, and it does not do so because, abstracted from a positive, by and large effective, coercive order, it has no content. '*X* constitution ought to be applied and obeyed' is merely an empty form, the '*X*' being a blank space that can only be filled in by a positive, by and large effective, norm. Any content that a basic norm can have it can only receive from a positive, by and large effective, coercive order. Indeed, until such 'filling' is effected, we do not strictly have a basic norm at all; all we have is *the form of a basic norm*.

Finally, the restriction involved in, or justified by, the conditioning thesis may help us to understand how a basic norm can be basic. It seems a fairly obvious question to ask of the so-called basic norm of some order, 'Why ought we to do things as it prescribes?'—perhaps seeking the answer in some theory of political morality. Kelsen, however, will not allow this question to be asked or, in so far as he does allow it to be asked, he will treat it as an attempt to evaluate a legal order from some moral viewpoint rather than as an attempt to extend the reason for legal valid-ity. This may seem arbitrary; but as soon as Kelsen is armed with the restriction provided by the conditioning thesis, the refusal to extend the reason for legal validity further may seem to be justified. If we do attempt to extend the reason, we imply that the basic norm may receive a content from, for example, a theory of political morality or whatever provides the reason for the 'basic norm', (which implies that the 'basic norm' is no longer basic). This, however, would contradict the moral formalism held to be justified by the conditioning thesis. To avoid this we must treat the basic norm as truly basic, as the end of the chain of reasoning involved in the search for the reason for legal validity.

If we interpret the significance of the conditioning thesis in this way we can see why Kelsen attaches so much importance to it; on this interpretation it is absolutely central to his attempt to combine Legal Positivism with the doctrine of presupposition involved in the doctrine of the basic norm.

But are Kelsen's arguments for the conditioning thesis valid? Kelsen's argument for effectiveness being a condition of legal validity in the required sense is defective on at least two counts. First, from a purely factual point of view, it is highly questionable that norms that are not obeyed are never regarded as valid. So-called 'dead-letter' laws are commonly regarded as valid are they not? Secondly, why is it important, or even relevant, what people (which people?) regard as a condition for the validity of a norm? And, if we delete 'regarded' from the formulation of the argument, then how is the fact that a norm is not obeyed supposed to render it as a norm that ought not to be obeyed?

For a norm to be valid (whether it be a legal norm—as contrasted with a non-legal norm—or a moral norm) is, on Kelsen's own account, for the norm to be one that ought to be obeyed, subjective attitudes to the contrary or otherwise notwithstanding (that is, for the norm to be 'objective'). The suggestion that no one regards a norm as an 'objective' norm because it is nowhere obeyed simply contradicts the fact that there are moral idealists, reformers, and revolutionaries in the world. In any case, even if, at the moment Kelsen was writing, no one did regard any norms never obeyed as valid, this is no longer true—for we, at least, do not agree with this assertion.

But why in any case is it relevant to the 'objective' status of a norm whether or not anyone regards a norm as such a norm?[53] Indeed, were it relevant then the idea of an 'objective' norm would be incoherent; for, to

---

[53] Kelsen claims that 'the doctrine of the basic norm is not a doctrine of recognition as is sometimes erroneously understood. According to the doctrine of recognition positive law is valid only if it is recognized by the individuals subject to it, which means: if these individuals agree that one ought to behave according to the norms of the positive law,' *PTL* § 34(i) (p. 218 n.83). But the doctrine Kelsen propounds *is* a doctrine of recognition of a different sort—it is necessary for someone (who?) to regard the norms as effective for the order to be legal, and maybe even sufficient. See the passage cited in n.50 above. Why the opinions of other states, adherents of the Pure Theory or whoever—Kelsen does not explain precisely who matters—should count, but not the opinions of those who are subject to enforcement of the norms, is not explained. We consider this to be wholly arbitrary, and it tends (does it not?) to have the effect that since a positive, by and large effective, coercive order can never be held to be invalid the presupposition of the basic norm is really redundant. Someone (who?) *can always* presuppose the basic norm in relation to such an order, so all that really matters is effectiveness. Is this really any different from realism?

repeat, an 'objective' norm is one that ought to be obeyed, subjective attitudes to the contrary or otherwise notwithstanding. If it is relevant to the 'objective' status of a norm that someone does not regard the norm as one to be obeyed (because it is not effective, or for any other reason) then Kelsen cannot define an 'objective' norm as he has done without contradiction.

If we delete 'regarded' from the argument then it states that a norm that is not effective ought not to be obeyed. If this remains an argument then Kelsen must hold that it follows from the fact that the norm is not effective that it ought not to be obeyed. But on Kelsen's own terms this is again absurd. For Kelsen, an 'ought' cannot follow from an 'is' (unless the 'is' contains an 'ought'). This is the basis of Kelsen's arguments against 'realism'. Without 'regarded', however, the 'argument' is a realist argument that Kelsen cannot employ.

Of course, it may be objected that this misunderstands Kelsen's position. Kelsen's position is that a norm that is not effective cannot be a valid *legal* norm, though it may be a valid moral or otherwise non-legal norm. This is because a legal norm is a norm of a legal order (versus non-legal order), and a legal order (versus non-legal order) is a by and large effective (and positive, coercive) order of norms.

However, this rejoinder will not do. We agree that effectiveness is a condition (a definitional condition) of stable positivity. But this does not make it a condition of legal validity unless legal (versus non-legal) orders must be stably positive orders—which really amounts to saying that they must be by and large effective orders. This is just what Kelsen's thesis of the conditioning of validity by effectiveness is supposed to establish. Kelsen, in fact, defines the legal (versus non-legal) in terms of coercion, not effectiveness.[54] If he intends effectiveness to be an additional necessary defining condition, then an argument must be presented for this. Otherwise the definition of the legal (versus the non-legal) is a definitional fiat that is question-begging in the present context.

By rejecting Kelsen's argument for the conditioning of validity by effectiveness, we do not wish to assert that there is no connection between validity and effectiveness. There is one very strict connection between *possible* effectiveness and validity (legal or moral). This is based on the principle usually expressed by the dictum, '"Ought" implies "can".' If a person cannot do something (x) then it seems senseless to demand that person ought to do x. Perhaps if x can be done (perhaps by some other person) then it still makes sense to say that x ought to be done, but not that the person who cannot do x ought to do x. Thus, a

---

[54] See *PTL* § 6(b) (at pp. 33–4), and at § 9 (p. 62).

norm that cannot be effective (applied and obeyed) cannot be a valid norm (one that 'objectively' ought to be applied and obeyed).

This principle may be used as an argument against legal idealists *if* idealists are persons who deny *any* connection between effectiveness and validity. Kelsen possibly has Natural Law Theory in mind when he refers to 'idealism'. However, we see no reason why Natural Law Theory should deny that 'ought' implies 'can'. But what is most important to note in the present context is that the principle that 'ought' implies 'can' in no way supports a conditioning thesis that is intended as the basis of restricting the employment of the basic norm to an actually effective order of norms.

Kelsen has much less to say about positivity than about effectiveness. This is probably because to be actually effective a norm must already be positive in some sense. He presumably thinks that if validity is conditioned by effectiveness then it must also be conditioned by positivity. Positivity is then, however, logically the more basic condition. So, if Kelsen could show positivity to be a condition of legal validity then the coupling of positivity with *possible* effectiveness would provide an adequate restriction for his Legal Positivism.

In order to assess positivity as a condition of validity, we must first of all note that Kelsen can quite rightly claim that positivity is a condition of the validity of a *positive* legal order, in the sense that a positive legal order can only be valid (or anything else for that matter) if it exists, that is, if it is positive. This is analogous to the fact that the King of France can only be bald (or anything else) if there is a King of France. His existence is a condition of his baldness.

But this fact is not enough to establish the conditioning thesis that Kelsen's Legal Positivism requires. What he must show is that a legal order must be positive, and not merely assert the tautology that a positive legal order must be positive. He must show that a legal order cannot exist as an ideal order of norms.

Secondly, we must note that there is more than one sense in which a norm may be said to be positive or posited, namely:

(a) the norm is posited by (that is, the product of) an imaginary will;
(b) the norm is posited by a real act of will;
(c) the norm is posited according to the constitution of an actually existing, by and large effective, coercive order.

Kelsen sometimes calls a norm a positive norm if it fulfils requirement (b),[55] as well as more customarily referring to positivity in sense (c). In sense (a), even the basic norm is posited, but in relation to (b) or (c) it is only presupposed.

---

[55] See e.g. *PTL* § 4(b) (at p. 9).

Finally it is to be noted that a norm need not be only the meaning of a real act of will; it can also be the content of an act of thinking. This is the case if the norm is only presupposed in our thinking. Just as we can imagine things which do not really exist but 'exist' only in our thinking, we can imagine a norm which is not the meaning of a real act of will but which exists only in our thinking. Then, it is not a positive norm. But since there is a correlation between the ought of a norm and a will whose meaning it is, there must be in our thinking also an imaginary will whose meaning is the norm which is only presupposed in our thinking—as is the basic norm of a positive legal order.[56]

For the purposes of his Legal Positivism, Kelsen requires validity to be conditioned by positivity in sense (c) above. Ideal orders and moral blueprints for legality could be positive in senses (a) or (b).

But, as far as we can discern, if Kelsen has any argument for conditioning by positivity that does not follow from conditioning by effectiveness, then this is that an 'ought' can only exist as a product of an act of will (in a very broad sense that regards norms posited in sense (c) as products of acts of will). But, even if this is valid,[57] it covers too much for Kelsen's purposes, and can only be turned into an argument for conditioning by positivity in sense (c) by employing the age-old stratagem of equivocation.

We must conclude that Kelsen's 'arguments' for conditioning by positivity and effectiveness are highly unsatisfactory, and if he is to marry the doctrine of the basic norm with Legal Positivism he needs a different matchmaker.

B. Kelsen's Moral Relativism.

Kelsen uses a thesis of moral relativism in two ways to support his Legal Positivism. He maintains that moral relativism entails the negation of Natural Law Theory, and that this requires Legal Positivism. He also argues that moral relativism supports moral formalism and this (via moral-neutrality/the Separation Thesis) amounts to Legal Positivism.

Kelsen's View that Rejection of Natural Law Theory Entails Legal Positivism. Kelsen argues that moral relativism is correct. Consequently, Natural Law Theory (Objectivistic Legal Idealism) is incorrect, *and therefore* Legal Positivism is correct.

We are concerned, here, not with the correctness or otherwise of moral relativism, but simply with whether moral relativism justifies Legal

---

[56] *PTL* § 4(b) (pp. 9–10).

[57] This creates problems inasmuch as the basic norm is supposed to be presupposed only and not posited, see *PTL* § 34(c) (at p. 200). Sense (a) will allow the basic norm to be posited. Sense (c) will not.

Positivism. For this reason, we will not attend to Kelsen's arguments against Natural Law Theory,[58] but will concentrate exclusively on the contention that if Natural Law Theory is mistaken then Legal Positivism must be correct.

Kelsen actually defines Legal Positivism as the denial of *Objectivistic* Legal Idealism.

The demand for a separation between law and morals, law and justice, means[59] that the validity of a positive legal order is independent of the validity of this one, solely valid, absolute moral order, 'the' moral order, the moral order *par excellence*. If only relative moral values are presupposed, then the postulate that the law *ought* to be moral, that is, just, can only mean that the formation of positive law ought to conform to one specific moral system among the many possible [moral] systems. This, however, does not exclude the possibility of the postulate that the formation of positive law ought to conform with another moral system— and actually perhaps conforms with it—while it does not conform with a moral system that is different from it.[60]

Such a definitional move, however, entirely trivializes the issue, because in requiring a relativized Legal Idealism to be labelled Legal Positivism, it leaves it open that 'Legal Positivism' might not require the Separation Thesis.[61]

Furthermore, such a move is inconsistent with Kelsen's ultimate intentions, which are to present Legal Positivism as a position incompatible with what we term 'Relativized Legal Idealism'.

If it is assumed that law *is* moral by nature, then, presupposing an absolute moral value, it is meaningless to demand that the law *ought* to be moral. Such a postulate is meaningful only (and the presupposed morality represents a yardstick for the law only) if the possibility of the existence of an immoral law is admitted—if, in other words, the definition of law does not include the element of moral content.[62]

---

[58] Which, to some extent, we do in *Law as a Moral Judgment* (n.1 above).

[59] It is important that Kelsen only claims that Natural Law Theory presupposes absolutism, and that he does not claim that absolutism entails Natural Law Theory. Converting relative values into objective ones cannot, by itself, forge a link between law and morality. The objectivism has to be of a specific kind.

[60] *PTL* § 12 (p. 66).

[61] Supposing moral relativism to be correct, it certainly follows that Objectivistic Legal Idealism is mistaken. Objectivistic Legal Idealism has, however, two components. It maintains that there is a conceptually necessary connection between law and morality, such that judgments of legality must be made in terms of judgments of moral legitimacy (the idealistic component) and that the criteria of moral legitimacy are rationally necessary or objective (the objectivistic component). Moral relativism clearly has a bearing in denying the objectivistic component, but it is altogether less clear what bearing it has on the idealistic component, and if it has none, then all that moral relativism can show is that *Objectivistic* Legal Idealism is mistaken, leaving it open that a relativized Legal Idealism is still an option to Legal Positivism.

[62] *PTL* § 12 (p. 66).

The target, here, is not just a position of the kind attacked that presupposes an absolute value. Were the argument valid, it would apply just as well to a position that held that the definition of law includes an element of *relative* moral content. What Kelsen is really after is the denial of any position that makes legal validity depend upon a moral content, whether this be absolute or relative. And this *is* Legal Positivism, not 'Relativized Legal Idealism'.[63]

However, another possibility that must be considered derives from Kelsen's view that Objectivistic Legal Idealism and Legal Positivism represent the only alternatives *if an objective science of law is to be secured*. Perhaps Kelsen's reasoning is that, given moral relativism (which rules out Objectivistic Legal Idealism), Legal Positivism is the only path to an objective science of law.

However, although we consider such a view to be correct (section II, C, below), it does not follow that Relativized Idealism must be rejected, because such an implication requires the premiss that an objective science of law is possible, which is just what Relativized Legal Idealism denies *on the grounds of moral relativism and denial of the Separation Thesis*. In short, it would appear that Kelsen must rely on an entailment between moral relativism and the Separation Thesis to make the rejection of Natural Law Theory relevant as an argument for Legal Positivism.

Kelsen's Argument that Moral Relativism Entails the Separation Thesis. Kelsen maintains that moral relativism in relation to legal values implies moral formalism. His argument is contained in the following passage.

All moral orders have only one thing in common: namely, that they are social norms, that is, norms that order a certain behavior of men—directly or indirectly—toward other men. All possible moral systems have in common their form, the 'ought': they prescribe something, they have normative character. Morally good is that which conforms with the social norm that prescribes a certain human behavior; morally evil that which is opposed to such a norm. The relative moral value is established by a social norm that men ought to behave in a certain way. Norm and value are correlative concepts.

Under these presuppositions the statement 'law is moral by nature' does not mean that law has a certain content, but that it is norm—namely a social norm that men ought to behave in a certain way. Then, in this relative sense, every law is moral; every law constitutes a—relative—moral value. And this means: The question about the relationship between law and morals is not a question about the content of the law, but one about its form. . . .

If, presupposing only relative values, the demand is made to separate law and morals in general, and law and justice in particular, then this demand does not

---

[63] Note that this argument is invalid, for Legal Idealism (whether Objectivistic or not) does not say the law ought to be moral: it says that norms, etc., ought to be moral (or better, not immoral) *if* they are to count as law.

mean that law and morals, law and justice, are unrelated; it does not mean that the concept of law is outside the concept of the Good. For the concept of the 'good' cannot be defined otherwise than as that which ought to be: that which conforms to a social norm; and if law is defined as norm, then this implies that what is lawful is 'good'. The postulate, made under the supposition of a relativistic theory of value, to separate law and morals and therefore law and justice, merely means . . . the validity of a positive legal order does not depend on its conformity with some moral system.[64]

This is ambiguous. On one reading, it is actually a statement of a relativized Legal Idealism. On another reading, it contains an argument for Legal Positivism, which excludes both Relativized and Objectivistic Legal Idealism.

Which interpretation we give depends on how we interpret the statement that the relationship between law and morals is not a question about the content of the law, but one about its form, and how we interpret the statement that the validity of a positive legal order does not depend on its conformity with some moral order.

Kelsen's contention that law is formally moral because it does not have a certain content might be either an assertion that

(a) law is 'formally moral' because it does not have to be determined by a unique (absolute) moral order; or that
(b) law is 'formally moral' because the 'ought' of a legal norm has no content of its own; it receives its content entirely from positive practice.

His contention that the validity of a positive legal order does not depend on its conformity with some moral order might be either an assertion that

(a) the validity of a positive legal order does not depend on its conformity with a unique (absolute) moral order; it depends on conformity with relative moral orders; or that
(b) the validity of a positive legal order does not depend on its conformity with any relative or absolute moral order; 'validity' is not conditioned by any relationship to morality.

If the interpretations labelled '(a)' are given then we do not have Legal Positivism, we have Relativized Legal Idealism, whereas under the interpretations labelled '(b)', we do have Legal Positivism.

The crucial question is whether the argument under (b) is valid. Given what Kelsen himself says, its validity is well-nigh inconceivable. If what is lawful is 'good', then lawfulness (legal validity) implies 'goodness', and by

---

[64] *PTL* §§ 11–12 (pp. 65–7).

modus tollendo tollens, what is 'not-good' is not-lawful and what is 'bad' is unlawful. The fact that what is good according to one moral order may be bad according to another provides no basis for revising the laws of logic.

We have yet to discern any valid argument by which moral relativism requires us to espouse Legal Positivism.

C. The Non-Prescriptive Nature of Legal Interpretation by the Science of Law.

As we see it, if the possibility of applying legal categories rests upon the presupposition that an order for creating and enforcing norms is morally legitimate, then anyone who identifies an order as legal must presuppose that this order is morally legitimate, and this means that the identifier must regard the order as morally legitimate. A person who does not regard an order as morally legitimate does not presuppose that it is legal. Furthermore, if the person regards it as morally illegitimate then he regards the order as illegal.

Kelsen's view is that a person who does not presuppose that an order is morally legitimate does not view it as legally valid. *But* he denies that a person who regards an order as morally illegitimate thereby views it as illegal; and he also denies that *to presuppose* that an order is morally legitimate *is to regard* it as morally legitimate. These are his theses of 'the exclusion of positive invalidity' and 'moral-neutrality' respectively.

Kelsen claims that the purpose of legal science is to describe the law, and that such description does not involve prescription, even though, in order to describe the law, the science of law must presuppose the basic norm.[65] One possible argument for this may be dismissed quite swiftly. This argument connects the idea of prescription with the positing or creation of norms within a context characterized as a legal order. Legal scientists are not essentially authorized as norm-creators, therefore they cannot prescribe.[66] Any validity that this argument has, however, rests on the idea that prescription involves, or means, authorized norm-creation. We are not specifically interested in the idea that legal scientists prescribe norms in such a sense, but only in the sense that by holding X to be law the legal scientist (or anyone else) assents to the prescriptive (normative) content of X.

Kelsen does, however, claim that 'rules of law',[67] which are 'the

---

[65] See *PTL* § 34(d) (at p. 204 n.72).   [66] See *PTL* § 47 (at p. 355).

[67] Stanley L. Paulson has pointed out to us that 'rule of law' is a poor translation of '*Rechtssatz*', a better translation being 'legal sentence' or 'legal proposition'. As with the translation of '*Rechtsordnung*' (see n.1 above) we are reluctant to alter the expression in quotations from the translation we are employing, and consider it to be confusing to use different locutions in text and quoted text. For this reason, and also because we did so in *Law as a Moral Judgment* (n.1 above), we will stick with 'rule of law'.

sentences by which the science of law describes its object, the law',[68] are to be distinguished from legal norms, which are prescriptions. This distinction is pivotal in his attempt to marry moral-neutrality with the doctrine of the basic norm.

Kelsen provides the following examples and 'definition' of a 'rule of law'.

If an individual commits a crime, he ought to be punished; or: If an individual does not pay his debt a civil execution ought to be directed into his possessions; or: If an individual contracts an infectious disease he ought to be interned in an institution. Generally formulated: Under conditions determined by the legal order a coercive act, determined by the legal order, ought to take place. This is the . . . basic form of the rule of law.[69]

Why does a statement of a rule of law not involve prescription?

By using the word 'ought', the rule of law formulated by the science of law does not assume the authoritative meaning of the legal norm described by the rule; the 'ought' in the rule of law has only a descriptive character. . . . Specifically, the rule of law is not an imperative; it is, rather, *a judgment, a statement about an object of cognition*.[70] Nor does the rule of law imply any approval of the described legal norm. The jurist who describes the law scientifically does not identify himself with the legal authority enacting the norm. The rule of law remains objective *de*scription; it does not become *pre*scription. . . .

Although the object of the science of law is legal norms and therefore the legal values constituted by these norms, the rules of law are nevertheless . . . a value-free description of their object. This means, that the description has no relation to a meta-legal value and does not imply any emotional approval or disapproval. If a jurist, describing, from the point of view of legal science, a positive legal order, asserts that under a condition determined by the legal order a sanction ought to be executed determined by this order, he asserts this even if he regards the imputation of the sanction to the condition as unjust, and therefore disapproves of it. The norms that constitute the legal value must be differentiated from the norms according to which the formation of the law is evaluated. If the science of law is called upon at all to answer the question of whether a concrete behavior does or does not conform to the law, the answer can only be an assertion to the

---

[68] *PTL* § 18 (p. 76).   [69] *PTL* § 18 (pp. 76–7).

[70] Our emphasis. This is, we think, to be interpreted via the distinction between subjective and objective value judgments noted earlier, remembering that only objective value judgments are, for Kelsen, properly designated as judgments. The most significant passage in Kelsen's discussion is the following.

If the statement that a behavior conforms or does not conform with an objectively valid norm is designated as 'value judgment', then this value judgment must be distinguished from the norm that constitutes the value. The value judgment can be true or untrue, because it refers to a norm of a valid order. For example, the judgment that according to Christian morality it is 'good' to love one's friends and to hate one's enemies is untrue because a norm of the valid Christian morality commands to love not only one's friends but also one's enemies. The judgment that it is legal to inflict upon a thief the penalty of death is untrue if the valid law in question commands to punish a thief by deprivation of freedom but not by deprivation of life. A norm, however, cannot be true or untrue, but only valid or not valid.

PTL § 4(e) (p. 19).

effect that this behavior, in the legal order described by the science of law, is commanded or prohibited, authorized or not authorized, permitted or not permitted—regardless of whether this behavior is judged by the one who makes the assertion to be morally good or bad, and whether he approves or disapproves of it.
    . . .[T]he rule of law by using the word 'ought' expresses merely the specific meaning in which condition and consequence, particularly delict and sanction, are connected by the legal norm . . .[71]

Within the present context, we are to read this as an argument that shows that the doctrine of the basic norm, coupled with moral relativism, does not amount to a relativized Legal Idealism, but is compatible with Legal Positivism.

Now, the thought that for a person to presuppose that *X* is morally legitimate is for the person to regard *X* as morally legitimate should, on the face of it, be quite disturbing for any moral relativist (even a relativistic legal idealist) *if* this moral relativist is someone who believes that an objective (truth-determinate) science of law is possible.[72] Such a science attempts to describe and explain legal phenomena. But in a relativized Legal Idealism (which couples the disturbing thought with moral relativism) the object of these descriptions and explanations can only be identified by evaluating it as morally legitimate, and such evaluations (given moral relativism) are truth-indeterminate, they have no truth-value. Descriptions of law would thus vary according to which object was 'constituted' by which evaluation. No evaluation could be preferred to any other on rational grounds; so no description could claim to be the description of *the* law, and whether or not a description was to be taken as a description of law would depend on evaluations with no truth-value. No one need take seriously what a so-called 'legal scientist' said about 'the law' unless he shared the legal scientist's moral evaluations, and there could be no conclusive reason why he should. Quite simply, the position of Relativized Legal Idealism seems, by making truth-determinate descriptions of law impossible, to make an objective science of law impossible.

If this reasoning is accepted then there are two lines of escape that may suggest themselves to a moral relativist who holds that the concept of law is the concept of morally legitimate power.

(i) The moral relativist may claim that presupposing that a norm is morally legitimate, as a necessary condition for characterizing it as law, does not entail regarding it as morally legitimate. This involves eschewing Relativized Legal Idealism.

---

[71] *PTL* § 18 (pp. 78–80).
[72] Not everyone believes in the possibility of a truth-determinate science. Relativism may extend to all forms of reason. It is not restricted to the practical sphere.

(ii) The moral relativist may admit that, in the sense described above, an objective science of law is indeed impossible, but claim that there are nevertheless activities with truth-determinate results in which a person with an interest in legal phenomena may engage and in terms of which the idea of an objective legal science may be re-conceptualized. Thus, the relativistic legal idealist may, for example, point to the following.

(a) 'Law' cannot be 'constituted' in a truth-determinate way. But the 'legal scientist' can make truth-determinate assertions about the way in which people, by making presuppositions of moral legiti-macy, 'constitute' what they characterize as law. He may, for exam-ple, describe who characterizes what as law without thereby making a judgment of moral legitimacy himself.[73]

(b) Having determined that someone (who may be himself or some-one else) 'constitutes' something as legal by presupposing its moral legitimacy, he may describe the consequences of this presupposition (what the presupposition validates, or does not validate), again with-out implicating the judgment of moral legitimacy in *this* description. He may also describe such consequences on a purely hypothetical assumption of legality.[74]

In (a), the object of the descriptions is not law as such, but the presup-positions through which people constitute 'law'. The descriptions do not involve making these presuppositions in any sense.

In (b), the reasoning is essentially this: *If* the presupposition X is made, then Y is to be characterized as law. Identify, or just suppose 'for the sake of argument', that X presupposition is made. As a straightforward matter of fact (logic) X validates Y. Given the supposition that X is presupposed (or relative to the identification of X being presupposed), it is correct to describe Y as law. That Y is to be described as law follows from the mak-ing of X presupposition. But our 'legal scientist' does not make X presup-position. What he does do is make the hypothetical supposition that X presupposition is made. He presupposes X only 'for the sake of argu-ment'. He does not actually describe Y as law; his truth-determinate assertion is that *if* X presupposition is made then Y is to be described as law. This assertion is a statement of what follows from making X presup-position. The assertion makes no moral evaluation of Y because X is not *actually* presupposed, only hypothetically presupposed.

Now, the activity that Kelsen characterizes as 'stating a rule of law' is undoubtedly truth-determinate, and it does not involve prescription. As

---

[73] This is an example of a transferred ascription.
[74] This is an example of a bracketed or hypothetical ascription.

we interpret it, the activity is essentially as follows: The constitution authorizes norm-creation according to specific procedures. Norms that are created by these procedures are legally valid. Norms that are legally valid provide that, under specified conditions, certain sanctions ought to be inflicted for certain delicts. When the legal scientist describes what the law is, he states that it is a fact that it follows from the constitution authorizing what it does that, under specified conditions, certain sanctions ought to be inflicted for certain delicts. It is a fact that this norm is validated by the constitution.

What is the difference between this activity and the corresponding descriptive activity ((b) above) permitted by Relativized Legal Idealism? We submit that there is no difference at all between these activities apart from the characterization provided of the role of presupposition of a basic norm (or moral legitimacy) in the description. Kelsen holds that the basic norm is presupposed in the description; but since the description is value-free this shows that presupposition of the basic norm does not involve prescription. The relativistic legal idealist holds that the description does not involve direct prescription because the basic norm is not presupposed, it is only supposed to be presupposed. The basic norm is hypothetically presupposed. If the latter is the correct interpretation, and we contend that it is, then Kelsen's appeal to 'stating a rule of law' as a value-free descriptive activity will not succeed in freeing his doctrine of presupposition from prescriptive implications, and will fail as a support for his Legal Positivism.

As we emphasized in our discussion of Kelsen's theory of presupposition, the presupposition of the basic norm is hypothetical. The theory never permits anyone to adopt an assertoric mode of thinking and say categorically that X *is* law. The basic norm is always employed in a hypothetical 'dialectical' mode—*if* X is characterized as (claimed to be) law, then the basic norm must be presupposed. It must be presupposed, because only then can a reason for the validity of a norm be given.[75]

Kelsen, however, has a persistent tendency to drop the hypothetical and generally refers to the existence of law rather than to a hypothetical characterization of something as law. This, as we have already noted, is quite permissible as an elliptical form of expression, where the

---

[75] Perhaps Kelsen does think that he can write out the hypothetical, by employing his thesis that the basic norm only applies to a positive, by and large effective, coercive order. If he does, however, then this involves defining a legal order as a positive, by and large effective, coercive order without any reference to the basic norm. A legal norm then simply becomes a norm of a legal order so defined, and the doctrine of the basic norm then becomes redundant. In any event, we have already explained why we do not think that Kelsen can restrict legal predication to a positive, by and large effective, coercive order. We, of course, think that the hypothetical can be written out—but only by showing that a presupposition is not merely presupposed but true.

hypothetical nature of ascription is suppressed but always understood as present. But it is not acceptable if meant to be taken literally, for then, apart from anything else, the doctrine of the basic norm becomes an idealistic doctrine whereby the presupposition of a basic norm actually creates legal validity rather than just being involved in a reason for it.

The description that is value-free is so because it is made on a supposition, not of the basic norm, but of the presupposition of the basic norm. If, however, an assertoric mode of expression is adopted, then it may become possible to forget that the presupposition of the basic norm is already implicated in the characterization of a norm as a legal norm, a constitution as the constitution of a legal order, and to think that the supposition that makes a value-free description possible is the presupposition of the basic norm. In fact, the presupposition of the basic norm is already present in characterizing the constitution as legal, and the supposition that makes a value-free description possible is an additional supposition that serves to bracket off the moral judgment that is involved in the presupposition of the basic norm itself.

Kelsen admits that he has on occasion expressed doubts that the science of law makes the presupposition of the basic norm.[76] We consider that he was right to do so. On his characterization, the science of law is not founded on the presupposition of the basic norm but on a different supposition, and even this different supposition does not enable him to square his doctrine of the basic norm with Legal Positivism; for the restriction of 'legal science' to truth-determinate description thereby secured in the face of moral relativism is only necessary if the presupposition of the basic norm does involve prescription. What should also worry Kelsen and the relativistic legal idealist is that hypothetical ascription is not description of law but only description of hypothetical law (of 'as-if' law), and we do not see how the hypothetical can be written out without abandoning a doctrine of moral presupposition or else opting for an Objectivistic Legal Idealism.

III. CONCLUSION

In our opinion, any doctrine of presupposition that specifies

(i) that it is necessary to suppose that a constitution is morally legitimate in order to characterize norms created according to it as legally valid, and

(ii) that to characterize a norm as legally valid is to characterize the norm as binding upon those whose behaviour it addresses (as imposing a moral obligation to obey the norm),

[76] See *PTL* § 34(d) (at p. 204 n.72).

must specify that if such norms are not morally legitimate then they are not legally valid. The claim that such norms are legal/illegal does not just rest on a moral judgment, it is a moral judgment.

It follows that if moral relativism is correct, then law has only a 'relative existence'. What this means is simply that whether or not a particular set of norms is legally valid is relative to the moral principles that validate it.

It follows, also, that if a theorist desires an objective science of law, one in which statements of legality can be true or false independently of moral judgments that cannot themselves, in the final analysis, be true or false, then the theorist must eschew moral relativism. Given a doctrine of presupposition, only moral objectivism can ground an objective science of law.

From this it follows that a theorist who both desires an objective science of law, and espouses moral relativism, must be a legal positivist.

However, a doctrine of presupposition precludes Legal Positivism. Moral relativism does not make a doctrine of presupposition compatible with Legal Positivism. The only import of moral relativism, when coupled with a doctrine of presupposition, is to make an objective science of law impossible, for objective statements that are permissible, given moral relativism, are not objective statements about law, but objective statements about who characterizes what as law, and what may/should be characterized as law given the hypothetical supposition of specified moral values.

Thus moral relativism, by itself, does not establish Legal Positivism, and is irrelevant to the choice between Legal Idealism and Legal Positivism.

Since Kelsen adheres to a doctrine of presupposition, yet wishes to be a legal positivist, our dismissal of his arguments for this marriage entails that there is a radical inconsistency in the Pure Theory. The doctrine of presupposition, coupled with moral relativism, entails that Kelsen should espouse a relativized Legal Idealism. But this means giving up the aim of an objective science of law. The aim of an objective science of law, coupled with moral relativism, entails that Kelsen should espouse Legal Positivism. But this means giving up the doctrine of presupposition (by adopting an amoralist relativism incompatible with the doctrine of presupposition). Kelsen's attempt to steer a middle-course between 'idealism' and 'realism' is simply an attempt to synthesize three elements—a doctrine of presupposition, moral relativism, and the aim of an objective science of law. Any two of these elements may be paired to produce a coherent position: presupposition with relativism entails Relativized Legal Idealism; relativism with science entails Legal Positivism; presupposition with science entails Objectivistic Legal

Idealism. But in each case the third element must be rejected. The conjunction of all three is simply inconsistent.[77]

The radical inconsistency between the doctrine of presupposition and Legal Positivism within the Pure Theory arises, principally, from the way in which Kelsen argues for the doctrine of presupposition, on the one hand, and the way in which he argues for its compatibility with Legal Positivism, on the other.

When arguing for the need to presuppose a basic norm, Kelsen assumes that the meaning that people attach to norms is an 'ought' of a particular kind; it is the kind of 'ought' that can only be justified by another 'ought'. It is not an 'ought' that can be derived as a conclusion to a set of 'non-ought' premises. For example, from (1) 'X wants to do Y' and (2) 'If X wants to do Y, X must do Z', we can deduce (3) 'X ought to do Z'. It is a straightforward fact that X ought to do Z given (1) and (2). That X ought to do Z simply means that Z is the necessary means for achieving Y, and X wants to do it. Only if he begins with the assumption that the 'ought' of legal validity is not a hypothetical 'ought' of this kind is there any need to presuppose his basic norm. It is not just that Kelsen explicitly accepts that his 'ought' has moral meaning that leads us to the interpretation that his concept of law is the concept of morally legitimate power. It must be if a basic norm must be presupposed in order to interpret norms as objectively valid.

When arguing for the limitation of the principle of validity/legitimacy by that of effectiveness, however, the base line for analysis becomes the actual views and practices of people (most specifically 'black-letter' lawyers) about what they call 'law'. Legitimacy must be limited by effectiveness because people (it is alleged) *do not regard* ineffective orders as legally valid. Black-letter lawyers, qua black-letter lawyers, *do not question* that norms created in a particular way are legally valid, and so on. But people who act in this way do not necessarily attach any moral meaning to what they call law. They may view the 'ought' of norms in relation to something more akin to H.L.A. Hart's variegated internal attitude, which permits 'X ought to be obeyed' to be derived from attitudes of expediency, or even habit.[78]

---

[77] There is a structural similarity between the arguments presented by Hart in *The Concept of Law* [see the Table of Abbreviations] and Kelsen. Hart essentially tries to steer a middle-course between Natural Law Theory and Imperativism, just as Kelsen tries to steer a middle-course between 'idealism' and 'realism'. As we see it, both attempts are failures for much the same reasons. There is no middle-course between Legal Idealism and a form of Legal Positivism that does not centre on practical reason, that is, a Non-Normative Legal Positivism (represented by Hart's 'Imperativism' and Kelsen's 'realism'). See Deryck Beyleveld and Roger Brownsword, 'Normative Positivism: The Mirage of the Middle-Way', *Oxford Journal of Legal Studies*, 9 (1989), 463–512.

[78] See Hart, *CL*, at 198, 2nd edn., at 203.

Now, whereas argument from the latter basis cannot produce any-thing other than positivistic results, argument from the former basis begins with a stipulation that cannot produce anything other than the results of Legal Idealism. The irony is that Kelsen introduces the Pure Theory by claiming that one of its central aims is to avoid an 'uncritical mixture of methodologically different disciplines (methodological syn-cretism) which obscures the essence of the science of law and obliterates the limits imposed upon it by the nature of its subject-matter.'[79]

We, however, are led to conclude that Kelsen has failed to avoid a methodological syncretism (of method, rather than discipline) in his own work, and that the 'Pure' Theory is, as a result, decidedly impure.

[79] *PTL* § 1 (p. 1).

7

Validity and the Conflict between Legal Positivism and Natural Law*

ALF ROSS

About a year ago I had the honour of delivering at the University of Buenos Aires several lectures on the conflict between legal positivism and natural law. This conflict is often treated as the most fundamental issue in legal philosophy, dividing the field into two hostile and irreconcilable camps. Positivists characterize natural law doctrines as beliefs based on metaphysical or religious ideas incompatible with the principles of scientific thought. Proponents of natural law theory, for their part, accuse their antagonists of failing to understand the realm of spirit and value, a realm that is real enough, although it cannot be discovered or described by means of sensory experience.[1] Natural lawyers have even gone so far as to accuse the positivists of moral torpidity, and of complicity in the abominations of the Hitler regime.[2]

I in no way intended in my lectures to minimize the importance of the issue. I tried, however, to point out that to some extent the discussion has been confused owing to a lack of clarity as to the meaning of 'legal positivism', a term rarely if ever defined with precision. I especially tried to show that the most acute aspect of the controversy—namely, criticism of the attitude reflected in the German slogan, '*Gesetz ist Gesetz*' ('a law is a law'), as an attitude lacking in morality and partially responsible for the

* *Editors' note*: This paper first appeared in a bilingual printing in *Revista Jurídica de Buenos Aires* (1961), no. 4, pp. 46–93. Minor changes in the English have been made by the editors.
    [1] See Giorgio Del Vecchio, 'Divine Justice and Human Justice', *The Juridical Review*, 1 (N.S.) (1956), 147–57, at 148.
    [2] See Gustav Radbruch, 'Gesetzliches Unrecht und übergesetzliches Recht', *Süddeutsche Juristenzeitung*, 1 (1946), 105–8, repr. in Radbruch, *Rechtsphilosophie*, 8th edn., ed. Erik Wolf and Hans-Peter Schneider (Stuttgart: K.F. Koehler, 1973), 339–51, and repr. in Radbruch, *Gesamtausgabe*, 20 vols. projected, ed. Arthur Kaufmann, vol. III: *Rechtsphilosophie III*, ed. Winfried Hassemer (Heidelberg: C.F. Müller, 1990), 83–93, 282–91 (editorial notes); Lon L. Fuller, 'Positivism and Fidelity to Law', *Harvard Law Review*, 71 (1957–8), 630–72, at 648–61.

Hitler regime—has nothing to do with legal positivism rightly understood. Rather, it is in reality a controversy between two divergent schools
of natural law.

In this paper, I want to take up once again the same line of enquiry,
elaborating on it in a way impossible in oral presentation. My observations will be concerned in particular with the meaning and the function
of the concept of validity in the theory of law.

I. WHAT IS MEANT BY 'LEGAL POSITIVISM'?

The term 'legal positivism', although frequently used, has never acquired
any generally accepted meaning. It is most often used loosely, without
any definite connotation at all. If the term is to designate a view that contrasts with natural law philosophy, it must be taken to mean not a specific doctrine but a broad, general approach to the problems of legal
philosophy and jurisprudence. Correspondingly, the opposing term
'natural law' must also be understood broadly, as designating a general
point of view or attitude.

Considering how the term 'positivism' is used in general philosophy, it
seems to me reasonable to take the term 'legal positivism' in a broad
sense to mean an attitude or approach to the problems of legal philosophy and jurisprudence, an approach based on the principles of an
empiricist, antimetaphysical philosophy. By contrast, the term 'natural
law' is taken in a broad sense to designate an attitude or approach to the
problems of legal philosophy and jurisprudence, an approach based on
the belief that the law cannot be exhaustively described or understood in
terms of empiricist principles, but requires metaphysical interpretation,
that is, interpretation in light of principles and ideas inherent in the
rational or divine nature of man, *a priori* principles and ideas transcending the world of the senses.

The vague term 'empiricist principles' may, of course, be interpreted
in various ways. I understand empiricist principles as leading to two fundamental theses that constitute for me the kernel of legal positivism.

First, the thesis that the belief in natural law is erroneous: No such law
exists, all law is positive law. This is of course a thesis that pertains to the
general field of moral philosophy or ethics, for it denies that ethical
(moral, legal) principles or judgments are the expression of truths to be
discovered and established objectively by some process of cognition.
Ethics (or morality in a broad sense) is usually divided into two parts by
the proponents of cognitive theories: morality in a narrower sense, and
natural law. Morality, it is commonly assumed, is concerned with the
ultimate ethical destiny and end of man, whereas natural law deals with

the principles and norms that must govern the life of man in civil society (the state) to make possible the realization of his moral destiny.[3] Ethical principles are, then, either principles of morality or principles of natural law. The positivist's denial of the existence of natural law is implicit in the more general doctrine denying the existence of any ethical cognition at all: There is no natural law, just as there is no natural morality.

The second fundamental thesis of legal positivism is a doctrine pertaining to the theory or methodology of legal science. It asserts the possibility of establishing the existence and describing the content of the law of a certain country at a certain time in purely factual, empirical terms based on the observation and interpretation of social facts (human behaviour and attitudes). And it asserts, especially, that there is no use in appealing to ideas or principles taken over from natural law or natural morality.[4] This applies in particular to the idea of validity. In so far as the term 'validity' is taken to mean that the law possesses an inherent moral force ('binding force'), so that subjects are constrained by appeal to morality, to conscience, as well as by the threat of sanctions, then validity has no meaning or function in the doctrine of law. Validity, in this interpretation, is an *a priori* idea not reducible to empirical terms determined by observable facts.[5] If, now, legal science—and by this I understand the activity directed toward describing the law that is actually in force in a certain country at a certain time—is to be understood as an empirical science, there can be no place in it for any concept of this kind.

When one goes from one country to another, it is easy to observe changes in topography and climate, and no one would doubt that these facts can be described without it being necessary to transcend empiricist principles. In the case of a country's law, although the facts are more complicated, and more difficult to grasp and describe, the situation is the same. It is a fact, easy to observe, that Switzerland is mountainous whereas Denmark is flat. It is no less a fact that according to Danish law, women have the right to vote for members of Parliament, whereas this is not so in the Swiss Federation. It may, however, be rather difficult to indicate exactly *what* facts we refer to when we state the existence of a legal rule. This may be ultimately explained in various ways by means of distinct positivist doctrines. What is common to them as positivist theories is the conviction that to state the existence of a legal rule as belonging to

---

[3] See e.g. Alfred Verdross, *Abendländische Rechtsphilosophie*, 1st edn. (Vienna: Springer, 1958), at 248.

[4] H.L.A. Hart takes legal positivism to mean 'the simple contention that it is in no sense a necessary truth that laws reproduce or satisfy certain demands of morality, though in fact they have often done so.' Hart, *CL* 181–2, 2nd edn. 185–6. This, I believe, comes rather close to my second thesis.

[5] Frede Castberg, *Problems of Legal Philosophy*, 2nd Eng. edn. (Oslo: Oslo UP, and London: George Allen & Unwin, 1957).

the law of a certain country at a certain time is to state a set of observable social facts.

The postulate contained in this second thesis of legal positivism has the same meaning as the Austinian battle cry, 'The existence of the law is one thing; its merit or demerit another.' This means, exactly, that the law is a fact, and that a fact is and remains a fact whether you happen to like it or not, and whether you consider it in harmony or conflict with natural law principles whose truth is presupposed. It is highly misleading, however, when this doctrine is characterized—as it often is—as a doctrine of the separation of law and morality. It is obvious that legal and moral facts are interrelated in various ways.[6] Moral ideas are, without a doubt, one of the causal factors influencing the evolution of law, and the law, for its part, influences in turn prevailing moral ideas and attitudes. It is also well known that moral evaluations are not infrequently incorporated into the law by way of so-called legal standards. There is no reason for a positivist to deny this mutual dependence or any other possible relationship between the law and morality (positive morality, moral facts). If this had always been understood, a great deal of irrelevant criticism and discussion would have been avoided.

We would also have been spared other questionable discussions if it had been recognized that a legal positivist cannot be held responsible for every view propounded in the name of positivism, just as a natural lawyer cannot answer for every doctrine advanced as a doctrine of natural law. For my part, I want especially to dissociate myself from a set of doctrines derived from a too elementary conception of the social facts constituting a legal system. I am referring to the Austinian interpretation of law as commands emanating from a powerful will that, in case of disobedience, enforces them by exercising physical force. And I am referring in particular to various doctrines derived from this model of law, namely, the imperative theory, the theory of a force 'behind' the law, and the mechanical theory of the judicial process.

This last theory especially, denying that law has sources other than legislation (and custom) and describing the judge's activity in logico-mechanical terms that leave no room for intelligent discretion or for the exercise of social or moral evaluations, has often been attacked as a positivist dogma.[7] Such a theory, however, does not derive from empiricist premises. If it is nevertheless considered to be a positivist doctrine, this is either a misunderstanding, or a manifestation of an ambiguity in the

---

[6] See Hart, *CL*, at 198–9, 2nd edn. at 202–4.

[7] 'If we ignore the specific theories of law associated with the positivistic philosophy, I believe we can say that the dominant tone of positivism is set by fear of a purposive interpretation of law and legal institutions, or at least by a fear that such an interpretation may be pushed too far.' Fuller (n.2 above), 669.

notion of positivism. A narrow theory of the sources of law, and a theory of judicial interpretation that adheres to the words used, to 'logical' deductions and conceptual constructions, might be called 'positivist' where the term refers to 'what has been expressed in definite phrases, established in arbitrary decisions', but not where it refers to 'what is based on experience and the observation of facts.' It is perfectly possible to welcome an evolution toward a theory of more intelligent, value-directed judicial interpretation, without joining the clamor for a return to natural law. 'Away from formalism' is by no means identical with 'back to natural law'.[8]

II. WHAT IS MEANT BY 'NATURAL LAW'?

It is, I believe, less difficult to explain what is meant by 'natural law'. From the days of Aristotle and on up to our own time, we find an unbroken tradition of natural law theories, as well as great variations, of course, in the theoretical foundation and practical tenor of this philosophy. Sometimes natural law theory has been based on theological concepts, at other times, on rationality. The 'nature' from which universal principles are derived has been the nature of the cosmos, or of God, or of society and history, but most often it has been the nature of man as a rational being. Thus, we can distinguish a theological, a sociological, a historical, and a rational, anthropocentric natural law. From a politico-practical point of view, natural law theories have been just as conservative as they have been evolutionary or revolutionary. In the province of political philosophy, all political systems, from extreme absolutism to direct democracy, have been justified by natural law philosophers.

Despite manifold divergencies, there is one idea common to all natural law schools of thought: The belief that there exist universally valid principles governing the life of man in society, principles that have not been created by man but are discovered, *true* principles, binding on everyone, including those who are unable or unwilling to recognize their existence.[9] The truth of these laws cannot be established by the methods of empirical science, but presupposes a metaphysical interpretation of

---

[8] See Alf Ross, *A Textbook of International Law* (London: Longmans, Green, 1947), at 95; Roberto Ago, 'Positive Law and International Law', *American Journal of International Law*, 51 (1957), 691–733, at 728.

[9] 'On the affirmative side, I discern, and share, one central aim common to all the schools of natural law, that of discovering those principles of social order which will enable men to attain a satisfactory life in common. It is an acceptance of the possibility of "discovery" in the moral realm that seems to me to distinguish all the theories of natural law from opposing views.' Lon L. Fuller, 'A Rejoinder to Professor Nagel', *Natural Law Forum*, 3 (1958), 83–104, at 84.

the nature of man.[10] For this reason, the *validity* of these laws and the *obligations* deriving from them do not imply anything observable. The validity of the laws stemming from natural law has nothing to do with their acceptance or recognition in the minds of men, and the obligations they create have nothing to do with any sense of being duty-bound, any sanction of conscience, or any other experience. The unconditional validity of the laws, and the non-psychological character of the obligations, are simple consequences of the point of departure, namely, that these laws are discovered, objectively given, a reality, although not the reality of sensory observation. While the process of cognition whereby these laws are discovered and stated is different from the empirical process, the outcome is the same: knowledge, insight, truth. The 'universal' validity of these laws means the same as the universality of true, logical, or empirical statements, namely, that they are independent of varying subjective conditions.

As mentioned above, 'natural law' is considered to be the part of general ethics that deals with the principles governing the life of man in organized society with his fellows, making it possible for him to attain his moral destiny.

III. WHAT IS THE EXTENT OF THE CLASH BETWEEN LEGAL POSITIVISM AND NATURAL LAW?

That natural law and what I have called the *first* thesis of legal positivism are antagonists is obvious, for this thesis specifically denies the existence of any natural law at all. It ought to be noted, however, that the conflict takes place not within the field of *legal* philosophy, but within the general field of ethics or *moral* philosophy. Natural law is only a part of ethics, and the positivist denial of the existence of natural law is based on the general denial of any ethical cognition whatsoever. Although everyone has a right to present an opinion on this issue, as on anything else, I believe it must be admitted that a serious discussion is possible only among those sufficiently acquainted with the modern philosophical debate on the logical status and the truth-value of moral judgments.[11]

The interesting problem is whether or not there is a conflict between natural law doctrines and the *second* positivist thesis, asserting that a legal system is a social fact that can be described in purely empirical

[10] See e.g. Del Vecchio (n.1 above), at 148–9.

[11] The question of the possibility of moral cognition is the theme of my book *Kritik der sogenannten praktischen Erkenntnis* [Critique of So-Called Practical Cognition], trans. Hans Winkler and Gunnar Leistikow (Copenhagen: Levin & Munksgaard, and Leipzig: Felix Meiner, 1933). See also my article 'On the Logical Nature of Propositions of Value', *Theoria*, 11 (1945), 172–210.

terms. It is commonly assumed that such a conflict exists. I shall try to show that this is not so or, at any rate, that the divergencies of opinion reflect nothing more than a question of classification and terminology.

To be sure, natural law is usually presented in a way that is apt to evoke the impression of a serious conflict with empiricist postulates. It is usually said that the principles of natural law, especially the idea of justice, are necessarily implied in the concept of law. This means that no system can be recognized as a legal system unless it embodies, at least to some degree, these principles. A system that is in no way inspired by the ideas of justice, that makes no attempt, however inadequate, to carry out the principles of natural law, is not a legal system but a system of brute force, a gangster regime. A gangster may succeed in establishing a regime of terror, and you may find yourself forced to obey his orders, but a regime of terror, since it is not based on justice, lacks *validity* or *binding force*. A legal system, on the contrary, is invested with validity or binding force precisely because it is based on the idea of justice.

This is the current tenor of natural law theory. It seems clearly to contradict the positivist position, in that it appeals to natural law, and to the *a priori* notion of validity as inherent in the concept of law, a notion that is fundamental to the description of a legal system.

Now let us examine more closely the 'validity' or 'binding force' that is said to characterize the idea of a legal system. 'Binding force', it is said, means that you are duty-bound to obey the law. What kind of duty is meant here?

It seems obvious that the duty to obey the law cannot mean, here, a legal duty or obligation in the same sense in which these terms are used to describe the legal situation arising in certain circumstances governed by a legal norm—for example, the obligation of the debtor to pay a contracted debt. An obligation in this technical sense means that the debtor runs the risk that legal sanctions will be carried out against him. For the act of 'not obeying the law', however, there is and can be no sanction different from the sanction for not paying the debt.

I can put it another way. A duty is always a duty to behave in a certain way. In this case, the required behaviour is 'to obey the law'. How do we obey the law? By fulfilling our legal obligations—for example, by paying our debts. It follows that the obligation to obey the law does not prescribe any behaviour that is not already prescribed by the law itself. And it follows in turn that if the duty to obey the prescriptions of a legal system is to mean something different from the obligation prescribed directly by this system, then the difference cannot consist in the *required behaviour—what* we are bound to do—but must consist exclusively in *how* we are bound. The meaning of the binding force inherent in a legal system is that the legal obligations corresponding to the rules of the system—for example, the obligation to pay a debt—are not merely legal duties deriving from the threat of legal sanctions. They are also *moral duties* in the *a priori* sense of true moral obligations deriving from the natural law principles that endow the legal system with its validity or binding force. The duty to obey the law is a moral duty *toward* the legal system, not a legal duty *conforming* to the system. The duty toward the system cannot derive from this system itself, but must follow from rules or principles that are outside the system.[12]

This means that validity or binding force is not really a quality inherent in the legal system, but is derived from principles of natural law. To assert that a legal system possesses validity or binding force is not to say anything about legal obligations or facts, but is to express our moral obligations. Such a statement belongs to a lecture on moral philosophy, and has nothing to do with describing the legal system.

I submit that there is no reason a natural law philosopher should not admit the positivist thesis and recognize that a legal system is a social fact to be described in purely empirical terms without reference to the concept of validity. The natural lawyer is concerned with the question of whether a certain factual system also binds people morally (in conscience, if they have sufficient understanding of what true morality requires). But before one can answer this question, one must know *that* a certain factual system exists and *what* its content is. Thus, the question of validity necessarily presupposes the positivist thesis, namely, that the existence of a certain legal system can be established, and its content described, independently of the ideas of morality or natural law.

The only issue that might separate natural lawyers from legal positivists is one of classification and terminology: Should a factual system in complete discordance with the principles of justice—for example, the Nazi regime under Hitler—be classified as a *legal* system? Or should this term be reserved for those systems that are, to some extent at any rate, based on the principles of natural law?[13]

The importance of this issue should not be overestimated. If a natural lawyer wants to reserve the term 'law' for a system having some moral value, it is because he wants to emphasize terminologically the moral difference between different systems.[14] And if a positivist prefers to classify as a legal system any factual system, whatever its moral value, that has

---

[12] See e.g. Johannes Messner, *Das Naturrecht*, 4th edn. (Innsbruck: Tyrolia, 1960), at 355–6.

[13] See Ross, *LJ*, at 31–2.

[14] Lon L. Fuller requires 'a definition of law that will make meaningful the obligation of fidelity to law.' Fuller (n.2 above), 635. The positivist's rejoinder is that it is preferable to define law in non-moral terms, and to understand that the moral idea of fidelity to law is not absolute, but contingent on the moral quality of the positive law.

the same structure as a typical legal system, it is because he wants to emphasize, also terminologically, the factual, structural similarity between diverse systems, whatever their moral qualifications. A system like the Nazi regime can be described using the same concepts and the same technique as those used to describe typical legal systems.

Personally, I prefer a conceptual criterion based on scientific convenience and not on moral considerations, just as I find it reasonable to include black swans under the zoological concept of swan, although some might think black swans lack aesthetic value. If everyone nevertheless clearly understands the terminological character of the issue, there is no reason to take the discrepancy in opinion seriously.

Summing up, I maintain that a natural law philosopher as such has no reason to deny that law is a social fact describable in purely empirical terms. As a natural law philosopher, he is concerned with a branch of moral philosophy. When speaking about the *validity* of a certain factual system, he is concerned especially with the question of whether or not there is a *moral* duty to comply with the rules of this system. Before this question can be answered, he must know what the rules of the system are, that is to say, he must have a description of it as observable fact. The natural law philosopher has no reason to deny that social facts, like other facts, are the object of empirical cognition obtained by means of empirical methods. It is of no great importance whether or not the expression 'legal system' is used to designate a factual system whose norms are conceived in a spirit repugnant to the ideas of justice and humanity, as long as its structure is similar to that of well-established legal systems.

IV. QUASI-POSITIVISM AS A TYPE OF NATURAL LAW

It is satisfying to note that the view defended in the preceding section has been accepted by some contemporary natural law philosophers trained in general philosophy. One example is Professor Alfred Verdross. In his book *Western Legal Philosophy*, he writes:

The defender of natural law cannot deny the possibility of the existence of norms that, although clashing with natural law, are actually efficacious and for this reason suitable as an object of scientific investigation. The defender of natural law is even obligated to seek cognition of all positive law as such, because he will not be able to evaluate efficacious norms until he has established their existence and ascertained their scope and content—for evaluation presupposes prior cognition of the object of evaluation.[15]

---

[15] Verdross (n.3 above), 254 (my translation) [trans. altered].

With these words, Verdross accepts the second positivist thesis. And when he recognizes further that it might be reasonable to reserve the term 'law' for systems of positive norms[16] (meaning that 'natural law' is not 'law'), he has fully accepted the positivist doctrine that all law is positive law. But he remains an ardent defender of natural law.[17]

On the other hand, we find in Verdross a misunderstanding arising from the ambiguity of the word 'positivism'. Because this misunderstanding is so common and has consequences for evaluating in terms of morality the true positivist attitude, it should be considered in some detail.

Verdross distinguishes between what he calls *dogmatic* (or *extreme*) and *hypothetical* (or *moderate*) legal positivism.[18] The first term is applied to the school of thought that denies the existence of specific ethical cognition, and so, in particular, denies the existence of a natural law composed of ethical principles that can be discovered and established by human reason. The second term designates the attitude that leaves open the question of the existence of natural law, and confines itself to asserting that the answer to this question is of no importance for legal science. The subject-matter of this legal science is efficacious normative systems whose existence can be established and whose scope and content defined without appeal to natural law principles.

The reader can easily see that the kind of positivism I define and defend in this article and in previous writings must undoubtedly be classified as 'dogmatic' or 'extreme' according to Verdross. This is why I feel called upon to object passionately to Verdross's mistaken interpretation of the positivist position.

In the view of dogmatic legal positivism, says Verdross, positive law possesses absolute validity or binding force. This means that the dogmatic positivist uncritically recognizes and accepts the moral authority of any established system as such. Verdross stamps this attitude '*Kadavergehorsam*' (stupid, blind obedience), and draws the conclusion that no adherent of dogmatic legal positivism can, without contradicting himself, take a firm stand against any political system, no matter how abominable.[19]

---

[16] Verdross (n.3 above), 252, quoting Pope Pius XII in support.

[17] Johannes Messner, too, the Roman Catholic author of the most modern and comprehensive exposition of natural law philosophy, recognizes the independence of positive law as the subject-matter of a legal science based on purely empiricist principles of cognition. Legal science, according to Messner, belongs to the empirical sciences, whose subject-matter is the reality given in external experience. The subject-matter of legal science is the determination of the factual rules of reciprocal human relations. Messner (n.12 above), 370.

[18] Verdross (n.3 above), 251–2.

[19] Ibid. 246, 252, 254.

The reasoning behind this line of thought is obvious. When the positivist denies that the validity of positive law derives from natural law, he must acknowledge that validity is inherent in the positive law as such, that is to say, it is unconditional, absolute.

This is a grave mistake. The consequence of denying natural law is to deny that positive law possesses validity in the same sense in which this term is used by natural law, where 'validity' designates a true moral claim on obedience, a claim that is independent of any recognition from subjects. Such a claim can only be based on ethical principles. The term has no meaning whatsoever for a doctrine that denies all ethical truths. It has no place in the positivist's vocabulary. For him, evaluating a political regime in terms of morality is a question of personally and subjectively accepting values and standards.

I would be pleased if my friend and colleague were to recognize that it is perfectly possible, without any self-contradiction, to deny the objectivity of values and morals, and, at the same time, to be a decent person and a reliable companion in the struggle against a regime of terror, corruption, and inhumanity. The belief that moral judgments are not true (or false), that they are not the outcome of a cognitive process or an insight comparable to logical or empirical cognition, is in no way incompatible with such judgments emanating from solid moral attitudes. The positivist position is concerned not with morality but with the logic of moral discourse, not with ethics but with meta-ethics.[20]

One thing is true, however, and should be emphasized in an effort to explain the misunderstanding. A number of writers usually considered to be 'positivists' have held the view described by Verdross, namely, that the established system has, as such, a claim on obedience. Verdross cites Bergbohm, the well-known representative[21] of a whole school of 'positivist' jurists who, while denying natural law, still cling to the idea that positive law possesses 'validity', derived now from the authority of the state.

This attitude, however, has nothing to do with empiricism (true positivism). It is itself a doctrine of 'validity', a moral philosophy marked by the derivation of validity not from abstract principles inherent in human reason, but from historical evolution and from established institutions.[22]

As far as I can see, this kind of moral philosophy has several roots. One, I think, reaches back to the teachings of Martin Luther, who gave new

---

[20] No moral judgment or principle can be deduced from the meta-ethical proposition that moral judgments are neither true nor false. See Alf Ross, *Why Democracy?* (Cambridge, Mass.: Harvard UP, 1952), at 94.

[21] See Karl Bergbohm, *Jurisprudenz und Rechtsphilosophie* (Leipzig: Duncker & Humblot, 1892, repr. Glashütten im Taunus: D. Auvermann, 1973).

[22] See Ross, *Kritik* (n.11 above), at ch. 12; Ross, *LJ*, at 149–50.

scope to St. Paul's words to the effect that all state authority comes from God. Another is to be found in the philosophy of Hegel, condensed into the famous slogan, 'What is real is valid, and what is valid is real.'[23] And there is consonance with the conservative ideology that what succeeds is justified, because God has permitted it to succeed. These diverse tendencies seem to have created, especially in Germany, an uncritical deference and submissiveness toward official authority, toward anyone in uniform. It is this attitude that is revealed in the slogan noted above, '*Gesetz ist Gesetz*' ('a law is a law'), meaning that every legal system is law and, as such, must be obeyed whatever its spirit and tendencies. If there is any truth in the belief that 'positivism' paved the way for the Hitler regime, it must refer to this type of 'positivism', this school of natural law, and not to true positivism understood as an empiricist theory in the field of moral philosophy.

To avoid confusing this school of thought with true positivism, I propose to name it 'quasi-positivism'.

V. THREE DIFFERENT FUNCTIONS AND MEANINGS OF 'VALIDITY'

To prepare the way for later sections, I want to point out that the term 'validity' is used in (at least) three different ways, that is, it has three different meanings performing three distinct functions.[24]

First, the term is used in current doctrinal expositions of prevailing law to indicate whether or not a legal act—say, a contract, a last will and testament, or an administrative order—has the desired legal effect. The act is said to be invalid or void if this is not the case. It is an internal function, for to state that an act is valid or invalid is to state something *in accordance with* a given system of norms. The statement is a legal judgment applying legal rules to certain facts.

Second, the term is used in general legal theory to indicate the existence of a norm or a system of norms. The validity of a norm in this sense means its actual existence or reality, contrary to the case of a rule merely imagined or that of a mere projection. This is an external function, for to state that a rule or a system of rules exists or does not exist is to state something *about* the rule or the system. The statement is not a legal judgment, but a factual assertion referring to a set of social facts.

I understand, however, that this use of 'validity' may appear odd in English. In Danish as in German, a distinction is made between *gyldig* (*gültig*) and *gældende* (*geltend*). A contract is said to be *gyldig* or *ugyldig*

---

[23] See Ross, *Kritik* (n.11 above), at 409–10; Ross, *LJ*, at 251–2.
[24] See Verdross (n.3 above), at 246.

(valid or invalid, void), but we use another term to speak of the law, namely, '*gældende*', to mean prevailing law, law actually in force, actually existing. It is noteworthy that for the negation of '*gældende*', there is no word corresponding to the negating '*ugyldig*' ('invalid'). Unable to find an English equivalent for '*gældende*', I have used 'valid' in the English versions of my writings to cover not only the function of '*gyldig*', but also that of '*gældende*'. I understand now that this translation might be confusing.[25]

Third, 'validity' in ethics and in natural law, as we have seen, is taken to mean a specifically moral, *a priori* quality, also called the 'binding force' of the law, which gives rise to a corresponding moral obligation.

VI. KELSEN AS QUASI-POSITIVIST

It follows from what is said above that if the term 'valid' (Danish '*gældende*') is used to indicate that a rule or a system of rules is a reality (and not simply a projection or something imagined), then, according to empiricist principles, the term must be taken to refer to observable social facts and nothing else. It may be difficult to define exactly which facts and which observations are suitable for verifying the assertion that a rule exists, but broadly speaking the existence (validity) of a norm is the same as its efficacy. To state that a rule or a system of rules exists is the same as to state the occasion of a complex of social facts—understanding 'social facts' broadly, to include psychological conditions too. In this context, then, the term 'validity' has nothing to do with any normative statement of a duty (in the moral sense) to obey the law. Such an idea of duty, characteristic of quasi-positivist and natural law thinking, has no place in a theory of law based on empiricist principles.

Validity in the normative sense has no function in describing and explaining reality. Its function is to reinforce the legal system by proclaiming that the legal obligations of the system are not merely legal obligations backed up by sanctions, but also moral duties. The normative notion of validity is an ideological instrument supporting the authority of the state. When this notion is used by a quasi-positivist, support is unconditional; when used by a natural law philosopher, support is conditioned by some degree of harmony with the presupposed standards of natural law.

In this respect, Kelsen's Pure Theory of Law is a continuation of quasi-positivist thought. Kelsen has never overcome the idea that an established legal system, as such, possesses validity in the normative sense of

---

[25]   I have discovered this from H.L.A. Hart's criticism, see § VII below.

the word. According to Kelsen, the existence of a norm is its 'validity', and to say that a norm possesses validity means 'that individuals ought to behave as the norm stipulates.'[26] But if the norm itself expresses in its immediate content what individuals ought to do, then we question the meaning of saying that individuals ought to do what they ought to do. I have analysed this idea above, in section III. We have seen that the idea of a duty to obey the law (to fulfil legal obligations) only makes sense on the supposition that the duty spoken of is a true moral duty corresponding to the 'binding force' inherent in the law.

Although this interpretation is not in harmony with the admittedly empiricist programme of the Pure Theory of Law, it is inevitable and ought to be taken as the survival of natural law philosophy of the quasi-positivist kind.

The interpretation is supported by the way Kelsen tries to explain the significance of the reiterated admonition to behave as the norm requires. The significance, he says, is that the subjective meaning of the norm is objective as well.[27] And this is the same as saying that the norm expresses a *true* obligation: Individuals are not only 'commanded' to behave in a certain way, but they also 'really', 'in truth', 'objectively' ought to behave as required by the norm. The idea of a true norm or an objective duty, however, is exactly the idea that is operative in natural law philosophy, an idea that has meaning only on the assumption of objective, *a priori*, moral principles from which true duties are derived.

Kelsen's concern with the traditional problem of the moral quality that distinguishes a legal system from a gangster regime is apparent in the way he illustrates the idea of validity as having objective, normative meaning. He writes,

Not every act whose subjective meaning is a norm is objectively one as well. For example, a robber's command to hand over your purse is not interpreted as a binding or valid norm.[28]

This interpretation alone makes it possible to understand the view, peculiar to Kelsen, that it is logically impossible to regard a particular legal rule as valid, and at the same time to accept as morally binding a moral rule prohibiting the behaviour required by the legal rule.[29] Kelsen's view here, puzzling in light of empiricist principles, gains a foothold if legal validity is understood as a moral quality inherent in the established system. It should be noted that the presupposition of the

[26] See Hans Kelsen, 'Value Judgments in the Science of Law', *Journal of Social Philosophy and Jurisprudence*, 7 (1942), 312–33, at 317, repr. *WJ* 209–30, at 214; *GTLS*, at 115–16, 369; *Phil. Fds.* § 4 (at pp. 395–6).

[27] See Hans Kelsen, 'Why Should the Law be Obeyed?', *WJ* 257–65, at 257 (the first appearance of this paper is in *WJ*).

[28] Ibid.   [29] *GTLS* 373–5; *Phil. Fds.* § 14 (pp. 408–10).

basic norm as investing the factual system with validity is attributed by Kelsen to what is called 'juristic thinking'. The presupposition is simply revealed—and accepted—by legal science.[30] 'Juristic thinking' refers, I suppose, to ideas and beliefs commonly held by lawyers, but it is not a reliable guide for logical analysis. It is possible, and highly probable in both the field of law and that of morality, that the usual way of 'thinking' is saturated with ideological concepts that reflect emotional experience but have no function in describing reality, which is the task of legal science. In that case, the job of the analyst is to reject, not to accept, the idea of validity.[31]

VII. COMMENTS ON HART

Emerging from the preceding sections are my main theses on the meaning and the function of the concept of validity. They are:

(1) If the term 'validity' is taken in the sense in which it is used in natural law (including quasi-positivism), that is, if it is used to designate a moral quality of a legal system, the quality that invests the obligations of the system with binding force, then it has no place in a legal science based on empiricist principles;

(2) If the term 'valid' (Danish '*gældende*', German '*geltend*') is used to designate the existence (the reality, the occasion) of a norm or a system of norms, it must be understood as an abbreviated reference to a complex of social facts, namely, those social facts that are considered in legal science to be necessary and sufficient to verify a proposition on the existence of the rule or the system of rules. In my book *On Law and Justice*, I develop this idea,[32] trying to show that in the final analysis verification is concerned with the future behaviour of judges (and of other law-enforcing authorities) under certain conditions; and that for this reason the proposition, '*D* (a certain directive or rule) is valid Danish law', is equivalent to the predictive proposition that the courts, in certain circumstances, will base their decisions (also) on the directive *D*. Such a prediction is possible only on the basis of a whole complex of social facts (including psychological facts of behaviour and attitude).

---

[30] *GTLS* 116; Kelsen, 'Value Judgments in the Science of Law' (n.26 above), 324, 326–7, repr. *WJ* 221, 224.

[31] I have presented a similar critique of Kelsen in my review of *What is Justice?*, in *California Law Review*, 45 (1957), 564–70. Kelsen, for his part, has propounded a penetrating analysis and critique of my views in his article 'Eine "realistische" und die Reine Rechtslehre', *ÖZöR*, 10 (1959), 1–25.

[32] See Ross, *LJ*, at 29–50.

In his article 'Scandinavian Realism', Professor H.L.A. Hart propounds a criticism of my analysis of 'validity'.[33] It might be of interest to ascertain to what extent, if any, Hart disagrees with my views as I have stated them here.

As far as I can see, there is virtually no disagreement at all. The objections advanced by Hart rest on a misunderstanding of my intentions, partly caused by the linguistic fact (which I have understood only recently) that the English 'valid' can hardly be used in the same way as the Danish '*gældende*'.

The term 'valid' is used by Hart in the first sense[34] and in the third sense[35] mentioned above, in section V. Since, however, he uses the word in the third sense (as a moral quality) only in the exposition of natural law views and not of his own, we shall limit ourselves here to Hart's analysis of the term as it occurs and functions in current legal thinking.

The concept of validity analysed by Hart is the concept as it functions when a certain contract, will, or other legal act is said to be valid or invalid (void). A legal act is said to be valid when it has been performed in such a way that it fulfils the conditions—established in a legal norm— necessary for it to have the intended legal effect.

This concept of validity is well known to every lawyer, and my own analysis of it is in complete harmony with Hart's views.[36] When, however, in *On Law and Justice*, I discuss at some length the meaning of the assertion, '*D* is valid Danish law', my concern is not that concept fulfilling that function. The way the problem is raised and treated leaves no doubt that the issue discussed is what Hart treats under the heading of the *existence* of a legal rule or a legal system.[37] As mentioned above, I am now aware that the Danish '*gældende ret*' should not have been translated into English as 'valid law'. I regret my lack of sufficient feeling for English usage, but, at the same time, I believe that had Hart been a little more attentive, he would have noticed that the problem I treat under 'validity' is altogether different from the problem he considers under the same heading. Had he understood this, there would have been no basis for his criticism, namely, that statements about legal validity have nothing to do with predicting judicial behaviour.

It is interesting to note that when these misunderstandings are eliminated, there seems to be no disagreement between our views as to what is involved in the question of the *existence* of a legal system. In clear

[33] H.L.A. Hart, 'Scandinavian Realism', *Cambridge Law Journal*, 17 (1959), 233–40, repr. Hart, *Essays in Jurisprudence and Philosophy* (Oxford: Clarendon Press, 1983), 161–9.

[34] Hart, *CL* 22, 28–31, 68, 70–1, 100–2, 2nd edn. 22, 28–32, 69–70, 71–3, 103–5.

[35] Hart, *CL* 152, 182, 195–207, 2nd edn. 156, 186, 200–12.

[36] Ross, *LJ* 204, and see at 32, 79.

[37] Hart, *CL* 106, 109, 117, 245 (note), 2nd edn. 109–10, 112–13, 120–1, 292–3 (note).

opposition to Kelsen, Hart rejects the idea that the existence of a legal system is its validity, expressed in a basic norm that exhorts individuals to obey the law. He rightly calls it mystifying to speak of a rule that pre-scribes that another rule be obeyed.[38] Hart's own position is put forward with all desirable precision in this statement:

The question whether a rule of recognition exists and what its content is, i.e. what the criteria of validity in any given legal system are, is regarded throughout this book as an empirical, though complex, question of fact.[39]

Anyone acquainted with the special terminology used by Hart will eas-ily see that he is concerned here with the existence of the supreme norm or of the legal system as a whole. His view that this issue is to be treated as a question of empirical fact is in complete harmony with the idea basic to my book *On Law and Justice*. Hart writes further that when we assert that a legal system exists, 'we in fact refer in compressed, portmanteau form to a number of heterogeneous social facts', and he writes that the truth of this assertion can 'be established by reference to actual practice: to the way in which courts identify what is to count as law, and to the gen-eral acceptance of or acquiescence in these identifications.'[40] The simi-larity here between Hart's position and my own is still more striking.

[38] Hart, *CL* 246 (note), 2nd edn. 293 (note).
[39] Hart, *CL* 245 (note), 2nd edn. 292–3 (note).
[40] Hart, *CL* 109, 105, 2nd edn. 112, 108.

PART III

The Normativity Problematic, continued: Kantian Doctrines versus Kelsen without Kant

A. A Neo-Kantian Dimension
in the Pure Theory of Law?

8

The Pure Theory of Law, 'Labandism', and Neo-Kantianism. A Letter to Renato Treves*

HANS KELSEN

Professor Dr. Hans Kelsen
Strobl, near Ischl
Villa Lechner
[Austria]
3 August 1933

Dear Dr. Treves,

I thank you very much indeed for your kind letter of 25 July. I am delighted that the translation of my manuscript on the methods and basic concepts of the Pure Theory of Law[1] is complete, and in particular that you are the one who did the translating. For I know how thoroughly you have grasped the spirit of my theory.

This is confirmed by the remarks you intend to make in your own manuscript on the Pure Theory.[2] The comments you convey to me are

* *Editors' note*: Kelsen's 1933 letter to Renato Treves was first published in French, translated by Michel Troper, in *Droit et Société*, 7 (1987), 333–5. The German original and an Italian translation by Agostino Carrino appeared, thanks to Carrino's initiative, in Hans Kelsen and Renato Treves, *Formalismo giuridico e realtà sociale*, ed. Stanley L. Paulson (Naples: Edizioni Scientifiche Italiane, 1992), 55–8, 51–4 respectively. The present translation is by the editors. The numbering of paragraphs is Kelsen's, the notes (which fill in Kelsen's references) are the editors'.

[1] *La dottrina pura del diritto. Metodo e concetti fondamentali*, trans. Renato Treves (Modena: Società Tipografica Modenese, 1933). Kelsen's German original, 'Grundriß einer allgemeinen Theorie des Staates' (Brno: Rudolf M. Rohrer, 1926), a printed manuscript as distinct from a published work, is a summary statement of doctrines in *ASL*.

[2] The manuscript in question is Renato Treves, 'Il fondamento filosofico della dottrina pura del diritto di Hans Kelsen', *Atti della Reale Accademia delle Scienze di Torino*, 69 (1933–4), 52–90, repr. in Hans Kelsen and Renato Treves, *Formalismo giuridico e realtà sociale*, ed. Stanley L. Paulson (Naples: Edizioni Scientifiche Italiane, 1992), 59–87. See also Treves, *Il diritto come relazione. Saggio critico sul neo-kantismo contemporaneo* (Turin: Presso l'Istituto Giuridico della R. Università, 1934), repr. in Treves, *Il diritto come relazione. Saggi di filosofia della cultura*, ed. Agostino Carrino, with a preface by Norberto Bobbio (Naples: Edizioni Scientifiche Italiane, 1993), where Treves takes up this and related themes at greater length.

Renato Treves (1907–92) was an influential figure in Italian legal philosophy and legal fully correct in every respect. Permit me, however, to give voice to a few additional thoughts.

(1) The claim of some that the Pure Theory of Law amounts to nothing other than 'Labandism' is especially absurd because of Laband's utter failure in his effort to separate the depiction of the positive law from politics.[3] In reality, Laband's theory of public law is an ideology of the monarchical principle, which Laband, entirely without warrant, considered contradictory to the positive law. As to the requirement, acknowledged by Laband, that the positivist theory of public law be separated from politics, the Pure Theory of Law is of course a continuation of the tradition that begins in Germany with Gerber, who simply extends to public law a fundamental principle that was self-evident in the field of private law for a long time.[4] The main distinction, however, between the Pure Theory of Law and Laband's position is that Laband did not establish a legal theory based on principle at all. Strictly speaking, he confined himself instead to an interpretation of the Constitution and, in the absence of a theoretical foundation, asserted the difference that exists in principle between public and private law. Similarly, Laband's position holds fast to the dualism of international law and state law, a dualism defended even today by Triepel[5] and, with him, by a great number of

sociology, and along with Norberto Bobbio (see this volume, ch. 23), he introduced Kelsen to an Italian audience. On Treves's life and work, see Vincenzo Ferrari and Nella Gridelli Velicogna, 'Philosophy and Sociology of Law in the Work of Renato Treves', *Ratio Juris*, 6 (1993), 202–15; bibliography, ibid. 216–25; see also *Diritto, cultura e libertà. Atti del convegno in memoria di Renato Treves*, ed. Vincenzo Ferrari et al. (Milan: A. Giuffrè Editore, 1997).

  [3] Paul Laband (1838–1918), the leading German public law theorist of his day. See generally Michael Stolleis, *Geschichte des öffentlichen Rechts in Deutschland*, 3 vols. projected (Munich: C.H. Beck, 1988–), vol. II (1992), at 341–50 *et passim*; Walter Pauly, *Der Methodenwandel im deutschen Spätkonstitutionalismus* (Tübingen: J.C.B. Mohr, 1993), at 177–208 *et passim*. The expression 'Labandism' stems from Hermann Heller (1891–1933), a gifted public law theorist in Weimar Germany. In the course of a scathing critique of the German theory of public law, he writes: 'The Pure Theory of Law is the heir, born too late, of a logicistic legal positivism, the logically inevitable fulfillment of the programme of Labandism, which was alien both to sociology and to questions of value.' Hermann Heller, 'Die Krisis der Staatslehre', *AöR*, 55, N.F.16 (1926), 289–316, at 300 (note omitted), repr. in Heller, *Gesammelte Schriften*, 2nd edn., ed. Christoph Müller, 3 vols. (Tübingen: J.C.B. Mohr, 1992), vol. II, 3–30, at 15–16.

  [4] Carl Friedrich von Gerber (1823–91), leading German public law theorist. As Kelsen points out, Gerber adopted the conceptual method of private law (the method of Pandectism, as reflected in the work of Puchta and the early Jhering) and then transferred it to public law, thereby ushering in what became known as the modern German *Staatsrechtslehre*, the 'Gerber-Laband-Jellinek Theory of Public Law'. See generally Stolleis (n.3 above), at 330–58 *et passim*, and Pauly (n.3 above), at 92–167, 177–245, *et passim*.

  [5] Heinrich Triepel (1868–1946), theorist in the fields of public law and international law. His treatise *Völkerrecht und Landesrecht* (Leipzig: C.L. Hirschfeld, 1899, repr. Aalen: Scientia, 1958) was for many decades the standard work on dualism. A guide to Triepel's work is Ulrich M. Gassner, 'Heinrich Triepel. Leben und Werk', which has not yet been published.

Germany's current theorists of public and international law—but also, regrettably, by Anzilotti,[6] whose theoretical work certainly ranks far above Triepel's. I should also like to mention, in passing, that even my early treatise, *Main Problems in the Theory of Public Law*,[7] was most emphatically directed against the political tendencies—albeit cleverly concealed—of Laband's theory of public law, and, therefore, that my Pure Theory of Law actually originated in the struggle against 'Labandism'. Furthermore, it is curious that the charge of 'Labandism' is levelled against me by the very people who never tire of warning that my theory is dangerous to the state. Laband himself, the decidedly conservative crown jurist of the Prussian dynasty, would no doubt spin in his grave if he were to learn that he is being held accountable for the Pure Theory of Law.

(2) It is altogether correct that the philosophical foundation of the Pure Theory of Law is the Kantian philosophy, in particular the Kantian philosophy in the interpretation that it has undergone through Cohen.[8] A point of special significance is that just as Cohen understood Kant's *Critique of Pure Reason* as a theory of experience, so likewise I seek to apply the transcendental method to a theory of positive law. If one understands the 'positive' law as 'empirical' law, law in experience, or 'legal experience', as Sander[9] has termed it, then the Pure Theory of Law is indeed empiricistic—but empiricism in the same sense as Kant's

---

[6] Dionisio Anzilotti (1867–1950), leading Italian proponent of a dualistic approach to the relation between international law and state law. See his treatise *Corso di diritto internazionale*, 3rd edn. (Rome: Athenaeum, 1928), 4th edn. (Padua: CEDAM, 1964) (first published in 1912).

[7] See bibliographical entry, at *HP*, in the Table of Abbreviations.

[8] Hermann Cohen (1842–1918), the leading figure in the Marburg School of Neo-Kantianism. See generally Geert Edel, *Von der Vernunftkritik zur Erkenntnislogik. Die Entwicklung der theoretischen Philosophie Hermann Cohens* (Freiburg and Munich: Karl Alber, 1988); Ulrich Sieg, *Aufstieg und Niedergang des Marburger Neukantianismus* (Würzburg: Königshausen & Neumann, 1994); Jürgen Stolzenberg, *Ursprung und System* (Göttingen: Vandenhoeck & Ruprecht, 1995); Andrea Poma, *The Critical Philosophy of Hermann Cohen*, trans. John Denton (Albany: State University of New York Press, 1997) (Italian original first published in 1988). The question of Cohen's influence on Kelsen remains controversial. In addition to Kelsen's own statements, both here and in his 'Foreword' to *HP*, in this volume, ch. 1, at § VI, see Geert Edel, 'The *Hypothesis* of the Basic Norm: Hans Kelsen and Hermann Cohen', in this volume, ch. 10; Stanley L. Paulson, 'Kelsen and the Marburg School: Reconstructive and Historical Approaches', in *Prescriptive Formality and Normative Rationality in Modern Legal Systems. Festschrift for Robert S. Summers*, ed. Werner Krawietz et al. (Berlin: Duncker & Humblot, 1994), 481–94.

[9] Fritz Sander (1889–1939), the *enfant terrible* of the Vienna School of Legal Theory in the early 1920s. Sander wrote initially as a neo-Kantian (see the first three of his papers collected in *RNK*), then became an acerbic critic of Kelsen (see the article cited in this note, below) and commenced work on a version of legal realism. In the present text, Kelsen takes the expression 'legal experience' from Sander's article 'Rechtsdogmatik oder Theorie der Rechtserfahrung?', *ZöR*, 2 (1921), 511–670, also published as a monograph (Vienna and Leipzig: Franz Deuticke, 1921), repr. *RNK* 115–278. In 'RWR', Kelsen replies at length to Sander.

transcendental philosophy. And just as Kant's transcendental philosophy energetically opposes all metaphysics, so the Pure Theory of Law takes aim at the natural law, which, in the field of social reality generally and the field of positive law in particular, corresponds exactly to metaphysics. I have elaborated on this in my monograph, *Philosophical Foundations of Natural Law Theory and Legal Positivism*, Lecture 31 of the Kant Society.[10] Precisely because the Pure Theory of Law was the first to try to develop Kant's philosophy into a theory of positive law (and did not get bogged down in a theory of natural law, as Stammler[11] does), it marks in a certain sense a step beyond Kant, whose own legal theory rejected the transcendental method.[12] Nevertheless, the Pure Theory of Law has been a more faithful custodian of Kant's intellectual legacy than any of the other legal philosophies that draw on Kant. The Pure Theory of Law first made the Kantian philosophy really fruitful for the law by developing it further rather than clinging to the letter of Kant's own legal philosophy. If one recognizes in Kant's work a truly German philosophy, then the Pure Theory of Law is the most German of all the legal philosophies developed in Germany since Kant. I address this to those who do not understand the Pure Theory of Law and therefore believe that they can successfully combat it in the politically polluted atmosphere of our time by describing it as 'un-German'. I should like to invite attention here, *en passant*, to the radically universalistic character of the Pure Theory of Law, which—the first theory to do so—takes as its point of departure the whole of the law, the legal system, in order to comprehend from this standpoint all other phenomena as parts of the whole. Thus, the doctrine of the reconstructed legal norm (*Rechtssatz*)[13] is at the core of the Pure Theory of Law. Even Hegel's legal philosophy—biased toward the natural law theory of its time—failed, notwithstanding its notion of

---

[10] For the full bibliographical reference, see the Table of Abbreviations.

[11] Rudolf Stammler (1856–1938), legal theorist and philosopher, with ties to Paul Natorp of the Marburg School of Neo-Kantianism. Many in legal science, philosophy, and sociology—e.g. Max Adler, Julius Binder, Hermann Cohen, Georg Jellinek, Hermann Kantorowicz, Siegfried Marck, Adolf Julius Merkl, Georg Simmel, Max Weber, and Franz Weyr—found a good bit to criticize in Stammler's work, and Kelsen was no exception; along with the present text, see *HP*, at 58–62, and *SJSB*, at § 25 (pp. 143–9). In one respect, however, Kelsen praises Stammler, writing that it was Stammler who brought 'Kant's transcendental philosophy to bear on legal science', *PS*, p. viii; see also 'RWR', at 104, repr. *RNK*, at 280, where Kelsen mentions both Stammler and Hermann Cohen in this connection. Stammler was prolific, and one of his treatises, *Die Lehre vom richtigen Recht* (Berlin: J. Guttentag, 1902), is available in English: *The Theory of Justice*, trans. Isaac Husik (New York: Macmillan, 1925, repr. New York: Kelley, 1969).

[12] Kelsen's expression 'transcendental method' ('*transzendentale Methode*') is not an expression that Kant himself used; see Edel, '*Hypothesis* of the Basic Norm' (n.8 above), § I, at n.3.

[13] See 'Foreword' to *HP* (n.8 above), § I, at n.5; *LT*, Appendix I, at Supplementary Note 5 (pp. 132–4).

objective thought, to approach the level of objectivity attained by the Pure Theory of Law. For the Pure Theory liberated from absolutism not only the opposition between public and private law, but also the opposition between objective and subjective law, thereby throwing over a host of completely indefensible positions in legal theory.

(3) What actually distinguishes the Pure Theory of Law from the Cohennian legal philosophy is that Cohen, in this field, was not in a position to overcome the natural law theory, primarily because he was simply unfamiliar with the positive law and with what he correctly invoked as 'the fact of legal science'. The deciding factor here was that Cohen lacked the courage to draw from the Kantian transcendental philosophy ultimate conclusions in the field of social reality, that is, with reference to existing social systems: the existing state, the positive law, the prevailing morality. He was unable to forgo the assumption of a contentually constituted, materially determined *a priori*. With reference to those positive norms determining social life, he could not rest content with purely formal categories of *a priori* validity. For that would inevitably have led to ethical relativism, something that Cohen—exactly like Kant on this point—was not prepared to accept, if only because of his religious convictions. Thus, the Cohennian legal philosophy, like Stammler's, is a theory of natural law, not a theory of positive law, which alone is, in the ideal system of the Kantian philosophy, the proper counterpart to the theory of nature qua experience. It is true that Kant himself was not sufficiently consistent to extend the splendid idea of his transcendental philosophy also to cognition of the state, the law, and morality—that is, to social theory—and that here metaphysics survives, which he had completely surmounted in the field of cognition of nature. The appeal to Kant made by the Pure Theory of Law, then, can of course be contradicted by those who look upon his ethics as the true Kantian philosophy. It is easily shown that the ethics is utterly worthless, a claim that can be made even by those who look upon the Kantian transcendental philosophy as the greatest philosophical achievement of all.

(4) Although it is altogether correct that the theory of the basic norm finds a certain support in Mach's principle of economy of thought[14] and

---

[14] Ernst Mach (1838–1916), physicist and philosopher, known, *inter alia*, for his principle of economy of thought (*Denkökonomie*): 'the greatest possible part of . . . truth with the least possible labour, in the shortest possible time, and even with the least possible thought', *Populär-wissenschaftliche Vorlesungen*, 4th edn. (Leipzig: Johann Ambrosius Barth, 1910), 16, and Eng. edn., *Popular Scientific Lectures*, trans. Thomas J. McCormack (La Salle, Ill.: Open Court, 1943), 16. 'Economy of thought' served Mach as a rationale for simplicity in science and the philosophy of science; an example is his idea that '[a]ll physical knowledge can only mentally represent and anticipate compounds of those elements we call sensations'; Mach, *Die Mechanik in ihrer Entwicklung*, 6th edn. (Leipzig: F.A. Brockhaus, 1908), at 554, and Eng. edn., *The Science of Mechanics*, trans. Thomas J. McCormack (La Salle, Ill.: Open Court, 1960), at 611–12. Kelsen takes up Mach's principle

in Vaihinger's theory of fictions,[15] nevertheless, owing to various misunderstandings that have arisen from these references, I no longer wish to appeal to Mach and Vaihinger. What is essential is that the theory of the basic norm arises completely from the Method of *Hypothesis*[16] developed by Cohen. The basic norm is the answer to the question: What is the presupposition underlying the very possibility of interpreting material facts that are qualified as legal acts, that is, those acts by means of which norms are issued or applied? This is a question posed in the truest spirit of transcendental logic.

In the resolution of the concept of person, the Pure Theory of Law also distinguishes itself from Cohen's legal philosophy, which retains the concept because there are concealed behind it those very ethico-metaphysical postulates that Cohen is unwilling to forgo. The Pure Theory of Law, recognizing the concept of person as a substantive concept, as the hypostatization of ethico-political postulates (freedom and property, for example), resolved this concept in the spirit of Kantian philosophy, where all substance is to be reduced to function. Cassirer, one of the best of the Kantians—while he was a Kantian—has shown this in his fine book.[17]

With these remarks, my dear Dr. Treves, I have scarcely said anything new to you. Perhaps, however, they will serve to reinforce your own views on the essence of the Pure Theory of Law.

of economy of thought in *PS*, § 24 (at pp. 98–101). See also Leonidas Pitamic, 'Denkökonomische Voraussetzungen der Rechtswissenschaft', *ÖZöR*, 3 (1917–18), 339–67, repr. *33 Beiträge*, 297–322; on Pitamic, see Marijan Pavčnik, 'An den Grenzen der Reinen Rechtslehre', *ARSP*, 81 (1995), 26–40. Of course Kelsen is not suggesting that 'economy of thought' could serve as the '*only* determining principle' of the law; such a principle, qua basic norm, would undermine the normative character of the law; *PS* § 24 (p. 100) (Kelsen's emphasis). See also Alfred Verdross, *Die Einheit des rechtlichen Weltbildes auf Grundlage der Völkerrechtsverfassung* (Tübingen: J.C.B. Mohr, 1923), at 79.

    [15] Hans Vaihinger (1852–1933), Kant scholar and philosopher. Vaihinger's interpretation of Kant came to be known as the 'patchwork theory'. His best-known work in systematic philosophy, *Die Philosophie des Als-Ob* (Berlin: Reuther & Reichard, 1911), is available in English: *The Philosophy of 'As If'* (London: Kegan Paul, Trench, Trubner & Co., 1924), a translation, by C.K. Ogden, of Vaihinger's '5th and 6th edition'. Kelsen's paper 'Zur Theorie der juristischen Fiktionen', *Annalen der Philosophie*, 1 (1919), 630–58, repr. *WS II* 1215–41, is a lengthy review article on Vaihinger's treatise. In his late, sceptical phase (after 1960), Kelsen returns to Vaihinger; see, above all, *GTN*, ch. 59.i.D. (at p. 256), on the basic norm qua fiction.

    [16] On the Method of *Hypothesis*, see Edel, '*Hypothesis* of the Basic Norm' (n.8 above), at §§ II-III.

    [17] Ernst Cassirer (1874–1945), in his earlier years the leading second-generation figure in the Marburg School of Neo-Kantianism. Kelsen's reference to Cassirer's 'fine book' is to *Substanzbegriff und Funktionsbegriff* (Berlin: B. Cassirer, 1910, repr. Darmstadt: Wissenschaftliche Buchgesellschaft, 1990), discussed by Kelsen in 'Staat und Recht im Lichte der Erkenntniskritik', *ZöR*, 2 (1921), 453–510, at 464–7, repr. *SJSB* §§ 33–45, § 35 (at pp. 212–14), and repr. *WS I* 95–148, at 105–8. Cassirer's book is also available in English: *Substance and Function*, trans. William Curtis Swabey and Marie Collins Swabey (Chicago: Open Court, 1923, repr. New York: Dover, 1953).

As you may already have learned, I was ousted from my position at the University.[18] In the fall, I am going to the University Institute for International Studies in Geneva, where I have made a three-year commitment and will be lecturing mainly on the theory of international law. If you ever happen to be in Geneva, I should be very pleased indeed to be able to welcome you there.

With warmest good wishes, I remain,

Yours sincerely,
Hans Kelsen [signature]

---

[18] On the authority of the notorious 'Law for the Restoration of the Professional Civil Service', Kelsen was dismissed in April 1933 from his university post in Cologne; for details see Frank Golczewski, *Kölner Universitätslehrer und der Nationalsozialismus* (Cologne and Vienna: Böhlau, 1988), at 114–23.

9

A Neo-Kantian Theory of Legal Knowledge in Kelsen's Pure Theory of Law?*

STEFAN HAMMER

INTRODUCTION

Unlike other legal theorists of a positivist bent, Kelsen placed essential reliance on epistemological arguments in defending legal positivism. For him, strictly limiting legal science and legal reasoning to the positive law counted as a corollary of a sound theory of knowledge. And it is this particular feature of Kelsen's theory that is especially deserving of our attention, presenting as it does a pointed argument in reply to those who would reject the view that the jurist's focus be restricted to the positive law.

In reconsidering the limits that Kelsen's Pure Theory of Law imposes on what a jurist may justifiably say, we have to concentrate on the doctrine of the basic norm as the keystone of his theory of a legal science that has been purged of metaphysics and methodological syncretism. Taking as their point of departure Kelsen's epistemological claim and his critique of legal method, a number of recent writers in the field have considered once again the question of the neo-Kantian roots of his concept of the basic norm and, thus, of his legal theory in general.[1] Indeed, it is

---

* *Editors' note*: This paper first appeared in *Untersuchungen zur Reinen Rechtslehre*, ed. Stanley L. Paulson and Robert Walter (Vienna: Manz, 1986), 210–31, and was translated by the editors and the author, who has made extensive changes in the present version. Minor alterations in quotations from existing English-language translations of Kelsen's works have been made *sub silentio*.

[1] See e.g. Wolfgang Schild, *Die reinen Rechtslehren* (Vienna: Manz, 1975); Hermann Klenner, 'Kelsens Kant', *Revue internationale de philosophie*, 138 (1981), 539–46; Gerhard Luf, 'On the Transcendental Import of Kelsen's Basic Norm', in this volume, ch. 11; Horst Dreier, *Rechtslehre, Staatssoziologie und Demokratietheorie bei Hans Kelsen* (Baden-Baden: Nomos, 1986), 56–90; Stanley L. Paulson, 'The Neo-Kantian Dimension of Kelsen's Pure Theory of Law', *Oxford Journal of Legal Studies*, 12 (1992), 311–32. For older writings on the subject, see e.g. Gamschei Abraham Wielikowski, *Die Neukantianer in der Rechtsphilosophie* (Munich: Beck, 1914), 132–75; Gottfried Hohenauer, 'Der Neukantianismus und seine Grenzen als Gesellschafts- und Rechtsphilosophie', *Blätter für deutsche Philosophie*, 2 (1928–9), 302–36, at 327–36.

this perspective that fundamentally informs one's answers to the following central questions: To what extent, if at all, can the Kelsen of the Pure Theory of Law appeal to the *theory of knowledge* in making a case for legal science? And to what extent, then, do the methodological limitations he imposes on legal science turn on claims stemming from the theory of knowledge?

Enquiring into the role of neo-Kantianism in Kelsen's theory of the basic norm, I do not lay emphasis on matters historico-textual or exegetical, where the question would be the extent to which it can be shown, on the basis of Kelsen's writings, that in the course of developing his idea of the basic norm, he was in fact influenced by certain neo-Kantian authors. Rather, taking as my point of departure a systematic approach, I focus on whether the Kelsenian doctrine of the basic norm can be *reconstructed* in neo-Kantian terms as the central element in a transcendental theory of legal knowledge.[2] The first question, then, is whether the problematic that underlies Kelsen's doctrine of the basic norm can be regarded, structurally speaking, as epistemological in the neo-Kantian sense at all. I defend a positive answer to this question in section I of the paper. I then enquire, in section II, as to how far the concept of the basic norm actually satisfies the requirements of a neo-Kantian argument on behalf of the cognition of objects. Finally, in a closing remark, I revisit the question of the adequacy of an epistemological approach in making a case on behalf of legal science generally.

I. KELSEN'S NEO-KANTIANISM

The first of the questions posed above, that pertaining to the neo-Kantian character of Kelsen's own question about the foundations of legal science, can only be answered after one has determined what qualifies as 'neo-Kantian' in this context. The common approach taken by the various philosophers falling under the rubric of neo-Kantianism is perhaps best clarified—as already suggested by the label 'neo-Kantian'—in terms of their particular understanding of Kant, that is, the particular orientation reflected in their reception of Kant. For them, Kant served as

---

[2] On the distinction between historical and reconstructive enquiry in the present connection, see Stanley L. Paulson, 'Kelsen and the Marburg School: Reconstructive and Historical Perspectives', in *Prescriptive Formality and Normative Rationality in Modern Legal Systems*. Festschrift *for Robert Summers*, ed. Werner Krawietz et al. (Berlin: Duncker & Humblot, 1994), 481–94, at 485–94, showing that a significant historical influence of neo-Kantianism on Kelsen can be traced to the Heidelberg School of neo-Kantianism but not to the Marburg School. For an illuminating example of reconstructive enquiry, see Wolfgang Stegmüller, 'Towards a Rational Reconstruction of Kant's Metaphysics of Experience', in Stegmüller, *Collected Papers on Epistemology, Philosophy of Science and History of Philosophy*, 2 vols. (Dordrecht and Boston: Reidel, 1977), vol. I, 66–136.

a point of departure for a programme establishing the possibility of scientific cognition in all those forms that had been developed in the various specialized disciplines.[3] The natural sciences set the tone here, not only because progress in those fields was seen as dominant at the time, but also because this had clearly been the case in Kant's own day; as a result, Kant had also developed his theory of knowledge as a theory of empirical cognition in natural science, for which Newtonian physics was regarded as the paradigm.[4]

To the neo-Kantians, however, Kant's theoretical philosophy appears to be an answer to the question of the possibility of scientific cognition as such. This answer, although in the first instance confined to the natural sciences, also contains a programmatic function vis-à-vis the foundations of other fields of scientific enquiry. In other words, Kant's transcendental enquiry into the conditions for the possibility of empirical knowledge is now to be extended to fields outside the realm of cognition in natural science, namely, to such phenomena as history, culture, morals, and the law, in so far as these are themselves the subject-matter of various species of scientific cognition (historical enquiry, humanities, ethics, legal science.)[5]

---

[3] See e.g. Heinrich Rickert, *Kulturwissenschaft und Naturwissenschaft*, 4th & 5th edn. (Tübingen: J.C.B Mohr, 1921), at § 2 (pp. 6–12), appearing in English under the title *Science and History*, translated (from the 6th & 7th German edn.) by George Reisman (Princeton, N.J.: D. Van Nostrand, 1962), at § 2 (pp. 5–9). (The first edition appeared in 1898, the last, termed the '6th & 7th', in 1926.) See also Cohen, *LrE*, at 11–13 together with 38–45. For the programmatic point of departure of the neo-Kantians in Kant's theory of knowledge, see Hermann Cohen, *Kants Theorie der Erfahrung*, 1st edn. (Berlin: Ferd. Dümmler, 1871, repr. Hildesheim: Georg Olms, 1987). On the importance of this work for the neo-Kantian programme, see Paul Natorp, *Hermann Cohens philosophische Leistung unter dem Gesichtspunkte des Systems* (Berlin: Reuther & Reichard, 1918), at 4–11. For an application of Kant's 'Copernican turn' to the theory of knowledge itself, see Emil Lask, *Die Logik der Philosophie und die Kategorienlehre* (Tübingen: J.C.B. Mohr, 1911), at 23, repr. Lask, *Gesammelte Schriften*, 3 vols., ed. Eugen Herrigel (Tübingen: J.C.B. Mohr, 1923), vol. I, 1–282, at 25: 'Now that Kant has instructed us in the "Copernican turn" taken by the natural sciences, it is time to prove its worth over its entire range of application.'

I might add that I take up only the basic thrust of the neo-Kantian movement, with an eye to its use as the point of departure for a reconstruction of Kelsen's theory. I do not consider here the very real differences within *fin de siècle* neo-Kantianism, most prominently between the Marburg and Heidelberg schools.

[4] See Heinrich Rickert, *Der Gegenstand der Erkenntnis. Einführung in die Transzendentalphilosophie*, 4th & 5th edn. (Tübingen: J.C.B. Mohr, 1921), ch. V, § 5 (at pp. 355–6); Cohen, *LrE*, at 7–9.

[5] See Rickert (n.4 above), ch. V, § 5 (at pp. 356, 367); see also Rickert's discussion of the application of a 'theory of the cognition of experience' to the historical sciences, in Heinrich Rickert, *The Limits of Concept Formation in the Natural Sciences*, abridged translation by Guy Oakes (from the 5th edn. of *Die Grenzen der naturwissenschaftlichen Begriffsbildung*) (Cambridge: Cambridge UP, 1986), at ch. V, § 2 (pp. 195–207). (The first edition of *Grenzen* appeared in 1902; the fifth and last in 1929.) Compare Wilhelm Windelband's standpoint in 'History and Natural Science' (Strasburg lecture, 1894), trans. Guy Oakes, *History and Theory*, 19 (1980), 169–185. On the necessity of a philosophy of legal science as an empirical science, see Emil Lask, 'Legal Philosophy', in *The Legal Philosophies*

Thus, the question underlying Kant's theoretical philosophy, 'What can I know?',[6] is the pivotal point for the neo-Kantians' approach and, at the same time, for their reception of Kant. Their reading of this question in terms of a general theory of science makes it possible for them to pose the question in the normative disciplines as well. Thus, a consideration of morals and the law within the purview of the question 'What ought I to do?',[7] which flags the rubric of practical reason under which Kant himself had considered these fields, can at the same time be avoided. From the standpoint of the neo-Kantian philosopher, Kant's own perspective, that of practical reason, would count as 'unscientific' or metaphysical. In other words, a scientific enquiry into norms is a matter not of justifying them as binding imperatives but rather of analysing them qua objects of cognition.[8]

Seen in this way, the important role that Kant's theory of knowledge assigns to the conditions for the experiencing of objects corresponds to the anti-metaphysical orientation of scientific positivism[9] toward positively 'given' objects. In both perspectives, objective knowledge is confined to the field of empirical data. By establishing transcendental conditions for the individual fields of scientific enquiry, the neo-Kantian seeks both to avoid scientific positivism's crude identification of all empirical disciplines with natural science, and to establish the specific autonomy of the normative and cultural disciplines qua epistemologically grounded empirical sciences.[10]

---

of Lask, Radbruch, and Dabin, trans. Kurt Wilk (Cambridge, Mass.: Harvard UP, 1950), 1–42, esp. ch. II (23–40). (Lask's work was first published in 1905.) On the transformation of legal philosophy that is implied in Lask's (and Rickert's) work, see Alexander Somek, 'The Concept of Value and the Transformation of Legal Philosophy into Legal Theory: Lask's Silent Revolution', *Diritto e cultura*, 2 (1992), 161–92, at 180–8. Finally, see Hermann Cohen on ethics as an independent field of scientific enquiry and as a form of theoretical cognition, on legal science as 'the mathematics of the human sciences', and also on the human sciences themselves as 'the methodological analogue to the natural sciences' ('*das methodische Analogon der Naturwissenschaften*'), in Cohen, *ErW*, at 22, 48, 67, and 230 respectively.

   [6] Kant, *CPR* A805/B833.   [7] See n.6 above.

   [8] As Rickert writes: 'There is *no* science that, qua science, tells us what we *ought* to will or *ought* to do.' Heinrich Rickert, *Die Grenzen der naturwissenschaftlichen Begriffsbildung*, 3rd & 4th edn. (Tübingen: J.C.B. Mohr, 1921), ch. 5, § 5 (at p. 540), 5th edn. (1929), ch. 5, § 5 (at p. 708) (Rickert's emphasis). (This text does not appear in the abridged translation of Rickert's treatise; see at n.5 above.) See also Cohen, *ErW*, at 228–30. For Cohen's earlier attempt at a 'theoretical' interpretation of Kant's own ethical theory, see Hermann Cohen, *Kants Begründung der Ethik*, 2nd edn. (Berlin: Cassirer, 1910), at 12–18, 137–8. (The first edition appeared in 1887.) On the expansion of the Kantian concept of experience that is implied in Cohen's *Begründung*, see Natorp (n.3 above), at 11–15.

   [9] See generally Auguste Comte, *Cours de philosophie positive*, 6 vols. (Paris: Bachelier, 1830–42, repr. Paris: Hermann, 1975).

   [10] See in this connection Rickert's critique of Comte in *Limits* (n.5 above), ch. 5, § 1 (at pp. 181–7).

The characteristics sketched here of the neo-Kantian programme and the specific reception of Kant that is implied therein reappear in Kelsen's work on the problem of establishing legal science as an objective science. For Kelsen, too, the essence of Kant's transcendental theory of knowledge lies in establishing the possibility of a science—for Kant, natural science. Kelsen writes:

The question in which Kant frames his problems, 'How are synthetic *a priori* judgments possible?', means the same as the question, 'How is experience, as science, how is science, as cognition, how is cognition possible?'[11]

As far as legal science is concerned, Kelsen sees himself as having undertaken a task analogous to that of Hermann Cohen, who 'tried to apply the transcendental method beyond the field of natural science and to constitute ethics transcendentally'.[12] Thus, Kelsen for his part appeals to the transcendental method in the theory of legal science— where, as he points out, Kant himself had 'rejected the transcendental method'.[13]

Kant asks, 'How, without appealing to metaphysics, can the facts perceived by our senses be interpreted in the laws of nature, as these are formulated by natural science?' In the same way, the Pure Theory of Law asks, 'How, without appealing to meta-legal authorities like God or nature, can the subjective sense of certain material facts be interpreted as a system of objectively valid legal norms that are describable in legal propositions?'[14]

This question clearly reflects Kelsen's primary methodological interest, namely, how it is that the law can be viewed normatively, that is, in terms of 'ought' or *Sollen*, as utterly distinct from the empirical facts captured in terms of 'is' or *Sein*, without thereby falling prey to the familiar metaphysical or 'natural law' confusion of reading moral precepts into

---

[11] 'RWR' 128, repr. *RNK* 304. Thus, for Kelsen 'the relation to the fact of a science (*Faktum einer Wissenschaft*), a field of enquiry, is the be-all and end-all of the transcendental philosophy'. Here he can refer directly to Cohen: 'This reference to the fact of the sciences (*Faktum der Wissenschaften*) counts, for us, as that which is eternal in Kant's system.' Cohen, *ErW* 67.

[12] 'RWR' 128, repr. *RNK* 304.

[13] *Phil. Fds.* § 40 (at p. 445); see also Hans Kelsen, 'Letter to Treves', in this volume, ch. 8, at numbered para. 2. This, although 'Kant's transcendental philosophy is especially well-suited to provide a foundation for a positivistic theory of law and politics.' Thus, Kelsen's theory is not supported by Kant's ethics and legal philosophy; rather, 'the Pure Theory of Law takes its support solely from Kant's theory of knowledge.' Hans Kelsen, 'Allgemeine Rechtslehre im Lichte materialistischer Geschichtsauffassung', *Archiv für Sozialwissenschaft und Sozialpolitik*, 66 (1931), 449–521, at 463 n.14, repr. Kelsen, *Demokratie und Sozialismus*, ed. Norbert Leser (Vienna: Wiener Volksbuchhandlung, 1967), 69–136, at 82 n.14.

[14] *PTL* § 34(d) (p. 202) (trans. altered).

the positive law for the sake of normativity.[15] At the same time, it becomes clear that this fundamental methodological problem of 'purity' is in fact a genuine neo-Kantian problem[16] in that it turns on the question of *how* the Kantian theory of knowledge is to be applied in establishing the foundations of legal science: To what extent must the transcendental argument for legal science differ from Kant's transcendental argument for natural science in order to save the normativity of the law in the face of the facticity of nature?[17] And, on the other hand, to what extent must the transcendental argument for legal science resemble Kant's argument for natural science in order that norms as positively given—by analogy to the objects of nature given in experience—be the subject-matter of legal science qua 'empirical' science, thereby avoiding a lapse into metaphysics?[18]

In his efforts to resolve this problem, Kelsen does not adapt any of the theories of his neo-Kantian predecessors, whom he regards as having for the most part failed in their effort to apply Kantian transcendental philosophy to cultural and normative sciences generally, and to legal science in particular.[19] Rather, he claims for himself the first *successful* application of Kantian transcendental philosophy to legal theory. In other words, Kelsen's own 'original' neo-Kantianism consists in his independent effort to carry out a programme that he shares with the other neo-Kantians, namely, to apply the Kantian transcendental theory of

---

[15] *LT* § 11(b) (pp. 23–4); see also Hans Kelsen, 'Foreword' to Second Printing of *HP*, in this volume, ch. 1, at § I; Kelsen, 'Geschichtsauffassung' (n.13 above), at 462, repr. at 80–1. On the neo-Kantian preparation for this rejection of the 'imperative theory' of norms, see text at n.8 above.

Paulson has offered a precise reconstruction of this fundamental problem in the form of a basic jurisprudential antinomy, which the Pure Theory of Law attempts to resolve; see Paulson (n.1 above), at 313–22. For Kelsen's own brief statement on the antinomical character of the problem, see *Phil. Fds.* § 3 (at p. 394, carryover para.).

[16] On 'purity', see Cohen, *LrE*, at 5–9; Cohen, *ErW*, at 29, 99, *et passim*.

[17] This difference is something Kelsen uses especially in his case against Sander, who in Kelsen's view mechanically follows Kant's theory of experience. See 'RWR' 132–3 *et passim*, repr. *RNK* 308–9 *et passim*.

[18] In this connection Kelsen goes so far as to accept Sander's expression 'legal experience'. See Hans Kelsen, 'Staat und Recht im Lichte der Erkenntniskritik', *ZöR*, 2 (1921), 453–510, at 467, repr. *SJSB* §§ 33–45 (pp. 205–53), § 35 (at pp. 214–15), and repr. *WS I* 95–148, at 108. In the 'Letter to Treves' (n.13 above), at numbered para. 2, Kelsen writes: '[J]ust as Cohen understood Kant's *Critique of Pure Reason* as a theory of experience, so likewise I seek to apply the transcendental method to a theory of positive law. If one understands the "positive" law as "empirical" law, law in experience, or "legal experience", as Sander has termed it, then the Pure Theory of Law is indeed empiricistic—but empiricism in the same sense as Kant's transcendental philosophy. And just as Kant's transcendental philosophy energetically opposes all metaphysics, so the Pure Theory of Law takes aim at the natural law, which, in the field of social reality generally and the field of positive law in particular, corresponds exactly to metaphysics.'

[19] On Cohen's theory, see 'RWR', at 128, repr. *RNK*, at 304; 'Letter to Treves' (n.13 above), at numbered para. 3. On the theories of Rickert and Lask, see generally 'RWNKW'.

knowledge as a theory of science to fields outside the natural sciences. Thus, 'Kelsen's Kant'[20] is the Kant of the neo-Kantians, that is to say, the Kant of the *Critique of Pure Reason* and of the *Prolegomena*. The epistemological standards of Kant's critical philosophy must be the measure of Kelsen's effort to provide a 'logico-transcendental argument for the validity of the positive law'[21] if one wants to take his effort seriously rather than simply dismissing as a bluff the philosophico-transcendental label Kelsen attaches to his theory. Thus, in the course of my effort to reconstruct Kelsen's theory, I seek to follow his own arguments in so far as it is possible to formulate them in terms of a Kantian theory of legal knowledge.

II. THE BASIC NORM AND THE TRANSCENDENTAL THEORY OF KNOWLEDGE

Kelsen's initial attempt to answer the question of how a normative, as distinct from a causal, sphere of objects is epistemologically possible is carried out by means of an appeal to Kant's 'Copernican turn',[22] which Kelsen regards as the epistemological core of transcendental philosophy.[23] This is the insight, namely, that all knowledge of objects depends on formal, constitutive conditions of theoretical cognition. Thus, cognition is not determined by objects that exist independently of it; rather, objects exist only within—and are determined by— the transcendental forms (categories) of cognition itself. The categories of understanding, which constitute cognition qua experience of objects in nature, are now to be juxtaposed with the '"ought" qua transcendental category'[24]—a category different in kind from the Kantian categories but, like them, originating in reason—for constituting legal norms as objects of cognition.

Analogous to the Kantian argument, in which the experience of objects of nature is constituted through the categorial function of causality, Kelsen further specifies the category of the 'ought' as the function of imputation: Imputation makes it possible to connect one sensibly perceptible material fact to another, not causally, but normatively, thereby providing for a 'normative interpretation' of these material facts.

The connection of the punishment to the delict, of the execution of the lien to the material fact of an unlawful civil act, has normative import, not causal import.[25]

---

[20] See Klenner (n.1 above), at 542–3.

[21] Hans Kelsen, 'On the Basis of Legal Validity' (first published 1960), trans. Stanley L. Paulson, *American Journal of Jurisprudence*, 26 (1981), 178–89, at 189.

[22] Kant, *CPR* Bxv–xviii (Foreword to 2nd edn.).

[23] *Phil. Fds.* § 34 (pp. 434–5); see also 'Foreword' to *HP* (n.15 above), at § VI.

[24] *LT* § 11(b) (pp. 23–5).   [25] *LT* § 11(b) (p. 24).

According to the function of causality—operative in the 'law of nature' (*Naturgesetz*)—an object of cognition is necessarily the effect of some other object qua cause. Similarly, according to the function of imputation—operative in the 'law of normativity' (*Rechtsgesetz*)—an object of cognition is the legal consequence of some other object qua legal condition.[26]

This categorial determination of the sphere of the 'ought' qua embodiment of the cognition of objects determined by the function of imputation serves, now, as an initial specification of the concept of the basic norm. Thus, the basic norm as the 'basic scheme of the law of normativity' (*Grundform des Rechtsgesetzes*)[27] is the formal embodiment of all imputative functions having the structure, 'if *a* is, then *b* ought to be', that is, the basic form of the hypothetical 'ought'-judgment. By virtue of this hypothetical structure, as applied to the law in its entirety, the validity of any particular 'ought'-judgment is made dependent on the condition that it give expression to a legal norm emanating from a particular legal authority in a given legal system. The basic norm, then, initially specified simply as the specific hypothetical form of all legal cognition, means that legal cognition can only refer to the conditions for the *positive-law* 'ought', the 'ought' in which valid norms are given hypothetically, namely, under legally imposed conditions. By the same token, cognition of nature, according to Kant, can only refer to the conditions for possible experience, experience in which objects are given only as conditioned, namely, as causally conditioned. Thus, in keeping with Kant's critical theory of knowledge as Kelsen applies it to the law, the cognition of an absolute—that is, unconditioned—'ought' (for example, 'justice' in the tradition of natural law) is no less precluded from scientific cognition than is the cognition of absolute—that is, unconditioned—being (*Sein*) (the 'thing in itself'). For Kelsen, the anti-metaphysical character of the Pure Theory of Law is documented in this parallel.[28]

However, the hypothetical character of the basic norm qua imputative function is, for Kelsen, not exhausted in the fact that legal cognition can only be relative or hypothetical, that is, non-metaphysical in the sense described. Rather, in Kelsen's conception the basic norm itself acquires the status of a simply relative, hypothetical presupposition for legal cognition:[29] It is only for one who presupposes the basic norm that legal science, as objective legal cognition, acquires validity. Thus, the possibility

[26] *LT* § 11(b) (pp. 23–5); see also 'Foreword' to *HP* (n.15 above), at § I.

[27] *Phil. Fds.* § 12 (p. 406).

[28] For the foregoing, see *LT* § 8 (at pp. 16–17), § 11(b) (at p. 25); *Phil. Fds.* § 3 (at pp. 393–4, carryover para.), and at §§ 34–5 (pp. 434–7).

[29] See e.g. *Phil. Fds.* § 3 (at p. 395), § 4 (pp. 395–6), § 9 (at p. 401, 2d para.); *LT* § 16 (at p. 34) together with § 29 (p. 58).

of legal science as a normative discipline is understood, in the end, to be dependent on a position taken by the legal scientist, namely, his presupposing the basic norm.[30] This seems odd, however, in view of the conception of a transcendental presupposition for cognition in legal science, since the very concern of a transcendental theory of knowledge is to demonstrate *a priori* necessary and therefore universally valid presuppositions for the cognition of objects. It is a transcendental theory of knowledge, then, that is supposed to satisfy precisely those epistemological requirements that metaphysics does not satisfy, and it is the presuppositions in metaphysics that, in light of the transcendental philosophy, must appear to have only been assumed, for they are now revealed to be without foundation.

By contrast, Kelsen appears to think that it is precisely the hypothetical character of the basic norm—in so far as it is not demonstrable but can only be assumed—that serves to express its epistemologico-transcendental character in contradistinction to a metaphysico-transcendent character.[31] The transcendental nature of a Kantian theory of knowledge does not, however, overcome metaphysical pseudo-certainty simply by presenting indemonstrable presuppositions as, so to speak, problematic objects. Rather, conditions that are prior to any theoretical reference to objects must be shown, lest the possibility of such reference not be established at all. In the transcendental sense, then, presuppositions for the cognition of objects are not problematic assumptions about fictitious objects; they are necessary conditions for the possibility of making cognitive reference to objects, or—in the parlance of the neo-Kantians—conditions that constitute the 'value of truth' in the scientific cognition of objects.[32]

A. The Basic Norm qua Category of the 'Ought':
   An *a priori* Necessary Category or a merely Relative Category?

Kelsen appears compelled, however, to declare the presupposition of the basic norm to be a merely hypothetical assumption. Why so? Because, first of all, it seems as if the presupposition of the basic norm, in so far as it is understood to be nothing other than a normative category

---

[30] See also Hans Kelsen, 'Die Selbstbestimmung des Rechts', *Universitas*, 18 (1963), 1087–95, at 1094–5, repr. *WS II* 1445–53, at 1452–3.

[31] In this connection, Kelsen moves the transcendental theory of knowledge in the direction of positivistic relativism, thus taking leave of his own standard. As he puts it: 'Positivism and (epistemological) relativism belong together just as much as natural law theory and (metaphysical) absolutism.' *Phil. Fds.* § 4 (p. 396, last para.).

[32] See Rickert, *Limits* (n.5 above), ch. 5, § 4 (at p. 220). For a polemical statement against a relativistic curtailment of the theory of knowledge, see Rickert (n.4 above), at 264–71.

of imputation, could not be established as *a priori* necessary in a way that would correspond to the categorial presuppositions of empirical cognition in natural science. For Kant, the pure forms of intuition (*Anschauungsformen*) and categories of understanding, including causality, are necessary conditions for the possibility of any cognition of objects whatever, and this necessity lends to the cognition of objects an objective validity free of all metaphysics. Without these presuppositions, no concept at all of an empirical world would be possible. Since theoretical cognition, however, necessarily takes place in the form of cognition of a world of objects that are given in experience, the formal structures necessary for such empirical cognition must also be recognized as universally valid. And since natural science, for Kant, is simply systematic empirical cognition of the concrete world of objects *par excellence*, he is able to demonstrate that the transcendental conditions for *any* cognition of objects are at one and the same time necessary conditions for valid *natural science*.

Kelsen, by contrast, faces a major difficulty in showing that the category of the 'ought' or *Sollen* is indispensable as a necessary condition for legal cognition and, thus, for legal science. His category of imputation offers an additional interpretation of natural facts—coming, as it were, on top of their interpretation as causally determined objects. This 'second-order' standing of the category of imputation implies, *inter alia*, that the interpretation of natural facts provided by this category is not necessary to their existence as objects, but represents a merely optional interpretation.[33]

Kelsen, then, does not have at his disposal a concept of legal science that is as unproblematic as Kant's concept of natural science. Kelsen is not in a position to show precisely why legal science has validity *only* as normative science. Why would it not be possible to proceed, say, with a description and analysis of 'law qua officials' behaviour'? Thus, where the normativity of the law is concerned, Kelsen appears to be compelled from the outset to supplant transcendental necessity with an *assumed* premiss: *Whoever aspires* to treat the law as something normative can do so only if he presupposes a basic norm, understood simply in terms of a normative *category* of the hypothetical 'ought'-judgment. This premiss, however, can be established neither transcendentally nor in any other way; it remains a simple assumption.[34]

It might well be argued that Kelsen's position is plausible simply as that of a neo-Kantian who takes as his point of departure 'the fact of legal

---

[33] See *LT*, at §§ 1–5 (pp. 7–12), and at § 7 (pp. 13–14).

[34] See *LT* § 16 (at p. 34); see also references at nn.29–30. According to Paulson's reconstructive interpretation of this difficulty, Kelsen cannot establish a progressive argument for normative legal science, and therefore cannot compel the legal sceptic to accept his normative interpretation of the 'given' legal material. See Paulson (n.1 above), at 327–9, 331–2.

science',[35] where the required presuppositions are unquestioned and the task of bringing these presuppositions to light is all that remains.[36] Such an interpretation, however, would reduce Kelsen's effort, together with that of his neo-Kantian predecessors, to a mere analysis of scientific method, with the result that their common claim to establishing the epistemological *validity* of scientific knowledge, as it is given in the various sciences, is in effect dismissed.

It is precisely in light of Kelsen's neo-Kantian statement of the problem, then, that one comes to see the epistemological task of demonstrating *a priori* necessary conditions for legal science as the actual task of a transcendental theory of law. For Kelsen, all that remains here is to point out that in every methodological variation at work in legal science—in so far as legal science still occupies itself with what is ordinarily taken to be 'law'—a normative category qua presupposition must necessarily be in effect; without it, the law could not be identified or delimited as a field of enquiry at all. This counts as a presupposition, too, for treating the normativity of the law as, say, simply a socio-psychological mechanism.[37] In any case, this is Kelsen's argument against the various 'two-sides' theories of the state: Lacking a normative dimension, the state as such—never mind that it may serve as the subject-matter of enquiry in the social sciences—could scarcely be distinguished from other empirico-factual events or phenomena.[38]

Now this is what can be regarded as Kelsen's neo-Kantian argument from the fact of the legal sciences, taken as the totality of disciplines that have as their common subject-matter a given material that is identified as 'legal': In all their methodological variations, they somehow presuppose the category of imputation as a necessary condition, even if it plays only a concealed or subordinate role in what is consciously done in the course of the specific enquiry at hand. In this more modest sense, then, the category of the 'ought' is now, indeed, the necessary condition for *all legal science*.[39] Thus, the claim could be made that the imputative

[35] See 'Letter to Treves' (n.13 above), at numbered para. 3; see also *LT* § 16 (at pp. 34–5), and n.11 above.

[36] See *LT* § 29 (p. 58). This corresponds to Paulson's suggestion that Kelsen only intended to establish an argument that could be reconstructed as the regressive version of a transcendental argument, which, then, is carried out by its various neo-Kantian proponents independently of the Kantian progressive version of the argument. See Paulson (n.1 above), at 322–32. Yet—a point Paulson underscores, ibid. 331—'this independent use of the regressive version of the argument . . . robs it of its transcendental force'.

[37] Kelsen's reflections in *LT* §16 (at p. 33) seem to point in this direction. In any case, Rickert (see n.10 above) employs a similar argument against Auguste Comte's scientific positivism of history.

[38] See *ASL* § 5(d) (at pp. 19–20). For greater detail, see *SJSB*, at §§ 18–21, 27 (pp. 105–32, 156–70).

[39] To put it in Paulson's reconstructive terms (see n.34 above), the legal sceptic would be 'caught' by that argument once he agreed to an identification of any given material as

function of the 'ought' is, as Kelsen says, a 'transcendental' or 'relative *a priori* category'.[40] In light of his own neo-Kantian statement of the task at hand, Kelsen at this point would not yet be compelled to yield altogether, declaring the category of the 'ought' to be a mere 'assumption'— that is, a decision—rather than showing it to be epistemologically necessary. If there still remains at least a chance of meeting the neo-Kantian transcendental requirements that are self-imposed on a theory of legal science, where then does the real reason lie for the fact that in the end Kelsen must nevertheless abandon the status of the basic norm qua transcendental, necessary condition for legal science?

B. The Basic Norm qua Hypothetical 'Thing in Itself'?

In answering this question, it is well to begin by recalling that the basic norm is intended to function as the embodiment of the conditions for a science of the positive law.[41] To be sure, as a simple normative category of imputation alone, the basic norm can be regarded—in the sense characterized above—as a *necessary* condition for legal science, but since it is not yet *sufficient* for the determination of an *object of cognition* in legal science, it remains a mere category and is, for now, 'empty'. An additional difficulty arises here for a theory of legal knowledge by contrast to a theory of empirical knowledge of objects in the natural sciences. Kelsen himself sets out the problem in thematic terms:

How are norms *given*, that is, given to cognition? How are they an object of cognition, and thus a possible object about which statements can be made that have the character of judgments? Obviously norms are not given in the same way as sensibly perceptible facts, which *exist*.[42]

For if norms were 'given' in the same way as 'sensibly perceptible facts', if they 'existed', they would not be norms, and legal science would not be a normative science. Thus, the Kantian theory of experience in the natural sciences cannot easily be transferred over in its schematic entirety to legal science, as Fritz Sander[43]—at least in Kelsen's eyes—attempted to do. And for that reason, according to Kelsen, Sander's concept of legal experience is to be handled gingerly.[44] But how, on the other hand, can the positivistic, non-metaphysical character of legal science nevertheless

---

'legal', while still denying the necessity of a normative method for the analysis of such material.

[40] *LT* § 11(b) (pp. 23, 24–5 respectively).

[41] See *Phil. Fds.* § 11 (at pp. 405–6, carryover para.), § 12 (at pp. 406–7, carryover para.); see also *LT*, at § 29 (p. 58).

[42] Kelsen (n.21 above), 180.

[43] See, in particular, Fritz Sander, *Rechtsdogmatik oder Theorie der Rechtserfahrung?* (Vienna and Leipzig: Franz Deuticke, 1921), repr. *RNK* 115–278.

[44] See nn.17–18 above.

be maintained? How can a reference to 'given facts' be preserved in its 'material'?[45] Certain facts are supposed to be normatively interpreted in legal science, and legal norms are supposed to be cognized as the meaning of these facts. The question, then, of just what these facts are, calling for this normative interpretation by means of the category of imputation, is properly the question of the subject-matter of legal science. In other words, the positive law that has already been presupposed as the subject-matter to which the category of imputation is to be applied[46] has yet to be established as the object of legal cognition. If the basic norm is to fulfil its function of constituting object qua subject-matter, it must be enriched with additional determining elements toward that end. And in determining the subject-matter of legal science, the basic norm must distinguish it from the subject-matter of other normative cognition, for example, from that of theology, of ethics, reaching all the way to grammar.[47]

What are the criteria, then, that the basic norm sets out in order to identify those facts that are to be normatively interpreted by legal science (namely, as legal norms)? Kelsen writes:

There are two. The one is that the law must be *issued, set down (ius positivum)*, by means of acts qualified in a certain way. The other is that the law must be *efficacious* to a certain degree.[48]

If the concept of the basic norm is thus enriched with these determinants (including the further qualification of those acts whereby the law is issued),[49] the basic norm makes it possible to identify the facts that are to be interpreted as norms of the positive law, those facts, namely, that are acts of will directed to the behaviour of other human beings, acts of will that exhibit the form of the hypothetical 'ought'-judgment and are for the most part efficacious. The implications of such a refinement of the basic norm must now be measured against the requirements of the programme underlying the basic norm, that for establishing an epistemologico-transcendental foundation for legal science.

By means of the basic norm, the category of imputation can now be applied to acts of will that themselves have the form of the hypothetical 'ought'-judgment.[50] And this application makes it possible to see that the normative import of these acts lies in their creating, in turn, a legal

[45] Hans Kelsen, 'Was ist juristischer Positivismus?', *Juristen-Zeitung*, 20 (1965), 465–9, at 465, repr. *WS I* 941–53, at 942.

[46] See text at nn.27–8 and 38–9 above.

[47] On this theme, see Wolfgang Schild, 'Die zwei Systeme der Reinen Rechtslehre', *Wiener Jahrbuch für Philosophie*, 4 (1971), 150–94, at 159 (with further references).

[48] Kelsen (n.45 above), 465, repr. *WS I* 942 (Kelsen's emphasis).

[49] See *Phil. Fds.*, at §§ 11–12 (pp. 404–7).

[50] See *Phil. Fds.* § 11 (at p. 404), § 12 (at p. 406, first para.).

'ought'-linkage of material facts. Thus, the validity of a particular norm that creates such a legal 'ought'-linkage can appear as the legal consequence that a higher-level norm has attached to an act of will that has for its part the form of a hypothetical 'ought'-judgment and has been issued in a certain way. The structure of the empowerment is thereby constituted, with the result that what was initially, in the hypothetical 'ought'-judgment, a two-party imputative relation can now be expanded to an indefinitely extensible series of empowerments.[51] Thus, the function of imputation can serve as the interpretative schema of a chain of delegation that can in principle be infinitely extended, as it were, backwards:[52] For every norm, one can enquire into its delegating authority, just as for every empirical object in the natural sciences, one can enquire into its cause.

To be sure, these two types of regress are essentially different from one another, and the difference is traceable to the respective ways in which 'is' and 'ought', *Sein* and *Sollen*, are given as objects of scientific cognition. According to the Kantian theory of experience in the natural sciences, every empirically given object has as its condition a cause that, like the object itself, is both necessarily conditioned and empirical. Although it need not be known in concrete terms, the cause is in any case *a priori* accessible to empirical enquiry. Without its being conditioned empirically, the object itself cannot be given empirically: The empirical condition, through the *a priori* category of causality, is inherent in the concept of the object. The categorial conditions for understanding alone are sufficient to constitute the 'world of being' as the embodiment of knowable objects, enabling Kant to speak of objectively valid empirical cognition without requiring that chains of causal conditions be empirically concluded. Kant develops this point in his well-known doctrine of the antinomies of pure reason, where he examines the status and function of concepts such as freedom and absolute being (the 'transcendental ideas') within a transcendental theory of knowledge.[53] The former of these concepts designates the representation of the totality of a series of causes, under natural laws, to any *single* given empirical event, namely, by way of a first cause, a cause that is not itself caused ('causality from freedom'); the latter concept designates the representation of the totality of the conditions for *all* the events in the world, that is, the representation of the necessity (noncontingency) of the world of being *in its entirety*. Now these postulates, namely, of the totality and unconditionality of being, stand in contradiction to the categorial (conditioned by

---

[51] See *LT* § 31(a) (at pp. 63–4); see also *Phil. Fds.* § 8 (at pp. 399–400, carryover para.).

[52] See *Phil. Fds.* § 4 (at pp. 395–6, carryover para.); *LT* § 28 (at p. 57).

[53] On this and on what follows, see Kant, *CPR*, at A405–565/B432–593, esp. A444–61/B472–90; Kant, *Pro.*, at §§ 51–4, 56.

understanding) impossibility of concluding a causal regress empirically. According to Kant, however, this is revealed as merely an apparent contradiction. It is thus revealed, specifically, as soon as one comes to see that these ideas of pure reason, as concepts of unconditioned being (the 'thing in itself'), can never be successfully applied in experience; it is only conditioned phenomena—and never unconditioned being—that can be the object of empirical cognition. The concept of an empirical absoluteness and totality of being is therefore a false ('transcendent') use of these transcendental ideas. By contrast, these ideas of unconditionality and totality take on a transcendental-regulative function within a critical theory of knowledge, a function that goes beyond any empirically conditioned cognition of objects, only to direct any claim of cognition of objects onto the path of experience that cannot be brought to conclusion.[54] In the end, this lends itself to an interpretation akin to modern philosophy of science, according to which hypotheses must always remain subject to possible empirical falsification and thus can never be claimed to have passed a test of definitive empirical verification.[55]

The import, in Kant, of the regulative ideas of reason requires no further explication here; Kelsen's regress of empowerment in the field of normative cognition has to be represented, from the beginning, in an altogether different way. The material of legal cognition was first acquired here through a 'selection' of certain material facts from a vast reservoir of empirical material. With that, however, it is not necessary that material facts in every concrete empirical situation be found that correspond to the *criteria* of that selection. That is to say, it is by no means certain that for each and every material fact that can be interpreted as a positive-law norm there stands—in the appropriate relation to that material fact—a further material fact that can be interpreted as the empowering norm. Rather, it is probable that in every normative regress of empowering norms, one will sooner or later stumble onto a norm that cannot—even upon the closest examination of the material in question, the prospective material facts—be traced back to a material fact that, reflecting the criteria sketched above, could be interpreted as the conditioning norm. This is Kelsen's problem of the 'historically first constitution'.[56] Since the categorial presupposition of a validity condition necessary for every 'normative object' cannot simply be suspended for this phenomenon, the validity condition for such a historically first constitution is, as Kelsen writes, to be presupposed if the historically first

[54] See generally Kant, *CPR*, at A508–17/B536–45; Kant, *Pro.*, at §§ 56–7.
[55] For a reconstruction, in terms of the problem of empirical verification, of the role that Kant attributes to experience, see Stegmüller (n.2 above), at 84–93, 114–21.
[56] See e.g. *Phil. Fds.*, at § 4 (pp. 395–6); *LT* § 28 (at p. 57).

constitution and the entire normative system based on it are to be maintained as the subject-matter of legal science.

The basic norm has to assume this function, too, in so far as it is supposed to constitute the cognitive object of legal science. The basic norm does this, in the formulation in the *Introduction to the Problems of Legal Theory*, as follows:

Coercion is to be applied under certain conditions and in a certain way, namely, as determined by the framers of the first constitution or by the authorities to whom they have delegated appropriate powers . . .[57]

Together with the definition of the 'historically first constitution' as the 'material fact creating that system to which actual behaviour (of the human beings addressed by the system) corresponds to the system to a certain degree',[58] the basic norm contains, at least in embryo, all the elements pertaining to the conditions for a science of the positive law.

As the validity condition for the historically first constitution, the basic norm not only delimits the field in which objects related to one another in the way familiar from the imputation connection can be cognized as obligatory (valid). With that, the basic norm also constitutes the totality of delegation conditions for any single norm cognized as valid, just as it constitutes generally the totality of the conditions for the entire normative sphere of legal science; it is the basis of the validity of *all* norms of a legal system. In these two totality-functions, the basic norm, when seen in light of the Kantian critical theory of knowledge, undergoes a portentous shift in the direction of a transcendent, metaphysical employment of the ideas of reason (as sketched above, namely, unconditionality and absolute essence). Kelsen, however, must conceive of the basic norm as an unconditioned validity condition in these two functions, for he cannot otherwise focus on any object of legal science at all. Structurally speaking, the concept of an absolute totality of the regress of conditions is, therefore, thoroughly *constitutive* vis-à-vis Kelsen's world of the normative, in contrast to the regulative function of this concept in Kant's world of being. In a word: The category of the 'ought' or *Sollen* remains altogether empty, unless a 'thing in itself' qua object is given to it. And that is what distinguishes it from the category of the empirical 'is' or *Sein*.

Therein lies the actual reason Kelsen must extol so greatly the merely hypothetico-relative status of the basic norm. Since, for the constituting of the cognitive object 'law', the basic norm must be more than a merely

---

[57] *LT* § 28 (at p. 57); see also *Phil. Fds.* § 11 (at pp. 405–6, carryover para.).
[58] *LT* § 30(a) (at p. 59).

transcendental category of imputation, namely an *unconditioned valid-ity condition*, it thereby assumes the character of a normative 'thing in itself', which as such could be claimed to be *apodictic* only in the face of its metaphysical character. It must—in any case in this function—be 'downgraded' from the position of cognitive necessity to the position of a merely assumed premiss: One who wishes to conduct legal science as a science of valid norms must then assume their validity. Beyond a mere tautology, this argument—carried out in detail—may serve as a struc-tural clarification of what those engaged in legal science have tradition-ally done. As an argument for a cognitive, logico-transcendental case on behalf of legal science, it is, however, unquestionably a failure. For the basic norm, if it is meant to be anything more than an arbitrary assump-tion, takes on a metaphysical character, a point conceded by Kelsen him-self when he speaks of it as being akin to a 'norm of natural law'.[59] But contrary to what Kelsen would have us believe, the basic norm does not share this metaphysical character with the 'categories of transcendental philosophy'.[60] While the transcendental categories make possible a nat-ural world of objects that are given in experience, the basic norm actually has to create as such the objects of the normative world, objects that are otherwise not given in 'legal experience' at all. And thus, contrary to hypotheses in natural science, hypotheses in legal science do not, in the end, lend themselves to an empirical test of falsification. With that, how-ever, the metaphysical character of the entire 'cognitive' object of the Pure Theory of Law may be regarded as settled. In the Kantian terms of theoretical reason, the law qua object of legal science thus turns out to be a mere 'object of imagination' (*Gedankending*).[61]

CONCLUDING REMARK

A reconstruction of Kelsen's concept of the basic norm as the keystone of a transcendental theory of legal cognition, modelled after Kant's theory of knowledge, has proven, then, to be impossible. Contrary to the tran-scendental categories and regulative ideas in Kant's theory of experi-ence, the basic norm must also generate the material of normative experience through a selection of those types of material facts that are to be singled out as 'legal material'. No such specific selection, however, can ever be established as *a priori* necessary, that is to say, as the only

[59] *Phil. Fds.* § 9 (p. 401), and see § 36 (at p. 437), where Kelsen speaks of 'the minimum . . . of natural law' in his theory.
[60] See *Phil. Fds.* § 36 (at pp. 437–8).
[61] See Kant, *CPR*, at A565–6/B593–4, in relation to A292/B348. But see *Phil. Fds.* § 36 (at p. 438n.).

selection that would make legal science possible.[62] A delimitation of positive law as the 'empirical' object of legal cognition is thus left without any epistemological foundation.

Is there any other option for establishing the positive law as the subject-matter of legal science, and at the same time as the basis of reference for objective legal reasoning? So long as the law is thereby recognized as having normative import, it is, I believe, altogether misleading to conceive of the 'positivity' of the law in terms of its 'being given in experience', and, thus, it is also misleading to conceive of legal positivism as an empirical science. One might then proceed along altogether different lines. In particular, Kant's own approach suggests that we conceive of the law, not least of all the positivity of the law, as a matter not of theoretical reason but of practical reason.[63] In establishing and delimiting what both legal science and legal practice are to recognize as the positive law, one would then have to proceed on the basis of arguments moral in nature, not epistemological.[64] In any case, as a fundamental alternative a Kantian approach along these lines has not been ruled out by anything in Kelsen's theory.

[62] To take up Paulson's reconstructive terms one more time, the legal sceptic, even if he should acquiesce to the necessity of the category of imputation for legal science (see n.39 above), need not accept any particular set of selection criteria for generating the relevant 'legal material'.

[63] Compare Immanuel Kant, *The Metaphysics of Morals*, trans. Mary Gregor (Cambridge: Cambridge UP, 1991), 'Introduction to the Metaphysics of Morals', at 50–1 [Akademie edn., at 224], and 'Introduction to the Doctrine of Right', at § B, 55–6 [Akademie edn., at 230]. (The first part of Kant's *Metaphysik der Sitten*, namely the *Rechtslehre*, was first published in 1797.)

[64] For details see Luf, 'Transcendental Import' (n.1 above).

10

The *Hypothesis* of the Basic Norm: Hans Kelsen and Hermann Cohen*

GEERT EDEL

INTRODUCTION

To make the effort to determine more precisely the specifically neo-Kantian dimension of Hans Kelsen's Pure Theory of Law is to be confronted with a great maze of problems. They stem in part from the complex theoretical constellation in question and in part from the undifferentiated preconceptions, as sweeping as they are mistaken, that still surround both Kelsen's legal theory itself as well as so-called neo-Kantianism. If, for example, Kelsen's legal positivism is precipitately reduced to a mindless legal empiricism, then there is no longer any way at all to tell how it is supposed to have acquired Kantian—that is, idealistic and transcendental—elements. And if, on the other hand, something termed neo-Kantianism is identified straightaway with the philosophy of the 'historical' Kant, then from the outset precisely those theoretical components are filtered out that underlie the neo-Kantian reformulation and further development of Kant's philosophy, but that, in this form, are nowhere to be found in Kant's own work.

In view of this compendium of problems, I am limiting myself in the present enquiry to a very narrowly defined goal. My aim is not to set out comprehensively the neo-Kantian dimension of Kelsen's thought as a whole; rather, it is limited to the question of Kelsen's relation to Hermann Cohen, the founder of and leading figure in the Marburg School of Neo-Kantianism. Specifically, the enquiry proceeds in three

* *Editors' note*: Geert Edel's essay, written especially for this volume, was translated by the editors, working in close collaboration with Edel. Throughout the essay, the expression 'Hypothesis', used as the transliteration of the Greek 'ñ ﬁ ÂÛÈ~', appears in italics and is distinguished in this way from the familiar term 'hypothesis' in modern natural science; Edel introduces and explains the distinction in § II. For the sake of uniformity, titles of German-language works referred to by Edel appear in German in the text.

steps. First of all, I shall briefly consider the most important of Kelsen's own express statements of a connection between his legal theory and the philosophy of Cohen. Second, I shall argue that, in terms of substance, Cohen's interpretations of Kant as well as his own 'System of Philosophy' actually differ profoundly from the historical Kant, thus showing the key theorem of Cohen's system to be not Kantian in origin but Platonic. Third and last, I shall consider the centrepiece of Kelsen's legal theory, the doctrine of the basic norm. Here I aim to show that Kelsen's solution to the problem of establishing legal validity by appeal to the basic norm represents a direct application of the key theorem of Cohen's system, and that this theorem offers one plausible possibility—albeit not the only one—for resolving the problem of validity on the basis of a concept of law that refers neither to natural law nor to any metajuridical source.

I. KELSEN ON COHEN

If one takes as one's point of departure Kelsen's own statements on the matter, there can be no doubt whatever that he was greatly influenced by Kantian or, as the case may be, neo-Kantian thought. To make this claim is not to minimize, let alone to deny altogether, either the independent originality of Kelsen's work in legal theory or the effect of other influences on him, in particular the definitive influence of the tradition in German public law theory during the period from Carl Friedrich von Gerber to Georg Jellinek. Only by impartially examining the sources and analysing the substance of the theories in question can one make a balanced judgment about the extent and limits of the influences on Kelsen.

The most prominent of Kelsen's own statements on the putative influence of Cohen has been quoted again and again in the literature. It is found in the 'Foreword' to the Second Printing, in 1923, of Kelsen's *Main Problems in the Theory of Public Law* (*Hauptprobleme der Staatsrechtslehre*), which was originally published in 1911. Since the passage in question, contrary to first impressions, is far from unambiguous, I quote it here in full. Kelsen writes:

It was by way of Hermann Cohen's interpretation of Kant, in particular Cohen's *Ethics of Pure Will* (*Ethik des reinen Willens*), that I arrived at the definitive epistemological point of view from which alone the correct employment of the concepts of law and of state was possible. In 1912 in the *Kantstudien*, a review of *Main Problems* appeared in which my book was recognized as an attempt to apply the transcendental method to legal science, and this brought to my attention the wide-ranging parallels that existed between my concept of legal will and Cohen's views, which at that time were not known to me. I came to appreciate as the consequence of Cohen's basic epistemological position—according to which the epistemic orientation determines its object, and the epistemic object is generated logically from an origin (*Ursprung*)—that the state, in so far as it is the object of legal cognition, can only be law, for to cognize something legally or to understand something juridically means nothing other than to understand it as law.[1]

If one carefully examines this declaration of Kelsen's, several ambiguities are immediately apparent, of which the most important has led on occasion to confusion in the literature. Kelsen quite clearly cannot have arrived by way of Cohen at the 'definitive epistemological point of view' for the 'correct employment' of the concepts of law and of state if it is the case that the parallels he mentions between his views and Cohen's were not known to him at all in 1911, at the time he completed the *Hauptprobleme*, but were only brought to his attention thereafter. Seen in this light, Kelsen's declaration appears to offer far more support for his own originality and independence than for Cohen's influence on him. It would nevertheless be a mistake to dismiss the question of Cohen's influence on Kelsen as having been thereby answered *in toto* in the negative. For Kelsen's express and altogether unmistakable profession of allegiance to Cohen's 'basic epistemological position' remains completely untouched by the fact that the parallels he mentions between his own concept of will and Cohen's were unknown to him at the time he wrote the *Hauptprobleme*. Thanks to the 1912 review, Kelsen began in his writings to take account of parallels between his views and Cohen's. As for these later works, in particular as for the works from his later, classical phase, Kelsen's declaration here will have to be understood rather in terms of a heuristic maxim for determining how Cohen's basic epistemological position, or Kelsen's profession of belief in Cohen's position, finds expression in the later works.

Scarcely less central than this first point are the second and third ambiguities contained in Kelsen's declaration. Kelsen claims to have acquired the 'definitive epistemological point of view' for the 'correct employment' of the concepts of law and of state from Cohen's interpretation of Kant, referring, 'in particular', to Cohen's *Ethik des reinen Willens*.[2] This work, however, is in no way, shape, or form an interpretation of Kant; rather, it is the second part of Cohen's own System of Philosophy, which in various respects is distinctly unkantian. What is more, while Cohen's specifically epistemological point of view—precisely that view for which he himself coins the title 'transcendental method'[3]—is indeed developed in his

---

[1] Hans Kelsen, 'Foreword' to Second Printing of *HP*, in this volume, ch. 1, § VI. In the text following the quotation, Kelsen indicates that he was also influenced by Hans Vaihinger's analysis of personifying fictions.

[2] Cohen, *ErW* (for bibliographical data, see the Table of Abbreviations).

[3] The expression 'transcendental method' occurs in Kant's own works only sporadically—and only in his handwritten, unpublished writings; the expression does not appear at all in his published writings.

interpretations of Kant, it is *not* to be found in the *Ethik des reinen Willens*. The latter does contain observations that one might designate in the broadest sense as 'epistemological', but only where Cohen is explicating its relation to the *Logik der reinen Erkenntnis*,[4] which forms the first part of his System of Philosophy. The epistemological position, however, that serves as the point of departure for the *Logik der reinen Erkenntnis* and, thus, for the Cohennian System itself as a whole is not to be identified straightaway with the transcendental method. This method proceeds from 'science qua fact' and raises the question as to the conditions for the possibility of science, whereas the logical generation of the epistemic object from an origin, carried out by the Cohennian logic, is a specific, further development of the transcendental method. More precisely, it is a specific way of answering the question as to the conditions for possibility—a way that is merely sketched and alluded to in Cohen's interpretations of Kant, where it is completely absent in its elaborated form. These two methods or, one might well say, epistemological positions of Cohen's are related to each other, to be sure, but a closer look reveals that they are also to be distinguished from each other. To which of them does Kelsen profess allegiance? Or ought one to assume instead that he perhaps does not maintain as sharp a distinction between them as envisaged here, and that his allegiance, therefore, is to both?

One comes a good bit closer to an answer here by turning to a second statement of Kelsen's expressly professing his allegiance to Cohen's philosophy, but now at the same time distinguishing his own views from Cohen's. I have in mind Kelsen's letter of 3 August 1933 to Renato Treves.[5] In the first of four numbered paragraphs, Kelsen sharply distinguishes his own views from those found in Paul Laband's public law theory; in the three remaining paragraphs, Kelsen considers Cohen's views in some detail, and for that reason excerpts from the essential claims in those paragraphs are quoted here. First of all, Kelsen restates his allegiance to Cohen's interpretation of Kant:

(2) It is altogether correct that the philosophical foundation of the Pure Theory of Law is the Kantian philosophy, in particular the Kantian philosophy *in the interpretation* that it has undergone *through Cohen*. A point of special significance is that just as Cohen understood Kant's *Critique of Pure Reason* (*Kritik der reinen Vernunft*) as a theory of experience, so likewise I seek to apply the transcendental method to a theory of positive law.[6]

---

[4] Cohen, *LrE* (for bibliographical data, see the Table of Abbreviations).
[5] Hans Kelsen, 'Letter to Treves', in this volume, ch. 8.
[6] 'Letter to Treves' (n.5 above), numbered para. 2 (emphasis by G.E.).

Here Kelsen clearly states that the philosophical foundation of the Pure Theory of Law is to be sought not in Kant himself, but in Cohen—not, then, in the *Kritik der reinen Vernunft*, but in Cohen's interpretation of that work, entitled *Kants Theorie der Erfahrung*.[7] Thus, where Kelsen refers to Kant, he is referring for the most part not to the historical Kant but to the picture of Kant that Cohen had developed in his book.[8] (The differences between Kant's critique of reason and Cohen's theory of experience will be discussed below.)

No less instructive than this connection between the two, however, is the distinction Kelsen makes between his views and Cohen's.

(3) What actually *distinguishes* the Pure Theory of Law from the Cohennian legal philosophy is that Cohen, in this field, was not in a position to *overcome the natural law theory*, . . . that Cohen lacked the courage to draw from the Kantian transcendental philosophy ultimate conclusions . . . with reference to . . . the existing state, the positive law, the prevailing morality. He was unable to forgo the assumption of a *contentually constituted, materially determined a priori*. With reference to those positive norms determining social life, he could not rest content with purely formal categories of *a priori* validity. For that would inevitably have led to ethical relativism, something that Cohen . . . exactly like Kant . . . was not prepared to accept . . .[9]

The limits of the Cohennian influence on Kelsen are unambiguously drawn here. When Kelsen charges that Cohen, in the field of legal philosophy, failed to overcome natural law theory and held fast to a contentual *a priori*, he strikes first of all at Cohen's specifically jurisprudential observations in the *Ethik des reinen Willens*. These observations, then, obviously do not account for Cohen's influence on Kelsen. This is true quite apart from the fact that there are nevertheless certain contentual parallels between Cohen and Kelsen (like that already mentioned with reference to the concept of will). And it is also true apart from whether or not Kelsen's charge that Cohen held fast to natural law is correct from Cohen's own perspective.[10] If, however, one considers that this charge also applies to Kant, that in the text following the cited passage Kelsen charges not only Cohen but also Kant with having failed fully to

---

[7] Hermann Cohen, *Kants Theorie der Erfahrung*, 1st edn. (hereafter '*TE 1*'), (Berlin: Ferd. Dümmler, 1871), repr. as vol. 1.3 in Cohen, *Werke* (Hildesheim: Georg Olms, 1987); Cohen, *Kants Theorie der Erfahrung*, 2nd edn. (hereafter '*TE 2*'), (Berlin: Ferd. Dümmler, 1885); Cohen, *Kants Theorie der Erfahrung*, 3rd edn. (hereafter '*TE 3*'), (Berlin: Bruno Cassirer: 1918), repr. as vol. 1.1 in Cohen, *Werke* (Hildesheim: Georg Olms, 1987).

[8] See, in particular, 'RWR', at 127–8, repr. *RNK*, at 303–4.

[9] 'Letter to Treves' (n.5 above), numbered para. 3 (emphasis by G.E.).

[10] What is of significance in this connection is solely the fact that Kelsen understood Cohen in this way. Whether Cohen, on the basis of what little he says in the *Ethik des reinen Willens* about natural law, can in fact be regarded as a natural law theorist is a question that need not be taken up here.

follow through on the application of the basic idea of the transcendental philosophy 'to cognition of the state, the law, and morality', and that Kelsen even goes so far as to characterize Kantian ethics as 'utterly worthless',[11] then the conclusion is inescapable: Kelsen's critique of the *contentual a priori* is to be evaluated not only as a means of distinguishing his own position from Cohen's specifically juridico-philosophical observations, but also as speaking to the contentual provisions of Cohen's ethics as a whole.[12] Putting a sharp edge on it, this is to say that Cohen's influence on Kelsen does not lie in Cohen's legal and moral philosophy. Indeed, it does not stem from the continuum of practical philosophy at all. Rather, it is to be sought first and foremost in Cohen's theoretical philosophy, in the sphere of epistemological or logico-methodological foundations.

This conclusion is expressly confirmed when one takes into account the last of the numbered paragraphs in Kelsen's letter to Treves. There Kelsen withdraws his earlier appeal to Hans Vaihinger, made in the 'Foreword' to the Second Printing of the *Hauptprobleme*, in favour of an unqualified connection to Cohen. Kelsen means to leave no room for misunderstanding.

(4) Although it is altogether correct that the theory of the basic norm finds a certain support in [Ernst] Mach's principle of economy of thought and in Vaihinger's theory of fictions, nevertheless, owing to various misunderstandings that have arisen from these references, I no longer wish to appeal to Mach and Vaihinger. What is essential is that the theory of the basic norm arises *completely* from the *Method of Hypothesis* developed by Cohen. The basic norm is the answer to the question: What is the presupposition underlying the very possibility of interpreting material facts that are qualified as legal acts, that is, those acts by means of which norms are issued or applied? This is a question posed in the truest spirit of transcendental logic.[13]

The doctrine of the basic norm is the centrepiece proper of the Pure Theory of Law, its theoretical core and systematic focal point. When Kelsen, with an eye to the basic norm, appeals to Cohen, and when he traces the basic norm 'completely' back to Cohen's 'Method of *Hypothesis*', then all questions about other parallels pale by compari-

---

[11] See 'Letter to Treves' (n.5 above), at numbered para. 3.

[12] In the course of the controversy with Fritz Sander, Kelsen clearly dissociates himself from the greater theory of Cohen's *Ethik des reinen Willens*. Characteristic of the greater theory is Cohen's effort, following his transcendental method (see § II, below), *first*, to formulate by analogy to the theory of knowledge a science qua fact of reference for ethics, and thereby, *second*, to address the human sciences, in particular legal science, so that, *third*, ethics becomes the logic of the human sciences generally and of legal science in particular. Kelsen remarks: 'Whether Cohen succeeds in this effort need not be considered here.' At the same time, Kelsen allies himself with Sander's opposition to Cohen's enterprise. 'RWR' 128, repr. *RNK* 304.

[13] 'Letter to Treves' (n.5 above), numbered para. 4 (emphasis by G.E.).

son—parallels, for example, with reference to subordinate conceptual constructions such as that of the legal will, of the legal person, and the like, however important these may be for realizing a fully developed theory of law. Without the doctrine of the basic norm, the Pure Theory of Law loses its logico-transcendental fundament. Before this problem can be more closely examined, however, and the Method of *Hypothesis* can be brought to bear on the doctrine of the basic norm, it is necessary to consider Cohen's philosophy itself—its differences from the historical Kant, as well as the relation between Cohen's Kant interpretations and his own later System of Philosophy.

II. COHEN'S THEORY OF KNOWLEDGE

Hermann Cohen, the leading figure in the Marburg School of Neo-Kantianism, owes his prominence primarily to his Kant interpretations, which are philosophically among the most distinguished—and therefore among the most controversial—of the fruits of the Kant movement in the latter half of the nineteenth century. Cohen's prominence is also owing to his later philosophy of religion, which today continues to play a role in Jewish studies in the philosophy of religion, thanks to the work of Franz Rosenzweig, the last and, with Ernst Cassirer, the most eminent of Cohen's students. On the other hand, Cohen's System of Philosophy, published between 1902 and 1912, when Cohen was at the height of his philosophical powers and his school had reached the zenith of its influence, remained caught up in the odium of the so-called 'professors' philosophy' of the nineteenth century: if known beyond the circle of direct disciples at all, then only in academe, and even there scarcely finding a serious or an unbiased reception. The baroque quality of Cohen's thinking, his metaphysical terminology, and most importantly the very reputation that he had acquired as an interpreter of Kant all stood in the way of a genuine exchange of ideas on Cohen's System, which nevertheless represents his seminal statement in philosophy—unless the philosophy of religion is acknowledged as the supreme domain of all philosophy.

Viewed from the perspective of historical development, Cohen's System of Philosophy is the result of a train of thought that begins, to be sure, with the effort to 'reestablish the authority of Kant',[14] but that increasingly incorporates Leibniz and, most of all, Plato until it leads in the end away from, and even beyond, the historical Kant. The most telling illustration is Cohen's massive critique of the Kantian dualism of intuition and thought, of sensibility and reason. This dualism is the

---

[14] Cohen, *TE 1* (n.7 above), p. vi.

principle of construction of the positive part of Kant's *Kritik der reinen Vernunft*, whose carefully balanced theoretical framework collapses without it. Nevertheless, it is now rejected by Cohen as a 'deficiency in the laying of the foundation' (*Grundlegung*), a 'defect', even as a 'basic mistake at the heart of things', a mistake 'not to be corrected by means of Kantian terminology'.[15] Kelsen's statements, quoted above, are also illustrative, for neither the generation of the epistemic object from the origin, accomplished by Cohen's *Logik der reinen Erkenntnis*, nor the Method of *Hypothesis*, made prominent by his *Ethik des reinen Willens*, has a terminological point of reference or an immediate substantive model in Kant's own work.

At the beginning of this train of thought of Cohen's, in the First Edition of *Kants Theorie der Erfahrung* (1871), the point was primarily to appropriate the Kantian theory in order to arrive at an accurate understanding of its content. This understanding should proceed from the Kantian texts themselves, that is, it ought to meet the standards of historico-philological exactitude while at the same time reflecting a spirit of systematic partisanship vis-à-vis Kant.[16] To be sure, even here Cohen is already putting his own stamp on things, namely, with regard to the concept of the *a priori*, the doctrine of consciousness or self-consciousness, and his conclusive definition of the concept of experience. On the whole, however, this interpretation—Cohen's first—of Kant's *Kritik der reinen Vernunft* is primarily confined to conveying Kant's theory by means of report and commentary. Cohen, here, is not yet moving ahead in utter clarity toward the 'epistemological point of view', mentioned by Kelsen, that will later be conceptualized under the rubric 'transcendental method'.

It is not until *Kants Begründung der Ethik* (1877)[17] and then, more importantly, the Second Edition of *Kants Theorie der Erfahrung* (1885) that Cohen moves in this direction. Indeed, the latter work became the basic text of the Marburg School, determining not only the School's interpretation of Kant, but also its systematic theoretical programme. The 'transcendental method', unadorned, comes down to this basic idea: Experience is *given*; what is *to be discovered* are the *conditions* on which the *possibility* of experience rests. This question as to the conditions for possibility is the basic question of transcendental philosophy and thus in seamless agreement with the historical Kant.[18] The distinctly Cohennian profile emerges only with the second element of the transcendental method, namely, 'science qua fact' as the point of departure,

---

[15] Cohen, *LrE* 12, 27.   [16] Cohen, *TE 1* (n.7 above), p. v.
[17] Hermann Cohen, *Begründung der Ethik* (hereafter '*BE*'), (Berlin: Ferd. Dümmler, 1877).
[18] Here there is a close tie between Kant's explanations of the transcendental and Cohen's own effort. See Kant, *CPR*, at B25, 40, 80. Needless to say, this alone is hardly a full articulation of the interconnection of the various aims of Kant's *Kritik der reinen Vernunft*.

that is, the equation of *experience* and *science*. Cohen's illustration here is offered repeatedly: It is not in the heavens that stars are given, but rather in the science of astronomy.[19] This specifically scientific cast to the orientation and contour of Cohen's theory of experience distinguishes it trenchantly from Kant's theories in the *Kritik der reinen Vernunft*.

To begin with, Kant's point of departure is primarily pre-scientific or extra-scientific experience. In the *Kritik der reinen Vernunft*, he introduces simply 'a capacity for cognition generally', and takes aim at the original seeds and sources of reason by enquiring into 'reason itself'.[20] Here, first of all, he specifies space and time as pure forms of our sensibility that explain why it is that whatever appears to us is spatially and temporally structured. He goes on to derive from the forms of judgment found in traditional logic the categories as 'original primary concepts' of pure reason, which stem not from experience but, *a priori*, from reason itself. These sources of cognition—sensibility and reason—are initially analysed separately, and how it is that they can come together, and why it is that only together do they yield objectively valid cognition, are matters explained in the end by the doctrine of the original synthetic unity of consciousness. Thus, for Kant, the unity of consciousness is the highest point of transcendental philosophy, the point to which the possibility of all experience is ultimately traced.[21]

Cohen, on the other hand, first regards experience, then reason itself, and finally, in his System of Philosophy, the whole of cognition as being objectively manifest in science—and never mind the protestations of those representing Kant philology and orthodoxy. The transcendental question as to the conditions for possibility is thereby directed exclusively to those conditions that make experience *as science* possible. This approach, however, challenges science's claim to validity, a claim culminating in the formulation of objectively valid laws. Their validity remains, in Cohen's view, fundamentally unexplained, indeed utterly inexplicable, if and as long as the epistemological effort is exhausted in tracing this validity back to pure forms of subjective sensibility or to the supposed primary concepts of human reason. In the Second Edition of *Kants Theorie der Erfahrung* (1885), which continues to be presented as an interpretation of the *Kritik der reinen Vernunft*, Cohen not impartially shifts the emphasis from the transcendental aesthetic and the analytic of concepts to the analytic of principles, which he now specifies as the actual transcendental conditions for the validity of experience qua

[19] Hermann Cohen, *Das Prinzip der Infinitesimal-Methode und seine Geschichte* (Berlin: Ferd. Dümmler, 1883), repr. as vol. 5.1 in Cohen, *Werke* (1984), 127, and see Cohen, *BE* (n.17 above), at 20.

[20] See Kant, *CPR*, at B91; see also Kant, *Pro.* § 4, at para. 3.   [21] Kant, *CPR* B134.

science. The theory of experience becomes, then, a system of principles. And in that system, the unity of consciousness, which Kant once designated as 'reason itself',[22] is resolved into a principle, namely, the highest principle, at the apex of the entire system, establishing the validity of those particular principles that for their part provide the transcendental fundament for mathematics and the natural sciences.[23]

The highest principle, then, is the ultimate or the most basic transcendental condition for scientific experience, a condition that cannot itself be established by means of a still higher condition or traced back to a still deeper foundation. This theorem of the highest principle represents a prototype of the theorems of origin and *Hypothesis* in Cohen's later System of Philosophy. As early as the Second Edition of *Kants Theorie der Erfahrung*, however, important theoretical motifs are already emerging that Cohen then uses in his Method of *Hypothesis*, to which Kelsen appeals for the doctrine of the basic norm. I shall examine this doctrine in the third section of the paper, but I want first to consider the grounds for taking as the point of departure science qua fact. These grounds, in the end, drive Cohen beyond his position in the Second Edition of *Kants Theorie der Erfahrung* to those epistemological problems that mark the beginnings of his own later System, in particular his *Logik der reinen Erkenntnis*.

It is sometimes claimed that proceeding from science qua fact as the point of departure is merely the reflection of an undiminished faith in science, a faith considerably shaken by the First World War and, in any event, passé today, perhaps even dangerous, given the incalculable consequences of dealing uncritically with the findings of modern science. This is not, however, a plausible claim. For there are, above all, philosophical grounds, specifically, epistemological grounds for proceeding from science qua fact. Doing so is the consequence of a fundamental comprehension of the task of philosophy within the overall ambit of human knowledge, an understanding that at the same time points the way to accomplishing the task. Philosophy is neither to design a more or less diffuse world view in the manner of Schopenhauer or Nietzsche, nor to design an ontology, both of which might enter into competition or even into conflict with modern, scientific cognition of the world. Where this is the case, philosophy exceeds the limits of its competence and becomes metaphysics. Not the world itself, immediate, and therefore understood, say, as the totality of material things, but rather cognition of the world is the theme of philosophy, its object and its subject-matter. Philosophy is, therefore, first and foremost epistemology. For if the problem of knowledge is not clarified, all other philosophical disciplines—

22 Kant, *CPR* B134.
23 See Cohen, *TE 2* (n.7 above), at 137–43, 589–92; *TE 3* (n.7 above), at 182–91, 748–53.

ethics, aesthetics, legal philosophy, the philosophy of history, and so on—are lacking a theoretical fundament.

Now every theory of knowledge, whatever its particular formulation, is sooner or later confronted with the famous sceptical question of whether knowledge is possible at all. The reference to science qua fact is the answer: Science is a fact of the real, empirical world, a fact confirming by its very existence that the world is in principle cognizable, thereby exposing a radical epistemological scepticism as metaphysical fundamentalism. This fact, to be found 'on the printed page', as Cohen puts it,[24] cannot be denied by anyone who accepts the technology that results from scientific knowledge, anyone who, for example, boards an airplane and relies on its usually reaching its destination. And science qua fact certainly cannot be denied by anyone who warns that the consequences of scientific knowledge are beyond control and dangerous, for example, in the civil or military application of knowledge acquired in nuclear physics. Implicit in such a warning is the claim, always conceded, that it is possible to formulate objective laws—that is to say, laws that are actually valid, according to which, for example, nuclear fission and fusion can be accomplished technically. And this is so not only for the human being in the empirical world he lives in, but 'for every x' 'in every possible world'. As long as this claim to validity is not clarified, as long as there is no philosophical agreement on it, the task of epistemology remains undone, its most philosophically pressing problem remains open.

Here, and not in some unexamined affirmation, lie the ultimate grounds for taking science qua fact as the point of departure. For Cohen, it is in principle impossible to understand science's claim to validity by following Kant back to the capacity for cognition, that is, by analysing the cognitive apparatus of the cognizing subject. Specifically, if one traces the validity of cognition back to elementary structures or functions of the cognitive apparatus, then this validity becomes dependent upon them. And even if one were to postulate, with Kant, a transcendental subject over and above the empirical subject, cognition would remain within subjective brackets, having validity not 'in every possible world', but only for such subjects as are constituted and organized in the appropriate way. Kant's dualism of appearance and the thing in itself—the doctrine that there is an utterly uncognizable thing in itself behind the appearance—is the necessary consequence of every attempt to understand the validity of cognition psychologically, that is, by appeal to the cognizing subject and his specific constitution. According to Cohen, however, this dualism does not hold its own against modern science's claim to validity.

[24] Cohen, *BE* (n.17 above), 27.

At one point, he designates the uncognizable thing in itself outright as a 'rumour',[25] adding, at another point, by way of explanation:

One has the law of nature at hand, one acknowledges in it . . . the existence and the effects of nature, and *still one asks* about the thing in itself. . . . So it is that bread is transformed into stone.[26]

The philosophical theory of knowledge is faced, then, with a hopeless situation. Those transcendental conditions are to be found that make it possible to understand the validity of the laws of cognition, objectively manifest in science. To revert to the cognizing subject is barred. Analysing the subject's cognitive apparatus is a task for empirical psychology and neurophysiology, not philosophy, and these findings, whatever they might be, can perhaps explain the genesis of particular pre-scientific insights, but they cannot explain precisely what is in question here. Reverting to the subject inevitably binds the validity conditions to the subject, leading necessarily to the metaphysical dualism of appearance and the uncognizable thing in itself. This contradicts precisely what is supposed to be understood, namely, that the world is, in principle, cognizable, and that this cognizability finds its highest expression in science's claim to validity. Nevertheless, it is clear that science—and thus the validity claimed for the laws of scientific cognition—can be understood, if at all, only as a product, as something generated by means of the cognitive effort of human beings, and therefore it must be understood as such. Science is not the gift of a divine revelation or even of a revelation of nature; to trace science back to revelation would be to capitulate before the task at hand. How, then, can one satisfy both requirements, which on the surface are diametrically opposed to each other: how understand the whole of science as something generated by human cognitive activity, without thereby rendering the laws of science subjective, relative, undermining their objectivity—and so, in the end, sacrificing science's very claim to validity?

Precisely this is the problem addressed by Cohen in his *Logik der reinen Erkenntnis*. First of all, he draws the pivotal conclusion that the sought-after conditions for validity can be found, if at all, only in science, that is to say, only in cognition itself, and thus they are only to be sought there. The *Logik der reinen Erkenntnis* strictly maintains, then, the immanence of cognition, neither returning to the specific constitution of the cognitive apparatus of the cognizing subject, nor reaching beyond to the world of material things. If there is talk about 'thought', then it is simply in terms of an activity that, to be sure, brings about and generates cognition, but that also, as such, only becomes comprehensible through this cognition, through the judgments and concepts that make up

---

[25] Cohen, *TE 2* (n.7 above), 502.   [26] Cohen, *ErW* 25–6 (emphasis by G.E.).

science and that science employs. And if there is talk about 'subject-matter', then it is simply in terms of something already scientifically determined and cognized, subject-matter that is itself, then, cognition—and not in terms of the substantive, so-called 'real' thing in its material, prescientific indeterminacy.

Thus, logically generating the epistemic object from an origin, to which Kelsen refers in the first of his statements above, is emphatically not to be understood in the notorious metaphysical sense according to which the pre-scientific qualities of so-called 'real' material things, or even the things themselves, can be derived from sheer thought.[27] What Cohen logically generates from the origin—while casting a covert glance, to be sure, at the history of philosophy and of science—are those concepts and types of judgment that must be assumed and presupposed as the ultimate basic concepts and logical foundations of scientific cognition, lest one be unable to speak of an object at all in the various scientific fields (mathematics, physics, chemistry, and the like). This, the subject-matter of science—for example, a galaxy—is of course not to be reduced to the pure sense-datum—for example, the dim flicker of light in the heavens, or whatever can be perceived without the help of optical or radio-astronomical instruments. Rather, this subject-matter only becomes accessible in—and to the same extent also consists of—the totality of all related astronomical knowledge, including presuppositions derived from knowledge in other fields (mathematics, physics, and so on). That it is in every case a question of judgments is summarized by Cohen this way: 'The unity of the judgment is the generation of the unity of the subject-matter within the unity of cognition.'[28]

The *Logik der reinen Erkenntnis* amounts to nothing other than the development of a sequence of basic concepts and kinds, types, or classes of judgment that are manifest, in the various disciplines, in an indeterminable number of individual judgments. They are the sought-after conditions for the validity of scientific cognition, its logical foundations, because and to the extent that they are already efficacious and in force there. And they are—Cohen's credo—*pure cognition*, emerging from thought alone, since merely sensible perception is insufficient for the formation of judgments, let alone for the formation of abstract theoretical concepts, a point familiar in philosophy ever since Plato. Sensible perception, which even simulates a false orbital relation between the

---

[27] Cohen makes this unmistakably clear when he describes thought qua generation this way: 'Thought itself is the goal and the subject-matter of the activity of thinking. . . . This activity does not change into a thing; it does not go outside itself. In so far as it comes to an end, it is complete and ceases to be a problem. The activity itself is the thought, and the thought is nothing but thinking.' Cohen, *LrE* 29.

[28] Ibid. 68.

earth and the sun, is not the solution; rather, it is itself the problem. All concepts, all judgments, and especially the ultimate basic concepts and foundations of scientific cognition must therefore be understood, in the end, as products, as something generated by means of thought, which is, then, their logical origin, the place of their provenance. Where else do concepts and cognition come from, if not from thought?

It is on this point that, in the *Ethik des reinen Willens*, the theorem of origin from the *Logik der reinen Erkenntnis* is extended to the notion that Kelsen termed Cohen's 'Method of *Hypothesis*'. This method, this theorem of *Hypothesis*, is the result of Cohen's examination of Plato, who moves up in Cohen's System of Philosophy alongside Kant, indeed even ahead of Kant, to become Cohen's main authority. One must keep this Platonic provenance in mind if one wants to understand the theorem of *Hypothesis* properly. For the Platonic *Hypothesis*, which is not beholden to experience and therefore not subject to empirical scrutiny, has nothing whatever to do with a 'hypothesis' in the sense familiar from modern natural science. Platonic *Hypotheseis* are, rather, the mathematical definitions and axioms that form the presuppositions, the foundations of abstract mathematical deductions and proofs, whose truth therefore depends on these presuppositions. These *Hypotheseis*, according to Plato, can be distinguished from the *Anhypotheton*, the idea of the good, representing the unconditional, the presuppositionless, in short, representing a metaphysical absolute whose dialectical cognition—unlike cognition in the mathematical sciences—also leads to an unconditional, presuppositionless, valid knowledge.[29]

According to Cohen, however, there cannot be unconditional, presuppositionless, valid knowledge. All concepts and all judgments must be understood as products, as something generated by means of thought. This is the purport of the theorem of origin. And this is true, in particular, for the highest concepts and for what appear to be the ultimate foundations of scientific cognition. To be sure, these serve as basic concepts and as foundations in science, whose conditions for validity they are, but they forfeit the rank and dignity that have so often been accorded them in the history of philosophy. They are not eternal truths, not absolute foundations given in and of themselves, but rather something generated by means of thought, and they serve, therefore and to that extent, as the laying of foundations, so to speak, subject in principle to revision, as are all thoughts, all cognition. Precisely this is the content and the core of the *Hypothesis* theorem.

Cohen repeatedly and with increasing emphasis sets out the *Hypothesis* theorem in his System of Philosophy. This is already evident

---

[29] See Plato, *Politics*, at 509b, 511a–e, 533b–e.

in the *Logik der reinen Erkenntnis*, and then above all in the *Ethik des reinen Willens*, of which Kelsen makes special mention alongside his reference to Cohen's interpretation of Kant. In the *Ethik des reinen Willens*, Cohen discusses the *Hypothesis* theorem in the chapter dealing with the relation between ethics and logic, and in this context, he designates it the 'ultimate totality', the 'centre' and 'focal point' of logic.[30] Of great significance is the fact that this chapter is entitled 'The Basic Law of Truth'. The definitive passage reads:

We know from logic that the ultimate foundations (*Grundlagen*) of cognition are, rather, the *laying of foundations* (*Grundlegungen*), whose formulations must change in keeping with the development of problems and insights. It is sheer madness [to suppose] that therefore the law, the *a priori*, the eternal, would be rendered volatile and subjective; rather, it is in the historical context of the laying of foundations that the perpetuity of reason is confirmed. . . . *The foundations are the laying of foundations.*[31]

Anticipating the problem of applying this theorem to the field of law—to its use, then, in legal theory—I cite here a passage from the last part of the System, accentuating the same basic idea a little differently:

All scientific enquiry, all thinking and cognizing that must be directed to all the material facts of culture, every individual enquiry as well as all research in general, has as its methodological presupposition not so much a foundation (*Grundlage*) as, rather, *the laying of a foundation* (*Grundlegung*).[32]

A few pages later, Cohen sharpens the claim by adding '*that all laws are only the laying of foundations*, that they can only be the laying of foundations'.[33]

III. COHEN'S ROLE IN THE PURE THEORY OF LAW

Against this background, it very quickly becomes clear how and in what sense Kelsen can subscribe to Cohen's basic epistemological position and trace the theory of the basic norm completely back to Cohen's Method of *Hypothesis*, while at the same time charging that Cohen failed to follow through in applying the Method to law and state, and held fast to natural law instead, that is, to a material, contentual *a priori*. In other words, it becomes clear how Kelsen can profess allegiance to Cohen's epistemological position, while at the same time rejecting not only the

---

[30] Cohen, *ErW* 84–5. [31] Ibid. 85 (Cohen's emphasis).
[32] Hermann Cohen, *Ästhetik des reinen Gefühls*, vol. 1 (Berlin: Bruno Cassirer, 1912), repr. as vol. 8 in Cohen, *Werke* (1982), 73 (emphasis by G.E.).
[33] Ibid. 88 (emphasis by G.E.).

contentual provisions of Cohen's *Ethik des reinen Willens* but, beyond that, its entire conceptual framework as well.

Just as science is a fact of the real, empirical world, so likewise is the positive law, which first takes on external form in sensibly perceptible acts of human behaviour (for example, the judge's pronouncement of a verdict), but which is found primarily 'on the printed page', as Cohen puts it, in the texts of statutes, in trial protocols, in the published opinions of the courts, and the like, and which is, then, systematically investigated by legal science. Theoretically, one can argue about whether individual provisions (say, of family law, public law, or international law) are desirable and good, whether they are 'just' in an ethical or a moral sense. In practical terms, however, one cannot deny the existence of this fact, the positive law, in particular when one holds that certain of its applications (say, the judge's determination of a support payment) are not good and just, or when one rejects on ideological grounds the institution of the positive law altogether. For to deny the positive law qua fact, and therefore to disregard it, is to come into direct conflict with it, to be exposed to the various sanctions and coercive measures that the state has at hand in order to enforce the claim to validity of individual provisions of the law, that is, of legal norms.

The task of a philosophical theory of positive law is exclusively cognition of the law, not the practical shaping of the law, which is the province of legislators and judges.[34] If there is any appeal at all made to transcendental philosophy, there will be the altogether general question as to the conditions for the possibility of positive law. If, as Kelsen expressly states in paragraph 2 of his letter to Treves, there is an attempt, in particular, to apply Cohen's transcendental method to a theory of positive law, then the question becomes the specific enquiry into the conditions for the validity of positive law, that is, into the presuppositions and foundations underlying—and to the same extent establishing—the claim of the positive law to validity.

The immediate corollary here—namely, the question of whether the point of departure is to be the law itself in the form of a particular legal experience, or whether it is to be legal science—was indeed among the main controversies in the dispute between Kelsen and Fritz Sander.[35] Strictly speaking, however, the question simply reflects the difference between the historical Kant and Cohen's interpretation of Kant. Cohen's equation of experience and science—his view that, for epistemology, experience is given only in science, only as science—serves to temper at first the apparently acute question of choosing between legal experience and legal science. At the same time, though, one asks how it should still

[34] *LT* 1 (Preface), and see § 1 (at p. 7), §§ 9, 24(b) (at p. 44), § 25 (at pp. 46–7), *et passim*.
[35] See generally the papers collected in *RNK*.

be possible that a particular legal experience be given to philosophy for consideration independently of legal science. By means of philosophical consideration alone, one could do no more than construct such an experience, but philosophy, restricted by Kant to critique, would thereby overstep the boundaries of its competence, becoming what Cohen rejects as metaphysics. So it is that Kelsen unequivocally and repeatedly points out to Sander that a transcendental theory of law is not viable without reference to legal science.[36]

Kelsen emphasizes still more vigorously the distinction between law and nature, between legal science and natural science. It stems from Kant's distinction between *Sein* and *Sollen* ('is' and 'ought'), resolutely maintained by Cohen as well. I shall take up at a later point how Kelsen transforms the Kantian *Sollen* into the concept of the legal norm and links it to the concept of imputation as the 'particular lawfulness, the autonomy, of the law'.[37] What is vital at this point is simply that nature is as it is, before and even entirely independently of whether its laws are cognized by science. Not nature, but natural science is a product, something generated by human cognitive activity, whereas the positive law itself is a product, something generated by human activity and, moreover, something eminently changeable. The question, then, in the transcendental enquiry into the conditions for the validity of positive law is not a question as to the conditions for the validity of legal science; rather, it is a question as to the claim of the law itself to validity, a claim immediately and practically manifest in coercive acts of the state. This claim can be clarified in philosophical terms only by appeal to legal science, which for its part acquires thereby a new, transcendental fundament and, with that, becomes *pure* legal theory.

Legal theory, enquiring transcendentally into the presuppositions and foundations of the claim of the positive law to validity, is pure only if its explanation of this claim to validity is drawn exclusively from the positive law itself. Here there is an important methodological parallel to Cohen. Just as Cohen, in the *Logik der reinen Erkenntnis*, considers cognition exclusively in terms of cognition, so likewise Kelsen, in the *Reine Rechtslehre*, considers the law exclusively in terms of the law.[38] Only thus

---

[36] See 'RWR', at 127–33, repr. *RNK*, at 303–9; see also Hans Kelsen, 'Was ist die Reine Rechtslehre?' (hereafter 'WRR'), in *Demokratie und Rechtsstaat. Festgabe zum 60. Geburtstag von Zaccaria Giacometti*, ed. Max Imboden et al. (Zurich: Polygraphischer Verlag, 1953), 143–62, at 143–4, repr. *WS I* 611–29, at 611–12.

[37] *LT* § 11(b) (p. 23), and see generally at §11(a)–(b); see also 'Foreword' to *HP* (n.1 above), at § I.

[38] Compare Kelsen's formula that 'to cognize something legally or to understand something juridically means nothing other than to understand it as law', 'Foreword' to *HP* (n.1 above), § VI. Altogether similar is the formulation that appears in both editions of the *Reine Rechtslehre*; see *LT* § 5 (at p. 11); *PTL*, at § 14.

is an undistorted view possible of 'the *autonomy of the law* as against nature or a social reality patterned after nature'.[39] This autonomy—that is, how the positive law as law is distinguished from nature and from all other phenomena of cultural reality—must be understood lest the claim of the positive law to validity not be understood either.

The positive law initially presents itself to legal science and thereby to philosophical theory as, generally speaking, nothing other than the totality of all its individual provisions, in particular its statutes. From this material alone, according to Kelsen, the propositions are to be formed that legal science uses in describing its subject-matter.[40] The law is manifest in its specific autonomy, then, in these legal propositions. And here there is another parallel to Cohen: Just as Cohen, in the *Logik der reinen Erkenntnis*, considers natural science as a system of judgments, so likewise Kelsen, in the *Reine Rechtslehre*, considers legal science as a system of legal propositions.[41] And these, too, are judgments that are systematically related to one another, like the judgments of natural science, whose validity is Cohen's concern in the *Logik der reinen Erkenntnis*. But legal propositions differ radically from the judgments of natural science in one absolutely decisive respect.

The judgments of natural science are directed to a *Sein*, to what is, to nature *per se*, which is described in these judgments in terms of causality, that is, the necessary linking of cause and effect. The positive law, in contrast to nature, is not a *Sein*, not what is, but a *Sollen*, what ought to be,[42] and as such—to use a formulation of Cohen's intended for the constructions of geometry—it is 'not existent in nature at all',[43] but is, rather, a product, something generated by human activity. Its laws—the individual provisions of the positive law, in particular statutes—are to be distinguished, therefore, in the specific quality of their lawfulness from the laws of nature. As laws of the *Sollen*, the 'ought', they do not describe in causal terms what happens, but prescribe what ought to happen. They are, in other words, norms. Thus, the question as to the claim of the positive law to validity becomes the more precise question as to the claim of individual norms of the positive law to validity, that is, the claim of legal

---

[39] 'Foreword' to *HP* (n.1 above), § I (Kelsen's emphasis). That Kelsen's first concern is with this distinction is something he emphasizes repeatedly in formulations that vary only slightly. See his definitions of 'purity', ibid., at § I; *LT*, at 1 (Preface), §§ 1, 26, *et passim*; Kelsen, 'WRR' (n.36 above), at 148, repr. *WS I*, at 616. See also Kelsen's description of the 'actual objective' of his theoretical work subsequent to the *Hauptprobleme*, in 'RWR', at 105, repr. *RNK*, at 281.

[40] See *PTL*, at § 16.   [41] See ibid.

[42] See 'Foreword' to *HP* (n.1 above), at § I; *LT* § 11(b) (at p. 24); *PTL*, at § 16; Kelsen, 'WRR' (n.36 above), at 145–6, repr. *WS I*, at 613–14.

[43] Hermann Cohen, 'Platons Ideenlehre und die Mathematik', in Cohen, *Schriften zur Philosophie und Zeitgeschichte*, ed. Albert Görland and Ernst Cassirer, 2 vols. (Berlin: Akademie-Verlag, 1926), vol. I, 336–66, at 356 (Cohen's emphasis omitted).

norms to validity. And this question, for its part, culminates in the question as to the character and the basis of the *Sollen*, the 'ought'.

According to Kelsen, the claim of legal norms to validity rests, strictly speaking, on a single pillar. The condition *sine qua non* is, above all, that individual norms be systematically related to one another; plainly, a norm incapable of integration into this systematic relation—into the legal system qua system of all valid legal norms—cannot be a valid legal norm. In terms of the positive law, this means: Within a certain legal system, a norm is valid only if it has been created or produced in accordance with the norms of the system that provide for norm creation. Kelsen describes this 'special property unique to the law' in these terms:

[T]he law governs its own creation. In particular, it is a legal norm that governs the process whereby another legal norm is created, and also governs—to a different degree—the content of the norm to be created.[44]

And here there is a third parallel to Cohen: Just as Cohen considers cognition as a generative relation whose philosophical systematization first constitutes the unity of nature qua unity of the ideal collective object of cognition, so likewise Kelsen considers the law as a generative relation, a 'chain of creation'[45] that ultimately becomes a 'unified, consistent system'[46] only by means of juridico-scientific systematization. The legal system turns out to be, then, not a linear juxtaposition of like-ordered legal norms, but a 'hierarchical ordering of various strata of legal norms' whose systematic relation 'emerges as one traces the creation of norms, and thus their validity, back to other norms, whose own creation is determined in turn by still other norms'.[47] If one stays with the figure of the hierarchical ordering, then the validity of any norm whatever is traced back to the validity of a higher-level norm, whose validity is traced in turn back to the validity of a still higher-level norm, and so on.

Logic dictates that this process of establishing the validity of a norm by tracing it back to the validity of a higher-level norm cannot be continued *ad infinitum* and must at some point come to an end. This end, which from an inverted perspective must be considered as, rather, the origin of all valid norms, is the '*Hypothesis* of the basic norm'.[48]

To be sure, a more precise statement is required to support the claim that the basic norm is a *Hypothesis*, that, more pointedly, it does not merely stem from Cohen's Method of *Hypothesis*, but actually is—indeed can only be—a *Hypothesis* through and through, the laying of a

---

[44] *LT* § 31(a) (p. 63); see also *PTL* § 15 (at p. 71).
[46] *PTL* § 16 (p. 72).
[48] *Phil. Fds.* § 11 (p. 405) (emphasis by G.E.).

[45] *LT* § 28 (p. 56: § title).
[47] *LT* § 31(a) (p. 64).

foundation (*Grundlegung*). (And it is, therefore, expressly if not uni-formly so named by Kelsen himself.)[49]

It is well to bear in mind, first, the necessity and the limits of transcen-dentally establishing the validity of positive law. Neither the basis for nor the aim of such an enterprise lies in somehow elevating the positive law philosophically or legitimating it ideologically. The point, here, is not to evaluate the positive law at all, that is, to show its provisions to be just or unjust from a moral standpoint, or to show them to be politically useful or socially wise.[50] These would all be abstract controversies, which are certainly admissible theoretically, even indispensable in the context of personal ethics, but which affect the positive law's factual claim to valid-ity not one iota. Not legitimation, not affirmation, but *cognition* is the aim of transcendentally establishing the validity of positive law, and the facticity of the positive law's claim to validity is the immediate basis for such an enterprise, which is necessary because the positive law *is* valid, not in order to render it valid. Thus, the question is compelling: What is this *Sollen*, this 'ought', whose validity is immediately and practically manifest in coercive acts of the state? And where does it originate?

The condition *sine qua non*—that a norm be capable of integration into the systematic relation of all valid legal norms—offers no answer to the question, because it takes as its point of departure the existing valid-

---

[49] This is especially evident in the work *Philosophische Grundlagen*, but is also seen in the 'Foreword' to the Second Printing of the *Hauptprobleme* (n.1 above), § V, where Kelsen speaks of the basic norm as a [*Hypothesis*] 'by analogy to the hypothesis in the natural sci-ences'—notably an analogy, not an identity. In the *Reine Rechtslehre* itself, Kelsen charac-terizes the basic norm as a 'hypothetical foundation', *LT* § 29 (p. 58), and as a 'logico-transcendental presupposition', *PTL* § 34(d) (p. 201: at § title); in both cases, pre-cisely what is meant is captured by the expression '*Hypothesis*'.

[50] Kelsen writes repeatedly and with great emphasis that a *constitutive* element of the purity of legal theory is freedom from all considerations of value, that this is, specifically, the negative counterpart of his aim to explain the positive law's claim to validity by draw-ing exclusively on the positive law itself. The following especially penetrating passage is representative: 'The separation of *legal science*—oriented to the value of truth alone—from *legal policy* qua the willful shaping of the social order—directed to the realization of values other than truth, in particular that of justice—is the second postulate, which guarantees the *purity* of a legal theory. . . . The science of law can and must be separated from policy if it is to lay claim at all to being a science. . . . The Pure Theory of Law is a *pure theory* of the law, not a theory of *pure law*, [which could] only mean correct law, law that is just. The Pure Theory of Law, however, does not and cannot aim to be a theory of correct or just law, *for it does not presume to answer the question of what is just*. As a science of the positive law, the Pure Theory is . . . a theory of real law, of law as it is actually created through custom, legis-lation, and adjudication, and as it is efficacious in actual society, without regard to whether this positive law, from the standpoint of some value—that is, from some political stand-point—is judged to be good or bad, just or unjust; and every positive law can be judged from some political standpoint to be just, and at the same time, from another, equally polit-ical standpoint, to be unjust; not, however, by the science of law, which like every genuine science does not evaluate, but describes, does not emotionally justify or condemn, but rationally explains its subject-matter.' Kelsen, 'WRR' (n.36 above), 152–3, repr. *WS I* 620–1 (the last of the emphases is by G.E.).

ity of the legal system. The process of establishing the validity of a norm by tracing it back to the validity of a higher-level norm must, as already noted, at some point come to an end, lest there be no possibility at all of establishing the positive law's claim to validity, or of rendering intelligible the law qua law, qua 'ought' and norm. The law qua law—its specific autonomy—consists, according to Kelsen, in the imputation of the legal consequence (the consequence of an unlawful act) to the legal condition.[51] Imputation means that a conditioning material fact (a delict) is necessarily linked to the legal consequence (the sanction), more precisely, ought to be linked. This linkage, according to Kelsen, cannot be explained by appeal to causality, for in fact the sanction may very well not be enforced—where, say, the lawbreaker succeeds in escaping it. Imputation has, rather, normative import. It links conditioning and conditioned material facts through an 'ought' that is no less rigorous[52] than the linkage of causality and 'just as inviolable', since 'in the system of the law, that is, owing to the law, punishment follows always and without exception from the delict, even if, in the system of nature, punishment may fail to materialize for one reason or another.'[53] This linkage alone—no more, but also no less—is the meaning of the legal 'ought', 'expressing the specific existence, the validity, of the law'.[54]

The question as to the basis of the validity of legal norms, taken as a question as to the basis of the legal 'ought', is aimed, therefore, not at some transcendent value in a merely postulated, metaphysical great beyond, but precisely and exclusively at this linkage. Where, then, does the legal 'ought', thus understood, originate? Where does the necessity originate that links legal condition with legal consequence in the system of the law? The theoretical alternatives to which one might appeal here are familiar from the philosophical tradition. In a word, the definitive concepts are nature, man, and God. Since Kelsen appeals several times to Cohen's interpretation of Kant, it is both reasonable and legitimate to draw on Cohen's 'theory of experience' in order to clarify these alternatives. As mentioned above, Cohen's theory of experience traces the validity of scientific experience back to a system of principles whose own validity stems in turn from the highest principle, at the apex of the system. Cohen discusses a problem entirely analogous to the problem considered here when he poses the question: What is it that makes possible or establishes the highest principle? He answers:

Nothing except itself. There is no authority above the highest principle: There is no necessity beyond the idea that we want to acknowledge necessity in that area of our consciousness that is characterized as science, as mathematical natural

---

[51] See *LT* § 11(b) (at pp. 23–4); Kelsen, 'WRR' (n.36 above), at 144, repr. *WS I*, at 612.
[52] See 'Foreword' to *HP* (n.1 above), at § I.   [53] *LT* § 11(b) (p. 25).
[54] Ibid. (p. 24).

science. Where else should necessity come from, if not from this determination in favour of a content of consciousness that is so characterized, if, not, then, *from the fact itself* that is sought by our question? One who expects, who considers possible, another necessity, another guarantee of necessity, takes his stand beyond the interest pursued by our question—whether he expects it from heaven or from his own body. One who recognizes the *source of the law* in a *supernatural revelation* is regarded as lacking the virtue of philosophical assiduity.[55]

That this statement applies to the question as to the origin of the *Sollen*, the 'ought', is clear. To trace the *Sollen* back to God, back to a 'supernatural revelation', would mean quite simply to replace philosophical cognition with faith. It is also clear that no bridge leads from *Sein* to *Sollen*,[56] neither from the reality of nature nor from man as he is, from his psychophysical nature. For this, too, in terms of Cohen's figure, would amount to a revelation—in this case, on the part of nature—of the sort whose unacceptability in the philosophy of our own day is captured in the label 'naturalistic fallacy'.[57] If one understands the *Sollen* not as a transcendent value but as a *transcendental category*, then it is no more to be found in nature than any other category, and must for this reason, exactly as with all other concepts, be understood as something generated by means of thought.

This category—the pure thought of the legal *Sollen*—can only be drawn by philosophical theory *from the law itself*, therefore, where it is, qua transcendental category, already efficacious and in force, that is, already functioning. It is extracted by means of a logical analysis of the legal propositions that legal science uses in describing legal norms.[58] It is found in every single norm, quite apart from whatever other content the norm may have, as the element that turns content into norm, and in this capacity it can, therefore, also be cognized, that is, it can be drawn from the norm. This element of the legal *Sollen*, the expression of the validity of the law, is carried over from norm to norm, from the higher-level norm to the lower-level norm, in the process of norm-creation in accordance with legal norms, that is, in the process of norm-issuance.

To establish validity philosophically is to trace this 'chain of creation' all the way back to its logical endpoint, to the idea of an 'ultimate' or a

[55] Cohen, *TE 2* (n.7 above), 139; Cohen, *TE 3* (n.7 above), 185 (emphasis by G.E.).

[56] Kelsen explains unequivocally: 'That something *ought* to be cannot follow from the fact that something *is*; likewise, that something *is* cannot follow from the claim that something *ought* to be. The basis of the legal validity of a norm can only be the validity of another norm.' *PTL* § 34(a) (p. 193) (trans. altered).

[57] Kelsen offers the following diagnosis of the 'naturalistic fallacy': '[A] metaphysical theory of law also maintains the belief that a natural law can be found in nature qua manifestation of God's will, which is to say, however, that a *Sollen* can be logically drawn from a *Sein*. This is a fallacy, and the *natural law theory* is based on this fallacy.' Kelsen, 'WRR' (n.36 above), 146, repr. *WS I* 613 (Kelsen's emphasis).

[58] Kelsen, 'WRR' (n.36 above), 144, repr. *WS I* 612.

'highest' norm, whose validity is not traced back to a still higher-level norm and which is, therefore and in this respect, the basis of the validity of all lower-level norms. This is the *basic norm*. It is different from other norms, whose validity it establishes in that they are created in accordance with legal norms and so in accordance with the basic norm, that is, they are issued. The basic norm qua ultimate or highest norm, however, cannot be created in accordance with legal norms, that is, issued; rather, it must be *presupposed*.[59] Since the basic norm qua norm cannot be existent and hidden somewhere in nature, and cannot have fallen from the heavens in some mysterious way either, it must be laid down as the ultimate basis of validity underlying legal norms. Thus, it is not a foundation (*Grundlage*) given in and of itself in nature or by God, but the laying of a foundation (*Grundlegung*), that is, a *Hypothesis*. Not, however, an empirical hypothesis, which could be verified or falsified through experience, for norms do not describe what is, and thus they cannot be true or false; rather, they prescribe behaviour (what ought to be), and thus they are either valid or invalid.[60] The basic norm is, in a Platonic and Cohennian sense, *Hypothesis* through and through. It is the transcendentally necessary presupposition that must be assumed, must be laid down as a foundation, if any directive at all is to be conceived of and intelligible as a valid norm, as a legal norm. The basic norm is in no way whatever, then, a 'product of free invention',[61] an assumption that would be capricious or arbitrary. Rather, the basic norm will be claimed *de facto* as a foundation and thus presupposed—in legal thought just as in philosophical cognition—whenever and wherever objective validity is attributed to a norm or to the legal system as a whole.[62] Yet the basic norm is not itself a particular positive norm 'contained' in the legal system.[63] For, according to Kelsen, the positivity of the law and of all its norms—existing alongside its factual efficacy, which is manifest in state coercion—consists alone in

---

[59] See *LT*, at § 29; *Phil. Fds.* § 11 (at pp. 405–6); *PTL*, § 34(a) (at pp. 194–5), § 34(c)–(d) (at pp. 200–4).

[60] See *PTL* § 16 (at pp. 71, 73–4). This does not mean that in reality there would be—or would have been—no actual course of events that would be comprehended, described, and interpreted by means of the *Hypothesis* of the basic norm. Kelsen attests to this when he illustrates the significance of the basic norm by appeal to the example of a revolution replacing an old legal system with a new one; see *LT* § 30(a) (at p. 59). The sense of the basic norm as the ultimate basis of validity, however, is precisely not dependent on the concrete circumstances that constitute such a course of events. The basic norm is not a hypothesis in historical terms whose significance would be exhausted in the reconstruction of historico-real events, through which the hypothesis could, then, also be shown to be false.

[61] *PTL* § 34(d) (p. 201).

[62] Thus, Kelsen remarks that with 'the doctrine of the basic norm, the Pure Theory analyses the actual process of the long-standing method of cognizing positive law, in an attempt simply to reveal the transcendental logical conditions of that method.' *LT* § 29 (p. 58); see also *Phil. Fds.* § 12 (at p. 406); and *PTL* § 34(d) (at pp. 204–5).

[63] *RR 2* § 34(c) (p. 201n.) (regrettably, the footnote is missing in the English translation).

the fact that the law has been issued, that is, created in accordance with legal norms.[64] This does not apply to the basic norm qua ultimate, highest, or first norm. It is the 'ultimate basis of validity', which is itself nothing other than the 'basic rule' of norm-creation and thus 'establishes the unity of [the] chain of creation'[65] that the legal system represents.

Along with the logico-epistemological status and the function of the basic norm, there is also its purely formal content. Its formality ensures that legal science can, by appeal to this *Hypothesis*, comprehend, understand, and cognize any and all concrete legal systems.[66] As noted above, the basic norm, as the ultimate basis of validity, is itself nothing other than the basic rule of norm-creation. As such it consists of only two components. It connects the idea of the law—that is, of the legal 'ought' qua linkage of legal condition and legal consequence—with the idea of a highest authority, for purposes of creating law. As Kelsen puts it in the First Edition of the *Reine Rechtslehre*:

The basic norm confers on the act of the first legislator—and thus on all other acts of the legal system resting on this first act—the sense of 'ought' (*Sollen*), that specific sense in which legal condition is linked with legal consequence in the . . . legal norm . . .[67]

Again, this time in the Second Edition of the *Reine Rechtslehre*:

[T]he basic norm confines itself to delegating power to a norm-issuing authority—that is, it sets out a rule—according to which the norms of the legal system are to be created.[68]

Thus, the basic norm comprehends the law's coercive character, which immediately and practically manifests the claim of the law to validity in that it renders the claim externally visible in the real, empirical world, in the system of nature. Likewise, the basic norm comprehends the specific autonomy of the law, which distinguishes the law qua *Sollen* from the *Sein* of nature. Precisely for this reason the basic norm itself has

the basic form of the law of normativity. . . . And because this *Hypothesis* of every positive legal system has the form of the basic normativity of all law, the idea of lawfulness itself is set down with the *Hypothesis*. This is the idea that a certain consequence is attached to a certain condition. . . . The basic norm says that

---

[64] *RR 2* § 34(d) (p. 207n.) (again, the footnote is missing in the English translation). See also Kelsen, 'WRR' (n.36 above), at 147, repr. *WS I*, at 614.

[65] *LT* § 31(a) (p. 64).

[66] On this issue, see Kelsen's response to the charge of formalism, 'WRR' (n.36 above), 159–60, repr. *WS I* 627, which, significantly, refers to a passage in Cohen's *Logik der reinen Erkenntnis*. Also of interest here is Kelsen's claim, *LT* § 29 (p. 58), that the basic norm is 'simply the expression of the necessary presupposition of every positivistic understanding of legal data'; see also *Phil. Fds.* § 12 (at pp. 406–7).

[67] *LT* § 29 (p. 58).   [68] *PTL* § 34(b) (p. 197) (trans. altered).

under certain conditions (or under conditions to be specified) a certain consequence (or a consequence to be specified) is set down as obligatory.[69]

The content and the form of the *Hypothesis* of the basic norm correspond, therefore, to each other. The positive law is not the necessary
effect of a cause in nature, but simply the obligatory consequence of the
condition that a first legislator, a norm-issuing authority, has achieved
sufficient power to lend validity to the law, that is, actually to enforce its
coercive character. If the content of the basic norm—the connection of
the idea of the law with the idea of a highest authority, for purposes of
creating law—were interpreted not normatively, not in accordance with
the legal 'ought', but in accordance with causality, then that very power
factor would be ignored without which the positive law, to put it collo-
quially, is not born and does not survive. For the positive law is valid only
if its claim to validity can also be enforced.[70] And because the content
and the form of the *Hypothesis* of the basic norm correspond to each
other, because the basic norm has, then, simply the basic form of the law
of normativity itself as its content (which it breaks down into its constitutive components), the basic norm establishes only the validity of individual legal norms, not their particular variable content.[71] Which
concrete content actually becomes a legal norm is not predetermined in
and with the basic norm, but can only be set down by means of creation
in accordance with legal norms, that is, in accordance with the basic
norm.

One could say that with the *Hypothesis* of the basic norm, the claim of
the positive law to validity is, in truth, not established at all but simply
described—or, at best, explained. As correct as this view is, it would be
out of place if it were meant as an objection. For philosophical theory can
only cognize the positive law. It does not itself produce the positive law,
and it is not in a position to demonstrate the necessity of the positive law
either. Philosophical theory can only demonstrate the transcendentally
necessary presuppositions on which the claim of the positive law to
validity rests. If philosophical theory recognizes the limits on its competence and its scientific credibility, and so forgoes a speculative exercise
in metaphysics, then the ultimate basis to which it traces the validity of
the positive law can, in accordance with the logico-epistemological status of this basis, only be a *Hypothesis*, a foundation (*Grundlage*) that is
the laying of a foundation (*Grundlegung*). Salient in this *Hypothesis* is
simply what the positive law is, not how it ought to be.

---

[69] *Phil. Fds.* § 12 (p. 406) (trans. altered) (Kelsen's emphasis).
[70] On this issue, see Kelsen's statement on the relation between the validity and efficacy
of the legal system, in *LT*, at § 30(b).
[71] *PTL* § 34(b) (d); Kelsen, 'WRR' (n.36 above), 148–9, repr. *WS I* 616.

11

On the Transcendental Import
of Kelsen's Basic Norm*

GERHARD LUF

I.

In the enquiry into the import and the function of the basic norm in Hans Kelsen's legal theory, those interpretations are of special interest that deal with the notion of the basic norm as a 'logico-transcendental' condition for cognition in legal science, or with the relation of Kelsen's juridico-scientific method to Kant's practical philosophy. Two thinkers in particular have written along these lines, Norbert Leser and Ralf Dreier respectively.

Leser underscores the close methodological connection between the Pure Theory of Law and Kant's theoretical philosophy.[1] According to Leser, it is only with the help of the transcendental method developed by Kant that Kelsen is able to avoid the extremes of both an uncritical positivism and a metaphysical theory of natural law, neither of which is tenable in laying a foundation for the legal sciences. Leser writes:

Philosophically, the position of the Pure Theory of Law in confrontation with positivism as well as with the various versions of natural law doctrine can be summarized as follows. The Pure Theory of Law is transcendental in terms of Kantian philosophy in so far as it does not ground experience in experience and therefore does not proceed in accordance with positivism; on the other hand, however, it is not transcendent and therefore not metaphysical either.[2]

What is more, as Leser goes on to emphasize, conceiving of the basic norm as a logico-transcendental presupposition guarantees that 'the

* *Editors' note*: This paper first appeared in *Theorie der Normen. Festgabe für Ota Weinberger zum 65. Geburtstag*, ed. Werner Krawietz et al. (Berlin: Duncker & Humblot, 1984), 567–81, and was translated by the editors, who wish to thank Alexander Somek (Vienna) for helpful suggestions. For the present version, the author has made a handful of minor changes.

[1] Norbert Leser, 'Die Reine Rechtslehre im Widerstreit der philosophischen Ideen', in *Die Reine Rechtslehre in wissenschaftlicher Diskussion* [no editor] (Vienna: Manz, 1982), 97–104.

[2] Ibid. 100.

transcendental programme, both preceding and applicable to all experience, is carried out and ensured, that the legal system is comprehended as a unity of norms and not merely as a concatenation of fact under-girded by power.'[3] Thus, the transcendental structure of the basic norm is directly linked in unbroken continuity to Kant's philosophy. Leser goes on in this vein:

The basic norm, as logico-transcendental presupposition for comprehending legal reality, is comparable to the categories as well as to the pure forms of intuition in Kant's philosophy, which have *a priori* character and first make possible the constituting of experience. Without themselves falling under the conditions of the context of experience, the categories shape sensory material, thereby condensing it into the unity of the world and making it accessible to the experiencing subject. So, likewise, the basic norm is the condition that makes possible the interpretation of acts of will as legal acts, being itself, nevertheless, in no way the sense of an act of will but, rather, a self-contained *a priori* assumption, independent of any constituting act of will.[4]

Thus, Leser draws a vivid analogy between the transcendental conditions for constituting experience generally and for the *a priori* comprehension of empirical legal reality to be made possible by the basic norm. And he justifies this analogy as methodologically successful and systematically faithful to Kant's philosophy.

The relation between Kelsen and Kant is also taken up by Dreier,[5] who defends the central thesis that 'it is reasonable to interpret and to develop further the theory of the basic norm in terms of Kant's practical philosophy.'[6] Dreier's methodological concern, in a word, is systematically to follow through on Kelsen's effort. With this in mind, he begins by distinguishing three different concepts of validity: a legal concept geared to the proper issuance of the positive law in the law-creating process, a sociological concept that has reference to social efficacy, and an ethical concept that addresses to the positive law the moral requirements of legitimacy. According to Dreier, Kelsen did consider in his conception of the basic norm both the legal and the sociological aspects of validity, but, owing to his rejection of the Kantian concept of practical reason, which he saw as a relic of metaphysics and theology, he improperly neglected the ethical aspect of validity.

As Dreier argues, if the objections against the scientific defensibility of the concept of practical reason were met, it would be 'possible to put the

[3] Leser (n.1 above).
[4] Ibid. 102.
[5] Ralf Dreier, 'Bemerkungen zur Theorie der Grundnorm', in *Die Reine Rechtslehre in wissenschaftlicher Diskussion* (n.1 above), 38–46.
[6] Ibid. 39.

theory of the basic norm once more into the context of Kant's practical philosophy and thereby to interpret it in connection with the contemporary debate in ethics, a debate characterized in large part by the appeals made to Kant.'[7] Seen in this way, then, the basic norm is to be understood as a command of practical reason, namely, that one act 'in a way that corresponds both to what is by and large an ethically justified constitution and to the norms issued in accordance with the constitution, in so far as these exhibit in their own right a minimum of social efficacy or the prospect of efficacy, and a minimum of ethical justification or the possibility of justification.'[8] Thus, Dreier is suggesting that the concept of the basic norm be brought into line with the law of reason, a modification that he believes to be compatible in principle with Kelsen's conception of the basic norm.

As the quoted passages make clear, the positions taken by the two authors are very different. The argument adduced by Leser is in keeping with the assumption of an unbroken continuity between Kant and the neo-Kantians. Dreier's argument is precisely the opposite: By systematically appealing to Kant, and, indeed, to an up-to-date understanding of Kant as developed in the current discussion in ethics, Dreier seeks to criticize and to modify the theory of the basic norm as substantially shaped by neo-Kantianism.[9]

Following up on these introductory comments, I should like to ask, first, whether in terms of Leser's thesis it is in fact possible to maintain the notion of the transcendental character of the basic norm. Then I turn to Dreier's suggested reinterpretation of the basic norm by appeal to the law of reason, examining the suggestion from the point of view of Kant's philosophy.

II.

Kelsen, over the course of his juridico-scientific development, attempted in very different ways to define the basic norm,[10] and within the framework of these various approaches, it is the characterization of the basic norm as a logico-transcendental premiss that plays an altogether central

---

[7] Ibid. 44.   [8] Ibid. 45–6.

[9] On Kelsen's relation to neo-Kantianism, see Wolfgang Schild, 'Die zwei Systeme der Reinen Rechtslehre', *Wiener Jahrbuch für Philosophie*, 4 (1971), 150–94; Schild, *Die Reinen Rechtslehren* (Vienna: Manz, 1975), 10–11, 14–15.

[10] On the various characterizations of the basic norm, see Ota Weinberger, *Normentheorie als Grundlage der Jurisprudenz und Ethik. Eine Auseinandersetzung mit Hans Kelsens Theorie der Normen* (Berlin: Duncker & Humblot, 1981), at 132–5.

role.[11] Here, Kelsen draws an analogy between his own basic norm and Kant's transcendental philosophy in the *Critique of Pure Reason*:

Kant asks, 'How, without appealing to metaphysics, can the facts perceived by our senses be interpreted in the laws of nature, as these are formulated by natural science?' In the same way, the Pure Theory of Law asks, 'How, without appealing to meta-legal authorities like God or nature, can the subjective sense of certain material facts be interpreted as a system of objectively valid legal norms that are describable in legal propositions?'[12]

It is with the help of the basic norm, then, that the objective validity of a positive legal system is to be established, that is, the subjective sense of acts of will (whose import obviously corresponds to the sensory material constituting experience) is to be interpreted as objectively valid. Just as the empirical material of the sensory world of appearances, the phenomenal world, is objectively constituted through the productive role of the cognizing subject appealing to an original categorial synthesis, so the presupposition of the basic norm is to make possible

the interpretation of the subjective sense of the material fact giving rise to the constitution, and the subjective sense of the material facts set down in accordance with the constitution, as their objective sense—that is, as objectively valid legal norms.[13]

Transcendental cognition is characterized by Kant as cognition that is concerned 'not so much with the objects of cognition as with how we cognize objects, in so far as this may be possible *a priori*'.[14] So, likewise, according to Kelsen, the assumption of the basic norm is not to help establish legal norms in their specific content, but to offer beforehand the condition for the possibility of comprehending the empirical material of norms as belonging to a unified system of legal norms, and thereby the possibility of creating *a priori* the object, law, as an object of enquiry in legal science.[15]

According to Kelsen, one proceeds regressively[16] here in order to demonstrate structurally whatever is already presupposed or must be presupposed when one takes up the law from the standpoint of legal science. In this vein he explicitly emphasizes that the theory of the basic

---

[11] An excellent study of the problem is Hans Köchler, 'Zur transzendentalen Struktur der "Grundnorm"', in *Auf dem Weg zur Menschenwürde und Gerechtigkeit. Festschrift für Hans R. Klecatsky*, ed. Ludwig Adamovich and Peter Pernthaler, 1 vol. in 2 pts. (Vienna: Braumüller, 1980), vol. I.1, pp. 505–17, repr. (in part) in Köchler, *Philosophie, Recht, Politik* (Vienna and New York: Springer, 1985), 15–24.

[12] *PTL* § 34(d) (p. 202) (trans. altered).   [13] *PTL* 201 (trans. altered).

[14] Kant, *CPR* B25 (trans. altered).

[15] On this and other functions of the basic norm, see Schild, *Die Reinen Rechtslehren* (n.9 above), at 20–1.

[16] On the 'regressive' argument, see Kant, *Pro.*, at § 5 (long note) (p. 31).

norm 'by no means inaugurates a new method of legal cognition', but, rather, merely raises to the level of consciousness 'what all jurists do, for the most part unwittingly, when, instead of comprehending the designated material facts as causally determined facts, they interpret the subjective sense of these facts as objectively valid norms.'[17] Elsewhere Kelsen writes that with the basic norm as 'the basic form of the law of normativity', the 'logical presuppositions of the method long practised are revealed by analysing the actual scientific process.'[18]

III.

The issue at hand is the analogy between the transcendental synthesis in Kant's *Critique of Pure Reason*—the enquiry into both its original forms of activity as well as its capabilities—and the directed, *a priori,* regressively demonstrable laying of a foundation for the object, law, by appeal to the conception of the basic norm. How is this analogy to be evaluated? Is it methodologically defensible at all? Or does it represent an indefensible linking of reason directed to different areas of subject-matter or active in different forms? On the one hand, there is the constituting of the object and experience of empirico-sensory, phenomenal reality by means of the categories, within the framework of the 'theoretical' use of reason. And, by appeal to practical reason on the other hand, there is the laying of a foundation for an 'ought'-system that is also apparent to the senses and therefore empirically accessible, but at the same time is shaped by determinations of will. Can the basic norm, then, be ranked alongside the categories? Does not 'transcendental' necessarily mean something different in the practical sphere than in the perspective of theoretical reason, drawn upon here as an analogue?[19]

Kelsen's methodological approach becomes more plausible if one sees it in connection with his negative comments on the concept of practical

[17] *PTL* § 34(d) (pp. 204–5) (trans. altered).

[18] *Phil. Fds.* § 12 (p. 406) (trans. altered). [On this reading of the 'law of normativity' ('*Rechtsgesetz*'), see Hans Kelsen, 'Foreword' to Second Printing of *HP*, in this volume, ch. 1, at § I.]

[19] See Köchler (n.11 above), at 509, repr. at 20, who characterizes the difference between Kant's question and Kelsen's as follows: 'The transcendental conditions for the possibility of cognition are formal as such—and here there is an analogy to Kelsen's model—but they ground each and every concrete experience or cognition. In contrast, the act of thought with which the basic norm is presupposed as the ultimate condition for the validity of a concrete system of norms does not result in the manifestation of a structure that is given as *Faktum*. . . . The presuppositional character of the assumption of a basic norm lies at a categorially, fundamentally different level: It is not that a factual "given" is manifest qua condition for the possibility of a concrete act of thought, but, rather, it is that an obligation is postulated qua necessary presupposition for recognizing the binding character of a concrete norm.'

reason in general, whose own notion of its task—the demonstration of fundamental, plainly valid, and universally binding conditions for action—Kelsen dismisses as scientifically indefensible, a relic of meta-physics.[20] Entirely in keeping with neo-Kantian tradition, Kelsen takes as his point of departure the idea that Kant developed his critico-transcen-dental method in the *Critique of Pure Reason* alone, while failing to assert his philosophico-transcendental programme in his practical philoso-phy—here, in particular, in his legal theory.[21] For here, Kelsen contends, Kant remained committed to a 'juridico-metaphysical' enquiry reflect-ing a programme of pre-critical natural law.

The main reason, according to Kelsen, lies in the continuing influence of Christianity, with its absolute, metaphysically transcendent claim to truth, an influence that had shaped Kant's thought in precisely the prac-tical sphere and hindered him in also developing his transcendental logic here. As Kelsen writes, it was precisely in practical philosophy,

where of course the greatest emphasis of Christian doctrine lies, that metaphys-ical dualism, which Kant fought against so tenaciously in the field of theoretical philosophy, completely invaded his system. Here Kant abandoned his transcen-dental method . . . So it happens that Kant, whose transcendental philosophy was eminently qualified to provide the foundation for a positivistic legal and political theory, remained, as a legal philosopher, mired in the rut of natural law theory.[22]

The view here endures even today, especially among jurists, and in its apparent obviousness it goes largely unquestioned as well. This wide-spread view may be characterized in terms of the methodological ten-dency to reduce practical philosophy to a scientific theory of the normative disciplines. When Kelsen, as quoted above, somewhat regret-fully opines that Kant, with his critical method, was eminently qualified 'to provide the foundation for a positivistic legal and political theory', he, Kelsen, quite obviously does not have in mind laying a genuinely philo-sophical foundation for the concept of law. Rather, he is looking to a theory of the legal sciences that has reference to the law in its empirically demonstrable positivity. It is this theory alone, in Kelsen's view, that merits the appellation 'critical'.

---

[20] For a more detailed exploration of Kelsen's criticism of the concept of practical rea-son, see Gerhard Luf, 'Überlegungen zum Verhältnis von Entscheidung und Rechtfertigung im Recht', in *Überlieferung und Aufgabe. Festschrift für Erich Heintel zum 70. Geburtstag*, ed. Herta Nagl-Docekal, 1 vol. in 2 pts. (Vienna: Braumüller, 1983), vol. I.2, pp. 229–43, at 233–6.

[21] For a convincing critique of this position, see Friedrich Kaulbach, *Studien zur späten Rechtsphilosophie Kants und ihrer transzendentalen Methode* (Würzburg: Königshausen & Neumann, 1982), at 9–54, 75–87.

[22] *Phil. Fds.* § 40 (pp. 444–5) (trans. altered).

IV.

Kelsen's objection—that Kant abandoned in his practical philosophy the standpoint of the critical method—cannot be maintained, for it is itself in the end the expression of a broad misunderstanding of the foundations as well as the tasks of Kant's practical philosophy. Kelsen to the contrary notwithstanding, there are very substantial indices that Kant also developed his critical programme of transcendental philosophy in the sphere of ethics generally and of legal philosophy in particular.[23] In order to follow this, one must pay attention to the difference between the questioning in theoretical reason and that in practical reason. What emerges is different theoretical and practical perspectives on the transcendental—perspectives that must also be taken into account in reflecting on the foundations of law.

While transcendental questioning in the sphere of the theoretical use of reason is directed to demonstrating the conditions for possible knowledge and its limits, the critique of the practical use of reason is directed elsewhere. In the question, 'What ought I to do?', practical questioning is directed to a 'practical object', namely, to fundamental purposes of will and action. Questioning is 'transcendental' when it calls for a demonstration of the plainly valid conditions for will and action within the scope of an unconditioned moral claim. This transcendental questioning necessarily applies also to the sphere of the law, for, while the law is indeed distinguished from morality, it does reach to the sphere of normative rules of action. Here the questioning calls for a demonstration of the conditions for the possibility of finite rational beings shaping their 'external' communal life in accordance with unconditioned, universally binding principles.[24]

This question as to the conditions for the very possibility of good will and action has, then, in the sphere of practical reason the same methodological—namely, transcendental—status as the question as to the conditions for the possibility of objective experience has in the framework of theoretical reason. What prevents Kelsen from acknowledging the critical character of the practical use of reason is the fact that Kant appeals in

[23] The argument for this view is found in Kaulbach (n.21 above), in particular in the opening chapter (ibid. 9–54), namely, on the 'juridico-philosophical presuppositions of the transcendental deduction'.

[24] On transcendental questioning in legal philosophy, see Otfried Höffe, 'Transzendentale Ethik und transzendentale Politik. Ein philosophisches Programm', in *Prinzip Freiheit*, ed. Hans Michael Baumgartner (Freiburg and Munich: Karl Alber, 1979), 141–70, at 163; Gerhard Luf, 'Naturrechtskritik im Lichte der Transzendentalphilosophie', in *Das Naturrechtsdenken heute und morgen. Gedächtnisschrift für René Marcic*, ed. Dorothea Mayer-Maly and Peter M. Simons (Berlin: Duncker & Humblot, 1983), 609–23, at 611–12.

his criticism to a concept of intelligibility apart from phenomenal reality. He aims to comprehend in this way the mediating function of thought in the process of constituting experience, as well as in that of determining will in accordance with principles. In order to perform this function, reason transcends the bonds of empirical reality. This transcending character of reason, addressed in the concept of the 'intelligible' or 'noumenal', leads to differing theoretical and practical consequences, something to be paid special attention in coming to terms with Kelsen.

From the theoretical perspective, the world of the intelligible or noumenal, because it is not apparent to the senses and therefore not empirically demonstrable, is not an object of possible experience and therefore of theoretical knowledge. From the practical perspective, the world of the intelligible or noumenal becomes a practical reality. That is, it becomes, in practical reality, a presupposition that must be postulated in order that moral determinations of will conform to reason. In the dialectic between natural causality and freedom, the postulate addressed in the intelligible or noumenal character of human action is the postulate conceptualizing the human being as free, that is, as called to responsible self-determination. Kant expressly emphasizes that 'in practical purpose, the footpath of freedom is the only path on which it is possible to make use of reason in our conduct.'[25] Thus, for Kant, freedom as the central concept of practical reason, while not a concept that, in terms of theoretical knowledge, can be experienced or empirically demonstrated, is nevertheless a concept that, in terms of practical purpose, is necessary to guarantee that reason be in a position to become reality in the context of human action.

This is by no means to say, however, that according to Kant a world of moral values, a transcendent sphere apart from empirical reality, should be established. This idea of an intelligible or noumenal world is simply a 'standpoint', a world 'into which the thinking, acting agent places himself . . . in order to comprehend himself as an independent, free subject of action and, in this capacity, to act.'[26] Thus, freedom, mediated by way of reflection on human motives for action or on the setting of practical goals, ought always to be brought into the phenomenal reality of human practice and there made historically concrete—without, however, ending in a system of absolute moral values. Kant very clearly meets this requirement, too, in his deduction of the concept of law, a concept he also defines by appeal to the law of freedom qua sole plainly valid principle of legitimization. '*Freedom* (independence from pressure exerted

[25] Immanuel Kant, *Foundations of the Metaphysics of Morals*, trans. Lewis White Beck (Indianapolis: Library of Liberal Arts, 1959), § 3, p. 75 [Akademie edn., 455–6]. (Kant's *Grundlegung* was first published in 1785.)

[26] Kaulbach (n.21 above), 15.

through another's discretion), in so far as it can coexist with every other person's freedom in accordance with a universal law', is expressly qualified as the 'only original right belonging to every man by virtue of his humanity.'[27]

This moral concept of law is the legitimizing foundation of every further formation of law, while, at the same time, the reference to the principle of freedom in its necessary formality is precisely what prevents the constituting, by way of natural law, of a canon of ultimate, absolutely valid, material purposes of law. One takes leave, then, of the traditional, natural law approach, with its claim of deriving fundamental legal norms from human nature.

V.

As already noted, Kelsen, owing to his own understanding of reality, cannot digest and accept such a concept of practical reason in the law, a concept shaped by the idea that nature is intelligible or noumenal, the idea of a 'causality stemming from freedom'. He is, therefore, in no position to distinguish with sufficient clarity between a concept of law grounded in traditional natural law and a freedom-oriented concept grounded in the law of reason. Rather, he classifies both, without differentiation, as reflecting a 'metaphysical' view of the law. This is understandable from the standpoint of Kelsen's own system, for he identifies reality—also the reality of human practices—with the facticity of objective existence in terms of a mechanico-causal model of explanation. This model is essentially a value-neutral ordering of the empirical material at hand, including legal material in positive form, an ordering to be undertaken in accordance with logico-formal criteria. The source of these logico-formal ordering categories remains, however, largely unexamined. In any case, they are seen as instrumentally available qualities, independent of any subject, and requiring no further legitimization in the rational action of human beings.

Based on this phenomenalistic understanding of reality, this reduction of reality to appearances, Kelsen comprehends the character of the intelligible or noumenal in the rational action of human beings, not in terms of transcendental difference—that is, being beyond the empirical world of objects and at the same time mediating hands-on in that world—but, rather, as something analogous to material objects,

---

[27] Immanuel Kant, *The Metaphysics of Morals*, trans. Mary Gregor (Cambridge: Cambridge UP, 1991), 'Division of the Doctrine of Right', §B, 63 (Kant's emphasis) (trans. altered) [Akademie edn., 237–8]. (The first part of Kant's *Metaphysik der Sitten*, namely the *Rechtslehre*, was first published in 1797.)

something equally 'thing-like'. In this way, Kelsen turns the idea of an intelligible or noumenal world into the idea of a transcendent 'counter-world', which, shaped by an irreconcilable dualism of fact and value, must of course be seen, correctly, as a phenomenal form reflecting the very metaphysics he criticizes. And thus seen, even freedom as the central concept of practical reason is problematic, at best an irrelevant concept and in any case useless in scientific enquiry.

Seen from an empiricist point of view, freedom can only be characterized as 'causal non-determinacy', which, owing to the equation of motivation and causal determination, stands then 'in evident contradiction to the facts of social life'[28]—a point Kelsen emphasizes, altogether in consonance with his theory. For within the framework of this empiricist point of view, looking to the simple alternative of determined or undetermined action, freedom necessarily enters into an antagonistic relation with every form of coercion. Every limitation of individual discretion represents a restriction of freedom. And it is precisely within the legal sphere, where the application of organized legal coercion looms large, that freedom, understood in this way, is not applicable. Freedom is simply a complementary remainder, the aggregate of all those spheres of action not comprehended by legal coercion and therefore left to subjective discretion. In no case is freedom thereby in a position to be the basis for unconditioned moral legitimization, a basis from which the claims of the positive law to validity might be derived.

VI.

All of these methodological presuppositions have of course far-reaching consequences for Kelsen's conception of the basic norm. In particular, if one were to understand the basic norm in terms of Kant's practical philosophy, as a transcendental presupposition of the validity of positive law, then, as Dreier correctly remarks, the basic norm would have to be conceived of and applied as a 'command of practical reason',[29] that is, as a principle of practical reason. Interestingly, it is by following a train of thought similar to Kelsen's deduction of the basic norm that Kant, too, expressly addresses this consideration. In the course of laying a foundation for the validity of positive laws, he writes:

One can . . . imagine external lawgiving that contains only (positive) laws; but then preceding it would have to be a natural law establishing the lawgiver's authority (that is, giving him the authority to bind others by the simple use of his discretion).[30]

---

[28] *PTL* § 23 (p. 94).   [29] Dreier (n.5 above), 44.
[30] Kant, *The Metaphysics of Morals* (n.27 above), Introduction, at §IV ('Preliminary Concepts'), 51 (trans. altered) [Akademie edn., 224].

To be sure, Kant uses traditional natural law terminology here. Seen in terms of his own system, however, this 'natural law' establishing the validity of legislation in the positive law is nothing other than the freedom-based moral concept of law. And this concept—thanks to the universality and formality guaranteed by its connection to freedom—is to fulfil the transcendental requirement (understood in the practical sense) of formulating institutional rules of community life that are unconditionally and universally binding, and that are to be taken into account as a permanent requirement in the shaping of the law as part of the historical process of making law reality.

A basic norm understood as a principle of practical reason cannot, then, refer simply to the correctness of the process of law creation or to the presence of a minimum level of social efficacy as establishing or conditioning validity. Rather, it must of necessity also incorporate substantive factors, namely, those serving the ethical justification of the positive law. These criteria of juridico-ethical legitimization are not to be understood, however, as a complex of absolute norms of justice that are based on natural law, norms that would form a kind of deductive meta-legal system. Rather, these criteria are basic moral requirements that demand of the positive law not only that fundamental guarantees of free and independent self-determination be recognized in the shaping of the law's content, but also that attention be paid to the historical dimension of the legal standards that are to be concretely applied.[31] If, then, one were to postulate here a duty of unconditional obedience to law reaching even to unjust norms, such a claim to obedience would not have to be seen as unconditionally given, as no longer justifiable in legal science, but, rather, would have to be legally legitimized by appeal to the basic norm (as represented in, say, the legal dictates of peace).

Since, however, Kelsen seeks to understand the basic norm—contrary to the practical system—as a logico-transcendental presupposition from the standpoint of theoretical reason, his conception of the basic norm lacks from the very beginning any reference to the practical dimension of establishing the law. Thus, from this methodological standpoint, it is impossible for Kelsen to establish normatively a legal *Sollen* or 'ought' in the context of the greater sphere of human practices. The *Sollen* or 'ought' becomes, then, nothing other than a form of logical connection within the context of a concept of imputation that is understood analogously to causality and that substantially reflects a mechanico-causal

---

[31] See Kaulbach (n.21 above), at 106. It is in the historical dimension of the legal standard that Kaulbach sees the essential difference between a transcendental legal philosophy and those neo-Kantian approaches that 'have left themselves open to the objection that value standards and norms are only to be understood in a formal sense' (ibid).

model of cognition.[32] In any case, this *Sollen* or 'ought' is not a moral concept, which would remain tied to the foundations of human will and action. Eliminating the ethico-practical dimension of establishing the law brings to the forefront the effort to formulate a scientific theory of law equivalent to a theory of legal cognition.

Such a theory of law is not, however, in a position to demonstrate any *a priori* structures of the law. For it is unwittingly dependent on the empirically given legal material that is to be systematized, as well as on the juridico-historical understanding behind this material, and it is confined to drawing from this empirical material, by way of abstraction, general empirical concepts at a high level of formalization, and then applying these concepts in accordance with formal, ordering points of view. Gottfried Hohenauer saw this abstract point of view very clearly, and emphasized that what counts for this legal theory, 'despite its strictest logical objectification, is in the end simply the abstract scheme of an empirical legal theory.'[33] Within this legal theory, the basic norm has the function, *inter alia*, of marshalling empirical legal material into a unified basis of validity and thereby creating a unified object of juridico-scientific enquiry. Thus understood, the basic norm is not a concept of transcendental standing. It is not demonstrated regressively by appeal to a plainly valid moral principle (like the principle of freedom) in keeping with a juridico-ethical claim of ultimate foundation. Rather, it functions as a hypothetical general empirical concept, arrived at by way of abstraction.

VII.

If one sees the basic norm as a general empirical concept, then its pretense of value neutrality—say, its independence of juridico-ethical criteria—cannot be maintained. All law, in its historico-phenomenal form, has been shaped by a variety of normatively significant factors: notions of justice, social conditions, problem-solving requirements, constellations of interests, and many more. If one abstracts from these factors in order to be able to refer to more fundamental structures of the law, the result is a concept of law that is, to be sure, contentually poorer but still not purely formal, since what remains decisive for each abstraction is points of view that provide normative guidance. And so it is with the con-

---

[32] For a critical evaluation of Kelsen's concept of *Sollen* or 'ought', see Schild, *Die Reinen Rechtslehren* (n.9 above), at 27–8; Günther Winkler, 'Sein und Sollen', *Rechtstheorie*, 10 (1979), 257–80, repr. in Winkler, *Theorie und Methode in der Rechtswissenschaft* (Vienna and New York: Springer, 1989), 233–59.

[33] Gottfried Hohenauer, 'Der Neukantianismus und seine Grenzen als Gesellschafts- und Rechtsphilosophie', *Blätter für deutsche Philosophie*, 2 (1928–9), 302–36, at 336.

cept of law that underlies the basic norm. The familiar formulation of the basic norm, that 'coercive acts ought to be imposed under the conditions and in the manner established by the historically first constitution and the norms issued in accordance with it',[34] and, furthermore, the express exclusion of 'transcendent values'[35] of justice from the positive law, or the focus on an efficacy that is 'by and large' given[36]—all these factors point to an altogether specific concept of law, a concept that is dependent on provisional methodological determinations and that does not possess a timeless quality at all.

In this concept of law, it is altogether obvious first of all that the coercive element plays a central role, and that, by comparison, all other, equally important social functions of the law fall very much into the background. Of significance, too, is an idea decisive for the theory of the sources of law, the idea of the all-encompassing positivity of the law, which excludes recognition of presupposed principles of justice that take priority over positive legal norms. And an important function is performed by abstract appeal to the effectiveness, 'by and large', of the legal system, for such an appeal excludes the question as to the presuppositions justifying the duty to obey the law. Seen in this way, generally speaking, the pre-eminent picture of the law is a picture that, marked by an interest in technico-practical cognition, is substantially shaped by the notion of instrumental control, the notion of an organization of social processes that is as trouble-free as possible. Seen historically, this understanding of the law is substantially shaped by industrial society with its special performance requirements, as well as by the idea of the liberal constitutional state, the rule of law.

Notwithstanding these inadmissible abstractions, Kelsen's conception of the basic norm has, without a doubt, great pragmatic value. As the basis of a formal concept of validity, centred in terms of a 'dynamic' norm type[37] on the process of law creation, this conception of the basic norm is capable of carrying out important tasks and facilitating cognition, for example, with an eye to structurally understanding positive legal material or responding to problems of validity by appeal to derogation. Equally manifest, however, are the limits of this approach. They are especially evident, to conclude with a single example, when one seeks to comprehend validity within the framework of an expanded understanding of the sources of law and, to this end, incorporates not only legal regulations in positive statutory form but also other sources of law, say, legal

[34] *PTL* § 34(c) (p. 201) (trans. altered).

[35] 'In the presupposition of the basic norm, no value transcending the positive law is endorsed.' *PTL* § 34(d) (p. 201) (trans. altered).

[36] *PTL* § 34(g) (p. 212).

[37] For the distinction between the 'static' and the 'dynamic' norm type, see *PTL*, at § 34(b) (pp. 195–8).

principles. In this case, it is not simply the abstract collection of positive legal regulations that can be characterized as the 'specific existence' of norms, a designation ascribing to these regulations the quality of being part of a comprehensive, valid legal system. Rather, 'validity' must grasp legal norms in their concrete, practical reality, as these are actualized and thereby first take on concrete form—through the application of law or through legal science incorporating the weighing of juridico-ethical principles and values. While one begins, then, with the assumption that the law cannot in practice do without such a weighing of juridico-ethical principles, Kelsen's basic norm is in no position to comprehend this aspect of the validity of juridico-ethically legitimized principles, for precisely this aspect violates the idea of the closed context of law creation in a system of positive law.

Nothing in all of this would change if, as Dreier attempts to do, one extended Kelsen's basic norm to include an ethical component of validity in order to limit by means of moral criteria—in line with Radbruch's view of 'statutory non-law'[38]—the claim of legal norms to validity. For the extreme case of terror through legal norms that lack a minimum possibility of ethical justification, this extension of the basic norm may have the greatest importance, but it has only limited significance for the everyday case of making the law concrete and taking juridico-ethical principles into account to do so. When Dreier, then, postulates a reinterpretation of the basic norm in terms of the law of reason, one fully supports him in his concern 'to rehabilitate the practical philosophy' also in the law. At the same time, one must note that such a modification in no way represents a mere extension of Kelsen's conception of the basic norm. Rather, it depends on the inclusion of altogether different systematic presuppositions that cannot be squared with Kelsen's effort at all.

---

[38] See Gustav Radbruch, 'Gesetzliches Unrecht und übergesetzliches Recht', *Süddeutsche Juristenzeitung*, 1 (1946), 105–8, repr. in Radbruch, *Rechtsphilosophie*, 8th edn., ed. Erik Wolf and Hans-Peter Schneider (Stuttgart: K.F. Koehler, 1973), 339–51, and repr. in Radbruch, *Gesamtausgabe*, 20 vols. projected, ed. Arthur Kaufmann, vol. III: *Rechtsphilosophie III*, ed. Winfried Hassemer (Heidelberg: C.F. Müller, 1990), 83–93, 282–91 (editorial notes).

B. Kelsen without Kant, and 'Validity qua Bindingness'

12

The Purity of the Pure Theory*

JOSEPH RAZ

Kelsen's range of interests and creative impulses were prodigious. In constitutional law, international law, moral philosophy, political theory, and the philosophy of law he kept a lively interest throughout his life. To all those areas he made valuable contributions, bringing to them the fruits of his incisive and uncompromising reflections. On many issues his contributions are of lasting value and will continue to stimulate students and scholars for many years to come.

Some commentators have expressed exasperation in the face of what they regard as Kelsen's obscurities and have dismissed some of his central doctrines as confused. I myself have not escaped the occasional feeling of despair in struggling to fathom the meaning of some of his theses. But I have always had the sense that he was a philosopher grappling with some of the more difficult problems of legal philosophy, problems the complexity of which he often understood better than anyone. All too often I have discovered that my sense of puzzlement at some of his doctrines was due to my failure to grasp the difficulties which Kelsen tackled and was striving to solve. His central doctrines have acquired for me a somewhat haunting character. Every time I return to them I discover new depths and new insights which had escaped me before. It is, therefore, as a personal tribute to his work's continuing fertilizing influence that I have chosen to return once more to review some of Kelsen's fundamental doctrines.

I.

Kelsen's reputation for obscurity contrasts with his reputation for logical rigour. Logical rigour he certainly respected and aspired to achieve.

* *Editors' note*: This paper was first published in *Revue internationale de philosophie*, 138 (1981), 441–59, and was reprinted in *Essays on Kelsen*, ed. Richard Tur and William Twining (Oxford: Clarendon Press, 1986), 79–97.

There is a fascinating sense of great austerity about his work. Of course this austerity did not remain a matter of personal style. It became the cornerstone of his legal theory, the purity of it.

Kelsen's theory is, as is well known, doubly pure. It is free of sociological and psychological investigations and it separates law from morality.[1] The first purity has attracted much criticism and is generally regarded as having been completely discredited. The criticism is based on one or the other of two quite separate objections. First is the objection that the content of the law cannot be established without regard to the actions and intentions of legal institutions be they legislative or adjudicative.[2] Second, there is the objection that the law and its significance cannot be appreciated unless one studies it in its social context, with an emphasis on its actual effects in practice. Both objections are familiar and I will not discuss them in detail. Let me, though, make a couple of observations about the second one.

It is beyond doubt part of the task of legal philosophy to explain the methods by which the existence and content of the law are ascertained. If it is true that they cannot be ascertained without regard to the practices and manifested attitudes of legal institutions, then the first objection is— as I believe it to be—an important valid objection to Kelsen's theory. It is less clear that the second objection is an objection at all. Kelsen did not deny the possibility of sociological jurisprudence. He was content to maintain four theses. First, that beside sociological jurisprudence there is also an independent enquiry, normative jurisprudence, whose subject is different. Normative jurisprudence is the study of legal norms, that is, the study of how people ought to behave according to law. It is not an enquiry into how they actually do behave. Second, normative jurisprudence is no less empirical than sociological jurisprudence, since it is concerned exclusively with *positive* law, that is, law as the product of the activity of social custom and of legislative and adjudicative institutions. Thirdly, normative jurisprudence enjoys in an important way a logical priority over sociological jurisprudence. The very definition of the subject-matter of sociological jurisprudence presupposes an understanding of law as provided by its normative study, since sociology of law is the study of those aspects of human behaviour which are related to the law. Here 'the law' must be normatively interpreted. Fourthly, normative jurisprudence is presupposed by sociology in another important way as well. The explanation of human behaviour related to law has to take account of the way people's beliefs about the law, normatively understood, affect their behaviour.[3]

---

[1] See e.g. *PTL*, at § 1 (p. 1).   [2] See H.L.A. Hart, 'Kelsen Visited', in this volume, ch. 4.
[3] For a detailed discussion, see *GTLS*, at 162–78.

I think Kelsen was essentially right in all four theses. They show that he was not hostile to sociological jurisprudence, though admittedly his own interests did not take him that way. Though these views have since been independently explored and developed by both social scientists and philosophers, I do believe that Kelsen has anticipated many of the arguments used by other thinkers and that we can still benefit from his explanation of the relations between the normative and the sociological study of the law. Both his emphasis on the explanatory importance of people's beliefs concerning what they are normatively required to do and his insistence on the autonomy and distinctness of normative concepts are a valuable and lasting contribution to a subject which has been for years dominated by reductive attempts to provide eliminative definitions of normative terms in favour of non-normative, descriptive ones.

II.

Kelsen's semantic anti-reductivism is of course intimately connected with the other purity of Kelsen's theory: its being free of moral elements. Here the antagonists were not the sociological theorists but the natural lawyers. The opposition to natural law was a major preoccupation of Kelsen's and he wrote extensively on the subject throughout his life. His views place him in the historical tradition of legal positivism.

Three major theses have been traditionally associated with legal positivism.[4] First is the reductive semantic thesis which proposes a reductive analysis of legal statements according to which they are non-normative, descriptive statements of one kind or another. Second is the contingent connection thesis according to which there is no necessary connection between law and moral values. Third is the sources thesis which claims that the identification of the existence and content of law does not require resort to any moral argument.

The three theses are logically independent and one is free to accept any one of them while rejecting the others. They were, however, collectively endorsed by many leading positivists such as Bentham, Austin, Holmes, and Ross among others. Where does Kelsen stand on these issues? The question is of the utmost importance to the understanding of his theory of law. In many ways it is the most important set of problems that any philosophy of law has to face since it raises the problem of the

---

[4] See my discussion of these problems in *Practical Reason and Norms* (London: Hutchinson, 1975, 2nd edn. Princeton: Princeton UP, 1990), at § 5.3 (pp. 162–70) and in Raz, *AL*, at 37–52. See also H.L.A. Hart, 'Positivism and the Separation of Law and Morals', *Harvard Law Review*, 71 (1957–8), 593–629, repr. in Hart, *Essays in Jurisprudence and Philosophy* (Oxford: Clarendon Press, 1983), 49–87.

double aspect of law, its being a social institution with a normative aspect. The supreme challenge for any theory of law is to do justice to both facets of the law.

Kelsen's solution is to reject the reductive semantic thesis and to embrace the contingent connection and the sources theses. Kelsen regards the law as positive law. It is based on social sources identifiable without any reference to moral argument. On this Kelsen never had any doubt. He never wavered in his endorsement of the two aspects of the thesis. The existence or non-existence of a legal system as a whole is a matter of social fact. It depends entirely on its efficacy in the society in question. Moreover, the test determining for every individual rule whether it belongs to a legal system in force in a certain country is equally a matter of social fact. It turns on whether or not it was posited in the appropriate way: whether or not it can be traced to an authorized social source.

Equally firm is Kelsen's belief in the contingent connection thesis. Kelsen insists that (1) to claim that there is a necessary connection between (the content of) law and morals either presupposes absolute moral values to which the law necessarily conforms or assumes that all the divers relativistic moralities have some values in common and that the law conforms to those. He further argues that (2) there are no absolute moral values and there is no content common to all the relativistic moralities. Hence he concludes that there is no necessary connection between law and morals.[5]

Kelsen's departure from the traditional positivist view is in his rejection of the semantic reductive thesis. Reductive positivists have variously argued that legal statements are statements about commands, or predictions of the likelihood of sanctions or of courts' decisions, etc. Kelsen is adamant in rejecting all reductive analyses of legal statements. He holds that 'a norm . . . is "valid" means that it is binding—that an individual ought to behave in the manner determined by the norm.'[6] Kelsen regards legal statements as fully normative statements. This view of his, as has been often noted, is difficult to reconcile with his acceptance of the sources and the contingent connection theses which leads him to say at the same time that 'juristic value judgments are judgments which can be tested objectively by facts'.[7] It is in his handling of the tension between his non-reductive semantic views and the sources and the contingent connection theses that one finds his most original contribution to the general theory of law. It is this tension which leads directly to his best-known doctrine, that of the basic norm.

---

[5] See *PTL* §11 (at pp. 63–5).   [6] *PTL* § 34(a) (p. 193).

[7] Hans Kelsen, 'Value Judgments in the Science of Law', *Journal of Social Philosophy and Jurisprudence*, 7 (1942), 312–33, at 332, repr. *WJ* 209–30, 389 (notes), at 229.

III.

Before we turn to an examination of this aspect of Kelsen's contribution it has to be conceded that Kelsen's own espousal of the two positivist theses leaves a lot to be desired. Kelsen's defence of the sources thesis is largely dependent on the view that the 'scientific' study of law would not be possible if the identification of law turned on moral argument.[8] But this argument is clearly fallacious. The study of law must be adjusted to its object. If its object cannot be studied 'scientifically' then its study should not strive to be scientific. One can learn from the nature of an object how it should be investigated but one cannot postulate that the object has a certain character because one wishes to study it in a certain way.

Nor is Kelsen's defence of the contingent connection thesis more convincing. Not only has he failed to establish that there are no absolute values nor even that there is no ground common to all relativistic moralities, he has failed to perceive the nature of the problem and addressed himself to the wrong question. Four elements contribute to this failure. First, from a relativistic point of view the right question for a person to ask is whether the morality which he shares does lead to the conclusion that there is a necessary connection between law and *this* morality, that is, whether *this* morality is such that all legal systems whatever they may be do necessarily enshrine some of the values which it proclaims. For a relativist this question is of practical and theoretical importance. Clearly an affirmative answer to it does not require an affirmative answer to Kelsen's question whether there are values common to *all* relativistic moralities which are respected by all legal systems.

Second, the question whether the law by its content necessarily conforms to moral values is not the only pertinent question to ask. Another is whether obedience to law is always morally required regardless of the content of the law. Possibly it is required because it is expected by others or because it will reciprocate their obedience. After all, Kelsen regards law as existing only if efficacious. I do not wish to maintain that this fact gives rise to any moral obligation. But it must be acknowledged that if it does, this will show a necessary connection between law and morals which does not depend on the content of the law.

Third, Kelsen's discussion is coloured by his conception of natural law as a theory which maintains that unjust laws are not valid laws at all. But many natural law theories do not conform to this view. Consider three prominent recent examples. Fuller, Dworkin, and Finnis maintain that

---

[8] See *GTLS*, at 5.

there is a necessary connection between law and morality. But none of them denies that there may be valid unjust laws.[9]

Finally, Kelsen here as elsewhere considers only conclusive moral force and neglects the possibility of a connection between law and morality which lends to the law a prima-facie moral character which may be overridden by conflicting moral considerations.

When we examine the views of the three authors I mentioned, we find that they tend to emphasize a connection between law and morality resting on various content-independent features of the law which does not exclude the possibility of valid unjust laws and which endows the law with only a prima-facie moral force. Kelsen's arguments for the contingent connection thesis are inadequate against such theories. The inadequacy of Kelsen's arguments does not, of course, mean that the views he thus tried to justify are themselves misconceived. But it is not my intention here to examine these theses.[10] Instead let us return to the question of their compatibility with a non-reductive semantic view of the analysis of legal statements. The question is crucial to the success of the second purity of the Pure Theory, its being free of moral elements. This purity seems to be guaranteed by the sources and the contingent connection doctrines. But isn't that purity undermined by the view that legal statements are ordinary normative statements just like moral statements?

IV.

I have already mentioned that Kelsen's rejection of semantic reductivism was a departure from traditional positivist views. Another legal philosopher who shares his anti-reductivism is H.L.A. Hart, and it may help clarify Kelsen's position briefly to describe Hart's first.

As is well known, Hart distinguishes two kinds of statements standardly made by the use of deontic sentences, which he calls internal and external statements.[11] External statements are statements about

---

[9] Lon L. Fuller, *The Morality of Law* (New Haven: Yale UP, 1964); Ronald Dworkin, *Taking Rights Seriously* (London: Duckworth and Cambridge, Mass.: Harvard UP, 1977); John Finnis, *Natural Law and Natural Rights* (Oxford: Clarendon Press, 1980). Incidentally while all three reject the contingent connection thesis only Dworkin rejects the sources thesis. Fuller's and Finnis's writings are consistent with a weak version of the sources thesis. For a distinction between a weak and a strong version of this thesis, see Raz, *AL*, at 37–52.

[10] In *AL* I have defended the sources thesis. Regarding the contingent connection issue one has to be more specific. I have argued that whatever moral character the law has it is not enough to establish a prima-facie obligation to obey the law. This leaves open the possibility of a necessary connection between law and morals of a lesser force.

[11] See Hart, *CL*, at 56–8, 86–8, 244, 2nd edn., at 56–8, 88–91, 291. For a discussion of Hart's anti-reductivism, see G.P. Baker, 'Defeasibility and Meaning', in *Law, Morality and Society. Essays in Honour of H.L.A. Hart*, ed. P.M.S. Hacker and Joseph Raz (Oxford: Clarendon Press, 1977), 26–57.

people's behaviour and attitudes and need not concern us. Hart's notion of internal statements is fraught with difficulties. I will outline without detailed textual argument my understanding of it when applied to the law and I will refer to such statements as legal statements.[12] The law is for Hart an immensely complex social practice or set of practices. In part the meaning of legal statements can be given a truth-conditional analysis. Legal statements are true if and only if certain relations obtain between them and the complex legal practices. But it would be wrong to say that legal statements are just statements about the existence of those practices. The truth-conditional analysis does not exhaust the meaning of legal statements. To understand them one must also understand their standard uses and what they express. Their typical use is to provide guidance by criticizing, commending, demanding, advising, approving, etc., and they express acceptance by the speaker of standards of behaviour towards conformity with which the statement is used to guide its addressee.

This view of legal statements is meant to accommodate both their social-factual and their normative aspects. The factual aspect is captured by a truth-conditional analysis. The normative one is accounted for by an explanation of the illocutionary force of the statements and by the fact that they express not only the speaker's beliefs but also his practical attitude, his willingness to be guided by certain standards.

One would expect Kelsen to propound a view of legal statements rather like Hart's since Hart's account shares three of the most important features of Kelsen's doctrine of the law and of legal discourse. First, the existence of law can be objectively ascertained by reference to social facts. Hence Hart says, and one would expect Kelsen to agree, that legal statements are either true or false and that their truth conditions are their relations to complex social practices. Second, Hart, like Kelsen, regards legal statements as having a normative dimension which cannot be reduced to an assertion of any social facts. Third, Hart's account of the normative dimension in terms of the illocutionary and expressive force of legal statements avoids any reference to moral facts and does not presuppose the existence of moral values. Since Kelsen denies the existence of absolute moral values one might have expected him to provide an analysis of legal discourse along lines similar to Hart's.

Despite these similarities Kelsen's view of legal statements is radically different from Hart's, because Kelsen advances a cognitivist interpretation of all normative discourse. He rejects expressive explanations such as Hart's. For him a normative statement, be it legal, moral, or other, expresses a practical attitude only in that it expresses a belief in the

---

[12] A similar analysis can be applied to his views of moral statements of duties but not to other normative statements.

existence of a valid norm, and a norm constitutes a value.[13] Hence the normative aspect of legal statements is not to be explained by their illocutionary force nor by the fact, taken by itself, that they express an acceptance of a standard of behaviour. It has to be explained by the fact that such statements state or presuppose the existence of a value or a norm, that is, a normatively binding standard and not merely a social practice.

This understanding of Kelsen's position is not without its difficulties. He says, for example, that '[t]here is not, and cannot be, an objective criterion of justice because the statement: something is just or unjust, is a judgment of value . . . and these value judgments are by their very nature subjective in character, because based on emotional elements of our mind, on our feelings and wishes. They cannot be verified by facts, as can statements about reality. Ultimate value judgments are mostly acts of preference . . .'.[14] This passage suggests a non-cognitive interpretation of moral statements. But for the most part Kelsen adopts a cognitive view and regards every normative statement, legal or otherwise, as a statement of a binding norm or of the value it institutes. Such a semantic view is of course consistent with value-scepticism. It will merely lead the sceptic to the belief that all normative statements are false. Kelsen, however, is not a sceptic. He is a subjectivist or a relativist. Normative statements can be true or false. It is merely that their truth depends on the existence of relative rather than absolute values: '[R]elativistic . . . positivism does not assert that there are no values, or that there is no moral order, but only that the values in which men actually believe are not absolute but relative values.'[15]

Unfortunately, Kelsen's version of relativism is the familiar and incoherent one by which relativism is the non-relativist position that each person's values apply only to himself and each society's values to itself.[16] It is, of course, Kelsen's semantic doctrine rather than his theory of morals that I am concerned with. But the troubles with this kind of relativistic morality infect the interpretation of moral statements. It seems to suggest the oddity that sincere moral statements of a person about his own conduct are always true. Since he believes that there is a norm that he ought to perform a certain action, there is, in virtue of the relativistic morality, such a norm and his statement is true. Insincere moral statements about oneself are always false. The person does not believe that there is such a norm and therefore it does not exist and the statement is false. Normative statements about other people would be on this view

---

[13] Hans Kelsen, 'A "Dynamic" Theory of Natural Law', *Louisiana Law Review*, 16 (1955–6), 597–620, at 602, repr. *WJ* 174–97, 388 (notes), at 179.

[14] Hans Kelsen, 'Law, State and Justice in the Pure Theory of Law', *Yale Law Journal*, 57 (1947–8), 377–90, at 384, repr. *WJ* 288–302, 390–3 (notes), at 295.

[15] Kelsen (n.13 above).   [16] See e.g. *PTL*, at §§ 7–13 (pp. 59–69).

true if and only if they accord with those other people's beliefs about themselves. Thus it is true that a racist should behave in a racist way.

None of this is acceptable and Kelsen does not explicitly draw such conclusions. He simply avoids talking of truth as applied to moral statements though he has no alternative account consistent with the rest of his doctrine. I believe that it is possible to provide a coherent relativist account of morality and that it can serve as a basis for a cognitivist interpretation of moral statements. But this is obviously not a task for this occasion. All that one can derive from Kelsen himself is the view that normative statements should be given a cognitivist interpretation, that they state the existence of duties, rights, powers, or permissions and do not merely express the speaker's attitude. Whatever other speech acts are performed in normative discourse, the one speech act common to it is that of stating what is alleged to be the case.

V.

Legal statements are normative statements in the same sense and in the same way that moral statements are normative. This is as we saw the gist of Kelsen's semantic anti-reductivism. The implication of his persistent emphasis is that legal statements are 'ought' statements, not to be confused with 'is' statements. The threat that this view poses to the purity of one's theory of law is evident. If legal statements are as normative as ordinary moral ones, if they are moral statements, then the law and its existence and content, which is what legal statements state, seem to be essentially moral facts. But the study of moral facts and their identification cannot be free of moral considerations and arguments.

Kelsen's solution is threefold. First, he points out that the existence of law can be established and its content ascertained without the use of normative statements. The law can be described in sociological terms, be described as a power structure in a society, etc. Such a description is not synonymous with a normative description of the law. If it were then it would amount to a reductive analysis of the normative description. But such a description will convey all the social facts which form the factual basis of the law, all the social practices which Hart regards as constituting the existence of law. What will be left out is the claim that these social facts are 'objectively valid', that they give rise to rights and duties and to other normative consequences. Some people have the appropriate moral beliefs and they regard the law as a normative system and describe it using legal statements. Those who do not share these moral views deny that the law is normative. But they can acknowledge its existence as a social fact.

But this first answer to the problem is not enough. It shows the possibility of a pure study of law as a complex social fact but it does not by itself establish the possibility of a pure study of law as a *normative* system. Therefore, Kelsen reinforces the first move with a second one. People have many moral beliefs. It is likely that for any individual in a society some of his moral beliefs coincide with the law and some diverge from it. But imagine a man whose moral beliefs are identical with the law. He does not add nor detract one iota from it. Furthermore assume that his moral beliefs all derive from his belief in the moral authority of the ultimate law-making processes. For him, in other words, his belief in the validity of all and only the legal norms is not a haphazard result of chance but a logical consequence of one of his beliefs. Let us call this person the legal man. Legal science, says Kelsen, studies the law as a normative system but without committing itself to its normativity. Basically the legal statements of legal science are conditional legal statements: if the legal man is right, they say, then this is what you ought to do. 'The Pure Theory', he says, 'describes the positive law as an objectively valid normative order and states that this interpretation is possible only under the condition that a basic norm is presupposed according to which the subjective meaning of the law-creating acts is also their objective meaning. The Pure Theory thereby characterizes this interpretation as possible, not necessary, and presents the objective validity of positive law only as conditional—namely conditioned by the presupposed basic norm.'[17] Therefore all the legal statements of legal science are hypothetical.[18]

My legal man is one who endorses the basic norm and all that follows from it and nothing else. Scientific legal statements, being conditional statements of the form 'if the legal man is right then one ought to . . .' or 'if the basic norm is valid one ought to . . .' etc., are value-neutral. They are free of any moral presuppositions. By using them legal science can both be pure and describe the law as a normative system.

The problem with this second answer is that although it allows legal science to describe the law as a normative system it does not allow it to use categorical statements, for they state that the law is a system of valid norms. It merely enables legal science to state what the law is *if it is valid*. This may be all that legal scholars need do. But it is not all that legal practitioners, barristers and solicitors, do. They do not merely talk about the law. They use it to advise clients and to present arguments before courts. Kelsen does not distinguish between the scholar and the practitioner. His analysis of legal discourse is meant to apply to both. But the practitioner does not state what the law is if it is valid. He states that it is valid. Yet if legal theory is pure such statements cannot be moral statements.

[17] *PTL* §34(i) (pp. 217–18).   [18] See *PTL* §16 (at p. 71).

They cannot be full-blooded normative statements. Kelsen requires a value-neutral interpretation of categorical legal statements. He solves this problem by making his third move. Legal scientists, he says, do not merely describe what the law is if the basic norm is valid. They do actually presuppose the basic norm themselves. They assume its validity. '[T]he basic norm really exists in the juristic consciousness.'[19]

Kelsen sometimes draws obscurely on a distinction between positing and presupposing the basic norm,[20] to suggest that legal scientists (by which he refers to practitioners as well) presuppose but do not posit it as do people who actually believe in the moral validity of the law. This terminological distinction is not a happy one. His idea seems to be that not all scientific legal statements are hypotheticals of the type analysed above. Some or most are categorical statements based on a presupposition of the basic norm as a fiction.[21] Categorical legal statements are therefore of two types, which I have called elsewhere committed and detached.[22] Committed statements are those of ordinary people who use normative language when stating the law because they believe or purport to believe in its binding force. Detached statements are typical of legal science, which assumes the point of view of the legal man without being committed to it. It describes the law in normative statements, but this is a description from a point of view which is not necessarily accepted by the speaker. He talks as if he accepts the basic norm and this pretence is what Kelsen refers to as presupposing the basic norm as a fiction. Detached statements state the law as a valid normative system; they do not merely describe what would be valid if the basic norm is valid. But they do so from a point of view, that of the legal man, to which they are not committed. Therefore, legal science is pure, free of moral commitment despite its use of normative language.

VI.

I have ascribed to Kelsen the view that there are three types of legal statement.

(1) Statements conditional on the validity of the basic norm, which are morally uncommitted since their normative force depends on the unasserted condition: if the basic norm is valid then . . .

(2) Detached statements, which are also morally uncommitted since they are statements from a point of view. They state what rights and

[19] *GTLS* 116.   [20] *PTL* § 34(d) (p. 204 n.72).
[21] See Hans Kelsen, 'On the Pure Theory of Law', *Israel Law Review*, 1 (1966), 1–7, at 6.
[22] See Raz, *AL*, at 146–59, see also at 122–45.

duties there are on the assumption that the basic norm is valid but without commitment to that assumption.

(3) Committed statements, which are ordinary moral statements about what ought to be done, what rights and duties people have because of the law.

Legal theory contains statements of the first two kinds only and is therefore pure.

It has to be admitted, of course, that this is more a reconstruction than a straightforward interpretation. Kelsen does not distinguish clearly between the three classes and he himself confessed to confusing the last with the other two on occasion.[23] Worse still, while I believe that he was generally aware of the distinction between the committed statements and the others, he appears to have been completely unaware of the difference between the detached statements and those conditional on the validity of the basic norm. Here I think it is fair to accuse him of confusion and equivocation. He does shift from one position to the other without noticing the difference. I have tried to separate the strands of thought as clearly as I can. But such a reconstruction is bound to remain tentative and controversial.

Interpretation aside, the question arises, how illuminating are these distinctions? I ask 'how illuminating' and not 'are they true' for it is clearly a programme for an explanation rather than a full explanation that Kelsen provides. We may approach the problem by comparing Kelsen (or should I say the reconstructed Kelsen?) with Hart.

Committed statements are essentially the same as Hart's internal statements with two important differences. First, Kelsen's is a cognitivist whereas Hart's is a non-cognitivist interpretation of the normativity of a statement. For Kelsen such statements are normative because they express a belief in the validity of a norm. For Hart they are normative because they express an attitude of willingness to be guided in a certain way. Second, Kelsen tends to identify all normative attitudes and beliefs as moral ones. Hart takes pains to explain that moral reasons are only one type of reason for accepting rules and for having the kind of practical attitude manifested in internal statements.

I will disregard the first difference for the moment. The second is sometimes thought to explain why Hart need not resort to Kelsen's distinction between committed and detached statements. All that Hart has to establish to be consistent with his own doctrine of the separation of law and morals[24] is that ordinary legal discourse does not commit one to a moral approbation of the law. Ordinary legal discourse consists of

---

[23] *PTL* § 34(d) (p. 204 n.72), § 34(i) (p. 218 n.82).
[24] See Hart, *CL*, at ch. 9, and Hart (n.4 above).

internal statements, and these, though expressing a practical attitude of acceptance of the law as a guide for behaviour, do not necessarily express acceptance on moral grounds. Even if one accepts that the interpretation of legal discourse has to be freed only of moral evaluation and not of other kinds of normative evaluation Hart's position is still difficult to maintain. The crucial point is that much legal discourse concerns the rights and duties of others. While one can accept the law as a guide for one's own behaviour for reasons of one's own personal preferences or of self-interest one cannot adduce one's preferences or one's self-interest by themselves as a justification for holding that other people must, or have a duty to, act in a certain way. To claim that another has to act in my interest is normally to make a moral claim about his moral obligations.

There are to be sure reasons on which claims about other people's duties and rights can be based which are neither moral reasons nor the speaker's self-interest or preferences. But none of them nor any combination of them is likely to explain the widespread use of normative language in legal discourse. I find it impossible to resist the conclusion that most internal or committed legal statements, at any rate those about the rights and duties of others, are moral claims.[25]

This conclusion creates a dilemma. Either most legal statements express moral endorsement of the law or not all legal statements are internal statements as understood by Hart or committed statements à la Kelsen. Hart rejects the first horn of the dilemma and he is surely right to do so. Clearly many legal statements do not express a moral position either way. This fact need not be disputed by natural lawyers and is indeed accepted by Finnis.[26] Hart is therefore bound to conclude that not all legal statements are internal. They cannot plausibly be said to be external statements since these are not normative statements but statements about other people's actions and beliefs. Hart has no alternative account. Kelsen has his doctrine of detached statements which provides the framework for a solution to the dilemma by explaining a class of statements which are normally made by the use of normative language, which are not about behaviour or beliefs but about rights and duties and which are none the less not committed and not internal statements.

VII.

I have said in my introductory remarks that Kelsen's most celebrated doctrine, that of the basic norm, is a direct result of the purity of the

---

[25] I am not saying that people who make such statements have the moral beliefs they express. They may be insincere.
[26] See Finnis (n.9 above), at 234–7.

theory of law. Let me conclude by commenting on the connection between the theses. First, the ground for the doctrine of the basic norm is prepared by Kelsen's cognitivist interpretation of legal statements. A person who believes that one should behave in accordance with a certain social practice does not merely have an attitude which inclines him to demand conformity to and criticize deviation from the practice. He is so inclined to behave because he believes in the validity of norms requiring such behaviour.

Norms can be divided into two types. Some are dynamically derivative while others are not. A norm is dynamically derivative if its validity depends on the occurrence of an action which creates it. Actions can create norms if they are authorized to do so by some other norms. Those other norms may themselves be derivative ones. But any normative system must contain at least one non-derivative norm and all its derivative norms must be subsumed under non-derivative norms. Both these conclusions are immediate results of Kelsen's principle of the autonomy of the normative, of his insistence that 'ought' cannot be derived from 'is', values cannot be derived from facts.

Laws are, as we have emphasized above, positive norms. That is, they are all dynamically derivative norms. But this means that the legal system will not be complete unless it also contains a non-derivative, that is, a non-positive, norm which authorizes, directly or indirectly, all the positive laws of the system. That norm is the basic norm, that is, a norm authorizing the creation of the historically first constitution and thus indirectly of all the other norms of the system.[27]

I have said that the basic norm has to be non-derivative, non-positive. This calls for further explanation. Individuals who do not regard the law as normatively valid do not, of course, believe in the validity of the basic norm at all. Those who accept the validity of the law may still not believe in its basic norm. Some may, for example, believe that many but not all of its norms are intuitively self-evident. Some but not all of the others may be believed by them to have been authorized by divine command and the rest to be binding because it was their parents' will that they should obey them. Such people while accepting the validity of all the law do not attribute it to the basic norm described by the theory of law. Others may believe in the moral validity of some but not all the laws of the system. They too do not believe in the validity of the basic norm (which authorizes all the laws). They derive the validity of those laws they believe in from some other norm(s) which do not entail the validity of the laws they do not believe to be valid.

---

[27] See J.W. Harris, 'Kelsen's Concept of Authority', *Cambridge Law Journal*, 36 (1977), 353–63; Stanley L. Paulson, 'Material and Formal Authorization in Kelsen's Pure Theory', *Cambridge Law Journal*, 39 (1980), 172–93.

The point is that norms relativistically understood are always to be looked at from the point of view of some person or group and that every person or group is likely to believe in more or less than the validity of all positive law. Very few people are like the legal man postulated above. But legal men are the only ones likely to accept the Kelsenian basic norm as their ultimate non-derivative norm. Despite this the basic norm is the key to the scientific understanding of the law. The reason is that legal theory to remain pure cannot study the law in so far as it is embedded in the moral beliefs of one person or another. That would violate the sources thesis by making the identification of the law dependent on a particular set of moral beliefs. To be pure, legal theory must strictly adhere to the sources thesis and identify the law by social facts alone. Hence to describe it normatively it must non-committally or fictitiously accept the basic norm of the legal man, that is, the Kelsenian basic norm, for it is the only one to give validity to the *empirically established* law and to nothing else. This, then, is the sense in which the basic norm is the scientific postulate of legal thought.

This claim clarifies the dual role of law-creating facts in the law. On the one hand they establish the character of law as a social fact. All the norms created and identified in a certain way which are by and large efficacious constitute a complex social practice by which members of the society guide and co-ordinate their actions. This is the function of law-creating facts as establishing the membership of certain norms in a system which is socially practised. On the other hand those facts transmit normative force from the authorizing norm to the authorized one. Since the authorizing norm is valid and since it endows those acts with law-creating status the norm they are meant to create is also valid. This is the role of law-creating acts as conferring validity, transmitting binding force from one norm to another.

Moreover, it is not accidental that law-creating facts fulfil both roles. Legal theory is the normative study of a social normative system. Therefore, given its purity it represents as norms only those rules which belong to the effective social order. In other words it is the character of law-creating acts as criteria for membership in a socially effective system which qualifies them to serve as facts transmitting validity from one norm to another.

Once more we can improve our understanding of Kelsen's meaning by comparing it with Hart's. Hart's focus of interest is on the character of law as complex social practice. He describes the existence conditions of social rules and then he turns to normative social systems and introduces the notion of criteria of validity as a test of membership in a social practice tying legal rules indirectly to the complex practice. He is not specifically interested in the descent of normative force from one norm to another. Validity for him indicates just membership in a system established in a certain way. It has little to do with binding normative force.

Therefore from Hart's point of view there is no difference between the role of legislative acts and the social practice which establishes the existence of a rule of recognition. Both are relevant as establishing the membership of certain rules in a legal system. Not so for Kelsen: he emphasizes the fact that a legislative act not only establishes membership, it also confers normative force on the norm created. But the social practice which ties the ultimate legal rules to social reality, while it too is relevant to establishing membership of the rule in an effective legal system (and also to establishing the effectiveness of the system), does not fulfil the other role of transmitting normative force. To assume otherwise is to regard law as consisting of derivative laws alone, which is, for Kelsen, a logical impossibility. If the judicial practices which according to Hart establish the existence of the rule of recognition were also to endow it with normative status this could only be in virtue of yet another norm which would then become itself the ultimate rule of the system.

I believe that this argument correctly reflects our unreflective thinking about the law. Judges regard the fact that a statute was enacted by Parliament as a reason to regard it as binding and to hold the litigants to be bound by it. But they do not necessarily regard the judicial practice of enforcing Parliamentary enactments as a reason for enforcing them, that is, as a reason for accepting the rule of recognition as binding. They may accept the rule of recognition because they believe in Parliamentary democracy or in some law and order argument, etc. But those norms which make them accept the binding force of the rule of recognition are not themselves part of the law. From the point of view of the study of law the ultimate rule is the rule of recognition directing the courts to apply Parliamentary legislation. The judicial practice of following the rule identifies it as part of a system effective in that society and helps establish the social existence of the whole system. Hart is right about this and Kelsen is guilty of overlooking or oversimplifying many of the facts which establish the social character of the law. But Kelsen is right in pointing out that these judicial social practices do not confer binding force on the ultimate legal rules and are not generally believed to do so. In this they differ from other law-creating acts. From the point of view of a pure study of law the validity of ultimate legal rules is simply (non-committally) assumed.

13

Some Confusions surrounding Kelsen's Concept of Validity*

CARLOS SANTIAGO NINO

I.

Many writers assume that Kelsen's concept of validity is primarily related to such issues as the identity of a legal system, the membership of particular norms in a legal system, its internal consistency, and so on. The result is that, for many, Kelsen's concept of validity bears no affinity to the idea of validity prevailing in traditional legal philosophy, where the main concern has been with the justification of law. I believe, however, that this reading of Kelsen's concept of validity is mistaken. Proponents of this reading have been led to disregard important aspects of Kelsen's theory, formulating unwarranted and tortuous interpretations of it in order to show how it deals with issues that are erroneously supposed to be primarily connected to its concept of validity.

No doubt the peculiarities of Kelsen's theory help to explain how this confusion has been generated. In particular, Kelsen's strong positivistic bent makes it seem altogether implausible to attempt to associate his concept of validity with the concept familiar from traditional theories inspired by natural law. What is more, Kelsen does deal in his theory with problems like membership in a way that deceptively gives rise to an identification with the problem of validity.

By means of the following very general propositions, one can, I believe, provide a reasonably accurate summary of the recurrent

* *Editors' note*: Nino's article first appeared in *ARSP*, 64 (1978), 357–77. The first part of the article, at 357–65, appears with minor revisions here. Occasional alterations in quotations from existing English-language translations of Kelsen's works are made *sub silentio*.

features of the concept of validity employed in the justification of law in works as different as those of Aquinas,[1] Suárez,[2] and Puchta.[3]

(a) To predicate validity of a legal system, or of a particular legal rule, is to assert that it has binding force, that its prescriptions constitute conclusive reasons for action.

(b) When the validity of a legal system, or of a legal rule, is contested, this is tantamount to denying its existence, since the lack of validity is taken to imply that the system, or the rule, does not have the normative consequences that it claims to have. (Thus, for example, if an invalid rule purports to prohibit a certain act, that act would not thereby be prohibited; the rule would be as ineffectual in establishing *normative* relationships as if it had never been issued.)

(c) Even when the ascription of validity depends on certain facts (as, for example, in some conceptions, where the efficacy of a system is a necessary or even a sufficient condition for the ascription of validity), the meaning of 'validity' is nevertheless not descriptive but normative; that is, to say that a system or a particular legal rule is valid is to endorse it, to maintain that its application and observance are obligatory and justified. (This last-mentioned feature of the traditional notion of validity permits us to hold that the different authors whose views I am adumbrating employed the same concept of validity, notwithstanding wide discrepancies in their criteria for ascribing validity.)

It seems clear to me that these features are present in Kelsen's concept of validity, too. Under A, B, and C below, I offer support for this contention, showing that Kelsen's theory, like traditional philosophical accounts of law, equates the validity of the law with its binding force and its existence, and that it conceives of the ascription of validity as a normative judgment.

---

[1] See St Thomas Aquinas, *Summa Theologiae* (Blackfriars, 1966), *Primae-Secundae*, question 9, question 95 art. 2, question 96 arts. 4 and 5.

[2] See Francisco Suárez, *De Legibus*, Libro VI (Madrid: Instituto Francisco de Vitoria, 1971). [For bibliographical details on Suárez, see ch. 14 in this volume, at n.17.] For a very interesting analysis of the concept of validity in Suárez and a comparison of it with Kelsen's concept and that of other theorists, see Ernesto Garzón Valdés, 'Algunos modelos de validez normativa', *Revista Latinoamericana de Filosofía*, 3 (1977), 41–68, repr. in Garzón Valdés, *Derecho, Etica y Política* (Madrid: Centro de Estudios Constitucionales, 1993), 73–105, [appearing (in abridged form) in this volume as ch. 14].

[3] See Georg Friedrich Puchta, 'Outlines of Jurisprudence as the Science of Right', in *Outlines of the Science of Jurisprudence*, ed. and trans. William Hastie (Edinburgh: T. & T. Clark, 1887), 1–134, at 41; Hastie's translation is taken from §§1–35 of *Cursus der Institutionen*, first published in 1841–2.

A. Validity as Equivalent to Binding Force.

In *General Theory of Law and State*, Kelsen writes:

To say that a norm is valid is to say that we assume its existence or—what amounts to the same thing—we assume that it has 'binding force' for those whose behavior it regulates.[4]

Kelsen then goes on to distinguish legal norms from commands, asserting that only legal norms, issued by authorized organs, obligate the individuals to whom they are directed. In the *Pure Theory of Law*, Kelsen writes:

The legislative act, which subjectively has the meaning of 'ought', also has that objective meaning—that is, the meaning of a valid norm—because the constitution has conferred this objective meaning upon the legislative act. The act whose meaning is the constitution has not only the subjective but also the objective meaning of 'ought', that is to say, the character of a binding norm, if—in case it is the historically first constitution—we presuppose in our juristic thinking that we ought to behave as the constitution prescribes.[5]

A bit further on in the same work, Kelsen writes:

To say that the behavior of an individual is commanded by an objectively valid norm amounts to the same as saying that the individual is obligated to behave in this way.[6]

Still further on in the *Pure Theory of Law*, Kelsen writes:

It was observed earlier that the validity of a norm (which means that one ought to behave as the norm stipulates) should not be confounded with the efficacy of the norm . . .[7]

B. Validity as Equivalent to Existence.

This feature of Kelsen's concept of validity, the notion that validity is equivalent to existence, is evident in the first quotation of the foregoing subsection, taken from the *General Theory of Law and State*. And it is still more evident in the preceding remark in that work: 'By validity we mean the specific existence of norms.'[8] In the same work, Kelsen writes:

The existence of a legal norm is its validity; and the validity of a legal norm, although not identical with certain facts, is conditioned by them.[9]

---

[4] *GTLS* 30.   [5] *PTL* § 4(b) (p. 8).   [6] *PTL* § 4(d) (p. 15).
[7] *PTL* § 6(c) (p. 46).   [8] *GTLS* 30.   [9] *GTLS* 48.

And, at a later point in the work, he writes: '[N]ormative jurisprudence asserts the validity of a norm, and that means its existence.'[10]

There are similar remarks in the *Pure Theory of Law*, where there is also an interesting explanation of what is involved in identifying the binding force of a norm with its existence:

It is, however, necessary to distinguish the subjective and the objective meaning of the act [of will]. 'Ought' is the subjective meaning of every act of will directed to the behavior of another individual. But not every such act has also objectively this meaning, and only if the act of will has also the objective meaning of an 'ought', is this 'ought' called a 'norm'. If the 'ought' is also the objective meaning of the act, the behavior to which the act is directed is regarded as something that *ought* to be, not only from the point of view of the individual who has performed the act, but also from the point of view of both the individual to whose behavior the act is directed and a third individual not involved in the relation between the two.[11]

C. Validity as a Normative Concept.

Validity qua normative concept is the crucial point in understanding Kelsen's concept of validity. For until the normative character of Kelsen's concept is fully grasped, interpretations that identify it with, for example, the membership of norms in a legal system will still command attention. In such interpretations, the assumption is made that when Kelsen equates validity with binding force, he is using 'binding force' in a special sense (to refer, for example, to the circumstance prescribed by another norm of the system, namely, that the norm in question be obeyed), and that when he equates validity with existence, 'existence' just means the membership of the norm in question in the legal system.

That the ascription of validity to a legal norm does not exhaust itself in the description of certain facts is something Kelsen asserts repeatedly. For example:

[That a] norm referring to the behavior of a human being is 'valid' means that it is binding—that an individual ought to behave in the manner determined by the norm. It has been pointed out in an earlier context that the question of why a norm is valid, why an individual ought to behave in a certain way, cannot be answered by ascertaining a fact, that is, by the statement that something *is*. The reason for the validity of a norm cannot be a fact. From the circumstance that something *is* cannot follow that something *ought* to be; and that something *ought* to be cannot be the reason that something *is*.[12]

But perhaps this feature of the Kelsenian concept of legal validity can be more firmly established if, instead of relying on Kelsen's explicit

---

[10] *GTLS* 170.   [11] *PTL* § 4(b) (p. 7) (Kelsen's emphasis).
[12] *PTL* § 34(a) (p. 193) (Kelsen's emphasis).

remarks, I show that a normative concept of validity is understood in the general structure of Kelsen's theory.

In Kelsen's theory, the validity of a legal rule requires that its issuance must be authorized by another rule, one that is itself valid. The judgment that a certain rule is valid presupposes, therefore, a judgment that another rule, which authorizes the creation of the former, is valid. Legal judgments of validity—judgments, namely, about rules that stand in a certain relation of 'derivation' to one another (constituted by the fact that one authorizes the issuance of the other)—themselves stand in a certain relation of 'derivation' to one another. Whereas one rule 'derives' from another when the latter authorizes the creation of the former, a legal judgment that a rule is valid 'derives' from the judgment that another rule is valid when the former judgment presupposes the latter. This can be illustrated as two parallel chains of 'derivation', one of rules and the other of judgments, formulated typically by jurists, of the validity of these rules:

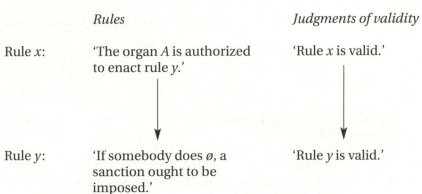

	Rules	*Judgments of validity*
Rule x:	'The organ A is authorized to enact rule y.'	'Rule x is valid.'
Rule y:	'If somebody does ø, a sanction ought to be imposed.'	'Rule y is valid.'

Now, when it is the case that the rule to which a judgment of validity refers is the highest-level positive norm of a legal system, Kelsen states that its validity or binding force is presupposed and that the formulation of that presupposition *is* the basic norm of the system.[13] He also says that 'since the reason for the validity of a norm can only be another norm, the presupposition must be a norm; not one posited (i.e. created) by a legal authority, but a presupposed norm.'[14] Following this remark, Kelsen offers a well-known formulation of the basic norm, namely: 'One ought to behave as the constitution prescribes.'[15] From assertions such as these, it is easy to infer that the basic norm is not a norm that belongs to the chain of derivation of rules, but is part of the chain of derivation of

[13] See *GTLS*, at 115.   [14] *PTL* § 34(c) (p. 200).
[15] *PTL* § 34(c) (at p. 201); see also *GTLS*, at 116.

judgments of validity. In other words, the basic norm *is* a judgment of validity. It is the fundamental judgment of validity which must serve as the basis of all other judgments about the validity of rules whose creation is directly or indirectly authorized by the constitution. The obvious conclusion is that if the fundamental judgment of validity, according to Kelsen, is itself a norm—the basic norm—and if from norms nothing but norms can be derived, then all further judgments of validity about rules other than the constitution must themselves be norms. Judgments of validity (including the basic norm) prescribe that what is stipulated by the rules referred to in the judgments ought to be done. If the rule in question stipulates that some act is obligatory, to predicate of that rule that it is valid implies the statement that *there is* an obligation to perform that act. (This is not the same as merely saying that there is a rule that prescribes such an obligation; rather, it entails the statement that the rule succeeds in creating the obligation it prescribes.) Ascribing validity to a rule (which thereby comes to be conceived of as a *norm*) marks the shift in Kelsen's theory from an 'inverted-commas' normative language to a direct normative language for describing the content of the law.[16]

II.

As I have already remarked, many contemporary theorists disregard the normative character of Kelsen's concept of validity, explicitly or implicitly assuming that it describes features of a legal system or of a particular legal norm, features that are for the most part related to the criteria for identifying a legal system, distinguishing it from others, and for establishing that a legal norm belongs to a certain legal system. It is true that Kelsen relates the question of the validity or the binding force of a legal system or norm to the question of the identification of legal systems and to the question of the membership of norms in those systems. He writes:

The legal order is a system of norms. The question then arises: What is it that makes a system out of a multitude of norms? When does a norm belong to a certain system of norms, an order? These questions are closely connected to the question as to the reason for the validity of a norm.[17]

But Kelsen's assertion that validity is closely connected to identification and membership by no means warrants the conclusion that questions of

[16] See the distinction between 'inverted-commas' and 'direct normative language', in R.M. Hare, *The Language of Morals* (Oxford: Clarendon Press, 1952), at 124.
[17] *GTLS* 110.

validity, in Kelsen's theory, are reducible to questions of identification and membership.

This impression has undoubtedly been caused by the fact that Kelsen's solutions to both kinds of problems can be stated in a superficially similar way. That is, Kelsen's answer to the question about what makes a legal system valid can be taken to be 'the basic norm', and he seems to give the same answer to the question of what identifies a given set of norms as a unitary legal system different from other such systems. It is, however, easy to see that the two answers are in fact substantially different. Kelsen's solution to the problem of the validity of a legal system might be paraphrased as follows: 'A legal system is valid when we presuppose a basic norm that prescribes that what the system's rules stipulate ought to be done.' A similar answer to the problem of the identity of a legal system would be not merely wrong but, indeed, absurd and wrongheaded. In fact, Kelsen's solution to this problem might be paraphrased as follows: 'A set of norms constitutes a unitary legal system if validity can be ascribed to these norms on the basis of one and the same basic norm.' To be sure, this is not a paraphrase of the basic norm or of any other norm, but a formulation of a criterion of identification that points to the circumstance that one and the same basic norm is presupposed when we ascribe validity to all the norms of the same legal system. Thus, authors like Carlos E. Alchourrón and Eugenio Bulygin[18] are mistaken when they criticize Kelsen's basic norm on the ground that what is needed for the identification of a legal system is a criterion and not a norm. Kelsen's basic norm establishes the obligatoriness of a legal system; the identity of that system is determined by a criterion that takes into account the fact that one and the same basic norm is presupposed when obligatoriness is ascribed to all the norms of the system. As a criterion of identity, however, the foregoing is vacuous, for the content of each basic norm (and, consequently, its own identity) cannot, in the context of Kelsen's theory, be established apart from comprehending the norms that belong to the legal system to which the basic norm ascribes binding force.[19]

Kelsen also seems to resolve the question of the validity of a particular norm and the question of its membership in a legal system in an identical way. His answer to both questions can be stated as follows: 'A norm is valid or belongs to a legal system when it derives from a valid norm of that system.' This way of presenting his answer to those questions is, however, misleading. The answer can be broken down into two parts,

---

[18] See Carlos E. Alchourrón and Eugenio Bulygin, *Normative Systems* (Vienna and New York: Springer, 1971), at 72–7.
[19] See this criticism in Raz, *CLS*, at 102.

each of which deals with one of the two questions at stake: (a) 'A norm is valid when it derives from a valid norm,' and (b) 'A norm belongs to a legal system when it derives from a norm that belongs to that system.' The latter statement endorses a 'genetic' criterion of membership, which has not enjoyed a great deal of discussion in modern legal theory. (Of course, it would have to be completed with a clause dealing with the membership of the fundamental norms of the system, a clause not provided by Kelsen.) The genetic criterion of membership is quite independent of the validity of the norms in question; nowhere in Kelsen's works is it suggested that this criterion applies to valid legal norms alone.

Despite the fact that the criterion of membership of non-fundamental norms and the criterion for 'transmitting' validity from the constitution referred to by the basic norm to norms not directly referred to by the basic norm are independent of one another, both criteria are based on the same notion of 'derivation', according to which one norm 'derives' from another when its issuance is authorized by the other. The result is that when the fundamental norms of the system are held to be valid, the class of norms that are valid according to a certain basic norm is coextensive with the class of norms that belong to the system to which that basic norm applies. Kelsen, quite obviously, is much in favour of maintaining this coextensivity (which many authors have confused with identity), and it is this feature of his theory that brings so many unwelcome results. The fact is that while, in relation to membership, the derivation of one norm from another (in the sense explained) seems a prima-facie sound criterion, it is clearly insufficient in relation to the 'transmission' of validity. If we accept the validity of a certain set of legal norms, we are committed to accepting the validity of certain other norms, not only when the norms whose validity we accept authorize the issuance of these other norms, but also when they 'recognize' or establish the obligation to obey these other norms. Thus, it has been argued[20] that a legal system could recognize as valid the rules of other legal systems or of private associations without thereby implying that those rules become part of the legal system in question. But the insufficiency of Kelsen's criterion for 'transmitting' validity is best manifested in his treatment of another problem: that of invalidatable norms.[21]

Norms that have been issued in violation of the conditions established by valid norms of the system are, in some circumstances, considered to be obligatory until some competent organ declares them invalid. According to the genetic criterion of membership, these norms are not part of the legal system in question. Whether or not this is a sound solu-

[20] See Joseph Raz, *Practical Reason and Norms* (London: Hutchinson, 1975), 2nd edn. (Princeton: Princeton UP, 1990), at 152–4.
[21] [On this terminology, see *LT* § 31(h) (at p. 73 n.56).]

tion may be in dispute. If, however, validity were equivalent to membership, there would not be any inconsistency whatsoever in the proposition that a norm that is not valid in a legal system is, nevertheless,
obligatory according to that legal system (just as in the case of norms of
another legal system that are deemed obligatory by rules set down in the
field of conflicts of law).[22] The fact that Kelsen does worry about this
problem suggests again that he identifies validity not with membership
but with obligatoriness or bindingness. Given this identification, a norm
that is obligatory must obviously be valid. But Kelsen considers a norm
to be valid only if its issuance is authorized by a valid norm. Thus, he is
compelled to adopt the absurd view that invalidatable norms are, in fact,
authorized by the applicable higher-level norms, since the latter have,
along with the explicit content violated by the invalidatable norm, a tacit
clause authorizing the creation of any norm, with any content whatever
and issued by means of any procedure whatever.[23] Of course, the clear
escape from this problem would be to recognize that validity or obligatoriness is transmitted from one norm to another not only when the former authorizes the creation of the latter, but also when the former
imposes the obligation to obey or to apply the latter. Thus, an invalidatable norm would be a norm that, not having been authorized by valid
norms of the system in question (and so not belonging to that system), is
held by other norms of the system to be obligatory, and therefore valid,
until some special procedure providing for invalidation has been carried
out. This solution would undermine the claim of the coextensivity of
legal validity and membership in a legal system—but that is all to the
good, since the defence of coextensivity is one of the most remarkable
weaknesses in Kelsen's theory and the source of the recent confusion,
among interpreters of that theory, between legal validity and membership.[24]

[22] See this analogy in Eugenio Bulygin, 'Sentenza giudiziaria e creazione di diritto',
RIFD, 44 (1967), 164–80.

[23] See *GTLS*, at 153–62.

[24] For a more extensive treatment of the problem of conflicts between norms at different levels in the Kelsenian legal system, see my paper 'El concepto de validez y el problema
del conflicto entre normas de diferente jerarquía en la Teoría Pura del Derecho', in
Derecho, Filosofía y Lenguaje. Homenaje a Ambrosio L. Gioja, ed. Genaro R. Carrió (Buenos
Aires: Editorial Astrea de Alfredo y Ricardo Depalma, 1976), 131–44.

14

Two Models of Legal Validity:
Hans Kelsen and Francisco Suárez*

ERNESTO GARZÓN VALDÉS

In section I of what follows, I should like to undertake a schematic presentation of Hans Kelsen's position on the problem of the validity of both legal norms and the legal systems constituted by such norms. I then turn, in section II, to a comparison of Kelsen's position with that of another jurist, Francisco Suárez, whose approach to the same problem is strikingly similar to Kelsen's despite stemming from a very different juridico-philosophical tradition. The comparison is instructive, I believe, for it sheds light on the epistemological problems connected with, *inter alia*, the identification of the validity and the existence of legal norms. As I shall attempt to show in section III, both thinkers take similar premises as their respective points of departure, and the internal coherence of their theories brings them to similar conclusions and renders them susceptible to similar critiques. In my concluding section, I suggest that this comparative model may also have application to other theories on the validity of legal norms and legal systems.

I.

A synthesis of Kelsen's position on the validity of norms and of systems constituted by norms can be expressed, as I understand it, in terms of four basic postulates:

(1) *The validity of a norm cannot be inferred from, or based on, facts.* Norms belong to the realm of *Sollen* or 'ought', and for reasons of

* *Editors' note*: The full paper from which this discussion is drawn first appeared in *Revista Latinoamericana de Filosofía*, 3 (1977), 41–68, and was reprinted in Ernesto Garzón Valdés, *Derecho, Ética y Política* (Madrid: Centro de Estudios Constitucionales, 1993), 73–105. The translation is by Ruth Zimmerling, working in close collaboration with the author and the editors. For the present version of the paper, the author has made a handful of minor changes.

logic, there is an insuperable abyss between this realm and the realm of *Sein* or 'is'. In Kelsen's own words:

> No one can deny that the statement, 'something is'—that is, a statement that describes a fact—is essentially different from the statement 'something ought to be'—that is, a statement that describes a norm; and, likewise, it cannot follow that because something is, something ought to be, just as it cannot follow that because something ought to be, something is.[1]

> The opposition between *Sein* and *Sollen*, between 'is' and 'ought', is a logico-formal opposition, and in so far as the boundaries of logico-formal enquiry are observed, no path leads from one to the other; the two worlds are separated by an insuperable abyss. Logically speaking, enquiring into the 'why' of a concrete 'ought' can only lead to another 'ought', just as the answer to the 'why' of an 'is' can only be another 'is'.[2]

And with specific reference to the problem of validity, Kelsen asserts that 'the basis of the validity of a norm cannot be fact.'[3]

(2)	*The validity of a norm is its specific form of existence.* That a norm is valid means simply that it exists; and, vice versa, if a norm exists, then it is valid. Thus, 'existence of a norm' and 'validity of a norm' are equivalent expressions. Kelsen formulates this postulate repeatedly.

> To say that a norm is valid is to say that we assume its existence . . .[4]

> With the word 'validity' we designate the specific existence of a norm.[5]

(3)	*When a norm is valid (that is, exists), it ought to be obeyed; and if it is disobeyed, the competent organs ought to impose a sanction.* The structure of a norm is that of a command. A command that must be obeyed on pain of suffering a sanction imposed by a state organ is an (individual or general) norm that, as such, is valid (exists).

> To say that a norm is valid is to say that we assume its existence or—what amounts to the same thing—we assume that it has 'binding force' for those whose behavior it regulates.[6]

Kelsen even goes a step further. According to him, 'individuals ought to behave as a norm stipulates'.[7] And he adds:

> Similarly, the basic norm of a legal system prescribes that one ought to behave as the 'fathers' of the constitution and the individuals—directly or indirectly—authorized (delegated) by the constitution command.[8]

---

[1] *PTL* § 4(b) (pp. 5–6) (trans. altered).			[2] *HP* 8.
[3] *PTL* § 34(a) (p. 193) (trans. altered).			[4] *GTLS* 30.
[5] *PTL* § 4(c) (p. 10) (trans. altered).			[6] *GTLS* 30.
[7] See Hans Kelsen, 'Value Judgments in the Science of Law', *Journal of Social Philosophy and Jurisprudence*, 7 (1942), 312–33, at 317, repr. *WJ* 209–30, 389 (notes), at 214.
[8] *GTLS* 115–16.

There is, then, a three-way equivalence of the expressions 'validity', 'existence', and 'duty to obey'. The three terms are analytically interdependent.

(4) *A norm is valid if it has been issued by a competent organ in accordance with the appropriate procedure.* The content of a norm plays no role—or, at most, a secondary role— in the validity of the norm. Which organ is competent and what procedure should be followed for the issuance of a norm are matters determined in higher-level norms, which, as norms, also exist, that is, are valid and ought to be obeyed.

A legal norm is valid not because it has a certain content, that is, not because its content can be logically derived from a presupposed basic norm, but because it has been created in a certain way, a way that is ultimately determined by a presupposed basic norm.[9]

Norms . . . of the law . . . are not valid by virtue of their content. Any content whatever can be law; there is no human behaviour that would be excluded simply by virtue of its substance from becoming the content of a legal norm. The validity of a legal norm cannot be called into question on the ground that its content fails to correspond to some presupposed substantive value, say, a moral value. A norm is valid qua legal norm only because it was arrived at in a certain way—created according to a certain rule, issued or set according to a specific method.[10]

From those four postulates, Kelsen draws the following conclusions:

(a) The concept of validity is relative, in the sense that the validity of a norm always has reference to another norm or, more precisely, to the validity of another norm.

The basis of the validity of a norm can only be the validity of another norm.[11]

The norm that serves as the basis of the validity of another norm is at a higher level in the normative hierarchy; thus, the legal system has a hierarchical structure.

(b) If the validity of a norm depends on the validity of the norm that establishes the competent organ and the appropriate procedure for the corresponding norm creation, then the chain of validity, if it is finite (which must be conceded in the case of positive norms), necessarily leads to a first positive norm, to the 'historically first constitution'.

The search for the basis of the validity of a norm cannot go on indefinitely, unlike the search for the cause of an effect.[12]

---

[9] *PTL* § 34(c) (p. 198) (trans. altered).   [10] *LT* § 28 (p. 56).
[11] *PTL* § 34(a) (p. 193) (trans. altered).   [12] *PTL* § 34(a) (p. 194) (trans. altered).

(c) Now, when we reach the historically first constitution, its basis of validity must be yet another norm (*postulate 1*). Since there is no higher-level *positive* norm, however, the existence of the required norm must be presupposed, and we must grant that norms can be not only *willed* (that is, issued by means of an act of will), but also *thought* (that is, presupposed in legal reasoning).[13] This presupposed norm will then be the basic norm of the system, that is, the basis of the validity of the system as well as of all the positive norms constituting the system. With respect to this basic norm, Kelsen asserts:

> As the highest-level norm, it must be *presupposed*, for it cannot be *issued* by an authority whose competence would have to be based on a still higher-level norm.[14]

(d) It is logically impossible to consider a particular norm valid and to accept at the same time as binding a moral norm that prohibits the behaviour prescribed by the legal norm.[15] '[T]wo contradictory norms cannot both be valid . . .'[16]

III.

Let us look now at another model, which, although stemming from an author who appears on first glance to be quite different from Kelsen, has a structure very similar to the one outlined above. I will call this the 'Suárez model', for it is based primarily on the theses of Francisco Suárez.[17]

The Suárez model accepts *postulate 1* of the Kelsenian model, and looks for the basis of the validity of norms not in facts but in the sphere of the norms themselves, that is, in the realm of *Sollen* or 'ought', rather

[13] See *PTL*, at § 34(d) (pp. 201–5).

[14] *PTL* § 34(a) (pp 194–5) (Kelsen's emphasis) (trans. altered).

[15] See *GTLS*, at 373–6, and *Phil. Fds.*, at 407–12.   [16] *GTLS* 375.

[17] The legal and political theory of Francisco Suárez was 'rediscovered' in 1927, with the publication of two books: Heinrich Rommen, *Die Staatslehre des Franz Suárez* (Munich-Gladbach: Volksvereins-Verlag, 1926), and L. Recaséns Siches, *La filosofía del derecho de Francisco Suárez* (Madrid: V. Suárez, 1927). Among later studies of his political and social thinking, Reijo Wilenius, *The Social and Political Theory of Francisco Suárez* (Helsinki: Societas Philosophica Fennica, 1963), deserves special mention. I limit my presentation to the *Tractatus de legibus ac Deo legislatore* (hereafter: *De legibus*). For the reader's convenience, I have sought to include page references (indicated by 'Eng. edn.') to the English translation of *De legibus*, in Suárez, *Selections from Three Works*, trans. Gwladys L. Williams, Ammi Brown, and John Waldron (Oxford: Clarendon Press, 1944), 1–646; this plan, however, met with only limited success, for the English translation is drastically abridged. See generally the unabridged Spanish edition of Consejo de Investigaciones Científicas, 6 vols. (Madrid: Instituto Francisco de Vitoria, 1971); volume and page references are to this edition.

than in that of *Sein* or 'is'.

With respect to *postulate 4*, the Suárez model accepts the necessity of a competent organ and of appropriate procedures for the creation of norms. As Suárez puts it, 'in order to dictate laws, one must have jurisdictional power'.[18] He writes:

[B]y itself, the correctness or justice of the action prescribed by the law is not sufficient for a norm to be binding, and, therefore, although prudence is desirable when issuing laws, and the advice of wise men should, and usually does, intervene, this advice is not sufficient if the will from which the law receives the force and character of law is missing.[19]

The Suárez model also introduces into *postulate 4*, however, a third essential condition, namely, that the law must be just.

[T]he human lawmaker . . . does not have the power to bind through unjust laws, and, therefore, were he to command unjust things, such prescriptions would not be law, because they have neither the force nor the validity necessary to bind.[20]

At a later point, he adds:

[F]or a law to be genuine law, it must . . . be just and reasonable, because an unjust law is not law . . .[21]

Thus, according to this model, an unjust law is equivalent to an invalid law—that is to say, a non-existent law. On the other hand, 'valid' ('just') law and 'existing' law are analytically equivalent terms. This means that the Suárez model also recognizes *postulate 2*.

Now, according to the Suárez model, every law is prescriptive. In other words, every law has the structure of a command, guiding action by threatening to impose sanctions. Even those laws giving expression to a permission imply a command. Laws that confer privileges or immunities on certain persons are actually commands directed to all other persons.

[A]s commands, they are directed not at those particular persons [that is, the holders of the privilege or immunity], but at the community and at all subjects of the lawmaker, who are obligated to respect some such immunity in favor of those persons.[22]

[P]ermissory laws are laws insofar as they implicitly entail commands, without which the permission could not be understood to have been especially ordered by the law.[23]

[18] *De legibus* (n.17 above), Book I, ch. VIII, § 6 (vol. I, 152).
[19] Ibid., Book I, ch. VIII, § 10 (vol. I, 157).
[20] Ibid., Book I, ch. IX, § 4 (vol. II, 6) (Eng. edn. 107).
[21] *De legibus* (n.17 above), Book III, ch. XXII, § 1 (vol. VI, 84).
[22] Ibid., Book I, ch. VI, § 14 (vol. I, 117) (Eng. edn. 83).
[23] *De legibus* (n.17 above), Book I, ch. XIV, § 5 (vol. II, 84).

Unjust laws—which are actually not laws at all—ought not to be obeyed.

[O]nce the injustice has been recognized, it is not permitted to obey, for any reason whatsoever, not even to avoid some harm or scandal . . .[24]

By contrast, valid law must be obeyed. This can not only be inferred *a contrario sensu* from the illegitimacy of obeying an unjust (invalid) law, but it is also stated explicitly by Suárez:

In fact, although civil law is not deduced speculatively, so to speak, by a rigorous inference from the principles of natural law, but is, rather, given by the lawmaker's will as something he determines, still, once this determination has been made, one can—in actual practice—deduce from natural principles that this human law ought to be obeyed . . .[25]

Again:

[I]t seems self-contradictory that a man should give a genuine law, and that this should not bind internally . . . If it is genuine law, then it is given with the intention to bind and with the power thereto, for in order to bind, power and will are sufficient; thus, it is contradictory to say that such law does not bind internally . . . The obligation follows intrinsically, by its nature, from the reality of a genuine law. Thus, even though it is left to the lawmaker to determine whether or not he wants to issue a law, it is not left to him to want to give a law that should, however, not bind internally . . .[26]

Postulate 3 of the first model is, therefore, also accepted by the second model.

With these revised postulates, the Suárez model warrants the following conclusions:

(a') Since a just content is a necessary condition for the existence or validity of a law, it is indispensable to have a standard or criterion for the justice or injustice of human laws. And since *postulate 1* has been affirmed, this criterion can only be found in other laws of a higher order than positive law. These are *lex naturalis* and *lex aeterna*. *Lex aeterna* is the 'essence' of law, 'and all other laws are law only by participation; thus, all law must be the effect of the eternal law.'[27]

(b') It is the human lawmaker who gives 'virtue and efficacy' to positive civil law. His authority stems ultimately from God himself, and his commands have binding force 'because of the divine law' that tells us that 'superiors ought to be obeyed'.[28] Divine law here is the equivalent of *lex aeterna*.

---

[24] *De legibus* (n.17 above), Book I, ch. IX, § 20 (vol. II, 25) (Eng. edn. 121).
[25] *De legibus* (n.17 above), Book II, ch. IX, § 12 (vol. III, 145) (Eng. edn. 230).
[26] *De legibus* (n.17 above), Book III, ch. XXII, § 2 (vol. VI, 84).
[27] Ibid., Book II, ch. IV, § 5 (vol. III, 51) (Eng. edn. 173).
[28] *De legibus* (n.17 above), Book II, ch. IV, § 8 (vol. III, 53) (Eng. edn. 175).

(c') Since every law is morally good,[29] there can be no conflict between
moral and legal norms. If the latter contradict the former, they are,
quite simply, not law at all; it would be 'contradictory' to hold that a
law is given but not morally binding.[30]

(d') The ultimate basis of the validity of all human law, therefore, is eternal law. It is the standard for the just content of laws as well as the
source of the sovereign's power.

The Kelsenian position (*Model I*) and the position defended by Suárez
(*Model II*) can now be presented in schematic terms (the numbers on the
left refer to the four postulates presented above):

	Model I	*Model II*
(1)	+	+
(2)	+	+
(3)	+	+
(4)	organ + procedure	organ + procedure + content

IV.

What these two models have in common is, first of all, the necessity of an
appeal to extra-positive norms to provide a basis for the validity of norms
and of the positive legal system. This means that the nature of the norm
or norms that serve as the ultimate basis of validity is different from the
nature of the norms based on them. The basic norm or norms must be
valid, lest the norms based on them not be valid. But validity means different things in the two cases. In *Model I*, it is the basic norm that makes
it possible to speak of validity, for the basic norm is the 'logico-transcendental condition' for the validity of positive law and therefore has an
'epistemological character'.[31] But then one can pose the question formulated by Eugenio Bulygin: 'What meaning can the word "validity"
have when it is applied to the norm that allows us to speak of validity in
the first place?'[32] In *Model II*, one must accept the existence of an eternal
law and of a law-giving God. The enquiry into the basis of the validity of
positive legal norms thus falls within the field of theology. As Suárez himself says: 'The law, with respect to its general nature as well as to all its
specific consequences, belongs to the sphere of theology.'[33]

---

[29] See *De legibus* (n.17 above), Book III, ch. XXII, § 2 (vol. IV, at 85).   [30] Ibid.

[31] See *RR 2*, second appendix: 'Die Naturrechtslehre', 402–44, at 443–4.

[32] Eugenio Bulygin, 'Sobre el fundamento de validez', *Notas de filosofía del derecho*
(Buenos Aires), 1 (1964), 23–33, 32.

[33] *De legibus* (n.17 above), Preface, 17.

Another feature common to both models is the identification of existence and validity, as well as the genetic character of the latter. A norm is
valid if it stems from another valid norm. Validity is a kind of hereditary
trait possessed by all norms. All norms belonging to one and the same
system have the same basis of validity—the same 'last name', so to speak.
In the case of *Model II*, this basis is ultimately one and the same for all
positive systems. In the case of *Model I*, each positive system, according
to Kelsen, has its own basic norm. (The question of the content of this
basic norm is, of course, a complicated matter. If the basic norm merely
says, 'One ought to behave as the constitution prescribes,'[34] it does not
seem to be very different from the command of divine law in *Model II*,
which says, 'Obey your superiors!' And then one is tempted to think that
the basic norm has the same content in all systems, which would make it
difficult if not impossible to distinguish the basic norm of system *A* from
that of system *B*. If, on the other hand, the content of the basic norm is
'determined by the facts' that accompany each act of creation in a positive system of norms, then it becomes hard to understand the sense in
which the basic norm can be seen as a Kantian category.[35]) Alternatively,
it would also be possible to speak of a single common basic norm if international law were taken into consideration, but in order not to compli-
cate the issue unnecessarily, let us leave this alternative aside and simply
consider a single-state, positive legal system.

Both models identify 'validity' with 'duty to obey'. This identification
seems more acceptable in *Model II* than in *Model I*, for the latter claims
to be a purely positivistic representation of the question of the validity of
norms. I therefore think Alf Ross is right to qualify the Kelsenian model
as 'quasi-positivistic'.[36]

The fact that Kelsen's basic norm has been criticized by a number of
authors with respect to its functions as well as its character and content
is a good indication that there is something about his model that is less
than satisfactory. Where *Model II* is concerned, it does seem extravagant
that the explication of the validity of norms is dependent on the existence
of God; it would no doubt be difficult to convince atheists that the question of validity is a theological problem, as Suárez holds.

[34] *PTL* § 34(c) (p. 201).
[35] See Bulygin (n.32 above), at 31.
[36] See Alf Ross, 'Validity and the Conflict between Legal Positivism and Natural Law', in
this volume, ch. 7, at § VI.

V.

Legal theory has offered a great many other solutions, of course, to the problem of the validity of legal norms and legal systems. I think that, in any case, each must give an answer to the questions posed in the four postulates presented above. The number of logically possible models that can be constructed by asserting and/or rejecting one or more of those postulates is 2^4 or 16. Interested readers may undertake for themselves the exercise of constructing these models and affixing to each the names of the legal theorists committed to it. I have in fact already done so.[37] And this work made it possible for me, even though looking only at models that address the positive law of legislation, to shed light on the ambiguity of the word 'validity' as reflected in its partial synonyms— 'existence of a norm (or a system)', 'bindingness', and 'duty to obey'. This ambiguity is not resolved, however, and the question becomes even more complicated if, in addition, we consider the validity of customary law or of the norms created by judicial decision. Precisely because of this it seems advisable to proceed with a modicum of caution when comparing models of validity and drawing conclusions about their degree of plausibility.

[37] [See the longer version of this paper, cited in the editors' note at the outset.]

15

The Reception of Norms, and Open Legal Systems*

JOSÉ JUAN MORESO AND PABLO E. NAVARRO**

INTRODUCTION: THE PROBLEM OF THE RECEPTION OF NORMS

Legal theorists and legal philosophers have often claimed that even if a revolution changes the political authorities and the grounds of validity in a legal system, many earlier norms—that is, norms belonging to the pre-revolutionary legal system—are legally binding in the new system brought about by the revolution.[1] In this connection, the following question arises: How is it that norms issued by the new authorities can be regarded as the foundation of the validity of the earlier norms? If there are no systematic relations between the new, revolutionary constitution and the earlier norms, it would then appear that the latter cannot belong to the new legal system. The problem adumbrated here is familiar under the rubric of *the reception of norms*. Many legal philosophers, in order to resolve the problem, have sought to establish structural relations between the earlier norms and the new system. For example, in his *General Theory of Law and State*, Kelsen writes:

If laws which were introduced under the old constitution 'continue to be valid' under the new constitution, this is possible only because validity has expressly or tacitly been vested in them by the new constitution. The phenomenon is a case of reception (similar to the reception of Roman law). The new order 'receives', i.e., adopts, norms from the old order; this means that the new order gives validity to (puts into force) norms which have the same content as norms of the old order. 'Reception' is an abbreviated procedure of law-creation.[2]

* *Editors' note*: This paper was written for the present volume.
** The authors wish to thank Andrei Marmor, Stanley L. Paulson, Joseph Raz, and Cristina Redondo for helpful comments on a draft of the paper. They would also like to acknowledge the financial support of the Ministerio de Educación y Ciencia de España.
[1] By 'earlier norms' we mean those legal norms that were valid in the legal system preceding the revolutionary break. In our use of 'revolution' we mean to refer, too, to the so-called *coup d'état* and to other irregular changes in the constitution.
[2] *GTLS* 117; see also *PTL*, at § 34(f) (pp. 208–11).

Kelsen's solution presupposes answers to two questions: What does *tacit adoption* mean, and how does the mechanism of adoption work? Since Kelsen made no explicit effort to answer these questions, he overlooked important objections to the concept of the adoption of norms.

The notion of tacit adoption was employed by Jeremy Bentham and John Austin as an explanation of how norms issued by an earlier sovereign can still be regarded as valid laws.[3] Thus, norms issued by Rex I are tacitly adopted by Rex II unless Rex II has expressly repealed them. In *The Concept of Law*, H.L.A. Hart raises strong objections to this mechanism, maintaining that tacit adoption is dispensable. According to Hart, the application of earlier norms does not imply adoption; rather, courts identify them as law in accordance with a rule of recognition, for example 'The norms issued by Rex I and his descendants are valid law.'[4]

Suppose, however, that after a revolution Brutus I becomes sovereign in direct violation of the accepted norms of succession. In such a case, the doctrine of the rule of recognition, which purports to explain the continuity of law, cannot explain the persistence of an important part of legislation after a revolutionary change. Thus, Lon Fuller argues that according to Hart's view, either the earlier norms are no longer valid or they have been tacitly adopted by Brutus. As Fuller writes, referring to the revolution carried out by Brutus:

Are we to say that it is a necessary consequence of this event that all previous laws—including those of property, contract, and marriage—have now lost their force? This is the result demanded by Hart's analysis, yet it violates the experience of history. In this case Hart would have to employ, presumably, some such argument as that Brutus I, by saying nothing about the matter, tacitly re-enacted the previous law—the very argument Hart himself criticizes in Hobbes, Bentham, and Austin and an argument Hart's analysis is intended to render unnecessary.[5]

In his reply to Fuller, Hart maintains that Kelsen's solution was suitable—which seems to bring us back to our starting point: The mechanism that explains the post-revolutionary validity of earlier legislation is the reception or adoption of norms. According to Hart, the earlier norms would have to be mentioned *eo nomine* in any description of the validity criteria employed by judges (that is, their rule of recognition). So it is that

---

[3] See Jeremy Bentham, *Of Laws in General*, ed. H.L.A. Hart (London: Athlone Press, 1970), at 21–2; John Austin, *Lectures on Jurisprudence*, 2 vols., 5th edn., ed. Robert Campbell (London: John Murray, 1885, repr. Glashütten im Taunus: Detlev Auvermann, 1972), vol. II, at 521.

[4] See Hart, *CL*, at 61–4, 2nd edn., at 62–5.

[5] Lon L. Fuller, *The Morality of Law*, rev. edn. (New Haven: Yale UP 1969), 142.

the earlier norms are received or adopted into the new system; their validity comes to rest on a new rule of recognition.[6]

The question of the membership of earlier norms in the new legal system was not in dispute among Kelsen, Hart, and Fuller; indeed, the persistence of earlier norms in new legal systems brought about by revolution may be regarded as the kernel of their respective resolutions of the problem of the reception of norms. In this paper we should like to challenge this traditional resolution of the problem of legal reception, offering in its place an alternative account. Specifically, we analyze, in section I, the extent to which certain analytical distinctions on loan from contemporary theories of legal systems can shed new light on the problem of the reception of norms, and, in section II, whether the notion of the legal system as an *open normative system* can provide a satisfactory resolution of the problem of the reception of norms. As is well-known, a legal system can provide criteria for enforcing both foreign norms and other, different types of non-legal norm, for example, regulations of commercial companies, contracts, and the like. These norms are adopted by the legal system, and, as Joseph Raz emphasizes, the more such a system adopts 'alien' norms, the more open it is.[7] In the same vein, we will argue that where revolutionary changes have taken place, earlier norms are adopted by the revolutionary law—that is to say, they can retain their binding force or applicability even though it is hardly possible to regard them as members of the new legal system. We shall also seek to show that a sharp distinction between membership and applicability is an important analytical tool whose use yields a better understanding of the authoritative character of law.

I. LEGAL SYSTEMS AND THE PERSISTENCE OF LEGAL NORMS

In legal theory the expression 'legal system' is used in a variety of ways. In order to avoid certain common misunderstandings, it is well to draw certain conceptual distinctions. First, one must appreciate that a legal system differs from a mere set of norms. And, in addition, one must be aware of the complex relations that exist between and among the temporal dimension of legal norms, the dynamic content of legal systems, and the identity of law.

---

[6] See H.L.A. Hart, Book Review: Lon L. Fuller, *The Morality of Law*, in *Harvard Law Review*, 78 (1964–5), 1281–96, at 1296, repr. in Hart, *Essays in Jurisprudence and Philosophy* (Oxford: Clarendon Press, 1983), 343–64, at 363.

[7] See Raz, *AL*, at 119.

A set of isolated elements, no matter how important they may be, can scarcely be regarded as a system. An ordinary shopping list is not a system, for its elements are not related to each other in a certain way that is deemed appropriate to them; that is, elements can be considered a *system* only if they are structured in a specific way. In contrast to a set of norms that lacks a systematic character, the structure of a legal system is given by certain specific relations.[8] These relations not only define the structure of the legal system, but also provide a criterion of membership in the system. Legal theorists and legal philosophers have often employed two relations as criteria for identifying norms in a legal system: a deductive relation and a genetic relation.

According to the deductive criterion, a norm belongs to the legal system *LS* if it can be deduced from other norms in *LS*. A norm that is a logical consequence of other norms plays a role similar to theorems in axiomatic systems and can for this reason be called *derived* or *implicit*. The admission of a deductive criterion allows us to reconstruct legal systems as deductive systems, closed by means of the notion of logical consequence. According to this criterion, a legal system is a set of norms that contains all the logical consequences of the set.[9]

The genetic criterion says that a norm N_j belongs to a legal system *LS* if another norm N_k, which belongs to *LS*, authorizes its existence. The genetic criterion can be applied only to *issued norms*, that is to say, a norm meets the genetic criterion only if its issuance is positively permitted by other norms in the legal system. In this respect, it is often asserted that the law regulates its own creation:[10] the introduction and the elimination of legal norms are determined by higher-level norms in the legal system.

It is not the case, however, that all norms belonging to a legal system *LS* can be regarded as derived or legally issued norms in virtue of other norms that are themselves members of *LS*. To avoid circularity in reconstructing the systematic structure of the law, it is necessary to distinguish between two types of norm, which will be termed independent and dependent norms.[11] A norm N_j is *independent* in a certain system *LS* if and only if it does not have a systematic relation within *LS* and its membership in *LS* is not based on the fact that another norm is already a member of *LS*. A norm N_k is *dependent* in a system *LS* if and only if its membership in *LS* presupposes that another norm N_j already belongs to *LS* and a systematic relation exists between N_k and N_j.

---

[8] See Raz, *CLS*, at 24.

[9] See generally Carlos E. Alchourrón and Eugenio Bulygin, *Normative Systems* (Vienna: Springer, 1971), at 54–60.

[10] See e.g. *LT* § 31(a) (at p. 63); *PTL*, at § 35(a) (pp. 221–4).

[11] See Ricardo Caracciolo, *El sistema jurídico. Problemas actuales* (Madrid: Centro de Estudios Constitucionales, 1988), at 31.

The problem of the reception of norms is directed primarily to the dynamic character of law, and genetic relations among legal norms lend this character to the legal system. According to the genetic criterion, the content of legal systems is changed by the acts of issuance and derogation of norms. Thus, the content of a legal system at a particular time, say, the English legal system in 1996, differs not only from the English legal system in, say, 1940, but also from the English legal system as a non-momentary legal system. It is worth asking here whether the identity of a set of norms can, then, be a function of the content of the set. The answer seems clearly to be a negative one. Such a reconstruction of the identity of a legal system would be at odds with another widely accepted thesis, namely: Even if the content of the law changes as a consequence of the issuance or derogation of norms, legal systems—for example, the English legal system—will maintain their identity over time. Various questions concerning the identity of legal systems and their temporal dimension may well be obscured by the ambiguity of the expression 'the content of a legal system'. In the interest of clarity, we shall introduce a technical distinction between *legal systems* and *legal orders*.[12] Legal systems are *momentary* normative systems, and each time a norm is issued or derogated by a competent authority, the result is a different legal system. Legal orders are *sequences* of legal systems.[13]

---

[12] For a more exhaustive analysis, see Carlos E. Alchourrón and Eugenio Bulygin, 'Sobre el concepto de orden jurídico', *Crítica. Revista Hispanoamericana de Filosofía*, 8 (1976), 3–21; Alchourrón and Bulygin, *Sobre la existencia de las normas jurídicas* (Valencia, Venezuela: Universidad de Carabobo, 1979, repr. Mexico City: Distribuciones Fontamara, 1997); Alchourrón and Bulygin, 'The Expressive Conception of Norms', in this volume, ch. 21.

[13] The concepts of legal system and legal order can be regarded as a new formulation of Joseph Raz's distinction between momentary and non-momentary legal systems; see Raz, *CLS*, at 34–5.

Three differences, however, are worth mentioning: First, Raz's characterization of the logical relations between momentary and non-momentary legal systems is ambiguous. On the one hand, he claims that momentary legal systems *belong* to non-momentary legal systems (see Raz, *CLS*, at 35). On the other, he maintains that momentary legal systems are *subclasses* of non-momentary legal systems (see ibid.). Since membership and inclusion are very different relations, the logical nature of non-momentary legal systems is not clearly captured by Raz's distinction; that is, non-momentary legal systems can be either a set of norms or a set of systems. See also Eugenio Bulygin, 'Time and Validity', in *Deontic Logic, Computational Linguistics and Legal Information Systems*, ed. Antonio A. Martino (Dordrecht: North-Holland, 1982), 65–81. A second difference is this. According to Raz, a momentary legal system contains only laws that judges are bound to apply. In our distinction between legal systems and legal orders, however, we are not assuming that all laws of a system at a moment *t* are, at this particular moment, legally binding. As we argue at some length below, a norm can belong to a legal system even if it is not applicable. For example, a norm in the period of *vacatio legis* belongs to the legal system but is not yet applicable. Finally, a third difference is this. Raz's non-momentary legal systems seem to coincide with the law of a certain state—for example, England. Our notion of legal order does not, however, commit us to this conception. For example, a system brought about by revolution and

The identification of particular legal systems and legal orders depends on the application of a conceptual rule that will be termed a *rule of identification* (hereafter '*RI*'). *RI* not only allows us to identify both independent and dependent norms within a legal system, but also serves as a criterion for determining whether two legal systems belong to the same legal order. Thus, the identification of a legal order *LO* requires that the first system of a sequence be identified (hereafter 'LS_0' or 'the originating system'); other systems LS_1, LS_2, . . . , LS_n belong to *LO* if and only if they meet certain criteria of membership in *LO*.

Since we are not interested in a particular legal order, we shall confine ourselves to the general structure of a conceptual rule of identification and provide only a definitional scheme. It is well to bear in mind, however, that in order to grasp the content of a *real* rule of identification, the independent norms of the originating system must be explicitly identified. The general structure of a rule of identification can be shown by means of the following scheme, drawn from Eugenio Bulygin:

(1) *Independent norms.* The norms N_1, N_2, . . . , N_n are valid in the legal system LS_0. LS_0 is the originating system of a legal order LO_j, and the norms N_1, N_2, . . . , N_n are the first constitution of LS_0.

(2) *Introduction of norms.* If a norm N_j is valid in a system LS_t that belongs to LO_j, and N_j empowers the authority x to issue the norm N_k, and x issues the norm N_k at time t, then N_k is valid in the system LS_{t+1} (the system at the moment following t) that belongs to LO_j.

(3) *Elimination of norms.* If a norm N_j is valid in a system LS_t that belongs to LO_j, and N_j empowers the authority x to derogate the norm N_k that is valid in LS_t, and x derogates N_k at time t, then N_k is not valid in the system LS_{t+1} (the system at the moment following t) that belongs to LO_j.

(4) *Persistence of norms.* Valid norms in a system LS_t that belongs to LO_j, so long as they have not been derogated at time t, are valid in the system LS_{t+1} of LO_j (at the moment following t).

(5) *Derived norms.* All logical consequences of the valid norms in a system LS_t that belongs to LO_j are also valid in LS_t.[14]

Some comments on this rule of identification:

a) Independent norms of a system are identified *extensionally*, and they do not meet either a genetic or a deductive criterion in the originating system LS_0. Dependent norms are identified *intensionally* through the satisfaction of certain conditions—that is, deducibility or genetic relations.

the old system do not in many cases belong to the same legal order, but even if we must distinguish in these cases between two different legal orders, we are not committed thereby to recognizing two non-momentary legal systems.

[14] See Eugenio Bulygin, 'Algunas consideraciones sobre los sistemas jurídicos', *Doxa*, 9 (1991), 257–79, at 263–4.

b) The independent norms of a system—that is, the first constitution—must be sharply distinguished from *RI*, for this conceptual rule of identification cannot be an independent norm. *RI* provides a *recursive definition* of valid norms in the legal systems that are members of a certain legal order, while the first constitution is a *set of valid legal norms*. It makes no sense to assert that *RI* is valid or invalid, and since by 'validity' we mean membership in a legal system, *RI* cannot belong to any legal system.

c) Legal systems are *static* normative systems, closed under the notion of logical consequence.[15] Once the constitution of LS_0 is identified, the scope of the originating system is given by the logical consequences of the first constitution.

d) The introduction and the elimination of norms provide an explanation of the genetic relations among legal norms. The dynamic character of law is reconstructed by genetic relations among norms belonging to an ordered pair of some subsequent static systems in a legal order. Thus, genetic relations are *intersystemic*.[16]

e) A legal system is a set of *norms*, and a legal order is a set of *legal systems*. Since the relation of membership is not transitive, legal norms do not belong to a legal order; the only elements of a legal order are static legal systems.

f) The expression 'legal order' is not tantamount to 'municipal law' or 'law of the state'; municipal law can normally be reconstructed as a set of successive legal orders.[17]

g) The continuity of law is usually regarded as an essential feature of legal dynamics. For this reason *RI* also includes a clause on the persistence of legal norms, that is, clause (4).

h) A conceptual rule of identification like *RI* is not to be confused with a social *norm* addressed to judges, prescribing that the norms to be applied are to be identified by certain criteria. This social norm is usually termed a 'rule of recognition', and we are by no means denying its existence.[18] We wish only to point out the following. Even if the existence of a rule of recognition is beyond doubt, it will still be necessary to distinguish between this regulative norm and the conceptual criteria that define the sources of legal validity in a legal system.[19]

[15] See Michael Hartney, 'The Confusion in Kelsen's Final Rejection of a Logic of Norms', in *Praktische Vernunft, Gesetzgebung und Rechtswissenschaft* (*ARSP* Beiheft 52), ed. Waldemar Schreckenberger and Christian Starck (Stuttgart: Franz Steiner, 1993), 77–81, at 81.

[16] See Raz, *CLS*, at 184–5; Caracciolo (n.11 above), at 67–73.

[17] This idea was adumbrated by Adolf Julius Merkl in 'Das Problem der Rechtskontinuität und die Forderung des einheitlichen rechtlichen Weltbildes', *ZöR*, 5 (1926), 497–527, at 499–500, repr. *WS II* 1267–300, at 1269–70.

[18] See Raz, *CLS*, at 200.

[19] For a classical discussion on this distinction between conceptual rules and prescriptive norms, see von Wright, *NA*, at 1–16.

According to our distinction between legal systems and legal orders, the problem of reception comes to this: To what extent does the content of legal systems belonging to a legal order LO_t determine the content of the originating legal system LS_0 in a subsequent legal order LO_{t+1}? Any successful revolutionary change is a break in the legal order, and if a new constitution arises as a result of the revolutionary change, then this constitution is the beginning of a new legal order. Still, there are questions arising from this state of affairs: Do earlier norms meet any criteria of membership in the new system, that is, can they be either independent or dependent norms in the new system? And what explanation is there for the fact that earlier norms are still regarded as valid in the first system of the new order? A postulate in legal theory has it that legal norms, once they have been created in a bona fide legal way, remain valid until they are explicitly or tacitly derogated.[20] Since this idea of legal continuity is deeply embedded in legal theory, this solution to the reception of norms will be termed the traditional doctrine. It is important to note that we are describing not a particular, historical doctrine, but a conceptual position that intrinsically relates the binding force of earlier norms to their membership in the legal system brought about by revolutionary change. This position can be reconstructed by means of the following postulate:

If a norm Nj belongs to a system LS that is a member of an order LO, then it belongs to all legal systems successive to LS in all legal orders successive to LO until its elimination.

This clause, which can be regarded as a reformulation of the principle of persistence in a certain legal order, implies that earlier norms that are not derogated in the revolutionary transition also belong to the originating system in the new order.[21] In other words, even if constitution A is illegally replaced by constitution B, the only change that occurs is in the law-making organs: the power to create and to derogate norms belongs henceforth to organ B instead of organ A. Nothing else changes; in particular, all of the norms that were created under constitution A continue to be valid.[22] Thus, according to this doctrine, it is the case that earlier norms are a part of the new system stemming from the revolutionary change, just as it is the case that legal norms remain valid after a lawful change in the constitution. Once a norm is legally issued, it belongs to all

---

[20] See e.g. John Finnis, *Natural Law and Natural Rights* (Oxford: Clarendon Press, 1980), at 268.

[21] See John Finnis, 'Revolutions and Continuity of Law', in *Oxford Essays in Jurisprudence, Second Series*, ed. A.W.B. Simpson (Oxford: Clarendon Press, 1973), 44–76, at 63; Neil MacCormick, *H.L.A. Hart* (London: Arnold, 1981), at 110.

[22] We are indebted to Michael Hartney for illuminating comments on this point.

successive legal systems in all successive legal orders until it is explicitly or tacitly eliminated.

The traditional doctrine is not, however, free of problems. We shall confine ourselves here to three objections that are closely related to the determinacy of legal material and its identification.

i) *Derogation and the Determinacy of Normative Powers.* Were the traditional doctrine accepted, the originating system in a legal order could not be regarded as the set of all logical consequences of the first revolutionary constitution, for this first system must also include the earlier norms. Therefore, the identification of the originating system would require determining which earlier norms are eliminated in the course of the revolutionary transition. It may be suggested that a norm is eliminated if it is derogated by the new authorities. For example, when earlier norms are explicitly rejected, they are eliminated from the new systems in the new legal order. Sometimes earlier norms are not explicitly repealed but are tacitly derogated by the new authorities. 'Tacit derogation' usually means the elimination of a norm from a system as the solution to a norm conflict. Thus, an earlier norm is tacitly derogated if it *contradicts* the new constitution brought about by the revolution. The notion of a contradiction between norms is often applied to mandatory norms in the following way: A norm N_j contradicts norm N_k if and only if it is logically impossible to obey both norms at one and the same time. The case of permissory norms is, to be sure, more complex, for they can be neither obeyed nor disobeyed; a permissory norm and a mandatory norm are *inconsistent*, however, if it is logically impossible to obey the command and to observe the permission at one and the same time.[23] New difficulties arise when we try to define a notion of norm contradiction that is appropriate for conflicts between competence norms. For example, does an earlier norm N_j that empowers the authority A_j to issue norms addressed to a certain object O actually contradict another norm, N_k, brought about by the revolutionary change and empowering the authority A_k to issue norms addressed to the same object O?[24] There is, prima facie, no conflict between these two competence norms, and consequently the principle of the persistence of valid law prompts one to grant that both norms belong to the legal system brought about by the revolutionary change. To be sure, this conclusion seems counter-intuitive, for it means that the earlier authorities retain their normative powers. What is more, since no

---

[23] See von Wright, *NA*, at 141–60.
[24] For a discussion of contradiction with respect to competence norms, see ibid. at 203–7.

sufficiently clear notion of contradiction between norms is at hand, the adopted norms (and *a fortiori* the normative basis of the first legal system) cannot be precisely identified. This situation, needless to say, reflects a serious difficulty in the traditional doctrine, which would have one reconstructing the law as a legal system.

ii) *The Logical Indeterminacy of Legal Systems.* Even if we could provide an appropriate reconstruction of the notion of 'tacit derogation', there is another source of indeterminacy in the identification of the first system, namely, the logical indeterminacy of the adopted set of norms. If an earlier *derived* norm contradicts the new 'first constitution', this norm can no longer be regarded as valid law and is eliminated from the new system. But in order to remove a derived norm N from a system, it is necessary to eliminate all those sets of norms that imply N. Since a number of norms are members of the sets that imply a derived norm N, the derogation of N leads to the logical indeterminacy of the legal system.[25]

iii) *Legal Orders and Recursive Definitions.* The first system in the new order can be indeterminate in another important way. A conceptual rule of identification *RI* is a scheme for deciding in a *finite* number of steps whether a certain norm is valid in a legal system, and this mechanism of recursion always terminates in some independent norm (for example, the first constitution). If earlier norms belong to the legal system *LS*, which was brought about by the revolutionary change, they must be either independent or dependent norms in *LS*. Since only norms compatible with the revolutionary constitution are adopted into the new legal system *LS*, it is clear that these adopted norms cannot be regarded as independent, for they presuppose the existence of other norms in *LS*. Moreover, earlier norms cannot be regarded as dependent in the new legal system either, for they are

---

[25] Let us assume that the normative basis of the pre-revolutionary system of a legal order is as follows: (N_1) If one is over eighteen years of age, then one is an adult. (N_2) All adults ought to vote.

As a logical consequence of N_1 and N_2, a norm N^* can be derived: (N^*) If one is over eighteen years of age, then one ought to vote.

Let us also assume that the following norm is issued by the revolutionary authorities: (N_3) People over eighteen years of age ought not to vote.

N^* is tacitly derogated by N_3 and cannot be a member of the new, revolutionary system. In order to remove N^*, it is also necessary to eliminate either N_1 or N_2 from the new system. However, since both $\{N_1, N_3\}$ and $\{N_2, N_3\}$ are consistent sets, the subtraction of N^* from the new system leads to a logical indeterminacy in the basis of the legal system.

See Alchourrón and Bulygin, 'Sobre el concepto de orden jurídico' (n.12 above); Alchourrón and Bulygin, 'Expressive Conception' (n.12 above); David Lewis, 'A Problem about Permission', in *Essays in Honour of Jaakko Hintikka*, ed. Esa Saarinen et al. (Dordrecht: Reidel, 1979), 163–79; Risto Hilpinen, 'On Normative Change', in *Ethics: Foundations, Problems, and Applications*, ed. Edgar Morscher and Rudolf Stranzinger (Vienna: Holder-Pichler-Tempsky, 1981), 155–64.

neither norms issued by authorities of the new legal system nor logical consequences of other norms of the new legal system. It can be argued that earlier norms were legally issued although their authorities are not competent in the new legal system. To identify the adopted set of norms, then, we must first determine not only the new, revolutionary constitution, but also which norms belonged to the last system of the old order. We cannot identify this last system, however, without resorting again to the mechanism of recursion, which leads us to the originating system of the old order. This originating system may contain an adopted set of earlier norms, and so on. Thus, to include in the rule of identification a clause of persistence in legal systems of different legal orders can lead to a *regressus ad infinitum*, a never-ending process in the effort to determine whether a certain norm belongs to a certain legal system.

We advance these arguments not as a decisive objection to the traditional doctrine, but simply to suggest that it be considered more carefully. However, although we do not analyze the basic assumptions of this classical solution, we fail to see why legal theorists seem to find the traditional doctrine compelling. The doctrine is constructed for the most part around two premises: Only valid norms are legally binding; and earlier norms are legally binding. From these premises, it is quite easy to reach the conclusion that earlier norms are legally valid. Thus, in the case of the reception of norms, the traditional doctrine seems to provide a compelling explanation of the binding force of legal norms. There exists, however, a certain tension between these two premises, a tension clearly manifested in the fact that legal philosophers often distinguish the persistence of earlier norms from other problems of legal continuity. For example, in *General Theory of Law and State*, Kelsen contends that a legal norm is valid only if its issuance is provided for by another, higher-level legal norm, but once a norm is legally issued, its validity is not affected by the elimination or derogation of the higher-level norm. In accordance with the so-called principle of legitimacy, legal norms 'remain valid as long as they have not been invalidated' in a way determined by the legal system itself.[26] Thus, although a higher-level norm of competence must exist at the moment the lower-level norm is created, the validity of the lower-level norm is not dependent on the continued existence of the norm of competence.

In his analysis of legal dynamics, Kelsen does not maintain that earlier norms, legally issued and not derogated by norms resulting from the revolutionary change, remain valid in the new legal system. Instead, he argues that the principle of legitimacy is limited by the principle of

[26] *GTLS* 117.

efficacy, and he follows through by introducing the doctrine of the reception of legal norms, which is actually an abbreviated procedure of law creation. Indeed, although neither of the above-mentioned premises of the traditional doctrine is rejected in *The Pure Theory of Law*,[27] Kelsen was perfectly aware that earlier norms can represent a theoretical problem: Earlier norms are deprived of their validity by revolution and not by means of the principle of legitimacy. In *General Theory of Law and State*, he writes:

No jurist would maintain that even after a successful revolution the old constitution and the laws based thereupon remain in force, on the ground that they have not been nullified in a manner anticipated by the old order itself. Every jurist will presume that the old order . . . has ceased to be valid, and that all norms which are valid within the new order receive their validity exclusively from the new constitution. It follows that, from this juristic point of view, the norms of the old order can no longer be recognized as valid norms.[28]

Thus, it follows from the revolutionary elimination of a constitutional norm, unlike the derogation of other norms, that those norms grounded in this constitutional norm will also lose their validity. For this reason, the 'reissuance' of earlier norms in accordance with the new legal foundation is required in order to explain why they are still regarded as binding norms. In other words, the concepts of legal reception, tacit adoption, and so on are introduced to account for both the systematic character of law and the binding force of earlier legal norms in new legal systems brought about by revolutionary change. It is easy to see why the traditional doctrine has had considerable influence on the thinking of jurists and legal theorists. At least two reasons can be proferred. The idea of preserving a systematic reconstruction of the law seems to be a necessary constraint, for a basic function of the concept of a legal system is to provide a conceptual scheme enabling legal theorists to distinguish between legal norms and other, non-legal norms—for example, moral norms. Furthermore, recognition of the normative force of earlier norms seems to be required in order to provide a sound reconstruction of a widely accepted legal practice that treats these norms as legally binding.

In summary, if the law is reconstructed as a system, legal norms seem to be binding in so far as they are valid in a legal system. A norm is valid in a legal system if and only if it is either an independent or a dependent norm. Earlier norms cannot be regarded as independent in the originating system LS_0 of a legal order, for they presuppose the membership of the norms in LS_0, which has been brought about by the revolutionary change. Since earlier norms do not satisfy the conditions marked by

---

[27] See *PTL*, at § 34(f) (pp. 208–11).   [28] *GTLS* 118.

the relations defining the membership of dependent norms in a legal system, the traditional doctrine introduces a clause of persistence as a means of explaining the membership of earlier norms in new systems. If, however, earlier norms do not belong to a new legal system, how might one explain their authoritative force? The relation between legal force and validity (membership) deserves closer attention here. If it were possible to distinguish sharply between the binding force of earlier norms and their membership in a new legal system, the traditional doctrine would no longer be regarded as an inevitable explanation of legal continuity. In section II, we argue that while we are not committed to accepting the membership of earlier norms in a new legal system, we seek to reconcile the systematic structure of law and the binding force of earlier legal norms.

II. LEGAL SYSTEMS AS OPEN NORMATIVE SYSTEMS

Our solution to the problem of the reception of norms requires that we distinguish *binding* norms from *valid* norms or, in other words, from independent and dependent norms in the legal system. A legally binding norm has legal effects (is applicable), and, from a positivistic point of view, the binding force of a legal norm is relative to the existence of other norms. If a norm N_i is *applicable* at moment t, then it is true that another norm N_j is *valid* in the legal system LS at this particular moment and prescribes how N_i is to be applied.[29] It should be noted that there is no necessary one-to-one relation between N_i and N_j, for N_j can also prescribe the application of several other norms, say, N_h, N_k, N_l. It must be emphasized, however, that the applicability of a certain norm, say, N_i, always requires the membership of another norm, say, N_j, in the legal system. Norms such as N_j provide the criteria of applicability in a legal system LS, and they are addressed to certain authorities—for example, to judges.

The applicability of legal norms is closely related to the institutional character of law, for a certain norm will have legal effects only if it is enforceable in the courts. Legal systems are *institutional normative systems*, and one characteristic of these systems is the existence of norm-applying institutions. Thus, it makes sense to attribute applicability to certain norms only if there are norm-applying institutions. Moreover, it is sometimes emphasized that legal systems necessarily contain norms establishing norm-applying institutions, and that norms belong to a legal system only if norm-applying institutions have a duty to apply the

---

[29] See Bulygin (n.13 above), at 66; José Juan Moreso and Pablo E. Navarro, 'Applicabilità e efficacia delle norme giuridiche', in *Struttura e dinamica dei sistemi giuridici*, ed. Paolo Comanducci and Riccardo Guastini (Turin: G. Giappichelli Editore, 1996), 15–35.

norms.[30] It follows from both theses that a (momentary) legal system contains only those norms that judges are bound to apply.

If this approach were correct, however, the distinction between validity and applicability would in part collapse. There are, to be sure, a number of interesting relations between applicability and membership in a legal system, but these are nevertheless altogether independent properties of legal norms—that is, there is no necessary connection between the applicability of a legal norm and its membership in a (momentary) legal system. On the one hand, norms that do not belong to a legal system may nevertheless be applicable to certain cases. For example, in private international law, a norm N of a country C_i may be applicable in another country C_j, even if N does not belong to the legal system of the country C_j. On the other hand, a norm N, belonging to a certain legal system LS, may be inapplicable, namely, when another norm N_j forbids the application of N. For example, in many countries some constitutional rights and guarantees may be rendered temporarily inapplicable in accordance with the exercise of certain exceptional powers, say, emergency powers of the parliament. Or there may be a period of *vacatio legis*, as happened in Argentina in the 1920s. The Argentine Criminal Code was enacted in October 1921, but its article 303, in stipulating that the Code 'shall become the law of the nation six months after its promulgation', thereby established a temporal restriction on the applicability of other norms of the Code. Thus, although the Criminal Code was valid from the moment of its *promulgation* and criminal norms could be derogated, these norms were not applicable until April 1922 (except, of course, for article 303).

Once membership and applicability are sharply distinguished, we can say that a conceptual rule of identification *RI* identifies only the valid norms in a legal system. Indeed, the distinction is necessary in order to grasp a crucial feature of legal systems, namely, that they are *open* systems.[31] One important function of law is to provide support to other forms of social organization, and to this end, legal systems contain norms that lend binding force to other, non-legal norms.[32] But how are we to characterize these other, non-legal norms? Raz points out that it is necessary to distinguish between norms that are recognized as binding in virtue of their being part of the legal system and other norms that are recognized thanks to the fact that lending support to such norms—that is, to foreign norms, contracts, regulations of commercial companies,

---

[30] See Raz, *AL*, at 115.

[31] See ibid., at 119–20; Joseph Raz, *Practical Reason and Norms*, 2nd edn. (Princeton: Princeton UP, 1990), at 152–4. The distinction between membership and applicability of legal norms can also be found in Eugenio Bulygin (n.13 above), at 65–81.

[32] See Raz, *AL*, at 119.

and so on—is an important function of legal norms.[33] Raz's arguments on the open character of legal systems are illuminating, but they stand in need of certain refinements lest misunderstandings arise. For example, Raz claims that 'alien' norms are adopted by an open legal system if and only if

they are norms which belong to another normative system practised by its norm-subjects and which are recognized as long as they remain in force in such a system as applying to the same norm-subjects, provided they are recognized because the system intends to respect the way that the community regulates its activities. . . .[34]

This characterization is too narrow, however, for it only makes possible the recognition of 'other' norms that are still in force. There is no room for the common-sense assertion that judges are in certain instances bound to apply the norms of an extinct state—for example, the Soviet Union. Moreover, as often happens in cases of private international law, judges can apply foreign norms that were derogated long ago.

The *criteria* for identifying adopted norms in a legal system must be distinguished from the *reasons* that are adduced to justify the adoption of norms. On the one hand, a norm N_j, not belonging to a legal system LS, is adopted into LS if and only if another norm N_k, belonging to LS, prescribes that N_j be applied to certain cases. On the other hand, there are certain reasons that serve to justify the adoption of norms—for example, providing support to social groups, private institutions, and individual arrangements. Other reasons might include preserving peace and social order, or promoting legal certainty.

Examples can shed light on the distinction between the criteria for identifying adopted norms and the reasons for adopting norms. Suppose that the following norm *CN* belongs to a certain criminal code:

If the law in force at the time the crime was committed is different from the law in force at the time the sentence is imposed, the law more favourable to the accused shall be applied.

Put generally, *CN*, belonging to a legal system *LS*, requires that judges apply the less severe of two criminal norms arguably applicable to the defendant. Indeed, even a repealed norm may be applicable, provided it prescribes the less severe sanction; since this norm has already been derogated, it does not belong to the present system *LS* and could be regarded as adopted by the judge at the time of his decision. A judge's reasons for applying the less severe norm are clearly different from the reasons that prompted the legislators to issue the criminal norm *CN* in

---

[33] See ibid., at 120. [34] Ibid.

the first place. The judge's reasons are usually related to the issue of fidelity to law in deciding legal cases, whereas the legislators' reasons are normally related to principles providing justification for criminal norms generally—for example, a certain justification of punishment.

So-called unconstitutional norms are another interesting example. An unconstitutional norm is an invalid norm, for it fails to exhibit the appropriate systematic relations to the independent norms of a legal system,[35] but a court—say, a constitutional court—can mistakenly declare it to be valid. In order to come to terms with invalid norms, we must bear in mind the distinction between final judicial decisions and infallible ones. The constitutionality of a legal norm is not a matter that is determined solely by what a constitutional court decides;[36] that is, legal norms issued by an authority without competence are invalid even if a court takes the opposite position. Nevertheless, a final decision of a constitutional court does determine the applicability of such a norm. When a court (wrongly) states that a norm is constitutional, such a norm will be applicable, but it is not valid in the system.[37] A judge's reason for deferring to applicable unconstitutional norms may be fidelity to binding precedents or the necessity of meeting formal requirements of justice—such as, for example, treating like cases alike. Thus, unconstitutional norms can be regarded as adopted by a legal system, and the reason for such an adoption is an important feature of the law, namely, that it necessarily provide a mechanism for solving conflicts. The rules of adjudication can fulfil their functions only to the extent that they can settle legal disputes authoritatively.[38] To obtain the social advantages of the legal process requires that the possibility of mistaken judicial decisions be accepted. However, to avoid one of the major shortcomings of legal realism, the concept of a definitive judicial decision must be carefully distinguished from the concept of an infallible decision.

As we have already pointed out, many different norms can be adopted by legal systems, and where the reception of norms is concerned, we are not committed to accepting the membership of earlier norms in the new system. Earlier norms are no longer valid law, but they may still be applicable—that is, if they are adopted into the new legal system, which is to say, only if norms belonging to the new system establish the obligation to apply the earlier norms. The reasons for adopting the earlier norms include the need to preserve legal certainty—that is, to avoid a situation in which a certain area is not legally regulated at all, or to honour

[35] See generally José Juan Moreso, 'Verfassungswidrige Normen', *Rechtstheorie*, 25 (1994), 417–49.
[36] See Hart, *CL*, at 138–44, 2nd edn., at 141–7.
[37] See Bulygin (n.14 above), at 267.
[38] See Raz, *AL*, at 172–6.

certain legitimate expectations of citizens. For example, law, as John Finnis writes, employs a special technique in order to provide precision and predictability. Yesterday's legal acts are treated, today, as exclusionary reasons for acting in a way that was 'provided for' then. Finnis continues:

The convenience of this attribution of authoritativeness to past acts is twofold. The past is beyond the reach of persons in the present; it thus provides (subject only to problems of evidence and interpretation) a stable point of reference unaffected by present and shifting interests and disputes. Again, the present will soon be the past; so the technique gives people a way of now determining the framework of their future.[39]

We have shown that a sharp distinction between the validity and the applicability of legal norms can provide a novel picture of the problem of the reception of norms. This picture, dispensing with the implausible doctrines of tacit adoption and reissuance, both preserves the systematic reconstruction of the law and takes into account the practice of recognizing the binding force of earlier norms.

Although we believe that the concept of the open legal system may provide a basis for solving the problem of the reception of norms, we have by and large left out of our account thus far certain possible objections to our reconstruction. In closing, we turn to three such objections, with an eye to showing how they can be met.

i) Lawyers are not always prepared to distinguish binding norms from valid norms. Many legal norms that judges are bound to apply are, no less for that, no longer valid, but lawyers may not be willing to grant this proposition. In the reconstruction of the concept of a legal system, however, legal theorists are not committed to the reproduction of all aspects of legal discourse; rather, their concern is with an analysis of legal practices. Were legal parlance a conceptual constraint, then the idea of open normative systems would collapse, for jurists often refer to adopted laws as members of their own legal systems. Kelsen, for example, writes:

The rule obliging the courts of a state to apply norms of a foreign law to certain cases has the effect of incorporating the norms of the foreign law into the law of this state. Such a rule has the same character as the provision of a new, revolution-established constitution stating that some statutes valid under the old, revolution-abolished constitution should continue to be in force under the new constitution. The contents of these statutes remains the same, but the reason for their validity is changed.[40]

---

[39] Finnis (n.20 above), 269.
[40] *GTLS* 244. For criticism, see H.L.A. Hart, 'Kelsen's Doctrine of the Unity of Law', in this volume, ch. 30, at § IV.

If the applicability of norms and their membership in a legal system are kept separate, the quoted passage from Kelsen can be considered as an argument that the ground for applying both foreign laws and earlier norms is one and the same: A norm in the system—say, the new constitution—prescribes the enforcement of norms that do not belong to the system.

ii) Does our solution actually presuppose a constitutional norm that prescribes the application of earlier norms? To be sure, a criterion for applying legal norms is not necessarily found in statutory or constitutional law. For example, some criminal codes specify no express means of resolving conflicts between general and particular norms, and, in order to resolve such conflicts, courts usually apply the so-called *lex specialis* rule of normative priority. The applicability of earlier norms can result not only from an explicit constitutional norm, but also from the practices of courts when they deal with the binding force of earlier norms.

iii) It is tempting to assert that certain adopted norms, for example, foreign norms, differ in legal status from earlier norms. While authorities can derogate earlier norms, it makes no sense to claim that they can derogate foreign norms. Derogation, however, has several different uses in legal theory, in particular, two central readings of 'derogation' must be distinguished in order to avoid ambiguity. On the first reading, derogation is the elimination of norms from a legal system. On the second, derogation serves to cancel the applicability of a norm. Following this distinction, earlier legal norms cannot be eliminated from a legal system, but an act of parliament or a decision of a constitutional court can extinguish their binding force. In this case, earlier norms are derogated by legal authorities, which is to say that judges are no longer bound to apply them.

CONCLUDING REMARKS

It has been our aim to show that the problem of the reception of norms is closely related to the persistence of law and the validity of legal norms. Above all, we have criticized and offered an alternative to the traditional solution to the problem of the reception of norms, which has it that earlier norms are legally binding because they belong to the new legal system. Our purpose has been to challenge this traditional solution, and to consider the extent to which the notion of open legal systems provides a solution to the problem. We have drawn a distinction between the membership and the applicability of legal norms. Only valid norms are members of a legal system, though a large number of norms may be applicable despite not belonging to the system. We have claimed, therefore, that earlier norms do not belong to the new legal system even though they may be applicable and legally binding.

The significance of what we have termed the applicability of legal norms has not always been appreciated by jurists and legal philosophers. The lack of an adequate reconstruction of the concepts of membership, existence, and the binding force of legal norms is largely responsible for the confusion still encountered in connection with applicability and other properties of legal norms. In particular, the underlying conceptual differences between applicability and membership are often overlooked, and it is claimed, for example, that legal norms are applicable only if they belong to a legal system, or that repealed legal norms are no longer applicable.

Although we have pointed up shortcomings in the traditional view, there is nevertheless a grain of truth in the idea that a conceptual connection exists between membership and applicability. The applicability of a norm N_j at a time t always presupposes the membership of another norm N_k in a legal system LS, a norm that prescribes that N_j be applied at t. In this respect, the notion of membership enjoys a conceptual priority over the notion of applicability, for the identification of a set of applicable norms at t is always relative to the identification of certain norms (that is, to criteria of applicability) belonging to the system LS at t.

The open character of legal systems is intrinsically related to the institutional character of law. Law, a system of norms created and applied by specific social institutions, is both a social and a normative order. A proper solution to the problem of the reception of norms not only depends on a clear understanding of the institutional aspects of open systems, but requires, too, a careful enquiry into the authority of law.[41] This last topic is something we reserve for another occasion.

---

[41] See Joseph Raz, *Ethics in the Public Domain* (Oxford: Clarendon Press, 1994), at 210–37.

PART IV

Toward a Theory of Legal Norms

A. Ramifications of Kelsen's Late, Sceptical Phase

16

An Antinomy in Kelsen's Pure Theory of Law*

EUGENIO BULYGIN

Despite the fact that the idea of validity plays a very central role in Kelsen's Pure Theory of Law, there is no consensus among scholars about the exact meaning of this rather elusive notion. Even among those authors who are of one mind on what Kelsen's concept of validity comes to, there is widespread disagreement in the appraisal of the concept.

In a lecture delivered at the University of Buenos Aires some thirty years ago, Alf Ross pointed out that Kelsen faces serious difficulties owing to his use of the concept of validity qua binding force, a view that Ross characterized as 'quasi-positivism'.[1] In his treatise on legal validity, Carlos Nino returns to this issue, maintaining, like Ross, that Kelsen employs a normative concept of validity akin to that found in classical authors of the natural law tradition.[2] Nino's attitude towards this phenomenon, however, is diametrically opposed to Ross's. Whereas Ross maintained that the concept of validity qua binding force should be eliminated from legal theory and, in particular, from Kelsen's Pure Theory of Law, Nino believes that the only correct interpretation of Kelsen is that which stems from acknowledging that his concept of validity is normative and not descriptive. Unless we take this step, Nino argues, we cannot grasp Kelsen's ideas about the nature of law.

In view of such basic disagreement, it seems advisable to re-examine the relevant aspects of Kelsen's Pure Theory of Law with an eye to determining the exact role played in it by what Nino calls the normative concept of validity. This is what I propose to do in the present paper.

---

* *Editors' note*: This paper first appeared in *Ratio Juris*, 3 (1990), 29–45. The present version contains minor revisions. In consultation with the author, the bibliography of the original printing has been incorporated into the footnotes; minor alterations in quotations from existing English-language translations of Kelsen's works have been made *sub silentio*.

[1] Alf Ross, 'Validity and the Conflict between Legal Positivism and Natural Law', in this volume, ch. 7.

[2] Carlos Santiago Nino, *La validez del derecho* (Buenos Aires: Astrea, 1985); see also Nino, 'Some Confusions surrounding Kelsen's Concept of Validity', in this volume, ch. 13.

I. THE KANTIAN AND THE POSITIVISTIC
INGREDIENTS IN THE PURE THEORY OF LAW

It is not easy to draw a coherent picture of Kelsen's theory of law, owing mainly to two kinds of difficulties. In the first place, Kelsen's written work ranges over a period of nearly seventy years, a fact that makes it easy to understand that his views on certain central topics in legal philosophy underwent considerable change during his long life. This is why it is almost impossible to speak of *the* Pure Theory of Law; none of Kelsen's books, not even the monumental Second Edition of the *Reine Rechtslehre* (1960), published when he was nearly eighty, can be regarded as the final version of his thought. It is an astonishing fact that the last twelve years of his life (he died in 1973 at the age of ninety-one) are especially rich in new ideas that have far-reaching consequences for his theory of law.

In the second place, and this is a more serious problem, we find in Kelsen's thought two groups of ideas that stem from quite different philosophical traditions. These ideas are not only difficult to reconcile but, indeed, are—as I shall try to show in some detail—radically incompatible. Both the Kantian and the positivistic trends are vividly present in Kelsen's works, and some of his main tenets can be traced back to these two strongly opposed philosophical traditions. Being incompatible, some of his ideas stemming from one of these traditions have to be eliminated, this in order to render the Pure Theory of Law coherent.

Which of the two traditions is to be preferred is, I think, to a certain degree a matter of taste. Personally, I regard Kelsen's positivistic views as the more important development, and I shall adduce reasons in support of this choice. Kelsen's views here made him, along with Max Weber, one of the founding fathers of the positivistic approach to social sciences and perhaps *the* founder of modern legal positivism. What is more, in the last years of his life Kelsen himself showed an increasing preference for the ideas that I term positivistic, and although he as a matter of fact never explicitly rejected his Kantian heritage, his philosophical evolution exhibits a clear tendency in the direction of the positivistic components in his theory of law.

From a chronological standpoint we can distinguish, roughly speaking, three main periods in Kelsen's thought. In the first period, the Kantian and the positivistic elements coexist more or less harmoniously, and Kelsen seems to be unaware of their antagonism. This period corresponds approximately to the first thirty years of his philosophical production (1911–1940); it includes such books as *Hauptprobleme der Staatsrechtslehre* (1911), the *Allgemeine Staatslehre* (1925), and the *Introduction to the Problems of Legal Theory*, which is the First Edition of the *Reine Rechtslehre* (1934). (Only works directly concerned with philosophy of law will be mentioned in this connection.) The second period is a transition stage of about twenty years, from 1940, when Kelsen leaves Europe and settles in the United States, to 1960. The main publications of this period are *General Theory of Law and State* (1945), *Théorie pure du droit* (1953),[3] which is a French-language revision of the First Edition of the *Reine Rechtslehre*, and the Second Edition of the *Reine Rechtslehre* (1960). The third period, predominantly positivistic in spirit, includes such important papers as 'Derogation' (1962) and 'Law and Logic' (1965), and also his unfinished work *General Theory of Norms* (first published in 1979).[4]

Kelsen's main ideas of Kantian origin are: (1) the characterization of legal norms as ideal entities belonging to the world of *Sollen* ('ought'), distinct from the world of natural reality or the world of *Sein* ('is'); (2) the conception of validity qua binding force (which, following Nino, I call the normative concept of validity); (3) the normativity of legal science; and (4) Kelsen's well-known doctrine of the basic norm as a transcendental category.

All these theses are closely connected. It is because norms are ideal entities belonging to a world that differs radically from the real one that their existence is not a (natural) fact; the specific existence of norms is their validity, understood as binding force. A norm exists if and only if it is valid or binding, that is, when its addressees ought to behave as the norm prescribes. Legal science is normative not only in the sense that it is concerned with norms. Legal science is normative, above all, because the sentences in which it describes law are normative, and they are normative because they refer not to natural facts but to valid norms, that is, to their obligatoriness or binding force. On the other hand, the idea of validity as a binding force is based—as we shall see below in some detail—on the hypothesis of a basic norm, whose main role is to make the idea of validity compatible with Kelsen's positivistic ideal of *eine wertfreie Rechtswissenschaft* (a non-evaluative legal science).

Kelsen's ideal of a positivistic legal science is related to four fundamental theses: (5) a sharp separation between 'is' and 'ought'; (6) the non-cognitivist conception of norms and value judgments as prescriptions that are neither true nor false; (7) the positivity of law, the thesis that all law is positive, that is to say, is created and destroyed by human acts, or—putting it more cautiously—legal norms come into and pass out of existence as a consequence of certain human acts; and (8) a sharp

[3] Hans Kelsen, *Théorie pure du droit*, trans. Henri Thévenaz (Boudry-Neuchâtel: Éditions de la Baconnière, 1953).

[4] [See the Table of Abbreviations for full references to all of these works.]

distinction between description and prescription (or evaluation), between reason and volition, between the cognition of law and the creation of law, between the science of law and legal politics.

The non-cognitivist conception of norms as prescriptions that are neither true nor false (thesis 6) has far-reaching consequences; it means that there are no normative facts that would make norms true, that is, there is no reality corresponding to norms. This is the main difference between norms and propositions. Moreover, Kelsen adopts the same sceptic position regarding values: Value judgments, too, lack truth-values, with the result that there are no objective values. But though Kelsen had always been a sceptic in matters of values, the characterization of legal norms as prescriptions appears at a relatively late stage of his philosophical development. In the first period of his thought, norms are characterized as judgments or propositions,[5] and he strongly objects to their characterization as imperatives even as late as the *General Theory of Law and State* (1945). It is only in the Second Edition of the *Reine Rechtslehre* (1960) that Kelsen explicitly identifies norms and imperatives and at the same time extends the notion of 'ought' (*Sollen*) to all deontic modalities: obligation, prohibition, permission, and empowerment (*Ermächtigung*). Later he adds derogation to this list.

Thesis 7 states that all law is positive law; this means that it is created and destroyed by human acts (this holds for enacted law as well as for customary law). This thesis has two important consequences: first, there is no natural law, and, second, legal norms have a temporal dimension—they begin to exist at a certain moment and cease to exist at a later moment, that is to say, they are historical. This thesis was firmly maintained by Kelsen throughout his life.

A sharp distinction between the pairs of concepts, description and prescription, cognition and evaluation, science and politics (thesis 8), can be regarded as the core of the positivistic programme of a value-neutral science, whose champions in the field of the social sciences have been Kelsen and Weber.

The three pairs of concepts are closely related. If norms and value judgments lack truth-values, they are not subject to rational control. Valuations and norms simply express certain preferences, and there are no objective criteria for settling a conflict between ultimate preferences. The reason for this state of affairs is that there are no evaluative or normative facts. Instead, the descriptive propositions are true or false; their truth is objective in the sense that it depends not on the person who utters the proposition, but only on the fact that makes it true. So we must distinguish sharply between the cognition of law, expressed by true

---

[5] See generally *HP* and *ASL*; see also *LT* § 11(b) (at p. 23).

descriptive propositions, and the creation of legal norms, which is an expression of certain valuations. Thus, legal science, which aims at the cognition of law, can only describe it; legal science is not to evaluate law and, still less, to create legal norms. All activities that are aimed at the evaluation of the law, at the creation and modification of legal norms, correspond to legal politics and have nothing to do with science. Thus, thesis 8 leads to an important step in the 'purification' of legal theory: the removal of all evaluative (moral and political) elements.

Kelsen certainly did not ignore the fact that jurists generally, and specialists in various substantive fields of law in particular, often perform activities that are quite different from a mere description of existing law. He was not, however, concerned with describing what jurists actually do; rather, his concern was to shape a model of a legal science that would satisfy the requirements of this programme of a positivistic science, and to provide methodological foundations and conceptual tools for such an enterprise.

It is my contention that the 'Kantian' theses 1–4, and especially thesis 2, validity qua binding force, are incompatible with the ideal of a positivistic science of the sort expressed in theses 6–8. Only thesis 5 is to be found in both traditions and is, therefore, acceptable to both; thesis 5, however, lends itself to two different interpretations. On an ontological interpretation (predominant in Kelsen's early writings), the thesis of a sharp separation between 'is' and 'ought' is related to Kelsen's distinction between two radically different realms or worlds: the world of *Sollen* ('ought') and the world of *Sein* ('is') (thesis 1). Thesis 5, however, can also be given a more sober interpretation that, with due caution, might be termed semantic. On this interpretation, thesis 5 means that prescriptive propositions cannot be inferred from descriptive propositions alone and, conversely, that descriptive propositions do not follow logically from prescriptions alone.[6] In this form thesis 5 is fully acceptable to the most rigorous positivist.

II. THE THEORY OF TWO WORLDS

Both the Kantian tradition (as expressed in theses 1–4) and the positivistic programme of a non-evaluative science (*eine wertfreie Wissenschaft*) have co-existed in Kelsen's work for a very long time. In spite of his efforts, however, he never succeeded in reconciling the incompatible elements in his theory, which stem from these distinct traditions. Towards the end of his life the positivistic tendencies became dominant, and Kelsen came to

---

[6] See Georg Henrik von Wright, 'Is and Ought', in this volume, ch. 20.

reject, sometimes implicitly (as in the idea of two worlds and the notion of validity qua binding force) and sometimes explicitly (as in the theory of the basic norm), his main theses of Kantian origin.

The idea of a sharp separation between the 'world of *is*' and the 'world of *ought*' already appears in *Hauptprobleme der Staatsrechtslehre* (1911), Kelsen's second book. There he is anxious to isolate the 'proper object' of legal science, which, once determined, was supposed to make it possible for him to distinguish legal science from other sciences. (This approach rests on the assumption that every science must have its proper object. There are a number of reasons that count against this assumption, but I shall not take up the matter here.) Such a 'proper object' is the positive law, understood as a set of legal norms created by human acts. According to Kelsen, when a jurist states, for example, that one who commits murder ought to be punished, he is not interested in whether someone has actually committed a murder, and he is also not interested in whether the punishment will actually be carried out or not. He is concerned only with what *ought to be* the case, not with what *is* the case, that is, with the norm and not with any actual behaviour. And *Sollen* is a special category of thought (*Denkkategorie*) that is not reducible to *Sein*.[7]

Now it is easy to show that a sharp separation between the 'world of *ought*' and the 'world of *is*' cannot be, and as a matter of fact is not, maintained within the framework of the Pure Theory of Law, even in its classical formulation (Kelsen's second period). Both worlds are strongly intertwined, and a study of norms necessarily requires taking certain facts into account. Even if it were true that jurists are not interested in the actual behaviour of murderers and the officials who punish them (which is rather doubtful), there are other actions without which there would be no norms.

(i) There is the action of issuing the norm performed by the norm authority. Since all legal norms are positive norms (see thesis 7), the act of the authority issuing the norm is at least a necessary condition for its existence.

(ii) Acts consisting in cancelling or derogating a norm must also be considered, since the derogation of a norm brings its existence to an end (at least in some sense of this term). Thus, even a *very* pure theory of law must take into account the acts of lawmaking and the acts of cancelling norms.

(iii) Another necessary condition for the validity (that is, existence) of a norm, according to Kelsen, is the *efficacy* of the legal system to which this norm belongs: 'If a legal system is no longer efficacious, its norms cease to be valid, that is, cease to exist.'[8] Moreover, even a

---

[7] See *HP*, at 7–8.   [8] *PTL* § 34(g) (p. 212).

particular norm ceases to be valid if it ceases completely to be effi-cacious.[9]

This shows clearly that there never was such a sharp separation between the world of facts and the ideal world of norms, as is required by thesis 1. The existence of a positive legal norm (and according to thesis 7 there are only positive legal norms) cannot be ascertained without mak-ing reference to certain facts.

In Kelsen's third period this connection between norms and facts becomes far stronger, for he emphasizes that there can be no norm without the corresponding act of prescribing (*kein Imperativ ohne Imperator*). Other clear signs of his increasing preference for the ideas I call positivistic are:

(i)   Acknowledgement of the fact that there are no logical relations between norms, a thesis that Kelsen puts forward in 'Law and Logic' (1965) and in *General Theory of Norms* (1979).
(ii) Acceptance of the possibility of coexistence of incompatible or con-tradictory valid norms within the same legal order. Until 1965,[10] Kelsen refused to accept the possibility of normative conflicts, which was reasonable as long as he used the normative concept of validity; thus, I take this acceptance on Kelsen's part as a sign that he has adopted instead a descriptive concept of validity.
(iii) Rejection of the theory of the basic norm as a mere fiction.[11]

All this shows that theses 1 and 2, even if not explicitly rejected, have been implicitly abandoned in favour of doctrines that are incompatible with them.

III. NORMATIVITY OF LEGAL SCIENCE

Before we proceed to the analysis of the concepts of validity used in the Pure Theory of Law, a few words must be said about the normativity of legal science, that is, thesis 3, in which the Kantian influence is very evi-dent. This thesis played a very important part in Kelsen's thought, enabling him to draw a distinction between factual (causal) and norma-tive social sciences—that is, between sociology on the one hand and legal science on the other. The difference lies in the kind of proposition

---

[9] See *PTL* § 34(g) (at p. 213).   [10] See 'LL'.
[11] See e.g. Hans Kelsen, 'Die Grundlage der Naturrechtslehre' and (with others) 'Diskussionen', *ÖZöR*, 13 (1963), 1–37, 117–62, at 119–20, repr. under the title *Das Naturrecht in der politischen Theorie*, ed. Franz-Martin Schmölz (Vienna: Springer, 1963) (same pagination); 'Die Grundlage' alone is also repr. in *WS I* 869–912.

that each of these sciences employs for the description of its objects. As for legal science, the idea is this. Legal science is normative not only in the sense that it describes norms but also in the sense that its propositions are themselves normative. Clearly, however, they are normative in a different sense from the sense in which norms themselves are said to be normative. It is not at all easy to discover what this sense is. Kelsen's well-known distinction between legal norms (*Rechtsnormen*) and legal propositions (*Rechtssätze*), a term that is sometimes misleadingly translated as 'rules of law'[12] or '*règles du droit*',[13] appears in a relatively late stage of his philosophic development, namely in the second period.[14] In what I have called the first period, the two terms '*Rechtsnorm*' and '*Rechtssatz*' are used as roughly synonymous, following the terminological tradition of German legal theory, in which '*Rechtssatz*' is normally used to refer to legal norms. This is reflected in the title of the second book written by Kelsen, *Hauptprobleme der Staatsrechtslehre entwickelt aus der Lehre vom Rechtssatz* (1911), where the term '*Rechtssatz*' refers to a legal norm and not to a proposition of legal science. In the *Allgemeine Staatslehre* (1925) he speaks of '*Rechtsnormen* or *Rechtssätze*' as the 'objective law'.[15] The same lack of any distinction, either terminologically or conceptually, where '*Rechtsnorm*' and '*Rechtssatz*' are concerned is found in Kelsen's *Introduction to the Problems of Legal Theory*, the First Edition of the *Reine Rechtslehre* (1934). The only exception to this general rule regarding the lack of any distinction between '*Rechtsnorm*' and '*Rechtssatz*' in Kelsen's earlier work is his use of '*Rechtssatz*' at some points to designate the reconstructed or hypothetically formulated legal norm.[16] Many years later, Kelsen admitted that he had not distinguished terminologically between norms and propositions; at the same time, he claimed always to have had in mind the distinction between the creative function of legal authority and the cognitive function of legal science.[17] In view of the foregoing quotations, even this claim appears to be an exaggeration. Although the distinction appears, more or less clearly stated, in *General Theory of Law and State* (1945), one finds, even as late as Kelsen's *Théorie pure du droit* (1953), a statement that is entirely characteristic of Kelsen's early position:

---

[12] See *GTLS*, at 45.

[13] See Kelsen (n.3 above), at 42, 45.

[14] Specifically, in *GTLS* (1945).

[15] *ASL* § 10(a) (p. 47).

[16] See Eugenio Bulygin, 'Zur Problem der Anwendbarkeit der Logik auf das Recht', in *Festschrift für Ulrich Klug zum 70. Geburtstag*, ed. Günter Kohlmann, 2 vols. (Cologne: Peter Deubner, 1983), vol. I, 19–31, at 20; also in Spanish under the title 'Sobre el problema de la aplicabilidad de la lógica al derecho', trans. Jerónimo Betegón, in Hans Kelsen and Ulrich Klug, *Normas jurídicas y análisis lógico* (Madrid: Centro de Estudios Constitucionales, 1988), 9–26, at 11.

[17] See Hans Kelsen, 'Professor Stone and the Pure Theory of Law', *Stanford Law Review*, 17 (1964–5), 1128–57, at 1132–5, 1136–7.

We can thus state simultaneously that the rules of law (*règles du droit*) are judgments formulated by legal science and that the object of such a science is constituted by legal norms. Here there is no contradiction. Without a doubt, one can consider that the norms created and applied within the framework of a legal system have the character of legal norms only if legal science ascribes this character to them. It is the role of this science to attribute to certain acts the objective meaning of legal norms. But this does not prevent us from stating that legal norms form the object of legal science or, which is the same, that law is a system of norms. This definition is in full accord with Kant's theory according to which knowledge constitutes or creates it object, for what is in question here is an epistemological creation and not something created by man's work in the sense that the lawmaker creates a law. In the same way, natural phenomena which are the object of causal sciences are only created by them in a purely epistemological sense.[18]

This quotation highlights one of the central 'Kantian' ideas in Kelsen's early thought: the epistemological creation of its object by a science, in our case the 'creation' of legal norms by the science of law. It is only by means of their recognition by legal science that certain acts, like those of the legislator, become law-creating acts and give rise to legal norms. This is why legal science is a normative science.

Already, however, in *General Theory of Law and State* (1945) Kelsen writes that judgments of legal science (that is, 'rules of law') should not be confused with legal norms created by legal authorities. And he emphasizes that he uses the term 'rule of law' in a descriptive sense. In later works and especially in the Second Edition of the *Reine Rechtslehre* (1960), a clear distinction is drawn between *legal norms* issued by legal authorities, which are prescriptive and hence—according to thesis 6— lack truth-values, and *legal propositions* formulated by legal science, which are descriptive of norms and thus either true or false. In this way Kelsen gives up the idea of the epistemological creation of legal norms and assigns to legal propositions a more modest role, that of describing the norms created by legal authorities. This, together with the concept of the existence of a norm as an empirical fact (a concept already implied in thesis 4, but explicitly introduced in Kelsen's third period), leads to the rejection of thesis 3, a step that Kelsen did not take but that is implicit in his later writings.

Kelsen's change with respect to thesis 3 explains Hart's perplexities[19] in trying to find a coherent interpretation of the theory, in view of Kelsen's insistence on maintaining thesis 3 and his failure to realize that this thesis rises and falls with the Kantian idea of the epistemological creation of legal norms by legal science, a thesis that Kelsen explicitly gave up after

[18] Kelsen (n.3 above), 45 (English translation by Anne Collins).
[19] See H.L.A. Hart, 'Kelsen Visited', in this volume, ch. 4.

1960. The problem is this. Once the idea that legal propositions are mere descriptions of legal norms is introduced, then the thesis of the normativity of legal science in the special sense which Kelsen gave to it in his earlier work, namely as the normativity of propositions used by legal scientists, is deprived of all support and is left hanging in the air. Thus, in the period after the publication of the Second Edition of the *Reine Rechtslehre* (1960), the theory of the normativity of legal propositions became a self-contradictory doctrine. For if these propositions are descriptive, then they are not normative. The occurrence of the term 'ought' is immaterial; it is the meaning of this term that makes all the difference. In other words, even if the *sentences* formulated by legal science are 'ought'-sentences, the *propositions* these sentences express are descriptive and not normative. Kelsen's attempt to save the doctrine by introducing the distinction borrowed from Christoph Sigwart between the prescriptive and the descriptive 'ought'[20] only reveals his confusion between sentences as linguistic entities and propositions as their meanings.

IV. VALIDITY, MEMBERSHIP, AND EXISTENCE OF NORMS

Kelsen says repeatedly that validity is the specific existence of norms. Unfortunately, however, and contrary to what Nino seems to believe,[21] the term 'existence' in Kelsen's use is at least as ambiguous as 'validity'. In order to avoid the frequent ambiguities of legal language, I shall distinguish between four different concepts of existence. (Although the term 'existence' clearly belongs to philosophical parlance, the corresponding conceptual distinctions turn up in ordinary legal discourse.)

(A) *Factual existence.* When we say that a norm to such-and-such an effect exists in a certain social group, we mean that this norm is in fact in force in that group. The concept of factual existence or of being in force is explicated differently by different authors. Kelsen uses for it the term 'efficacy' (*Wirksamkeit*); a norm is efficacious if it is obeyed by legal subjects or applied by legal authorities. Alf Ross, at least in the English translation of *On Law and Justice* (which is not very felicitous), uses the term 'validity'.[22] A norm is valid in this sense when the prediction that it will be used in the future to justify judicial decisions is true.[23]

---

[20] See *RR2* § 16 (at p. 77n); Christoph Sigwart, *Logic*, trans. Helen Dendy, 2 vols. (London: Swan Sonnenschein, 1895), vol. I, at 17 n.1.

[21] See Carlos Santiago Nino, *Introducción al análisis del derecho*, 2nd edn. (Buenos Aires: Astrea, 1980), at 132–41.

[22] See Ross, *LJ*, at 72–4. Far better is the Spanish version, Alf Ross, *Sobre el derecho y la justicia*, trans. G.R. Carrió (Buenos Aires: Eudeba, 1963), in which the distinction between the expressions '*gyldig ret*' and '*gældende ret*' of the original Danish is preserved by means of the terms '*válido*' and '*vigente*'. See also Ross, 'Validity' (n.1 above), §§V–VII.

[23] See my analysis of this concept in Eugenio Bulygin, 'Der Begriff der Wirksamkeit', in

Perhaps the most illuminating analysis of factual existence is given by Hart in *The Concept of Law* in terms of the acceptance of the norm as a standard of behaviour by the social group; this means that members of the group regard conduct in conformity with the norm and reactions against those who violate the norm as required and justified by the norm.[24] This is to say that they regard the norm as obligatory or binding, a fact altogether characteristic of what Hart calls the *internal* point of view.

This factual concept of existence is descriptive (to say that a norm exists in a certain society is to state a fact), and it admits of different degrees of intensity: A norm can exist or be in force to a greater or lesser degree, which depends on the degree of its acceptance. What is more, this concept is relative to a certain social group and to a particular point in time.

(B) *Membership*. Sometimes a norm is said to exist when it belongs to a certain system of norms. Jurists usually accept a genetic criterion of membership: A norm is regarded as belonging to a given system if it has been created by a competent authority, and has not subsequently been derogated by the same authority or some other authority of the system.

This concept is often referred to by means of the term 'validity',[25] and, as we shall see presently, Kelsen uses the term 'valid' in this sense at least some of the time. The concept is also descriptive and relative (one and the same norm can be a member of one system and not of another, and it can belong to a system at one time and not at another time).

(C) *Existence as validity*. This is a *normative* concept: A norm exists or is valid in this sense if and only if it is obligatory or binding. (In order to avoid confusion, I shall use the term 'valid' only in this normative sense, unless otherwise indicated.)

It has been stressed by Nino[26] that the concept of validity as binding force is normative in the sense that to say a norm is valid is not to state a fact; rather, it is to prescribe an obligation to obey the norm in question. Hence, judgments of validity are themselves normative—that is, they are norms. But, according to Nino, binding force implies not only that one ought to do what the norm prescribes—that is, the norm succeeds in establishing the obligation it purports to establish—but also that the norm is justified. This presupposes a conception of 'justified normativity', which—according to both Nino and Joseph Raz[27]—Kelsen shares

Lateinamerikanische Studien zur Rechtsphilosophie (*ARSP* Beiheft 41, N.F. [new series] 4), ed. Ernesto Garzón Valdés (Neuwied am Rhein and Berlin: Luchterhand, 1965), 39–58.

[24] See Hart, *CL*, at 53–6, 86, and esp. 244, 2nd edn., at 54–7, 88–9, and esp. 291.

[25] See von Wright, *NA*, at 194–8.

[26] See Nino, 'Some Confusions' (n.2 above), at § 1; Nino, *La validez del derecho* (n.2 above), at 8.

[27] See Joseph Raz, 'Kelsen's Theory of the Basic Norm', in this volume, ch. 3.

with natural law theorists. Moreover, Nino maintains that not only is the use of this normative concept of validity supported by express quotations from Kelsen's writings, it is 'understood in the general structure of Kelsen's theory'.[28]

This concept of existence differs from the others not only in being normative but also in being an absolute concept.

(D) *Existence as formulation.* Jurists sometimes treat as existent norms those norms that are neither accepted nor efficacious, that neither belong to a system of norms (having not been issued by a competent authority) nor are regarded as binding. Such norms exist (in this broad sense) either if they have been formulated by somebody (who need not be a legal authority) or if they are a logical consequence of formulated norms. A typical case is the draft of a statute that has not yet been promulgated: Its norms do not exist in any of the first three meanings I have distinguished, for they are neither accepted nor binding, nor do they belong to the legal order, and yet it makes perfect sense to say that they are there.

This kind of existence, which for lack of a better term I called 'formal' existence in an earlier version of this paper, is a neglected child of the general theory of law; philosophers of law rarely take notice of it, and yet it is very important, for it is in a certain sense a basic notion concerning the existence of norms.[29] Obviously, neither this concept nor the concept of membership (which presupposes that of existence as formulation) is applicable to customary norms.

The four concepts of existence distinguished thus far are not, of course, incompatible: A norm can exist in all four senses, or only in some of them. Moreover, some of these notions are not independent of each other. I have already remarked that membership presupposes existence as formulation. Kelsen has (sometimes) maintained that validity implies efficacy (that is, factual existence). A norm can be in force in a given society without being formulated (this is the case with customary norms) and without being binding, although, in order to be in force, norms must of course be regarded as such by those who employ them. Thus, we see that some concepts of existence are independent, others are not.

While Kelsen pays little attention to concept (D), the other three can be traced to his writings, though he uses the same term 'validity' to refer to both membership and binding force, and that has given rise to a good bit of confusion. Nino, in his very interesting paper of 1978, has clarified

[28] Nino, 'Some Confusions' (n.2 above), § I(C).
[29] See Carlos E. Alchourrón and Eugenio Bulygin, 'On the Logic of Normative Systems', in *Pragmatik. Handbuch pragmatischen Denkens*, 5 vols., *Sprachphilosophie, Sprachpragmatik und formative Pragmatik*, ed. Herbert Stachowiak (Hamburg: Meiner, 1993), vol. IV, 273–94, where this concept of existence is analysed in detail.

some of these confusions, but at the same time contributed to new ones, which is why his title has an almost ironic ring to it: 'Some Confusions surrounding Kelsen's Concept of Validity'.[30]

Nino has perhaps developed the idea of normative validity further than any other writer; he not only emphasizes its role in Kelsen's theory, but assumes it as basic for his own views on law and morality.[31] He exaggerates, however, the importance of this concept for the Pure Theory of Law. The consequences that Nino draws from Kelsen's premisses go far beyond Kelsen's own statements and intentions, and show clearly that the concept of binding force is inconsistent with legal positivism as well as the task of legal science as envisaged by Kelsen. Kelsen would certainly not subscribe either to the view that 'the only conceivable type of normativity is justified normativity'[32] or to the view that to say of a norm or a system of norms that it is valid is tantamount to asserting its justifiability. Kelsen would also not accept the notion that judgments about the validity of legal norms are of the same logical nature as norms themselves, and he would not agree that he shares a concept of validity with traditional natural law theory. In fact, the concept of existence as binding force is connected with Kelsen's idea that norms are ideal entities belonging to the 'world of *ought*' (thesis 1). We have already seen that this idea, if not altogether abandoned, was at any rate considerably weakened in the last stage of Kelsen's thought. His late conception of norms does not require either the normative concept of validity or the idea of norms as ideal entities; rather, Kelsen's view is very close to the expressive conception of norms.[33]

Nino's suggestion that some authors, like Hart, Alchourrón, and Bulygin, have assumed 'that Kelsen's notion of validity is equivalent to membership', although they do not offer much by way of discussion on the matter,[34] is, to say the least, an overstatement. I cannot be sure whether Hart ever made this dogmatic assumption; I do know that the other two authors whom Nino mentions did not. What we intended to do in *Normative Systems* (1971) was to reconstruct the concept of membership—but without claiming, as Nino seems to believe, that this

[30] See Nino, 'Some Confusions' (n.2 above).

[31] See Nino (n.21 above); Carlos Santiago Nino, *Los límites de la responsabilidad penal. Una teoría liberal del delito* (Buenos Aires: Astrea, 1980); Nino, *Etica y derechos humanos* (Buenos Aires: Paidos, 1984).

[32] Carlos Santiago Nino, 'Some Confusions around Kelsen's Concept of Validity', *ARSP*, 64 (1978), 357–77, at 373 [portion not reproduced in ch. 13 of this volume].

[33] See Carlos E. Alchourrón and Eugenio Bulygin, *Normative Systems* (Vienna: Springer, 1971); Alchourrón and Bulygin, 'The Expressive Conception of Norms', in this volume, ch. 21; Alchourrón and Bulygin, 'Pragmatic Foundations for a Logic of Norms', *Rechtstheorie*, 15 (1984), 453–64; Bulygin, 'Norms and Logic. Kelsen and Weinberger on the Ontology of Norms', *Law and Philosophy*, 4 (1985), 145–63.

[34] Nino (n.32 above), 365 [portion not reproduced in ch. 13 of this volume].

is the only concept of validity in Kelsen's theory. Indeed, to identify Kelsen's concept of validity with the notion of binding force would be as mistaken as equating it with membership; behind the term 'validity' two different concepts are hidden. Despite the fact that Kelsen uses two different concepts of validity, one of them—precisely the normative notion of binding force—proves to be incompatible with his positivistic views, as I shall try to argue in the next sections of this paper. Thus, what is really imposed by the general structure of Kelsen's positivistic theory of law is the rejection of the normative concept of validity as binding force, something that had already been proposed by Alf Ross.

V. MEMBERSHIP AND THE DEFINITION OF LEGAL ORDER

For Kelsen there is a close connection between membership and validity.

The legal order is a system of norms. The question then arises: What is it that makes a system out of a multitude of norms? When does a norm belong to a certain system of norms, an order? This question is in close connection with the question as to the reason of validity of a norm.[35]

In fact, Kelsen seems to believe that the concepts of membership and binding force are coextensive, which may well explain why he uses the same term, 'validity', to refer to both of them. This would mean that all norms and only norms that are members of a legal system are binding. I agree with Nino that this is a serious mistake.

According to Nino, one must be careful in distinguishing between two quite different problems: the validity of a norm and its membership in a particular system of norms. When Kelsen says that a norm is valid when it derives its validity from a valid norm of the system, his formulation is misleading. This statement should be broken down into two statements: (a) A norm is a member of a given system when it derives from another norm that belongs to that system; and (b) A norm is valid when it derives from another valid norm.[36]

This, I think, is a sound strategy. Following it, Kelsen's concepts of validity should be analyzed in two steps. In the present section, I shall analyze statement (a), that is, Kelsen's criterion of membership, leaving for the next section the analysis of statement (b).

I shall try to show that no basic norm is needed either for the problem of establishing whether or not a given norm belongs to a certain system

---

[35] *GTLS* 110.   [36] See Nino, 'Some Confusions' (n.2 above), at § II.

(the problem of membership) or for the definition of the concept of a legal order.

In fact, the problem of membership is absolutely independent of any speculation about the binding force of legal norms. It makes perfectly good sense to ask whether a given norm is a member of a certain set of norms, even if we do not regard them as obligatory or binding. For instance, one may very well ask whether a certain norm belongs to the Mafia code or to the draft of a statute that has never been promulgated.

A satisfactory characterization of a certain legal order α can be provided by a recursive definition of membership along the following lines:

(i)   The set of norms C belongs to (or is a member of) α.
(ii) If there is a norm *p* that authorizes or confers power or competence on an authority *x* to issue a norm *q*, and *p* belongs to α, and *x* issues *q*, then *q* is a member of α, unless it is derogated by a competent authority.
(iii) All norms that are logical consequences of the norms belonging to α are members of α.[37]

Rules (i), (ii), and (iii) jointly determine the conditions under which a norm belongs to (or is a member of) the system of norms α. Rule (i) provides a criterion of membership for the primitive norms of the system by indicating which norms are contained in the first constitution (set C).[38] Rule (ii) lays down a criterion for the dynamic derivation of norms, making it possible to incorporate new norms into the system and to eliminate norms that belong to the system. It is in virtue of rule (ii) that legal systems are temporal (that is, they are relative to a certain time).[39] Rule (iii) states that α is closed under the notion of logical consequence, which is a general requirement for deductive systems.[40] So rules (i)–(iii) provide a *criterion of identification* for the norms of the system α.

At the same time, they define this system α: It is constituted by a certain (finite) set of primitive norms (the first constitution in Kelsen's sense), together with all those norms that derive either dynamically—rule (ii)—or logically—rule (iii)—from the primitive norms. So every constitution, that is, every set of norms containing at least some

---

[37] See Alchourrón and Bulygin, *Normative Systems* (n.33 above), at 73–6; Carlos E. Alchourrón and Eugenio Bulygin, *Sobre la existencia de las normas jurídicas* (Valencia, Venezuela: Universidad de Carabobo, 1979), at 73–6, repr. (Mexico City: Distribuciones Fontamara, 1997), at 67–70.

[38] A first constitution, according to Kelsen, is one that has been created not by a competent authority but 'by an individual usurper or a kind of assembly', *GTLS* 115.

[39] See Eugenio Bulygin, 'Time and Validity', in *Deontic Logic, Computational Linguistics and Legal Information Systems*, ed. Antonio A. Martino (Amsterdam: North-Holland, 1982), 65–81.

[40] See Alfred Tarski, *Logic, Semantics, Metamathematics*, trans. J.H. Woodger (Oxford: Clarendon Press, 1956), at chs. 5, 12.

power-conferring norms, can give rise to a system of norms or a legal order. The minimal condition that must be met by the primitive norms is that they must exist in the sense of merely formal existence (sense (D)), that is, they must be formulated. But they need not be either accepted or efficacious (though this, of course, is not excluded), nor need they be binding. We will require that the primitive norms should have factual existence (sense (A)) only if we are interested in a legal order that is actually in use.

This shows that the question of whether the constitution is a member of the system simply does not arise. It makes no sense to raise this question, for the system is defined in terms of a given constitution. We need not go beyond the constitution, for the chain of dynamic derivation begins with it; it is by definition the first member of this chain. Hence, the problem of membership and the identity of a legal system can be resolved without any recourse to Kelsen's basic norm.

VI. THE ROLE OF NORMATIVE VALIDITY IN KELSEN'S THEORY

I turn now to the problem of normative validity or binding force. It has been observed by von Wright[41] that the validity of a norm in its descriptive sense of membership is relative not to the *validity* of another norm, but to the *existence* of another norm. The situation is different with normative validity. Kelsen rightly says that the reason for the validity of a norm can only be the *validity* of the norm from which it derives its validity.[42] This implies that a norm p is valid if p has been created by a competent authority, say, x. That x is competent means that there is a norm q that confers competence or law-making power on x.[43] A competence norm prescribes an obligation to obey the norms issued by the competent (delegated) authority.[44] So q prescribes the obligation to obey p (which is issued by x). Of course, the mere fact that q commands that p be obeyed does not make p valid (binding, justified); p will be valid only if q is valid. Therefore, q must be valid.

Now, if the validity of a norm is relative to the validity of another norm, then the chain of validity must be infinite—unless we assume the existence of a norm that is valid in itself, that is, whose validity is not relative

---

[41] von Wright, *NA* 196.   [42] *PTL* § 34(a) (p. 193).   [43] See *PTL* § 34(a) (at p. 194).

[44] Ross, *LJ*, and Thomas Cornides, *Ordinale Deontik. Zusammenhänge zwischen Präferenztheorie, Normlogik and Rechtstheorie* (Vienna: Springer, 1974), share Kelsen's conception of competence norms as indirectly formulated commands or obligation norms. For a criticism of this conception, see Hart, *CL*, at 27–33, 2nd edn., at 27–33; the nature of competence norms is discussed in Eugenio Bulygin, 'On Competence Norms', *Law and Philosophy*, 11 (1992), 201–16.

to the validity of another norm but is absolute. This role cannot be played by the constitution, for even though it does not make sense to ask whether a (first) constitution belongs to a legal system, the question whether a given constitution is binding or justified is perfectly meaningful. Plainly, no norm can be binding by definition. This is the reason for Kelsen's appeal to the basic norm in reply to the question concerning the validity of the first constitution: The first constitution is valid in virtue of the basic norm.

The validity of this first constitution is the last presupposition, the final postulate, upon which the validity of all the norms of our legal order depends. It is postulated that one ought to behave as the individual, or the individuals, who laid down the first constitution have ordained. . . . That the first constitution is a binding legal norm is presupposed, and the formulation of the presupposition is the basic norm of this legal order.[45]

So the basic norm is the ultimate reason for the validity of all other norms; it fulfils this function by conferring competence on the author of the first constitution.

The whole function of this basic norm is to confer law-creating power on the act of the first legislator and on all the other acts based on the first act.[46]

Kelsen seems to believe that the mere fact that the basic norm confers law-creating powers on the first legislator and thus establishes an obligation to obey his norms is sufficient to make these norms valid (binding). This conclusion would be correct, however, only if the basic norm itself were valid, for as I have already emphasized, a valid norm can only derive its validity from another valid norm.

Now, the validity of the basic norm must be absolute and not relative to another norm. But Kelsen does not accept the possibility of absolutely valid norms; in order to be absolutely valid a norm should be self-evident, but this would imply the idea of practical reason, which is rejected by Kelsen. He is very emphatic that there are no self-evident norms.[47]

The basic norm is neither a self-evident norm nor does it justify any legal order,[48] for it is merely presupposed to be valid, but is not really binding.

The basic norm is not created in a legal procedure by a law-creating organ. It is not—as a positive legal norm is—valid because it is created in a certain way by a legal act, [rather,] it is valid because it is presupposed to be valid; and it is presupposed to be valid because without this presupposition no human act could be interpreted as a legal, especially as a norm-creating, act.[49]

---

[45] *GTLS* 115. [46] *GTLS* 116. [47] See *PTL* § 34(b) (at p. 196).
[48] See *PTL*, at § 34(i) (pp. 217–19). [49] *GTLS* 116.

If, however, the basic norm is not a valid norm, it follows that the first constitution is not a valid norm and that none of the norms that can be traced back to the first constitution is valid.

It is because the basic norm is a mere hypothesis of legal science that its acceptance does not commit jurists to a certain moral or political position, for it is compatible with any ideology whatever. Kelsen is very emphatic on this point and stresses that his basic norm has nothing to do with natural law: It validates any legal system, whatever its content may be.[50]

Then, however, one cannot speak seriously about the justifiability or obligatoriness of legal systems. A jurist who asserts the validity of a norm does not say that it is justified and ought therefore to be obeyed. What he says, according to Kelsen, is that *if* the basic norm is accepted, then it is obligatory to do what the norm in question prescribes, without asserting categorically that the basic norm is valid or binding.

It is not surprising that this solution à la Vaihinger did not seem satisfactory to most jurists. In fact, the theory of the basic norm (thesis 4) was always vigorously resisted by legal philosophers. Even its author recognized towards the end of his life the fictitious character of his basic norm, although he did not draw the unavoidable conclusion, namely, that the concept of validity as binding force should play no role at all in the Pure Theory of Law, once the theory is stripped of its purely rhetorical Kantianism.

VII. CONCLUDING REMARKS

The normative validity of legal norms cannot be based on mere hypothesis and still less on fiction. This is why those philosophers of law who take seriously the idea of validity as binding force cannot be satisfied with Kelsen's basic norm and must resort to more powerful substitutes. Nino, for instance, maintains that the validity of legal norms is based on absolute and objectively valid moral judgments. This way out is closed to Kelsen, owing to his conception of a positivistic theory of law. He cannot accept the view that there are objectively valid moral principles or true norms, for norms lack truth-values (thesis 6). This means that there is no objectively privileged set of norms. In order to give preference to a certain set, an act of will is required, that is, one must take a political decision. Kelsen, however, is anxious not to exceed the limits of knowledge; thus, political decisions lie outside the scope of a positivistic theory of law. Hence his efforts to make compatible the idea of validity as binding

---

[50] See *PTL*, at § 34(i) (pp. 217–19).

force with his positivistic conception of legal science by means of the doctrine of the basic norm. As we have seen, these efforts resulted in failure, a fact acknowledged by Kelsen himself. Therefore, in order to render the Pure Theory of Law consistent, it is necessary that one or the other of the two incompatible ideas be rejected. Either we will want to preserve the idea of normative validity (but then true principles or norms must be substituted for the basic norm, which implies the rejection of positivism and the acceptance of some sort of natural law),[51] or else we will choose to be thoroughgoing positivists (but then we must reject the idea of validity as binding force). It is only by choosing the second way that we can preserve a strict dichotomy between knowledge of law, the description of law, and legal science on the one hand, and evaluation of law, the creation of legal norms, and legal policies on the other. From Kelsen's positivistic perspective, legal science can establish which norms belong to a given legal order, but cannot prescribe the obligation to obey these norms, that is, it cannot assert their validity without trespassing the limits imposed by the positivistic ideal of a value-free legal science.

[51] Contrary to Nino, *Introducción al análisis del derecho* (n.2 above), at 37–43, both Kelsen and Ross maintain that legal positivism is incompatible with the acceptance of true moral or legal principles. See Kelsen's theses 6 and 7 (above) and Ross's definition of what he calls the 'kernel of legal positivism': 'First, the thesis that the belief in natural law is erroneous: No such law exists, all law is positive law. This is of course a thesis that pertains to the general field of moral philosophy or ethics, for it denies that ethical (moral, legal) principles or judgments are the expression of truths to be discovered and established objectively by some process of cognition.' Ross, 'Validity' (n.1 above), at § I.

17

Normativism or the Normative Theory of Legal Science: Some Epistemological Problems*

RICCARDO GUASTINI

I. 'NORMATIVISM'

By 'normativism' I have in mind, above all, certain tenets worked out by Hans Kelsen that have been widely disseminated in contemporary Continental legal theory. The main tenets of normativism or what might be termed the normative theory of legal science are these:

The law is a set of norms.

Given that the law is a set of norms, then:

Legal science is a science of norms.

Moreover:

Norms are altogether different from facts; they are entities not of the world of *Sein* ('is'), but of the world of *Sollen* ('ought').

Consequently (or so it is argued):

Legal science cannot express itself in factual language; rather, it must express itself in normative or deontic language ('permitted', 'obligatory', and the like).[1]

The thesis that the law is a set of norms appears, prima facie, to be obvious, and it has rarely been contested. In a sense, even proponents of

---

* *Editors' note*: Guastini's paper first appeared in *Analisi e diritto 1991. Ricerche di giurisprudenza analitica*, ed. Paolo Comanducci and Riccardo Guastini (Turin: G. Giappichelli Editore, 1991), 177–92, and, in a somewhat different form, in *Ratio Juris*, 4 (1991), 308–21. The present version of the paper draws on both earlier versions and reflects minor changes and revisions by the author in consultation with the editors.

[1] As I suggest at the outset, these notions are to be attributed, above all, to Hans Kelsen; see e.g. *PTL*, esp. ch. 3. Some of these notions may also be attributed to H.L.A. Hart in *CL*.

legal realism, notwithstanding their well-known scepticism about norms
or rules, could agree on this point. Legal realists, however, conceive of
norms as ordinary social facts (though nevertheless *sui generis*),[2] while,
in the normative theory of legal science, norms are understood not in the
manner of simple sensible objects (for example, linguistic entities or
utterances of prescriptive language) but, rather, as peculiar entities
inhabiting the world of *Sollen*, the realm of 'ought'. Such a realm, in turn,
is conceived of as a world unto itself, endowed with an independent existence—a sort of 'third world' in the sense introduced by Karl Popper.[3]

From the standpoint of the normative theory of legal science, certain
distinctions—and these are matters on which Kelsen insists—must be
observed. Specifically, *norms* are to be distinguished (a) from the human
act of *norm issuance*, (b) from the *norm-formulations* by means of which
norms are given expression, and (c) from the *actual behaviour* counting
as compliance with, or as enforcement of, norms. In a word, norms are in
no way reducible to 'facts' and are not, therefore, 'natural' (or social)
objects lending themselves to empirical knowledge.[4] Knowledge or cognition of norms is 'normative' knowledge, 'normative' cognition.

While facts can be described by means of indicative sentences, norms,
as entities of *Sollen*, can only be described by means of normative sentences, more precisely, by means of deontic sentences. There is no way
to describe, say, the norm according to which 'Thieves ought to be punished', except by saying 'Thieves ought to be punished'. Such sentences
as 'The legislator has commanded that thieves be punished', 'Thieves are
punished', and so on, describe *stricto sensu* not the norm itself, but only
certain facts that are connected with the norm in various ways.

Thus, proponents of normativism understand legal science as a 'normative' science[5] in two senses: it has norms as its subject-matter, and its
statements are (necessarily) formulated in normative (that is, deontic)
language.

Moreover, from the standpoint of the normative theory of legal science,
legal norms are created by the legislature—or, more generally, by state
organs exercising norm-creating powers or competences. Judges and
jurists for their part do not create legal norms; rather, they 'find' or 'discover' them. Legal norms, once created, await both judicial application

    [2] See Ross, *LJ*; Alf Ross, *Directives and Norms* (London: Routledge & Kegan Paul, 1968).
    [3] Karl Popper, *Objective Knowledge. An Evolutionary Approach* (Oxford: Clarendon
Press, 1972), ch. 4.
    [4] See Riccardo Guastini, *Lezioni di teoria analitica del diritto* (Turin: G. Giappichelli
Editore, 1982), at 19–38.
    [5] See Jerzy Wróblewski, 'Normativity of Legal Science', *Logique et analyse*, 9 (1966),
60–77; Norberto Bobbio, 'Essere e dover essere nella scienza giuridica', *Rivista di filosofia*,
58 (1967), 235–62, repr. in Bobbio, *Studi per una teoria generale del diritto* (Turin: G.
Giappichelli Editore, 1970), 139–73. See also n.10 below.

and juridico-scientific enquiry. So-called interpretation of legal norms (statutory construction) is, then, nothing other than the acquisition of knowledge or cognition of norms; the norms, for their part, exist independently of the interpretative attitudes and practices of judges and jurists.[6]

Normativism or the normative theory of legal science represents, then, an attempt to describe (and to rationalize) the actual practice and thinking of contemporary jurists. On the one hand, what jurists say (and think) they are doing when they interpret the materials that are usually termed 'sources of law' (statutes, judicial precedents, regulations, and the like) is nothing more than a description of norms; and the norms themselves are conceived of as 'data' that precede the interpretations offered of them. (Norms precede their interpretations, which is to say that their existence precedes the interpretative activity directed to them.) On the other hand, jurists in fact typically provide *statements* of norms in a deontic language—in a language, that is to say, that is syntactically indistinguishable from the language used to give expression to the norms themselves. And the normative theory of legal science recommends precisely this approach.

II. THE AMBIGUITY OF DEONTIC OR 'OUGHT'-SENTENCES

The normative theory of legal science finds confirmation of a sort in two theses that are quite widespread among legal theorists and deontic logicians. These theses concern the philosophical analysis of deontic language, the language of 'ought'-sentences.

First, 'ought'-sentences suffer from a characteristic ambiguity; that is to say, they can be used to perform different kinds of speech acts.[7]

Second, 'ought'-sentences are, so to speak, susceptible of 'double negation'.[8]

---

⁶ See Giovanni Tarello, *Diritto, enunciati, usi* (Bologna: il Mulino, 1974); Tarello, *L'interpretazione della legge* (Milan: A. Giuffré Editore, 1980).

⁷ See generally *PTL*; von Wright, *NA*; Georg Henrik von Wright, *Practical Reason* (London: Routledge & Kegan Paul, 1983); Carlos E. Alchourrón and Eugenio Bulygin, 'Pragmatic Foundations for a Logic of Norms', *Rechtstheorie*, 15 (1984), 453–64; Bulygin, 'Norms, Normative Propositions, and Legal Statements', in *Contemporary Philosophy. A New Survey*, ed. Guttorm Fløistad, 4 vols. (The Hague: Nijhoff, 1981–3), vol. III (1982), 127–52; Bulygin, 'Enunciados jurídicos y positivismo: respuesta a Raz', *Análisis Filosófico*, 1 (1981), 49–59; Tecla Mazzarese, *Logica deontica e linguaggio giuridico* (Padua: CEDAM, 1989).

⁸ See e.g. Alf Ross, 'Imperatives and Logic', *Theoria*, 7 (1941), 53–71; von Wright, *NA*; Carlos E. Alchourrón and Eugenio Bulygin, *Normative Systems* (Vienna: Springer, 1971); Alchourrón and Bulygin, 'Permission and Permissive Norms', in *Theorie der Normen. Festgabe für Ota Weinberger zum 65. Geburtstag*, ed. Werner Krawietz et al. (Berlin: Duncker & Humblot, 1984), 349–71.

The ambiguity alluded to here is neither syntactic nor semantic. Rather, it is a pragmatic ambiguity, affecting not the meaning-content of the sentence but its use; it is an ambiguity respecting the kind of act performed. Thus, an 'ought'-sentence may be used—by a legislator, for example—in order to prescribe or, more precisely, to formulate a prescription (a command, a prohibition). That same 'ought'-sentence, however, can also be used—say, by a jurist—to describe an existing legal norm.

Thus, one and the same 'ought'-sentence, depending on actual circumstances and the context of the utterance, can express either a norm or a normative statement. The latter is a statement, formulated in a meta-language, about the norm. The difference between the two—between norm and normative statement—follows straightaway: Norms, in contrast to normative statements, are neither true nor false.

Moreover, a negative 'ought'-sentence, for example,

It is not obligatory that p,

may, depending on circumstances and the context, express either a negative norm (a norm to the effect that p is not obligatory and is, hence, 'permitted' in the strong sense), or a statement denying the existence or validity of a positive-law norm altogether (the denial, namely, of the norm to the effect that p is obligatory, from whose non-existence it can be inferred that p is 'permitted' in the weak sense). In the first case, one speaks of 'internal negation', in the second, of 'external negation'.

My point here is not the ambiguity of deontic or 'ought'-sentences. This much is uncontroversial. That is, it seems obvious enough that an 'ought'-sentence uttered (or written) by a jurist is different in an important way from the same 'ought'-sentence uttered (or written) by a legislator. It seems obvious that jurists, like judges, do not—at least in ordinary circumstances—formulate new norms; rather, they enquire into and 'talk about' norms whose existence antedates the jurists' enquiries.[9]

Jurists' deontic or 'ought'-sentences—for example, Kelsen's *Sollsätze* and Hart's 'internal statements'—are not, however, restricted in their use simply to the various things that jurists say about norms. Rather—and this is the specific claim of the normative theory of legal science—deontic or 'ought'-sentences are used to *describe* norms. It is this notion that I want to examine more closely—specifically, the problematic idea that 'ought'-sentences can be used in a descriptive sense, and the claim

---

[9] Uberto Scarpelli, 'Le "proposizioni giuridiche" come precetti reiterati', *RIFD*, 46 (1967), 465–82.

that 'ought'-sentences provide, indeed, the only proper means of describing norms.[10] I should like to challenge Kelsen's view here.

III. 'DESCRIBING NORMS': IN WHAT SENSE?

Jurists' 'ought'-sentences are used to 'describe norms'. What does this mean? There are several possible answers.

According to the legal realist, to describe a legal norm is to describe certain social facts and instances of behaviour. For example, a norm is described when one points out that a certain act has been performed, say, that a particular legal regulation has been issued. Likewise for jurists' and judges' constructions of legal texts (reporting, say, on past judicial decisions that speak to a certain issue).

In the present context, however, 'describing norms' cannot be a matter of accounting for social facts or instances of behaviour at all, for norms are deemed in the normative theory of legal science to be non-factual entities (as explained in § I above). Describing such matters as legislators' enactments, jurists' constructions, and judges' decisions does not, then, amount to describing norms—not, at any rate, from the standpoint of the normative theory of legal science.

Within the normative theory of legal science, 'describing norms' can only mean either interpreting norms or stating that they are valid. I cannot see any other possibility. The first of these readings seems to be the one tacitly accepted, by and large, within the mainstream of legal thought. The second reading is the one defended by Kelsen.

The question then arises: Are deontic sentences or 'ought'-sentences a suitable instrument either for interpreting norms or for providing statements of their validity? I shall argue that they are not, and I take up each of the proposed readings in turn.

IV. INTERPRETING DEONTIC OR 'OUGHT'-SENTENCES

According to the first of the proposed readings, describing norms amounts to interpreting them. In analysing this proposal it is well to begin by asking what, exactly, 'norm' means in this context.

[10] On Kelsen's *Sollsätze*, see Alf Ross, Book Review: Kelsen, *What is Justice?*, *California Law Review*, 45 (1957), 564–70; H.L.A. Hart, 'Kelsen Visited', in this volume, ch. 4; Bobbio, 'Essere e dover essere nella scienza giuridica' (n.5 above); Joseph Raz, 'Kelsen's Theory of the Basic Norm', in this volume, ch. 3; Bulygin, 'Norms, Normative Propositions, and Legal Statements' (n.7 above); Bulygin, 'Enunciados jurídicos y positivismo' (n.7 above); Eugenio Bulygin, 'An Antinomy in Kelsen's Pure Theory of Law', in this volume, ch. 16. On Hart's 'internal statements', see Alf Ross, Book Review: Hart, *The Concept of Law*, *Yale Law Journal*, 71 (1961–2), 1185–90.

Termed 'norms' by those jurists and legal philosophers who accept the normative theory of legal science are both (a) norm-formulations, or sentences used to formulate, say, statutory provisions, and (b) their meaning-contents, that is, norms *stricto sensu.* As a matter of fact, jurists hardly ever distinguish between the two. The failure to distinguish them, however, can give rise to serious confusion, for there is no one-to-one correspondence between norm-formulation and norm. For this lack of correspondence there are a number of reasons.

First, norm-formulations are often vague or ambiguous—or, indeed, both. That is, the meaning of a norm-formulation—a sentence used to formulate, say, a statutory provision—is controversial, and such a norm-formulation or sentence can therefore be interpreted in different ways. From this point of view, one could say that no sentence used to formulate a statutory provision expresses a single norm. On the contrary, every such sentence expresses, disjunctively, two or more norms. Many norms, then, can be drawn from one and the same norm-formulation, depending on the different interpretative attitudes and evaluations of jurists and judges, and on the choices they make.

Second, leaving controversies of interpretation aside, one can say that many sentences used to formulate statutory provisions—perhaps, indeed, all such sentences—have a compound meaning. That is, they give expression not to a single norm but to several different norms. In other words, jurists usually draw a number of different norms from one and the same norm-formulation. (The case here is to be distinguished from the one considered above, where it was a matter of deciding on the meaning of a norm-formulation—choosing, that is, from a number of possible meanings. In the present case the meaning of the norm-formulation, the sentence used to formulate a statutory provision, has already been determined, but this determination reveals that the meaning in question amounts to a number of independent norms.)

Third, two different norm-formulations, sentences used to formulate, say, statutory provisions, might be perfectly synonymous. In such a case, one and the same norm is expressed by two different norm-formulations. Or there are two sentences of which the first gives expression, say, to the norms N_1 and N_2, and the second, say, to the norms N_1 and N_3; the norm N_1 is, then, identical in the two sentences. In that case, the respective meanings of the two sentences overlap.

The conclusion of this argument is that there is no one-to-one correspondence between the norm-formulation (the sentence used to formulate a statutory provision) and the norm.[11] The clear-cut separation of

---

[11] Moreover, there is a widespread consensus among jurists to the effect that a legal system includes not only the norms that can be drawn from the existing norm-formulations by means of plain interpretation, but also a great number of norms that do not correspond

the two is of great importance in the analysis of a number of topics—for example, validity (since the criteria of validity applying to norms are different from the criteria applying to norm-formulations) and derogation (since explicit derogation is addressed to the norm-formulation whereas implicit derogation is addressed to the norm).[12]

In the present context, my point is that when speaking about the interpretation of norms, the term 'norm' means a norm-formulation. In other words, in the context of norms qua subject-matter of legal interpretation, the object of enquiry is in fact the (uninterpreted) norm-formulation or sentence used to formulate statutory provisions (and the like). These are sentences in a natural language, and they have an undetermined meaning.

Having said this much, it remains to distinguish no fewer than three different senses in which 'interpreting a norm' can be understood.[13]

In the first sense, 'interpreting a norm' is interpreting a sentence that has been used to formulate, say, a statutory provision. Here the interpretative enterprise is devoted to ascertaining the range of possible meanings that might be attributed to the sentence. In this sense, legal science does not, properly speaking, 'interpret' norms (texts with normative import) at all; that is to say, it does not decide on or determine their meaning. Rather, legal science confines itself to recording and listing all their possible interpretations, without choosing any definite interpretation of its own. This, according to Kelsen, is the way 'juridico-scientific' legal interpretation ought to proceed.[14] As he writes:

If 'interpretation' is understood as discovering the meaning of the norm to be applied, its result can only be the discovery of the frame that the norm to be interpreted represents and, within this frame, the cognition of various possibilities for application.[15]

This task cannot, however, be accomplished by means of 'ought'-sentences. A legal sentence, such as

(1) Murderers ought to be punished by imprisonment,

is in no way suitable for listing the possible meanings of a norm. This task can only be accomplished by a straightforward indicative sentence, such as

---

to any norm-formulation whatever. In other words, legal systems include norm-formulations without norms, as well as norms without norm-formulations. Principles are usually seen as falling within this latter class. In a weak sense, a norm does not correspond to any norm-formulation when it is drawn not from some one isolated norm-formulation but from a set of norm-formulations. In a strong sense, a norm does not correspond to any norm-formulation when it is a merely implicit or unexpressed norm, that is, a norm not expressly issued by the legislature but constructed by jurists or judges, say, by analogy.

[12] See Riccardo Guastini, *Dalle fonti alle norme* (Turin: G. Giappichelli Editore, 1990), at chs. 13, 15.

[13] See Tarello, *L'interpretazione della legge* (n.6 above), at 61–7.

[14] See *PTL*, at ch. 8.   [15] *LT* § 36 (p. 80); likewise, *PTL* §45(d).

(2) To the norm N the meanings M_1, M_2, M_3 can be ascribed,

or

(3) The norm N can be understood according to readings R_1, R_2, R_3.

In the second sense, 'interpreting a norm' means accounting for the different interpretations a norm (that is, a text with normative import) has in fact been given by jurists or judges. In this sense, legal science confines itself to describing actual dogmatic or judicial developments in statutory interpretation.

Once again, however, legal science cannot accomplish this by means of 'ought'-sentences. Moreover, it must be stressed that to describe actual interpretations of a given norm-formulation—a sentence used to formulate, say, a statutory provision—is not to describe a norm in the sense stipulated by the normative theory of legal science. Rather, a description of actual interpretations amounts to a description of ordinary social facts—those bits of observable human behaviour (specifically, jurists' and judges' legal discourse) that represent the dogmatic or judicial development in question.

In the third sense, 'interpreting a norm' means deciding *the* meaning of a given sentence used to formulate a statutory provision. It is in this sense that legal science describes the 'true' (the 'proper', the 'one and only') meaning of norms. Two remarks are called for here.

First, such a task cannot be accomplished by means of 'ought'-sentences. The proper way of ascribing meaning to a given norm (norm-formulation, sentence) is not elliptically to say,

(1) Murderers ought to be punished by imprisonment,

but either to say,

(4) The norm 'Murderers ought to be punished by imprisonment' means M_1,

provided that 'Murderers ought to be punished by imprisonment' is the interpreted sentence, or to say,

(5) The norm N means that murderers ought to be punished by imprisonment,

provided that 'Murderers ought to be punished by imprisonment' is the result of interpretation. Interpretative sentences are not 'ought'-sentences. The standard form of interpretative sentences is, arguably, the following:

(6) The sentence S used to formulate a statutory provision means M_1,

or

(7) The sentence S expresses the norm N.

Secondly, interpretative sentences cannot in any way be considered descriptive sentences (that is, propositions), unless one accepts the mistaken belief according to which words and sentences carry a 'proper' intrinsic meaning that exists antecedent to both actual use and interpretation. As a matter of fact, such a belief—from which it would follow that for every norm, one could always find its 'true' interpretation—is often accepted by jurists, who without reflecting on the matter simply take legal interpretation to be a cognitive enterprise. If a legal scholar does not confine himself to listing the manifold possible meanings of statutory texts, but rather interprets *stricto sensu*, that is, recommends (to law-applying authorities) a certain interpretation, the enterprise is not legal science at all, but legal policy.[16]

Interpretation is not just description, but rather the ascription of meaning—at least in 'hard cases'. If it is appropriate to distinguish between, on the one hand, the norm-formulations or sentences in which the legislature formulates the law and, on the other, their meaning-contents, and if it is appropriate to use the term 'norm' to denote such meaning-contents, then one may conclude that to ascribe meaning to norm-formulations or sentences is *not* to describe pre-existing norms. There are no norms that antedate, that exist independently of, interpretation. In a sense, then, interpreting amounts to 'producing' or 'creating' norms—at any rate, in a weak sense of 'creating'.

V. STATING THE VALIDITY OF NORMS

According to the second of the proposed readings of 'describing norms' (readings set out in § III, above), the activity of describing norms amounts, simply, to stating the validity of norms. Accordingly, legal science should state the validity of norms by means of deontic sentences. For example, to state the validity of a norm to the effect that 'Murderers ought to be punished by imprisonment', it would be pointless to say,

(8) The norm 'Murderers ought to be punished by imprisonment' is valid.

The more concise statement, however,

(1) Murderers ought to be punished by imprisonment,

tout court, would be appropriate. To state the invalidity of the same norm, it would be pointless to say

(9) The norm 'Murderers ought to be punished by imprisonment' is not valid (invalid).

---

[16] See *LT*, at ch. 6; *PTL*, at ch. 8.

Rather, the legal scientist should simply say,

(10) Murderers ought not to be punished by imprisonment,

without any further qualification.

According to this view, validity statements preserve the syntactic structure—and hence, the logic—of norms themselves. Validity statements repeat, or iterate, the norms they talk about. I believe this view to be untenable, for 'ought'-sentences amount to unhappy formulations of validity statements—indeed, altogether unacceptable formulations.

The standard and, in my view, correct formulation of a validity statement is a sentence of the form,

(11) The norm N is valid/invalid.

Such a sentence clearly belongs to the meta-language. It expressly mentions the norm it refers to, and ascribes to it the predicate 'valid' or 'invalid'.

By contrast, 'ought'-sentences do not mention any norm whatever, and their formulation does not include the term 'valid' either. Such sentences have no meta-linguistic character; at any rate, their meta-linguistic character, if there be any, is well hidden. Prima facie, they simply deal with behaviour. As a consequence, 'ought'-sentences iterate norms without saying anything about them.

In standard use, 'ought'-sentences are suitable for formulating norms. They are not, however, statements about the validity or invalidity of norms.

VI. VALIDITY STATEMENTS AND CONFLICTS BETWEEN NORMS

If validity statements were provided with the same syntactic structure as the norms to which they refer, then their logical behaviour could serve as a mirror of the logical behaviour of the norms themselves. In other words, a validity statement, if true, would reflect a valid norm; if false, it would reflect an invalid norm. Thus, if the validity statement 'Smoking is forbidden' were false, then the underlying norm *Smoking is forbidden* could not be valid. Things do not work out this nicely in fact, however, and the point merits closer attention.

By hypothesis, one and the same 'ought'-sentence can express either a norm or a validity statement. If understood as a norm, it is neither true nor false. Hence, it does not permit the application of logical principles, since such principles turn on truth and falsity. Two sentences, for example, are contradictory if and only if they cannot both be true and cannot

both be false. The same 'ought'-sentence understood as a validity statement is understood as either true or false. It, therefore, does permit the
application of logical principles, for example the principle of contradiction.

As a consequence, contradictory validity statements, such as

(12) Smoking is forbidden,

and

(13) Smoking is not forbidden,

cannot both be true or both be false. For purely logical reasons, one must
be true, the other false. Hence, one of them truly states the validity of a
certain norm, while the other falsely states the validity of a different
norm. One of the underlying norms must be valid, whereas the other
must be invalid. Such is a matter of plain logic.

Or so proponents of the normative theory of legal science would have
us believe. Such a thesis was expressly defended by Kelsen, for example,
as follows:

Although the principles of logic, such as the law of contradiction and the rules of
inference, apply only to statements that can be either true or false, they are indirectly applicable also to legal norms, in so far as statements about norms, statements affirming the existence, that is, the validity, of legal norms, are subjected
to these principles. Two statements of which the one affirms the validity of a
norm prescribing that men ought to behave in a certain way, and the other the
validity of a norm prescribing that men ought not to behave in this way, contradict each other, just as do two statements of which the one affirms that something is, and the other that it is not. If the one is true, the other must be false. Two
conflicting norms can be described as valid norms only by [means of] statements
that contradict each other. In this sense we may say of conflicting norms that
they 'contradict' each other. Consequently, two conflicting norms cannot be
considered to be valid at the same time. Thus, legal science conceives of its object
as a logical unit: a system of noncontradictory norms.[17]

The soundness of Kelsen's conclusion depends entirely on the presupposed concept of validity. That is, Kelsen's argument is persuasive if and
only if 'validity' is understood here in the sense of 'binding force', such
that valid norms are held to be 'obligatory' and judgments of validity and
invalidity are conceived, in turn, as a species of normative attitude, that
is to say, as the approval or disapproval of norms.[18]

---

[17] Hans Kelsen, 'What is the Pure Theory of Law?', *Tulane Law Review*, 34 (1959–60),
269–76, 271.

[18] Thus, smoking is forbidden = the norm 'Smoking is forbidden' is valid = the norm
'Smoking is forbidden' is obligatory = I accept the norm 'Smoking is forbidden'.

As a matter of common sense, it seems that no one, at a given point in time, can both accept and reject one and the same norm, and likewise that no one can accept both the norm prescribing a certain course of behaviour and the norm prescribing the opposite course of behaviour.

Kelsen's position, however, is untenable, something he himself demonstrated in later work.[19] As a starting point, it is well to emphasize that in this context the term 'validity' cannot be understood in the sense mentioned above, that of 'binding force', for we are talking here about the description of norms, while approval or disapproval of norms routinely involves evaluations and commitments. Approving of a norm just amounts to iterating it. Hence, the sentences that express such normative attitudes cannot be understood as a part of descriptive language, for they are neither true nor false. If logical principles do not apply to norms on the ground that norms are neither true nor false, such principles do not apply to validity statements either, understood as expressions of normative attitudes.

---

[19] See 'Derogation', 'LL', and *GTN*. The theory of the indirect applicability of logic to norms, which Kelsen defended in *PTL*, presupposes a conception of norms according to which they are conceptual entities similar to propositions; that is to say, norms do not depend on the actual use of language. A norm can be 'existent' although it has never been issued (thanks to the logical rule of inference), and it can be 'non-existent' although it has been positively issued (thanks to the law of contradiction). The theory that Kelsen defends in papers written during the 1960s and in *GTN* represents an altogether different view. There it is a matter of conceiving of norms as entities similar to facts, namely, as language-dependent entities. A norm 'exists' if and only if it was created by a speech act performed by the appropriate authority (notwithstanding the rule of inference), and no issued norm can magically lose its 'existence' (notwithstanding the law of contradiction). The theory defended by Kelsen in *PTL* presupposes an analogy between the truth of propositions and the 'existence' of norms. The truth of a proposition is independent of the actual performance of the speech act of stating it. The same holds for the 'existence' of norms. According to the opposite theory, that held by Kelsen in *GTN*, there is no room for such an analogy. A non-issued norm cannot 'exist', just as an issued norm cannot disappear. The theory maintained by Kelsen in *PTL* presupposes that statements concerning the validity of norms are but *Sollsätze*, that is, deontic sentences with the same logical structure as the norms themselves. The opposite theory involves a different conception of validity statements, according to which such statements are not deontic sentences, but are, rather, indicative sentences expressly stating that the norm *N* is valid. In *PTL*, the usual deontic language of jurists is approved as the proper language of legal science, since there is no other way of describing (the existence of) legal norms. In *GTN*, a different model of legal discourse is (tacitly) defended. According to this model, legal sentences ought to be regarded as ordinary indicative sentences, quite different from the sentences of law-making authorities. Kelsen's theory in *PTL* entrusts legal science with the task of working out conflicts of norms by means of logic. Thus, such legal operations are justified in purely logical (that is, juridico-scientific) terms. According to the theory Kelsen defends in *GTN*, the matter of working out conflicts between norms is exclusively the concern of the law-making authorities themselves. It is not a matter of legal science or of logic. It is simply a matter of political decision. Legal science can bring such conflicts to light, but it does not itself provide any solution to them.

In the present context, the term 'validity' can be understood in two different senses.[20] In a strong sense 'validity' means membership: A norm is valid (or invalid) within a certain legal system, namely, as a member of that system. Within a given legal system, a valid norm is a norm that meets the criteria of identification that are peculiar to that legal system. In each legal system the criteria for identifying norms lie in meta-rules concerning the so-called sources of law, as well as in meta-rules concerning the solution of inconsistencies (for example, the rule *lex superior derogat legi inferiori*).

In a weak sense 'validity' means existence. Unfortunately, the concept of existence is not entirely clear. In the present context, however, an existing norm is, quite simply, a norm that actually was created, laid down, that is, was formulated and issued by an authority (a prima-facie competent authority).

In either case, whether it be the concept of validity qua membership or qua 'existence', the logic of validity statements does not reflect the logic of norms.

On the one hand, both the conflicting norms ('Smoking is forbidden', 'Smoking is not forbidden') may be valid. In such a case, the validity statements concerning these norms will, paradoxically, both be true, notwithstanding their (apparent) inconsistency. The appearance of inconsistency vanishes, however, once one sees that it is not a matter of logic that the legislature validly issued conflicting norms; it is simply a matter of fact.

Conflicts of norms are in fact quite common in actual legal systems. A conflict, however, does not involve the invalidity (either lack of membership or non-existence) of one or the other of the conflicting norms. To be sure, it may happen that one of the conflicting norms is invalid, but this does not turn on some sort of logical necessity. One of the conflicting norms is invalid if and only if its invalidity (lack of membership) stems from the positive law.

In actual legal systems, it is usually only a conflict between norms found at different levels in the hierarchy of legal sources that will involve the invalidity of one of the conflicting norms (the lower-level norm, of course). However, in this case, too, the ensuing invalidity is not the consequence of any logical principle. It is the result of the positive legal norms that determine the hierarchy of legal sources—for example, those norms that render the constitution 'rigid', and thereby render statutory norms that cannot be reconciled with the constitution invalid.[21]

---

[20] See Eugenio Bulygin, 'Time and Validity', in *Deontic Logic, Computational Linguistics, and Legal Information Systems*, ed. Antonio A. Martino, 2 vols. (Amsterdam: North-Holland, 1982), vol. II, 65–81; Bulygin, 'An Antinomy' (n.10 above); Guastini (n.12 above), at ch. 13.

[21] See ibid., at ch. 14.

On the other hand, both of the conflicting rules ('Smoking is forbidden', 'Smoking is not forbidden') may be invalid. This is the case if the legislature simply refrains from regulating, in any way whatever, the behaviour in question. In such a case, the validity statements concerning these rules will, paradoxically, both be false, notwithstanding their (apparently) contradictory character. That the legislature regulates, or fails to regulate, a given course of behaviour is not a matter of logic, it is simply a matter of fact.

The paradox lies in the fact that the two 'ought'-sentences, understood as validity statements, are inconsistent. Thus, they can be neither both true nor both false. At the same time, however, the two underlying norms can both be valid and they can both be invalid; as a consequence the two 'ought'-sentences can both be true and they can both be false. How can contradictory sentences be either both true or both false?

The way out of the paradox is to drop the tenet according to which validity statements are 'ought'-sentences that reproduce the syntactic structure of the underlying norms. There is no room left for the paradox as soon as validity statements are seen as ordinary indicative, non-deontic sentences. For example, there is no contradiction whatever between the sentences,

(14) The norm 'Smoking is forbidden' is valid

and

(15) The norm 'Smoking is not forbidden' is valid,

for they predicate one and the same attribute of two different subjects. Thus, such sentences can be both true as well as both false.

This argument shows that validity statements cannot be reduced to 'ought'-sentences iterating the norms to which they (are supposed to) refer.

From a different standpoint, one could also conclude that actual legal 'ought'-sentences cannot be understood as validity statements. Indeed, legal 'ought'-sentences seem to be but iterations of legal norms.[22] Iterating a norm amounts to an approval of such a norm.[23]

My general conclusion, then, is the following: The doctrine that legal 'ought'-sentences might be understood as descriptive sentences, hence propositions in the logical sense, is not sound. In so far as normativism or the normative theory of legal science presupposes this doctrine of 'ought'-sentences, the case against the doctrine counts against normativism, too.

---

[22] See Scarpelli (n.9 above).
[23] The analysis of validity statements sketched earlier in this section, where validity is understood as 'binding force', holds for such iterations, too.

18

Hans Kelsen's Deontics*

AMEDEO G. CONTE

1. DEONTIC VALIDITY AS EXISTENCE, AND THE LOGIC OF NORMS

1.0. A Thesis of Hans Kelsen's: Deontic Validity as Existence.

'*Simplex sigillum veri*', Ludwig Wittgenstein writes in his *Tractatus*.[1] And simplicity marks Kelsen's essay, 'Law and Logic' (1965), on the relation between logic and norms.[2]

For Kelsen, a prescriptive sentence (*Norm*) is either valid or invalid.[3] Now, by definition, deontic validity is existence, it is the specific existence of prescriptive sentences.[4] That a prescriptive sentence is valid or invalid signifies for Kelsen that it is existent or non-existent, it exists or does not exist. Kelsen's equation of deontic validity and existence has a twofold effect on the relation between law and logic.

1.1. Deontic Validity as Existence, and the Principle of Contradiction.

1.1.1. *In the first place*, the equation of deontic validity and existence affects, in Kelsen, the application of the *principle of contradiction* to prescriptive sentences. Take, in a normative system, a contradiction

---

* *Editors' note*: This paper first appeared as 'In margine all'ultimo Kelsen' in *Studia ghisleriana*, ser. I, 4 (1967), 113–25. The present version of the paper (incorporating minor revisions made by the author, including his English-language title and profuse use of italics) was translated by Michael Sherberg and Bonnie Litschewski Paulson.

[1] Ludwig Wittgenstein, *Tractatus Logico-Philosophicus*, ed. and trans. D.F. Pears and B.F. McGuinness, with an introduction by Bertrand Russell (London: Routledge & Kegan Paul, 1961), at 5.4541. (The work was first published in 1921.)

[2] 'LL'.

[3] I translate the German '*Norm*' as 'prescriptive sentence', '*Aussage*' as 'descriptive sentence'. Kelsen's discourse is limited to prescriptive sentences *in the law*, and it is useful to note that what he writes cannot necessarily be generalized, that is, extended from *legal* prescriptive sentences in particular to prescriptive sentences generally.

[4] I translate the German '*Geltung*' as 'validity', '*Existenz*' as 'existence'. In 'LL', there are also two synonyms of '*geltend*', namely, '*gültig*' and '*verbindlich*'. Since these three terms are synonymous for Kelsen, at least in 'LL', I translate all of them with a single term, 'valid'.

between two prescriptive sentences, an antinomy. In other words, assume that the system contains two contradictory (antinomic) prescriptive sentences. Is one of them invalid? Does the principle of contradiction apply to contradictory prescriptive sentences?[5]

1.1.2. At first glance, it would seem so. Just as one of two contradictory descriptive sentences is necessarily not true (false), so too, I repeat, one of two contradictory prescriptive sentences would seem necessarily to be invalid.

Yet Kelsen denies it. The principle of contradiction does not apply either *directly* or *indirectly* to the validity of prescriptive sentences.

1.1.2.1. It is obvious why the principle does not apply *directly*. If there are two contradictory prescriptive sentences in a normative system, then they both exist within it, which is to say (in keeping with Kelsen's equation of validity and existence) that they are both valid. The principle of contradiction does not apply directly (immediately), then, to the validity (existence) of prescriptive sentences.

1.1.2.2. Nor does it apply *indirectly* to the validity of prescriptive sentences. The principle of contradiction does not apply even indirectly (mediately) to contradictory prescriptive sentences by being applied to the descriptive sentences that affirm the validity (the existence) of two contradictory prescriptive sentences in a system. What would the indirect application of the principle of contradiction entail? Descriptive sentences on the validity of prescriptive sentences are—because they are descriptive—either true or false. Thus, the principle of contradiction applies to them: If two descriptive sentences on validity contradict one another, then one is false. Now, say the two descriptive sentences affirm the validity of two contradictory prescriptive sentences. Since it would be false to say that both of the antinomic prescriptive sentences are valid, then, if we were to apply the principle of contradiction, one of the descriptive sentences would be false, and the corresponding antinomic prescriptive sentence would therefore be invalid. Thus, the principle of contradiction would be applied indirectly to contradictory prescriptive sentences via its application to descriptive sentences affirming the validity of the contradictory prescriptive sentences.

But is this indirect application of the principle of contradiction possible? No, it is not. In fact, the two descriptive sentences about the contradiction are not themselves contradictory and, in turn, do not constitute a contradiction. They are not contradictory and cannot be contradictory,

---

[5] Kelsen defines the antinomy in terms of *efficacy*, not validity; that is, an antinomy is an incompatibility at the level of the *efficacy* of two prescriptive sentences, not at the level of their *validity*. See 'LL', at 230. For a definition of 'antinomy' in terms of *validity*, not efficacy, see Amedeo G. Conte, review of *Les antinomies en droit. Études publiées par Ch. Perelman* (Brussels: Bruylant, 1965), in *RIFD*, 43 (1966), 545–6.

for they have two different objects. The object of the one is the validity of a prescriptive sentence *p*, while the object of the other is the validity of another prescriptive sentence—the validity, precisely, of prescriptive sentence *q*, the contradictory of *p*. Since, in a normative system, the two descriptive sentences affirming the validity (the coexistence, the joint validity) of two contradictory prescriptive sentences are not themselves contradictory, they are not subject to the principle of contradiction. The principle of contradiction cannot, therefore, be applied even indirectly to antinomic prescriptive sentences.[6]

1.1.3. In short, the principle of contradiction does not apply either *directly* or *indirectly* to contradictory prescriptive sentences.

It does not apply *directly*, since, if two contradictory prescriptive sentences both exist, then, given the equation of validity and existence, both are valid.

And it does not apply *indirectly*, since the descriptive sentences about the validity of two contradictory prescriptive sentences do not have the same object and therefore do not constitute a contradiction.[7]

1.2. Deontic Validity as Existence, and the Rule of Inference.

1.2.1. *In the second place*, the equation of deontic validity and existence affects, in Kelsen, the application of what Kelsen calls the *rule of inference*[8] to prescriptive sentences. Take, in a system, a general prescriptive sentence, for example, 'All thieves ought to be punished'. Is the individual prescriptive sentence, 'The thief Schulze ought to be punished', also valid? In other words: Does the rule of inference apply to general prescriptive sentences?

1.2.2. At first glance, it would seem so. From the truth of the general descriptive sentence, 'All men are mortal', there follows logically the truth of the individual descriptive sentence, 'The man Socrates is mortal'. So too, I repeat, from the validity of a general prescriptive sentence,

---

[6] Kelsen had already asserted in 1962 that the principle of contradiction does not apply to prescriptive sentences. In his essay, 'Derogation' [see the Table of Abbreviations], Kelsen poses—and decides negatively—the question of whether, in resolving antinomies, the criterion usually expressed as '*lex posterior derogat priori*' is a *logical* principle.

[7] That the principle of contradiction does not apply to the contradiction between prescriptive sentences (to the *antinomy* of prescriptive sentences) is implicitly affirmed by those who deny the possibility of contradiction between prescriptive sentences, that is, who deny the subsistence of the first necessary condition for applying the principle of contradiction. The (paradoxical) difference between such a theory and that of 'LL' is this: For Kelsen, the principle of contradiction is inapplicable to the antinomy not because *there is no* contradiction, but because *there is* a contradiction, that is, because both terms of the antinomy are *existing* prescriptive sentences, which is to say (in keeping with the equation of deontic validity and existence) that they are *valid* prescriptive sentences.

[8] In German, '*Regel der Schlußfolgerung*'.

there would seem syllogistically to follow the validity of each individual prescriptive sentence.

But Kelsen says 'no'. The rule of inference does not apply either *directly* or *indirectly* to the validity of prescriptive sentences.

1.2.2.1. It is obvious why the rule of inference does not apply *directly*. If, in a normative system, a general prescriptive sentence is valid (exists), it is not for this reason that each individual prescriptive sentence is valid (exists) whose validity would seem to be logically implicit in (entailed by) the validity of the general prescriptive sentence. In order for an individual prescriptive sentence to be valid in a normative system, it must be issued, set into the normative system (for example, by means of a judicial decision).

1.2.2.2. Nor does the rule of inference apply *indirectly*. The rule of inference does not apply even indirectly (mediately) to general prescriptive sentences by being applied to the descriptive sentence that affirms the validity (the existence) of a general prescriptive sentence in a normative system. The reason is obvious. A descriptive sentence affirming the validity of a general prescriptive sentence does not entail a descriptive sentence affirming the validity of an implicit individual prescriptive sentence. For example, the descriptive sentence, 'The general prescriptive sentence p, according to which all thieves ought to be punished, is valid', does not entail the descriptive sentence, 'The individual prescriptive sentence r, according to which the thief Schulze ought to be punished, is valid'.

1.2.3. In short, the rule of inference does not apply either *directly* or *indirectly* to general prescriptive sentences.

It does not apply *directly*, since, given the equation of validity and existence, an individual prescriptive sentence must come into existence (that is, it must be set into the normative system) in order to be valid.

And the rule of inference does not apply *indirectly*, since the respective descriptive sentences affirming, in the normative system, the *validity* of the general prescriptive sentence and the *validity* of the individual prescriptive sentence are *logically* unrelated.

2. DEONTIC VALIDITY AS TRUTH, AND THE LOGIC OF NORMS

2.0. A Hypothesis of Mine: Deontic Validity as Truth.

2.0.1. It may seem paradoxical to claim that the principle of contradiction and the rule of inference do not apply (either directly or indirectly) to prescriptive sentences. To a vigilant reader, however, the apparent paradox becomes a tautology. The two theses formulated *negatively* by

Kelsen (first thesis, the principle of contradiction does not apply to prescriptive sentences; second thesis, the rule of inference does not apply to prescriptive sentences) can be reformulated *positively* as two logically necessary theses.

2.0.2. To wit: The negative thesis, 'The principle of contradiction does not apply to prescriptive sentences', can be reduced to the logically necessary thesis, '*If* a prescriptive sentence exists, it exists'.

The negative thesis, 'The rule of inference does not apply to prescriptive sentences', can be reduced to the logically necessary thesis, '*Only if* a prescriptive sentence exists does it exist'.

The conjunction of these two logically necessary theses is itself a logically necessary thesis: 'A prescriptive sentence exists *if and only if* it exists.'

Why, indeed, of two contradictory prescriptive sentences, is each one nevertheless valid? The reason is obvious: It is because validity is existence, and because the *sufficient* condition for the existence of a prescriptive sentence is the existence of this prescriptive sentence. (*If* a prescriptive sentence exists, it exists, and that it contradicts another is irrelevant to its existence.)

And why, indeed, is even the individual prescriptive sentence that is logically implicit in a general one nevertheless not valid? The reason is obvious: It is because validity is existence, and because the *necessary* condition for the existence of a prescriptive sentence is the existence of this prescriptive sentence. (*Only if* a prescriptive sentence exists does it exist, and that it is logically implicit in another is irrelevant to its existence.)

2.0.3. Thus, there is nothing paradoxical in what Kelsen claims. On the contrary, his claim is ultimately reducible to the tautology, 'A prescriptive sentence exists *if and only if* it exists'.[9]

To say, then, that the principle of contradiction and the rule of inference do not apply to the validity (understood as the existence) of prescriptive sentences is true, but tautological. It is a tautology that holds not only for the existence of prescriptive sentences in particular, but also for the existence of descriptive sentences in general. (Even two contradictory descriptive sentences, for example, if they exist, both exist notwithstanding their contradictoriness.)

---

[9] Reducible to the same tautology is also the thesis according to which the dual of the principle of contradiction, the *principle of the excluded middle*, does not apply to the *validity* of two contradictory prescriptive sentences.

I have discussed elsewhere, from another perspective, the applicability of the principle of the excluded middle to prescriptive sentences. See Amedeo G. Conte, *Saggio sulla completezza degli ordinamenti giuridici* (Turin: G. Giappichelli Editore, 1962), at 120–9; Conte, 'Incalificación e indiferencia', trans. (into Spanish) Alejandro Rossi, *Diánoia*, 9 (1963), 237–57.

2.0.4. The question of whether or not the principle of contradiction and the rule of inference apply is a legitimate question only for deontic validity conceived no longer as *existence*, but as *truth*. Are prescriptive sentences true or false? What is their semantic status? And how does their semantic status affect the applicability of the principle of contradiction and the rule of inference to them?

2.0.5. I shall not speak here of the semantic status of prescriptive sentences, not because I do not have opinions, but because I could not justify them here. Rather, I shall limit myself to discussing how the questions of the applicability of the principle of contradiction and the rule of inference to prescriptive sentences take shape according to whether it is affirmed or, instead, denied that prescriptive sentences are either true or false, that is (using Aristotelian terminology), whether or not they are *apophantic*. In other words, for each of the possible hypotheses here, I shall examine how each of the two questions treated by Kelsen takes shape. (There is in fact no reason at all to presume that the two questions are correlative. It is quite possible that the principle of contradiction but not the rule of inference applies to prescriptive sentences, and, vice versa, it is quite possible that the rule of inference but not the principle of contradiction applies to prescriptive sentences.)

2.0.5.1. *The first hypothesis*: Prescriptive sentences are *non-apophantic*, that is, they are not true or false. Within this first hypothesis (non-apophanticity), two subhypotheses can be distinguished.

First subhypothesis: Prescriptive sentences (considered non-apophantic) are also *non-semantic*, which is to say, lacking in meaning, non-significative. (They are non-significative, for example, for those who affirm the 'principle of verification'—which is to say, those who equate meaning with the method of verification—and at the same time deny the verifiability of prescriptive sentences.)

Second subhypothesis: Prescriptive sentences are non-apophantic but *semantic*, significative. (Aristotle writes that the prayer is λόγος σημαντικός [*lógos semantikós*], even though it is not λόγος ἀποφαντικός [*lógos apophantikós*].)[10]

2.0.5.2. *The second hypothesis*: Prescriptive sentences are *apophantic*, that is, either true or false.

'Apophantic prescriptive sentence' may seem to be an oxymoron (ὀξύμωρον), like 'boiling ice', if not indeed a *contradictio in adjecto*, like 'round square'. My intention here is not to say whether, and in what sense, prescriptive sentences are either true or false, but simply to show how the two questions posed by Kelsen (the applicability of the principle

---

[10] For the concept of apophantic discourse (λόγος ἀποφαντικός [*lógos apophantikós*]) as discourse that is either true or false, and for the assertion that the prayer (εὐχή [*euché*]) is not apophantic, see Aristotle, *On Interpretation*, at 17a.

of contradiction and the applicability of the rule of inference to prescriptive sentences) take shape according to the various hypotheses about the apophanticity of prescriptive sentences.

Nevertheless, I should like to mention a possible sense in which the thesis that prescriptive sentences are either true or false may be interpreted. (This is the sense in which I *interpret* the thesis, not a sense in which I *affirm* it. I intend simply to *interpret* the concept of the apophanticity of prescriptive sentences, not to *affirm* or to *deny* that prescriptive sentences are apophantic. Analogously, those who interpret the German sentence, '*Das Viereck ist rund*', as 'The square is round' do not thereby affirm that the square is round.)

The truth of *prescriptive* sentences is quite analogous to the truth of *descriptive* sentences: in both cases it is truth as correspondence. Take the *descriptive* sentence, 'It is raining today'. This *descriptive* sentence is true if it is actually raining today, and false if it is not raining today. A *descriptive* sentence is true or false according to whether or not it corresponds to its object (that is, according to whether or not its object exists).

Now, it is possible to speak in analogous terms of the truth of *prescriptive* sentences. A *prescriptive* sentence (for example, 'It is forbidden to smoke') is true or false according to whether or not its object (in our example, the prohibition on smoking) exists. We could give a name to the object (the deontic status) of a *prescriptive* sentence, say, the name 'norm'. Just as the *descriptive* sentence, 'It is raining today', is something other than today's rainfall, so too (it seems to me) the *prescriptive* sentence, 'It is forbidden to smoke', is not the prohibition on smoking itself. That a one-to-one correspondence holds, then, between the set of *prescriptive sentences* and the set of *norms* (since the existence of a prescriptive sentence is the necessary and sufficient condition for the existence of the norm) does not weaken the possibility of distinguishing in principle between prescriptive sentence and norm but, on the contrary, strengthens it. One-to-one correspondence is a relation, and relation presupposes distinction.

2.0.6. Thus, I have shown a possible sense in which to interpret the thesis of the apophanticity of prescriptive sentences (the thesis that prescriptive sentences are apophantic, that is, true or false). It goes without saying that to interpret this thesis is not to make it one's own.

Indeed, I am the first to see the many objections that can be made to the thesis of the truth or falsehood of prescriptive sentences. One of the possible objections is this: It is paradoxical to call prescriptive sentences either true or false, since it is they that produce their object, since it is through them that their object exists. (Returning to our example: The prohibition on smoking exists if and only if a prescriptive sentence, 'It is forbidden to smoke' exists.) Thus, it is paradoxical to call prescriptive sentences true or false, for in constituting their own object, they *verify themselves*, so that they are all necessarily true.[11]

2.0.7. In sections 2.1 and 2.2, I shall re-examine the question of the applicability of the principle of contradiction and the rule of inference to prescriptive sentences considered no longer from the point of view of *existence*, but from the point of view of *truth*.

Kelsen asked: Do the logical principle of contradiction and the logical rule of inference apply to the validity of prescriptive sentences, where validity is conceived as *existence*? Do they apply to the *existence* of prescriptive sentences?

I shall ask: Do the logical principle of contradiction and the logical rule of inference apply to the validity of prescriptive sentences, where validity is conceived as *truth*? Do they apply to the *truth* of prescriptive sentences?

2.1. Deontic Validity as Truth, and the Principle of Contradiction.

2.1.1. First, I shall re-examine the question of the applicability of the *principle of contradiction* to contradictory prescriptive sentences.

If the validity of prescriptive sentences is understood as *existence*, then the principle of contradiction undoubtedly does not apply. The reason is obvious: Of two prescriptive sentences, regardless of whether or not they are contradictory, one, both, or neither of them may exist. The fact that they are contradictory prescriptive sentences does not affect their *existence*. *What logic applies to is truth, not existence*. Thus, the logical principle of contradiction is not even considered if the validity of contradictory prescriptive sentences is conceived as the *existence* (coexistence) of contradictory prescriptive sentences.

---

[11] It is in this sense (in the sense that every prescriptive sentence is necessarily true) that it seems to me possible to reinterpret Kelsen's thesis: '*Eine nichtgeltende Norm ist eine nicht existente, also* keine *Norm*' ('A norm that is not valid is a norm that does not exist, therefore *it is not* a norm'). 'LL' 229. Analogously, *RR2*, at 271, *PTL*, at 267: '*Eine "normwidrige Norm" ist ein Selbstwiderspruch*' ('A "norm contrary to norm" is a self-contradiction'). In fact, a *normwidrige Norm* '*könnte nicht als gültige Rechtsnorm angesehen werden, sie wäre nichtig, und das heißt überhaupt keine Rechtsnorm*' ('. . . could not be regarded as a valid legal norm; it would be null and void, which is to say it would *not* be *a* legal *norm at all*') (trans. altered, emphasis added). Kelsen's thesis has the flavour of paradox: For the existence of the prescriptive sentence, Kelsen seems to return to that deduction of existence from essence that is the ontological proof of the existence of God. Actually, Kelsen does not mean to deduce existence from essence when he asserts that a non-existent prescriptive sentence is not a prescriptive sentence. What Kelsen means is simpler: A *descriptive* sentence can exist without being true; a *prescriptive* sentence, by contrast, cannot exist without being valid, since (in keeping with Kelsen's equation of validity and existence) a prescriptive sentence that exists without being valid would be a prescriptive sentence that exists without existing, which is logically impossible.

2.1.2. If the validity of prescriptive sentences is understood no longer as *existence*, but as *truth*, the answer is nevertheless the same: The principle of contradiction does not apply to contradictory prescriptive sentences in either case; that is, it does not apply (i) when they are considered to be neither true nor false (*non-apophantic*), and it does not apply (ii) when they are considered to be either true or false (*apophantic*).

2.1.2.1. *The first hypothesis*: If prescriptive sentences are considered to be neither true nor false (that is, *non-apophantic*), it is *a priori* excluded that the principle of contradiction applies to contradictory prescriptive sentences. In fact, the principle of contradiction dictates that, given two contradictory sentences, at least one of them must be false. Now, *ex hypothesi*, prescriptive sentences are neither true nor false, so the principle of contradiction does not apply to them. (If, in particular, prescriptive sentences are considered to be not only neither true nor false, but also non-significative, this is an additional argument against the applicability of the principle of contradiction to them. Since they signify nothing, since they say nothing, 'contradictory' prescriptive sentences cannot signify contradictorily, they cannot contradict. But if they are not properly contradictory, they do not satisfy the first condition for the applicability of the principle of contradiction, which applies precisely to sentences that signify contradictorily, that is, to contradictory sentences.)

2.1.2.2. *The second hypothesis*: If prescriptive sentences are considered to be either true or false (that is, *apophantic*), then, if contradictory, they would seem to be subject to the principle of contradiction, a principle that applies precisely to all true or false contradictory sentences.

But, paradoxically, this is not the case. In fact, each of the two contradictory prescriptive sentences (contradicting one another) necessarily corresponds to that norm for which it is the necessary and sufficient condition. And if each of the two contradictory prescriptive sentences, conceived as being apophantic, is true, then it is false that one of them is false (as, to the contrary, the principle of contradiction dictates).[12]

2.2. Deontic Validity as Truth, and the Rule of Inference.

2.2.1. Having re-examined (in section 2.1) the question of the applicability of the principle of contradiction to contradictory prescriptive sentences, I shall re-examine here (in section 2.2) the question of the applicability of the *rule of inference* to general prescriptive sentences.

---

[12] I shall leave open, here, the question of whether this paradox (sentences assumed to be either true or false [apophantic] are nevertheless not subject to the principle of contradiction) is an argument against the hypothesis that prescriptive sentences are true or false (apophantic).

If the validity of prescriptive sentences is conceived as *existence*, then the rule of inference undoubtedly does not apply. The reason is obvious: The rule of inference does not apply since the principles of logic do not apply to the existence of prescriptive sentences. In fact, *what logic applies to is truth, not existence.*

2.2.2. If the validity of prescriptive sentences is conceived no longer as *existence*, but as *truth*, the answer is not necessarily the same. Here one must distinguish instead between two hypotheses: (i) prescriptive sentences are neither true nor false (that is, *non-apophantic*);[13] (ii) prescriptive sentences are either true or false (that is, *apophantic*).

2.2.2.1. *The first hypothesis*: If prescriptive sentences are considered to be neither true nor false (that is, *non-apophantic*), it is *a priori* excluded that the rule of inference applies to general prescriptive sentences. In fact, according to the rule of inference, if a general sentence (that is, a universal sentence with a certain predicate about *all* the elements of a set) is true, then every sentence with that same predicate about *every one* of the elements of that set is true. In other words, the rule of inference establishes an entailment-relation between the *truth* of certain sentences and the *truth* of certain other sentences—more precisely, an entailment-relation between the *truth* of a general sentence and the *truth* of an individual sentence.[14] Now, *ex hypothesi*, prescriptive sentences are neither true nor false; therefore, the rule of inference does not apply to them.[15]

2.2.2.2. *The second hypothesis*: If, instead, prescriptive sentences are considered to be either true or false (that is, *apophantic*), they are therefore subject to the rule of inference. If a general prescriptive sentence is valid in the sense of being true, then each individual prescriptive sentence entailed by it is true.

That does not mean, of course, that the individual prescriptive sentence entailed by the general prescriptive sentence is, being *valid*, also *efficacious*. It *can* be inefficacious. Returning to Kelsen's example: If the general prescriptive sentence, 'All thieves ought to be punished', is true, it follows logically that the individual prescriptive sentence, 'The thief Schulze ought to be punished', is also true.

[13] Within this first hypothesis (non-apophanticity), two subhypotheses can be distinguished: Prescriptive sentences are considered *semantic* (significative); prescriptive sentences are considered *non-semantic* (non-significative).

[14] For the distinction between the semantic relation of *entailment* and the syntactic relation of *derivability*, see e.g. Ettore Casari, *Lineamenti di logica matematica* (Milan: Feltrinelli, 1959), at 45–51, 95–112, 212–26; Heinrich Scholz and Gisbert Hasenjaeger, *Grundzüge der mathematischen Logik* (Berlin and Heidelberg: Springer, 1961), at 21–5.

[15] The rule of inference does not apply to prescriptive sentences themselves. Obviously, however, the possibility is not thereby excluded that the rule of inference does apply to their *phrastic*. (The neologism 'phrastic' was coined by Richard Mervyn Hare; see Hare, *The Language of Morals* (Oxford: Clarendon Press, 1952), at 18 *et passim*.)

However, it is of course possible that this individual prescriptive sentence remains, so to speak, a dead letter, which is to say that no judge's decision renders efficacious at the *judicial* level the prescriptive sentence that is true at the *legislative* level. But it is impossible to infer invalidity from inefficacy without violating that separation of *Sein* and *Sollen*, of 'is' and 'ought', whose staunchest advocate was none other than Kelsen himself.[16]

[16] Obviously, the picture changes if one reinterprets the concept of the general prescriptive sentence in one of these two ways:

(i) as a *deontic* prescriptive sentence about the position of the individual prescriptive sentence;

(ii) as an *adeontic* prescriptive sentence that determines the conditions for the validity of the individual prescriptive sentence.

If one reinterprets the concept of the general prescriptive sentence in one of these two ways, it is clear that no individual prescriptive sentence can be logically entailed by a general prescriptive sentence. But, in this case, the syllogism is impossible not because the major premiss is prescriptive, but simply because no premisses hold for any syllogism at all.

I refer here to five deontic logicians who have written on the subject of prescriptive sentences about prescriptive sentences: Oskar Becker, *Untersuchungen über den Modalkalkül* (Meisenheim am Glan: A. Hain, 1952), at 37–50; Mark Fisher, 'A Logical Theory of Commanding', *Logique et analyse*, 4 (1961), 154–69; von Wright, *NA*, at 189–207; Nicholas Rescher, *The Logic of Commands* (London: Routledge & Kegan Paul, 1966), at 14–16; Ruth Barcan Marcus, 'Iterated Deontic Modalities', *Mind*, 75 (1966), 580–2.

19

Norm Conflicts: Kelsen's View in the Late Period and a Rejoinder*

BRUNO CELANO

In 'Law and Logic' (1965) and in the last chapters of *General Theory of Norms* (1979), Hans Kelsen argues that the principle of non-contradiction (hereafter *P*) and the rule of deductive inference (hereafter *R*) cannot, either of them, be applied to norms. There is no direct application, and no indirect application either—no application, that is to say, by means of statements describing norms.[1] My aim is to evaluate Kelsen's arguments with respect to the principle of non-contradiction; thus, my general concern is with his conception of norm conflicts. I confine my discussion to writings from Kelsen's late, sceptical period.[2]

* *Editors' note*: Adapted from ch. 5 of Celano's book, *Dover essere e intenzionalità. Una critica all'ultimo Kelsen* (Turin: G. Giappichelli Editore, 1990), this paper was translated by Michael Sherberg in close collaboration with the author and Stanley L. Paulson. (Minor alterations in quotations from existing English-language translations of Kelsen's works have been made *sub silentio*.)

[1] This formulation of Kelsen's view stems from Amedeo G. Conte, 'In margine all'ultimo Kelsen', in *Studia ghisleriana*, ser. I, 4 (1967), 113–25, rev. version in *Problemi di teoria del diritto*, ed. Riccardo Guastini (Bologna: Il Mulino, 1980), 197–208, and in Conte, *Filosofia del linguaggio normativo*, 2 vols., vol. I: *Studi 1965–1981* (Turin: G. Giappichelli Editore, 1989), 17–30, translated in the present volume, ch. 18, as 'Hans Kelsen's Deontics'. For a general examination of the evolution of Kelsen's views on the relation between logic and norms, see Mario G. Losano, *Forma e realtà in Kelsen* (Milan: Comunità, 1981), at 125–37; Losano, 'La dottrina pura del diritto dal logicismo all'irrazionalismo', in Hans Kelsen, *Teoria generale delle norme*, trans. Mirella Torre (Turin: Giulio Einaudi, 1985), pp. xvii–lxi, at pp. xix–xxxiii; Robert Walter, 'Das Problem des Verhältnisses von Recht und Logik in der Reinen Rechtslehre', *Rechtstheorie*, 11 (1980), 299–314; Letizia Gianformaggio, 'Hans Kelsen on the Deduction of Validity', *Rechtstheorie*, 21 (1990), 181–207. On norm conflicts in particular, see Stanley L. Paulson, 'Zum Problem der Normenkonflikte', *ARSP*, 66 (1980), 487–506; Ota Weinberger, *Normentheorie als Grundlage der Jurisprudenz und der Ethik* (Berlin: Duncker & Humblot, 1981), at 98–103; Weinberger, 'Der normenlogische Skeptizismus', *Rechtstheorie*, 17 (1986), 13–81, at 27–8; Tecla Mazzarese, *Logica deontica e linguaggio giuridico* (Padua: CEDAM, 1989), at 116–27; Mirella Urso, 'Hans Kelsen: Coerenza dell'ordinamento e teoria della scienza giuridica', in *Studi in memoria di Giovanni Tarello*, [no editor], 2 vols. (Milan: A. Giuffrè Editore, 1990), vol. II, 579–615.

[2] Hans Kelsen, 'Derogation' (1962); 'On the Concept of Norm' (1965), in *Essays*, 216–27; 'LL' (1965); 'Law and Logic Again' (1967), in *Essays*, 254–6; *GTN* (1979). [For full references to 'Derogation', 'LL', and *GTN*, and to the collection *Essays*, see the Table of Abbreviations.]

I begin, in section I, with a summary of the main tenets of Kelsen's conception of norm conflicts in his late period. I then turn, in section II, to an examination of his arguments to the effect that *P* does not apply to norms; and I raise objections to Kelsen's view of the matter. I move, in section III, to possible replies by Kelsen to my objections, and argue that they are inadequate. In a brief closing section, I place my criticism of Kelsen in a broader perspective, arguing that it is the background assumptions of his conception of *Sollen* or 'ought' that lead directly to the deep problems in his account of norm conflicts.

I. KELSEN'S VIEW

Kelsen's conception of norm conflicts is grounded in a fundamental thesis: Norms, unlike statements of fact (descriptive sentences, assertions, or statements), are not subject to *P*.[3] According to Kelsen, neither *P* nor *R* can be applied to norms. First, given two norms belonging to the same norm system, it does not follow from a direct conflict of one with the other that either of them is invalid (that the existence or membership in the norm system of either of them is undermined). And, second, the validity of a given norm cannot be logically derived from one or more higher-order norms in the norm system, not even in conjunction with statements of fact. According to Kelsen, to say that a norm belongs to a norm system—that is, is valid—is to say that it stems from an (authorized) act of will, of which the norm itself is the sense (*Sinn*, or *Sinngehalt*).

I do not wish to challenge these tenets, which I believe to be correct. Instead, I wish to make the following three claims:

First, Kelsen's rejection of the applicability of *P* to norms turns heavily on the assumption that if *P* were applicable to norms, this would be owing to an analogy between the 'truth' of statements and the 'validity' of norms. While rejecting the hypothesis that 'validity' stands to norms as 'truth' stands to statements, and also the hypothesis, closely tied to the former, that validity may be conceived as a function of logical relations between norms, Kelsen nevertheless fails to take into account the possibility that, granting that *P* does not apply to norms, a different kind of

---

[3] A statement (*Aussage*) is, according to Kelsen, the sense (*Sinn*) or sense-content (*Sinngehalt*) of an act of thought; a norm is the sense or sense-content of an act of will (aimed at someone else's behaviour). The sense-content of acts of thought and of acts of will are, respectively, *Sein* and *Sollen*. *Sein* and *Sollen*, for their part, are two elementary and indefinable 'forms' or 'modi', and their relationship is one of 'irreducible dualism'. See Kelsen, 'On the Concept of Norm' (n.2 above); *GTN* ch. 1, at §§ III–IV (p. 2), ch. 8, at § I (p. 26), ch. 16, at § I (pp. 58–60); and see generally Bruno Celano, *Dover essere e intenzionalità* (Turin: G. Giappichelli Editore, 1990), at 51–61.

connection might hold, all the same, between logical contradiction (of statements) and norm conflict.

Second, this approach has two consequences. Kelsen fails to see that a specific relation holds between logical contradiction and norm conflict—a relation, moreover, the understanding of which is a necessary condition both for understanding what a norm conflict is and for defining it. And Kelsen's discussion of the applicability of *P* to norms belies, in the end, its insightful point of departure, for he ends up by granting, paradoxically, that *P* and *R* do apply to norms in exactly the same way they apply to statements.

Third, the roots of the problem here are ultimately traceable to a set of assumptions making up the core of Kelsen's conception of *Sollen* or 'ought'.

In short, in arguing that 'validity' is not a function of logical relations between norms (unlike 'truth', which is a function of logical relations between statements), Kelsen puts forward his argument as if its conclusion were, by itself, sufficient to show that relations of logical contradiction between norms do not hold in any sense whatever, not even 'by analogy' ('*per analogiam*').[4] Contrary to Kelsen's view, I aim to show that a norm conflict is indeed something analogous, in a sense to be specified, to a logical contradiction.

Before showing in what sense Kelsen's arguments remain misleadingly tied to the idea of a supposed analogy between truth and validity, and before pointing to the consequences of this approach for the problem of the applicability of *P* to norms, I should like to offer certain additional observations on Kelsen's view of the relation between logic and norms.

Kelsen is not denying the possibility, in principle, of logical relations between norms; indeed, he explicitly grants such a possibility when he acknowledges that a norm, although not a concept, nevertheless 'contains' concepts, and that logical relations may therefore hold between the concepts contained in different norms.[5]

In particular, as far as *R* is concerned, and quite apart from the logical non-derivability of the validity of an individual norm from a general norm, Kelsen adduces arguments for two additional theses:

First, the possibility that an individual norm 'corresponds' ('*entsprechen*') to a general norm.

Second, the possibility that a norm of a lesser degree of generality is derived from a norm of a greater degree of generality.[6]

---

[4] 'LL' 230, 233.
[5] See 'LL', at 247–8; *GTN* ch. 50 (at pp. 192–3), at ch. 60 (pp. 266–7).
[6] See generally 'LL'; see also *GTN* ch. 58, at § XXII (pp. 249–50), at ch. 59 (pp. 252–65).

Thus, Kelsen's views about the applicability of R to norms are more differentiated than appears on first glance to be the case.[7] Not so, however, where P is concerned. The basic problem, which Kelsen takes as his point of departure, is

whether a conflict between two norms of morality or of law, one of which decrees that particular behaviour is obligatory and the other of which decrees that forbearance from this behaviour is obligatory, constitutes a logical contradiction that can be resolved by applying the principle of non-contradiction.[8]

Kelsen answers in the negative. In making a case on behalf of his negative response, he argues not only that a normative conflict is neither a contradiction nor reducible thereto but also that the case of a norm conflict is something 'altogether different' from a logical contradiction, just as the case of 'tension between opposing forces' is altogether different. Logical contradiction and norm conflict are not comparable in any respect whatever, and it is possible to identify and describe the latter without in any way presupposing or referring to the former. The conflict between two norms does not, in any sense, 'represent' ('*darstellen*') or imply a logical contradiction.[9]

Thus, Kelsen's view of the applicability of P to norms may be summarized in three main tenets. A norm conflict:

(1) is not a logical contradiction;
(2) it has nothing to do with (that is, does not represent, is not analogous to, not comparable to, and can be described without reference to) a logical contradiction; and
(3) it cannot be resolved by means of the application of P.

Kelsen's denial of the possibility of a logic of norms may be criticized from a number of perspectives. Everything turns, here, on what we mean by the word 'logic'. Kelsen repeatedly says that he wants to consider the role of a 'bivalent (true/false) logic' vis-à-vis norms; accordingly, his interpretation of P is strictly truth-functional.[10] One might object that

---

[7] For a general discussion of Kelsen's views on the applicability of R to norms, see Letizia Gianformaggio, *In difesa del sillogismo pratico* (Milan: A. Giuffrè Editore, 1987).

[8] *GTN* ch. 50 (p. 191).

[9] As Kelsen writes, a conflict between norms 'can be described without any contradiction'; it is 'something entirely different from a logical contradiction', 'LL' 235. Again: 'a conflict of norms is not a logical contradiction, or even something that can be compared to a logical contradiction', *GTN* ch. 29, § II (p. 124). '[A] conflict between norms is not a logical contradiction and cannot even be compared to a logical contradiction,' 'Derogation', 271. A conflict between norms cannot be 'anything analogous' to a logical contradiction, 'LL' 233. Rather, it is an 'antithesis or opposition', *GTN* ch. 57, § IV (p. 214), which, to the extent that it can be compared to something, is similar not to a logical contradiction but to 'two forces applied to the same point that are moving in opposed directions.' *GTN* ch. 29, § II (p. 125); see also 'LL', at 235.

[10] *GTN* ch. 50 (p. 189). 'The principle of non-contradiction asserts that when two statements contradict one another, only one of them can be true and when one of them is

uninterpreted logical calculi may be interpreted by assigning to formulae of such calculi values other than the pair 'true'/'false'. In such an interpretation, classical logic, conceived as a set of uninterpreted formal calculi, might then be shown to account for logical relations between norms.[11] And, it may be added, there remains the possibility of building new calculi, capable (given the appropriate logical values) of being interpreted as the syntactic framework of a logic of norms.

As we shall see presently, Kelsen's arguments against the idea that P and R are applicable *per analogiam* to norms are designed to undermine the idea that those interpretations of classical bivalent calculi—and, therefore, of P and R—in which appeal is made to logical values other than the pair 'true'/'false' could provide a showing of the applicability of logic to norms. The candidates Kelsen explicitly takes into account here are the two pairs 'valid'/'invalid' and 'obeyed'/'not obeyed'.[12] By themselves, however, Kelsen's arguments do not suffice to rule out the possibility either of finding new and more adequate logical values or of building new formal frameworks adequate to a logic of norms. Be that as it may, I shall not pursue this line of argument in raising objections to Kelsen's negative thesis concerning the applicability of P to norms. Specifically, I shall not appeal either to the hypothesis of a non-truth-functional interpretation of classical logic or to new and more sophisticated formal frameworks. Rather, following Kelsen's own approach, I shall rest content with the classical truth-functional interpretation of P and try to show, contrary to what Kelsen argues, that it is precisely in this sense that a norm conflict presupposes, or implies, P.

Finally, some qualifications are in order. In what follows, norm conflicts will be discussed in a highly simplified way. As a paradigm case of a norm conflict, I shall adopt the case of a norm that prescribes a given act as obligatory and another norm prescribing forbearance from the performance of that same act—a norm, then, proscribing the act in question. I shall not take into account the following: 1) conflicts between non-prescriptive norms (for example, constitutive or technical norms); 2) conflicts between prescriptive or proscriptive norms and permissory norms. Moreover, the analysis of conflicts between *legal* norms, when compared

---

true the other must be false.' *GTN* ch. 29, § IV, Note 83 (p. 325), and see ch. 54, n.141 (at pp. 383–4); see also Losano, 'La dottrina pura del diritto . . .' (n.1 above), at pp. li–v; Mazzarese (n.1 above), at 104.

[11] This is a standard argument in support of the possibility of a logic of norms; see e.g. Georges Kalinowski, 'Über die Bedeutung der Deontik für Ethik und Rechtsphilosophie', in *Deontische Logik und Semantik*, ed. Amedeo G. Conte et al. (Wiesbaden: Athenaion, 1977), 101–29; Weinberger, *Normentheorie* (n.1 above), at 95; Weinberger, ' "Is" and "Ought" Reconsidered', *ARSP*, 71 (1984), 454–74, at 458–9.

[12] See *GTN* ch. 57, at §§ III, VIII (pp. 212–13, 218–19).

with the analysis of norm conflicts in general, raises special problems (for example, problems pertaining to the possibility of conflict between norms at different levels in a hierarchically ordered system of norms, techniques of conflict resolution, and so on). And the solution to these problems turns on assumptions about the structure of the legal system and the interpretative practices shared in a particular legal culture. These issues, too, are no part of my concern here.

Why hold to a single form of norm conflict, a conflict between the obligation to perform an act and the obligation to forbear from performing that act? First, it is the simplest form of norm conflict, a feature making it possible to grasp more easily the core of the problem of the applicability of *P* to norms. Second, Kelsen himself, in denying the applicability of *P* to norms, considers this form of norm conflict to be paradigmatic. Third, building on this simplified version of our problem, we are in a position to understand more complicated cases.[13]

II. WHAT IS A NORM CONFLICT?

I shall not challenge Kelsen's claim that a norm conflict is something different from a logical contradiction. Rather, my interest is in his claim that the difference between norm conflict and logical contradiction is, as he himself puts it, *complete*—that, in other words, the identification, description, and definition of norm conflicts require no reference to logical contradiction (the second, then, of the three tenets listed in section I).

Why does Kelsen deny the applicability of *P* to norms? The main reason is apparent: *P* is to be understood truth-functionally, and norms, according to Kelsen, are neither true nor false; *P*, then, has no application to norms. One may suppose, however, that logical values analogous to the pair 'true'/'false' might well be applied to norms and that, in this instance, *P* could be applied 'by analogy' to norms. As I have already suggested, Kelsen rejects this hypothesis, too. His arguments directed against the attempt to resort to the values 'valid'/'invalid' and 'obeyed'/'not obeyed' are the following.

---

[13] It must be stressed that the problem of norm conflicts, as I consider it, is not to be identified with the problem of 'moral dilemmas' (the problem, namely, of whether and in what sense it is possible for one moral 'ought' to conflict with another). To identify these two problems would require identifying the moral 'ought' with positive norms. As I understand the term 'norm' here, *norms* are heteronomous; it is not, however, to be taken for granted that the moral 'ought' is to be understood as heteronomous. On Kelsen's affirmative answer to this question, see Bruno Celano, 'Il problema delle norme autonome', in *Sistemi normativi statici e dinamici*, ed. Letizia Gianformaggio (Turin: G. Giappichelli Editore, 1991), 333–66; I do not, however, pursue the question here.

A. Validity.

Given contradictory statements of fact, one of them must be true and the other false. Contrariwise for conflicting norms: As Kelsen argues, *both* conflicting norms are valid (both exist, both belong to a given norm system); a so-called invalid norm 'is one that does not exist, and is, therefore, *no norm* at all.'[14] Kelsen's point can be paraphrased in another way: On the one hand, it is impossible that two contradictory statements of fact are both true. On the other, it is not only possible but, indeed, necessary that two conflicting norms both be valid; that there is a conflict between them presupposes their joint validity.[15]

In a sense, then, the application of *P* makes it possible to resolve a contradiction between statements of fact, while a norm conflict cannot be resolved by means of the application of any logical principle whatever. If we are given two contradictory statements, then the inference that one of the contradictories is true and the other false is, in virtue of *P*, certain—that is to say, it is made on *a priori* grounds. In the case of two conflicting norms, no analogous criterion permits us to infer at all, let alone on *a priori* grounds, that one of the conflicting norms is invalid. Rather, as already suggested, it is a necessary condition of a norm conflict that the conflicting norms both be valid. A contradiction between statements of fact may be resolved by carefully examining the state of affairs to which they refer; even if *opinions* about a given state of affairs contradict each other, it remains the case that *knowledge* of the state of affairs in question would eliminate the contradiction. A conflict between norms, however, 'cannot, like a logical contradiction, be resolved by way of knowledge, with the aid, say, of legal science.'[16] In fact, according to Kelsen in his late period, norm cognition consists in being able to recognize that the norm in question belongs to the norm system, that is to say, it consists in the ability both to discriminate between norms that are valid and those that are not, and to describe the former. Owing to the 'irreducible dualism' of *Sein* ('is') and *Sollen* ('ought'), of thought and will, cognition of norms is something wholly different from the production or the suppression of valid norms. Knowledge or cognition of norms may lead one to see that two conflicting norms both belong to the norm system; whenever this happens, enquiries conducted in the name of legal science, being merely descriptive and not prescriptive in character, cannot eliminate the conflict in any way whatever. A norm conflict can be resolved only if one of the

---

[14] 'LL' 230 (Kelsen's emphasis).   [15] 'LL' 235; *GTN* ch. 29, § II (p. 124).
[16] 'LL' 235.

conflicting norms loses its validity, only if, in other words, one of the conflicting norms (in virtue of losing its validity) should vanish.[17]

By contrast, the truth of a statement of fact is not something that can somehow vanish. That is, if a statement of fact is true, it has always been true and will always be true. A norm, on the contrary, may be 'invalidated' by means of an abrogating norm, or its validity may be undermined owing to a loss of efficacy.[18]

B. Obedience.

(a) Given two contradictory statements of fact, the one, if it is true, has always been true and will always be true, and the same holds for the falsity of the other. Two conflicting norms, while they cannot both be obeyed or applied by the same agent at the same time, can be obeyed at the same time by different agents, and at different times by the same agent.[19]

(b) Second—and this is the main argument—'true' and 'false' are properties of statements, whereas 'obedience' and 'non-obedience' are properties not of norms themselves, but of behaviour that either conforms or does not conform to norms. The norm, qua 'ideal entity' a *Sollen*, makes no reference to, has no relation whatever to, its own obedience, which is, qua actual behaviour, a *Sein*.[20]

Of these arguments, addressed to validity and obedience, one may grant Kelsen's point that for a norm conflict to exist, it is necessary that both norms be valid, and also his point that norm conflicts cannot be resolved through theoretical enquiries that have as their subject-matter the norm system to which the norms in question belong. If the conflict is to be resolved, it is necessary that one or the other of the conflicting norms lose its validity. Both tenets are rooted in the idea that while a statement can be false only on condition of being exactly what it is, namely a statement, a so-called invalid norm is *no norm* at all.[21] Still, the

---

[17] And this, in turn, may happen either through loss of efficacy or by means of derogation, which Kelsen understands as the specific function of a third norm. The derogating norm does not conflict with the norm derogated; see generally 'Derogation', and see also 'LL', at 234; *GTN* ch. 29, at § III (pp. 125–6), ch. 57, at § XIII (p. 225). The idea that the proper task undertaken in cognizing norms—the task, then, of legal science—is merely the identification and description of the norms belonging to the system under examination (and not a Kantian regimentation of material, itself multiple and chaotic, into an objective unity) is one of the main differences, and probably the most important one, between the late Kelsen and the Kelsen of the earlier work, including the Second Edition of the *Pure Theory of Law*. On this change in Kelsen's conception of science, see Urso (n.1 above), Gianformaggio (n.1 above).

[18] 'LL' 230, 239.   [19] *GTN* ch. 57, § IX (pp. 219–20).

[20] See 'LL', at 239–40; *GTN* ch. 57, at § IX (pp. 219–20).

[21] From this point of view, Kelsen's thesis to the effect that *P* is not applicable to norms reduces to a tautology: '*If* a prescriptive sentence exists, it exists'. Conte, 'In margine all'ultimo Kelsen' (n.1 above), 117, rev. version, *Problemi di teoria del diritto*, 201, *Filosofia del linguaggio normativo*, 23, and in the present volume, ch. 18, § 2.02.

question arises: Is it possible, from these tenets, to draw the conclusion that a norm conflict is something *completely* different from a contradiction (the second of the three tenets listed in section I)?

The answer is negative. To appreciate why it is, it suffices to ask how Kelsen himself *defines* the concept of norm conflict. On the very first page of his paper 'Law and Logic', Kelsen offers a definition of 'norm conflict' as:

a situation in which two norms are valid, of which one prescribes a certain course of conduct, and the other a course incompatible with this.[22]

In the subsequent steps of his argument in 'Law and Logic', Kelsen repeats this definition with slight modifications, adding that the situation is such that 'he who obeys the one norm, violates the other.'[23] We have already granted to Kelsen that such a situation cannot be understood as a logical contradiction between the two norms; if the norms conflict with one another, it is necessary that both be valid. To say this, however, is tantamount to saying that there is no assimilation of logical contradiction and norm conflict—in other words, no assimilation of 'being valid' in the sense of being true (which pertains to statements) and 'being valid' in the strict and proper sense of the existence of a norm.[24]

Still, this argument does not, by itself, suffice to show that there is *no* sense in which a norm conflict might 'present' a contradiction. The question for Kelsen here is not whether a norm conflict may be assimilated to a logical contradiction, where it would be argued that just as, given two logically contradictory statements of fact, the one must be true and the other false, so likewise, given a conflict between norms, the one norm is necessarily valid and the other necessarily invalid. The question, rather, is this: Why and in what sense are the two acts prescribed by conflicting norms 'incompatible'? In other words: Why is it that an individual who complies with one of the conflicting norms *necessarily* violates the other?

---

[22] 'LL' 228.

[23] 'LL' 233. Again: 'A conflict exists between two norms when that which one sets down as obligatory is incompatible with that which the other sets down as obligatory, so that the observance or application of one norm *necessarily* or *possibly* involves the violation of the other.' *GTN* ch. 29, § I (pp. 123–4) (Kelsen's emphasis). The distinction between the case in which obeying one norm necessarily involves violating the other, and the case in which this is possible but not necessary, will not be taken up here and does not have relevant implications for our problem. The latter case turns on the possibility of conflicts between prescriptive and permissory norms (see § I above).

[24] Kelsen himself engages in a rhetorical exploitation of this ambiguity: 'as it is said in this case, only one [statement] can "be valid" (*gelten*), while the other must be false, that is to say, cannot "be valid".' 'LL' 233. The distinction between these two senses of 'validity'—the validity of a statement, namely its truth, and that of a norm—is clearly drawn in *GTN* ch. 44, at § IV (pp. 173–4).

It is the answer to this question that brings to light a specific relation between norm conflict and logical contradiction. The reason why an individual who complies with one of the conflicting norms must necessarily violate the other is that the conjunction of the descriptions of the acts constituting obedience to the two conflicting norms is a description of a logically contradictory state of affairs. In other words, the conjunction of the two statements of fact to the effect that a given agent actually carries out those acts that are prescribed by the two conflicting norms is a self-contradiction. (Following a well-trodden path, I shall call such statements 'obedience-statements'.[25]) An agent cannot both carry out and forbear from carrying out one and the same act at one and the same time.[26] In fact, it is difficult to imagine any other reasons that might explain why the acts prescribed by the two conflicting norms should be seen as 'incompatible': They are incompatible because their respective descriptions in 'obedience-statements' are logically contradictory. The norms conflict, then, *because* the corresponding obedience-statements are logically contradictory.

Kelsen himself explicitly acknowledges that the impossibility of complying with one of two conflicting norms without violating the other is related in some way to contradiction:

If one complies with a norm, the fact that one cannot, then, simultaneously comply with a norm conflicting with [the first norm]—that is, cannot both comply with the first norm and not comply with it—is indeed an application of the logical principle of non-contradiction. For this principle merely means that if it is true that a person behaves in a certain way, it cannot be true that he does not so behave.[27]

If, however, the fact that two norms conflict with one another entails that they prescribe incompatible acts, and if the acts are incompatible because, and to the extent that, carrying out both of them is logically impossible, then it is not true that a norm conflict in no sense 'presents' a logical contradiction.

How then are we to understand Kelsen's claim that a norm conflict 'can be described without any contradiction'? By saying that a norm conflict can be described without any contradiction Kelsen means, first of all, that it is possible to describe a norm conflict without contradicting

[25] See e.g. Bernard Williams, 'Consistency and Realism', in Williams, *Problems of the Self* (Cambridge: Cambridge UP, 1973) 187–206; Hart, 'Unity of Law' (n.29 below).

[26] Given a logic of action that includes the distinction between doing, not doing, and forbearing from doing a given act, this formulation of *P* lends itself to further developments; see e.g. von Wright, *NA*, at 64–6; Georg Henrik von Wright, 'Handlungslogik', in *Normenlogik*, ed. Hans Lenk (Pullach: Verlag Dokumentation, 1974), 9–24, at 14–15, 21–3. I do not take up these complications here.

[27] 'LL' 240.

oneself. This, however, only amounts to saying, once again, that both conflicting norms are valid, something that, as we have seen, may be granted to Kelsen.[28] It does not, however, go far enough. The crucial point is that Kelsen's arguments constantly slip from the claim that 'A norm conflict can be described without any contradiction', in the sense just specified (which corresponds to the first of the three tenets listed in section I), to a wholly different claim, namely, that a norm conflict can be described without in any way identifying a logical contradiction, and that its proper understanding requires no reference to a contradiction (the second of the three tenets listed in section I). As we have just seen, however, such a conclusion, in light of Kelsen's own definition of the concept of norm conflict, is simply false; the incompatibility in virtue of which two norms may be said to conflict with each other is the logical impossibility of both carrying out and forbearing from carrying out one and the same act at one and the same time.

In arguing that a norm conflict does not in any sense 'present' a contradiction, Kelsen defines the phrase 'norm conflict' by implicitly making reference to logically contradictory statements.[29] His emphasis on the heterogeneity of norm conflict and logical contradiction is not, contrary to the suggestion of one writer, the expression of a genuine species of 'norm irrationalism'.[30] It is, more simply, an implicitly self-defeating claim.

---

[28] In *PTL*, Kelsen tries to show that *P* is (mediately) applicable to norms thanks to the contradiction obtaining between the statements asserting the existence (validity) of each of the conflicting norms. He writes: 'Logical principles can be applied, if not directly, at least indirectly, to legal norms, namely, in that they are applicable to the legal propositions, which are true or false, that describe these norms.' *PTL* § 16 (p. 74), see also at § 34(e) (pp. 205–8). In the late period, Kelsen emphatically rules out this possibility; see *GTN* ch. 57, § XII, at Note 155 (p. 395). No contradiction obtains between the (descriptive) statements that assert the existence, or validity, of two conflicting norms, for both statements are trivially true.

I should perhaps add that I do not consider, here, the reasons that prompted Kelsen's shift. According to Urso (n.1 above), Kelsen's shift on the applicability (both direct and indirect) of *P* to norms should be understood as one of the results of a radical change in his conception of legal science, the 'shift from a productive to a descriptive task of science', ibid. 612, 614. See also Mazzarese (n.1 above), at 122–7; Gianformaggio (n.1 above).

[29] For an argument close to the one developed in the present section, but relating to Kelsen's works preceding 'Derogation' (1962), see H.L.A. Hart, 'On the Doctrine of the Unity of Law', in this volume, ch. 30, at § II, A; Hart, 'Kelsen Visited', in this volume, ch. 4, at § III.

[30] That Kelsen's conception of the relation between logic and norms is a form of 'norm irrationalism' has been maintained by Ota Weinberger, *Normentheorie* (n.1 above), at 98–9. In order to avoid the pejorative connotations of the term, he speaks, in later writings, of Kelsen's 'scepticism towards a logic of norms'. See Weinberger, 'Skeptizismus' (n.1 above), 13 (at Weinberger's n.1).

III. NORM CONFLICTS AND THE IDEA OF A MODALLY INDIFFERENT SUBSTRATE

It is not easy to say whether Kelsen appreciated that while maintaining that norms are not subject to *P*, he was at the same time presupposing the notion of logical contradiction (between statements) as the criterion by means of which one identifies, and defines, a norm conflict. To be sure, certain adumbrations and some sketchy arguments of Kelsen's suggest that he may well have seen the problem. For he actually tries to block the path that leads to the conclusion just drawn—the conclusion, namely, that a norm conflict 'presents' a logical contradiction or, better, that a logical contradiction (between possible states of affairs) is a condition for the possibility of a norm conflict. Kelsen explicitly acknowledges that the inclination to equate norm conflict and logical contradiction stems from one's awareness of the logical contradiction obtaining between the obedience-statements corresponding to conflicting norms.[31] He strives, however, to blunt the force of such an acknowledgment by going on to draw a sharp distinction between the *incompatibility* of the acts prescribed by two conflicting norms and the logical *contradiction* obtaining between the corresponding obedience-statements.

Thus, Kelsen writes that, in the case of a norm conflict, obedience to or the application of one norm involves non-obedience to or the non-application of the other norm, and this happens *because* what the one norm prescribes is incompatible with what the other norm prescribes.[32] He is apparently trying, in this passage, to distinguish between the impossibility of 'unifying' the prescribed acts and the logical impossibility of an agent's carrying out and forbearing from carrying out one and the same act at one and the same time—the logical necessity, in other words, that the two contradictory obedience-statements be neither both true nor both false. Elsewhere, Kelsen characterizes the impossibility of complying with both norms as an aspect of the 'situation created' by a norm conflict,[33] implicitly attempting to distinguish between such a 'situation'—a state of affairs concerning the courses of action open to the addressee of the norms—and the norm conflict itself.

It is not difficult to arrive at the reasons lying behind these verbal acrobatics. If the impossibility of complying with both norms were the criterion by means of which a norm conflict is identified and understood as such, then two points would have to be granted: first, that norms, as *Sollen*, stand in a determinate relation to the possibility of their being obeyed or not obeyed (that compliance with a norm, then, is not merely

---

[31] See *GTN* ch. 57, at § XI (pp. 222–3).   [32] See *GTN* ch. 29, at § I (pp. 123–4).
[33] 'The situation created by a norm conflict . . .', *GTN* ch. 57, § IV (p. 214).

a property of the actual behaviour conforming to it);[34] and, second, that reference to logical contradiction is a necessary aspect of the definition of the concept of norm conflict.

Verbal moves like those reported two paragraphs above will not suffice, however, to save Kelsen's view. In order to avoid such unwanted conclusions, Kelsen would have to clarify what the incompatibility of the prescribed acts could consist in, if not in the impossibility of an agent's performing and at the same time forbearing from performing one and the same act. Only on this condition would it be possible for Kelsen to distinguish between, on the one hand, the conflict obtaining between norms as *Sollen* and, on the other hand, the 'situation created' by the conflict itself at the level of the corresponding obedience-statements, that is, at the level of *Sein*.

The theoretical device by means of which Kelsen might draw a distinction between the incompatibility of the acts prescribed by conflicting norms and the logical impossibility of an agent's both carrying out and forbearing from carrying out a given act at a given point in time is the very device by means of which he tries to avoid qualifying as descriptive (or indicative) the non-imperative factor contained in a norm: the notion of a *modally indifferent substrate*.

According to Kelsen, a norm consists of two different elements: what is prescribed (certain behaviour) and its being prescribed. The first element is the 'content' of the norm, a content that appears, in the norm itself, in the form of *Sollen*; such a content, however, may also figure as the content of a statement—that is, it may also appear in the form of *Sein*. *Sein* and *Sollen* are 'purely formal concepts', that is, 'forms' or 'modi', 'which may have any content whatever, but which must, in order to make sense, have a determinate content'; 'it is something that is, and it is something that ought to be'. Such a 'something', which either *is* or *ought to be*, Kelsen terms the 'modally indifferent substrate'.[35] It is a given

---

[34] That a norm has no relation whatever to its being obeyed is a tenet to which Kelsen gives considerable emphasis; see 'LL', at 239; *GTN* ch. 57, at § VIII (pp. 218–19), see also ch. 16, at § II (pp. 60–1), ch. 51 (at p. 196), and at ch. 56 (pp. 208–10). For a critique of Kelsen's arguments on this point, see Celano (n.3 above), at 111–18.

[35] *GTN* ch. 16, §§ I–II (pp. 59, 60). The notion of the modally indifferent substrate does not appear for the first time in *GTN*; it does, however, play a fundamental role in this work. See Kazimierz Opałek, *Überlegungen zu Hans Kelsens 'Allgemeine Theorie der Normen'* (Vienna: Manz, 1980), at 27–9; Weinberger, *Normentheorie* (n.1 above), at 47–9; Gianpaolo Parodi, 'Sul concetto di "norma giuridica" nella *Allgemeine Theorie der Normen* di Hans Kelsen', *Materiali per una storia della cultura giuridica*, 15 (1985), 153–231, at 185–202. For a critical examination of the notion of the modally indifferent substrate, and the role it plays in Kelsen's rejection of any attempt to analyse norms (along the lines traced by Walter Dubislav, Jørgen Jørgensen, Richard M. Hare, and many others) into an imperative (normative etc.) and an indicative (descriptive etc.) factor, see Celano (n.3 above), at ch. 2. For a full statement of such an account of prescriptions, see Bruno Celano, *Dialettica della giustificazione pratica. Saggio sulla Legge di Hume* (Turin: G. Giappichelli Editore, 1994), at ch. 5.

content, which may appear either in the form of *Sein* or in the form of *Sollen*, but which is, by itself, neutral as between these two possibilities. A statement, qua sense of an act of thought, presents a modally indifferent substrate in the form of *Sein*; a norm, qua sense of an act of will, presents a modally indifferent substrate in the form of *Sollen*.

How could the idea of a modally indifferent substrate make it possible for Kelsen to avoid the conclusion that a norm conflict does indeed 'present' a contradiction? Two norms conflict to the extent that the acts prescribed by them are incompatible. Were it possible to understand such an incompatibility not as a relation holding between the acts as described by statements of fact corresponding to each of the conflicting norms (that is, obedience-statements), but as a relation holding between the acts taken as modally indifferent substrates, which in the conflicting norms would appear in the form of *Sollen* and in the corresponding obedience-statements in the form of *Sein*, then the unbridgeable separation between norm conflict and logical contradiction would hold. One could argue that if two modally indifferent substrates are incompatible, their appearance in the form of *Sollen* produces a norm conflict, while their appearance in the form of *Sein* produces a contradiction.

The question, however, is this: What could one mean by saying that the modally indifferent substrates of two norms are 'incompatible' if not that the corresponding obedience-statements are contradictory?

Kelsen in two crucial passages introduces a further distinction, the distinction between logical *contradiction*, which obtains only between statements, and *opposition*, which obtains not between statements or judgments but only between concepts. Here he seems to hint at the possibility that one might understand the incompatibility of the acts prescribed by two conflicting norms as an opposition (between concepts), so that it would be possible to avoid a definition of norm conflict that presupposes the notion of logical contradiction (between obedience-statements). In neither passage, however, is such an argument explicitly developed. The first passage is nothing more than a quotation in a footnote where Kelsen comments on his own statement in the text to the effect that a norm conflict is not a contradiction.[36] In the second passage, Kelsen, writing with even greater ambiguity, states that

---

[36] *GTN* ch. 29, § II (p. 124). The quotation stems from Arthur Drews, *Lehrbuch der Logik* (Berlin: G. Stilke, 1928), 229, and runs as follows: 'Concepts do not contradict each other, but only oppose each other. "Circle" and "non-circle" are mutually exclusive, but one of the two concepts does not make the other one impossible. This occurs only with two judgments, one of which asserts the opposite of the other. The principle of contradiction therefore expresses a relation between two judgments . . . When one of two judgments asserts what the other denies, then one of the two must be false.' Kelsen comments: 'The principle of non-contradiction is applicable only to the relation between statements and not to the relation between norms.' *GTN* ch. 29, § II (p. 124, at Note).

a logical contradiction may obtain only between true or false judgments, and therefore not between two concepts, which are neither true nor false, as for example, 'circle' and 'non-circle' (the one concept does not at all make the other impossible), *and not even* between two norms, which are neither true nor false.[37]

In this second passage, it is not clear whether Kelsen is suggesting that a norm conflict has as its basis the opposition between the concepts of the acts prescribed by the conflicting norms, or whether he is merely stressing instead an analogy that holds between the opposition of two concepts on the one hand and a norm conflict on the other.

We face, then, the following situation. In order to avoid logical contradiction between statements as the (implicit) basis of the definition of a norm conflict, Kelsen has to understand the 'incompatibility' between the acts prescribed by two conflicting norms as a relation holding between the modally indifferent substrates of the two norms. This, however, is possible only if the modally indifferent substrates are characterized as concepts, and their relation (both in the case of conflicting norms and in the case of a logical contradiction between statements) as a relation of opposition. Is such a view tenable? There are in fact two questions here: Is such a view tenable in and of itself? And is it consistent with Kelsen's general tenets about the modally indifferent substrate? The answers, I believe, to both questions are negative.

As for the first question, it will be enough to note the following. Kelsen invites express attention to the idea that the opposing concepts may be understood as fundamental to the incompatibility between the acts prescribed by two conflicting norms only to the extent that these concepts *mutually exclude* each other. The idea of mutual exclusion, however, depends on the notion of logical contradiction and cannot be understood independently of it. That two concepts are opposed does indeed mean that they mutually exclude each other, but it is not clear what this could mean if not that it is impossible for both concepts to hold at one and the same time for one and the same subject. In short, opposition between concepts cannot be understood independently of the idea of logical contradiction. The incompatibility that lies at the root of the concept of norm conflict depends on statements according to which a given act is or is not carried out; there is no 'principle of excluded opposition' in virtue of which a relation between two norms could be understood as a conflict between them *sans* reference to a contradiction. Resorting to the concept of opposition in order to avoid reference to the concept of contradiction is, in short, a blind alley.

What about the coherence of the thesis at hand vis-à-vis the general framework of Kelsen's concept of norm? Within this framework,

---

[37] *GTN* ch. 57, § IV (p. 214) (emphasis added).

understanding the incompatibility between modally indifferent sub-strates as an opposition between concepts would have some altogether unfortunate implications.

First of all, Kelsen assumes that no logical relation holds between modally indifferent substrates,[38] while the thesis at hand no doubt con-tradicts such an assumption.

Second, if one were to understand the modally indifferent substrate as a concept, and the incompatibility between modally indifferent sub-strates as the basis of norm conflict, then by the same token, this very same incompatibility would have to be understood as the basis of logical contradiction between statements. Apart from turning out to be non-sense from the point of view of classical truth-functional logic (to which Kelsen explicitly resorts in his interpretation of P), this thesis would once again involve an assimilation of norm conflict and logical contradiction. The difficulty, then, would only be deferred, not resolved.

Third, according to Kelsen, the obligation to forbear from doing x is fully convertible into the proscription to do x.[39] Thus, if one were to grant that between modally indifferent substrates a relation of opposition may hold, one would then also have to grant that such a relation may hold between norms, and that between norms there can, therefore, also obtain a relation of negation.[40] This conclusion, however, is explicitly rejected by Kelsen, who writes that '[w]hat can be negated is always . . . a *judgment*', and the only sense in which one could speak of the 'negation' of a norm is the negation of its validity, that is, the statement according to which a given norm is not valid.[41] (Once again, the idea of an analogy between truth and validity is implicitly at work.)

It is no wonder, then, that Kelsen confines—or 'relegates'—to the space of a footnote and to an ambiguous analogy the suggestion that norm conflicts are to be understood in terms of incompatibility between modally indifferent substrates, and that incompatibility, in turn, is to be understood in terms of opposition between concepts. In the passages quoted above, Kelsen does not explicitly *state* that a norm conflict has to be understood in terms of opposition between concepts, for that would amount to conferring on the modally indifferent substrate the status of a concept and characterizing the relation between a norm that prescribes an act and a norm that proscribes the same act as a relation of negation.

---

[38] See *GTN* ch. 16, at § II (pp. 60–1), ch. 57, at § II (p. 212).

[39] See *GTN* ch. 25, at § I (p. 96).

[40] See Kelsen's definition of norm conflict in *GTN*: 'A conflict of norms obtains when one norm decrees certain behaviour to be obligatory, and the other decrees forbearance from this behaviour to be obligatory.' *GTN* ch. 57, § IV (p. 213).

[41] See *GTN* ch. 23 (at p. 92) (Kelsen's emphasis); see also 'Law and Logic Again' (n.2 above), at 255–6.

Thus, notwithstanding these attempts, Kelsen cannot avoid the conclusions drawn in section II. To be sure, the impossibility of complying
with both conflicting norms is the 'situation created' by their conflict; it
is likewise true, however, that the relation holding between the two
norms may be understood as a conflict only if the impossibility of joint
compliance is indeed the case. The 'incompatibility' of the prescribed
acts, the pivotal element in Kelsen's definition of a norm conflict, cannot
be anything but the logical impossibility, for a given agent and at a given
point in time, of carrying them both out. Singling out a norm conflict and
defining the concept of norm conflict are tasks that both depend on the
idea of a (logical) impossibility inherent in the situation 'created by' the
conflict. It is not surprising, therefore, that in a passage in 'Derogation'
Kelsen simply ends up by equating the two perspectives:

a conflict between two norms occurs if in obeying or applying one norm, the
other one is necessarily or possibly violated.[42]

IV. CONCLUDING REMARKS

Kelsen, then, seems not to have been aware of the fact that the concept
of norm conflict crucially depends on the concept of logical contradiction, and that a logical contradiction between statements is the criterion
by means of which norms can be understood as conflicting. Owing to this
lapse, it is not surprising that in one of the last chapters of *General Theory
of Norms*,[43] when facing the objection that just as classical logic has as its
subject-matter not acts of thought but, rather, their sense-content, so
likewise a hypothetical logic of norms would have as its subject-matter
not the acts of will of which norms are the sense-content but, rather, the
norms themselves as sense-content, Kelsen grants, albeit hesitatingly,
the possibility that P and R are applicable to norms thus understood.

Commentators have been quick to point out that such a concession
is a sign of the weakness of Kelsen's views about the relation between
logic and norms.[44] In fact, Kelsen's concession belies his own claim
that a norm, understood as the sense-content of an act of will, cannot in
any way subsist in the absence of such an act; indeed, the act is a condition for the norm.[45] In light of the aforementioned concession, Kelsen's
claim that P and R are not applicable to norms means no more than that

---

[42] 'Derogation', 269.
[43] *GTN* ch. 58, § XXIII (pp. 250–1).
[44] See Opałek (n.35 above), at 34–5; Gianformaggio (n.7 above), at 98–103.
[45] On Kelsen's thesis to the effect that norms, unlike statements (*Aussagen*), cannot be
taken in abstraction from the acts of will of which they are the sense-content, see 'LL', at
230–1, 240; *GTN* ch. 44, at § I (p. 170). I do not take up the implications of Kelsen's thesis
here; for a general discussion, which also deals with the problem of 'merely thought', or
'fictive', norms, see Celano (n.3 above), at 55–61.

P and *R* are not applicable to the acts of will of which the norms are the sense; this, as Kelsen himself correctly acknowledges,[46] is trivially true also of the acts of thought whose sense-content is statements.

I shall not examine here the consequences of such a restatement of Kelsen's point for the coherence of Kelsen's theory of norms as a whole. For present purposes, it is enough to note that Kelsen, in granting, albeit hesitatingly, that *P* and *R* are applicable to norms as sense-content abstracted from the corresponding acts of will, not only implicitly belies his stated view on the possibility of a logic of norms, but also ends up denying that the question of whether *P* and *R* are applicable to norms (understood, precisely, as sense-content) constitutes a real problem. This question, however, *is* genuinely problematic;[47] and Kelsen's own arguments supporting a negative answer[48] do indeed hit the nail on the head. He starts in full awareness of the problem. His argument, however, is grounded in the assumption that if *P* and *R* were applicable to norms, this would be owing to an analogy between truth and validity.[49] Then, as soon as he faces the possibility that norms may be understood as sense-content (and, thus, in abstraction from their validity), he simply drops the question. This is why *P* and *R* are held, in the end, to be applicable to norms as abstract sense-content in exactly the same way as they are applicable to statements. Kelsen's argument on the inapplicability of *P* and *R* to norms ends, then, a step behind its insightful point of departure.

Why does Kelsen fail to see that contradiction between statements is a condition, in the sense specified thus far, for the possibility of norm conflicts?

The roots of his failure may be traced back to a set of strong background assumptions that make up the core of Kelsen's conception of *Sollen* (and of the 'irreducible dualism' of *Sollen* and *Sein*):

(1) A norm, as the sense-content of an act of will, does not include the description of a possible state of affairs, namely, an 'indicative' element.[50]

(2) A statement of fact asserting that the addressee of a norm carries out an act, namely, the act prescribed by the norm, does not

---

[46] 'Logic relates not to *acts* of thought, but to their sense', 'LL' 241–2 (Kelsen's emphasis).

[47] At least in so far as norms are held to be neither true nor false. For a full discussion of this tenet and its negative implications for the possibility of logical relations between norms, see Celano (n.35 above), at 156–66, 335–63, 704–13.

[48] See § II above.

[49] 'One could speak of a "contradiction" [between imperatives] only in some *analogical* sense. If there is such an analogy, it can only be between the *truth* of a statement and the *validity* of an imperative (or norm)', *GTN* Note 151 (p. 391) (Kelsen's emphasis).

[50] See 'LL', at 229–31; *GTN*, at chs. 51–6 (pp. 194–210).

'correspond' to the norm itself;[51] this is a corollary of the claim that compliance, as *Sein*, is merely a property of actual behaviour, not of the norm itself.[52]

(3) *Sollen* does not 'aim at' *Sein*, and it is not 'directed toward' *Sein* either. From this it follows that to say that something 'ought *to be*' is misleading; properly speaking, the sense-content of an act of prescribing is, simply, that something 'ought'.[53]

These tenets push Kelsen toward arguing not only that a norm conflict is not a logical contradiction and that no analogy holds between the validity of norms and the truth of statements, but also that a norm conflict does not in any sense imply, or depend on, or presuppose, a logical contradiction. It is these tenets that produce the slippage in Kelsen's discussion of the applicability of *P* to norms from the first to the second of the tenets listed in section I, namely, from the insight that a norm conflict is not a logical contradiction to the conclusion that it is something 'wholly different' from a logical contradiction.

These three tenets (and their strongly counter-intuitive consequences) are the main differences between Kelsen's conception of *Sollen* and an intentionalist account of normative discourse. The failure in Kelsen's analysis of norm conflicts, stemming from these tenets, provides a strong reason for rejecting them.[54]

---

[51] See *GTN*, at ch. 56 (pp. 208–10), and Note 138 (at p. 379); see also ch. 16, at § II (pp. 60–1), ch. 51 (at p. 196).

[52] See § II, text at n.20 above, § III, text at n.34 above.

[53] 'The common expression "Something ought to be" is misleading. It creates the impression that "ought" involves an "is". . . . People say that an "ought" aims at an "is". But that, too, is misleading. It is not the "ought" that "aims at" an "is", that is to say, has a certain intention. It is the person commanding that another is to behave in a certain way who, by means of his command, "aims at" the "is" of this behaviour. . . . If expressions to the effect that the "ought" "aims at" something or "is directed" to something refer to the *meaning* of the "ought", then "ought" "aims at" nothing but itself: "ought". As the goal of the positing of norms, the actually *existing* behaviour agreeing with the norm is the effect caused by the mental representation of the norm decreeing certain behaviour to be obligatory, acting as a motive in the norm-addressee. The expression "something ought to be" supports the erroneous assumption that an "ought" is directed to an "is", or that every "ought"-norm, every imperative, contains an "is"-statement. . . .' *GTN* ch. 16, § I (pp. 59–60) (Kelsen's emphasis). For variations on the argument, see *GTN*, at ch. 43 (pp. 168–9), ch. 51 (at p. 196), ch. 2, at Note 17 (p. 286).

[54] The three tenets may also be criticized on other, independent grounds, see Celano (n.3 above), at 83–93, 95–118, 182–6. By an 'intentionalist' account of normative discourse, I mean, very roughly, an account drawing (contrary to Kelsen's concept of *Sollen*, as defined by the three tenets under scrutiny) on the concepts of intention, aim, end, purposive action, and the like. Drawing on G.H. von Wright's work, I have tried to develop such an analysis of normative discourse, including an alternative account of norm conflicts, in Celano (n.3 above), chs. 4–5.

B. On Competing Conceptions of Norms

20

Is and Ought*

GEORG HENRIK VON WRIGHT

1. The two figures of this century who have most deeply influenced its social science are—there can be no doubt—Hans Kelsen and Max Weber. (A comparable influence has been exerted only by Karl Marx but he died long before the century was born.) Both represent a spirit which can, with due caution, be labelled 'positivist' although the philosophic tradition in which they were reared was neo-Kantianism rather than nineteenth-century positivism. Common to both was a passionate urge to 'purify' science of ingredients which they thought extraneous to an uncompromising pursuit of truth. Weber saw the threat to scientific purity in valuations and professed the ideal of a value-free science (*eine wertfreie Wissenschaft*). Kelsen's vision was of a *reine Rechtslehre*, a legal science uninfected by teleological and moralistic argumentation.

The climate of opinion which these two giants represented has changed and is much less characteristic of recent decades than it was of the mid-century years when 'logical positivism' was dominant in philosophy and exerted a strong influence on scientific methodology. Criticism of positivism was for some time a fashion, and if the *Positivismusstreit* no longer appears exciting this is because it has effected a change from which no return seems possible to the positions which were then attacked. But there is also a danger that some important clarity attained by the genius of men like Kelsen and Weber was obscured in the debate and will have to be regained through a new process of 'purification'. My paper is intended as a modest effort in this direction.

2. In a paper from the early 1950s called 'Was ist die Reine Rechtslehre?' ['What is the Pure Theory of Law?'], Kelsen emphasizes two features

---

* *Editors' note*: This paper first appeared in *Man, Law and Modern Forms of Life*, ed. Eugenio Bulygin et al. (Dordrecht: Reidel, 1985), 263–81.

of his 'pure theory'.[1] One is the sharp distinction between fact and norm, the other is the logico-analytical character of a 'scientific' jurisprudence.

'The logical distinction between *Sein* and *Sollen*', he writes, 'and the impossibility of proceeding from the one field to the other by means of a logical inference, is one of the essential positions of the Pure Theory of Law.' And, Kelsen adds, 'the logic that the Pure Theory of Law was the first to discover, so to speak, is the *general logic of norms*, that is: a logic of Ought or of Ought-sentences, the logic of a [form of] cognition directed to norms, and not to natural reality'. This logic of norms he also calls 'the presupposition for a correct theory of law'.

There is something problematic, not to say ironic, about Kelsen's juxtaposition of the two features. For the sharp distinction between Is and Ought is the very thing which makes it doubtful whether there *can be* a 'logic of norms' at all—particularly if, as is the case with Kelsen, the separation of fact and norm goes together with a so-called non-cognitivist conception of norms as directives or prescriptions which cannot be true or false. For a reason which I shall mention presently Kelsen seems to have been unaware then of the difficulties of reconciling with one another the sharp Is–Ought distinction, a non-cognitivist position, and the idea of a logic of the normative.[2] But I shall also argue that a reconciliation is, in fact, possible.

3. The history of the Is–Ought debate is often traced back to a well-known passage in Hume's *Treatise*[3]—and the idea that there is 'an unbridgeable gap' separating fact from value and norm is sometimes also referred to as 'Hume's guillotine'.[4] The attribution of the separation thesis to Hume may not be historically entirely fair.[5] But it was certainly forcefully defended by the neo-Humeans of the logical positivist movement who shared with Hume a phenomenalistic epistemology, the denial of natural necessity, and an emotive theory of morality.

[1] Hans Kelsen, 'Was ist die Reine Rechtslehre?', in *Demokratie und Rechtsstaat. Festgabe zum 60. Geburtstag von Zaccaria Giacometti* [no editor] (Zurich: Polygraphischer Verlag, 1953), 143–62, repr. *WS I* 611–29. Quoted here (in the text) from Ota Weinberger, 'Kelsens These von der Unanwendbarkeit logischer Regeln auf Normen', in *Die Reine Rechtslehre in wissenschaftlicher Diskussion* [no editor] (Vienna: Manz, 1982), 108–21, at 109–10.

[2] Towards the end of his life, however, Kelsen changed his views, moving towards a 'nihilistic' position, reminiscent of that of Hägerström, with regard to the possibility of a 'logic of norms' or 'deontic logic'. See the paper by Weinberger referred to in n.1 above, and see for further details Weinberger's book, *Normentheorie als Grundlage der Jurisprudenz und Ethik. Eine Auseinandersetzung mit Hans Kelsens Theorie der Normen* (Berlin: Duncker & Humblot, 1981).

[3] David Hume, *A Treatise on Human Nature*, bk. III, pt. I, § 1 (at the end).

[4] The title is an invention of Professor Max Black's in his well-known essay 'The Gap between "Is" and "Should" ', first published in *The Philosophical Review*, 73 (1964), 165–81, repr. in Black, *Margins of Precision* (Ithaca: Cornell UP, 1970), 23–40.

[5] See the paper by Alasdair MacIntyre, 'Hume on "Is" and "Ought" ', *The Philosophical Review*, 68 (1959), 451–68.

In this context, a saying by the French mathematician and philosopher of science, Henri Poincaré, is also often quoted to the effect that from premisses in the indicative, one cannot draw conclusions in the imperative mood.[6] Ought-sentences and value-judgements are then regarded as imperatives and exclamations in linguistic disguise, so to speak.[7] A more refined version of this view—associated above all with the name of the English philosopher Richard Hare[8]—says that from (purely) descriptive premisses one cannot draw prescriptive conclusions.

But if norms are imperatives or otherwise 'prescriptive', how can they enter into logical discourse at all? Relations of contradiction and of logical consequence (entailment) seem to presuppose that the related entities have truth-value. But imperatives certainly are neither true nor false, and the same presumably holds good of prescriptions of all kinds. Can even a simple subsumptive inference which a judge draws when he applies a general law to an individual case claim to be logically valid?

Axel Hägerström and some of his followers in Scandinavian jurisprudence had the courage to give a frank 'No' in reply to the question.[9] The logical positivists found this separation of norms from logic difficult to stomach, although they appreciated the problematic nature of any attempt to create a logic of norms. The difficulty is still sometimes referred to as Jørgensen's Dilemma after the Dane Jørgen Jørgensen, who gave a particularly clear expression to the difficulty of reconciling the sharp Is–Ought dichotomy with the aspirations of logicians to penetrate with their instruments also the realm of the normative.[10]

4. After the heyday of positivism in the mid-century years the climate of opinion in philosophy gradually changed.

The success of some logicians in the 1950s in creating a 'deontic logic' which, at least from a purely formal point of view, was easy to integrate into the mainstream of modern logical research, made it doubtful whether Hume's guillotine really constituted an obstacle to 'logicizing' the Ought-side, too, of the Is–Ought dichotomy. It was partly under the influence of these developments that Kelsen in his 1953 paper expressed

[6] Henri Poincaré, *Dernières Pensées* (Paris: Flammarion, 1913), 225.

[7] See Rudolf Carnap, *Philosophy and Logical Syntax* (London: Kegan Paul, Trench, Trubner & Co., 1935), at 23: 'It is easy to see that it is merely a difference of formulation, whether we state a norm or a value-judgment. A norm or rule has an imperative form. . . . [A]ctually a value statement is nothing else than a command in a misleading grammatical form.'

[8] R.M. Hare, *The Language of Morals* (Oxford: Clarendon Press, 1952).

[9] Axel Hägerström, *Till frågan om den objektiva rättens begrepp*, I, in the series *Skrifter utgifna af K. Humanistiska Vetenskaps-Samfundet i Uppsala* (Uppsala, 1917). Included in Hägerström, *Inquiries into the Nature of Law and Morals*, ed. Karl Olivecrona, trans. C.D. Broad (Uppsala: Almqvist & Wiksell, 1953).

[10] Jørgen Jørgensen, 'Imperatives and Logic', *Erkenntnis*, 7 (1937–8), 288–96.

his confidence in *Normenlogik*—although he was a bit too egocentric, I think, in attributing its discovery to the Pure Theory of Law.

However, with further changes in the philosophic climate some began to doubt even the *existence* of the infamous 'guillotine'. Perhaps the Is–Ought gap was just an illusion.

A forceful attack on the received doctrine was made by John Searle, first in a paper 'How to Derive "Ought" from "Is" ' and subsequently, with some modifications, in his very influential work *Speech Acts*.[11] I shall here present Searle's argument in a somewhat 'compressed' form which, nevertheless, should do justice to his main point:

First premiss: *A* promises to do *p*.
Second premiss: By promising to do *p*, *A* has placed himself under an obligation to do *p*.
Conclusion: *A* ought to do *p*.

The performance of actions and the existence of obligations are facts. Searle does not explicitly deny that it also is a fact that *A*, who gave a promise, ought to act accordingly. His point is rather that an Ought-statement has been derived from obviously factual statements. So there *is* a 'bridge' from Is to Ought.

Shortly after Searle's first paper, Max Black presented an even simpler argument against the Is–Ought separation.[12] His reasoning runs as follows:

A and *B* are playing chess. *A* wants to checkmate *B*. The situation is such that unless he makes a certain move he cannot mate his opponent. Therefore he should now make this very move.

Since Searle and Black wrote their papers the Is–Ought debate has been in full swing again—and there is no sign in recent years that it has abated.[13] Opinions are sharply divided. Also, the nature of the issue has become vastly more complicated. That Ought-sentences may be derived from Is-sentences does not necessarily show that normative conclusions are derivable from factual premisses. There is also the pos-

---

[11] John Searle, 'How to Derive "Ought" from "Is" ', *The Philosophical Review*, 73 (1964), 43–58, and Searle, *Speech Acts. An Essay in the Philosophy of Language* (Cambridge: Cambridge UP, 1969). Searle calls the Is–Ought dichotomy a distinction between Fact and Value (*Speech Acts*, 197). He does not explicitly contrast facts with norms, nor descriptions with prescriptions in the context of his discussion. This, however, does not change the issue. It is true that 'ought' sometimes is used as an evaluative term, but to call it evaluative in the example which Searle discusses, which is concerned with obligations arising from promises, seems to me not very natural.

[12] In the paper referred to in n.4 above.

[13] As witnessed, for example, by the collections *The Is–Ought Question. A Collection of Papers on the Central Problem in Moral Philosophy*, ed. W.D. Hudson (London: Basingstoke, 1979), and *Ethics. Foundations, Problems, and Applications*. Proceedings of the Fifth International Wittgenstein Symposium, ed. Edgar Morscher and Rudolf Stranzinger (Vienna: Hölder-Pichler-Tempsky, 1981).

sibility to be considered that Ought-sentences, or *some* such sentences, actually state facts—and the possibility that Is-sentences sometimes express norms. We have to consider here, not only the syntactical form of some sentences, but also the semantics of their interpretation.

5. As already hinted at (in § 3 above), the question of whether the alleged gap between Is and Ought can be bridged or not is crucially related to the question of whether norms can be true or false. One may distinguish two positions on this last question:

The first position I shall call cognitivist (or descriptivist). According to it, some norms are true, such that in their case one can truthfully say that something or other ought to or may be. One can, moreover, distinguish two forms of this position according to whether the truths are held to be contingent empirical facts to be ascertained through observation of the social reality or whether they are thought of as a kind of necessity to be grasped through reflection on the nature of law and morality. I shall call the two positions naturalist and non-naturalist cognitivism (descriptivism), respectively.

Various systems of normative ethics and ideas about so-called 'natural law' exemplify non-naturalist cognitivism. The norms of natural law may then be regarded as a measure whereby positive law, the law of the state, is judged adequate or inadequate in relation to a universally valid standard of justice. Thus Cicero in a well-known passage in his *Republic* (Bk. III, Ch. 32) wrote:

There is a true law . . . that conforms to nature; this law directs men to the good by its commands, and deters them from evil by its prohibitions, . . . It is impermissible to oppose it by other laws, or to derogate its precepts . . . It cannot be different in Rome or in Athens, and it will not be in the future different from what it is today; but one and the same law, eternal and immutable, will impose itself upon all peoples forever.

One may smile at the lack of a sense of 'cultural relativity' revealed in Cicero's words. The philosophic difficulties encountered by a natural law theory with such universalistic claims as Cicero's are all too obvious. But it would be quite wrong to think of the idea itself as obsolete, belonging only to the past. Thus an influential work on political theory from recent years, Robert Nozick's *Anarchy, State and Utopia*, opens with the statement: 'Individuals have rights, and there are things no person or group of persons may do to them (without violating their rights).'[14] The author does not mean rights actually conferred on people by (positive) legislation, but rights, presumably, 'eternal and immutable', which men have by virtue of being individuals and which set a standard for what the state and its officials may 'legitimately' do.

[14] Robert Nozick, *Anarchy, State and Utopia* (New York: Basic Books, 1974).

I think myself the tendency pernicious to try to remove the 'ought' and 'may' of norms from the realm of contingent facts of the world to a 'non-natural' realm of timeless truths. A removal of the norms from the world of facts is also a removal of them from the realm of truth.

The second position on our question I shall call non-cognitivism or prescriptivism. According to it, norms do not describe or state anything which is true or false, but prescribe what ought to or may be (or be done). This is a position usually taken by philosophers who would label themselves 'positivists'. But it is certainly not confined to philosophers of that particular denomination.

The term 'prescriptivism' suggests that norms are issued by some norm-*authority* as I shall call it and directed to some agents or groups of people, the norm-*subjects*. The basic pattern is that of a master imposing duties and giving permissions to his servants. But the master can also be a legislature, composed of members selected according to some rules (norms), and enacting laws (norms) in accordance with regulations (norms) for its procedures. Or the authority can be the group itself which, in the course of generations, has evolved customs and other precepts for the conduct of its members. He can also be a fictitious figure of a remote past, like Lycurgus, or a fictitious supernatural authority, like the Yahveh who handed to Moses the tablets on Mount Sinai.

6. It is an essential feature of norms that they should be expressible in language, in what I propose to call norm-formulations. Some norms may never be expressed and yet 'exist', for example in the form of 'instinctively' observed customs or taboos. And when formulated they need not be written.

There are standard forms of norm-formulation using deontic words such as 'ought', 'should', 'must(-not)', 'may'. But, in addition, forms of sentence whose primary use is for describing, and not for prescribing, are quite frequently used as norm-formulations. I have seen it stated that some legal codes have been deliberately written in the indicative mood, for example, using sentences of the type: 'Whoever does so-and-so will be sentenced to such-and-such.' This may be a pretty accurate description of what actually happens in a society, and a basis for reliable predictions. But as a fragment of a legal text, that is, as a norm-formulation, the form of words is neither descriptive nor predictive, but prescriptive. It says what ought to happen consequent upon such-and-such facts.

If norms, by definition, are to the effect that certain things ought to or may be, then all norms are also expressible in deontic language. And I think one may say that, from the point of view of understanding their logic, it is preferable that norms be thus expressed.

It is a great merit of the Swedish philosopher Ingemar Hedenius to have clearly noted and exploited an ambiguity which is characteristic of deontic sentences.[15] I shall refer to it as their descriptive and prescriptive interpretation; Hedenius himself called legal sentences in the descriptive interpretation 'spurious', and in the prescriptive interpretation 'genuine'. A legal sentence 'it ought to be the case that so-and-so' can be read as a norm or prescription, say, for the reader's own conduct: he is urged to behave in a certain way. But the same sentence can also be read as a statement that there is (exists) a norm to this effect. That a certain norm exists or does not exist is a fact. It may therefore be uncontroversially true that, according to, say, Finnish law such-and-such ought to be the case or be done.

To notice the ambiguity inherent in deontic sentences is, of course, not to 'bridge the gap' between Is and Ought. But it can be said to throw light on the distinction. In a certain sense the Is–Ought distinction *is* the difference between description and prescription, the difference which comes to light in the descriptive and the prescriptive use of a peculiar type of linguistic discourse, namely deontic sentences.

7. We can now give to the traditional Is–Ought problem a slightly new formulation: Can prescriptions follow logically from descriptions? We can supplement this with the converse question: Can descriptions follow logically from prescriptions? And we can add a third question: Can prescriptions follow from other prescriptions?

I think that the answer to all three questions is a firm 'No'. The reason is simple: Logical consequence is a truth-preserving relationship. If from *A* follows logically *B* then either *A* is false or *A* and *B* are both true. Since prescriptions are neither true nor false they can figure neither as premisses nor as conclusions in logically valid inferences. It is a consequence of this that no combination (conjunction) of descriptions and prescriptions can perform in these roles either.

These statements may sound dogmatic. They are certainly much more radical than the views usually held by authors on legal theory or argumentation—even by writers who take an otherwise guarded attitude to the problem of bridging the gap between Is and Ought. I must therefore try to argue in defence of my position.

Before considering the Is–Ought case I shall say something about what may be termed the Ought–Is and the Ought–Ought cases.

The former is the question, already raised, of whether a description can follow logically from a prescription. Some writers think this possible. They often use as a supporting example a famous principle associated with the name of Kant, namely, the principle that Ought entails or

15 See Ingemar Hedenius, *Om rätt och moral* (Stockholm: Tidens förlag, 1941), at 65–6.

implies Can. That something or other can be the case or can be done may be regarded as a factual statement. It could rightly be said that a law-giver who enjoined the impossible would behave irrationally, since his will could not be fulfilled. We may therefore make it a maxim of rational or reasonable law-giving that only possible things (actions) be subject to norm. But this maxim is itself a norm, or something norm-like, and the 'inference', 'you ought, so therefore you can', is not a logical entailment but an affirmation of the reasonableness of the command.

Of greater importance to our theme is the question of whether there can exist logical relations such as consequence and contradiction between prescriptions, that is, prescriptively interpreted norm-formulations. This question takes us to the topic of deontic logic or the logic of norms.

Deontic logic as a systematic study came into existence some thirty years ago. It can be said without exaggeration not only that it has acquired an established status as a branch of (modern) logic, but also that it has aroused unusual interest outside the circle of logicians, among social scientists and legal and moral philosophers.

It is, I hope, not too self-centered to tell here the following story. When Kelsen in 1952 made his first and only visit to Finland he was very excited about the prospects which deontic logic seemed to open for vindicating some basic tenets in his own 'pure' theory of law. In particular, he looked for support in logic for his idea that a legal order is of necessity closed, that is, that there are no 'gaps' in the law, and for the idea that a legal order must be free from 'contradictions'.

I do not remember exactly how I answered him, but presumably my reply was encouraging. I certainly believed myself then that, for example, 'it ought to be the case that p and it ought to be the case that not p' was a *logical* contradiction. And this in spite of the fact that I—and Kelsen, too—held norms to be neither true nor false. It seemed to me then that, with the invention of deontic logic, logic had somehow transcended the borders of truth and falsehood, and subjected a wider realm of conceptual entities to its laws.

But this opinion was premature—and, I now think, false.

We already noted that deontic sentences are characteristically ambiguous. They can be used for expressing norms, that is, prescribing modes of conduct. Or they can be used for describing or stating what norms or prescriptions there are. Under the second use deontic sentences are said to express norm-propositions.

The formulas of deontic logic are schematic representations of deontic sentences. Noting the ambiguity one can ask: Is deontic logic a logic of (genuine) norms, or of norm-propositions? If the second, there is no question of truth-values being transcended. For norm-propositions are true or false as the case may be.

I find it surprising that this problem has been but little discussed among logicians. (An exception are the writings of Carlos E. Alchourrón and Eugenio Bulygin.[16]) Authors generally regard it as clear what deontic logic is about and assume that standard logical techniques can be used for handling its formulas. My own view was for a long time that deontic logic is concerned with norm-propositions, although it also embodied some conceptual elements relating to norms proper.

If this opinion were correct it would indeed be the case, for example, that two norms could not coexist if the one enjoined something which the other norm prohibited. By suitably molding the notion of existence when applied to norms this could be made true by definition. But it would be in flagrant conflict with the fact that contradictory norms actually appear in legal orders[17]—not only in the sense that they are duly enacted by the same legislature but also in the sense that they are both applied—sometimes the one, sometimes the other—by the judiciary when deciding legal cases. Do they not then coexist? I think it would be absurd to deny that they do. But then the contradiction is not between norm-propositions. And if norms have no truth-value, then contradiction, it seems, cannot be between the norms either. So where *is* the contradiction? Is there a *logical* contradiction at all?

The last two questions are in fact quite easy to answer. There is a straightforward logical contradiction between the *contents* of the two norms. This is so because it is logically impossible for one and the same agent both to do and to refrain from doing the same thing on the same occasion. And this contradiction between the norm-contents is obviously the reason why we call the norms themselves (and the correlated norm-propositions) contradictory, although this is really a misnomer.

Calling norms contradictory is a signal that something is 'unsatisfactory' about them. In order to see what it is we must, I think, reflect on the purpose of norms and of norm-giving activity such as legislation.

The one who issues an order or prohibition—be it an individual commander or a legislative assembly—can normally be said to *want* or to '*will*' that things be as prescribed. And the one who gives permission is prepared, if not to encourage, so at least to *tolerate* that the permission-holders avail themselves of the permission. I think this is true and important—notwithstanding difficulties which in other respects may be encountered by a so-called 'will theory' of norms.

In order to enforce his will, the law-giver normally also prescribes various measures, such as punishment and fines, to be taken against those

---

[16] Carlos E. Alchourrón, 'Logic of Norms and Logic of Normative Propositions', *Logique et Analyse*, 12 (1969), 242–68; Carlos E. Alchourrón and Eugenio Bulygin, *Normative Systems* (Vienna and New York: Springer, 1971).

[17] See ibid., at 63–4.

who do not comply with his (primary) prescriptions. As has often been said, a legal order is a coercive order. Use of coercion and force are of its essence—even if some valid norms may be (legally) broken with impunity.

If a law-giver issued norms with mutually contradictory contents he would be acting *irrationally* in the sense that he wanted something to be the case which is logically impossible. *Ordering* something and its contradictory is possible, but having both orders *satisfied* is impossible. Similarly, if a law-giver permitted something of which—for reasons of logic—nobody could ever avail himself, the 'permission' could rightly be labelled irrational, silly, no permission at all.

Generally speaking: a legal order and, similarly, a coherent code or system of norms may be said to envisage what I propose to call an *ideal* state of things when no obligation is ever neglected and everything permitted is sometimes the case. If this ideal state is not logically possible, that is, *could not* be factual, the totality of norms and the legislating activity which has generated it do not conform to the standards of rational willing. Deviations from these standards sometimes occur—and when they are discovered steps are usually taken to eliminate them by 'improved' legislation.

I think this characterization is substantially correct—ignoring here some complications connected with the *unity* and possible *hierarchical* structure of normative codes. Any such code may be said to contain an implicit description of a state of affairs, namely the ideal state envisaged by the law-giver. This description is almost certainly *false* in the sense that it does not agree completely with reality, the factual state of things. But unless it *could be true* it cannot be *rationally willed* by the law-giver either. In order to be rational to entertain, the ideal must be a picture of a *possible world* which is, to use a happy phrase coined by Jaakko Hintikka, *deontically perfect*.[18]

Anything which is possible at all is logically possible, but not everything which is logically possible is also physically possible, that is, possible according to the laws of nature. And not everything physically possible is also humanly possible, that is, possible to achieve through human action. In view of the fact that (most) norms are rules of action it seems reasonable to demand that the ideal world envisaged by a system of norms should be not only logically but also humanly possible to realize, but such stronger demands we need not consider here.

---

[18] Jaakko Hintikka, 'Deontic Logic and its Philosophical Morals', in Hintikka, *Models for Modalities* (Dordrecht: Reidel, 1969), 184–214, and Hintikka, 'Some Main Problems in Deontic Logic', in *Deontic Logic: Introductory and Systematic Readings*, ed. Risto Hilpinen (Dordrecht: Reidel, 1971) 59–104.

Deontic logic, to put it in a nutshell, is the study of logical relations in deontically perfect worlds. The fact that norms are neither true nor false constitutes no obstacle to this study. Deontic logic is not concerned with logical relations between prescriptions (norms) but with logical relations between the ideal states the descriptions of which are implicit in norms.

I think it is a good characterization of the activity of the discipline called *legal dogmatics* to say that its task is to expound and make clear the exact nature of the ideal state of affairs which the law envisages. It clarifies the content of the law. Sometimes it is clear from the norm-formulations what this content is. But sometimes it is not clear, and the activity of the legal dogmatist has to assume a hermeneutic or interpretative character. He makes a proposal or recommendation about how the law should be understood. The proposed content is stated in true or false propositions—but the proposal itself cannot be assessed as true or false. It can, however, be justified by various means of legal argumentation, and it may be assessed as reasonable or not according to a variety of standards which need not, incidentally, mutually agree.

8. From the platform which we have now reached, new vistas open on the Is–Ought question.

First, I think we can demolish the myth of a separate Realm of the Normative—*ein Reich des Sollens* in which Oughts and Mays exist in isolation from the actual world. The myth demolished, what remains of the 'realm' is a description of an alternative, 'ideal' world constituted by the norm-contents of a given normative code or order. This description can, point by point, be compared with reality and will then normally be found to be partly true, partly false of our real world. Calling the description false does not mean that it describes what is sometimes called a 'false ideal'. It means that the actual world is not perfect, the ideal not realized.

The function of norms, one could say, is to urge people to realize the ideal, to make them act in such a way that the description of the real approximates the description of the ideal. In an important sense we could say that the purpose of norms is to 'bridge the gap' between Is and Ought, although *not* in the sense of establishing a deductive bond of entailment between the two. Such a bond is out of the question, cannot possibly exist—for the simple reason that norms are prescriptions, and relations of entailment can exist only between descriptions or, if you wish, between propositions expressed by descriptive sentences.

I am presumptuous enough to think that what has been said contains, *in nuce*, a solution to the much debated Is–Ought problem. It is a solution which both preserves the underivability of the ideal from the real *and* accords to the existence of norms the same robust reality as other (social) facts.

This said, there still remains a formidable task before us. It is to examine those arguments which have recently been brought forward to show that it *is* sometimes possible to derive an Ought from premisses which look undoubtedly factual.

9. Let us first consider Searle's argument. By performing a certain action which constitutes a promise, a man commits himself to a further action, namely, to fulfilling his promise. The statement that he gave the promise is a statement of a fact. From it follows logically, it seems, that now he ought to do a certain thing. Is this not deducing a norm from a fact?

It certainly is not—but to see this clearly is not all that easy.

There is a norm of promise-keeping. It goes as follows: It ought to be the case that, if someone promises to do something, he also does this thing. Or, which says the same: It must not be the case (that is, is forbidden) that someone gives a promise without fulfilling it. Now A promises to do *p*. It follows that he then ought to do *p*.

Since the conclusion was drawn from the factual statement that *A* gave a promise in conjunction with the norm of promise-keeping, one may feel inclined to say as follows: Searle has not shown that an Ought may be inferred from (just) an Is, but that it can be inferred from an Is in combination with an(other) Ought. So Searle is not entirely right, only half-right.

But this is to concede too much. First, one may doubt whether one premiss was normative. Was it not rather the norm-proposition to the effect that *there is* a norm of promise-keeping? If so, both premisses were factual. Secondly, it is not clear either whether the conclusion is normative. If it too were factual, Searle's argument would have no bearing at all on the Is–Ought issue, that is, on the question of whether *normative* conclusions can follow from (purely) *factual* premisses. It would only show that sometimes a factual statement to the effect that something ought to be (done) follows logically from some other factual statements one or several of which are to the effect that certain obligations under norms exist.[19] And that such entailments are possible nobody could ever seriously have doubted.

However, Searle's argument *is* much more interesting than this. We can leave unanswered the question of whether one of its premisses is a norm or a norm-proposition. We focus attention on the conclusion that *A* ought to do *p*. Of it I shall say that it is neither a norm—in the sense in which the rule of promising is a norm or the laws of the state are norms—nor a norm-proposition. So what is it then?

---

[19] It is perhaps revealing that Searle in one place (*Speech Acts*, n.11 above, at 182) should say that the Ought in the conclusion of his argument 'is relative to the *existence* of the obligation' (my emphasis).

We are here confronted, I maintain, with another 'ought'—equally common as the deontic or normative ought of moral or legal norms. I shall call it a *technical* Ought. When in this 'technical' sense it is said of something that it ought to be or to be done, this is an elliptical statement the full meaning of which is that *unless* this thing is (done), something else will (also) fail to be the case. For example: If I have given a promise, I ought to (must, have to) fulfil it *in order to* satisfy the obligation constituted by the norm which prohibits breach of the promise given.

The technical Ought expresses a requirement, a practical necessity, and it is also often—and perhaps better—rendered by the word *must*. The thing for which something is required can be called, quite generally, an *end*, and the thing required, a *means*. The formulation in language of the means-end relationship can also be called a *technical norm*; it is closely related to that which Kant called a 'hypothetical imperative'.

The technical Ought must not be confused with the Ought of genuine norms. There is a strong tendency to do so. It is nourished by the use of the same word 'ought' (or 'must') in both cases. It would be pedantic and contrary to sound linguistic practice to try to reserve the word 'ought' for the obligation imposed by norms and 'must' for the practical necessities stated in hypothetical imperatives. The fact is that both 'oughts' are intimately connected. The 'ought' of norms engenders 'oughts' of practical necessity—as witness Searle's example. And the 'ought' of a hypothetical imperative very often engenders 'oughts' of a normative character: when we want to make true that for which certain actions are practical requirements we urge people to perform those actions by telling them that they ought to be done. This last is norm-giving activity giving rise to genuine norms (commands, orders).

We can now see what is wrong with Searle's purported argument to show that one can deduce an Ought from an Is. From the fact that there exists an institution of promising, that is, a norm to the effect that promises given ought to be kept, and the fact that a person has given a promise, it follows logically that he ought to do a certain thing. That he ought to do this is then an elliptical formulation, short for the statement that unless he does it he will not satisfy his obligation. His obligation, however, is not to do the thing in question *simpliciter*; his obligation, that which he, in the normative sense, ought to do, is either not to promise or, once he has promised, to keep his word. By having promised he has created for himself a practical necessity of doing the thing promised in order to fulfil his obligation. This is true, a fact, not a norm. But *ought* he not then to keep his promise—in the normative sense of 'ought'? If he hesitates to do the thing he promised, someone else may urge him on, saying 'promises ought to be kept'. This is the prescriptive use of language. Or the promisee, who is interested in getting for himself the thing promised but perhaps does not care much about moral duties, may say 'you ought to do what you promised me'. This too is prescriptive activity. Such activity may occur after a promise has been given. But whether it does or not is contingent. At no stage is there anything which could rightly be called the deduction or derivation of an Ought from an Is, that is, of a norm from some facts.

10. We can now also deal with Black's example of the chess-player who is anxious to mate his opponent and will not (cannot) do this unless he makes a certain move. Does it 'follow logically' that he ought to make this move then? Black prefers to say 'should' rather than 'ought to' but admits that the difference between the two deontic verbs is immaterial here.[20] He, furthermore, does not say that the should-sentence which is the conclusion of the argument is prescriptive (nor that it is normative). But he says that it has a 'distinctively performative aspect'[21] and that it has the practical function of *advising* ('prodding') the player.[22] One can grant the correctness of these observations about the role of the should-sentence. They do not substantially affect the issue. But we must disagree with Black on the question of whether some non-factual conclusion here follows from factual premises. Advice does not 'automatically' follow from the facts of the case—as a propositional conclusion would do, even if there were nobody to 'draw' it. Advice requires an advisor and an advisee, and whether any advice is forthcoming or not in this case depends upon a number of facts other than those mentioned in the premises of Black's inference schema. What follows logically, however, is that unless player *A* makes a certain move he will forfeit his objective (in the game against *B*). This is a technical norm which can be expressed elliptically in the sentence '*A* should make move *M* now'. Also other things follow logically in the sense that they are true if the premises are true—for example, that if *C* is to give honest (correct) advice to *A* on how *A* shall mate *B*, he must advise *A* to make move *M* now. And this he can do by saying to *A* 'you should now make move *M*'. But whether *C* actually gives this advice or not depends on circumstances other than the facts that *A* wants to checkmate *B* and that the one and only way in which *A* can achieve this is by making move *M*.

　　Also in the context of chess-playing genuine *norm*-giving may occur. The captain of the chess team may tell one of the members never to make a certain move in such-and-such a situation. This is an order (a norm)— and there may even be some sanction attached to it. But the reason for giving the order may be the captain's firm conviction that if the member in question does not observe this norm the team is in for defeat. Here a technical Ought can be said to 'back' or to justify a deontic Ought. This is

[20] Black (n.4 above), 169, repr. 27.　　[21] Black (n.4 above), 171, repr. 29.
[22] Black (n.4 above), 173, repr. 31.

a common type of situation. It is also prominent in legislation. Laws are usually enacted with a view to some end or purpose which the legislator considers important. The purpose may be outlined in a preamble stating the motivation for the law. The purpose is often debated publicly. Do, for example, very strict regulations about speed limits for vehicles promote safety on the roads? If not, why issue them? Drivers tend not to observe them very strictly and this again may encourage disregard for regulations generally, including those which obviously serve important purposes. These are familiar arguments.

The question might be raised: Is it theoretically conceivable that all laws of the state could be given a backing in technical norms? So that every Ought of a legal norm could be, as it were, translated into the Ought of a technical norm which says that *unless* certain things are the case (citizens and officials observe certain conduct) the law-givers' aims will be forfeited?

To the best of my knowledge no law-code is written in the form of technical norms. Maybe a code could, 'in principle', be thus written. This would not show, however, that the normative 'Ought' is reducible to the 'Is' of technical 'Oughts'. For the law-code would not be 'meant' to be read as a description of what is required if certain aims are to be attained; it would be 'meant' to urge 'all those concerned' to live up to the ideal. Its 'meaning' qua *law* would be prescriptive, not descriptive.

11. I shall try to summarize my position on the Is–Ought issue.

Norms pronounce certain things (actions or states) to be obligatory, permitted, or forbidden. Such pronouncements are neither true nor false. Neither between norms mutually nor between norms and facts can there exist logical relations, for example, relations of contradiction or entailment. In this sense Is and Ought are separated by an 'unbridgeable gap'.

Norms prescribe something and do not describe anything. But the content of norms, that is, *that which* norms pronounce obligatory, permitted, or forbidden, may be said to describe an ideal world. Between the constituent parts of it logical relations can obtain. The formal study of such relations is the subject-matter of deontic logic, also called, somewhat misleadingly, the 'logic of norms'.

Given a norm, one may consider what has to or may be done in order to satisfy it. And the result of such considerations will be that unless such-and-such is done the norm is not satisfied. So therefore, if the norm is to be satisfied such-and-such ought to be done. This is a different kind of Ought from the one enunciated in the norm. It is what I have called a 'technical' Ought stating a fact which is *internal* to the assumed existence of a 'normative' Ought. The technical Ought, one could say, is an Is—and nothing normative 'follows' from it, although something normative may be presupposed in it.

12. The term 'legal positivism' embraces a variety of positions among which there is a family resemblance.[23]

A common feature of many members of the family is the idea of a sharp separation of Is and Ought. Another is the non-cognitivist view that norms are prescriptions and therefore neither true nor false. As a third we may count the view that norms are 'posited', that is, have come to exist and often also passed out of existence in the course of the history of societies—sometimes as a consequence of acts of legislation, sometimes as commandments of a trusted authority or leader, sometimes a result of gradually formed societal habits, customs, and traditions, to mention only a few of the sources of origin of norms.

At least in the above three respects I should myself wish to defend a 'positivist' position in the philosophy of norms, legal or moral. Some main arguments for this position I hope I have succeeded in presenting in this paper.

The impossibility of deriving an Ought from an Is is a *consequence* of the non-cognitivist view of norms. There is also another view which I mentioned and called non-naturalist cognitivism (in § 5 above). On this view, too, there is no derivation of norms from facts. But norms may be, in their own right so to say, true or false. We must still say something about this.

The law of the state says that we ought this and that. But ought we, without exception, to obey the law? The same question can be raised about morals: Ought we to be moral? And if so, why?

Such questions must be taken seriously. They concern the topic called civil disobedience and also, though less directly, human rights.

The person who says he ought not to do what the law commands usually claims to have a *right* to dissent. He would perhaps call it a moral right which overrides his legal duty. Or he may appeal to a principle of so-called natural law which the law of the state is thought to violate.

What is the logical nature of such a claim? Is it a truth-claim? So that the claimant could say that *it is true that* he ought not to obey the law, that is, true that he is free, permitted, has a right to disobey.

To construe the claim as a truth-claim would, in my opinion, be a serious mistake. The foundation of the claim is not truth but something which I propose to call *assent*.

A person who obeys the law may do so unreflectingly, just 'because it is the law'. Most conduct in conformity with law is, I presume, of this kind. Sometimes one obeys for reasons of expedience, thinking perhaps that being caught and punished for disobedience is a risk one better not

---

[23] See Aulis Aarnio, 'The Form and Content of Law. Aspects of Legal Positivism', *Archivum Iuridicum Cracoviense*, 13 (1980), 17–35, repr. in Aarnio, *Philosophical Perspectives in Jurisprudence*, in the series *Acta Philosophica Fennica*, vol. 36 (Helsinki, 1983), 76–93.

take. Sometimes, finally, one obeys thinking it *right* to do so—either because one considers the thing decreed right as such, or because one considers it right to obey the law of the state as such. Then one assents to the legal Ought.

One can refuse assent and still obey—for example, for reasons of expedience. Or one can refuse assent and disobey. In both cases one would say that one *ought* not to obey.

To assent to a norm is not to affirm a truth—and to dissent is not a denial (of truth). To assent (dissent) is more like an act of legislation or norm-giving itself. By assenting to the norm given him by some external norm-authority, the agent gives the same law unto himself so to speak—transforms it from heteronomous to autonomous. In this same sense of 'assent' a subject may also create norms for his own conduct. Assenting, one could also say, is prescriptive and not descriptive (mental) activity.

In assenting or dissenting a subject evinces his moral attitude to a norm, his conception of what is right and what is not. When legal matters are concerned what is right is said to conform to an ideal of *justice*.

Attitudes of assent to norms are also reflected in legislation and in the interpretation of law by jurists and lawyers. From the legislator's point of view it is *expedient* that the citizens should assent to the laws. The less assent, the more civil disobedience and the more complaints about injustice. This may even become a threat to the stability of the legal order. Therefore legislation usually tries to adjust to prevailing conceptions of what are the 'demands' of justice.

Such demands express the moral consciousness of a society. This consciousness is not uniform. It varies from one individual to another and it changes in the course of history. The prime movers of change are usually some outstanding individuals such as the founders and reformers of a religion, moral philosophers, or experienced and prestigious judges. These individuals may be said to 'mold' the notions of justice and morality which come to prevail in a society. Their role as 'molders' places them 'ahead of developments'—and sometimes in tragic conflict with the moral consciousness of the majority of their contemporaries.

Morality can be said to 'transcend' legality in the sense that it censures laws and the decisions of courts. For this reason morality can never be fully embodied in the kind of coercive order which the laws of the state constitute. In order to function as a standard whereby the rightness of law is judged, moral principles cannot be turned into positive law. If they were, this would be the end of morality.

Legal positivism is right when it maintains that law and morals are essentially different things and when it combats doctrines of 'natural law' which blur this distinction. But legal positivism is wrong if, in the name of the 'purity' of law, it insists on excluding considerations of a

moral nature from legislation, legal decision-making, and the hermeneutic aspects of legal dogmatics.

21

The Expressive Conception of Norms*

CARLOS E. ALCHOURRÓN AND EUGENIO BULYGIN**

I. TWO CONCEPTIONS OF NORMS

Questions concerning the ontological status and the logical properties of norms have been much debated in recent years, not only by legal and moral philosophers but also by a steadily increasing number of a 'deontic' logicians. In spite of this a number of very basic problems have apparently not been solved, and persist.

One such issue is the problem of the possibility of a logic of norms. Some authors think that there are logical relations between norms, and so favour the development of a specific logic of norms (sometimes called 'deontic logic', though 'normative logic' would perhaps be a more appropriate name).[1] Other writers deny the very possibility of such a logic because in their view there are no logical relations between norms. According to them deontic logic can only assume the form of a logic of normative propositions, that is, (true or false) propositions about (the existence of) norms.[2]

Another fundamental problem, or perhaps another aspect of the same problem on which there is no consensus, is the relation of norms to truth: whereas some writers readily ascribe truth-values to norms,[3] others emphatically deny that norms could conceivably be true or false. This issue is related to the first one, but not in a very clear way. Those authors

* *Editors' note*: This paper first appeared in *New Studies in Deontic Logic*, ed. Risto Hilpinen (Dordrecht: Reidel, 1981), 95–124. In consultation with Eugenio Bulygin, the authors' bibliography has been incorporated into the footnotes of the present printing.

** The authors express gratitude to David Makinson for his helpful remarks and corrections both of style and content.

[1] See Kalinowski's discussion of these terms in Georges Kalinowski, *Lógica de las normas y lógica deóntica* (Valencia, Venezuela: Universidad de Carabobo, 1978, repr. Mexico City: Distribuciones Fontamara, 1993).

[2] See Dagfinn Føllesdal and Risto Hilpinen, 'Deontic Logic: An Introduction', in *Deontic Logic: Introductory and Systematic Readings*, ed. Risto Hilpinen (Dordrecht: Reidel, 1971), 1–35.

[3] See, *inter alia*, Georges Kalinowski, *Le problème de la vérité en morale et en droit* (Lyon: Emmanuel Vitte, 1967), and Jürgen Rödig, *Schriften zur juristischen Logik* (Berlin and Heidelberg: Springer, 1980).

who believe that norms have truth-values will certainly accept the possibility of a logic of norms, but the converse does not hold: *accepting* that there are logical relations among norms does not commit one to the view that norms have truth-values.[4]

A third and apparently unrelated issue is the question concerning permissive norms. A great number of philosophers (especially philosophers of law) deny that there are permissive norms, admitting only one type of norm (mandatory norms, imperatives, commands). Logicians and lawyers—though probably for different reasons—are less inclined to defend a monistic conception, and see no obstacle that would prevent them from speaking of permissive norms (independently of the question of whether they are definable in terms of obligations or not).

To a large extent these discrepancies are due to the fact that authors often start from two quite different and incompatible conceptions regarding the nature of norms, which are seldom—if ever—made explicit. It may be illuminating to characterize briefly these conceptions in order to see why different writers maintain conflicting and even diametrically opposed views on some very basic features of norms. These two conceptions will be called the *hyletic* and the *expressive* conception of norms.

For the *hyletic conception*, norms are proposition-like entities, that is, meanings of certain expressions, called normative sentences. A normative sentence is the linguistic expression of a norm, and a norm is said to be the meaning of a normative sentence in much the same way in which a proposition is regarded as the meaning (sense) of a descriptive sentence. But normative sentences, unlike descriptive sentences, have *prescriptive meaning*: that something ought, ought not, or may be the case (or be done).

In this conception, norms are not language-dependent; they can only be expressed by linguistic means,[5] but their existence is independent of any linguistic expression. There are norms that have not yet been formulated in any language and that perhaps will never be formulated. A norm, on this view, is an abstract, purely conceptual entity.

But norms are not independent of descriptive propositions; they are the result of an operation on such propositions. So in a norm, say '*Op*', we find two components: a descriptive proposition p and a normative operator O, both of them belonging to the conceptual import of the norm. In this sense normative operators are similar to modal alethic

[4] See generally von Wright, *NA*; Ota Weinberger, 'Normenlogik und logische Bereiche', in *Deontische Logik und Semantik*, ed. Amedeo G. Conte et al. (Wiesbaden: Athenaion, 1977), 176–212.

[5] The term 'language' is to be understood in a wide sense; a gesture, a look, a traffic light are in this sense linguistic expressions.

operators, and a norm is a proposition in much the same sense in which a modal proposition like *Np* is said to be a proposition.

Norms must be distinguished from *normative propositions*, that is, descriptive propositions stating that *p* is obligatory (forbidden or permitted) according to some unspecified norm or set of norms. Normative propositions—which can be regarded as propositions about sets (systems) of norms—also contain normative terms like 'obligatory', 'prohibited', and so on, but these have a purely descriptive meaning.[6] In what follows the symbols 'O' and 'P' will be used to refer to these descriptive deontic operators.

For the *expressive conception*, norms are the result of the *prescriptive use* of language. A sentence expressing the same proposition can be used on different occasions to do different things: it can be asserted, questioned, commanded, conjectured, and so on. The result of the performance of these actions will be a statement, a question, a command, or a conjecture. It is only on the pragmatic level of the use of language where the difference between statements, questions, commands, and the like arises; there is no such difference on a semantic level. For instance, the proposition expressed by the sentence 'Peter puts the book on the table' can be used to make an assertion (Peter puts the book on the table.), to ask a question (Does Peter put the book on the table?), or to give a command (Peter, put the book on the table!).

The signs '⊢' and '!' will be used to indicate the kind of linguistic act (assertion or command) performed by an (unspecified) speaker. These signs are mere *indicators* of what the speaker does when uttering certain words; they do not contribute to the meaning (that is, the conceptual content) of the words uttered. They show what the speaker is doing, but in doing it he does not say what he is doing; so they are not part of what he says, or what his words mean. The expression '⊢*p*' indicates that *p* is asserted, and '!*p*' indicates that *p* is commanded, whereas '*Op*' expresses a proposition that *p* ought be (done). So '*Op*' is the symbol for a norm in the hyletic conception, whereas '!*p*' symbolizes a norm in the expressive conception.

It is important to stress the fact that the expressions '!*p*' and '⊢*p*' do not describe the fact that *p* has been commanded or asserted. The sentences '*A* asserts that *p*' and '*A* commands that *p*' certainly express propositions that describe certain speech acts, but they do not say what is done with them: they can in turn be asserted, questioned, commanded, and so on. But '!*p*' and '⊢*p*' do not express any proposition at all, although they are constructed with the help of the proposition *p*; so they have no truth-value and cannot be negated or combined by means of propositional

⁶ See Carlos E. Alchourrón and Eugenio Bulygin, 'Von Wright on Deontic Logic and the Philosophy of Law', in *The Philosophy of Georg Henrik von Wright*, ed. Paul A. Schilpp and Lewis E. Hahn (La Salle, Ill.: Open Court, 1989), 665–93.

operators.[7] What a speaker *does* on a certain occasion cannot be said by him (on the same occasion): it can only be shown by a gesture, a certain inflexion of the voice, or some special sign, but these devices only show the mood in which the sentence is used; they do not form part of what the sentence says (that is, its conceptual content).

For the expressive conception, norms are essentially *commands*, but they must be carefully distinguished from propositions stating that there is a norm to such-and-such effect or that *p* is obligatory or prohibited, which are normative propositions. Normative propositions are related to norms in the following way: if *p* has been commanded, then the proposition that *p* is obligatory is true. If ~*p* (the omission or forbearance of *p*) has been commanded, then it is true that *p* is prohibited or—what is the same—that ~*p* is obligatory.

The two conceptions of norms are radically different and incompatible; there is no room for any eclecticism. If norms are expressions in a certain pragmatic mood, then they are not part of the meaning; if they are meanings (propositions), they are independent of any use of language or pragmatic mood. And yet many authors do not clearly adhere to either of the two conceptions, or rather seem to adhere to both of them. It is symptomatic of the very intricate nature of the issue that among those who seem to oscillate between the two conceptions are those philosophers who have dug most deeply into these problems. Thus, C.I. Lewis appears to be a clear expressivist when he says:

the element of assertion in a statement is extraneous to the proposition asserted. The proposition is something assert*able*; the *content* of the assertion; and this same content, signifying the same state of affairs, can also be questioned, denied, or merely supposed, and can be entertained in other moods as well.[8]

Among these moods Lewis explicitly mentions the 'imperative or hortatory mode', including in his characterization the 'modal statements of possibility and necessity'.[9] But in his modal logic he treats the expression 'T*p*' as a proposition, where the modal operator of possibility is part of the content of the proposition.

In Georg Henrik von Wright, too, we find arguments that would permit us to classify him according to either of the two conceptions. On the one hand, he speaks of 'prescriptively interpreted deontic expressions' between which certain logical relations hold;[10] this seems to locate him

---

    [7] See Hans Reichenbach, *Elements of Symbolic Logic* (New York: Free Press, 1947), at 336–44.
    [8] Clarence Irving Lewis, *An Analysis of Knowledge and Valuation* (La Salle, Ill.: Open Court, 1946), 48–9 (emphasis by Lewis) (footnote omitted).
    [9] Ibid. 49 n.8.
    [10] Von Wright writes: 'The "fully developed" system of Deontic Logic is a theory of descriptively interpreted expressions. But the laws (principles, rules), which are peculiar to

among the adherents to the hyletic conception. On the other hand, he states that

it would be misleading to conceive throughout of the relation between norms and their expressions in language on the pattern of the above two 'semantic dimensions' [sense and reference]. At least norms which are prescriptions must be called neither the reference nor even the sense (meaning) of the corresponding norm-formulations. . . . The use of words for giving prescriptions is similar to the use of words for giving promises. Both uses can be called *performatory* uses of language.[11]

This seems to beckon more in the direction of expressivism.

What these quotations from the works of the founders of modal and deontic logic show is that both conceptions are plausible, with one perhaps more plausible than the other in some contexts and vice versa, so that it is not easy to take a decision concerning the two conceptions before exploring the whole range of their implications.

But as it stands, most legal and moral philosophers as well as deontic logicians share the expressive conception of norms; the most conspicuous and clear cases are those of Jeremy Bentham, John Austin, Hans Kelsen, Alf Ross, Richard Hare, Jørgen Jørgensen, Manfred Moritz, Bengt Hansson, Lennart Åqvist, Joseph Raz, and Franz von Kutschera.[12] Among

this logic, concern logical properties of the *norms* themselves, which are then reflected in logical properties of norm-propositions. Thus, in a sense, the "basis" of Deontic Logic is a logical theory of prescriptively interpreted *O*- and *P*-expressions.' von Wright, *NA* 133–4 (von Wright's emphasis).

[11] von Wright, *NA* 94 (von Wright's emphasis).

[12] See Jeremy Bentham, *On Law in General*, ed. H.L.A. Hart (London: Athlone Press, 1970); John Austin, *Lectures on Jurisprudence*, 2 vols., 5th edn., ed. Robert Campbell (London: John Murray, 1885, repr. Glashütten im Taunus: Detlev Auvermann, 1972); Kelsen, *PTL*; Ross, *LJ*; Richard M. Hare, *The Language of Morals* (Oxford: Clarendon Press, 1952); Jørgen Jørgensen, 'Imperatives and Logic', *Erkenntnis*, 7 (1937–8), 288–96; Manfred Moritz, 'Permissive Sätze, Erlaubnissätze und deontische Logik', in *Philosophical Essays Dedicated to Gunnar Aspelin on the Occasion of his Sixty-fifth Birthday the 23rd of September 1963*, ed. Helge Bratt et al. (Lund: C.W.K. Gleerup, 1963), 108–21, and Moritz, 'Kann das (richterliche) Urteil deduziert werden?', in *Festskrift till Per Olof Ekelöf*, ed. Henrik Hessler (Stockholm: P.A. Norstedt & Söner, 1972), 502–18; Bengt Hansson, 'An Analysis of Some Deontic Logics', *Nous*, 3 (1969), 373–98, repr. in *Deontic Logic: Introductory and Systematic Readings* (n.2 above), 121–47; Lennart Åqvist, 'Interpretations of Deontic Logic', *Mind*, 73 (1964), 246–53; Raz, *CLS*; Joseph Raz, *Practical Reason and Norms* (London: Hutchinson, 1975), 2nd edn. (Princeton: Princeton UP, 1990); Franz von Kutschera, *Einführung in die Logik der Normen, Werte und Entscheidung* (Freiburg and Munich: Karl Alber, 1973).

A less clear case—at least on first glance—is that of Castañeda, but one should not be misled by differences in terminology. What Castañeda calls 'norms' are normative propositions (in our sense); there is, then, a very interesting theory of normative propositions here, but he does not analyze norms, which he refers to as 'regulations', 'ordinances', or 'rules'. See Hector-Neri Castañeda, 'The Role of Science in the Justification of Norms', 16th World Congress of Philosophy, Düsseldorf, plenary session of 29 August 1979. See also Alchourrón's critical note on Castañeda's *Thinking and Doing* (Dordrecht: Reidel, 1975): Carlos E. Alchourrón, 'Prescripciones y normas. La teoria de Castañeda', *Crítica. Revista Hispanoamericana de Filosofía*, 13 (1981), 3–27.

the far less numerous representatives of the hyletic conception might be mentioned Georges Kalinowski and Ota Weinberger.[13]

It is not surprising that such antagonistic views on the nature of norms should lead to quite different answers to the three problems mentioned at the beginning of this paper. For the expressive conception there can be no logic of norms, because there are no logical relations among norms. Deontic logic can only assume the form of a logic of normative propositions.[14] For the hyletic conception, there are instead two logics: a logic of norms and a logic of normative propositions.[15]

Regarding the second issue, the situation is less clear. Adherents to the expressive conception are committed to the view that norms lack truth-values; but among the representatives of the hyletic conception there are two tendencies. Some believe that norms are true or false;[16] others maintain that they lack truth-values.[17] This question will not be discussed here.

Most expressivists deny that there are permissive norms (which does not amount to denying the existence of permissible states of affairs), because they only accept one kind of normative (prescriptive) action: commanding. This version of the expressive conception is the *imperative theory of norms*. But there are exceptions even among clear expressivists; some of them accept a peculiar normative act, that of permitting.[18] We shall consider later whether there are reasons for the expressive conception to accept other types of normative act besides commands and to accept the existence of permissive norms.

No such problems arise for the hyletic conception; hence the authors who share this conception accept at least two kinds of norm: mandatory or *O*-norms and permissive or *P*-norms.

Our purpose in this paper is to examine in some detail the expressive conception. On close inspection it proves to be much more powerful than might appear on first glance. When duly enriched by some new concepts (compatible with its spirit though usually ignored by its adherents), it is capable of capturing most if not all important features of a normative

---

[13]   See Kalinowski (n.3 above); Kalinowski (n.1 above); Weinberger (n.4 above).

[14]   Føllesdal and Hilpinen (n.2 above), 7–8.

[15]   See Carlos E. Alchourrón, 'Logic of Norms and Logic of Normative Propositions', *Logique et analyse*, 12 (1969), 242–68; Alchourrón, 'The Intuitive Background of Normative Legal Discourse and its Formalization', *Journal of Philosophical Logic*, 1 (1972), 447–63.

[16]   See Kalinowski (n.3 above); Kalinowski (n.1 above).

[17]   See Weinberger (n.4 above); von Wright, *NA*, and Georg Henrik von Wright, *An Essay in Deontic Logic and the General Theory of Action* (Amsterdam: North-Holland, 1968); Carlos E. Alchourrón and Eugenio Bulygin, *Normative Systems* (Vienna and New York: Springer, 1971).

[18]   See Manfred Moritz, 'Permissive Sätze, Erlaubnissätze und deontische Logik' (n.12 above).

phenomenon. But many expressivists, like Horatio, are bound to accept more things than are dreamt of in their philosophy.

In previous publications, especially in *Normative Systems*, we adhered to the hyletic conception. Norms were treated as abstract entities, as propositions with prescriptive meaning, capable of entering into logical relations. Since then, we realized that most writers share the expressive conception; thus, it seemed interesting to explore its possibilities in order to uncover its limitations and show the differences between the two conceptions. Such was the origin of this paper.

We now have the impression that the same conceptual distinctions appear in both conceptions, though, of course, expressed in different languages. The choice between them is motivated by ontological considerations regarding the nature of norms, but there seems to be no crucial test that would justify a decision in favour of one of them. So, after all, it looks more like a problem of philosophical style and even personal preference than a question of truth. As Rudolf Carnap puts it: 'Let us be cautious in making assertions and critical in examining them, but tolerant in permitting linguistic forms.'

II. NORMS AND NORMATIVE SYSTEMS

The expressive conception is primarily concerned with norms issued by some agent (norm-authority) and directed to other agents (norm-subjects), that is, norms that von Wright calls *prescriptions*.[19] So we shall take into account only this type of norm, of which many legal norms provide a clear example.[20]

We shall begin by examining the imperative theory of norms, which accepts only one kind of normative act, the act of commanding, and therefore only one type of norm, mandatory norms. (It is immaterial whether they are conceived of as establishing obligations or prohibitions.)

Commanding is essentially a linguistic activity, a speech act. It consists of formulating certain words (or other symbols) with a certain meaning. A norm is the meaningful sentence in its imperative use ($!p$). The content of the norm is the proposition expressed by 'p'. Thus the act of commanding can be described as the act of *promulgating* a norm. The act of promulgating has temporal, but instantaneous existence. Yet norms are said to exist continually during a certain period of time (this is clearly so

---

[19] See von Wright, *NA*, at 7–10.

[20] But the theory can also be adapted to customary norms. Their existence is dependent on certain dispositions, which are revealed by certain actions.

in the case of legal norms). How can this feature of norms be accounted for in the expressive conception?

In order to illustrate it we shall, following H.L.A. Hart, suppose a simplified situation in which a certain population living in a certain country is governed by an absolute monarch called Rex. Rex controls his people by general commands requiring them to do various things and to abstain from doing certain other things. Let us suppose further that Rex is the only legislative authority of that country.

From time to time Rex performs the action of commanding a certain proposition or a set of propositions. The propositions that have been commanded by Rex form a set, the *commanded set A*. Each time Rex issues a new command, this set is enlarged by the new proposition commanded by Rex, so that it becomes a new set, say A_1. Thus in the course of time we have not one set, but a *sequence* of sets ($A_1, A_2, \ldots A_n$). So far (that is, as long as the imperativist variety of expressivism is accepted) these sets can only be increased by the addition of new propositions, but there is nothing like subtraction.

A proposition becomes a member of some set of the sequence as a result of an act of commanding performed by Rex. Hence we can say that the norm !p exists from the moment at which p has been commanded and so the proposition p has become a member of the corresponding set. This is, of course, only a mode of speech. In fact, the norm !p has an instantaneous existence, exactly like the act of commanding p. The point, however, is that all the propositions that belong to the set A are regarded as obligatory in A. As one and the same proposition p can be a member of, for example, successive sets $A_2, A_3, \ldots A_n$ but not of A_1, so p is not obligatory in A_1 but is obligatory in A_2, and so on. As long as the successive sets can only be increased by new commands, p commanded at t_1 belongs to all sets subsequent to the set corresponding to t_1.

Thus the existence of a norm (= the membership of the norm-content) is dependent on certain empirical facts (acts of promulgation in the case of prescriptions, certain actions revealing dispositions in the case of customary norms). Therefore, as there are no logical relations between facts, there is no room for a logic of norms.

But this does not preclude the possibility of a logic of normative propositions. Indeed, as we have already pointed out, the proposition that p is obligatory in A is true if p has been commanded by Rex and so is a member of the commanded set A. Yet this is a sufficient but not a necessary condition for the truth of 'p is obligatory in A'. It may occur that Rex has never commanded that p, but has commanded, for example, that p & q. This is a different proposition, and so, according to our criterion, p would not belong to A. But as p is a consequence of p & q (for it is logically deducible from p & q), it is also true that p is obligatory in A. The obligatoriness of p is a consequence of the obligatoriness of p & q, because p is a consequence of p & q.

We can now define the concept of a normative system as the set of all the propositions that are consequences of the explicitly commanded propositions.[21] (Though we use the traditional expression 'normative system', it must be emphasized that for the expressive conception a normative system is not a set of norms, but a set of norm-contents, that is, propositions.) This enables us to distinguish between the set A (formed by all the explicitly commanded propositions) as the axiomatic *basis* of the system, and the normative system $Cn(A)$, which is the set of all the consequences of A.

We are in a position to correct our criterion for the truth of normative propositions: 'it is obligatory that p in A' is true if and only if p is a member of the system $Cn(A)$—that is, if and only if p belongs to the consequences of A. This means that p is obligatory in A if and only if p has been commanded or p is a consequence of the propositions that have been commanded. In this last case we say that $O_A(p)$ and that p is a *derived obligation*.

The notion of derived obligation is related to the notion of implicit command. This last concept, in its turn, is closely related to that of implicit assertion. Indeed, there are at least two different senses in which a person can be said to have made an assertion. In a psychological sense of 'assertion', what is asserted in an act of assertion is only the sentence uttered, and not even the proposition expressed by that sentence. In this sense of 'assert', if X asserted 'John kissed Mary', he *did not assert* 'Mary was kissed by John', because it is a different sentence, even if both sentences have the same meaning, that is, express the same proposition. But in another, non-psychological sense of 'asserting', if X asserted 'John kissed Mary', he explicitly asserted the proposition expressed by that sentence, and so he also asserted that Mary was kissed by John, and, moreover, he also implicitly asserted all those propositions—such as 'Somebody kissed Mary'—that are consequences of the proposition he asserted explicitly. This is a non-psychological sense of assertion, for it is clear that the person in question probably did not think of all such propositions and so had not the slightest intention of asserting them. It may even be the case that q is a consequence of p, and that the person who asserts p not only ignores this fact, but believes q to be false. If he is not prepared to assert q (for example, because he believes it to be false), then we can show that his position is inconsistent by proving that q is a consequence of p. This is a very common way of arguing. We often try to refute our opponent by showing that the propositions he asserts imply

---

[21] On the notion of consequence, see Alfred Tarski, *Logic, Semantics, Metamathematics*, trans. J.H. Woodger (Oxford: Clarendon Press, 1956), at chs. 3, 5, 12, and 16.

some proposition he is not willing to accept. This kind of argument is based on the notion of implicit assertion: in this sense, one asserts all the propositions that are a consequence of the explicitly asserted propositions.

A famous case might be mentioned in this connection. When Bertrand Russell found a contradiction in Gottlob Frege's system, this fact had a terrible impact on Frege. Why? Frege certainly did not assert any inconsistent proposition; but Russell showed that the self-contradictory proposition was a theorem (a consequence) of Frege's system. Frege did assert it implicitly by asserting the axioms of his system, and he could not maintain the axioms and reject that theorem.

The same kind of observation can be made regarding the act of commanding. Here, too, we have a non-psychological sense of implicit commanding. If a person commands something, he also commands all the consequences of what he has explicitly commanded (even if he is not aware of them). For instance, if a teacher commands that all his pupils should leave the classroom, he also implicitly commands that John (who is one of his pupils) should leave the classroom, even if he is not aware of the fact that John is there.

These considerations show that there are logical relations between normative propositions. In addition to obligation, we can also define the concepts of prohibition and permission for normative propositions:

p is prohibited in $A(\mathbb{O}_A(\sim p))$ = df. the negation of p ($\sim p$) is a member of the system $Cn(A)$.

p is permitted in A ($\mathbb{P}_A(p)$) = df. the negation of p ($\sim p$) is not a member of $Cn(A)$.

Even if for the imperative theory of norms there are no permissive norms, there are permitted propositions or states of affairs. According to the definition, p is permitted if and only if p is not prohibited in A. This shows that permissions have a normative status which differs from that of obligations and prohibitions. The permission of p is given by the absence of certain acts (acts of prohibiting that p or—what is the same—of commanding that $\sim p$), whereas the prohibition (obligation) requires the existence of certain normative acts.

The analyses of this section show that a careful distinction must be made between: (a) the act of promulgation of a norm (commanding), (b) the operation of adding new elements to a system as a result of such acts, and (c) the criteria that govern such an addition of elements. It is important to realize that what is added to the system A as a consequence of an act of promulgating a set of propositions B is not only the set B itself, but also all its consequences and, moreover, all those propositions that, without being consequences of B or consequences of A, are nevertheless consequences of A taken together with B. In other words, if to a set A we add a set B, the resulting system is not $Cn(A) + Cn(B)$, but $Cn(A + B)$. In most cases, this last set will be considerably larger than the first.

III. REJECTION

Suppose now that Rex realizes that the state of affairs p, that he prohibited some time ago, should not be prohibited now (perhaps because he committed a mistake in prohibiting p, or because the circumstances that made the prohibition of p convenient have changed). So he wants to permit p. How can he achieve it?

It is clear that once the act of commanding $\sim p$ has been performed, nobody can modify this fact. So it will always be true that p is forbidden in A. If Rex wants to permit p, he must change the system into a system where $\sim p$ does not obtain. But this change is impossible as long as there are only acts of commanding, which alone are accepted by the imperative theory of norms. By commanding, a permitted state of affairs may become prohibited, but not vice versa. The change from a prohibition to a permission requires an operation of *subtraction*; addition alone is clearly not sufficient. Therefore, in order to permit p, Rex must repeal or derogate the norm that prohibits p; more exactly, he has to eliminate $\sim p$ from the system. For this he must, first, identify what he wants to eliminate ($\sim p$) and, second, perform the operation of subtracting $\sim p$, so that as a result of this operation, $\sim p$ will be eliminated from the system. Here again a distinction must be made between the act performed by Rex, which will be called the *act of rejection*, the operation of eliminating certain propositions from the system, and the criteria that govern such elimination.[22] We shall begin with an analysis of the act of rejection.

In the same way as there are (among others) two types of propositional attitude—descriptive and prescriptive, that is, in this context, asserting and commanding—there are two types of the act of rejecting that may refer to the same proposition. We shall call them the descriptive and the prescriptive rejection. The content of both types of act is a proposition, but the two acts reject it in different ways. The first act of rejecting is opposed to asserting, the second to a command. We shall use the signs '⊣' and 'i' to symbolize the two kinds of rejection.

It is important to realize that rejecting is not the same as negating. When we negate a proposition, we assert another proposition that is the

---

[22] The literature on the concept of derogation is rather scarce. See the excellent paper by Thomas Cornides, 'Der Widerruf von Befehlen', *Studium Generale*, 22 (1969), 1215–63; Cornides is a true pioneer in this field. Weinberger's distinction between '*Begrenzungssatz*' and '*Tilgungsoperation (Streichung)*' seems to reproduce our distinction between rejection and elimination. See Weinberger (n.4 above), at 192.

negation of the first. Thus to negate p is to assert $\sim p$. Similarly, to negate the command that p can be regarded as commanding that $\sim p$: in this case the negation of the command that p would be the prohibition that p. Hence if Rex, in order to permit that p, were to negate the prohibition that p by commanding that p, the only thing he would achieve is to introduce a contradiction into the system: both p and $\sim p$ would belong to Cn(A), and both propositions 'p is obligatory in A' and 'p is prohibited in A' would be true, and neither p nor $\sim p$ would be permitted. This is not what Rex wants to do, if he wants to permit that p.

Therefore rejection is another type of speech act; he who rejects a proposition does not assert any proposition at all. It is the kind of difference that obtains between an atheist and an agnostic. The atheist negates the existence of God; he does it by asserting the proposition that God does not exist. The agnostic rejects the proposition that God exists without asserting the proposition that God does not exist. Incidentally, this shows also that the position of a sceptic need not be inconsistent. It would be self-refuting if the sceptic were to assert that nothing can be known, for he would then be claiming at least to know the proposition that nothing can be known. But if all he does is to reject all propositions, then he does not assert any proposition at all and his position becomes perfectly consistent.

Similarly, the (prescriptive) rejection of p is no prescription at all; in particular, it is not a prohibition of p. So the sign 'i' is a mere indicator of a certain speech act, and does not form part of the conceptual content of this act. ('ip' like '!p' does not express a proposition, but only indicates what is done with the proposition p.)[23]

When lawyers speak of derogation there is a rejection of a norm-content. No act of rejecting is required when what is derogated is not a norm-content but a mere formulation of a norm (a sentence). When the legislator becomes aware that there are two or more redundant formulations, that is, the same norm-content is expressed, for example, by different paragraphs of a statute, then he may be willing to derogate the redundant formulations, without eliminating the norm-content. In this case what he wants to do is to 'efface' the redundant formulations, leaving only one of them. No rejection of the norm-content is required to achieve this aim. But the removing of a norm-formulation should not be confused with the elimination of a norm-content. In this latter case what the authority wants to eliminate from the system is a certain conceptual

---

[23] Hare describes the difference between negation and rejection when he says that in a negation the term 'not' is part of the phrastic, but it can also occur in neustics: they then become 'not-yes' and 'not-please'. This seems to correspond to what we call rejection. Thus Hare's 'not-yes' is our descriptive rejection and 'not-please', the prescriptive rejection. See Hare (n.12 above), at 20–1.

content (a proposition), and, in order to achieve it, the performance of an act of rejection is necessary.

So expressivism must accept besides commanding another type of normative act, that of rejecting. The imperative theory of norms cannot account for the phenomenon of derogation, but expressivism is not bound to stand or fall with it. The acceptance of various types of normative act, in particular, acts of rejection, is perfectly compatible with the expressive conception.

If as a result of the rejection of a norm-content, it is eliminated from the system, the norm ceases to exist. Two important conclusions may be drawn from this fact: (1) norms not only begin to exist at a given time, they also cease to exist at a certain moment; (2) normative sets not only can be extended by the addition of new elements, they also can be restricted by the subtraction of elements.

Conclusion (1) is in need of some clarifying remarks. As we have already seen the temporal existence of norms is just a metaphor. What really happens is the performance of two types of act (commanding and rejecting): these are the only empirical facts relevant for the existence of a norm. There is no need for the occurrence of any further fact that would make true the proposition that a norm exists.[24] On the other hand, the assertion that a given norm ceases to exist at a certain moment is misleading. All there is, is a sequence of different sets of propositions, and a given proposition p may be a member of some of these sets and not of others. If it belongs to a certain set, it never ceases to belong to it, though it may occur that it does not belong to the next set. What we do is to take at different times different sets as points of reference for our assertions that certain propositions or states of affairs are obligatory, prohibited, or permitted: this gives the illusion of a temporal change. But in fact, normative propositions are timeless, for they always refer to some definite system. Hence the proposition 'p is obligatory in A_1' is either true or false, but if true, it is always true, even after the derogation of p. For if p is eliminated, we obtain a new system, say A_2. The proposition 'p is obligatory in A_2' is, in this hypothesis, false, but it is a different proposition. The first proposition (p is obligatory in A_1) continues to be true, though one is perhaps no longer interested in it. In this sense normative systems are instantaneous;[25] when jurists speak of a legal system as persisting through time (as for instance the system of French Law), what they mean is not one system, but a sequence of systems.

[24] See Carlos E. Alchourrón and Eugenio Bulygin, *Sobre la existencia de las normas jurídicas* (Valencia, Venezuela: Universidad de Carabobo, 1979, repr. Mexico City: Distribuciones Fontamara, 1997); for a different view, see von Wright, *NA*, at ch. 7.

[25] See Raz, *CLS*, at 34–5, who drew our attention to this fact. See Carlos E. Alchourrón and Eugenio Bulygin, 'Sobre el concepto de orden jurídico', *Crítica. Revista Hispanoamericana de Filosofía*, 8 (1976), 3–23.

IV. CONFLICTS OF PROMULGATION AND REJECTION

If X asserts that p and Y asserts that $\sim p$, the two assertions are said to be incompatible, not in the sense that they could not coexist, but in the sense that the two propositions asserted by X and Y are contradictory, that is, they cannot both be true (or false). The fact that two persons assert two contradictory propositions is certainly possible (and moreover extremely common); it is even possible for one and the same person to assert two contradictory propositions. But such assertions conflict. If we want to integrate them into a coherent whole, we must first resolve the conflict.

Analogously, the command that p and the command that $\sim p$ conflict because the norm-contents p and $\sim p$ are contradictory. This is the 'classic' notion of *normative inconsistency*. The concept of contradiction between propositions is extended to commands (norms), based not on the criterion of truth (commands lack truth-values) but on the notion of fulfilment (it is logically impossible to fulfil or to obey both commands $!p$ and $!\sim p$). Nevertheless, it is surely possible for two persons or even for one person to issue two conflicting commands. As long as they belong to different systems there is no difficulty; the need for resolving the conflict arises when they become members of the same system. It is the unity of the system that determines this need. A normative system that contains both p and $\sim p$ is *inconsistent*, and this is regarded as a serious defect of the system, for relative to it the propositions that p is obligatory and p is prohibited are both true.

Consider now the kind of conflict that would arise not between a theist and an atheist (who assert two contradictory propositions, 'God exists' and 'God does not exist'), but between a theist and an agnostic. An agnostic rejects the proposition that God exists, without affirming its negation. Here there is no inconsistency between two propositions, but a conflict between two propositional attitudes concerning the same proposition: assertion and rejection. In a certain sense, assertion and (descriptive) rejection are incompatible.

In a similar way promulgation of a norm and rejection of the same norm-content are incompatible: there is a kind of conflict between commanding that p and rejecting p. This conflict is different from that of commanding p and $\sim p$. In the latter case we have an agreement in attitude, but a disagreement in content; we call it *normative contradiction* or inconsistency. In the former case we have a disagreement in attitude and an agreement in content; this kind of conflict will be called, following Carnap,[26] *ambivalence*.

---

[26] Rudolf Carnap, *Introduction to Semantics* (Cambridge, Mass.: Harvard UP, 1942), 187.

The need for resolving the conflict of ambivalence arises when the same proposition is (directly or indirectly) commanded and rejected by the same authority or by different authorities in the same system.

In order to resolve conflicts of ambivalence certain criteria are used, which will be called *criteria or rules of preference*.[27] The rules of preference are designed to resolve conflicts between acts of promulgation and acts of rejection referring (directly or indirectly) to the same norm-content. They stipulate which of the acts prevails over the other. That the act of rejection of p prevails over the act of commanding p means that the set which does not contain p is to be preferred to the set that contains p as the point of reference of normative judgments of the form $\mathbb{O}_A(p)$ or $\mathbb{P}_A(p)$, and vice versa.

The rules of preference are seldom if ever explicitly stated, but they are in fact used by lawyers and by all those who have to manipulate normative systems. Three such rules are commonly used in legal practice; we shall call them rules *auctoritas superior*, *auctoritas posterior*, and *auctoritas specialis*. These names are an adaptation of certain other, analogous but different rules that lawyers explicitly use for resolving contradictions between norms (*lex superior*, and so on), to which we shall return in section VI.

The rule *auctoritas superior* stipulates that the act (be it promulgation or rejection) performed by an authority of a higher hierarchical level prevails over the act performed by an authority of a lower level. This means that when a higher authority, for example, a legislature, has issued a norm, it cannot be repealed by a lower authority, for example, by the executive. Even if it is rejected, the system does not change. On the other hand, when a higher authority rejects a norm-content, this act derogates it (that is, leads to its elimination from the system) if it had been issued earlier by a lower authority, and prevents its addition to the system by a later act of promulgation by a lower authority. This last case is especially interesting: it shows that rejection need not be temporally posterior to the act of promulgation.

If we distinguish between the *operation of eliminating* norm-content that has been rejected and the act of *rejecting* (which is frequently also called 'derogation'), then we become aware that it makes perfectly good sense to reject the norm-content p, even if p is not a member of the system. Though such rejection does not lead to an elimination of any norm-content, it may produce the important result of preventing the addition of p if p is issued later by an authority of a lower level. This is what happens with constitutional rights and guarantees: the constitution rejects in advance certain norm-content (that would affect basic rights),

---

[27] Here the term 'rule' does not mean a norm (command or commanded content) but a purely conceptual criterion.

preventing the legislature from promulgating this norm-content, for if the legislature promulgates such norm-content, it can be declared unconstitutional by the courts and will not be added to the system.

The other two rules operate in a similar way. The rule *auctoritas posterior* stipulates that a temporally later act prevails over an earlier act, whether it be promulgation or rejection. Obviously, this rule only applies to acts performed by authorities of equal hierarchy; thus, it is supplementary to the first rule.

Finally, the rule *auctoritas specialis* stipulates that an act of promulgating (rejecting) less general norm-content prevails over an act of rejecting (promulgating) more general norm-content.

It is important to stress the fact that these rules do not resolve all the possible conflicts between acts of promulgation and rejection. It can very well occur that the same authority or two authorities of equal hierarchy perform simultaneously the acts of promulgating and rejecting the same norm-content. In such a case clearly none of the three rules is applicable; such cases, though rare, sometimes do occur in legal practice. If such conflicts are to be resolved, further criteria of preference must be introduced. But it would be a mistake to regard the rules of preference (traditional or not) as *logical* rules.

V. IMPLICIT REJECTION AND DEROGATION

When Rex rejects a norm-content (or a set of norm-contents), this act identifies what he wants to be eliminated (subtracted) from the system. The set of the explicitly rejected propositions will be called, accordingly, the *derogandum*.

But if the derogandum alone is subtracted from the system, Rex may well fail to achieve his purpose. Indeed, suppose that p has been rejected, but the system contains not only p, but also p & q. Then to eliminate only p will simply not do, for as long as p & q is a member of the system, so is p. What the rejection of p would achieve in such a case is at most to change the status of p; if it was explicitly commanded and so a member of the basis, it will now be one of the consequences of the basis, but remain a member of the system. Hence p has not been derogated at all.

This argument makes it clear that the derogation of p requires not only the explicit rejection of p itself, but also the rejection of all those propositions of which p is a consequence. We shall say that these propositions are implicitly rejected by the act of rejecting p. Moreover, it may occur that two or more propositions (taken together) imply a rejected proposition, although none of them (taken alone) does so. Suppose, for example, that $q \supset p$ and q are members of the system and that p is rejected. The set $\{q \supset p, q\}$ implies p, so it must be (implicitly) rejected.

Generalizing this result, we can state the following *general criterion for implicit rejection*: The rejection of a set of propositions B implicitly rejects all propositions and sets of propositions that imply some of the propositions belonging to B.

It is worth noting that what is rejected by an act of rejection is not a set of propositions, but a *family* of sets. This fact determines an important difference between promulgation and derogation: it is always a *set* of propositions that is promulgated, but it is always a *family* of sets that is rejected. ('Rejected' means here 'explicitly or implicitly rejected'.)

What effects does an act of rejection produce? We must distinguish two cases:

(i) If none of the explicitly rejected propositions is a member of the system $Cn(A)$, then none of the rejected sets is included in A. Here the problem of subtraction does not arise. But if some of the rejected propositions or sets were promulgated later, this fact would give rise to a conflict of ambivalence. Such a conflict can only be resolved by the application of some rule of preference.

(ii) If some of the explicitly rejected propositions are members of the system $Cn(A)$, then some of the rejected sets are included in A. As the members of $Cn(A)$ are promulgated, we have a conflict of ambivalence and need some rule of preference to resolve it. If it is resolved in favor of promulgation, the rejection produces no effect whatsoever—no derogation takes place, and there is no change in the system. But if rejection prevails, certain propositions must be eliminated by subtraction from the system. Which are these propositions? What criteria determine the operation of subtraction?

It is clear that neither a rejected proposition nor a rejected set can remain in A; for in that case some of the members of the derogandum (that is, some of the explicitly rejected propositions) would continue to be members of the system $Cn(A)$. In particular, if a set is rejected, at least one explicitly rejected proposition is a consequence of it. Therefore, all rejected sets must be eliminated from A. But what does it mean to eliminate a set? If one of its elements is removed from the set, the set disappears as such: what we have in its place is another, less numerous set. On the other hand, as long as all of its members are there, it is the same set. So removing at least one of its elements is a necessary and sufficient condition for the elimination of a set.

Now if—as the hypothesis runs—at least one of the explicitly rejected propositions belongs to the system $Cn(A)$, the set A (that is, the basis of the system) is one of the rejected sets. Hence it must be eliminated; but if we remove all its elements, the whole system collapses. So by derogating one norm-content, we would succeed in derogating the whole system. This seems to be a little too drastic as a method of complying with the requirement that all the rejected sets should be eliminated from *A*.

This observation suggests the following *adequacy conditions* for the operation of subtraction: (i) no rejected proposition or set of propositions shall remain in the system, and (ii) the set of the subtrahend shall be *minimal*, that is, only those propositions shall be eliminated that it is strictly necessary to remove in order to comply with (i). In other words, the remainder of the operation must be the *maximal* subset of *A* consistent with the derogation.

A subset of *A* (that is, the explicitly promulgated propositions) that fulfils the requirements (i) and (ii) will be called a *derogans*. To each non-empty derogandum corresponds at least one derogans.

In order to construct a derogans corresponding to a derogandum, we must take at least one proposition out of all the rejected sets in *A*.[28] Since, however, some of such sets may have several members (none of which is rejected), any of them can be used for the construction of a derogans; so there are several ways of constructing a derogans, and consequently we have not one derogans but several derogantes. As each derogans is a set of propositions, the set of all derogantes is a family. But what we must subtract—if we want to satisfy the adequacy conditions—*is only one of them*, for if we remove one derogans, the remainder will contain no rejected set (and therefore no rejected proposition). On the other hand, if more than one derogans is removed, the remainder is no longer a maximal set and so condition (ii) fails to be fulfilled.

This shows that situations may arise where several derogantes correspond to one derogandum, and therefore there are several different ways of carrying out the subtraction corresponding to the same act of rejection. And what makes things even worse, we may have no criteria for preferring one of them. In such situations, there are several possible remainders instead of one; the remainder is not a set, but a family of sets. This is what we have called elsewhere the *logical indeterminacy of the system*.[29]

[28] We say 'at least one' instead of 'only one' because in the case of overlapping sets it is impossible to remove one and only one element from all of them. Consider, for example, the case of the three following sets: {*x*,*y*}, {*y*,*z*}, and {*x*,*z*}; if one element of two of them is removed, both elements of the third are removed as well.

[29] See Alchourrón and Bulygin (n.25 above); Alchourrón and Bulygin, 'Unvollständigkeit, Widersprüchlichkeit und Unbestimmtheit der Normenordnungen', in *Deontische Logik und Semantik* (n.4 above), 20–32; Alchourrón and Bulygin (n.24 above). This problem has already been seen by Cornides, though he seems not to lend it much importance; see Cornides (n.22 above), at 1241.

The problem of indeterminacy does not arise if the explicitly rejected propositions (the derogandum) are independent members of A. Then it is sufficient to eliminate from A the derogandum alone. In general: the derogation is univocal if and only if there is only one derogans and therefore only one remainder.

It may occur that the subtraction of a derogans carries with it the elimination of some other propositions that are a consequence of A (that is, they do not belong to A, but are members of the system Cn(A)), and are no longer consequences of A minus derogans. So the set of eliminated propositions may, after all, be larger than the set of subtracted propositions (a derogans). This makes it convenient to distinguish between subtraction and elimination.

To sum up: derogation, which leads to a new system (the remainder), has been analysed into two components: the act of rejection and the operation of subtraction. The act of rejection identifies a derogandum, and the resulting system is the remainder after subtracting a derogans (corresponding to the derogandum) from the original system. It should be emphasized, finally, that this kind of subtraction is—as our informal analysis shows—a much more complicated operation than the ordinary set-theoretical subtraction.[30]

VI. INCONSISTENCY

In section IV, we examined the conflicts of ambivalence that arise between two propositional attitudes: promulgating and rejecting the same norm-content. The two acts are incompatible because they tend to achieve incompatible results: the addition of a norm-content to a system and its subtraction from it. Our purpose in this section is to analyse the other kind of normative conflict: inconsistency between norm-contents (normative contradiction).

If both a proposition p and its negation $\sim p$ are members of a normative system, the system is said to be inconsistent. The trouble with an inconsistent system is that it is impossible, for reasons of logic, to obey all of its norms. At the very least, the norms $!p$ and $!\sim p$ cannot both be complied with. Moreover, if the classic notion of consequence is accepted, the effects of a contradiction are even more disastrous: all propositions belong to an inconsistent system. This is so because according to the classic notion of consequence, from a contradictory pair of propositions any proposition whatsoever can be derived. So all inconsistent systems are

---

[30] For a detailed analysis of the concept of derogation, see Carlos E. Alchourrón and David Makinson, 'Hierarchies of Regulations and their Logic', in *New Studies in Deontic Logic*, ed. Risto Hilpinen (Dordrecht: Reidel, 1981), 125–48.

equivalent: they contain the same consequences and are equally useless. Everything is obligatory according to such a system, and no one can ever possibly comply with it; thus, it cannot guide any action.

And yet it is extremely important to realize that inconsistent normative systems are perfectly possible, and their occurrence, at least in certain areas like law, is rather frequent. The reason for this is fairly clear. The selection of the propositions that form the basis of the system (the set A) is based on certain empirical facts: the acts of commanding or promulgating. Now, there is nothing extravagant about the idea that an authority commands that p, while another authority (or the same authority perhaps on a different occasion) commands that $\sim p$. Even one and the same authority may command that p and that $\sim p$ at the same time, especially when a great number of norms are issued on the same occasion. This happens when the legislature enacts a very extensive statute, for example, a civil code, which usually contains four to six thousand dispositions. All of them are regarded as promulgated at the same time, by the same authority, so that it is no wonder that they sometimes contain a certain number of explicit or implicit contradictions.

Nevertheless, many authors are extremely reluctant to accept this relatively simple fact. Some of them (especially deontic logicians and moral philosophers) are perhaps influenced by their (direct or indirect) interest in moral discourse, for it seems hard to accept that the same action may be morally good and wrong (obligatory and prohibited) at the same time. There is a grain of truth in this thought. It is probably true of rational morality, but very likely not true of positive morality, and it is plainly false of positive law. Strangely enough, there are also legal philosophers, that is, people whose primary interests concern positive law, who share this antiseptic conception. Kelsen is—or rather was—perhaps its most prominent representative among legal philosophers. In his *Reine Rechtslehre* (1960) he does not deny that legislators can enact contradictory laws, but he firmly maintains that the *system* of law is always consistent. This 'miracle' is achieved, according to Kelsen, by legal science; jurists eliminate all contradictions, and so 'the chaos becomes a cosmos', that is, 'the multiplicity of general and individual legal norms issued by different legal authorities becomes a unitary and consistent system, a legal order.'[31]

What Kelsen says here sounds perhaps a little too optimistic, but is substantially true. Yet far from supporting his contention that legal systems are always consistent, it proves it to be false. Indeed, if contradictions must be eliminated, then there is such a thing as a contradiction that must be eliminated. QED.

---

[31] *PTL* § 16 (p. 74).

This result is corroborated even by Kelsen himself. Indeed, in his latest publications, 'Derogation' (1962) and 'Law and Logic' (1965),[32] Kelsen changes radically his view concerning normative conflicts, a view that he had maintained in all of his previous writings.

Now, in 'Law and Logic' Kelsen clearly states that conflicts between norms are perfectly possible, where by 'conflicting norms' he understands two norms that prescribe incompatible actions, for example, p and $\sim p$. (So Kelsen's notion of a conflict of norms corresponds exactly to our 'inconsistency between norm-contents'.) According to the new doctrine, such conflicts differ from logical contradiction in so far as two contradictory propositions cannot both be true, whereas two conflicting norms can both be valid, in the sense of their having been issued by competent authorities. And such a conflict can only be resolved—on Kelsen's new view—by explicit or implicit derogation of one (or both) of the two conflicting norms. Thus, Kelsen's new position is in complete agreement with the views put forward in this paper.

It is, of course, a purely terminological matter whether the term 'system' will only be applied to sets of norm-contents once they are purged of their inconsistencies, or whether it will be applied to inconsistent sets as well. The important thing is to identify the inconsistencies and to examine the techniques used to remove them. This is what we propose to do in this section.

It is interesting to observe that lawyers (not contaminated by philosophy) readily accept the possibility of contradictions in law. This is shown by the fact that there are venerable principles designed to solve such conflicts. The principles *lex posterior*, *lex superior*, and *lex specialis* would have no application at all if there were no inconsistencies in legal dispositions. The very fact that lawyers often resort to such principles shows at least that they believe that normative contradictions are quite possible. And this belief is not mistaken.

How are cases of inconsistency treated in legal practice?

Two situations are to be distinguished: (i) When a legislative authority discovers a contradiction in a legal system, it may either derogate one or both of the two conflicting norm-contents, or leave things as they are, relying on the ability of judges to resolve the conflict. If the authority chooses to derogate one or both conflicting norm-contents, this solves the problem. The curious thing about derogation is the fact that a resolution to the conflict can be reached by a rather unexpected procedure (at least if the classic notion of consequence is accepted): by derogating any proposition you wish! This can easily be proved. Suppose that p and $\sim p$ are members of $Cn(A)$ and that the legislature rejects q; in this case

---

[32] In *Essays*. [For full bibliographical data on these papers, see the Table of Abbreviations.]

$\{p,\sim p\}$ is one of the rejected sets (for from a contradiction any proposition, including q, can be derived), and at least one of its members must be eliminated. It is enough that one proposition not be a member of a system for it to be consistent. Hence the derogation of any proposition ensures the consistency of the system. The only problem that may arise in this connection is the indeterminacy of the remaining system.

(ii) The situation of the judges seems to be different. Judges are supposed to apply the law, not to modify it. They lack competence or power to derogate laws enacted by the legislature (except perhaps in the case of unconstitutional laws). What can judges do when faced with an inconsistent system? What methods do they actually apply to deal with such situations?

We must remember at this point that legal systems are not just sets of norms, but hierarchical structures.[33] There are certain hierarchical relations among legal norms or, as we would say, between norm-contents belonging to a legal system. Such hierarchies may be established by the legislature (that is, by laws themselves) or determined by some general criteria based on the date of promulgation (*lex posterior*), the competence of the promulgating authority (*lex superior*), or the degree of generality of norm-contents (*lex specialis*). They may even be imposed by the judge himself, using his personal criteria of preference.[34]

As in the case of ambivalence, the three well-established traditional principles are not sufficient to resolve all possible contradictions. Sometimes, judges must resort to further criteria—based, for example, on considerations concerning justice or other values involved in the issue.

The hierarchical ordering of the system enables the judge to give preference to some norm-contents or sets of norm-contents over others and so to disregard the hierarchically lower sets. In such cases, lawyers tend to say that the conflict was an apparent one and that there was really no inconsistency at all.

This may be perfectly true, provided one understands by 'normative system' not a set but an *ordered set* of norm-contents, the ordering relations being intrinsic to the concept of a normative system. This shows that lawyers tend to use—at least in some contexts—the term 'normative system' in this special sense.

---

[33] This is emphasized by most legal philosophers—for example, Kelsen, Alf Ross, and Hart.

[34] From the logical point of view such an ordering is either a partial ordering (reflexive, transitive, and antisymmetric relation) or a weak ordering (reflexive, connected, and transitive, though not necessarily antisymmetric relation). The first alternative (partial ordering) is thoroughly studied in Alchourrón and Makinson (n.30 above).

But if by 'normative system' we understand an ordered set of norm-contents, then every modification of the ordering relations modifies *eo ipso* the system itself. The fact that as a result of a new ordering, the system provides different solutions for the same specific cases shows that it is another system, not identical with the original one, *even if it contains the same elements* (norm-contents).

In spite of this, there is a widespread idea that derogation (which removes altogether certain norm-contents) is a much more fundamental operation than simple ordering, and that therefore the judge, though he can impose a new ordering or modify the existing one, cannot derogate legislated norm-contents for the same reasons that he cannot promulgate new norms. The idea is that as long as the system contains the same elements it remains substantially identical, and so the judge who 'only' orders the elements of the system does not change it and hence does not trespass beyond his powers. Consequently, ordering is regarded as a much more elastic and less permanent operation than derogation.

But this idea is wrong. The impression that the removing of one or more propositions by derogation is somehow more fundamental and permanent than the imposing of an ordering on a system proves to be a mere illusion. A modification of the ordering is as fundamental as the removing of elements; indeed, *both procedures are substantially equivalent*.[35] Those norm-contents that are 'put aside' or disregarded by an ordering have as little application (as far as this ordering is concerned) as when they are derogated. As to the alleged permanence of derogation there is no difference either. A derogation made by a legislature may last for a very short time if the legislature changes its mind and promulgates again the derogated norm-content. On the other hand, an ordering imposed by a judge may enjoy a very long life if other judges adopt it as well. Thus, the question of temporal duration is quite irrelevant to this issue.

The much debated problem of whether judges 'create' law or only apply it can be settled in favour of the first thesis, at least in the sense that they modify the legal system by imposing an ordering on its elements when they have to resolve contradictions, disregarding some of the norm-contents (which amounts to derogating them).

Nevertheless, though these two methods lead to substantially identical results (and this is what justifies calling them equivalent), they are two distinct methods, applied by different kinds of authorities

---

[35] In the sense that to every derogation corresponds a (set of) ordering(s) and to every ordering corresponds a derogation. For a detailed proof, see Alchourrón and Makinson (n.30 above). But they are not quite identical: a partial ordering imposed on a system confers uniqueness upon otherwise indeterminate derogations by means of a process of ranking the various remainders.

(legislative authority in the case of derogation, judicial authorities in the case of ordering). Both are designed to solve the same problem: the inconsistency of a normative system. This shows that inconsistency is indeed treated as a problem that calls for a solution, and hence that there are contradictions and inconsistent systems.

VII. PERMISSION

For the imperative theory of norms (which is the most popular version of the expressive conception), there is only one type of normative act (commanding). Thus, there are only mandatory norms, prescribing acts and omissions and so giving rise to obligations and prohibitions. Permission appears to be a purely negative notion; it is the absence of prohibition. So there may be permitted states of affairs, but thus far there are neither permissive acts (that is, acts granting permission) nor permissive norms.

How can this theory explain acts granting permission or authorization? When Rex says 'I hereby allow (permit) that p', how is this speech act to be analysed?

There seem to be two possible ways out of this difficulty. (i) One way is to describe this act as the act of lifting a prohibition, that is, as the derogation of the prohibition of p. (ii) An alternative way is to accept a new kind of normative act, the act of giving or granting permission (in short, the act of permitting). If this is accepted, then it must also be accepted that there are two kinds of norm, mandatory norms and permissive norms (in the sense in which an expressivist uses the term 'norm'). A permissive norm is—like a mandatory norm—a meaningful sentence in its peculiar, that is, *permissive*, use. So the act of granting permission can be described as the act of issuing a permissive norm.[36]

These two proposals will be examined separately.

(i)　The second analysis entails the explicit acceptance of a new kind of normative act, which is probably the reason why it is less popular among expressivists who feel some affinity with Ockham, but, as has been argued in section III, the first analysis also leads implicitly to the acceptance of a new normative act: the act of rejection. Since philosophers and logicians have so far paid comparatively little attention to the concept of derogation, no full analysis of the act of

---

[36] There are relatively few expressivists who accept this second interpretation. See Moritz, 'Permissive Sätze, Erlaubnissätze und deontische Logik' (n.12 above), who is one of the few.

rejection has been elaborated thus far.[37] This is a serious shortcoming of current expressive theories, for only with the recognition of the act of rejection as a fundamental, independent normative act can the expressive conception give an account of such important issues as derogation and permission. Once this is done, there are two different concepts of permission: *negative permission* (absence of prohibition) and *positive permission* (derogation of a prohibition).

Positive permission is linked to a positive act, the act of rejection, and so to a conflict of ambivalence. This conflict may be actual or merely potential if p has not been thus far prohibited. Once this conflict is resolved by giving priority to the rejection, the prohibition is eliminated (by subtraction) and p is permitted in the positive sense.

The main difference between negative and positive permission (apart from their different origins) appears to be this: if p is negatively permitted, then if an authority prohibits p there is no conflict: $\sim p$ is added to the system, and in the new system it is no longer true that p is permitted. But if p is positively permitted, any act of prohibiting p gives rise to a conflict of ambivalence that calls for a resolution. It will be true that p is prohibited (in the new system) only if this conflict is resolved in favour of the act of prohibiting.[38]

(ii) We turn now to the second analysis of sentences granting permission. For this analysis there are two different acts: commanding and permitting, promulgation of a mandatory norm and promulgation of a permissive norm. Consequently, there are also two kinds of permission: the above-mentioned negative or weak permission (absence of prohibition) and *strong permission*, granted by a permissive norm. Strong permission, like positive permission, is incompatible with prohibition, but here the conflict seems to be not of ambivalence, but of a contradiction between two norms. Yet it must be observed that this contradiction is not the classic contradiction where p and $\sim p$ are both members of the commanded set. In our hypothesis $\sim p$ has been commanded, so $\sim p$ belongs to the commanded set, but p has not been commanded; it has been permitted. What happens with p as a result of its being permitted? It certainly

---

[37] There are some valuable remarks on this subject. For example, Hare writes: 'Modal sentences containing the word "may" could, it seems, be represented by negating the neustic; thus "You may shut the door" (permissive) might be written "I don't tell you not to shut the door" and this in turn might be rendered "Your not shutting the door in the immediate future, not-please".' Hare (n.12 above), 20–1. If the negation of the neustic is taken to be a rejection—as was suggested in n.23 above—then Hare's proposal amounts to analysing the act of permitting in terms of rejection.

[38] Some authors interpret permissions as exceptions in a prohibitive norm. Thus, to permit would mean to introduce an exception in a prohibition. This can be explained as a partial derogation of the norm-content, that is, as a derogation of some of the consequences of the prohibitive norm.

cannot belong to the commanded set, for in that case it would be true that p is obligatory. In other words: how are we to construct the system, once we accept two kinds of promulgation? We cannot put together all the promulgated norm-contents, for then we could not distinguish between obligations and permissions. (For an expressivist the difference can only lie in the kind of act of promulgating, not in the conceptual content of the act; if there were a difference in the proposition this would mean the acceptance of the hyletic conception!) The only way out seems to be to form two sets: the set of commanded propositions (the commanded set A) and the set of permitted propositions (the permitted set B). But then, if we want a non-ambivalent system, we must somehow unify both sets. It is clear that subtracting the permitted set from the commanded set will not do. What we want here is not to remove obligations but rather to remove prohibitions. Thus, if p is prohibited and hence $\sim p$ is a member of A, and p is permitted as well and hence a member of B, what we must subtract from A is not p, but its negation ($\sim p$). Therefore the operation of unification requires subtracting from the commanded set the negations of the propositions that are members of the permitted set.[39] Thus, if p is permitted, $\sim p$ must be subtracted (eliminated from A) and vice versa. Thus the permission of p gives rise to the same operation as the rejection of $\sim p$.

At this stage one feels tempted to ask: are there really two distinct analyses? What is the difference, if any, between issuing a permission and derogating a prohibition? What is the difference between the act of permitting p and the act of rejecting $\sim p$?

There are indeed very strong analogies between the two concepts:

(1) Commanding a proposition is incompatible with permitting its negation, exactly in the same way as commanding that p is incompatible with rejecting p. In both cases we have a conflict of ambivalence (two incompatible attitudes regarding the same proposition).

(2) The set of the negations of permitted norm-contents (which is to be subtracted from the commanded set) is formally identical to the set of rejected propositions, for it is constructed in the same way.

(3) The operation of subtraction is the same: the identity of the subtrahend determines the identity of the remainder.

(4) Strong permission proves to be the same as positive permission.

---

[39] It would be pointless to form two sets, a set of permitted propositions and a set of their negations, just as it would be pointless to separate the commanded from the prohibited propositions. In both cases we have the same attitude regarding two contradictory propositions.

One has the impression that both analyses are substantially equivalent in the sense that they are two different descriptions of the same situation. If this is so, it is a rather surprising result; it shows the fruitfulness of the concept of derogation and its importance for the theory of norms. The concept of a permissive norm can be dispensed with, a fact that justifies the position of those expressivists who only accept mandatory norms, provided they accept the existence of derogation.

VIII. CONCLUSIONS

We are in a position to draw some conclusions from the preceding analyses; we shall do it by comparing the hyletic and the expressive conceptions of norms (henceforth HC and EC).

(1) HC rests upon a very strong ontological presupposition of Platonic flavour: the assumption that there are prescriptive propositions. No such presupposition is needed for EC.

(2) The price that EC must pay for this advantage is the proliferation of illocutionary acts: it must distinguish between asserting and commanding on the one hand, and between two kinds of rejecting (descriptive and prescriptive rejection) on the other. For HC there are only two types of act, assertion and rejection, because commanding is just asserting an O-norm, and permitting is just asserting a P-norm. And there is only one kind of rejection. What varies is the content of this act; it may be a descriptive proposition or a prescriptive proposition, that is, a norm.

(3) EC can dispense with permissive norms, for an account of acts granting permission can be given in terms of derogation (rejection and subtraction). For HC there can be permissive norms on the same level as mandatory norms (O-norms).

(4) For EC there are two kinds of incompatibility: conflicts between norm-contents (normative inconsistency, $!p$ and $!\sim p$) and conflicts between acts of promulgation and rejection (ambivalence, $!p$ and $\mathrm{i}p$).

For HC there are two kinds of inconsistency between norms: the inconsistency between obligation and prohibition (Op and $O\sim p$) and the inconsistency between prohibition and permission ($O\sim p$ and Pp, or, what is the same, Op and $\sim Op$). Besides these two kinds of inconsistency between norms, there is the conflict of attitudes between promulgation and rejection (ambivalence). Whether the inconsistency between prohibition and permission is reducible to a conflict of ambivalence (as the analysis of section VII suggests) may be regarded as an open question.

(5) For HC there are two logics: a logic of norms and a logic of normative propositions (a logic of promulgation and of derogation). The logic of norms is concerned with logical relations of prescriptive propositions (norms); it is a peculiarly normative logic.[40] The logic of normative propositions is concerned with logical relations of descriptive propositions about normative systems. Its aim is the development of a comprehensive logic of normative systems that may be regarded as a special case of Alfred Tarski's logic of systems. Especially interesting would be a logic capable of rendering the dynamic character of normative systems, that is, their temporal development through acts of promulgation and derogation. (It scarcely need be added that at its present stage deontic logic is far from having reached this aim.)[41]

(6) For EC there is only one possible logic: the logic of (descriptive) normative propositions, in the same sense as for HC. This deontic logic looks very much like von Wright's 'classic' deontic logic,[42] but with two important differences: (i) Normative propositions are always relative to a definite normative system. Hence the subscripts in formulae like $\mathbb{O}_A(p)$. (ii) The law of deontic subalternation $\mathbb{O}_A(p) \supset \mathbb{P}_A(p)$—analogous to von Wright's theorem $Op \to Pp$—does not hold without restrictions.[43] It does not hold for inconsistent systems, and one of the main contentions of this paper is that normative systems can be inconsistent. But from what has been said in sections VI and VII, it follows that a system is consistent (i) if there is at least one derogated proposition, (ii) if the notion of consequence is restricted by an ordering relation imposed on the system,[44] and (iii) if there is at least one positively permitted proposition. (In fact, the three conditions amount to the same: derogation of at least one norm-content.) Thus, the conditions under which a system is consistent (and the law of deontic subalternation holds good) are extremely weak and easily obtainable.

[40] See Alchourrón (n.15 above); see also Alchourrón and Bulygin (n.17 above).

[41] Some hints in this direction are to be found in Alchourrón and Makinson (n.30 above).

[42] Georg Henrik von Wright, 'Deontic Logic', *Mind* (1951), 1–15, repr. in von Wright, *Logical Studies* (London: Routledge & Kegan Paul, 1957), 58–74; von Wright, *An Essay in Deontic Logic and the General Theory of Action* (n.17 above).

[43] See E.J. Lemmon, 'Deontic Logic and the Logic of Imperatives', *Logique et Analyse*, 8 (1965), 39–71.

[44] See Alchourrón and Makinson (n.30 above).

22

The Expressive Conception of Norms:
An Impasse for the Logic of Norms*

OTA WEINBERGER

INTRODUCTION

The recent development of the ontology of norms has taken a surprising turn. Some writers in the field of deontic logic (or, perhaps more appropriately, the logic of norms) and in the philosophy of law have adopted a conception of norms that stresses a close connection between norms and acts of commanding, and that either precludes any possibility of developing a logic of norms or leads to a transfer of logical relations and inference operations from the field of norms into the field of descriptive norm-contents, all of which looks rather similar to a proposal made by Jørgen Jørgensen in the 1930s.[1]

* *Editors' note*: From *Law and Philosophy*, 4 (1985), 165–98, at 165–91. The present version of the paper contains minor stylistic revisions, which were made in consultation with the author.

[1] Jørgensen contends:

It is not possible to issue a command without commanding something to be done or to express a wish without expressing a wish for something. Any imperative sentence may therefore be considered as containing two factors, which I may call *the imperative factor*, and *the indicative factor*, the first indicating *that* something is commanded or wished and the latter describing *what* it is that is commanded or wished . . .

Jørgensen concludes his paper with several theses:

I. Imperative sentences are not capable of being either true or false. According to the logical positivist testability-criterion of meaning they must therefore be considered meaningless. However, they are nevertheless capable of being understood or misunderstood and seem also to be able to function as premisses as well as conclusions in logical inferences.
II. This puzzle may be dealt with by analysing the imperative sentences into two factors: an imperative and an indicative factor, the first being merely an expression of the speaker's state of mind (his willing, wishing, commanding etc.) and therefore of no logical consequence, whereas the [latter] may be formulated in an indicative sentence describing the contents of the imperative sentences and therefore being capable of having a meaning and of being governed by the ordinary rules of logic.
III. The ordinary rules of logic being valid for the indicative sentences which can be derived from the imperative ones, and no specific rules for the imperatives being known (unless it should be the rule governing the derivation of the indicative sentence from the imperative one), there seems to be no reason for, indeed hardly any possibility of, constructing a specific 'logic of imperatives'.

Jørgen Jørgensen, 'Imperatives and Logic', *Erkenntnis*, 7 (1937–8), 288–96, at 291, 296. See also Ota Weinberger, *Studien zur Normenlogik und Rechtsinformatik* (Berlin: J. Schweitzer, 1974), at 103–10.

One will, of course, recall criticism of the imperative theory of legal norms—in particular, in the writings of Hans Kelsen and H.L.A. Hart.[2] It seems, however, that an immediate connection between norms and acts of will has now gained the assent of many philosophers of a positivist persuasion, namely: there is no imperative (or norm) without an act of commanding (positing a norm).[3] This view is not only positivistic in a straightforward way; it is also an argument for conceiving of norms as not lending themselves to the attribution of truth-values.

The main attempts in this direction include the following:

1. Hans Kelsen's last work, contained mainly in his posthumously published book, *General Theory of Norms*;[4]
2. Carlos E. Alchourrón and Eugenio Bulygin's distinction between hyletic and expressive norm ontologies and their effort to construct an expressive logic of norms;[5]
3. Georg Henrik von Wright's opening lecture at the 11th World Congress of the International Association for the Philosophy of Law and Social Philosophy (Helsinki, 1983), 'Is and Ought'.[6]

---

[2] See, in particular, *HP*, *LT*, *PTL*, and Hart, *CL*.

[3] Early in *GTN*, Kelsen refers to an essay by Walter Dubislav in which Dubislav speaks of the impossibility of an imperative without an imperator; see Walter Dubislav, 'Zur Unbegründbarkeit der Forderungssätze', *Theoria*, 3 (1937), 330–42, at 335. Kelsen writes: 'In order to exist—that is, to be *valid*—a norm must be posited by an act of will. No norm without a norm-positing act of will; or as this principle is usually phrased: No imperative without an imperator, no command without a commander.' *GTN* ch. 1, § VI (p. 6).

[4] His views were deeply influenced by Karel Engliš, *Malá-logika* (Prague: Melantrich, 1947); Engliš, *Das Problem der Logik* (Vienna: Rohrer, 1960); Engliš, 'Die Norm ist kein Urteil', *ARSP*, 50 (1961), 305–16; and Ota Weinberger, *Die Sollsatzproblematik in der modernen Logik* (Prague: Tschechoslowakische Akademie der Wissenschaften, 1958); Weinberger (n.1 above). Thanks both to Franz Weyr, whom Kelsen and Engliš counted as a close friend, and to my book *Die Sollsatzproblematik in der modernen Logik*, which Kelsen knew, Kelsen was familiar with the main ideas of Engliš concerning the impossibility of a logic of norms

Kelsen's transformation from an ardent proponent of the logic of norms into a norm irrationalist proceeded in a series of consecutive steps. See Ota Weinberger, *Normentheorie als Grundlage der Jurisprudenz und Ethik. Eine Auseinandersetzung mit Hans Kelsens Theorie der Normen* (Berlin: Duncker & Humblot, 1981), at 161–7.

[5] The authors do not use this term, but their analysis aims in effect at this goal even though they speak only of the logic of norm-contents, which they conceive of as propositions. See Carlos E. Alchourrón and Eugenio Bulygin, *Sobre la existencia de las normas jurídicas* (Valencia, Venezuela: Universidad de Carabobo, 1979, repr. Mexico City: Distribuciones Fontamara, 1997); Alchourrón and Bulygin, 'The Expressive Conception of Norms', in this volume, ch. 21; Eugenio Bulygin, 'Norms and Logic. Kelsen and Weinberger on the Ontology of Norms', *Law and Philosophy*, 4 (1985), 145–63.

[6] See von Wright, 'Is and Ought', in this volume, ch. 20; Ota Weinberger, '"Is" and "Ought" Reconsidered', *ARSP*, 70 (1980), 454–74.

I. TWO ONTOLOGIES OF NORMS

Alchourrón and Bulygin maintain that there are just two radically different and mutually incompatible conceptions of norms:

(i) The hyletic view conceives of norms as proposition-like entities; norms are conceptual entities, independent of language. They can be expressed by linguistic means, namely, by sentences having prescriptive meaning. Such sentences—let us call them 'norm-sentences'—are the result of a certain operation on (other) propositions.[7]

(ii) For the expressive conception, norms are essentially commands, the result of the prescriptive use of language. The authors—though not, I believe, all expressivists (for example Kelsen)—contend that on the semantic level there is no difference between statements, commands, questions, rejections, permissions, and the like; rather, there are differences only on the pragmatic level, for norms are nothing but propositions used in acts of commanding (or in acts of promulgation).[8]

Alchourrón and Bulygin's expressive conception of norms is evidently based on the theory of speech acts: prescriptiveness is an illocutionary feature of propositions, just as are asserting, asking, and so on, but also rejecting and permitting.

In any case, normative propositions, taken as descriptive, differ from norms (norm-sentences): beginning with the hyletic conception, Alchourrón and Bulygin define normative propositions as 'descriptive propositions stating that p is obligatory (forbidden or permitted) according to some unspecified[9] norm or set of norms'.[10] On the basis of the expressive conception Alchourrón and Bulygin define normative propositions as follows: 'if p has been commanded, then the proposition that p is obligatory is true.'[11]

Alchourrón and Bulygin's distinction between the two norm ontologies is not a fair description of the views actually held by contemporary philosophers, and it does not capture all of the essential differences

---

[7] See Alchourrón and Bulygin, 'Expressive Conception' (n.5 above), at § I.

[8] See Alchourrón and Bulygin, *Sobre la existencia de las normas jurídicas* (n.5 above), at 43, repr. at 49: 'The notion of normativity is essentially linked to the speech act of prescribing; without such an act, there is no norm.'

[9] It does not, I believe, make any sense to assert that p is obligatory (forbidden, permitted) according to an 'unspecified norm or set of norms'. It is only regarding a *given* norm (or a *given* set of norms) that such a statement is meaningful, and its truth depends, of course, on the norms to which the statement refers.

[10] Alchourrón and Bulygin, 'Expressive Conception' (n.5 above), § I.

[11] Ibid.

between the different ontologies of norms proposed by these thinkers either.

There are perhaps some authors who hold that norms are ideal entities existing *per se*, that is, conceptual (or Platonic) entities existing independently of any language. There are perhaps some logicians who conceive of norm-sentences as the result of an operation on propositions (or on descriptive sentences expressing propositions). Not everyone, however, who is unwilling to accept a strict connection between norms and acts of commanding (that is, who does not accept an expressive norm ontology) accepts a hyletic ontology of the kind described by Alchourrón and Bulygin. I do not hold the latter view myself. Indeed, I am strongly opposed to the view that meanings are Platonic entities, existing independently of any language. Meaning is an element of a language (or of languages) just as signs are elements of languages.

A linguistic system is a product of our linguistic capacity in both respects, namely: syntactically as a class of signs with the corresponding formation rules for well-formed sign series, and semantically as producing concepts and other 'units of meaning' and correlating them to the sign series.[12]

The concept of meaning should not be restricted to criteria for determining objects, that is, to features of possible objects that are used to refer to real or ideal objects. If we want to analyse the whole field of thought—including practical discourse, the interplay of questions and answers, and the great variety of speech acts—then we must overcome the reifying conception of semantics that restricts the concept of meaning of a sign to designators. There are sign series that do not characterize any objects—in particular, questions, exclamations, norm-sentences. It would therefore make no sense, for example, to define a concept of the following kind: 'All the x's that satisfy the question "Is it going to rain tomorrow?"'

We may argue that the very same unit of meaning may be expressed in different languages, and that meaning should therefore be conceived of as something existing beyond languages. I believe that the fact of interlinguistic synonymy does not prove in any way the language-independent existence of meanings, that is to say, their existence as Platonic entities. Even if some sign series in different languages—say the languages, $L_1, \ldots L_n$—should have the same meaning (are identical in meaning), the respective interlinguistic meanings are not yet proven to be language-independent. Rather, I suggest, they are concepts gained by

---

[12] This consideration concerns, of course, only interpreted languages. Abstract languages do not determine the meaning associated with the sign series, but they represent a general framework for different interpretations, that is, for the correlation of different systems of meaningful elements to the well-formed formulae.

abstraction based on the equivalence relation of synonymy from a set of languages $L_1, \ldots L_n$, embracing some sign series that have the same meaning.

Meanings are not performed and objectively given entities. Rather, they are constructs of our intellect, which produces concepts and other meaningful structures from the languages underlying our reasoning and discourse. And there are various ways of creating such linguistic (conceptual or meaning) systems. This, I believe, is the real sense of the so-called 'principle of tolerance',[13] and its foremost philosophical and methodological consequence.

To conceive of norms as the results of an operation on propositions may lead to misunderstandings. We should deal with the relation between descriptive sentences (and propositions as their meanings) on the one hand, and norm-sentences (and norms as their meanings) on the other, on two levels—namely, on the level of elementary sentences and on the level of complex sentences. On the level of elementary sentences, there is a coordination of content (that is, of descriptions of states of affairs) between descriptive sentences and norm-sentences. The notion of an operation on propositions could, however, evoke the idea that a proposition is, so to speak, contained in the norm-sentence. This, I believe, is an erroneous conception. And from a strictly logical point of view, the notion of an operation calls for a determination of the set of objects that are the results of the operation (in this case we should say explicitly that this is not a set of propositions, but a set of norms).

Even Alchourrón and Bulygin's definition of the expressive ontology is not univocal and free of problems. It is clear that all expressivists hold that norms are created through acts of commanding (or promulgation). If this notion is conceived very broadly, so that every institutionalization of normative rules is a case of commanding, then this view is fairly plausible. But the essential differences, in the view of expressivists, are brought to light by the following two questions:

(i)   What is the content of acts of commanding? Do these different speech acts have a specific content expressed in sentences different in meaning? Or are they only specific speech acts—kinds of use—of a propositional content, such that all speech acts (assertions, commands, questions, and so on) have exactly the same content, namely certain propositions?

(ii) What are the consequences of acts of commanding? Does commanding p produce the effect that p ought to be, but nothing else, or does it generate a realm of ideal normative entities with certain kinds

---

[13] See Rudolf Carnap, *The Logical Syntax of Language*, trans. Amethe Smeaton (London: Routledge & Kegan Paul, 1937), at 51: 'In logic, there are no morals.'

of internal logical relations and consequence relationships? (Even Alchourrón and Bulygin's conception that there is a set of propositions that is the set of the consequences of the commanded contents, namely the normative system, is of this kind. As a matter of fact, it actually provides in a roundabout way for a logic of norms!)

All of this reveals such far-reaching differences among the expressive conceptions that I cannot accept Alchourrón and Bulygin's characterization of this ontology of norms as a well-defined class of norm ontologies.

If we define commanding in a very broad sense as the bringing about of a norm, then I, too, am an expressivist. Kelsen and I would hold that a command has a specific nonpropositional content. Alchourrón and Bulygin hold that there is only one kind of content of speech acts, whether asserted, asked, or whatever. Kelsen denies that a command has any consequences, for he conceives of norms as strictly bound to real acts of commanding.[14] Alchourrón and Bulygin, and I, too—even if on different logical grounds—conceive of norms as having logical consequences such that not only the contents of valid imperatives but also the contents deduced from valid normative premisses are valid.

These considerations prove, in my view, that Alchourrón and Bulygin's systematization of norm ontologies is not workable, that is, that the two kinds of ontologies are neither mutually exclusive nor do they capture the essential differences between distinct theoretical views in this area.

It seems that the authors have no strong preference for one ontology or the other. The paper 'The Expressive Conception of Norms' is an attempt to show that the expressive ontology of norms, together with some ideas of speech act theory and a suitable conceptual apparatus for logical analysis (namely, the concept of a normative system, the idea of rejection, the notion of permissive acts, and so on), can be taken as a basis for the resolution of pressing problems of practical discourse and legal reasoning. Alchourrón and Bulygin's attempt is illuminating; I doubt, however, that it is successful. Still, even if their assumption that speech acts of different kinds (assertions, commands, questions, and so on) always have merely propositional content and differ only pragmatically but not in meaning is fundamentally mistaken, it is of considerable

---

[14] Kelsen is even surprised by the fact that norms are valid where the act of commanding no longer exists. As he writes:

The only qualification this principle suffers [the principle, namely, that no norm exists without an actual act of will whose meaning it is] is the fact that the *ought*, which is the meaning of the act of will about the behaviour of another person—that is, the norm—is valid, exists, even after the act of will of which it is the meaning no longer exists; and the existence of an act of will is, by its very nature, limited to the short period of time it is being performed.

GTN ch. 58, § XI (p. 235) (trans. altered).

interest to analyse the possibilities and implications of an expressive logic of norms (or, in Alchourrón and Bulygin's terminology, a logic of commanded propositions).

II. VARIETY OF SPEECH ACTS AND IDENTITY OF MEANING?

The technique of Alchourrón and Bulygin's expressivist analysis of norms is based on some surprising assumptions:

(a) Norms are results of a prescriptive use of language.
(b) There is, on the semantic level, no difference between assertions, commands, questions, rejections, permissions, and so on, for they all have as their content nothing but propositions.
(c) Differences between statements, commands, and the like exist only on the pragmatic level, namely in different speech acts (that is, different kinds of use of propositions).
(d) These pragmatic differences (illocutionary indications) are irrelevant from a semantic and logical point of view.

Let us first consider the general conception of speech acts and illocutionary force in Alchourrón and Bulygin's interpretation. Since we are now dealing not only with norm ontology but with the general conception that speech acts differ only on the pragmatic level (that is, in illocutionary force) and not in meaning (because their meaning is always a proposition), the difficulties of this conception in all fields of application are equally relevant for our argument.

It is, of course, true that the illocutionary force of a given series of signs may vary in different situations, depending on its use, but from this fact it does not follow that different speech acts—or their contents—never differ in meaning, and that the contents (or meanings) of all speech acts are of the same kind, namely propositions.[15]

It is easy to prove that logical relations are not solely determined by the propositional content of speech acts or, as we might more adequately put it, that not all speech acts are utterances of propositions. If Alchourrón and Bulygin were right in their conception of speech acts, then the contradiction between the propositions 'p' and '$\sim p$' would bring about:

(i)   a contradiction between assertions, '$\vdash p$'/'$\vdash \sim p$';
(ii) a contradiction between commands, '$!p$'/'$!\sim p$';

---

[15] The fact that a sign series can be used in different pragmatic roles is very important for my own conception of norm-sentences.

(iii) a contradiction between prescriptive rejections, '¡p'/'¡$\sim p$';
(iv) a contradiction between (positive) permissions, 'Pp'/'$P\sim p$';
(v)   a contradiction between questions, '?p'/'?$\sim p$'; and so on.

I doubt whether (iii) can be conceived of as a contradiction at all, but in any case the permission of p and the permission of $\sim p$ do not constitute a contradiction at all but are perfectly compatible. Their conjunction is often defined as 'indifference'. I am also not sure whether the concept of contradiction is applicable to questions: '?p' ('Is it the case that p?') and '?$\sim p$' ('Is it the case that not-p?') cannot be mutually contradictory, for both questions concern the very same state of affairs. For example, 'Is it the case that it is raining?'/'Is it the case that it is not raining?' are questions applicable to the same situation, and both may be answered by the same sentence 'It is raining'.

If we have a set A, which may be the set of

(i')   asserted propositions,
(ii') commanded propositions,
(iii') rejected propositions,
(iv') permitted propositions,
(v')   asked propositions,[16]

then we can always find the corresponding set of consequences $Cn(A)$. The interpretation of the role of $Cn(A)$ is different in the cases (i') through (v'); and it is, at least in cases (iv') and (v'), rather curious. In the case of permission, one indifferent state of affairs (namely the permissions 'Pp' and '$P\sim p$') would entail that everything is permitted. If the speaker asks 'Is it raining?' and also 'It's not raining?' then—in Alchourrón and Bulygin's view—not only is he guilty of having contradicted himself, he has also presented all the possible questions.

We see, then, that the assumption criticized here clearly leads to unacceptable consequences.

The authors deal with the sets of propositions that are asserted, commanded, and so on as distinct sets, and it is of course necessary to distinguish them carefully. In any process of communication, every participant must be informed about the character of the set of propositions under consideration. Specifically, the indication that the set in question is a set of commanded propositions (and not of asserted, permitted, etc. propositions) is relevant information, that is, information determining the meaning of the set under consideration. And the same is true, *mutatis mutandis*, for the other cases of pragmatic use. Unless

---

[16] This expression has a strange ring about it; it would be clearer to call this set 'the set of propositions correlated with questions'. Our language is not adapted to Alchourrón and Bulygin's strange conception of speech acts. To be sure, this fact does not count as a sound argument against their theory.

the participant in the communication situation is aware of the kind of use (the character of the respective speech acts or the illocutionary role of the set of propositions), the set of propositions carries no meaningful information at all. Can we hold the view that this element, essential for determining the meaning (and the role) of the set of propositions, is semantically irrelevant? To do so would be quite absurd.

Alchourrón and Bulygin's assumption implies that the same logical relations and the same entailments hold among assertions (or statements), commands, questions, and so on,[17] and since this is manifestly not the case, this linguistic theory and the logic based upon it seem to me to be disproven.

The proposed theory is unsatisfactory for another reason as well, namely, that it is in principle incapable of explaining the meanings of very important types of sentences. Examples are questions of the type 'Who did it?', since there is no proposition corresponding to this question,[18] and hypothetical norm-sentences ('If it is raining, stay at home', 'If you have money, you may buy the book').[19]

There is no proposition corresponding to a hypothetical norm-sentence that could be used to issue such a norm; and even a pair of propositions—one for the antecedent and one for the consequent—would not do. The pair as a whole should then be commanded, and the consequent should be regarded as 'conditionally commanded' (or should be regarded, as I would put it, as having normative meaning). And the set of all commanded propositions should embrace propositions, pairs of propositions, and so on. To find an acceptable way out of this mixture of propositions of different types (or pseudo-propositions, since the propositions corresponding to the consequents of hypothetical norm-sentences should be distinguished as having a normative role) seems to me to be impossible. To deal with a set of antecedent propositions and a set of consequent propositions is of no help either, for the normative conditional expresses a relation of just one element of the set of antecedents to one element of the set of consequents, and consequences drawn from the application of *modus ponens* cannot be established by a relation between the two sets.

---

[17] In the field of the logic of norms, 'ought' and 'permitted' would exhibit the same logical relations (for example, 'Pp' and '$P{\sim}p$' should be inconsistent, just as '$!p$' and '$!{\sim}p$' are), and no logical relation between 'ought' and 'permitted' would exist (for example, from '$!p$', 'Pp' would not follow).

[18] 'X did it' is not a proposition, but a propositional function.

[19] Hypothetical norm-sentences as the basic structure of legal rules are, of course, so important that a norm theory that is not able to deal with them is hardly of interest.

III. THE EXPRESSIVE LOGIC OF NORMS

Alchourrón and Bulygin say explicitly that there is no room for a logic of norms, while granting a logic of normative propositions.[20] It is not quite clear how this thesis is to be understood. If Rex has commanded p, then p is an element of A, that is, of the set of commanded propositions. But even in the context of the expressive conception, Alchourrón and Bulygin also speak of normative propositions in another sense. 'Normative propositions are related to norms in the following way: if p has been commanded, then the proposition that p is obligatory is true.'[21] Here the proposition 'p is obligatory' seems to be conceived of as the normative proposition, whereas the commanded p is a proposition *simpliciter*, used as a command ($!p$). I have no doubt that the view really intended by the authors is that

(a) the commanded set A is the set of propositions, describing states of affairs, that are used in the commanding acts;
(b) the normative system is the set of all the consequences of A; and
(c) all elements of the normative system are equally commanded contents.

These stipulations provide a path not only to implicit commands and derived commands, but also to inferred norms. Not only the contents of commands (or promulgated norms) are commanded (or, as one might put it, are the contents of valid norms), but also all of the implications of these contents. This procedure leads, indeed, to a form of a logic of norms, albeit an incomplete one.

To speak of a 'non-psychological sense of implicit commanding'[22]—as the authors do—will not suffice. The non-psychological conception of commands, that is, the conception of the contents of commands as ideal entities comprising their logical relations, is a necessary step on the way to a logical analysis, but along with this recognition we must see that the procedure introduced by Alchourrón and Bulygin is a kind of technique for analysing norm-logical relations and norm-logical inferences. This theory is, of course, only a very small part of the logic of norms (for neither inferences reflecting the application of *modus ponens* nor subsumptive conclusions are available), and it is a logic of norms with questionable consequences. ('$!(p \lor q)$' follows from '$!p$'—Ross's paradox; and from '$!(p \& q)$', there follow '$!p$', '$!q$'.)

Normative rejection is a type of normative act. Normative rejection, by itself, yields a set of rejected propositions. It is only on the basis of a

[20] See Alchourrón and Bulygin, 'Expressive Conception' (n.5 above), at § II.
[21] Ibid. § I.   [22] Ibid. § II.

special stipulation that the act of normative rejection can prevail over the act of commanding. The inconsistency between '$!p$' and '$¡p$' is not an inconsistency within a single set of propositions; therefore, it is not determined by propositional logic. Rather, it is an additional stipulation of Alchourrón and Bulygin's logic of norms; thus, we see that they are not following their own programme of building up solely a logic of normative propositions.

Alchourrón and Bulygin introduce (strong or positive) permission as another special kind of normative act, namely, the permissory use of propositions. The set of commanded propositions and that of permitted propositions have to be unified so that if 'p' is a member of the permitted set, then '$\sim p$' shall be eliminated from the commanded set. But in my view, this, too, is a special rule of normative logic and not an operation justified by means of propositional logic.

I can see no reason why the operation of 'subtraction' should not be performed in the opposite direction. Explicit (strong) permission may be eliminated (derogated) by the corresponding prohibition. In any case, the fact that the contents of two kinds of acts (that is, of two uses of propositions) contradict each other is not a relation that can be expressed within the logic of propositions: it depends on the indicator determining the character (and, I believe, the meaning) of the speech acts. It is a logical relation or, *stricto sensu*, a norm-logical relation, for it is determined by normative indicators and their mutual relationships.

Alchourrón and Bulygin succeed in explaining some incompatibilities on the basis of the notion of contradiction in propositional logic, namely, the contradiction '$!p$'/'$!\sim p$'.[23] Other kinds of incompatibilities, however, are stipulated without any justification from the field of propositional logic: '$!p$'/'$¡p$' (command and permission of opposite contents).[24]

Thus, Alchourrón and Bulygin's theory of norms is an expressive logic of norms, but not, as the authors contend, a logic of normative propositions.

IV. THE NON-PSYCHOLOGICAL SENSE OF ACTS

Alchourrón and Bulygin introduce the notion of a non-psychological sense of assertion and of commanding. This idea deserves more detailed consideration. They characterize this concept of acts (or of contents of possible acts, as I would put it) by means of two features:

[23] But they do not explain the compatibility of 'Pp'/'$P\sim p$'.

[24] Still other kinds of incompatibilities are not mentioned by Alchourrón and Bulygin in their paper, for example, 'If p, then q should be'/ 'If p, then $\sim q$ should not be'; and they are hardly definable in Alchourrón and Bulygin's theory.

(a) If a sentence *p* is asserted (or commanded), then all sentences with the same meaning are asserted (commanded) implicitly (their example reads 'John kissed Mary'—'Mary was kissed by John'); and

(b) all consequences of assertions (commands) are asserted (commanded) as well.

Basically, I agree with the authors' conception here. What is more, it is, I believe, only on this basis that the logic of norms and the logical analysis of norms become possible. We must analyse the content of (possible) acts detached from the acts themselves.[25] But then we cannot deny the existence of logical relations between the contents of acts—be they acts of assertion or normative acts, that is, acts of commanding, permitting, or rejecting. All the operations must be conceived of as taking place in the realm of idealized entities, that is, entities taken in a non-psychological sense.

If Alchourrón and Bulygin followed their non-psychologistic stipulation, there would be no difference between our standpoints save for the problems arising from their thesis that there is no difference in meaning (and therefore in logical relations and operations) between assertions, commands, permissions, rejections, and the like, since all of them have the same kind of content (namely propositions). This conception was criticized in the preceding section. Even if Alchourrón and Bulygin were correct in this assumption, and I have denied that they are, they should nevertheless acknowledge a form of the logic of norms as an immediate consequence of both the non-psychological sense of commanding and the introduction of the concept of normative system as leading to derived obligation (that is, to inferred norms). To make implicit commands explicit (or better, to command what has already been commanded implicitly) means nothing other than to establish normative conclusions, and this, in my view, is a part of the logic of norms.

V. NORMS AND TIME

There are objects that are absolutely timeless, and other objects to which we may meaningfully ascribe a temporal determination. For example, it makes no sense to ascribe temporal coordinates to numbers. We may also say that propositions are timeless, and Alchourrón and Bulygin contend the same with respect to normative propositions (or, as I would prefer to put it, norms as linguistic entities).

---

[25] See Edmund Husserl, *Logical Investigations*, 2 vols., trans. J.N. Findlay (London: Routledge & Kegan Paul, 1970), vol. I, at §§ 30–5 (pp. 327–33).

If we conceive of norms as bearing on social reality, that is, as institutional facts, then the problem of temporal determination becomes meaningful and relevant in practice. Institutionalized norms come into being, and their validity may also terminate at some point.

All analyses in which time is taken into consideration concern sets of norms that are ordered in a temporal series. The growth of the set of norms through successive acts of commanding also has the character of a temporal series of sets of norms. A set of norms can be constituted by a set of commands *uno actu*, but any change of a norm or of a set of norms—the addition as well as the subtraction of norms—produces a temporal series of normative systems. Norms as facts are not timeless, even if they do not change during the period in question. The change of a normative system in time depends on the rules of the dynamics of norms. Thus, I cannot accept Alchourrón and Bulygin's view that there is a fundamental difference between the addition and the subtraction of norms:[26] both are changes in a set of norms; both are established by the rules of change.

VI. REJECTION, DEROGATION, AND PERMISSION

One of the most interesting and subtle parts of Alchourrón and Bulygin's paper, 'The Expressive Conception of Norms', is the analysis of the concepts of rejection, derogation, and permission.[27]

Rejection is introduced as a special kind of a normative speech act. Alchourrón and Bulygin distinguish between descriptive and prescriptive rejection. Prescriptive rejection is the rejection of explicit or implicit commands. Acts of rejection of a certain kind, namely, of commands or assertions (perhaps also of permissions, and the like), constitute a set of rejected propositions. According to Alchourrón and Bulygin, the normative rejection of *p* does not presuppose that *p* is an element of a set of previously commanded propositions. We may also reject nonexisting normative propositions, and we may reject in advance propositions that could be commanded in the future. By an act of rejection the rejected proposition is not automatically eliminated from the set of commanded propositions, but the operation of elimination is given effect by a rule of preference. There is a conflict (a kind of incompatibility) between the command of *p* and the rejection of *p*.

Rejection is doubtlessly a relative notion. It makes sense only in relation to a set of propositions under consideration. Rejection refers to a certain set of propositions; and this set must be characterized by its

[26] See Alchourrón and Bulygin, 'Expressive Conception' (n.5 above), at § II.
[27] See ibid., at § III.

pragmatic (illocutionary) role, even in Alchourrón and Bulygin's teaching, for the distinction between descriptive and prescriptive rejection could not otherwise be maintained.

Alchourrón and Bulygin treat normative rejection as referring to commanded propositions alone, but I believe that in a system dealing with permissory acts and introducing the concept of a set of permitted propositions, the rejection of permission should also be taken into consideration. We might even raise the question of whether the rejection of a rejection makes sense, and if it does, we should explain how it should be handled.

It is neither useful nor consistent with our linguistic intuitions to relativize rejection solely to a set of propositions, together with their illocutionary indication, and not to a specific commanded (or permitted) content. It is, of course, logically possible to define rejection in such a way that rejection in advance, and even the rejection of propositions that will not ever be commanded in the future, becomes possible. But is it reasonable to conceive of rejection in this way? An act of rejecting p does not prevent a future act of commanding p, and it does not exclude the validity of such a future command either. In the usual terminology, we would say in such cases that p is explicitly permitted, rather than that p is rejected. It is reasonable, I think, to use the customary terminology, as the following considerations show. If rejection amounts to the elimination of the rejected content from a given set of propositions—and, at least in connection with the rules of preference, this is the main role of acts of rejection—then the rejection of propositions that do not belong to the set in question is void and ineffective even against future acts of commanding. It does not preclude the validity of future commands. It may lead to an inconsistency in the system if the principle of *lex posterior* is not institutionalized, or, if the principle of *lex posterior* is presupposed in relation to the rejection, a later command is *lex posterior* and its prior rejection will have no effect at all. Rejection in advance may have an effect only on the basis of certain hierarchical rules (rules of preference). But not every normative order contains hierarchical rules. If they are accepted, they not only prevent the efficacy of future commands of the rejected content but also prevent the validity of all future normative acts that are in conflict with higher-order norms.

Rejection is based on the dynamic conception of the normative order; it is meaningful only if we take into consideration changes in the order over time, that is, if we conceive of the order as a temporal series of normative systems.

The act of rejection is not by itself an operation—no speech act is. Rejection does, however, provide an input for the operation of elimination in a dynamic system of norms (or, according to Alchourrón and

Bulygin, a system of normative propositions). The elimination is deter-mined by the rules of preference, which may differ in different systems. I would stress, however, the thesis that according to the dynamic view of normative systems, there is a fundamental preference rule that is valid (in some sense) for all systems, namely, the priority of the *lex posterior* rule.

Logically there is, of course, the possibility of freezing a given norma-tive system, that is to say, precluding any change in the order. Normative orders as political institutions, however, involve the idea of evolution through acts of creating or transforming valid norms in the flow of time, that is, they contain some sort of rule to the effect that later normative regulations are preferred.

It is not easy to grasp Alchourrón and Bulygin's conception of deroga-tion, for (a) their semantics attaches meanings only to propositions, and (b) in some places they identify derogation with rejection, not with the elimination of norm-contents. They also explicitly accept Kelsen's con-ception of conflicting norms, as expressed in his later papers,[28] even though Kelsen's opinion on derogation is markedly different from their own view.

According to Kelsen, derogation is the effect of norms of a special kind: the effect of a derogating norm is the elimination of a heretofore valid norm from a normative order. Derogation as elimination does not pro-duce but rather eliminates conflicts, whereas Alchourrón and Bulygin's rejection of 'p' ('¡p') leads to a conflict if the normative system concerned embraces 'p' ('!p'). According to Kelsen, a derogated norm ceases to exist; it is no longer a norm of the system, and no normative determination stemming from the norm in question survives where that norm has been derogated.

Alchourrón and Bulygin write that '[w]hen lawyers speak of derogation there is a rejection of a norm-content',[29] and they hold that the elimina-tion is determined by rules of preference, the status of which is left unclear. Are they norms—as Kelsen contends—or methodological rules, or something else?

In Alchourrón and Bulygin's conception, derogation concerns the set of commanded normative contents A (why not also the set of permitted contents?) or the set of consequences $Cn(A)$, whereas Kelsen relates derogation to a given norm-content. Alchourrón and Bulygin's view leads to a very complicated theory according to which the system result-ing from a rejection may be logically indeterminate.

It behooves us to distinguish clearly (following Kelsen on this issue) between two cases: (a) the mere elimination of a norm (which may state

---

[28] See 'Derogation' and 'LL'. [For full bibliographical data, see the Table of Abbreviations.]
[29] Alchourrón and Bulygin, 'Expressive Conception' (n.5 above). § III.

an obligation or a permission) and (b) the creation of a new norm to the effect that a so-called material derogation has taken place. In case (a), there is no norm left after derogation, but in case (b), the *ought*-norm '!p' ('Op') is derogated by a norm of explicit permission 'Pp', or the permissory norm 'Pp' is derogated by the *ought*-norm '!$\sim p$' ('Fp'). It is only in the latter case that derogation may possibly bring about inconsistencies owing to the fact that a conflicting norm may come into being in the future.

According to Alchourrón and Bulygin's expressive conception, the notion of permission can be analysed in two ways, both of which are based on their concept of rejection and lead to nearly identical results.

(i) We may introduce a special kind of permissory use of propositions. This entails the existence of 'negative permission' (that is, the absence of prohibition) and of 'positive permission' (that is, the derogation of a prohibition).

(ii) Commanding as well as permitting are conceived of as forms of promulgation, namely, of a mandatory or of a permissory norm. In this case, Alchourrón and Bulygin distinguish 'weak permission' (that is, the absence of prohibition) from 'strong permission' (that is, the promulgation of a permissory norm).

I have some difficulties in understanding this distinction: in Alchourrón and Bulygin's theory promulgation is nothing other than a way of using a proposition. Permissory use is either the use of a sentence having a permissory meaning (this assumption contradicts Alchourrón and Bulygin's theory) or it is a use that cannot be distinguished from the rejective use. Thus, Alchourrón and Bulygin's conclusion, 'Strong permission proves to be the same as positive permission',[30] is not surprising.

In Alchourrón and Bulygin's theory the question arises as to why some kinds of acts are conceived of as normative acts. The authors, I believe, do not set out a complete list of normative speech acts,[31] and they do not explain the features that distinguish normative acts from other acts either.

The class of normative acts can be defined only if we take into consideration the different meanings of the contents of acts, but not if we presuppose, as Alchourrón and Bulygin do, that all speech acts have the same kind of content, namely propositional content.

I should like to introduce both a different terminology and a different conception of derogation and permission. Derogation is the elimination of norms belonging to a normative order that express an 'ought' (obliga-

---

[30] Alchourrón and Bulygin, 'Expressive Conception' (n.5 above), § VII.
[31] They do not mention either rejection of permission or rejection of rejection.

tion) or a 'may' (permission). Elimination is effected through normative acts of derogation, or is the result of the existence of conflicting norms (and thus the result of certain acts of normative promulgation), in accordance with the dynamic rules of the system. Derogation is relative to a certain norm of a given normative order. If a derogating norm states that the obligation (the permission) p is derogated but that the order does not contain the norm in question, the act of derogation is either senseless or void. Either of these stipulations is possible.

My analysis substantiates the following conclusions:

(i)   The thesis of the semantic and logical irrelevance of the norm-indicator (normative operator) is disproven.

(ii) Logical relations and logical inferences are, even in Alchourrón and Bulygin's theory, based on an idealization (or a non-psychological view) of the contents of acts, that is, they are obtained only by transcending the expressive conception in the strict sense, which ties normativity to the actual existence of normative acts.

(iii) The relations that Alchourrón and Bulygin accept as valid are not only relations among propositions, but also relations among different sets of propositions in different pragmatic roles, and the pragmatic (or illocutionary) character of the set determines these relations. Thus, it is not true that the authors provide only a logic of normative propositions.

(iv) The authors have presented very interesting analyses of the problems of rejection, derogation, and permission, but their results are vitiated by the untenability of the underlying ontology of norms criticized above.

(v)   Any derogation depends on extra-logical rules that establish a preference ordering of validity in relation to time. Not only can a permission derogate a proposition, but an explicit permission can also be derogated by a subsequent prohibition.

(vi) Explicit permission should be distinguished from derogation, although the meaning of permissory norms can be defined on the basis of their derogating capacity with respect to *ought*-sentences.

APPENDIX: GENERAL REMARKS ON PERMISSION

Recently, Alchourrón and Bulygin published an important new paper on the problems of permission, a paper not explicitly based on the expressive conception of norms.[32] There they offer a convincing analysis both

[32] Carlos E. Alchourrón and Eugenio Bulygin, 'Permission and Permissive Norms', in *Theorie der Normen. Festgabe für Ota Weinberger zum 65. Geburtstag*, ed. Werner Krawietz et al. (Berlin: Duncker & Humblot, 1984), 349–71.

of others' views on permission and of some conceptions of permission expressed in earlier papers of mine.[33] I do not intend to defend here the theses that I presented in these papers, but I should like to present a short account of my present views concerning permission and permissory sentences. I believe that we are now in a position to overcome the muddle concerning permissory sentences that arose in the early development of deontic logic.

I shall begin with some basic clarifications.

1. The field of prescriptive language and of norm-logical enquiry is primarily concerned with obligation, not with permission. Only *ought*-sentences, but not permissory sentences, can assume a regulative role. Regulation means determination (that is, the elimination of certain possibilities), whereas any form of behaviour is compatible with every permission, and no permission can be in conflict with any other permission. Only *ought*-sentences are directives for action; thus, a purely permissory system would not constitute a normative order at all.

2. It is important to introduce permissory sentences as a special kind of norm-sentence. Permissory sentences may be posited in acts of willing, or, as one might also put it, they are established and promulgated in the same way as *ought*-sentences (for example, as the content of legislative acts fulfilling the conditions for the creation of law).

3. Permissory sentences as a kind of normative sentence may have different pragmatic functions in different contexts, analogous to the different pragmatic roles of *ought*-sentences; in particular, they may be used in acts of promulgation as well as in speech acts that inform one about the normative situation without creating norms. I accept neither the doctrine of the duality of a descriptive and a prescriptive 'ought' nor the analogous duality of descriptive and prescriptive permission.[34] Instead, I conceive of the logic of norms as concerned with norm-sentences expressing 'ought' or 'may', notwithstanding the fact that there may also be descriptive sentences about a normative order or about norm-sentences. These sentences contain *ought*-sentences or permissory sentences in indirect speech, and the truth of these descriptive sentences is determined by the validity of the respective norm-sentences in the normative system in question.

[33] Ota Weinberger, 'Fundamental Problems of the Theory of Legal Reasoning', *ARSP*, 58 (1972), 305–36; Weinberger, 'Der Erlaubnisbegriff und der Aufbau der Normenlogik', *Logique et analyse*, 16 (1973), 113–42; Weinberger, 'Normenlogik und logische Bereiche', in *Deontische Logik und Semantik*, ed. Amedeo G. Conte et al. (Wiesbaden: Athenaion, 1977), 176–212.
[34] See Weinberger (n.6 above).

4. The distinction between open and closed normative systems is of crucial importance for the analysis of permissory sentences. A system NS is closed if and only if all obligations that are valid in NS are consequences of the explicitly stated norm-sentences. The system is an open system if and only if there may also be obligations or prohibitions that are not explicitly stated by the given norm-sentences. In the case of a closed system, the set of normative sentences provides complete information about the instances of 'ought' that hold in the system, whereas an open system admits of deontically undecided states of affairs.

5. If we accept the idea that permissions are not regulative norms and that therefore they can only play a secondary role in the field of prescriptive thought and discourse, we then have the task of explaining why such normative sentences are needed.

A. The Descriptive Concept of Permission.

We may even discuss the question of whether speaking about the permissory status of p is not simply a reflection of the fact that we find no prohibition of p in the normative system in question. An expressivist who restricts prescriptive discourse to commands may define permission as a descriptive notion by taking 'p is permitted' to mean exactly the same as the assertion that p is not forbidden in the system in question. In this case permissory sentences may be treated as descriptive sentences about a normative system NS. Such descriptive permissory sentences are, indeed, of two different kinds:

(i) the statement that p is permitted in NS means that p is definitely allowed in NS, for there is no prohibition of p in NS and NS is known to be a closed system, or

(ii) the statement that p is permitted in NS does not guarantee that p is definitely allowed, for NS is an open system such that we cannot be sure that the explicitly commanded duties (including consequences of explicit commands) express all duties valid in the normative system NS.

In closed systems, but only in such systems, the permission of p in this reflexive sense is a consequence of the absence of a prohibition of p, and vice versa: if p is permitted in NS, then p is not forbidden in NS. But reflexive permission in an *open system* does not justify the conclusion that if there is no explicit prohibition of p (that is, if there is only a reflexive permission in an open system, namely, reflexive permission), then p is definitely not forbidden in NS.

B. The Normative Concept of Permission.

There are good reasons for introducing another concept of permission, namely, one that is normative in character.

(i)   The practice of normative discourse usually contains explicit acts of permission that assume, as I will show, important pragmatic roles (see (ii)–(v) below). Thus, the language of the logic of norms should provide a rational reconstruction of such sentences.

(ii)   Permissory sentences may restrict prohibitions (that is, restrict the realm of applicability of *ought*-sentences) or state exceptions to more general prohibitions. (In these cases there is of course always the possibility of determining exactly the same normative situation without using permissory sentences, for the insertion of additional conditions may serve the same purpose.)

(iii)   Permissory sentences play an important role in the language of dynamic systems of norms: They can express a derogation (or partial derogation) of previously existing duties (obligations or prohibitions). This relation is a symmetric one. Permissory sentences may be used to derogate *ought*-sentences seen from the dynamic perspective (if they allow what has been previously forbidden), and *ought*-sentences may be used to derogate previously valid permissions.

(iv)   In open normative systems, permissory sentences are tools for removing uncertainty about the permissory status of states of affairs that are not explicitly characterized as either obligatory or forbidden.

(v)   In hierarchical systems, explicit permission is a tool for guaranteeing some kinds of normative freedom. Qualified permissions can be derogated only by means of suitably qualified acts.

(vi)   Permissory sentences may be used to provide information about what is permitted in NS, in that
        (a) the normative system embraces an explicit permissory sentence 'p is permitted', or
        (b) such a sentence can be deduced from the norm-sentences of the normative system (for example, from 'p is obligatory').

Thus, the concept of 'explicit permission' can be conceived of in two different ways, namely, (α) as given, if NS contains a sentence stating explicitly that p is permitted, or (β) as valid, if the sentence 'p is permitted' is deducible in NS. The latter view is of course more useful.

Reflexive permission does not entail, at least not in general, explicit permission. Only in a closed system NS can the absence of the prohibition of *p* justify the conclusion that *p* is permitted, for the closure of NS entails the rule that what is not explicitly forbidden in NS is allowed.

(vii) Deliberations about what is permitted are important for determining the range for action within the framework of a given normative system.

If we accept the view that permissory sentences should be introduced into prescriptive language, we must then find some method of defining the meaning of '*p* is permitted' and stating its relationship to *ought*-sentences.

We may define the meaning of '*p* is permitted' by means of the notion of derogating force. If the sentence '*p* is permitted' is used as a tool of derogation (elimination) or exclusion of *ought*-sentences, then we may say that '*p* is permitted' is a normative sentence that excludes the norm 'not-*p* ought to be'.

The conflict (logical exclusion) of '*p* is obligatory' ('$\sim p$ is forbidden') and '$\sim p$ is permitted' ('*p* is permitted') is a mutual one. If '*p* is permitted' belongs to NS, and '$\sim p$ is obligatory' is used on the basis of a rule with derogating force (that is, following the rule, say, *lex posterior derogat legi priori*), then '*p* is permitted' is eliminated from NS; and, vice versa, if '*p* is forbidden' ('$\sim p$ is obligatory') belongs to NS, then the norm '*p* is permitted' eliminates the previously valid 'ought'.

The definition of the notion of permission by means of the derogating capacity of permissory sentences does not prevent the existence of conflicts in normative systems; on the contrary, this definition is the logical reason for the conflict between '*p* is permitted' and '*p* is forbidden'.

It would be misleading to conceive of the relation between prohibition and permission as a relation of interdefinability. The derogating capacity used in the definition of permission is not a logical negation. In open systems—and most normative systems are open systems—there is no equivalence between the validity of the permission of *p* and the absence of the prohibition of *p*. What is more, interdefinability would be possible only in consistent systems. The apparatus of norm-sentences as a presupposed linguistic system for the logic of norms and for prescriptive discourse should be defined in such a way that even inconsistent normative systems can be given expression by means of it.

Generally, we assume that any norm-sentence whatever is deducible in an inconsistent normative system (*ex falso quodlibet*: from logically impossible premisses anything follows). The corresponding rules concerning descriptive language are clear from the fact that '$F \supset q$' and '$(p \& \sim p) \supset q$' are tautologies, and thus an impossible premiss such as '$p \& \sim p$' yields all possible consequences '*q*'. An analogous dictum concerning norm-sentences and normative inconsistency can be substantiated only if we introduce into the logic of norms analogous sentence structures (that is, a conditional of the type 'If (p & $\sim p$), then q should be') and rules of inference (that is, *modus ponens*).[35]

[35] See Ota Weinberger, 'Ex falso quodlibet in der deskriptiven und in der präskriptiven Sprache', *Rechtstheorie*, 6 (1975), 17–32.

PART V

Power, Legal Powers, and Empowerment

23

Kelsen and Legal Power*

NORBERTO BOBBIO

1. In general legal and political theory, norm and power are two sides of the same coin. In what sense? In the sense that if the law is understood, as it is in legal positivism, to be a collection of norms that are binding for an entire community in that they are enforced by ultimate recourse to coercion, then the existence of norms cannot be granted without pre-supposing the existence of individuals or collective entities that hold and regularly exercise power. And, conversely, if the state is understood, as it always has been in traditional political theory, to be an organization of power or organized power, then the existence of (state) power cannot be granted without presupposing at the same time the existence of norms that regulate the holding and exercise of this power, and that serve thereby to define the attributes of legitimacy and legality respectively.[1]

Of these two sides of the same coin, norm and power, some theories of the state emphasize the first, others the second. Indeed, general legal and political theories can be divided into two broad categories according to whether they affirm the primacy of power over norm or of norm over power. The classic theory of modern public law, which places at the apex of its construction the concept of sovereignty, understood as the highest power, having no other power above it, considers the state first of all from the standpoint of power. Hans Kelsen's theory, which places at the apex of the system the basic norm, not sovereign power, considers the state (and any other organized power) from the standpoint of normativity. Indeed, his theory can be interpreted as the most radical and

* *Editors' note*: This paper first appeared as 'Kelsen e il potere giuridico' in the collection *Ricerche politiche*, ed. Michelangelo Bovero (Milan: il Saggiatore, 1982), 3–26, and was reprinted in Norberto Bobbio, *Diritto e potere* (Naples: Edizioni Scientifiche Italiane, 1992), 123–39. The present version of the paper, in which a few minor changes have been made in consultation with Professor Bobbio, was translated by Michael Sherberg and Bonnie Litschewski Paulson.
[1] For the notions of legitimacy and legality, I am presupposing the analysis in my article, 'Sul principio di legittimità', in Bobbio, *Studi per una teoria generale del diritto* (Turin: G. Giappichelli Editore, 1970), 79–93.

thoroughgoing attempt (an attempt 'taken to extremes', which is not to say 'successful') to reduce the state to a legal or normative system, and to eliminate every form of dualism of law and state, truncating with one fell swoop the boring, sterile dispute over whether the state precedes the law or the law the state.[2]

In a rigorous normative theory like Kelsen's, the concept of the basic norm is exactly symmetrical to the concept, in political theory, of sovereign power. The basic norm is the norm of norms, just as sovereign power is the power of powers. These two concepts are perfectly symmetrical in that the basic norm and sovereign power both have the same function, that of closing the system of the state—the first in legal theory, the second in political theory. Kelsen understands the state as an organization of power. In public law, the state is understood for the most part as organized power, and, what is more, the reality of the modern state has been conceptually reconstructed as a state that affirms itself through the maximum concentration and centralization of power ever achieved over a determinate territory. Understood either as an organization of power or as organized power, the state is conceived of for the most part as an ordered and hierarchical system, that is to say, as a system comprising several planes or levels that are related to one another as superior to inferior or vice versa—not one alongside another, but one above or below another, like the stories of a building. A more appropriate metaphor might be the different strata of a pyramid, which takes into account not only the vertical dimension but also the fact that power, as it moves upward, is concentrated in a few hands. If one considers the various levels linked by the superior-inferior relation, in which a given level, superior in relation to its inferior, is at the same time inferior in relation to its superior, one sees clearly that the progression from inferior to superior level necessarily arrives—if one wishes to avoid an infinite regress— at a superior level that has no other level above it, and in relation to which all the other levels are, to different degrees, inferior. Starting at the bottom of the staircase and moving to the top, the traditional theory of public law takes as its point of departure a lower-level power and moves upward from power to power to arrive at sovereign power, the foundation of the authority of all other powers, while Kelsen's theory takes as its point of departure a lower-level norm and moves upward from norm to norm to arrive at the basic norm, the foundation of the validity of all other norms. The two staircases run alongside one another, but they are arranged so that the superior step of the one corresponds to the imme-

---

[2] For a clear position on the terms of the problem, see Miguel Reale, 'Law and Power and Their Correlation', in *Essays in Jurisprudence in Honor of Roscoe Pound*, ed. Ralph A. Newman (Indianapolis and New York: Bobbs-Merrill, 1962), 238–70.

diately inferior step of the other. For the normative theory, the superior step is the norm, for the traditional theory, the superior step is power.

Kelsen, when he proposes a description of the legal system in terms of levels, moves from lower-level norm to higher-level norm, to arrive at the highest-level norm, in what amounts to a 'backwards' or regressive process,[3] while, on the other hand, traditional political theory takes as its point of departure the superior level, that is, sovereign power. With that in mind, one can maintain that the same hierarchical order, made up of powers that create norms and of norms that authorize powers, changes according to whether one looks at it from bottom to top or from top to bottom. In the first case, one sees a gradation of norms, in the second, a cascade of powers.

2. Devoted to developing a normative legal and political theory, which dictates focusing on the norm rather than on power, Kelsen's work treated the problem of legal power as secondary. It is no accident that his writings conclude with the *General Theory of Norms* (posthumously published in 1979),[4] and not with a general theory of power like Max Weber's.[5] Still, it must be acknowledged that the problem of legal power took on ever greater significance in Kelsen's later work, not least of all in the Second Edition of the *Pure Theory of Law* (1960) and in the above-mentioned *General Theory of Norms*, where an entire chapter is devoted to legal power. For this reason, too, I believe that the time has come to begin to address the problem with the attention it deserves. (I say 'to begin', for I do not find in the immense body of secondary writings on Kelsen any treatment whatsoever of the theme.)

The object of the commentary that follows is not so much the problem of the relation between law and power qua coercion (which, in Kelsenian terms, resolves into the relation between the validity and the efficacy of the legal system). This problem has already been thoroughly discussed by critics of the Pure Theory of Law. Rather, my focus is the problem of legal power as an instance of subjective law, which Kelsen comes to define only in his later works.

3. In a legal and political theory that has as its point of departure the primacy of the norm over power, there cannot be any power other than legal power, that is, power regulated by law, where 'regulated' is understood to mean both authorized by an empowering norm (*ermächtigende Norm*) and, in certain cases, bound by imperative norms. In all his

---

[3] *PTL* § 35(a) (p. 222).

[4] *GTN*.

[5] The question of the relationship between Weber and Kelsen was the focus of my contribution to a meeting on 'Max Weber and the Law', held in Rome in October 1980; the paper appeared under the title 'Max Weber e Hans Kelsen', *Sociologia del diritto*, 8 (1981), 135–54.

writings, Kelsen returned repeatedly to this point with a constancy unassailable by any critique. The following passage is exemplary:

What distinguishes the relation characterized as state power (*Staatsgewalt*) from other power relations is the fact that it is legally regulated (*rechtlich geregelt*), which is to say that those who exercise power as the government of the state are authorized by the legal system to exercise that power by creating and applying legal norms, which is to say that state power has normative character.[6]

It is by means of the basic norm that Kelsen reduces to a legal power every power exercised in the sphere of the legal system. Understood precisely as the norm that, on the one hand, authorizes the supreme power to create law and, on the other, commands those addressed by the supreme power to obey the norms issued by the supreme power, the basic norm has the function, as Kelsen himself incisively puts it, of 'transforming power into law',[7] thereby permitting the distinction between a legal norm and a bandit's command.

Kelsen devoted one of the first sections of the Second Edition of the *Pure Theory of Law* to the problem—familiar from the tradition in legal and political theory—of whether and what kind of a difference exists between a legal community and a band of brigands. It is no accident that precisely here, in these pages, one of the first references to the basic norm is encountered.

The problem is posed in these terms: From the standpoint of their 'subjective sense', the command of an organ of the state and the bandit's command are not different. Only the first, however, has an objective sense in that we interpret the command of the legal organ, but not that of the bandit, 'as an objectively valid norm'.[8] But why, Kelsen asks, do we interpret in one case, and not in the other, the subjective sense of the act also as its objective sense? The answer is that in attributing an objective sense to the command of the organ of the state, our point of departure is a *presupposition*; specifically, we presuppose that, as we move from a lower-level regulated power to a higher-level regulated power, even the ultimate power—the so-called constituting power—is regulated by a norm 'according to which the act to be interpreted as the constituting act is to be regarded as an act establishing objectively valid norms, and those who carry out this act are to be regarded as the constituting authority.'[9]

Kelsen, taking to its extreme the thesis that, with respect to a legal system, there is no power other than legal power, goes so far as to negate the traditional dualism of law and state, formulating the well-known and controversial theory according to which the state is reduced to a legal

---

[6] *PTL* § 41(a) (p. 289) (trans. altered).
[7] *Phil. Fds.* § 35 (p. 437) [Kelsen's emphasis omitted by Bobbio].
[8] *PTL* § 6(c) (p. 45).   [9] *PTL* § 6(c) (p. 46) (trans. altered).

system. Having arrived at this conclusion, he does not miss the chance to argue with traditional theory, which identifies the state as power, and power as being behind the law, indeed, as establishing the law. For Kelsen, the existence of this power reduces to the fact that a determinate legal system is efficacious in the sense that the organs mandated to enforce legal norms succeed for the most part in doing so.

The power of the state is the power organized by positive law—is the power of law; that is, the efficacy of positive law.

Conclusion:

To describe the state as 'the power behind the law' is incorrect, since it suggests the existence of two separate entities where there is only one: the legal [system].[10]

The same polemic returns in Kelsen's critique of the distinction between private and public law that is made by distinguishing between private law relations understood as legal relations and public law relations understood as power (*Macht*) relations. Against the tendency to take this distinction to be an opposition between law and extralegal power (*Gewalt*), and, finally, between law and state, Kelsen maintains that

if one considers more closely the greater value conferred upon certain subjects, their superordination over others, one sees that it properly consists in a distinction between law-creating material facts.[11]

In what sense? The law can be created either by means of heteronymous norms, where the issuer of the norm and its addressee are two different subjects, or autonomously, where the subject to whom the norm is addressed is the same subject who creates the norm or collaborates in its creation. An example of the first type of law creation is the administrative order, an example of the second type is the contract and, in general, the commercial transaction. For Kelsen, the distinction between private and public law reduces for the most part to the difference between these two methods of creating law, a difference that is entirely resolved within the legal system and requires no reference to extralegal concepts. In sum, the Pure Theory of Law sees an act of the state in both the commercial transaction and the authoritative order, that is, in an instance—in both cases—of law creation that can be ascribed to the unity of the legal system considered as a whole.

  4. Returning to the passage quoted above,[12] according to which 'legally regulated power' is understood as power conferred by the system on certain individuals to create and to apply legal norms, one notes that, for Kelsen, the scope of the concept of legal power (while still very broad) is limited to the phenomena of creating and applying the law. The

---

[10] *GTLS* 190–1.   [11] *PTL* § 37 (p. 281) (trans. altered).   [12] See the text at n.6.

existence of legal norms (and other norms) requires that there be some- one whose act of will creates and enforces them. Although not until the Second Edition of the *Pure Theory of Law*, 'legal power' ('*Rechtsmacht*') does definitively become a technical term in Kelsen's language for indi- cating the capacity [*capacità*] conferred by the legal system on certain subjects to create and to apply legal norms. Correspondingly, the act of conferring this power [*potere*] is termed 'empowerment' ('*Ermächti- gung*'), defined as 'the conferral of a legal power, that is, the capacity [*Fähigkeit*] to create and to apply legal norms'.[13]

In the works preceding the Second Edition of the *Pure Theory of Law* and therefore preceding this definition of legal power (and of the corre- sponding conferral of capacity), where the respective terms '*Rechts- macht*' and '*Ermächtigung*' are used as technical terms, Kelsen proceeds by analysing subjective law. In the First Edition of the *Pure Theory of Law* (1934),[14] Kelsen already understood subjective law in a technical sense as the power conferred by some legal systems (in particular, capitalistic legal systems oriented to protecting private property) on the subject to bring an action in defence of his own violated right. Since the exercise of this power contributes to the creation of an individual norm (the judge's decision), subjective law thus understood could be interpreted as a form of participation, if only partial, in the creation of law. It followed that this right to bring an action came to be considered a species of a greater genus that also includes the right to vote, that is, the right conferred by some legal systems (in particular, democratic systems) on some subjects to participate—if only indirectly, by electing legislators—in the forma- tion of those general norms that are laws. This definition of subjective law in a technical sense includes, then, the private right to bring an action as well as the public right to vote, which are distinguished from one another only in that the first is taken as functioning to create an indi- vidual norm, the second, a general norm. Using this definition, Kelsen demonstrated the importance that he attached to the connection between some traditional instances of subjective law and the problem of law creation, or, according to the traditional theory, the problem of the sources of law.[15]

Still, one must go to the Second Edition of the *Pure Theory of Law* to find legal power (*Rechtsmacht*) as subjective law in a technical sense, and empowerment (*Ermächtigung*) as the corresponding authorization.[16]

---

[13] *RR 2* § 30(c) (p. 156) [this passage is not reproduced in *PTL*].

[14] [Translated into English under Kelsen's subtitle, *Introduction to the Problems of Legal Theory* (see the Table of Abbreviations, at *LT*).]

[15] I considered this problem in greater detail in an article on 'Kelsen et les sources du droit', *Revue internationale de philosophie*, 35 (1981), 474–86 (a special number dedicated to Kelsen and legal positivism).

[16] *RR 2* § 29(d) (pp. 139–42); *PTL* § 29(d) (pp. 134–7).

But now—and this is what matters—Kelsen went a step further in determining instances of subjective law; he linked them, not surprisingly, to the diverse functions of the legal norm, the focus of one of the first sections of the Second Edition. In the First Edition, Kelsen had distinguished the legal norm as imposition of an obligation from the legal norm as authorization, but he had understood this authorization ('*Berechtigung*', not '*Ermächtigung*') only as the conferral of a subjective right in the technical sense. And he had specified straightaway that he was dealing with a particular technique of determinate legal systems—more precisely, the capitalistic system in the case of the private subjective right, and the democratic system in the case of the public subjective right. In the Second Edition, three functions of the legal norm emerge, and they are command, permission, and empowerment (*Gebieten*, *Erlauben*, and *Ermächtigen*).

For the definition of empowerment, which is the function that interests us, two passages near one another may be cited, one more limited in scope, the other broader. The first:

(Certain human acts) are intentionally directed to the behaviour of another individual not only when, according to their meaning, they command (order) this behaviour, but also when they permit it and, in particular, when they authorize it, that is to say, when a certain power is conferred on the other individual—in particular, even the power to issue norms.[17]

Here, the notion of the legal power that derives from an authorizing norm is directly linked to the notion of law creation. The second passage:

Human behaviour is also governed positively [as opposed to negatively] when an individual is empowered by the normative system to bring about, by means of a certain action, certain consequences normatively regulated by the system—in particular, to create norms or to participate in their creation (if the system governs its own creation); or when a legal system that establishes coercive acts empowers an individual to carry out these coercive acts in accordance with the conditions established by the legal system.[18]

In this passage, the meaning of legal power as the power to create the norms of a system that regulates its own creation of norms (and the legal system is precisely this, as we shall see below) is extended to include legal power as the power to carry out coercive acts in order to enforce norms. (Among the different normative systems, the legal system, since it is a coercive system, is characterized by coercive acts.) In short, it turns out that from the very first pages of the Second Edition, the founder of the Pure Theory of Law concludes in a certain sense that 'legal power' must be understood technically as the power that a determinate normative

---

[17] *PTL* § 4(b) (pp. 4–5) (trans. altered).   [18] *PTL* § 4(d) (pp. 15–16) (trans. altered).

system confers on certain individuals to create and to apply the norms of the system. The normative system is understood here both as regulating its own creation of norms and as making use of coercive acts—that is, of ultimate recourse to coercion—to enforce the norms it creates (two characteristics of the legal system). Through this series of definitions at the beginning of the treatise, Kelsen renders the notion of legal power independent of the notion of subjective law in a technical sense. The contrast between the two is telling here. The subjective right, as defined by Kelsen, is a characteristic feature of some legal systems, as we have seen, and so there can be legal systems that do not provide for the conferral of subjective rights, for example, systems that are neither capitalistic nor democratic; legal power, understood as the power to create and to apply norms, is a constitutive element of every legal system. A legal system is defined here as a system that, in governing its own creation, must empower certain individuals to carry out norm-creating acts, and, at the same time, as a system that, in resorting to organized sanctions to govern compliance with the norms created, must empower certain individuals to carry out coercive acts.

5. That legal power became an independent, consistent theme in the later phase of Kelsen's work is borne out by its prominence in the posthumously published monograph of 1979.[19] Here an entire chapter is devoted to empowerment (*Ermächtigung*), with a title significant in and of itself since it shows that the problem of power is now separate from the specific treatment of subjective law: 'Empowering: Conferring the Power to Issue and to Apply Norms' ('*Ermächtigen: die Macht verleihen, Normen zu setzen und anzuwenden*'). And the chapter begins with this statement: 'Since the law governs its own creation and application, the normative function of empowerment plays a particularly important role in the law.'[20] Immediately following, in fact, the statement that 'only individuals on whom the legal system confers this power can create or apply legal norms.'

At this point, Kelsen's awareness of empowerment as a normative function independent of the functions of command and permission leads him to dwell primarily on the relation between empowering and commanding. First of all, the authorized act can be commanded or not; that is, the individual on whom power is conferred can be obligated or not to exercise it. Only in the case where he is obligated to exercise power does his failure to do so constitute a violation of law. Plainly, this is the instance of subjective law that jurists call obligatory power. Second,

[19] *GTN.* See generally Kazimierz Opałek, *Überlegungen zu Hans Kelsens "Allgemeine Theorie der Normen"* (Vienna: Manz, 1980), and Pier Paolo Portinaro, 'La teoria generale delle norme nell'opus posthumum di Hans Kelsen', *Nuovi studi politici*, 11 (1981), 45–70.
[20] *GTN* ch. 26, § I (p. 102) (trans. altered).

empowerment can imply a command, and always does so when—like the empowerment emphasized in Kelsen's work—it is an empowerment to create norms. The norm empowering the father to command his son also commands the son to obey the father. The constitution empowering legislative organs to create general legal norms also commands citizens to obey the laws. Consequently, the same norm has two simultaneous functions: It is an empowering norm with respect to the father and the legislator, an imperative norm with respect to the son and citizens. Third, while the command is obeyed and disobeyed, the empowerment is applied. The difference is that a command can be obeyed or disobeyed and either behaviour has a legal consequence, while power can only be exercised, and failure to do so does not imply any legal consequence—except in the case of obligatory power, where a legal consequence inheres in noncompliance with duty, that is, in a violation of law.

It is one thing, however, not to exercise a power that has been conferred on us, and something else to exercise a power that has not been conferred on us. These two situations can be expressed with statements like these: 'I am empowered to do something, but I do not do it,' and 'I am not empowered to do something, but I do it,' as opposed, respectively, to the two regular situations, which can be expressed with: 'I am empowered to do something, and I do it,' and 'I am not empowered to do something, and I do not do it.' In the case of failing to exercise power (I mean, here, non-obligatory power), the expected effect of the conferral of power does not follow, because the act that should produce this effect is missing. In the case of exercising nonexistent power, the effect follows, but it is legally null and void. Kelsen pauses to consider briefly the act that is not authorized. He limits himself to saying that carrying out an unauthorized act neither creates law nor applies it, even if the act, subjectively, is carried out with this intention. It is objectively null and void, which means 'legally nonexistent' ('*rechtlich nicht vorhanden*').[21] And, Kelsen adds, to say that an act is not authorized is not to say that it is prohibited. Unauthorized acts might be prohibited, like the act of someone who threateningly orders another to hand over money; and unauthorized acts might not be prohibited, like the act of someone who commands his followers to abstain from sexual relations. While an unauthorized act might not be legally prohibited, the norm produced by such an act is not a legal norm if the actor is not empowered to issue legal norms, that is, has not been invested with legal power. Kelsen stops here, however, not confronting the problem of nullity or annullability, which he had considered elsewhere. He does discuss whether nullity is or is not a sanction, a familiar question in general legal theory. For Kelsen, and for

---

[21] Ibid.

H.L.A. Hart as well, nullity cannot be numbered among the sanctions. In my opinion, the question here is in large part a question of words; settling it depends in one sense or another on a broader or narrower definition of sanction. If, for sanction, one means an unwanted, unintended consequence of behaviour, then both punishment (as the unwanted, unintended effect of behaviour that is not permitted) and nullity (which is the unwanted, unintended effect of behaviour that is not authorized) can be considered to be sanctions. The difference between the two is that punishment is a consequence other than what the agent intended, while nullity consists purely and simply in failing to accomplish what was intended. Nullity is the typical sanction, if you will, of technical norms or norms that prescribe an act not as an end in itself but as a means for accomplishing an end. An example is the will or testament, a means provided by the law to permit a person to declare his final wishes.

6. In the posthumous work, as I pointed out above, Kelsen finally acknowledged that 'the normative function of empowerment plays a particularly important role in the law.' He bases this assertion on the argument that the law is a normative system that governs its own creation. While acknowledging the importance of the argument, to which I return below, I believe it is useful to point out that in order to demonstrate the importance of the notion of legal power, understood in Kelsenian terms as the capacity to create norms, another argument—preliminary to Kelsen's own—can be adduced.

The Pure Theory of Law is a positivistic theory of law, not only in the sense that it is a theory of positive law, but also in the even more suggestive sense that it recognizes no law other than positive law. Now, according to Kelsen, what distinguishes legal positivism from the theory of natural law is its view of the law as man's creation. It is certainly not possible here to reconsider Kelsen's polemic against natural law; it suffices to call attention to the terms Kelsen uses to define the contrast between positive law and natural law. Close to the beginning of Kelsen's treatise, *Philosophical Foundations of Natural Law Theory and Legal Positivism* (1928), the contrast between an 'artificial' law, created by man, and so-called 'natural' law could not be neater:

Unlike the norms of positive law, which are valid because they are 'artificially' *issued* by a specified human authority, norms of the 'natural' order that govern human conduct are valid because, stemming from God, nature, or reason, they are good, right, and just. Precisely here—by comparison to natural law—lies the 'positivity' of positive law: that it is 'issued' by way of human will, a basis of validity wholly alien to natural law because, as a 'natural' order, natural law is not created by man and, indeed, cannot by definition be created by way of a human act.[22]

[22] *Phil. Fds.* § 2 (p. 392) (Kelsen's emphasis) (trans. altered).

On the basis of this contrast, Kelsen works out a theory of normative systems. He suggests that there are two types of normative system: Static systems are made up of norms that are deduced from one another on the basis of their content, dynamic systems are made up of norms that are produced by means of one another through a relation of delegation, that is, through the transmission of power from a higher level to a lower level. Legal systems, according to Kelsen, belong to the second category. Nothing demonstrates the central place that the notion of law creation occupies in Kelsen's theory better than his interpretation of the legal system as a dynamic system. A system of natural law is deduced, a system of positive law is produced.

As a theory of positive law, understood as law created by man and not existing in nature or created by God, the Pure Theory of Law cannot help but give maximum importance to acts that create legal norms. A legal system, composed of norms, exists in that it is created and continually recreated, in that there are individuals who create law—in different forms, as general norms or individual norms, and with different functions, the imperative, the permissive, or the empowering function. Now, once Kelsen goes so far as to include in the general category of legal power all law-creating acts, he cannot fail to acknowledge the centrality of this category in the system. Legal norms are man's creation; in order that these norms be created, it is necessary that the selfsame system confer on certain individuals the power to create norms. Thus, the existence of a legal system cannot be separated from the carrying out of certain acts, and legal power consists in precisely these acts.

7. What remains open—indeed, untreated—is the problem of custom, which might very well be considered positive law in that it is law created by man, but which cannot be assimilated to positive or written law on a par with general norms enacted by a parliament or individual norms set by judges as decisions in litigation. Favouring the view of custom as law created in the same way as that created by a sovereign will, Kelsen takes a clear position critical of theories—like the legal theory of the Historical School and the sociological theory of Léon Duguit—according to which custom has declarative not constitutive value, that is, custom has the function of revealing pre-existent law, not of creating law. Kelsen's objection to these two theories is the same as his objection to natural law theory. Noting that the two theories are simply variations of natural law, he states that

[f]rom the standpoint of a positivistic theory of law, which cannot assume the existence of either an imaginary *Volksgeist* or an equally imaginary '*solidarité social*', the constitutive or law-creating function of custom is as indubitable as that of legislation.[23]

<hr>

[23] *PTL* § 35(b) (p. 227) (trans. altered).

Thus, there is no difference between custom and legislation with respect to the definition of positive law as law that is created—'artificial' or customary law—and nonexistent in nature. The theory of the sources of law, or, in Kelsen's terms, the 'methods of law creation' ('*Methoden der Rechtserzeugung*'),[24] is unitary. As a source of law, custom, too, is one of the methods of law creation, a 'law-creating material fact' ('*ein rechtserzeugender Tatbestand*').[25]

In the later phase of Kelsen's thought, as we have seen, the theory of legal power as the power to create legal norms is closely linked to the theory of the sources or the creation of law. If custom can rightfully take its place among the material facts that create law, can it also be included in the definition of legal power? Can one say that the formation of custom is the effect of legal power? Can one say that the recognition of custom as a source of law in a determinate legal system—with reference to a statute or simply to the basic norm (as happens in international law)—amounts to the conferral of legal power, that this recognition is comparable to empowerment, and that the norm recognizing custom as a source of law is an empowering norm (*ermächtigende Norm*) equivalent to the constitutional norm that empowers parliament to issue general norms and the judge to issue individual norms? That the creation of legal norms is linked to legal power permits us to speak of constituent power in relation to constitutional norms, legislative power in relation to ordinary laws, administrative power with respect to the regulations of administrative authority, judicial power with respect to the decisions of judges, and negotiating power with respect to the creation of contractual and negotiated [commercial] norms in general. Can one speak, correctly, of customary power? When Kelsen introduces the expression 'legal power', he makes no specific reference to custom. In the posthumous work, in the chapter devoted to legal power, the examples of normative power all concern single individuals or organs, while custom is the product of an indiscriminate community. Nor does the expression 'legal power', for its part, turn up in the pages devoted to custom as a source of law. The problem of whether custom, beyond being a material fact that creates legal norms, can be included in the general category of legal power remains, as I said, untreated, since Kelsen does not discuss it explicitly, and open, since the solution is uncertain.

8. Finally, one cannot fail to comment on Kelsen's statement in the posthumous work, quoted above,[26] to the effect that the normative function of empowerment plays a particularly important role in a normative system that—like the legal system—governs its own creation.

---

[24] *PTL* § 35(e) (p. 233).   [25] *PTL* § 35(b) (p. 225).
[26] See text quoted at n.20 above.

That the law governs its own creation means, in Kelsenian terms, that a legal system is a normative system in which the creation of the system's norms is itself regulated by other norms of the system, in a process that begins, necessarily, with the basic norm ('necessity' must be understood here as logical, not factual, necessity), and moves from higher-level norm to lower-level norm, to arrive, finally, at the lowest-level norm. In that the legal system is created and continually recreated through the system's norms, it is, in an expression characteristic of Kelsen, 'self-creating'. 'The doctrine of the hierarchical structure of the legal system comprehends the law in motion, in the constantly regenerating process of its self-creation.'[27] Regulation of its own creation of norms by a normative system like the legal system, which has rules for the creation of rules, takes place by means of empowerment, starting from the basic norm and progressing all the way to commercial transactions. It follows that legal power is indeed of particular importance in such a system, just as Kelsen stated. The existence of so many legal powers that are linked to one another by relations of delegation permits the self-creation that is characteristic of a dynamic normative system.

9. The concept of legal power that Kelsen always defines in relation to the creation and application of norms may seem narrow by comparison to the concept of legal power that general legal theory uses primarily in determining instances of subjective law, one of which is power. I refer in particular to the table of fundamental legal concepts set out by Wesley Newcomb Hohfeld and accepted by Alf Ross, according to which the notion of power, in Manfred Moritz's interpretation, is extended to include all acts whose effect is a change in a legal relation.[28] In reality, when one considers the broad meaning of the term 'legal norm' in the language of the Pure Theory, Kelsen's definition of power is less narrow than it appears to be on first glance. By 'legal norm', Kelsen means not only general norms, but also individual norms, like the decisions of judges, not only norms of public law, like statutes or administrative measures, but also norms of private law, like contracts. The legal system, in conferring on someone the power to carry out commercial negotiations or to enter into a contract, is also conferring on that person the power, according to Kelsen, to create prescriptive legal norms. Since the function of prescriptive norms is to modify the behaviour of the subjects addressed, by ordering either an act or a forbearance, the conferral of power, even in a Kelsenian sense, has the function of making change

---

[27] *LT* § 43 (p. 92).
[28] See Wesley Newcomb Hohfeld, *Fundamental Legal Conceptions*, ed. Walter Wheeler Cook (New Haven: Yale UP, 1919); Ross, *LJ*, at 161–9; Manfred Moritz, *Über Hohfelds System der juridischen Grundbegriffe* (Lund: C.W.K. Gleerup, and Copenhagen: Ejnar Munksgaard, 1960), § 22 (on power) (at pp. 85–92).

possible in legal relations, whether this change takes place by means of general norms issued by legislative organs or by means of the agreement of private citizens.

Closer to the Kelsenian notion of power is the view proposed by Hart. As is well known, Hart divides norms into two broad categories, those that impose obligations and those that confer powers. He describes the latter as norms that define 'the ways in which valid contracts or wills or marriages are made [but that] do not require persons to act in certain ways whether they wish to or not.'[29] He then extends this category to include norms that confer public powers, like, for example, the power of a legislature to issue new norms or to modify or to abrogate existing norms, or the power of a judge to settle a controversy. 'Surely not all laws', Hart writes,

order people to do or not to do things. Is it not misleading so to classify laws which confer powers on private individuals to make wills, contracts, or marriages, and laws which give powers to officials, e.g. to a judge to try cases, to a minister to make rules, or to a county council to make by-laws?[30]

The difference between Hart and Kelsen is that for Hart, norms that impose obligations and norms that confer powers belong to two distinct classes, independent of one another, while for Kelsen, empowering norms are not independent since their function is simply to establish one of the conditions ultimately linked to the coercive act, which depends on the only norm that is truly primary and therefore independent: the norm establishing that a given (illegal) act must be followed by an act carried out by public officials (the sanction).[31] Hart repeatedly takes a position against Kelsen's theory of dependent norms, arguing that the price of the uniformity stemming from Kelsenian reductionism is the distortion of reality.[32]

10. I said at the outset that since norm and power are two sides of the same coin, the problem of law and state can be considered for the most part either from the standpoint of the norm, as Kelsen does, or from the standpoint of power, as the traditional theory of public law has always done. But now, in conclusion, I should like to add that neither of the two standpoints succeeds in being exclusive, because the two concepts are so interlaced and interdependent. The theorist *par excellence* of sovereignty, Jean Bodin, having defined sovereign power as absolute power in the sense of *legibus solutus*, cannot help but specify that 'absolute' must be understood here as independence from positive laws but not from natural and divine laws—as if to correct the idea that one can completely

---

[29] Hart, *CL* 27, 2nd edn. 27.   [30] Hart, *CL* 26, 2nd edn. 26.
[31] See *PTL*, at § 6(e) (pp. 54–8).
[32] See Hart, *CL*, at 35–8, 239 (notes), 2nd edn., at 35–8, 286 (notes).

separate power from law even at the apex of the system (power that must be legitimately held and legally exercised in order to be 'right' power and therefore distinguishable from the power of the tyrant). And the founder of the normative theory of law and state? Kelsen, as is well known, having arrived at a basic norm that closes the system, cannot help but specify that, notwithstanding the basic norm, the legal system is valid overall only if it is also efficacious, that is, only if those who have the power to create the norms of the system also have the power to enforce them, with the result that the norms of the system are by and large observed.

Thus, in a way that is both contrary and symmetrical to the traditional theory, the Pure Theory of Law makes it known that, at the apex of the system, law can no longer be separated from power, and, indeed, it becomes increasingly difficult to make out where one ends and the other begins. The jurist's maxim, *lex facit regem*, is continually converted into its opposite, the maxim always defended by the realist politician, *rex facit legem*.

24

Voluntary Obligations and
Normative Powers*

JOSEPH RAZ

The main thesis for which I shall argue is that a satisfactory analysis of voluntary obligations must be in terms of normative powers. To substantiate this claim it will be necessary to examine in some detail the concepts of a normative power and of a power-conferring norm (or *P*-norm). I shall start with an analysis of legal powers and then proceed to examine the applicability of the concept outside the law.

I shall refer throughout to 'norms' rather than 'rules'. Norms, unlike rules, can be particular as well as general. Some principles as well as rules are norms, but not all the types of rules and principles are norms. Technical rules, for example, are not norms. The sense in which 'norms' is being used will be explained below.

I. LEGAL POWERS

Legal writers, judges, and lawyers do not use the term 'legal power' as often as do legal theorists. They speak of the powers of the police, of courts, or ministers, but seldom refer to the power of a person to make contracts or wills, etc., where terms like 'competence' or 'capacity' are more often used. Legal theorists have given 'legal power' a wider and more technical meaning, not because they sought to elucidate the ordinary meaning of the words, but because they saw the need for a general concept to draw attention to important similarities between otherwise heterogeneous phenomena. The same must be true of an investigation of the role the concept should play in general normative theory. To be sure, the term is not often employed in ordinary discourse concerning

* *Editors' Note*: This symposium contribution (together with a contribution by Neil MacCormick, see n.8 below) first appeared in the *Proceedings of the Aristotelian Society. Supplementary Volume*, 46 (1972), 79–102.

voluntary obligations. The question is whether we shall gain in clarity and understanding from its employment to describe certain non-legal normative phenomena. I have no doubt that we shall.

Most of the textbook definitions of a legal power are derived from Hohfeld's famous analysis of the concept in *Fundamental Legal Conceptions*,[1] though by far the most thorough and penetrating analysis is Bentham's.[2] Not wishing to engage in a comparative study of various definitions of the concept, I shall take Hohfeld's analysis as my starting-point.

Hohfeld writes:

A change in a given legal relation may result (1) from some superadded fact . . . not under the volitional control of a human being . . .; or (2) from some superadded fact or group of facts . . . under the volitional control of one or more human beings. As regards the second class of cases, the person (or persons) whose volitional control is paramount may be said to have the (legal) power to effect the particular change of legal relations that is involved.[3]

Following Hohfeld most textbooks define legal power as the ability to effect a legal change, a change in the legal situation, by a voluntary act. Such definitions though helpful and in the main correct are not precise and may mislead. Let me add four points clarifying and modifying the traditional definition.

1. The Relation between the Act and its Legal Consequences.

A legal power is normatively, not causally, effective. It is not the ability 'to cause certain desired legal effects'.[4] I may be able to bring it about that my wife will make a gift of all her property to me, but it is she, not I, who has the power to make a gift of her property. I may be able to make all the voters of my ward vote for me in every local election, but I have the power to cast just one vote in each election. I have a legal power only if it is my act which is recognized by law as effecting a legal change.

2. The Power-Exercising Act.

Hohfeld's and most of the other explanations of a legal power are too sweeping. Not every voluntary act which effects a legal change is an exercise of a legal power. Every offence or civil wrong changes the legal

---

[1] Wesley Newcomb Hohfeld, *Fundamental Legal Conceptions*, ed. Walter Wheeler Cook (New Haven: Yale UP, 1919).

[2] See Jeremy Bentham, *Of Laws in General*, ed. H.L.A. Hart (London: Athlone Press, 1970). Bentham's analysis is discussed in detail by H. L. A. Hart, 'Bentham on Legal Powers', *Yale Law Journal*, 81 (1971–2), 799–822, repr. under the title 'Legal Powers', in Hart, *Essays on Bentham* (Oxford: Clarendon Press, 1982), 194–219.

[3] Hohfeld (n.1 above), 50–1.

[4] Ross, *LJ* 166.

situation. It usually makes, for example, the offender liable to a sanction, and imposes on the wrongdoer an obligation to compensate. There are many other acts which effect a legal change but are not the exercise of legal powers. By changing my residence from one town to another, or from one country to another, I change my rights and duties, but I do not have a legal power to effect these changes by such action. Salmond seems to meet the problem by defining power 'as ability conferred upon a person by the law to alter, by his own will *directed to that end*', the legal situation.[5] Unfortunately the added condition makes his definition both too wide and too restricted. It does not avoid the objection I raised, for people have been known to commit an offence in order to be punished, or to change residence in order to change their legal position. On the other hand, it is possible to exercise power and to make a contract or some other legal transaction with no intention to do so, if one does not correctly appreciate the legal consequences of one's action.

The solution of the difficulty lies not in the intention with which power-exercising acts are performed but in the reasons for which they are recognized as effecting a legal change. An action is the exercise of a legal power only if one of the law's reasons for acknowledging that it effects a legal change is that it is of a type such that it is reasonable to expect that actions of that type will, if they are recognized to have certain legal consequences, standardly be performed only if the person con- cerned wants to secure these legal consequences.[6]

This is a most important feature of legal powers, which is all too often neglected. It explains why they are exercised either by special formal and ceremonial acts as in making a deed or getting married, or by ordinary actions whose legal consequences approximate their non-legal and obvious consequences, as in making a contract. It also explains why most legal powers are exercised by acts with only negligible non-normative consequences, like signing, so that there are few reasons for or against doing them apart from their legal or other normative consequences.

3. The Nature of the Legal Consequences.

Hohfeld thought that every legal change is a change in someone's rights and duties. However, a legal change may consist in change of status or in the creation or liquidation of a legal person, and Hohfeld was mistaken in thinking that these are no more than bundles of rights and duties. A legal change should therefore be defined as a change in the existence,

[5] John Salmond, *Jurisprudence*, 12th edn., ed. P.J. Fitzgerald (London: Sweet & Maxwell, 1966), 229 (emphasis added).
[6] Lawyers have established procedures for determining what are the law's intentions or reasons. These need not be discussed here.

content, or application of a law or a legally recognized norm. The distinction between laws and other legally recognized norms will be discussed below.

Powers of legislation and of making contracts are, respectively, the paradigmatic examples of powers determining the content and existence of laws and of legally recognized norms. By their exercise a law is created or modified or repealed, or a contract is created or modified or rescinded. Such powers I shall call norm-creating powers. (Not every law is a norm, but those which are not are logically related to legal norms, and therefore there is no harm in calling powers determining their content and existence 'norm-creating' powers.) The powers to appoint a judge or to transfer ownership do not determine the content of laws or of legally recognized norms. They govern the application of such norms. The rights and duties of a judge or of a property owner are determined by laws, the validity and content of which are unaffected by the appointment or the transfer of title. The latter merely invest a person with these rights and duties and, in the case of change of ownership, divest some other person of them. I shall call such powers regulative powers.

4. Powers and Rights.

It is commonly thought that powers are a species of rights. This is a mistake. Though powers are essential to the explanation of rights, they are not in themselves rights. It is possible to speak of a power-right only if one is at liberty to use or not to use the power at will.[7] But often one has a power which one is obliged either to use or not to use, without having any choice in the matter. In Israel, Jews and Muslims have power to contract polygamous marriages. If they perform the marriage ceremony their polygamous marriage is valid. But they have no right to contract such marriages, and indeed they commit a criminal offence if they do so. In many countries a thief has the power, but not the right, to sell stolen property in the open market. Under the law of agency, an agent often has powers which he is under a duty to the principal not to exercise, or to exercise only under certain conditions. Public officials often have mandatory powers which they are under a legal obligation to use only when certain conditions obtain, and therefore their powers do not amount to rights. Company directors are often in a similar position.

---

[7] On this point, see H.L.A. Hart, 'Bentham on Legal Rights', in *Oxford Essays in Jurisprudence, Second Series*, ed. A.W.B. Simpson (Oxford: Clarendon Press, 1973), 171–201, repr. in Hart, *Essays on Bentham* (n.2 above), 162–93; here Hart discusses some exceptions to this rule.

II. LEGAL POWERS AND LEGAL NORMS

Let us agree, then, that an act is the exercise of a legal power only if it is recognized in law as effecting a legal change, and if it is so recognized because, among other things, it is an action of a type which it is reasonable to expect to be performed for the most part only when the person concerned wants to bring about the legal change. A person has a legal power to produce a certain legal change if and only if, when he behaves in a certain way, he produces this legal change by exercising a legal power. Let us now turn to the problem of the relations between legal powers and legal norms. Clearly legal powers can be conferred by legal norms, and they can be powers the exercise of which affects legal norms. But must all legal powers be related in both these ways to legal norms? Two questions should be examined:

(1) Are all legal powers necessarily conferred by legal norms?
(2) Does the exercise of every legal power determine either the existence or application of legal norms?

MacCormick[8] presupposes a positive answer to the first question: If there is a certain power there must be a rule conferring it. It is certainly true that most legal powers are conferred by laws. But it is interesting to notice that the analysis of the concept of a legal power suggested above did not include any reference to power-conferring laws. There are, no doubt, strong policy reasons to minimize legal recognition of legal powers not conferred by laws, but there is nothing in the concept of a legal power to necessitate an affirmative answer to the first question.

Let us first note as, I hope, an uncontroversial fact that a legal system may recognize powers which are not conferred by the laws of the system but by some other laws. Private international law, for example, includes laws whose purpose is to define the conditions under which such powers are to be recognized. Similarly, powers granted by social norms may be recognized by a certain legal system. A Muslim country, for example, may recognize the validity of Taleq divorce performed in a foreign country where such a divorce is not recognized and may even be illegal. (Whether we should call such powers 'legal powers' or 'legally recognized powers' need not concern us here.) I wish, however, to argue for a stronger thesis, namely, that legal powers may exist even if not conferred by any norm, whether legal or non-legal. It is worth our while to examine two cases of legal powers not conferred by norms in order to see the reasons for admitting the existence of such powers.

[8] See Neil MacCormick, 'Voluntary Obligations and Normative Powers', *Proceedings of the Aristotelian Society. Supplementary Volume*, 46 (1972), 59–78.

Austin's sovereign obviously has powers of legislation, but these are not powers conferred by a law. No law can apply to the sovereign. The fundamental reason for this was explained by Markby.[9] The powers of an Austinian sovereign are illimitable. All his general commands are law. His particular commands are not law, not because they are not binding, but because Austin erroneously thought that laws are necessarily general. There can be no law purporting to confer power on the sovereign, not because a person cannot grant powers to himself—this is possible and does occasionally happen—but because such a law would not guide the sovereign's behaviour, and would be empty and pointless. The sovereign has these powers regardless of any law purporting to grant them to him.

A second example. The first Israeli law, embodied in the Israeli declaration of independence, was made by a body called 'The People's Council'. In it this council granted to itself unlimited legislative powers and changed its name to the 'Provisional Council of State'. The Provisional Council of State had legislative powers derived first from this and later from other laws. The People's Council on the other hand was never granted powers by any law. Nevertheless it had and did exercise legislative powers by enacting the first law. The reason its powers were not granted by a law is obvious. There was no authority which could enact such a *P*-law at the time, and there was no point in enacting a retroactive authorizing law later. It could make no difference. It could neither guide the Council's actions nor affect their legality. Some might argue that in such cases it is the rule of recognition which, on Hart's theory at any rate, confers these powers. But, as I have argued at length elsewhere,[10] the rule of recognition is a law of a different kind. It imposes duties and cannot be interpreted as conferring powers. It is arguable whether or not there was in Palestine at the time a social norm which conferred powers on the People's Council. I doubt whether there was such a norm. The point is that the existence of such a norm does not affect the issue. It is possible for a legal power to be recognized in some such circumstances even if it is not conferred by a pre-existing social norm.

To conclude: A legal power may exist even if it was not conferred by any norm at all. Whenever the exercise of a power cannot be guided by a norm we should regard it as not conferred by one.

What about the second question posed above? Does the exercise of every legal power determine the existence or application of a legal norm?

---

[9] See William Markby, *Elements of Law*, 5th edn. (Oxford: Clarendon Press, 1896), at 93–4.

[10] Joseph Raz, 'The Identity of Legal Systems', *California Law Review*, 59 (1971), 795–815, repr. with revisions in Raz, *AL* 78–102.

I shall use the expression 'a power affects a norm' to refer both to cases where a norm is created, abrogated, or modified by the exercise of a power and to cases where the exercise of a power regulates the application of a norm. Is it necessary that all powers recognized by a legal system S_1 affect in one of these ways the laws of S_1? It seems to me that the answer is a qualified 'yes'.

The reason for the affirmative answer lies in the concept of legal recognition. A power is legal only if it is recognized by a legal system. As we have seen, to be recognized in S_1 does not mean to be granted by a law of S_1. It means that the courts of S_1 have a duty to apply the norm affected by the power, subject to the changes in its content or application made by the use of the power. Thus, the notion of a legally recognized power is parasitic on that of a legally recognized norm. A power is recognized only if the norms it affects are recognized as affected by it. A norm is recognized only if the courts are under a duty to apply it. It follows that if a power affects a recognized norm, it affects also the law imposing a duty to apply that norm. Consequently, to be a legally recognized power entails being a power regulating the laws of a system which determine which norms the courts ought to apply. In other words, every legally recognized power is a regulative power. The legislative powers of Parliament, for example, are also regulative powers. They regulate the duty of the courts to apply parliamentary legislation. Similarly the power to make a gift is regulative both by regulating the application of property laws and by regulating the application of the duty of the judges to apply these laws. One should distinguish between the direct and the indirect character of legal powers. All legal powers are indirectly regulative for if they are recognized in law they regulate the application of laws imposing duties on courts to apply certain norms. But they have this indirect character only because they affect norms directly either by making, changing, or repealing them or by regulating their application. To the question whether every power recognized in S_1 affects a law of S_1, the answer is affirmative, in so far as its indirect character is concerned. To be recognized in S_1 it must indirectly regulate laws of S_1 which impose duties on courts to apply certain norms.

But now we are faced with another question: Are the norms directly affected by the power also always laws of S_1? I agree with the implication in MacCormick's paper that they need not be.[11] As I have argued elsewhere,[12] the view that every norm which it is the duty of the courts to enforce is part of the system is mistaken. It is part of the function of a legal system to ensure the enforcement of some norms not belonging to it. Consequently, legal systems recognize powers which directly affect norms which do not belong to these systems.

[11] MacCormick (n.8 above).　　[12] See Raz (n.10 above).

Powers directly affecting norms which are not part of the system S_1 may be recognized in S_1 for two different types of reason. They may be recognized in S_1 because they are recognized by some other legal system or by social conventions or practices which S_1 wishes to respect and enforce. When this is the reason for recognizing these powers one can talk of derivative recognition.[13] But some powers not directly affecting the laws of S_1 may be recognized in S_1 for different reasons. A law may simply intend to create ways in which individuals may achieve certain results even though these ways are not recognized by some other norms. The powers to make and amend the regulations of private companies are an example of this kind of recognition. They are normative powers because they affect the company's regulations, which are norms. They are recognized in law since they indirectly affect the duties of the courts to enforce these regulations. But a company's regulations are not part of the legal system, nor are they recognized in law because they are conventional social rules. These powers are powers directly affecting norms which are not laws of the system, but they are given original rather than derivative recognition.

Powers which enjoy only derivative recognition in S_1 are not usually called legal powers in S_1 though they may properly be called powers recognized in S_1. All the powers which enjoy original recognition in S_1 are called legal powers even if they are not powers directly affecting the laws of S_1.

Concerning the legal status of powers to make contracts, MacCormick's view—formulated in this terminology—is that they are not really legal powers but, since they are derivatively recognized, merely powers recognized in law. They are recognized only because they are recognized according to sound moral principles. I agree with him that they are not powers directly affecting the laws of the system in which they are recognized. Contracts are not laws; they are merely legally recognized norms. But I disagree with his contention that they are recognized derivatively. Though the fact that many contracts are morally binding and, more important still, the fact that they are socially accepted as binding are part of the reason for their legal recognition, ultimately they are recognized in law because, regardless of moral and social norms, they are considered as a desirable means to achieve some legitimate ends. It may be that the facts which contribute to the argument for regarding promises as morally binding are also among the facts which make it desirable to make contracts binding in law, but it is these facts which count and not their results in morality.

---

[13] See H.L.A. Hart, 'Kelsen's Doctrine of the Unity of Law', in this volume, ch. 30, at § IV.

III. POWER-CONFERRING LAWS

The concept of a legally recognized power is logically connected with that of a norm because every legally recognized power is a power affecting one or more legally recognized norms, not because all such powers are conferred by laws. But most legal powers are conferred by laws, and something must be said about the nature of power-conferring laws (*P*-laws). What is the logical character of a *P*-law? Are all *P*-laws also duty-imposing (*D*-laws)? The answers to these questions depend on the principles of the individuation of laws, for they determine what counts as one complete law. Legal practitioners are not normally concerned with the doctrine of individuation, and ordinary legal discourse embodies only a very vague notion of what is one law. The problem is of considerable importance in jurisprudence, however, since it underlies any attempt to classify laws into distinct logical types; and this is a major jurisprudential concern. Let me explain briefly the nature of the problem and the kind of considerations involved.[14]

It is obvious that not every true legal statement describes one complete law. Of the three following statements

(1) Every male has a duty not to trespass;
(2) Every female has a duty not to trespass;
(3) Every person has a duty not to trespass;

only the third describes a law while the others are deductions from it. It might be thought that the formulation of the law in the statute or judgment which created it determines which statement describes one complete law and which does not. But this is a mistake as is explained by Bentham:

What is a law? What the parts of a law? The subject of these questions, it is to be observed, is the *logical*, the *ideal*, the *intellectual* whole, not the *physical* one: the *law* and not the *statute*. An inquiry directed to the latter sort of object could neither admit of difficulty nor afford instruction. In this sense . . . [s]o much as was embraced by one and the same act of authentication, so much as received the touch of the sceptre at one stroke, is *one* law . . . and nothing more. A statute of George II made to substitute an *or* instead of an *and* in a former statute is a complete law; a statute containing an entire body of laws, perfect in all its parts, would not be more so. By the word *law* then . . . is meant that ideal object, of which the part, the whole, or the multiple, or an assemblage of parts, wholes, and multiples mixed together, is exhibited by a statute.[15]

---

[14] For a detailed discussion, see Raz, *CLS*, at 90–2, 140–7.
[15] Jeremy Bentham, *An Introduction to the Principles of Morals and Legislation*, ed. J.H. Burns and H.L.A. Hart (London: Athlone Press, 1970), 301 (Bentham's emphasis).

In a word, we want the concept of a law to be determined by rationa. principles, not by the vagaries of legislative technique or judicial style.

An acceptable doctrine of individuation has to satisfy in the best possible way a set of partly conflicting desiderata. Three of these are important for the present discussions: (1) The laws individuated by the principles of individuation should be relatively simple. (2) It is desirable that every generic act that is guided by law should be the core of a separate law. (3) The laws individuated by the principles of individuation should, as far as possible, display important connections between various parts of a legal system. Consider the application of these desiderata to the following legal statements:

(1) A person has power to make a gratuitous promise binding in law by executing a deed.
(2) The promisee of a deed has a power to claim its performance.
(3) The courts ought to enforce the performance of duties at the instance of those who have a claim to their performance.
(4) If any promisor expresses his promise in a deed, it must be enforced by the courts at the instance of the promisee.

This is a much simplified and somewhat distorted statement of the law, but it will do for our purposes. Statement (4) is entailed by statements (1)–(3). It entails statements (1) and (2) but not (3), which ascribes a more general duty to the courts than the duty to enforce the deed mentioned in statement (4). MacCormick claims that statement (4) describes one complete law,[16] and, presumably, he regards the other statements as conclusions of law derived from it and (in the case of (3)) other laws. From this premiss he rightly concludes that the law described in (4) can be seen as both conferring powers and imposing duties.[17]

That some laws can be both power-conferring and duty-imposing is not a very startling conclusion. Every statement of the form (5), for example, entails and is entailed by a statement of the form (6):

(5) 'x has power to enact D-laws applying to members of population y.'
(6) 'Members of y ought to obey the enactments of x.'

Every statement ascribing powers to enact D-laws entails and is entailed by a statement ascribing a duty to obey. If one member of such a pair of statements describes one complete law so does the other member of the pair, and they both describe one and the same law. Such laws both confer powers and impose duties. It is, however, important to remember that most laws conferring norm-creating powers authorize the enactment of P-laws as well as of D-laws. When the same rules gov-

---

[16] MacCormick (n.8 above).   [17] Ibid.

ern the exercise of these powers we usually have sufficient reason to regard them as conferred by one law, and such a law cannot be completely described, without distortion, by a statement ascribing a duty to obey. Consequently, most laws conferring norm-creating powers can only be properly described as *P*-laws, even though their existence entails as a conclusion of law that certain persons have a duty to obey *D*-laws enacted by the exercise of these powers. Furthermore, even when laws confer only powers to enact *D*-laws we may still have reasons for regarding them as primarily power-conferring laws and for regarding statements of the form (5) as their proper description and statements of the form (6) as conclusions of law from them. This interpretation fits the ordinary way of talking about them better, and the laws can be said to guide the behaviour of the legislators more directly than that of the ordinary citizen, which is affected only if and after the legislator has exercised his legislative powers. But the arguments for this view are by no means overwhelming, nor do they always apply outside the law. We certainly refer more often to the child's duty to obey his parents than to the parents' power to command.

Our judgments concerning the proper description of a norm depend in such cases on pragmatic considerations which may vary from one context to another. In any case, they do not affect the conclusion that laws conferring powers to enact *D*-laws impose duties as well.

But MacCormick suggests not only that some laws may both confer powers and impose duties, but that all the laws which confer powers impose duties as well.[18] In this he is following Bentham and even more closely, as he himself said, Kelsen. For MacCormick is tempted by the idea that all the laws relating to voluntary obligations are directed to the courts and instruct them to perform certain acts if certain conditions obtain. Let me grant straight away that if MacCormick is right in thinking that statement (4) describes one complete norm then he is right in suggesting that *P*-laws are merely a subclass of *D*-laws. For Bentham demonstrated long ago that the complete content of a legal system can be described by statements each one of which asserts that a duty exists if certain conditions are fulfilled, using the same technique by which (4) is derived from (1)–(3). Furthermore, since it is the duty of the courts to enforce all legal obligations, provided that certain conditions are satisfied, it is possible to describe the complete content of a legal system by a set of statements every one of which describes an obligation imposed on the courts. The possibility of providing such descriptions is not in doubt. The only problem is whether each statement in the set really describes one complete law or 'an assemblage of parts, wholes, and multiples mixed together', to use Bentham's felicitous expression.

---

[18] Ibid.

That the mere possibility of providing a complete description of a legal system by means of such statements does not entail that each of them describes one complete law is a conclusion forced on us by the fact that not every true legal statement describes one complete law. To settle the question we need to resort to the doctrine of individuation. And the fundamental problem facing us is crystallized in our example of statements (1) to (4). If statement (4) describes one complete law then MacCormick and Kelsen are right, but if statements (1) to (3) each describes one complete law then they are wrong, and we must conclude that power-conferring laws are a distinct type of law.

There can be no doubt that according to the three requirements of a doctrine of individuation mentioned above every one of the statements (1)–(3) describes a law whereas statement (4) describes two laws and part of the content of a third. Statements (1)–(3) are simpler than (4). They each refer to one act guided by law, whereas statement (4) refers to three such acts (the act of the promisor making the deed, the act of the promisee lodging a claim against the promisor who did not keep his promise, and the action of the court in enforcing the deed). Statement (3) has the further advantage of satisfying the third requirement better. Since it refers to the court's duty to enforce many other types of duty apart from those arising out of deeds, it draws attention to the fact that it is the function of courts to enforce not only the laws regulating deeds but many other laws as well at the instance of a person having a claim that the duty shall be performed. Statement (3) thereby directs our attention to an important general function of courts and to a special legal technique of making the enforcement of a whole class of duties subject to the will of certain individuals.

It is true, of course, that the fact that according to these requirements of individuation statement (4) does not describe one complete law may be an argument against accepting these requirements. But this is so only if there are good reasons for thinking that statement (4) does describe one complete law. MacCormick provides no such arguments, and he fails to answer the criticism of Bentham's and Kelsen's theories made by Hart and myself.[19] Nor does he furnish any other grounds to question the soundness of the requirements. The justification of the requirements seems to me to be very obvious. The main purpose of dividing the enormous amount of legal material constituting one legal system into laws is to create simple units for easy reference. And it is desirable to direct our attention to acts guided by law by making each one of them the subject of a separate law. Our understanding of the working of the law is further promoted if we individuate laws in a way which draws attention to important connections between groups of laws.

[19] See Hart, *CL*, at 35–41, 2nd edn., at 35–42; Raz, *CLS*, at 70–92, 109–20.

Power-conferring laws form, therefore, a distinct type of law which is different from duty-imposing laws.

IV. NORMATIVE POWERS

Can the concept of a normative power be usefully applied outside the law? There can be little doubt that it can. Legally recognized powers are powers to affect legally recognized norms. To the extent that one can talk of non-legal norms which can be affected in the appropriate way by human action one can also talk of normative powers not recognized in law. There is indeed little difficulty in applying the concept to a discussion of the rules and principles of voluntary associations or to rules and principles which have become the practices of a community. Nor does MacCormick find fault with the use of the concept of a normative power in such contexts. He does, however, object to its application to norms which are recognized neither by an existing legal system nor by an existing association and which are not practices of a community. The problem we face, therefore, concerns the possibility and fruitfulness of giving a general account of the concept of a normative power which makes it applicable in a general theory of norms, regardless of whether these are the actual practices of any community, institution, or organization. Let us consider first the feasibility of such an account and defer to the next section consideration of its fruitfulness.

There are two ways of challenging the feasibility of such an account of normative powers. It might be claimed that the concept of a norm can only be used to refer to actual practices of groups or institutions. Alternatively, admitting the applicability of the notion of a norm in other contexts as well (for example, to moral or prudential reasoning in general), one may claim that norms which are not practices cannot be affected by human acts in a way which allows one to regard these acts as the exercise of normative powers. I have tried elsewhere[20] to meet the first challenge and will not deal with it here. Instead I shall try to show how one type of norm, namely mandatory norms, can be affected by the exercise of powers.

Mandatory norms are norms requiring that an agent behave in a certain way in certain circumstances. Duty-imposing norms, both legal and non-legal, are the most important species of mandatory norms. Given an account of power to affect mandatory norms, there is no difficulty in generalizing it to provide a general account of normative powers, that is,

[20] Joseph Raz, 'Reasons for Action, Decisions and Norms', *Mind*, 84 (1975), 481–99, repr. (in part) in *Practical Reasoning*, ed. Raz (Oxford: Oxford UP, 1978), 128–43.

powers to affect any type of norm be it mandatory, power-conferring, or permissive.

An act is the exercise of a legal power only if it effects a legal change—that is, creates, extinguishes, or modifies the application of a legal norm. It is obvious that non-legal norms are similarly affected by human action. If I intentionally slap John in the face, my action affects the application of the norm prescribing that one should apologize and compensate for intentionally inflicting harm on others, and I, therefore, incur a duty to compensate and apologize.[21] If I move to a new house my action affects the application of the norms obliging me to certain modes of behaviour towards my neighbours. I consequently incur new obligations to my new neighbours and am relieved of my obligations to my old neighbours. When I promise to do *A*, I create a new norm requiring that I do *A*, and consequently I incur an obligation to do *A*. However, we have seen that not every act affecting a legal norm is an exercise of a legal power, and it is equally clear that not every act affecting non-legal norms is an exercise of a non-legal normative power.

Two conditions must be fulfilled if an act affecting a legal norm is to be regarded as an exercise of a legal power. First, it must be normatively and not merely causally effective. Second, it must be acknowledged in law as normatively effective for reasons of a special kind. If non-legal norms can be affected by the exercise of normative powers, then analogous conditions must be fulfilled. Let us examine each of them in turn.

An act is an exercise of normative power only if it affects a norm normatively and not causally. The distinction turns on the distinction between the results and the consequences of acts. As Anthony Kenny writes:

The result of an act is the end state of the change by which the act is defined. When the world changes in a certain way there may follow certain other changes . . . In that case we may say that the second transformation is a consequence of the first and of the act which brought the first about. The relation between an act and its result is an intrinsic relation, and that between an act and its consequences is a causal relation.[22]

That John wakes up is the consequence of my turning on the light but the result of my waking John, which I may have done by turning on the light. An act affects a norm causally if its consequences regulate the application of the norm. It affects a norm normatively if the act itself or its result affects the existence or application of the norm. Raising my hand with the

---

[21] This and other norms mentioned in the sequel are meant as illustrative examples. My case does not depend on agreement that they are binding moral or prudential norms.

[22] Anthony Kenny, 'Intention and Purpose in Law', in *Essays in Legal Philosophy*, ed. Robert S. Summers (Oxford: Blackwell, 1968), 146–63, at 150. See also Von Wright, *NA*, at 39–42.

intention of slapping John in the face and with the consequence that he is hit, causally affects the norm concerning intentionally inflicted harm. Slapping John affects the same norm normatively. Similarly, bullying somebody to promise to do *A* with the consequence that he does make the promise is causally effective in creating the norm that he ought to do *A*, but only his act of promising affects this norm normatively.

As is clear from my examples not every act which normatively affects a norm is an exercise of a normative power. Intentionally inflicting harm on a person and changing residence are examples of acts which normatively affect norms but which are not the exercise of powers. To be an exercise of a normative power the act must be recognized as affecting a norm for reasons of a special sort. Whose reasons and what kind of reasons are these? In the case of powers to affect norms which are the practices of institutions or groups, the answer to the first question is simple enough: The reasons of the institution or the group for recognizing the normative effects of the act determine its character as a power-exercising act. When dealing with norms which are not practices the relevant reasons are those because of which the norm is binding, the reasons which justify the norm, because of which one should respect and follow the norm. If a norm which can be affected by human action is to be respected then the reasons for respecting it reveal also why it ought to be respected as created and regulated by human action. It is the nature of the reasons justifying the norm which determine whether acts affecting its existence or application are power-exercising acts.

Arguments justifying norms are of different types. Some are based on reasons establishing the desirability of performing the norm-act. These are content-dependent justifications. They establish that the norm-act is desirable because its performance secures desirable consequences or contributes to the realization of some value. For the justification to be complete it has to do more than that. But it is the fact that the justification is based on the desirability of the norm-act which determines that it is a content-dependent justification. Some justifications are content-independent. Sometimes there are reasons justifying a norm which do not bear directly on the desirability of the norm-act. The justification of the mandates of authority are of this nature. They depend not on the desirability of acting as commanded or advised in the particular instance but on the fact that the instruction was issued by authority.

Jeremy, John's teenage son, is told by his father to return home before midnight. There may or may not be a content-dependent justification for this command, but in any case if it is true that parents have authority in such matters over their children then there is a content-independent justification for the command. It does not justify the making of the command but it explains why Jeremy ought to follow it once made. It is important to notice that the content-independent argument justifies the particular norm—John's command that Jeremy be home by midnight. The reasons for his general authority may also be content-independent (God gave parents authority over their children, etc.) or they may be content-dependent (acting on parents' instructions will, on the whole, have the best consequences, etc.). But this is a separate question. One should further notice that the identification of the reasons for the various norms does not necessarily presuppose that the norms are followed or believed to be justified either by John or Jeremy or by the community at large. It depends solely on the availability of the justifying reasons.

Content-independent justification is to be distinguished from conservative justification. A conservative justification establishes that even though there may not have been adequate reasons justifying a norm in the first place, since it is followed and has become a practice it should not be changed, for changing it will have worse consequences than preserving it. A conservative justification applies only to norms which are practices. Content-independent justifications apply both to norms which are practices and to those which are not.

Given these distinctions and clarifications our task is complete. An act is the exercise of a norm-creating power if and only if it normatively affects the content or existence of a norm which is justified by content-independent arguments. An act is the exercise of a regulative power if and only if it normatively affects the application of a norm and there are content-independent arguments for respecting the norm as affected by such acts. This explanation does not presuppose that normative powers are themselves conferred by norms. But it makes plain that sometimes they are. The problem of the conditions under which a normative power should be regarded as conferred by a norm raises interesting issues which cannot be examined here. The account proposed of the concept of a normative power is over-simplified because it overlooks the possibility of justifications of norms which combine content-independent and content-dependent arguments. But this further complication does not raise new problems of principle and need not detain us here.

V. NORMATIVE POWERS AND VOLUNTARY OBLIGATIONS

Having attempted to provide the outline of a general analysis of the concept of a normative power, it is time to demonstrate the importance and usefulness of the concept. It has been suggested above that the concepts of a norm and of a normative power provide the key to the notion of authority. A person has authority to the extent that he has power to affect norms. Instead of developing this suggestion, let us turn to the problem of voluntary obligations.

I agree with MacCormick's main thesis, namely, that the analysis of the concept of a voluntary obligation does not entail that only social practices can give rise to binding voluntary obligations. MacCormick is, however, mistaken in thinking that this entails that voluntary obligations can be explained without reference to normative powers.

MacCormick restricts his attention to promises, but promises are not the only source of voluntary obligations. Among the other sources of voluntary obligations which some people regard as binding one should mention the private vow or oath. I do not wish to consider to what extent and on what ground private vows, promises, or other sources of voluntary obligations are to be regarded as binding. My point is that any adequate account of the concept of a voluntary obligation should be wide enough to explain all the sources of voluntary obligations, regardless of whether one believes that they ought to be recognized as binding. A man does not necessarily make a private vow intending to induce others to rely upon it, or knowing that his act betrays such an intention. Consequently, so far as the obligatoriness of a vow can be justified, this must be in a manner different from the justification of promises. Promises do, whereas private vows do not, create claims for other people on the behaviour of the persons under obligation. This explains the difference in the way these voluntary obligations are created and justified. Since MacCormick has confined himself to an examination of promises we must conclude that he has not provided us with a general explanation of the concept of a voluntary obligation.

Not every obligation created for a person by his own voluntary action is a voluntary obligation. By locking John up Tom has imposed upon himself an obligation to release John, to explain his behaviour, apologize, and, sometimes, compensate John. But his is not a voluntary obligation. The only way in which voluntary obligations can be distinguished from other obligations which a person imposes on himself by his own action is by reference to their justification. Voluntary obligations are characterized by having content-independent justification. The agent is under a voluntary obligation to perform an act only if the reasons because of which the act is obligatory bear not on the desirability of performing the act but on the manner in which the obligation was incurred.

Obligations imposed by authority and voluntary obligations are the two main types of obligation justified by content-independent arguments. This leads to the conclusion that the concept of a normative power applies to voluntary obligations. Those who are entitled to bind themselves by voluntary obligations have normative power to do so.

Since we regard every person as having equal power to bind himself we do not have much need to refer to these powers. If we believed that only certain categories of persons had these powers, we should have more reason to refer to them. But this does not mean that the concept does not apply or that its examination does not clarify the structure of practical reasoning.

Because all types of voluntary obligations are characterized by being mandatory norms with content-independent justification, they are justified by the justification of the general norm that promises or private vows ought to be respected; they are not justified by giving reasons for the desirability of each obligatory act in its particular circumstances. MacCormick is, therefore, wrong in rejecting the two-level procedure of justification—first justifying the obligatoriness of the act in terms of the general norm that promises, etc. ought to be respected, and then justifying that norm itself. The two-level justification does not presuppose, as MacCormick thinks it does, that the general norm is a social norm.

VI. NORMATIVE POWERS AND PROMISES

It follows from the discussion above that to the extent that promises are a source of voluntary obligations they are made by the exercise of normative powers. The obligatoriness of many promises can no doubt be explained on other grounds which do not depend on the fact that promises yield voluntary obligations. But such explanations, correct and useful as they are, miss the essential point in the common conception of promises. It may be that the common conception is morally indefensible, and that we should abandon or reform the common belief which regards promises as a source of voluntary obligation and justified as such. It is important, however, not to confuse reform with elucidation.

It seems to me that MacCormick, while professing to elucidate and defend the common conception of promises, is actually proposing to reject it and to elucidate a different type of obligation which is not a voluntary obligation at all. That this is the effect of his account is intimated in his explanation of the promising act and is made clear by his justification of the binding force of promises. I shall comment on each of these points in turn.

Strictly speaking there is nothing in MacCormick's account of the promising act which conflicts with the explanation given above of the role of normative powers in the analysis of voluntary obligations. If his account is correct we need only conclude that acts intended to induce reliance constitute the exercise of the normative power which creates a binding promise. Nevertheless, I doubt whether intentionally inducing reliance or acting in a way which suggests such an intention is either necessary or sufficient for promising.

Can one intentionally induce reliance without promising? Imagine that John wants to know whether he can rely on Harry giving him a lift to town tomorrow. Harry tells him: 'I am almost certain to offer you a lift to town tomorrow. In the circumstances it would be far wiser for you to rely on me rather than make alternative arrangements, but remember—I do not promise anything, I am merely advising you.' Harry is intentionally inducing John to rely on him but he does not promise anything. Promising is surely more than inducing reliance; by promising I bind myself and confer a right on the promisee. Harry in my story makes clear that he does not wish to bind himself or to give John any rights.

Can one promise without intending to induce reliance or acting in a way which suggests such an intention? Suppose that Colin tells David, 'I promise to make you a gift of a million pounds on your 21st birthday, but I beg of you: Until the time comes act as if I had not promised. It would ruin your character if you should now start behaving in anticipation of your gift.' We may well think that Colin was ill-advised to make the promise, because once made, David may have reasonable grounds for relying on it and may disregard Colin's advice. But we cannot say either that Colin intended David to rely on his promise or that he behaved in a way which created the impression that he had such an intention.

I have followed MacCormick in interpreting 'inducing reliance' as meaning encouraging action in reliance upon the promised act. One may interpret the expression as including the inducement of a belief. However, the only belief that the promisor need always intend to induce or be taken to have the intention of inducing is the belief that he (the promisor) intends to undertake an obligation and to confer a right on the promisee. It is, indeed, both a necessary and a sufficient condition of making a promise that the promisor behave in a way which is either intended or can reasonably be taken to indicate the promisor's intention to bind himself to perform an act and to give the promisee a right against the promisor.

On this account of the promising act it is plain that in normal circumstances acting with an intention to induce reliance is making a promise, but the account also allows for special circumstances in which this is not so. This explanation of the nature of the promising act also helps to clarify one aspect of the relevance of social convention to promising. I agree with MacCormick that the concept of a promise does not presuppose that of a social practice of regarding promises as binding. It may be, though I do not wish to express an opinion on the matter, that there are adequate reasons for regarding promises as binding even in a society which does not have any such practice. But it is clear that social convention may nonetheless determine what acts can reasonably be taken to express an intention to undertake an obligation and to confer a right. In our culture, communicating an intention to act in a certain way to a person who is known to be interested in the action is conventionally regarded as an act expressing an intention to undertake an obligation to act in that way and to confer a right on the person concerned. Since this is our social convention anyone wishing to express such an intention and yet not wishing to undertake the obligation must make his intentions clear by saying that he is not promising or words to that effect. But for this convention, communicating an intention to perform an act in these circumstances would not normally amount to promising, though there would still be other ways of promising.

The fact that MacCormick thinks that communicating an intention to induce reliance is logically, and not merely contingently, related to promising, suggests that he does not regard promises as a case of voluntary obligation at all. This is borne out by his justification for the obligation to keep promises. MacCormick derives the obligation to keep a promise from the principle that one 'must not act as to disappoint the reliance of others when we intentionally or knowingly induce them to rely on us'.[23]

But this principle in itself is not sufficient to explain the binding force of promises. As illustrated above, it fails to distinguish them from certain cases of advising or even merely informing, and, more important still, it does not explain why promises once made and understood are binding even if not relied upon. MacCormick mentions this feature of promises but fails to account for it. In fact he regards promises as a case of estoppel. The doctrine of estoppel does rest on the principle he mentions, but duties arising from estoppel are not voluntary obligations. Though many cases are cases of both estoppel and promising, the two notions are distinct. This is clear from the fact that estoppel applies only if the person concerned relied on the other person, whereas promises are binding even in the absence of reliance. The reason for this difference is that promises are binding because it is desirable to make it possible for people to bind themselves and give rights to others if they so wish. It is desirable, in other words, to have a method of giving grounds for reasonable reliance in a special way, not necessarily by intending to induce reliance, but by intending to bind oneself. It is because of this feature that we regard promises as a source of voluntary obligations, and it is because of this feature that making a promise or undertaking any other voluntary obligation is exercising a normative power.

---

[23] See MacCormick (n.8 above) at 68, 71.

25

Legal Powers*

DICK W.P. RUITER

I. THE CLASSICAL VIEW

If one took the classical view of legal norms as one's model, it would then be true to say that *deontic norms* enjoy a fundamental status in the legal system—that is, all legal norms are reducible to deontic norms. Deontic norms are distinguished by a deontic modality. By analogy to the alethic modalities—necessity, possibility, contingency, and impossibility—four deontic modalities can be distinguished: prescription, permission, indifference, and proscription.[1] Deontic modalities are reflected in modal verbs, such as 'must' and 'may', which function as deontic operators in sentences expressing deontic norms.

Traditionally, it is held that the deontic modalities of 'permission' and 'indifference' are derived from the modalities of 'prescription' and 'proscription' by means of the operation of negation, such that unilateral permissions as well as bilateral permissions (cases of indifference) are nothing but negations of prescriptions or proscriptions.[2] In a different way, 'empowerment', expressed by the modal verb 'can', is also derived from the prescriptive modalities—it is, at any rate, if one is prepared to defend the view that empowering norms are obligations not to violate the obligations created by appealing to the empowering norms.[3] Thus, on this view, *all* the norms of a legal system are correctly understood in the end as variations on the concept of legal obligation.

The classical view exhibits major deficiencies. It leaves the nature of 'empowerment' in the dark. And to characterize 'empowerment' as a non-deontic modality, as some writers have done, only serves to point

---

* *Editors' note*: Ruiter's paper, written especially for this volume, reflects themes developed in his book, *Institutional Legal Facts. Legal Powers and their Effects* (Dordrecht: Kluwer, 1993).

[1] Georg Henrik von Wright, 'Deontic Logic', *Mind*, 60 (1951) 1–15, repr. in von Wright, *Logical Studies* (London: Routledge & Kegan Paul, 1957), 58–74.

[2] von Wright, *NA* 7.

[3] *GTN* ch. 26, § IV (pp. 103–4); Alf Ross, *Directives and Norms* (London: Routledge & Kegan Paul, 1968), 118.

out what 'empowerment' is not. Moreover, power-conferring norms are only one among a variety of non-deontic norms that play a role in legal systems, a variety that includes authoritative statements of fact, formal recommendations, and legal institutions; thus, there appears to be far more here than the classical view can account for.

In a word, the traditional assumption that all legal norms are reducible to deontic norms is, at the very least, open to question.

II. SYSTEMIC VALIDITY

In order to make a fresh start, we must break the spell cast by the deontic modalities. This can be done by considering, first of all, the manner in which all legal norms exist irrespective of their content.

The mode of existence of legal norms is that of 'systemic validity', a term coined by Jerzy Wróblewski. Reducing his definition of 'systemic validity' to its bare bones, we can say that a norm is valid in a legal system if it is issued according to the norms valid in the system and is consistent with them.[4] This definition is in fact recursive in character. It states that a norm is valid if its validity is warranted by a prior norm. The same applies to the prior norm and so on. Ultimately, one arrives at a construction such as Hans Kelsen's basic norm or H.L.A. Hart's rule of recognition in order to stave off the threatening infinite regress.[5] Although a great part of recent legal theory is concerned with the seemingly irresolvable problems relating to these constructions, I shall assume for present purposes that the chain of validity can be terminated in an acceptable way, restricting myself to problems concerning the existence of issued norms qua elements of the legal system.

III. ISSUANCE

According to Wróblewski, valid norms are issued norms. To issue a norm is to declare it valid. Simply declaring a norm valid, however, does not suffice to convey validity to it. To that end, appeal must be made to *another* valid norm, in particular, to a norm determining that the party making the declaration is capable of conveying validity to the first-mentioned norm in this manner. The capacity to convey validity to a

---

[4] Jerzy Wróblewski, *The Judicial Application of Law*, ed. Zenon Bankowski and Neil MacCormick (Dordrecht: Kluwer, 1992), 32, 77.

[5] See Dick W.P. Ruiter, *Institutional Legal Facts. Legal Powers and their Effects* (Dordrecht: Kluwer, 1993), at 14–20, and Ruiter, 'Economic and Legal Institutionalism: What Can They Learn from Each Other?', *Constitutional Political Economy*, 1 (1994), 99–115, at 101–6.

norm by declaring it valid is termed a 'legal power'. A legal power derives from a 'power-conferring norm'. The basic structure of legal powers and of the underlying power-conferring norms can be clarified with the help of an example.

Suppose that John and Mary want to name their new-born daughter 'Louise'. In organized society it will be necessary for them to appeal to a legal power to give this name to their daughter. The legal power in question can be represented as:

If John and Mary name their daughter Louise, then her valid name is Louise.

Using square-cornered brackets to designate validity, we can formalize this legal power as follows:

$(\text{LOUISEdaughter})_{\text{john\&mary}} \rightarrow [\text{LOUISEdaughter}]$

The underlying power-conferring norm can be represented as follows:

If its parents give a child a name, then that name is the valid name of that child.

Formalized:

$(\text{NAMEchild})_{\text{parents}} \rightarrow [\text{NAMEchild}]$

'Can' appears to be shorthand for a linguistic construction of the following structure:

If a linguistic content C is declared valid by certain individuals i, then C is valid.

In symbols:

$(C)_i \rightarrow [C]$

This is what we mean when we say that certain parties *can* give commands, conclude contracts, appoint officials, establish companies, or declare wars. Even when we say that certain parties can empower other parties to issue certain norms, 'can' has this meaning, for what we are actually saying is:

$((C)_i \rightarrow [C])_a \rightarrow [(C)_i \rightarrow [C]]$

Restating this scheme:

If a linguistic content (If C is declared valid by certain individuals i, then C is valid) is declared valid by certain agents a, then (If C is declared valid by certain individuals i, then C is valid) is valid.

It appears that the modal verb 'can' does not reflect a non-deontic modality that bears a resemblance to the deontic modalities. Rather, legal powers are reminiscent of dispositional concepts employed in descriptive language. A dispositional concept such as 'fragile' in 'Glass is fragile.' makes it possible to speak of a potentiality as an actual property. Here 'fragile' means that glass breaks if it is not handled with proper care. Likewise, John and Mary's legal power to give their daughter a name means that if they give her a name, then that is the child's name.

'Legal power' is a normative dispositional concept. It is used in power-conferring norms to create acts whose performance yields valid norms. Acts created by power-conferring norms are termed 'legal acts'.

Performing legal acts is logically dependent on power-conferring norms.[6] Put abstractly, a power-conferring norm serves to constitute a legal act-type. Every performance of a legal act of this type counts as an instance thereof. The term 'act' will be employed to designate act-types. Instances of act-types will be termed 'individual acts'.[7]

The relationship between power-conferring norms and legal acts is a specific case of the general relationship between *declarative* speech acts and *constitutive* rules as conceptualized in speech act theory. Following John Searle, a constitutive rule has the form 'x counts as y in context c'.[8] In this formula, x stands for a specification of a speech act while y represents a specification of the type of result individual acts answering to the former specification have in the institutional context c, of which the constitutive rule is a part. Searle's famous example is the constitutive rule of promising: 'Promising counts as the undertaking of an obligation to do some act.'[9] It does not take a great deal of imagination to recognize a constitutive rule, too, in the provision of the Dutch Civil Code incorporating into the Dutch legal system the concept 'legal act': 'A legal act requires a will that is directed to a legal effect and has been divulged in a declaration.' This can be rephrased as: 'Declaring a will directed to a legal effect (x) counts as performing a legal act (y) in the Dutch legal system (c).'[10]

Legal acts are specific declarative speech acts. The consequences of this conclusion deserve closer scrutiny. With this in mind, I should like to invite attention to some key concepts in recent speech act theory. These concepts are drawn from the theory propounded by Searle and Daniel Vanderveken.[11]

---

[6] See John R. Searle, *Speech Acts. An Essay in the Philosophy of Language* (Cambridge: Cambridge UP, 1969), at 34; Ross (n.3 above), at 53; Amedeo G. Conte, 'Idealtypen für eine Theorie der konstitutiven Regeln', in *Reason and Experience in Contemporary Legal Thought* (*Rechtstheorie*, Beiheft 10), ed. Torstein Eckhoff et al. (Berlin: Duncker & Humblot, 1986), 243–50, at 244; Ruiter, *Institutional Legal Facts* (n.5 above), at 33–6.

[7] von Wright, *NA* 37; Amedeo G. Conte, 'Fenomeni di fenomeni', *RIFD*, 63 (1986), 29–57.

[8] Searle (n.6 above), 36; John R. Searle, *The Construction of Social Reality* (Harmondsworth: Allen Lane, and New York: Free Press, 1995), 43–51.

[9] Searle (n.6 above), 63. [10] Art. 3:33, Dutch Civil Code.

[11] John R. Searle and Daniel Vanderveken, *Foundations of Illocutionary Logic* (Cambridge: Cambridge UP, 1985); Daniel Vanderveken, *Meaning and Speech Acts*. vol. I: *Principles of Language Use* (Cambridge: Cambridge UP, 1990).

IV. SPEECH ACT THEORY

Speech acts have an internal purpose or, in Searle and Vanderveken's terminology, an *illocutionary point*. Since there are five illocutionary points, speech acts divide into five classes.[12]

Assertive Speech Acts

The purpose internal to asserting is to provide a faithful representation of a part of reality. This assertive illocutionary point is distinctive of assertive speech acts. Assertive speech acts have a word-to-world direction of fit, for individual assertive speech acts achieve success of fit only if their content is true—that is to say, corresponds to reality. 'It is raining.' achieves success of fit just in case it is raining.

Commissive Speech Acts

The purpose internal to promising is to undertake an obligation to perform some act. This commissive illocutionary point is distinctive of commissive speech acts. Commissive speech acts have a world-to-word direction of fit, for individual commissive speech acts achieve success of fit only if the speaker sees to it that reality is changed to correspond to their content. 'I shall come.' achieves success of fit just in case I come.

Directive Speech Acts

The purpose internal to ordering is to oblige someone else to perform some act. This directive illocutionary point is distinctive of directive speech acts. Directive speech acts, too, have a world-to-word direction of fit, for individual directive speech acts achieve success of fit only if the addressee sees to it that reality is changed to correspond to their content. 'Come!' achieves success of fit just in case the ordered person comes.

Expressive Speech Acts

The purpose internal to congratulating is to communicate one's pleasure in the achievement, success, or good fortune of another. This expressive illocutionary point is distinctive of expressive speech acts. Expressive

---

[12] Searle and Vanderveken (n.11 above), 13–15; Vanderveken (n.11 above), 105–10; Ruiter, *Institutional Legal Facts* (n.5 above), 43–7.

speech acts have a null or an empty direction of fit, for individual expressive speech acts serve to express attitudes of speakers. Although it is presupposed that that which the attitudes are about exists, the attitudes themselves are part of the speaker's mind and not of reality. In the exclamation 'Happy birthday!' it is assumed that it is the addressee's birthday. However, the conveying of congratulations relates not to reality but to a psychological state of the speaker.

Declarative Speech Acts

The purpose internal to appointing a committee is to transform a collection of persons into a single unitary body by presenting them as thus transformed. This declarative illocutionary point is distinctive of declarative speech acts. Declarative speech acts have a double direction of fit, for individual declarative speech acts change reality in conformity with their content by presenting reality as thus changed. 'I appoint you chairman.' achieves success of fit when the appointed person becomes chairman by virtue of the declaration.[13]

V. CLASSES OF DECLARATIVE SPEECH ACTS

Of the five classes of speech acts that Searle and Vanderveken distinguish, declarative and commissive speech acts are the most problematic. With respect to assertive, directive, and expressive speech acts, reality is conceived of as standing apart from the content of the individual speech acts of these classes. That is to say, reality is not changed by making assertions. Demands must be met to achieve success of fit on the directive illocutionary point; in other words, something must actually be done in order to change reality according to the content of individual directive speech acts. And in the case of individual expressive speech acts, reality is taken for granted. In contrast, declarative and commissive speech acts appear to relate to a kind of reality that can be changed through their performance. Individual declarative speech acts produce facts by declaring them existent. In the same way, individual commissive speech acts produce obligations on the part of the speakers.

  How can language change reality? In order to answer this question, one must appreciate that Searle and Vanderveken use the term 'world' to refer indiscriminately to two wholly different kinds of reality. The first kind I

---

[13] John R. Searle, *Expression and Meaning. Studies in the Theory of Speech Acts* (Cambridge: Cambridge UP, 1979), 3, 12; Searle and Vanderveken (n.11 above), 92–8; Vanderveken (n.11 above), 105–10; Ruiter, *Institutional Legal Facts* (n.5 above), 47–9.

shall term 'a real world'. A real world is a part of reality as it is. The second kind I shall term 'an institutional world'. An institutional world is the meaning-content of an institutionalized normative system. A meaning-content of this kind offers an over-all picture of a real world with an eye to bringing about a social practice in which that picture is actualized. Thus, institutional worlds aim at effectuating congruent real worlds.

Real worlds stand just as far apart from individual declarative and commissive speech acts as they do from the individual speech acts of the other three classes. Declarative and commissive speech acts can be performed in order to add elements to the institutionalized normative system to which they belong and in this way to change the institutional world that the system constitutes. The mode of existence of these elements, however, is no more than systemic validity. Just as something must be done to adapt reality to a request, for example, so something must be done to adapt a real world to an individual declarative or commissive speech act. To that end, social practice must change in accordance with the content of these speech acts. In this wider sense, declarative and commissive speech acts have a world-to-word direction of fit as well.

Elements created by individual declarative speech acts are 'institutional facts'. Actually, institutional facts are not facts at all; rather, they are verbal presentations of facts having systemic validity in the institutionalized normative system of a community. From the systemic validity of such verbal presentations it follows that they purport to be made true by general acceptance. General acceptance takes the form of a social practice that can be interpreted as resulting from a shared belief in the facts presented by the verbal presentations.[14] For example, John and Mary's giving their daughter the name 'Louise' is an individual declarative speech act creating the institutional fact that their daughter's name is Louise. Creating this institutional fact is tantamount to achieving success of fit on the double direction of fit that is characteristic of the declarative illocutionary point. It is only the first step, however, for the institutional fact that the daughter's name is Louise is meant to achieve additional world-to-word success of fit on the declarative illocutionary point by virtue of the fact that the daughter is generally called Louise. The practice of calling her Louise forms the social realization of the institutional fact that her name is Louise.

Individual commissive speech acts, too, produce institutional facts. These institutional facts, however, are of the special kind usually called

---

[14] See Roger A. Shiner, 'The Acceptance of a Legal System', in *Wittgenstein and Legal Theory*, ed. Dennis M. Patterson (Boulder: Westview Press, 1992), 59–84, at 77–84; Eerik Lagerspetz, *The Opposite Mirrors. An Essay on the Conventionalist Theory of Institutions* (Dordrecht: Kluwer, 1995), at 9–14.

'obligations'. An obligation is a valid verbal presentation of an order. An order, in turn, is the result of ordering—that is, of telling someone to do something under threat. The standard example is the gunman's order to hand over money. His order achieves success of fit on the directive illocutionary point if his victim is obliged to do as he is told. Plainly, a promise is not the result of a promisor's telling himself to do something under threat. Yet, a promise binds the promisor. How is this possible? The puzzle is solved when one sees that promises are valid presentations of orders to the promisors that are established by the promisors themselves. Being institutional facts, promises purport to be made true by a social practice that can be interpreted as resulting from a shared belief that promisors are obligated to keep their promises. Thus, although we cannot order ourselves, we are quite capable of committing ourselves to something.

Declarative and commissive speech acts are performable only in the context of institutionalized normative systems that include their respective constitutive rules. By contrast, assertive, directive, and expressive speech acts are normally used in a purely linguistic way. For example, the speech acts marked by the verbs 'assert', 'warn', and 'congratulate' can all be performed by simply using the natural language. However, each of these three classes also includes speech acts whose performance must take place in the context of an institutionalized normative system. The umpire's authoritative assertion 'You're out.' establishes the institutional fact of your being out. The sergeant's command to the soldier to dig a foxhole establishes the soldier's obligation to dig a foxhole. President Clinton's letter of condolence to the government of North Korea on the occasion of Kim Il Sung's death establishes the institutional fact of presidential sympathy for the bereavement of the North Korean state. The objectives of the individual speech acts in these three examples are similar to the objectives of individual declarative and commissive speech acts. The umpire's decision purports to be made true by being generally accepted as truthful. The sergeant's command has the purpose of being made true by the military community's acceptance of the fact that the soldier is obligated to dig a foxhole. President Clinton's letter of condolence aims at being made true by international recognition of the sympathy it expresses.

Assertive, directive, and expressive speech acts can be either purely linguistic or declarative forms. In contrast, commissive speech acts can only be declarative forms. The reason is that commissive speech acts are declarative forms belonging to a larger class of speech acts that also includes purely linguistic forms. This larger class consists of all speech acts that can be performed in order to express speakers' purposes of taking certain courses of action, irrespective of whether or not the speakers are subsequently committed to taking them. The individual speech act marked by 'I'll see whether I can come tomorrow.' achieves success of fit on a world-to-word direction of fit when I turn up the next day. The phrasing is so chosen, however, that I am not committed to coming tomorrow. The class of speech acts to which commissive speech acts belong shall be termed 'purposive speech acts'.

In fact, commissive speech acts are not the only declarative forms of purposive speech acts. Noncommittal declarative forms occur, too. For example, a certain state formally threatens another state with lawful retaliation. Under public international law the threat is a valid presentation of the first state's purpose of taking some action to the detriment of the latter state. Recognition of the threat by the international community does not, however, obligate the first state to carry out the threat.

The preceding commentary on Searle and Vanderveken's general classification of speech acts leads to a classification of declarative speech acts consisting of seven classes.

Exclusively Declarative Speech Acts

The constitutive rule of an exclusively declarative speech act determines that the performance of the act brings about a valid presentation of a state of affairs. The presentation requires realization in the form of a general practice that can be interpreted as resulting from a shared belief that the state of affairs does exist. Manchester United exists for as long as all concerned act upon the belief that it exists.

Commissive Speech Acts

The constitutive rule of a commissive speech act determines that the performance of the act brings about a valid presentation of an order to the performer to carry out a certain course of action. The presentation requires realization in the form of a general practice that can be interpreted as resulting from a shared belief that the performer is obligated to carry out the course of action. An oath of allegiance obligates for as long as it is generally believed to do so.

Purposive Declarative Speech Acts

The constitutive rule of a purposive declarative speech act determines that the performance of the act brings about a valid presentation of the performer's purpose of carrying out a certain course of action. The presentation requires realization in the form of a general practice that can be interpreted as resulting from a shared belief that the performer has the purpose of carrying out the course of action. President Kennedy's formal announcement that the United States would go to the moon did not obligate the Presidency to follow through on what had been announced.

Imperative Speech Acts

The constitutive rule of an imperative speech act determines that the performance of the act brings about a valid presentation of an order to another person to carry out a certain course of action. The presentation requires realization in the form of a general practice that can be interpreted as resulting from a shared belief that the other person is obligated to carry out the course of action. A fatherly admonition obligates for as long as the family accepts that it does.

Hortatory Declarative Speech Acts

The constitutive rule of a hortatory declarative speech act determines that the performance of the act brings about a valid presentation of a non-binding exhortation to another person to carry out a certain course of action. The presentation requires realization in the form of a general practice that can be interpreted as resulting from a shared belief that the other person is given a serious incentive to carry out the course of action. A formal recommendation by a governmental advisory board need not be taken seriously by the government if it is generally treated as a meaningless compromise.

Expressive Declarative Speech Acts

The constitutive rule of an expressive declarative speech act determines that the performance of the act brings about a valid presentation of an attitude about something. The presentation requires realization in the form of a general practice that can be interpreted as resulting from a shared belief in the attitude. Official celebrations are founded on a general acceptance of the fact that there is something worth celebrating.

Assertive Declarative Speech Acts

The constitutive rule of an assertive declarative speech act determines that the performance of the act brings about a valid representation of a state of affairs. The representation requires realization in the form of a general practice that can be interpreted as resulting from a shared belief in its truthfulness. Theological dogmas are made true in the form of their general acceptance.

VI. A CLASSIFICATION OF LEGAL ACTS

A legal act is a declarative speech act that is constituted by a power-conferring legal norm. Performance of a legal act produces a legal presentation demanding general acceptance by the legal community owing to its systemic validity. Legal presentations of all classes exert this general pressure on members of the legal community who are in a position to contribute to the realization of the legal presentations in question—and thereby to contribute to the general effectiveness of the legal system. Therefore, they can all be qualified as legal norms directed at the regulation of social behaviour.

The preceding classification of declarative speech acts offers a point of departure for a general classification of legal acts. Previously, the linguistic structure of power-conferring norms was symbolized as follows:

$(C)_i \rightarrow [C]$

Using this formula, one can symbolize the general structure of power-conferring norms underlying legal acts of all seven classes distinguished above.

Declarative Legal Acts

$(state\_of\_affairs)_{performer} \rightarrow [state\_of\_affairs]$

Example: The government can designate an area in which noise pollution occurs or is expected to occur as a noise zone, to which the provisions of this chapter apply.[15]
Legal act: to designate as a noise zone.

Commissive Legal Acts

$(ORDER(ACTperformer))_{performer} \rightarrow [ORDER(ACTperformer)]$

or

$(ORDER(\sim ACTperformer))_{performer} \rightarrow [ORDER(\sim ACTperformer)]$

Example: Every State possesses the capacity to conclude treaties. Every treaty in force is binding upon the parties and is to be performed by them in good faith.[16]
Legal act: to conclude treaties.

---

[15] Art. 108, sec. 1, Dutch Act on Noise Pollution.
[16] Arts. 6 and 26, Vienna Convention on the Law of Treaties.

Purposive Legal Acts

$(PURPOSE(ACTperformer))_{performer} \rightarrow [PURPOSE(ACTperformer)]$

or

$(PURPOSE(\sim ACTperformer))_{performer} \rightarrow [PURPOSE(\sim ACTperformer)]$

Example: The Council of Ministers issues plans with respect to certain aspects of national environmental policy.[17]
Legal act: to issue plans.

Imperative Legal Acts

$(ORDER(ACTaddressee))_{performer} \rightarrow [ORDER(ACTaddressee)]$

or

$(ORDER(\sim ACTaddressee))_{performer} \rightarrow [ORDER(\sim ACTaddressee)]$

Example: All members of the United Nations, in order to contribute to the maintenance of international peace and security, undertake to make available to the Security Council, on its call, armed forces, assistance, and facilities.[18]
Legal act: to call for armed forces, assistance, and facilities.

Hortatory Legal Acts

$(HORTATION(ACTaddressee))_{performer} \rightarrow [HORTATION(ACTaddressee)]$

or

$(HORTATION(\sim ACTaddressee))_{performer} \rightarrow [HORTATION(\sim ACTaddressee)]$

Example: In order to carry out their task the Council and the Commission shall make recommendations in accordance with the provisions of this Treaty. Recommendations shall have no binding force.[19]
Legal act: to make recommendations.

Expressive Legal Acts

$(ATTITUDE(state\_of\_affairs))_{performer} \rightarrow [ATTITUDE(state\_of\_affairs)]$

Example: After taking the oath, the King is inaugurated by the States General whose chairman pronounces the following declaration, which is

---

[17] Art. 2a, Dutch Physical Planning Act.
[18] Art. 43, sec. 1, UN Charter. [19] Art. 189, EC Treaty.

then confirmed by all members: 'In the name of the Dutch People and by virtue of the Constitution, we receive and pay homage to you as King.'[20]
Legal act: to pay homage.

Assertive Legal Acts

$(ASSERTION(state\_of\_affairs))_{performer} \rightarrow [ASSERTION(state\_of\_affairs)]$

Example: The determination that the offence has been committed by the accused must rest on those justificatory facts and circumstances to which reference is made in the verdict.[21]
Legal act: to determine that an offence has been committed.

Negative Legal Acts

In principle, all legal acts have negative counterparts.[22] The structure of *negative* legal acts will be illustrated with the example of the negative counterpart of imperative legal acts: *permissive* legal acts. Performance of a permissive legal act produces a legal permission, that is, a valid presentation of the absence of an order. For instance, a fishing licence is a valid presentation of the absence of an order to forbear from fishing. A legal permission to perform some act can be symbolized as:

$[\sim ORDER(\sim ACTaddressee)]$

A legal permission not to perform some act, as:

$[\sim ORDER(ACTaddressee)]$

Accordingly, power-conferring norms specifying a permissive legal act are of the form:

$(\sim ORDER(\sim ACTaddressee))_{performer} \rightarrow [\sim ORDER(\sim ACTaddressee)]$

or

$(\sim ORDER(ACTaddressee))_{performer} \rightarrow [\sim ORDER(ACTaddressee)]$

The legal permission requires realization in the form of a social practice that can be interpreted as resulting from a shared belief that the permission-holders are free to carry out the permitted course of action.[23]

---

[20] Art. 54, former Dutch Constitution (1972).
[21] Art. 359, sec. 3, Dutch Code of Criminal Procedure.
[22] Ruiter, *Institutional Legal Facts* (n.5 above), 103–14.
[23] von Wright, *NA* 90–120; Ruiter, *Institutional Legal Facts* (n.5 above), 105–14.

VII. PERFORMANCE OF LEGAL ACTS

A legal act is constituted by a power-conferring legal norm that also specifies the class of individuals capable of performing it. All individuals of that class have the legal power to perform the legal act in question. When they exercise their legal power, they thereby create valid legal norms. Created legal norms, by virtue of their validity, require general acceptance. This sequence can be represented as follows:

Symbolic	Verbal	Example
$(C) \rightarrow [C]$	legal act	to vote
$(C)_i \rightarrow [C]$	power-conferring norm	all citizens over eighteen have the right to vote
$(C)_a \rightarrow [C]$	legal power	citizen Alfred's right to vote
$(c)_a$	exercise legal power	Alfred votes
$[c]$	legal norm	Alfred's vote
$\vdash(c)$	acceptance	Alfred's vote is counted

As far as declarative and expressive legal acts are concerned, general acceptance of the validity of the legal norms resulting from their performance is all that is called for. With respect to legal acts of the other classes, complete success of fit requires more. For each of these classes, the completing sequence starting with $\vdash(c)$ is presented below.

Commissive and Imperative Legal Acts

Symbolic	Verbal
$\vdash(\text{ORDER}(\text{ACTalfred}))$	acceptance of obligation
$\vdash(\text{ACTalfred})$	fulfilment of obligation
or	
$\vdash\sim(\text{ACTalfred})$	violation of obligation

As H.L.A. Hart points out, general acceptance of rules giving rise to legal obligations is expressed in the form of an insistent general demand for conformity and serious social pressure brought to bear on those who would depart from the rules.[24] Public censure transforms legal obligations into orders or, seen from a different perspective, transforms legal authority into social power. Nevertheless, it is an essential characteristic of legal obligations that their violation be a real possibility. Thus, such violations, even if they occur frequently, do not threaten the effectiveness of obligatory norms. When non-conforming behaviour no longer meets with public censure, however, obligatory norms cease to be effective.

[24] Hart, *CL* 84, 2nd edn. 86–7.

Purposive and Hortatory Legal Acts

Symbolic	*Verbal*
⊢(PURPOSE/HORTATION(ACTalfred))	acceptance of purposive/ hortatory norm
⊢(ACTalfred)	purpose achieved/hortation adopted
or	
⊢∼(ACTalfred)	failure

It is perhaps true that any performance of a purposive or hortatory speech act results in a sort of commitment. Empty threats are ineffective. Constant disregard of well-intended advice may irritate the advisor. Such commitments, however, lack the 'institutional force' of legal obligations.[25] Purposive and hortatory acts are used when the kind of social pressure associated with legal obligations is considered too strong. Purposive legal acts accord expressions of intended behaviour a legal status while keeping open the possibility of reconsideration in light of the reactions of others or changing circumstances. Sending letters of intent and making offers free of engagement are examples of purposive legal acts. Hortatory legal acts are important components of legal procedures. One may think of applications for decisions, official expert judgments, formal recommendations, and nominations. Common to all hortatory legal acts is the fact that they serve to make explicit what is expected from the addressees without presenting them as obligated to meet these expectations.

Assertive Legal Acts

Symbolic	*Verbal*
⊢(ASSERTION(state_of_affairs))	acceptance of assertive norm
⊢(state_of_affairs)	truth of assertive norm
or	
⊢∼(state_of_affairs)	falsity of assertive norm

Performance of assertive legal acts is directed at producing valid verbal representations of reality as it is. Being representations, assertive legal norms purport to be true. If, however, they happen to be false, their validity prevails. The paradoxical consequence is that even false assertive legal norms claim general acceptance of their truthfulness. As a rule, legal systems include procedures for redressing false assertive norms. It is entirely possible, however, that a false assertive norm will be upheld.

[25] W. J. Waluchow, *Inclusive Legal Positivism* (Oxford: Clarendon Press, 1994), 168–74.

Failing this possibility, World Championship Soccer 1994 would quite possibly never have produced a world champion.

VIII. EMPOWERING LEGAL ACTS

Power-conferring norms are created through the performance of legal acts of a special kind, which I shall term 'empowering legal acts'. Empowering legal acts are constituted in turn by power-conferring norms of a higher order. To determine which class empowering legal acts belong to, we must clarify the nature of legal powers. A legal power can be conceived of as a valid presentation of the fact that if a certain agent performs a certain specified speech act, then he creates a valid presentation. One may well ask what the general acceptance of a legal power looks like. In order to answer this question I must introduce the concept 'scope of validity'. The scope of validity of a legal power is the set of cases with respect to which the power may be exercised. The set divides into two subsets. The first is the set of cases with respect to which the legal power has in fact been exercised. I shall term this the 'consumed' scope of validity. The second subset is the set of cases with respect to which the legal power has not been exercised. I shall term this subset the 'unconsumed' scope of validity.

As far as its consumed scope of validity is concerned, a legal power requires acceptance in the form of a social practice that can be interpreted as resulting from a shared belief that the legal norms that have been issued by appeal to it are valid. As far as its unconsumed scope of validity is concerned, a legal power requires acceptance in the form of a social practice in which the possibility of its exercise is taken into account. Anticipation of the possible exercise of a legal power can take different forms. One may think of calls for the exercise of a legal power. One may also think of arrangements to prevent such an exercise or, indeed, of other social strategies in which the possible employment of a legal power plays a role. In their own special way, legal powers function analogously to social power: latent power is often more effective than manifest power.

In general, a legal power requires general acceptance in the form of a social practice that can be interpreted as resulting from a shared belief in the validity of legal norms that have been or may be issued by appeal to it. Accordingly, an empowering legal act can be said to have the purport that the validity of the norms created by the exercise of the legal powers conferred by the power-conferring norm created by the performance of the empowering legal act will be accepted. Since empowering legal acts have no further purport, they are declarative in character.

Disqualifying Legal Acts

The negative counterparts of empowering legal acts are *disqualifying* legal acts. Performance of disqualifying legal acts produces legal *incompetence*:

$(C)_i \rightarrow [\sim C]$

Example: Minors are incapable of performing legal acts.[26]

IX. LEGAL ACTS ABOUT LEGAL NORMS

Legal norms of all the different types distinguished above were found to be valid presentations of a part of reality that stands apart from the legal system. However, a legal system may also contain norms that are valid presentations of elements of the system itself. The most important types are produced through the performance of revocatory and invalidating legal acts respectively. Both kinds of act are negative in character, so it stands to reason to assume that they have positive counterparts. The assumption is correct. The positive counterparts of revocatory legal acts are consolidatory legal acts. The positive counterparts of invalidating legal acts are endorsing legal acts.

Revocatory Legal Acts

Performance of a revocatory legal act produces a valid presentation of a valid presentation as prospectively invalid. When a public authority repeals a statute, it does so by presenting it as no longer existent. The revocatory act performed can be symbolized as:

$(\sim[C])_i \rightarrow [\sim[C]]$

In words: if *i* declares valid norm *C* invalid, then a presentation of *C* as invalid becomes valid. The presentation achieves direct success of fit on a double direction of fit: *C* becomes invalid by being validly presented as invalid.

Consolidatory Legal Acts

Performance of a consolidatory legal act produces a valid representation of a presentation as valid. A solemn reconfirmation of a pledge produces a restatement of the pledge's validity. The consolidatory act performed can be symbolized as:

---

[26] Art. 1:234, sec. 1, Dutch Civil Code.

$(\vdash[C])_i \rightarrow [\vdash[C]]$

In words: if *i* formally asserts that norm *C* is valid, then a representation of *C* as valid becomes valid. The representation achieves direct success of fit on a double direction of fit: the validity of *C* is consolidated by being validly represented as valid.

Invalidating Legal Acts

Performance of an invalidating legal act produces a valid representation of a presentation as invalid. When a higher public authority declares null and void a statute issued by a lower public authority, it formally asserts that the statute was devoid of legal validity from the outset. The invalidating act performed can be symbolized as:

$(\vdash \sim[C])_i \rightarrow [\sim[C]]$

In words: if *i* formally asserts that norm *C* is invalid, then a presentation of *C* as invalid becomes valid. The representation achieves direct success of fit on a double direction of fit: *C* is invalidated by being validly represented as invalid.

Endorsing Legal Acts

Performance of an endorsing legal act produces a valid presentation of a presentation as legally valid. A higher public authority, by approving a statute decided upon by a lower public authority, conveys validity to it. The endorsing act performed can be symbolized as:

$([C])_i \rightarrow [[C]]$

In words: if *i* declares norm *C* valid, then a presentation of *C* as valid becomes valid. The presentation achieves direct success of fit on a double direction of fit: *C* is validated by being validly presented as valid.

X. COMPREHENSIVE LEGAL POWERS

The previous analysis may have created the impression that all legal acts must be separately specified in a power-conferring norm. This impression would be mistaken, for in actual legal practice power-conferring norms usually provide parties with rather unspecified abilities to perform a great variety of legal acts of different classes. Legal powers of this kind we shall qualify as 'comprehensive'. The provision of Article 1 of the United States Constitution, to the effect that all legislative powers shall be vested in the Congress, invests that body with a comprehensive legal power to perform legal acts of all classes, provided that they be of a legislative nature. Similar provisions are to be found in the constitutions of other democratic states. To my knowledge, none of these states is in possession of a conclusive legal doctrine with respect to substantive criteria for distinguishing 'legislative' legal acts from other legal acts. The doctrine of the 'formal concept of legislation' (*formeller Gesetzesbegriff*), which prevails on the European continent, boils down to the maxim that whatever the legislature enacts is valid. At lower state levels, too, legal powers are usually comprehensive. With respect to so-called private legal powers, a similar comprehensiveness is evident. The principle of contractual freedom enables private citizens to perform legal acts of any kind considered opportune, except where the act counts as a violation of public policy.

Consequently, the question of whether or not a certain class of legal act is included in a legal system cannot be answered merely by determining whether the system contains power-conferring norms that explicitly constitute legal acts of that class. In most cases, a positive answer will have to be based on the fact that norms of the type in question are valid within the system. Their validity demonstrates that the legal power exercised in issuing them includes the corresponding legal act.

XI. LEGAL INSTITUTIONS

A special and important class of legal powers are powers to establish legal institutions. Legal institutions are relatively independent systems of legal norms that can be dealt with as distinct entities. Associations, rights of property, public authorities, and marriages are examples of such relatively independent systems of legal norms that are valid within a covering legal system.

Legal institutions are usually established by the performance of a legal act. Legal acts of this kind are specified in what Neil MacCormick has termed 'institutive rules'.[27] Institutive rules are of the form:

'If a person having qualifications *q* performs an act *a* by procedure *p* and if the circumstances are *c*, then a valid instance of the institution *I* exists.'[28]

The formula makes it clear that we must distinguish between 'legal institutions' in the sense of legal categories on the one hand, and 'legal

---

[27] Neil MacCormick, 'Law as an Institutional Fact', *Law Quarterly Review*, 90 (1974), 102–29, repr. (with minor revisions) in Neil MacCormick and Ota Weinberger, *An Institutional Theory of Law. New Approaches to Legal Positivism* (Dordrecht: Kluwer, 1986), 49–74; on 'institutive rules', see at 106–7, repr. at 52–3.

[28] MacCormick (n.27 above), 119, 126, repr. 65, 71.

institutions' in the sense of instances of such categories on the other. MacCormick illustrates the distinction by means of the true proposition that the trust is an institution that does not exist in French law.[29] This proposition represents the fact that in the French legal system there is no constitutive rule for the legal category 'trust', and that consequently no trusts can be established in France. The example shows that the names of legal institutions are employed indiscriminately to designate legal categories as well as instances of such categories. Here we shall term the former, 'legal institutions', and the latter, 'individual legal institutions'. Marriage is a legal institution; John and Mary's marriage is an individual legal institution.

Legal institutions are associated with three kinds of rules. First, *institutive* rules determine that through the performance of a certain act an individual legal institution of the category in question becomes valid. Second, *terminative* rules determine that through the performance of a certain act a valid individual legal institution ceases to be valid. Third, legal institutions are accompanied by sets of *consequential* rules. An operative fact of the consequential rule is that an individual legal institution is valid. The consequential rules of a legal institution determine the legal consequences of establishing an individual legal institution of the category in question. In other words, the set of consequential rules of a legal institution determines the legal regimes of the individual legal institutions that are established by appeal to the institutive rule.[30]

Institutional legal regimes may consist of norms of all the types distinguished above. The legal regime of an individual institution provides an over-all picture of the practice required to transform the latter into a social institution. For example, the lawful marriage of John and Mary is an individual legal institution that provides a valid picture of John and Mary as being married with the purpose of effectuating a practice of John and Mary living the life of a married couple. The practice required is not restricted to John and Mary's fulfilling their marital duties; it also includes acceptance of their marriage by the legal community at large.

Legal institutions designate a category of legal systems fit to provide over-all pictures of a certain kind of practice. Once such an institutional legal system is established and put into practice, the result is a set of social relations functioning as a separate entity. In this way, we are able to deal with legal persons as if they were natural persons, to deal with

---

[29] MacCormick (n.27 above), 108, repr. 54.
[30] MacCormick (n.27 above), 106–7, repr. 52–3; Ruiter, *Institutional Legal Facts* (n.5 above), 208.

legal rights as if they were natural objects, and to treat legal qualities as if they were natural properties.[31]

Individual legal institutions are declarative norms that are elaborated in the legal regimes applying to them under the consequential rules of the corresponding legal institution. Therefore, institutive rules specify declarative legal acts of a very special kind. Performance of *institutive* legal acts does not simply yield valid presentations of states of affairs; it brings about, in addition, the emergence of entire institutional legal systems consisting of legal norms of all imaginable types, which in turn require general acceptance in accordance with their own specific illocutionary forces.

XII. CONCLUSION

The classical approach pictures legal systems as structures consisting of deontic norms and norms conferring powers to issue deontic norms. Challenging the classical approach, I have sketched a picture in which deontic norms are no longer the only type of primary legal norm. Moreover, the notion of 'empowerment' as a non-deontic modality is replaced, in my scheme, with the idea of legal powers as normative dispositional concepts. The reader will have seen, too, that certain norms relate not to social reality but to the legal system itself. The availability of norms of this type renders legal systems self-adaptive. Finally, legal systems are systems of individual legal institutions. Individual legal institutions are valid over-all pictures of social reality as it ought to be. The variety of linguistic devices required for drawing such legally valid pictures is no less numerous than the variety of linguistic devices required for *describing* the world surrounding us. Of course, readers will decide for themselves whether or not such devices qualify as 'legal norms', but they should at the same time keep in mind the fact that devices not found worthy of the qualification will not for that reason disappear from the legal system.

---

[31] See Ota Weinberger, *Law, Institution, and Legal Politics. Fundamental Problems of Legal Theory and Social Philosophy* (Dordrecht: Kluwer, 1991), at 20–1; Dick W.P. Ruiter, 'A Basic Classification of Legal Institutions', *Ratio Juris*, 10 (1997), 357–71.

26

Powers and Power-Conferring Norms*

NEIL MACCORMICK

I. INTRODUCTION: NORMATIVE ORDER

Normative order is exhibited in human activities, that is, in assemblages of human actions and interactions, wherever these are properly to be explained as responding to relatively stable ideas of right and wrong conduct, ideas about what ought to be or ought not to be. 'Responding to' such ideas is not, of course, a matter of showing perfect conformity. All it requires is that people attempt seriously to orient their conduct to such ideas, at least partly succeed in doing so, and deem it a matter for justified regret and criticism when someone's conduct falls short of the right, or defies it. 'Responding to' ideas of right and wrong is closely related to 'appealing to' them. When I call on someone to act in a certain way because it's the right thing to do, or not to do something else because it would be wrong, I hope that the person in question will respond to the ideas of right and wrong that I have thus called to attention.

Appealing to ideas of right and wrong presupposes that these ideas have general applicability and acceptability, if not indeed general acceptance. To make such appeal in an interpersonal context is to imply that the other does or should already accept the idea of right to which appeal is made, on the ground of its being interpersonally valid for guiding action. There is no implication, however, of any particularly systematic or structured character in the ideas of right we use. Normative order does not have to be envisaged or reconstructed as some systematic set of structured 'norms', 'rules', or 'principles'. To reconstruct interpersonal normative order in terms of some implicit system and structure is something it may be possible to do, something there may be stronger or weaker reason to try to do in one special context or another, but an already-implicit conception of system and structure is not presupposed

* *Editors' note*: MacCormick's paper is an original contribution to the present volume. An earlier version was delivered at the Fifth Siena Kelsen Symposium (June 1993), devoted to powers.

in normative order as we envisage it here. The possibility of systematization is one that will be considered later.

For the moment I wish merely to record this idea of normative order as constituted by ideas of right and wrong, and the possibility that humans may appeal to these ideas interpersonally and respond to them in their conduct. I do wish, however, to emphasize the idea of normative order as involving 'relatively stable' ideas of right and wrong conduct. This is to accept in effect Lon Fuller's[1] point that an 'order' of moment-by-moment changing ideas of right and wrong (or of so-called 'rules' that change moment by moment) would be no real order at all. On the other hand, absolute stability would scarcely be more acceptable, nor in fact commonly to be found. The common idea that it is right for people to keep their promises presupposes also that they can make promises and, by making them, can change what it is right or wrong to do. Likewise the idea that one ought to obey one's parents, to the extent that it is believed, makes it possible for parents to change what it is right for their children to do, by varying the directives issued to them. Indeed, notwithstanding the necessary relative stability of any normative order, almost any such order that we can imagine will contain some possibility for making deliberate changes in the normative situation as it affects individuals.

II. POWER

The idea of change which we have just introduced is an idea essential to the discussion of power. Power in its widest sense is the ability to cause or to prevent change in some prevailing state of affairs. As between human beings, power of one over another is the ability within some determinable context to take decisions that bring about changes affecting that other's interests regardless of his or her consent or dissent. People frequently do act, and always have reason to act, in accordance with their interests. Hence, when one has power over another in the sense of being able to affect that other's interests regardless of consent, this amounts to having the ability unilaterally to affect the other's reasons for action. Someone who has power over another is able to impose on that other reasons for action or inaction that would not otherwise have existed. Since people often act in accordance with the reasons they have for acting, it follows that having power means being able to get people to do things, to act as they might not otherwise have acted; conversely, it can mean being able to get them to refrain from doing things they would otherwise have done. Exercises of power affect the way in which it is rational for people to act.

---

[1] See Lon L. Fuller, *The Morality of Law*, rev. edn. (New Haven: Yale UP, 1969), at ch. 2.

Interpersonal power is hence a factor in practical reason; it is a factor relevant to the practical deliberations of both the power-holder and the person subjected to the power. By contrast with physical and perhaps psychological power (charisma, personal magnetism), it operates through reason, and accounts for human action and behaviour only to the extent that rational and motivational accounts are adequate to explain that. To say that the power of the moon's gravitational field causes the tides to rise and fall does not imply that anyone thinks of the sea as responding to the moon's demands. Some would argue, with Michel Foucault, that social structures are endowed with an analogous form of power extraneous to practical reason, a power which, like physical power, operates without regard to reason and deliberation, and enables us to explain social events and outcomes in terms of the operations of the social structure regardless of individual motivation or decision. Power in that social-structural sense is largely excluded from the present discussion, yet it should be borne in mind as one possible source or ground of the interpersonal power that is here analysed. For if we were to ask how it comes about that one person is able to act in ways that affect another's interests regardless of consent, it seems probable that some account of social-structural aspects of the situation of the parties would be highly relevant.

Hitherto, our discussion of power has considered mainly power-in-fact, power actually to change the factual situation so that another's interests are affected and thereby his or her reasons for action or inaction altered. In the prior discussion of normative order, however, brief mention was made of the possibility to bring about change in the ways in which it is right or wrong to act, or in the demands that can be made for action or inaction. Since ideas of right and wrong belong within the range of reasons for action, it follows that we must acknowledge the possibility of normative power as a special form of interpersonal power. This exists when one is able to change ways in which it is, within a certain normative order, right or wrong to act, or able to change possibilities of change of that simpler sort.

To summarize: Normative power is the ability to take decisions that change what a person ought or ought not to do, or may or may not do, or what a person is able or unable to do, in the framework of some normative order, with or without the other person's consent to this change.

Normative order is a pervasive feature of human life, whether considered in isolated or individualistic mode, or in a context of community or society. There is an important difference between non-institutional and institutional normative order. The former is the sphere of moral deliberation, characterized as that is above all by the autonomy of moral agents.[2] The latter exists whenever questions about the interpersonally correct interpretation of what is right and wrong, both generally and in individual cases, are of regular and standing practice handled by particular persons, and where their doing so is regarded as right, at least in certain circumstances attended with certain procedural ways of acting, so that it is in turn held to be wrong for others to ignore the interpretative decisions they give.

Law is institutional normative order. It has a specially significant instantiation in the modern state, but state law is in fact only one type of legal order, not the whole of it.[3] Legal order being a special form of normative order, legal power is a special form of normative power. Legal order, as everyone knows, abounds in illustrations of normative power so defined. Legal powers are powers to change, or to block changes in, what some person or persons are legally obligated to do or to refrain from doing, or are legally at liberty to do or to refrain from doing, or are legally empowered to do. Legal power, in short, is the legally conferred ability to make changes that affect another person's legal position regardless of his or her consent or dissent. Particular examples are the power to make general rules or particular executive decisions imposing duties or conferring powers on other persons, and the power to pass judgment on alleged breaches of such rules or on the validity or invalidity of other acts that purport to exercise legal power. There are also powers exercisable by private persons with regard to the operations of such institutions of private law as contract, trust, property, marriage, and the like.

Discussion of power in this sense has become a commonplace of modern jurisprudence. Law has as much to do with enabling as with obligating. In large part, H. L. A. Hart's *The Concept of Law*[4] is an exploration of the theoretical significance of this truth. Law gives powers as well as duties, and these can be powers exercisable in a private capacity, as in contracting a marriage, forming a partnership, making a will, buying and selling stocks and shares, or in a public capacity, as in voting upon legislation, judging a lawsuit, issuing a notice of demand for the payment of taxes, granting planning permission for property development under a zoning law, issuing payment of a social security benefit.

It is worth repeating that such power, as normative power, remains distinct from power-in-fact. This provides the ground for the distinction of legal power from a closely related, and indeed intertwined, form of power: political power. Political power is power over the conditions of

[2] See Neil MacCormick, 'The Relative Heteronomy of Law', *European Journal of Philosophy*, 3 (1995), 69–84.

[3] The point is more fully argued in my Brusiin Lecture, 'Law as Institutional Normative Order', Helsinki, 1994, awaiting publication in a volume of the Brusiin Lectures to be edited by Jyrki Uusitalo.

[4] See especially at chs. 4 and 5. [For bibliographical data, see the Table of Abbreviations.]

life in a human community or society. It is the ability to take effective decisions on whatever concerns the common well-being of the members, and on whatever affects the distribution of the economic resources available to them. The taking of such decisions has important bearing on the reasons that guide the actions of people in their social intercourse with each other. Political power is power-in-fact concerning what can actually be brought about by the decisions of power-holders.

However, since the ability to do such things depends to a considerable extent upon the opinion of members of a society, especially their opinion about the legitimacy of a decision-maker's decisions, it follows that political power is rarely independent of legal power. For legitimacy is largely dependent on the possession of power or authority conferred by legal order, so far as it is not a matter of purely traditional respect, or of personal magnetism or charisma. Conversely, the stability of any institutional normative order must be dependent to a considerable extent on the possibility of exercising power-in-fact in the political setting. Hence, although it is important to distinguish political from legal power, it seems improbable that either can endure without the support of the other, certainly not in any society whose members aspire to co-exist in a state organized under the rule of law, that is, in a *Rechtsstaat*.

III. POWER-CONFERRING NORMS?

Normative orders characteristically allow for change in normative positions, and in law this takes the form of acknowledging legal powers. How then ought we to analyse this feature of law? Some scholars would perhaps suggest that it arises from the fact that law includes norms of competence or power-conferring rules as part of its raw data. Presumably the same would then have to be said about moral powers like the power to bind oneself by making a promise. One of Hans Kelsen's greatest contributions to the theory and philosophy of law was to have shown the incorrectness of such a suggestion. The systematized character of law (where it exists) is a product of legal science and legal theory, not a datum for it.[5] It is by constructing practical legal thought, with its raw ideas about right and wrong, duty and obligation, capacity and competence, into a rationally ordered scheme of knowledge that we endow law (or other normative order) with a systematic character. This is a process well described as

---

[5] I read this as the basic message of Kelsen's *Reine Rechtslehre* in its various editions and translations. It is difficult to cite any particular passage for what is a pervasive element in the whole idea of the relation between legal practice and legal science as Kelsen envisaged these, but particular attention should be paid to the way in which Kelsen differentiates 'nomostatics' and 'nomodynamics'. See e.g. *PTL*, at § 15 (pp. 70–1).

'rational reconstruction'.[6] Speech and grammar provide an analogy. Successful communicative speech must precede any systematizing grammar reconstructing the spoken language as an ordered sum of differentiated 'parts of speech'. The theorization of 'norms of competence' or 'power-conferring rules', and their individuation[7] as a distinct class of rules within a system, is one contribution to the process of systematization of law.

Such systematization was historically achieved through a combination of legal science (legal dogmatics, legal doctrine) and legal theory. It involves conceptualizing the normative order of law as based upon a statable set of legal rules or norms which can be ordered and expounded in a structured and systematic way. The rules or norms are understood as differentiated in terms of content and their bearing on human conduct, but as interrelating in complex unities of differentiated and individuated rules. In some way, the totality of legal rules is a complex unity of complex unities, unified by some ultimate '*Grundnorm*' presupposed in legal scientific thought or by some ultimate 'Rule of Recognition' entrenched in legal practice.[8]

According to a widely held, though at best over-simplifying, view—that of legal voluntarism—all (or nearly all) rules or norms of law owe their existence to acts of will, whether of the legal community at large, in the case of custom, or of the legislature, in the case of statute law, or of the courts, in the case of precedent. 'Written' statute law (and 'written' constitutional law) may give the appearance of determining the system element in law. For legislation is arranged in chapters, parts, and sections, and broken down into grammatically convenient units, with explicit and implicit linkages and connections made between different sections. So it may be said that legislative practice, not juristic reconstruction of legal materials, is what constitutes the system element in law.

Even in countries of codified law, this claim seems to me unconvincing. It is true that legislators in modern times are guided significantly by the system-conception of law, and approach their task with every effort to produce well-systematized and intelligible statutes. In this, they are guided by the skills of trained and experienced legislative drafters. But drafters and legislators alike respond to an idea of system which they do

[6] I attempt to give a further explanation of this idea in 'Reconstruction after Deconstruction: a Critique of CLS', *Oxford Journal of Legal Studies*, 10 (1990), 539–58; the original idea, for me, comes from Martin P. Golding's excellent study, 'Kelsen and the Concept of "Legal System"', *ARSP*, 47 (1961), 355–86, at 356–61, repr. in *More Essays in Legal Philosophy*, ed. Robert S. Summers (Oxford: Blackwell, 1971), 69–100, at 70–5.

[7] See Raz, *CLS*, *passim*, on the 'individuation of laws'.

[8] The references to *Grundnorm* and Rule of Recognition are, of course, to the central ideas of the above-cited works of Kelsen and Hart.

not themselves make. Legislation is systematic to the extent that it measures up to some presupposed notion of system given in a prevailing paradigm of legal thought. Such paradigms emerge from legal science and legal theory, not from the efforts of the legislator, not even Napoleon. As Max Weber pointed out, the rationalization of law has not been a universal feature of law as normative order at the practical level; it has been a special historical feature of certain forms of law.[9] Whether in the work of the great Roman systematizers starting with Gaius, or in the work of the institutional writers of modern legal systems from the seventeenth century onwards, or in the work of those who advised in the great codifications, or in the particular contributions of analytical jurisprudence, one can see this process at work. Law acquires the quality of a system and becomes a systematic body of knowledge through its scholarly (or 'scientific') reconstruction in those terms.

IV. POWERS, RULES, INSTITUTIONS, AND VALIDITY

Given that understanding of the task of legal theory and its special contribution to the systematization of law, let me now apply it in presenting a study of the norms or rules that confer power. I do this from a particular point of view, that of the 'normativist institutionalism' proposed in broadly similar terms by Ota Weinberger and myself over recent years.[10]

The starting point must lie in a basic understanding of law as imposing requirements about conduct in society. Law is normative in that it differentiates wrong from right, and prescribes abstention from wrongdoing. However simple and unanalysed a normative order might be, that is the basic distinction which it necessarily enshrines in being normative. Wrongdoing is held to be excluded, and the fact of an act's being wrong is held to exclude legitimate deliberation about the general balance of reasons for and against doing the wrongful act. We find at the conceptual ground floor of any normative order an appeal to what Joseph Raz has called 'exclusionary reasons'.[11] A more commonly understood terminology in this context is that of 'duty'. Avoiding wrongful acts on the ground that they are wrong is doing one's duty. Acting from a sense of duty is

[9] See Max Weber, *On Law in Economy and Society*, ed. Max Rheinstein and trans. Edward Shils (from *Wirtschaft und Gesellschaft*) (Cambridge, Mass.: Harvard UP, 1954), at 61–4, 301–20.
[10] The basic ideas are stated in Neil MacCormick and Ota Weinberger, *An Institutional Theory of Law. New Approaches to Legal Positivism* (Dordrecht: Reidel, 1986); see also Ota Weinberger, *Law, Institution and Legal Politics* (Dordrecht: Kluwer, 1991).
[11] See Joseph Raz, *Practical Reason and Norms* (London: Hutchinson, 1976), 2nd edn. (Princeton: Princeton UP, 1990); compare Frederick Schauer, *Playing by the Rules* (Oxford: Clarendon Press, 1993).

behaving rightly on the ground of the rightness of what one does. Thus 'duty' belongs with 'right' and 'wrong' at the ground floor of our grasp of law as normative order.

It is therefore quite natural that any attempt to provide a systematic structure for the analytical understanding of law, aimed at providing a rational framework within which to comprehend simple responses or appeals to simple ideas of right and wrong, should postulate in the first place a set of rules or norms requiring certain conduct (or, indeed more frequently, prohibiting it), and these can be considered as norms of obligation, duty-imposing rules. Voluntaristic analyses of law can then represent these norms of obligation as commands or prohibitions issued by the sovereign, or at any rate by the legislature. Kelsen points out,[12] however, that the simplest versions of voluntarism confuse 'command' with 'binding command'; only on the presupposition of the rightness, indeed rightfulness, of the issuance of the command can it constitute a source of obligation or duty. In this sense, some foundational norm or *Grundnorm* is always presupposed in the ascription of obligatory quality to the positive norms issued by purported authorities for any normative order.

The representation of the most basic elements of law as formulable in specific rules or norms that impose duties also makes possible a differentiation of powers and an explanation of powers as resultant from particular rules that confer them. This is a parasitic interpretation of powers. The power-conferring aspect of law involves a legally-conferred ability to alter the legal situations or relationships of legal persons. Legal powers in their simplest form are powers to vary in some way the incidence of duties; for example, by consenting to take part in a boxing match with *B*, *A* (validly) waives *B*'s duty not to assault *A* (so far as concerns those forms of physical attack allowable under the rules of boxing). But vastly more complex powers can also be envisaged, including power to confer, vary, or restrict powers and cognate relations, as well as powers to confer, vary, or restrict duties and rights.

To ascribe this aspect of law to some special and distinct set of rules or norms is to propose a focus on those elements of law that give guidance on what we are able to do in the way of bringing about normative change. Here, the notion of 'validity' has considerable importance. For acts aimed at bringing about change may be ineffectual to that end. The law may prescribe conditions for validly achieving change of a certain kind (and may also prescribe that certain changes can validly come about regardless of, or in opposition to, the aim or intention of an acting subject). Validity is a concept special to institutional normative orders, since

---

[12] See *GTLS*, at 30–3.

it is the conceptual tool for distinguishing between that which is operative within the system and that which is not. Hence, to the extent that it can be a reasonable and intelligible aim in practical reasoning to bring about some normative change that will count as operative within a given normative order, we can regard the elements of law that regulate the bringing about of valid change as genuinely normative, that is, as genuinely and distinctively action-guiding from the point of view of practical reasoning.

Valid exercises of power are effective in changing the legal situation in some way, and indeed they often bring about complex sets or series of changes. Whatever reason one has for bringing about such changes, these are reasons to observe the law's requirements for validity; hence such requirements are in the Kantian sense hypothetical in character. Public powers are, however, quite often subject to a categorical duty to exercise them in certain circumstances, for example, when a valid request or complaint of some kind is made through some person's exercise of private power. A court which has the power to hear and to determine a certain kind of issue between citizens, subject to the adoption by a plaintiff of the appropriate procedures, has also the duty (sometimes itself legally enforceable) to hear and to determine according to law once the appropriate steps to initiate an action have been taken.

A complete understanding of any particular power (and, generalizing, an adequate understanding of the concept 'legal power' in its institutional setting) therefore depends on adequate awareness of the whole range of circumstances required for validly exercising power. The conditions of legal enablement are always in some measure complex, and in each case must cover the following points:

(a) Which person or persons, having
(b) What general capacity or particular position
(c) Subject to what required circumstances, and
(d) In the absence of what vitiating circumstances
(e) By what special procedures or formalities, and
(f) By what act
(g) In respect of what if any other persons
(h) Having what general capacity
(i) In respect of what thing or activity,
(j) Can create a valid instance of institution I.

What all this adds up to is that the exercise of a power requires there to be a person with appropriate capacity or competence performing a specified act in a specified form (procedure), and in addition there have to be appropriate background circumstances, such as prior possession of a property right one proposes to transfer, or the giving of due notice, for example, in the case of marriage, or having an appropriate intention, for example, intention to create legal relations (contract), intention to create an irrevocable trust (trust), or the like; such 'positive' conditions are within the knowledge and, to a degree, the control of the party who seeks to exercise a power. To some extent they contrast with the 'negative' conditions envisaged in (d), circumstances which must be absent for the valid exercise of power, circumstances whose presence vitiates the otherwise valid exercise of power, such as mistake (error) of one or both parties, or fraud, or unintended contravention of some collateral provision of the law, or illegal or immoral purpose of one or both parties. As can be illustrated from many branches of law, this kind of vitiating factor may depend upon a background principle of law, not necessarily upon an explicit rule or explicit condition or exception specified in a rule-formulation.

Characteristically, such vitiating factors are often of a sort which lie outside the control, and perhaps even the knowledge or reasonably discoverable knowledge, of the person who exercises the power. Difficulties of a similar sort might affect questions of capacity both of the power-exerciser and of the other party in case of a strictly bilateral power. So whenever a person acts with a view to exercising a certain power, though he or she (and his or her legal advisers) can take all possible steps to secure regularity in matters within his or her own control or knowledge and can exercise considerable diligence to check on the absence of vitiating circumstances, yet even so there remains some risk, often only the faintest risk, that events as they unfold will reveal some defect such that the ostensibly valid exercise of power has been defective, and is hence either a nullity *ab initio* or nullifiable (voidable) in its effects as from the moment of discovery of the defects or from some earlier or later date determined by appropriate legal provisions.

The concept of validity, in the sense of valid exercise of a power, is thus a moderately complex one. The correct personal and contextual circumstances must be present, and all potentially vitiating ones absent, before the power to establish a particular instance of some institution can be exercised effectually, through performance of the appropriate act and having regard for the content of the act (the contractual terms specified, the postulated trust purposes, the objectives of the company according to the memorandum and articles of association, or whatever). Moreover, as I have pointed out here and elsewhere,[13] if we interpret the conferment of power as achieved through such a rule or set of connected rules, these rules must in turn be interpreted as operating against a back-

---

[13] See MacCormick, 'Law as Institutional Fact', *Law Quarterly Review*, 90 (1974), 102–29, repr. in MacCormick and Weinberger (n.10 above), ch. 2.

ground of legal principles having to do, *inter alia,* with the overall purposes and values imputed to the various institutions of the law, read alongside fundamental values such as justice and the rule of law. Hence any formulation of rules of this kind is subject to a general qualification, whereby the validity conditions specified in the rules are to be understood as ordinarily necessary and presumptively sufficient for, not absolute guarantees of, validity.

V. THE NORMATIVITY OF POWERS

A question that remains open at this stage concerns the normativity of powers, or of power-conferring rules as we have analysed those here. If the present analysis of power in its legal-institutional setting is sound, are power-conferring rules truly normative? To put it more arrestingly: are norms of competence really norms?

Kelsen has shown in the *General Theory of Norms*[14] that wherever one envisages the power to create an obligation, the power-conferring rule in question is susceptible of alternative modes of statement.

(a) 'A parent can impose an obligation upon a son or daughter by ordering him or her to act in a certain way';

or

(b) 'If a parent orders a son or daughter to act in a certain way, then he or she has an obligation to act in accordance with the order'.

The latter formulation is clearly normative in respect of the son or daughter. It posits an obligation, lays down what a person ought to do or must do in certain circumstances. The former formulation is thus at least indirectly normative in implying, but without directly positing, what the son or daughter ought to do.

The assumption that an 'ought'-formulation betokens normative quality can pass with little argument. The 'ought' indicates a standard whereby conduct may be guided and appraised *ex ante*, and evaluated or appraised *ex post*. Here, if anywhere, the fundamental distinction of right and wrong is invoked. But does the 'can'-formulation indicate any similar standard for guidance, appraisal, or evaluation?

The answer seems to be, as pointed out above, that the 'can' guides conduct only hypothetically. If one has some purpose or project towards realization of which imposition of the 'ought' would be instrumental, one has then reason to carry out the appropriate action—give an appropriate order, in this case. But the ability in question remains something

[14] See *GTN*, ch. 26, at § IV (pp. 103–4).

of a blank cheque. What order shall be given, with what content? And then on the other hand there comes in view a question of appraisal: over what range of issues, and perhaps by what procedural steps, can a parental order be given? Would such-and-such an order, if issued, be valid? The validity judgment and the implicit guidance that the power-exerciser must attend to conditions for validity as well as, or in interaction with, the demands of the given project are of some significance even in the simple moral situation envisaged here.

All the more must the issue of validity bulk large in institutional normative orders, that is, in the legal setting. I have already pointed out at some length just how complex may be the conditions of validity attaching to powers formally conferred by a legal system, by contrast with the rather bare and simple moral power that Kelsen draws to our attention. The point about validity in the legal setting is that it introduces the ideas of right and wrong in a new form. At the basic level of duty, we are concerned with certain forms of conduct as categorically wrong, wrong regardless of other reasons or projects. In the context of the hypothetical imperative of legal power, the project of the actor is what gives legal validity its action-guiding significance. For the exercise of power, the invocation of the legal institution is the chosen means to realization of the project. My aim is to acquire a new house in the country for holiday and leisure use; very well, I shall have to go about validly securing title to the chosen house, assuming indeed that I can induce the seller to enter into a contract with me unsullied by force or fraud at the price I am willing to pay. The bearing of the law on this project of mine is to indicate that there is a right and a wrong way of going about achievement of its essentials; and if I do not act in the right way, interacting with a competent co-contractor also acting rightly, my project will fail. So I must take guidance from the validity-conditions laid down by law, and/or instruct a professional legal adviser whom I can trust to do this on my behalf.

We may conclude that power-conferring rules are then normative in the following sense: they do differentiate right from wrong ways of acting, albeit hypothetically or instrumentally, presupposing some project which is at least partly extraneous to the law. That is, they pose conditions for validity that are distinctive (but partial) guides to conduct as well as grounds for appraisal and evaluation of possible courses of action or of acts actually performed.

It may be asked from what point of view such guidance and evaluation operates. Here, I should like to re-introduce an idea which I put forward in a recent paper, that of '*homo juridicus*'.[15] *Homo juridicus* is envisaged as playing a role in legal science similar to that which *homo economicus*

---

[15] See Neil MacCormick, 'Further Thoughts on Institutional Facts', *International Journal for the Semiotics of Law*, 5 (1992), 3–15.

plays in economic theory. That is to say, *homo juridicus* is an ideal-typical person whom we suppose always to act with regard to legal requirements, permissions, and empowerments. It is posssible to imagine a person who acts only with rational economic motives of the kind handled by economics; likewise it is possible to imagine someone who exactly observes all the constraints of the law and always enquires into all the possibilities and competences for action, as well as any special privileges or permissions, while engaged in any course of conduct, whatever other motives may be presupposed as determining the person's activities and projects. As with *homo economicus*, we need not suppose that any actual human being ever acts solely with regard to this scheme of guidance and values; it is enough that we acknowledge the possibility that a person could carry on in this way and the probability that most people do so some of the time, especially in regard to transactions of special significance whose legal character is rather salient, as in the case of making a will or getting married or buying or selling a house.

In my earliest essay exploring the institutional approach, 'Law as Institutional Fact' (1974),[16] I criticized the way in which, without any systematic investigation of empirical evidence, Hart argues in *The Concept of Law* for a differentiation between power-conferring and duty-imposing rules on the basis of how (he claims) these are 'thought of, spoken of, and used' in social life. This is at best a highly speculative point, given that we know very little indeed about the plain person's understanding of law. It would in my view be a better understanding of Hart's point to say that we can imagine a person or persons who do differentiate in the way mentioned, thereby achieving a certain clarity of thought. In effect, Hart argues from the style of thought of *homo juridicus*, making the assumption that ordinary people in their law-talk approximate to this juridical way of considering matters.

But why is the differentiation of rules one that promotes clarity of thought? The answer is to be found in those very works of legal science that constitute the best attempts of scholars to systematize law. It is law in books rather than law in action that provides the basis for this general approach. When I postulate a structure of 'institutive, consequential, and terminative rules' as that which structures our understanding of concepts like contract, trust, corporation, marriage, and the like, I can certainly bring forward the massive consensus of a huge range of works of legal dogmatics in many languages and legal traditions in my favour. Books on the law of contract characteristically describe first the conditions for formation of contracts, second the rights and duties arising from contracts, and finally the conditions for discharge (termination) of

---

[16] See n.13 above.

contractual obligation. Likewise with the other subjects. Thus, institutions as I have analysed them belong first and foremost to the law as structured—as rationally reconstructed—through doctrinal legal studies, 'legal science' or 'legal dogmatics' as we sometimes call it.

In 1973–4, the focus of my attention was on a puzzle in relation to analytical legal positivism, concerning Hart's picture of law in 1961 as comprising primary rules (of obligation) and secondary rules (mainly power-conferring), as further elucidated in Raz's rediscovery of the need to produce articulate 'principles of individuation' of normative material into distinct rules or types of rule. In that setting, it did not seem clear to me exactly how we were supposed to be able to differentiate, for example, between rules concerning power to contract and rules imposing obligations on those who make contracts. The explanation of the structure of institutions seemed to me to give a satisfactory answer to the problem of individuation, moreover one that was really anchored in legal usage, not in rather untested assertions about the ordinary speech of ordinary persons. It also tied in with a distinct interest in applying the concept of 'institutional fact' in the legal setting. Again, the anchoring in legal usage was for me important; but I can see in retrospect that the decisive legal usage to which I was referring was that of legal scholarship and legal science, not, or not directly, that of legal practice.

Nevertheless, if *homo juridicus* belongs particularly to the implicit view of human concerns and human motivation expressed in legal science, it should be acknowledged that the motivational schema implied is one that makes good sense in terms of general practical reason. We do have to have some basic schemes of right and wrong within which to frame the activities and projects of our lives, and in complex societies these projects also have to have procedural conditions attached to them if they are to receive collective support through institutional agencies. The hypothetical guidance of valid/invalid can be quite as important as the categorical guidance of right/wrong. So a representation of law that makes this clear is a rationally satisfying one. In turn, those concerned with the practice of law and in particular those acting as judges have available, to assist the structuring of their reasoning upon claims and complaints laid before them, the framework of thought suggested by legal science. There is doubtless always a gap between the law in action and the law in books, but there is also an interaction between them.

27

Reflections on Legal Science, Law, and Power*

AGOSTINO CARRINO

A theory can be assessed either for its practical results, that is to say, its technical utility, its uses, or for its logical rigour, its formal coherence, its freedom from contradiction. Even if virtually no one is inclined, today, to contest the significance of Hans Kelsen's Pure Theory of Law, the question remains: Is the significance of the Pure Theory found in its practical results or in its 'logical rigour'? Or—going beyond these alternatives—does the interest and significance of the Pure Theory lie in the fact that it represents an attempt to meet the acute crisis of European culture, a desperate attempt, after the collapse of metaphysics, to preserve the 'ethos' reflected in the 'autonomy of the scientific enterprise'?[1]

It may be clear that a theory is part of a specific and particular 'world', a world of ideas, and that a theory is an aggregate of propositions or utterances addressed to an 'object' or a 'complex of objects', with an eye to analysing first and foremost the formal structure of this object. This aspect can be set aside for the time being, however, in order to concentrate on the ultimate practical effects of theory, its efficacy in a world of experience of which the law is a part.

If, in particular, one considers Kelsen's constructions of the separation of *Sein* and *Sollen*, the hierarchical structure (*Stufenbau*) of the legal system, the legal norm qua hypothetically formulated objective judgment, the identity of law and state, and so on—constructions on which he was busy at work over a period of some seventy years—the question arises:

---

* *Editors' note*: This paper is drawn from chapter 2 of Carrino's book, *L'ordine delle norme*: *Stato e diritto in Hans Kelsen*, 3rd edn. (Naples: Edizioni Scientifiche Italiane, 1992), 31–50. The present version contains a number of minor changes in the text and notes. It was translated by Michael Sherberg in close collaboration with the author and editors.

[1] Franz Wieacker, *Privatrechtsgeschichte in der Neuzeit unter besonderer Berücksichtigung der deutschen Entwicklung*, 2nd edn. (Göttingen: Vandenhoeck & Ruprecht, 1967), 589. [This passage is not fully captured in the recent translation: see Wieacker, *A History of Private Law in Europe*, trans. Tony Weir (Oxford: Clarendon Press, 1995), at 465.]

To what do these constructions lead? What is their point? It is, as I see it, essentially a matter of affirming the relativity and conventionality of the law and, likewise, of the state. For Kelsen, the law, as expressed in '*Sollen*', '*Norm*', and the like, is a value; the 'content' of the law is relative, however, not absolute. Far from having a 'holier than thou status', as in Hegel,[2] the law is nothing other than a specific ideology through which man's effort to realize particular interests is given effect.

However different human beings may be and however diverse their settings, they are inevitably and unavoidably tied to a historico-anthropological constant—the distinction, namely, between those who command and those who are commanded, between those who rule and those who are ruled, between those who hold the sword and those who fear its blow. As Kelsen writes:

The difference between the will of the individual, which is the starting point in the quest for liberty, and the state system, opposed to the individual qua extraneous will, is inevitable.[3]

And this inevitability is evident even in the most broad-based democracy. Kelsen writes that the 'idea of a social condition not regulated by any coercive system' is utopian; it ignores 'the innate urge to aggression in man'.[4] In their normative identification, law and state are the specific forms that seek, constitute, and guarantee social peace, the dominion of rational knowledge, the will to know as found within the conflicts of the social world, and the unresolvable tension between opposed instincts in the individual: 'Social reality', Kelsen writes, 'is in fact power and command.'[5]

The law is a complex of norms, but it is more than that. It is a system that determines the organs of power, hierarchically ordered. In Kelsen's view, the law does not have as its sense the idea of serving truth, and—*contra* Gustav Radbruch—it does not have as its sense the idea of serving

[2] The law is 'something *utterly sacred*, for the simple reason that it is the existence of the absolute concept, of self-conscious freedom.' G.W.F. Hegel, *Elements of the Philosophy of Right*, ed. Allen W. Wood, trans. H.B. Nisbet (Cambridge: Cambridge UP, 1991), § 30 (Hegel's *Grundlinien der Philosophie des Rechts* was first published in 1819). In the first lecture of 1817–18, recorded in Heidelberg by Peter Wannenmann, one reads that the law is 'sacrosanct because it rests on the freedom of will; and this also follows from the basic determination of the essence of God.' Hegel, *Lectures on Natural Right and Political Science*, intro. Otto Pöggeler, trans. J. Michael Stewart and Peter C. Hodgson (Berkeley and Los Angeles: University of California Press, 1995), § 8 (p. 56).

[3] Hans Kelsen, *Vom Wesen und Wert der Demokratie*, 2nd edn. (Tübingen: J.C.B. Mohr, 1929, repr. Aalen: Scientia, 1981), 11; see also *ASL* § 44(b) (at p. 325).

[4] Hans Kelsen, 'The Law as a Specific Social Technique', *University of Chicago Law Review*, 9 (1941–2), 75–97, at 84, repr. *WJ* 231–56, at 241.

[5] Hans Kelsen, 'Demokratie', *Verhandlungen des 5. Deutschen Soziologentages* (meeting of 26–9 September 1926, in Vienna) (Tübingen: J.C.B. Mohr, 1927), 37–68, 113–18, at 55, repr. *WS II* 1743–76, at 1759.

justice either.[6] Rather, it is presented solely as an instrument, a means, a 'specific technique' for social coexistence and the control of human behaviour by those who hold effective political power. If, for Kelsen, the law is found entirely in the sphere of validity, of the ideal *Sollen*, of value, and not in the sphere of fact, of 'things', of the sensorily perceptible *Sein*, this is not to say that between these two opposing spheres there is no point of contact, no possibility of translation or exchange whatever. Indeed, without a point of contact it would not even be possible to pose the 'problem' of the law. There also exists for Kelsen (perhaps more than for others) something behind the positive law, something that the positive law itself, in the final analysis, manifests. This 'meta-legal' *quid*, this 'thing in itself', is not the eternal law of nature, of God, or of Reason, nor is it some absolute ideal value of material justice. Rather, it is simply that which is habitually understood as power, as dominion. As Kelsen writes:

The problem of natural law is the eternal problem of what lies behind positive law. And one who still seeks an answer will find, I fear, neither the absolute truth of metaphysics nor the absolute justice of natural law. One who raises the veil without closing his eyes will confront the gaping stare of the Gorgon's naked power.[7]

The emphasis Kelsen places on the impossibility, so to speak, of considering power from the standpoint of natural law has a precise sense for him: to preserve, somehow, the freedom and autonomy of those who would know the law, that is to say, to preserve their autonomy from the inexorable tendency toward the absolute dominion of power, with its inherent will to control us, wrapping us in an ever tighter net of norms, rules, and relations that qualify anything in conflict with this power as 'illegal', and imposing sanctions upon it. Only through the 'existence' of the illegal act does power affirm its specific *Sein*, its specific characteristic qua sovereign, coercive system. To the oft-discussed Kelsenian theory of a 'basic norm', which is not a part of the positive law but is the basis of a purely normative structure, the basis, then, of 'legal norms', Carl Schmitt objected that this course abandons the *Sollen* altogether, paving

---

[6] '[L]aw is the reality the meaning of which is to serve [justice].' Gustav Radbruch, *Legal Philosophy* (first published in 1932), in *The Legal Philosophies of Lask, Radbruch, and Dabin*, trans. Kurt Wilk (Cambridge, Mass.: Harvard UP, 1950), 43–224, § 4 (p. 73). Raffaele De Giorgi, *Scienza del diritto e legittimazione da Kelsen a Luhmann* (Bari: De Donato, 1979), at 81, observes in this connection that Kelsen 'succeeds in constructing the positivity of law as a normative contingency, eliminating once and for all the problem of truth, and recognizing the empirical foundation of *Sollen*.'

[7] Hans Kelsen, 'Aussprache' [statement in discussion following lectures on the theme:] 'Die Gleichheit vor dem Gesetz im Sinne des Art. 109 der Reichsverfassung' (annual meeting of the German Society of Public Law Teachers, held on 29–30 March 1926, in Münster), *Veröffentlichungen der Vereinigung der Deutschen Staatsrechtslehrer*, 3 (1927), 2–62, 53–5 (Kelsen), at 55.

the way for 'facticity', a concatenation of 'raw fact'.[8] Schmitt, however, seems to be taking too seriously Kelsen's statements on the insuperable abyss existing between *Sein* and *Sollen*,[9] almost as if the programme of the Viennese jurist simply favoured one side of the abyss rather than pro-faning the *sancta sanctorum* or the *arcana imperii*, with an eye to new possibilities of power and its exercise, held in any event to be a fact of life and not eliminable.

What is this coercion that enters into the very definition of the law if not that which is initially given politically? The legal system delineated by Kelsen is a system of norms, pure *Sollen*. It is a system, however, addressed only to the determination of legal organs' power, not to the discrete facts of subjects' behaviour. It is, in sum, both a pyramid of norms and a 'cascade of powers',[10] political powers. To be sure, the same legal norm can be termed 'subjective law',[11] which marks the possibility, granted to the legal subject, of activating the coercive process against whoever 'violates' the law provided by the system; but this, too, is nothing other than a power, albeit a partial power (just as the legal person is a 'partial legal system', a 'legal subsystem'). 'This power of the subject', Kelsen writes, 'is a political power, a public function *par excellence*.'[12] Thus, the 'specifically "political" element consists in nothing but the element of coercion'.[13]

It is true that the law, for Kelsen, is a system of norms that the instruments of power use to spread and to impose their own will. One sees this very clearly in connection with his theory of interpretation.[14] In the Pure Theory, interpretation has a peculiarly Kelsenian import. Kelsen's break with the tradition means, here, a break with a type of legal thought that conceals, mystifies, smacks of the ideological. The judge—and likewise the legislative and executive organs—does not, in Kelsen's view, 'interpret' the norm, he creates it, authoritatively resolving an individual case

---

[8] Carl Schmitt, *Verfassungslehre* (Munich and Leipzig: Duncker & Humblot, 1928), 9.

[9] *HP* 8; and see Hans Kelsen, 'Foreword' to 2nd Printing of *HP*, in this volume, ch. 1, at § I.

[10] Norberto Bobbio, 'Kelsen and Legal Power', in this volume, ch. 23, § 1.

[11] *HP* 663. See also 'RWR', at 103–4, repr. *RNK*, at 279–80; 'Foreword' to *HP* (n.9 above), at § II.

[12] Kelsen (n.4 above), 90, repr. 248.

[13] Ibid. 82, repr. 239.

[14] The theme of interpretation in Kelsen, central for a deeper understanding of the political plan underlying the Pure Theory of Law, is at the same time the basis of comparison for delineating the true significance of his legal method. It is not by chance that Kelsen's theory of interpretation (apparently playing only a marginal role in the system) can be made to function 'in such a way as to subvert the Kelsenian concept of the structure of the legal system'. Michel Troper, 'Kelsen, la théorie de l'interprétation et la structure de l'ordre juridique', *Revue internationale de philosophie*, 138 (1981), 518–29, at 520, repr. in Troper, *Pour une théorie juridique de l'état* (Paris: Presses Universitaires de France, 1994), 85–94, at 86.

and issuing an individual command. The judge, in other words, interprets 'authentically', for the technique of legal production is finalized in
effective power, in the concrete command, the decision; and this is a
political decision, since the sentence of the judge, the individual norm, is
linked 'with an act of will'.[15] As Kelsen puts it,

even the judge creates law, even he is relatively independent in this capacity. And
precisely for this reason, it is a function of will to arrive at the individual norm in
the process of applying a statute, provided that the frame of the general norm is
filled in thereby.[16]

Thus, Kelsen's theory of interpretation, opposed to the myth of the
certainty of law, has the fundamental task of revealing that all the intermediate passages between legislator and judge, the gradual production—ever more complex—of the law, are uniquely the outcome of a
historical evolution.[17] Despite its pretence of separating legislative, executive, and judicial powers according to a specific historico-political,
social ideology, this process has failed to undermine the reality of the
qualitative identity of legislator, executive, and judge. Legislation and
adjudication are 'diverse stages of a single, autonomous process . . .
which is precisely the law itself.'[18]

It is only for specific historico-political reasons, wholly independent of
the nature of the law (and of power), that we claim to be able to posit a
fictitious separation between legislation and execution (administration
and adjudication).[19] The task of legal science, according to Kelsen, is to
show that the distance between one function and the other is, in the official terms of the theory of the traditional state, only a historical result, an
ideology unmasked by legal science. Behind the 'appearance'[20] of the
separation of powers there is the fact of the mere superordination and
subordination of just two functions in the production of law.[21] The
law in its essence is always the same thing, in the feudal 'state' and in the
liberal state: a technique for social control, an instrument of power. One
can imagine an indefinite number of steps in the concretization of the

---

[15] *PTL* § 46 (p. 353).   [16] *LT* § 38 (p. 83).

[17] See Hans Kelsen, 'Die Lehre von den drei Gewalten oder Funktionen des Staates',
ARWP, 17 (1923–4), 374–408, at 389, repr. *WS II* 1625–60, at 1640; *GTLS*, at 281–2.

[18] Kelsen, 'Die Lehre von den drei Gewalten' (n.17 above), 384, repr. 1635. For the theory
of the qualitative identity of the legislative and judiciary functions, see Adolf Julius Merkl,
Das Recht im Lichte seiner Anwendung (Hanover: Helwing, 1917), at 17, repr. *WS I*
1167–201, at 1179.

[19] 'The historical significance of the principle called "separation of powers" lies precisely
in the fact that it works against a concentration rather than for a separation of powers.'
GTLS 282.

[20] *GTLS* 272.

[21] See Kelsen, 'Die Lehre von den drei Gewalten' (n.17 above), at 398–9, repr. at 1650; see
also *GTLS*, at 269–70.

legal norm, but the result does not change. There are many ways, Kelsen seems to be saying, of leading people by the nose—faking the divine election of a king, for example, or pretending that the parliament effectively represents the will of 'the people'. The result, however, does not change for the legal scientist, the only one who cannot be deceived without his being aware of it, for whom the king is always and irremediably naked.[22] As Kelsen writes:

If there is effectively a point at which one can put oneself outside the sphere of power, of force, this point is science, perhaps the science of power, which then becomes a pure theory of the state and of law.[23]

The Kelsenian legal scientist knows that the particular content of a legal norm and the issuance of that norm are altogether different matters; that is, the fact of issuance places no constraints on the possible content of the norm. The content of a norm in a particular case is simply a reflection of what the sovereign aims to bring about—within, to be sure, certain historically established limits. This is why the Kelsenian legal scientist, qua legal scientist, cannot be directly concerned with any given, historically determined content. In his role, he is only to identify the 'laws' of a phenomenon, in a manner analogous to that of the natural sciences, and he cannot (must not) legitimize any particular act of will as being, say, morally required. From the standpoint of the legal subject, certain behaviour may well possess a 'double obligatoriness', counting, then, as an 'enhanced obligatoriness',[24] but if it is legally required, this is only because it is legal, that is, negatively sanctioned (according to the sanctions of this world). As Kelsen explains in the *Hauptprobleme* of 1911:

[T]he juridico-obligatory nature of legal norms, their normative character, derives from a completely different source than the obligating force of ethical laws. In its normative character, each is fully independent of the other. Whatever the origin of moral commands, the source of the binding legal norm, from the juridico-formal standpoint of modern law, is exclusively and alone the will of the state, which of course, qua authority of the state, can never come into consideration for the norms of morality.[25]

---

[22] Two essays of Kelsen's from 1933, on Plato and on Aristotle, are both strongly marked by a critique of ideology and must be read in this key: 'Die platonische Liebe', *Imago. Zeitschrift für psychoanalytische Psychologie*, 19 (1933), 34–98, 225–55, repr. *AI* 114–97, and repr. in Hans Kelsen, *Die Illusion der Gerechtigkeit*, ed. Kurt Ringhofer and Robert Walter (Vienna: Manz, 1985), 46–132; 'Die hellenisch-makedonische Politik und die "Politik" des Aristoteles', *ZöR*, 13 (1933), 625–78, repr. *AI* 293–357.

[23] Hans Kelsen, 'Juristischer Formalismus und reine Rechtslehre', *Juristische Wochenschrift*, 58 (1929), 1723–6, at 1726.

[24] *HP* 56.

[25] Ibid. On this problem, see Georges Davy, 'Le problème de l'obligation chez Duguit et chez Kelsen', *Archives de Philosophie du droit et de Sociologie juridique*, 3 (1933), 7–36.

Thus, a legal norm is obligatory not in virtue of being materially just, but only because it is produced by the 'will of the state', because it is valid, because it is sanctioned. The individuals subject to the law—and they alone—are responsible for deciding, according to criteria that are wholly independent of and extraneous to science (in particular normative legal science) and its judgments, whether or not they are required, based on a variety of psychological motives, to conform to the norm or, alternatively, to perform an illegal act. The recognition theory,[26] the imperative theory,[27] and the theory of the social contract[28] are all rejected by Kelsen as making no sense from a legal point of view. Where the validity of the legal system is concerned, the jurist cannot proceed with enquiries addressed to the material basis of the law. What must interest him is 'not the reason, the "why", but only the "how".'[29] The jurist's problem is: 'What are the norms that must be applied by the organs of the state as legal norms and complied with by the subjects?'[30] Everything else is ideology or pure fiction. Kelsen dissolves the concept of legal obligation into that of the valid legal norm, radically excluding every extension of morality into the field of law:[31] '[B]etween "unjust" and "just" law no relevant juridico-formal distinction is to be found.'[32] Thus, Kelsen continues, once it has been recognized

that the legal obligation is not an autonomous case in point, distinct from the legal norm, but is the same legal norm in the relation of subjectivization, then the question of the 'birth' of the legal obligation becomes the question of the birth of

---

[26] This rejection assumes a politically relevant meaning in the discussion of the dogma of sovereignty, inasmuch as it rules out the possibility that the existence of an 'objective ... world legal system', a *civitas maxima*, can be made to depend on a form of 'recognition', *PS* § 63 (p. 316). On the Kelsenian rejection of the recognition theory, see Adriano Giovannelli, *Dottrina pura e teoria della costituzione in Kelsen* (Milan: A. Giuffrè Editore, 1979), at 38–47; Agostino Carrino, *Kelsen e il problema della scienza giuridica* (Naples: Edizioni Scientifiche Italiane, 1987), at ch. 2.

[27] See *HP*, at 210–12 *et passim*; 'RWR', at 105–13, repr. *RNK*, at 281–9.

[28] See *ASL* § 7(c) (at pp. 35–7); Kelsen, 'Die Lehre von den drei Gewalten' (n.17 above), at 400–2, repr. at 1652–4.

[29] *HP* 353. See also Siegfried Marck, *Substanz- und Funktionsbegriff in der Rechts-philosophie* (Tübingen: J.C.B. Mohr, 1925), at 8.

[30] *HP* 353.

[31] *HP* 405, see also at 321–46; *ASL* § 13 (at p. 62). In that validity is perhaps one of the most debated points in Kelsen's thought, the resolution (and dissolution) of the concept of obligation has been subject to tightly-knit critiques by, above all, Alf Ross, but also by other general theorists of law. On the problem of validity and efficacy—'one of the most important and at the same time most difficult problems for a positivistic theory of law', *PTL* § 34(g) (p. 211)—see Virgilio Giorgianni, 'Il fondamento della validità nella teoria generale del Kelsen', *RIFD*, 29 (1962), 102–9; Uberto Scarpelli, *Cos'è il positivismo giuridico* (Milan: Comunità, 1965), at 63–9; Mauro Barberis, 'La norma senza qualità. Appunti su "validità" in Hans Kelsen', *Materiali per una storia del pensiero giuridico*, 11 (1981), 405–38; Giacomo Gavazzi, 'Validità e effettività', in *Hans Kelsen nella cultura filosofico-giuridica del nove-cento*, ed. Carlo Roehrssen (Rome: Istituto della Enciclopedia Italiana, 1983), 77–86.

[32] *HP* 375.

the legal norm, that is, simply, of the law, a question that no longer fits within the confines of legal science.[33]

The practical result of this theory is germane. By bringing itself fully within the tradition of realistic political thought,[34] the Pure Theory demystifies the will of the sovereign, revealing his nakedness. Positive law is neither just nor unjust; in the case of Kelsen, we witness the most complete laicization of the legal phenomenon, fully belonging to the particular conception that lays the foundation for the new world of science and reaching to the absolute and definitive secularization of what is 'law'—or of what we think is 'law'. The 'elimination of transcendent elements by means of the transcendental element'[35] turns out to be not only 'Kelsen's true and proper philosophical theme',[36] but, indeed, at the very core of his political philosophy and epistemology, his theory of legal science, and his prescriptive methodology on how legal phenomena are cognized.[37]

Despite repeated discussions on the classification of the sciences, on the distinction between causal sciences and legal (normative) science, and the like, Kelsen never tells us explicitly what 'science', in his view, comes to. Nonetheless, one can arrive at his concept of science without great difficulty. 'The concept of science', he writes in an essay of 1916, 'is based on the concept of lawfulness.'[38] A characteristic of science is, moreover, that it describes its object in its specific lawfulness or conformity to law: Science has as its 'immanent aspiration . . . the unveiling of the object of its cognition.'[39]

To have cognition of, to know, the object—'to conduct scientific enquiry'—means to describe it in its lawfulness, without prescribing anything, without falling into a surreptitiously subjective valuation of it. To assess subjectively and to know are different activities of human

---

[33] *HP* 405, see also at 321–46; *ASL* § 13 (at p. 62). On the other hand, the jurist 'can never assume the results of his explicative considerations (history, sociology, psychology) in his normative conceptual constructions,' *HP* 42.

[34] The thought goes back to Pareto; see Ernst Topitsch, 'Einleitung' to *AI* 11–27, at 19; Norberto Bobbio, *Dalla struttura alla funzione. Nuovi studi di teoria del diritto* (Milan: Comunità, 1977), at 199–202.

[35] William Ebenstein, *The Pure Theory of Law* (Madison: University of Wisconsin Press, 1945, repr. New York: Kelley, 1969), 85. See also Czesław Martyniak, 'Le problème de l'unité des fondéments de la théorie du droit de Kelsen', *Archives de Philosophie du droit et de Sociologie juridique*, 7 (1937), 166–90.

[36] Wolfram Bauer, *Wertrelativismus und Wertbestimmtheit im Kampf um die Weimarer Demokratie* (Berlin: Duncker & Humblot, 1968), 83.

[37] On the Pure Theory of Law as a meta-science of law, see Günther Winkler, 'Sein und Sollen', *Rechtstheorie*, 10 (1979), 257–80, at 270–1, repr. in Winkler, *Theorie und Methode in der Rechtswissenschaft* (Vienna and New York: Springer, 1989), 233–59, at 247–9. Winkler also points to the way in which the distinction between the object of knowledge and the object of experience is obscured in Kelsen.

[38] 'RWNKW' 1183, repr. *WS I* 39.   [39] *LT* § 9 (p. 19).

endeavour. Without a doubt, 'science'—for Kelsen, too—means first of all the natural sciences, which throughout the nineteenth century celebrated their extraordinary accomplishments by banishing and deriding metaphysics. Seen from this standpoint of the natural sciences, all that addresses society, history, and the like seems to be of an inferior order. Thus, Kelsen's effort, which presupposes this view, is in some measure analogous to Max Weber's[40] in the field of sociology: Kelsen seeks to liberate jurisprudence from its 'unhealthy isolation',[41] and to elaborate a model of legal science that is comparable in explanatory force and logical perspicuity to the natural sciences,[42] in particular to mathematics—that is, legal science qua formal science and paradigm of knowledge.

From this perspective, and accepting science as an ethical value, Kelsen distinguishes 'sciences of *Sein*' from 'human sciences' or 'sciences of *Sollen*', the 'normative sciences'.[43] He distinguishes between reality and ideality, reality and value, between two clearly distinct worlds: the world of that which takes place in time and space, and the world of value, of validity, of that which does not belong to the first world and has its own specific existence, an ideal existence. Every science has, first of all, an ideal character. In a certain sense, one could apply even to Kelsen the Popperian theory of the three worlds:[44] scientific thought has nothing 'real' in the physico-naturalistic sense; every science is a world unto itself. But within science, which is a complex of judgments, it is necessary to distinguish the way the knowing intellect observes the object, that is, whether according to the category of reality or that of ideality. The distinction between reality (*Sein*, nature) and ideality (*Sollen*, value, category) is the consequence of the intellect's initial way of observing. On this subject,[45] Kelsen cites a passage from Johann Friedrich Herbart's *Metaphysics*: 'Implicitly, one can expect that unadorned reason, in

[40] On Weber and Kelsen, see Norberto Bobbio, 'Max Weber e Hans Kelsen', *Sociologia del diritto*, 8 (1981), 135–54; Agostino Carrino, 'Weber e la sociologia del diritto nella critica di Kelsen', ibid., vol. 14 (1987), 31–49. See also Hans Kelsen, 'Der Staatsbegriff der "verstehenden Soziologie"', *Zeitschrift für Volkswirtschaft und Sozialpolitik*, 1 (1921), 104–19, repr. *SJSB* § 27 (pp. 156–70).

[41] Kelsen, 'Foreword' to *HP* (n.9 above), concluding paragraph. See on this point, Bobbio (n.34 above), at 195–201.

[42] See Ralf Dreier, 'Sein und Sollen. Bemerkungen zur Reinen Rechtslehre Kelsens', *Juristen-Zeitung*, 27 (1972), 329–35, at 335, repr. in Dreier, *Recht-Moral-Ideologie. Studien zur Rechtstheorie* (Frankfurt: Suhrkamp, 1981), 217–40, at 231.

[43] On the sense, the problem, and the admissibility of a 'normative' science, see Georges Kalinowski, *Querelle de la science normative. Une contribution à la théorie de la science* (Auzias: Pichon et Durand, 1969).

[44] See Karl Popper, *Objective Knowledge. An Evolutionary Approach* (Oxford: Clarendon Press, 1972), at ch. 4.

[45] 'RWNKW' 1181, repr. *WS I* 37. It is, however, in the *Hauptprobleme*, at 8, that Kelsen, on the basis of Georg Simmel's *Einleitung in die Moralwissenschaften*, offers the clearest

seeking the *Sein* and *Sollen*, originally reflects by looking in two altogether different directions.'[46] Kelsen comments:

> Herbart, who grasped the opposition of *Sein* and *Sollen* in terms of principles and
> logical consistency even more [firmly] than Kant had, perspicaciously grounds
> the fundamental dualism on an *original reflection*, and—correctly, from an epis-
> temic standpoint—resolves it into the total divergence of the *directions this*
> *reflection takes.*[47]

The distinction between *Sein* and *Sollen* is proper to the intellect, more
precisely to the knowing intellect. And, with that, it would seem that one
could give an exact philosophical foundation to the Pure Theory of Law,
specifically a foundation that is in some way Kantian or neo-Kantian.
Why, then, does an Italian critic of Kelsen, one who is well versed in
Kantian philosophy, argue precisely the opposite, namely that 'Kelsen's
Reine Rechtslehre is neither Kantian nor neo-Kantian'?[48] It appears to be
a paradoxical thesis, as we shall see, but it must be kept in mind in order
to appreciate just how much of Kelsen's theory is a reflection of his own
enterprise, his own overall theoretical construction, which often begins
with radical and irrepressible dualisms, only to arrive a bit later at reconciliation or even confusion. This happens—I choose my example in order
to avoid repeating objections and polemics that are already well known—
with the introduction of Adolf Julius Merkl's *Stufenbaulehre* into the Pure
Theory of Law.[49] According to Merkl's doctrine of hierarchical structure,
the law is transformed from mere normativity into a real, effective process
of acts of law creation[50] that 'is no longer a *Sollen* but a system of psychophysical acts in relation to norms and determined by norms',[51] inasmuch as an act that is not only a fact, *Sein*, 'but is also due the character

---

and most radical formulation of the 'insuperable abyss' between *Sein* and *Sollen*, affirming
the strictly formal character of the legal norm. And, at 42: the legal theorist, like the judge,
'neither explains materially the actual legal behaviour of individuals nor provides explicative reasons for the phenomena of the life of the law; rather, he comprehends them normatively. Explanation is the task of the sociologist and the psychologist, the description of
what exists and the exposition of what is to come are the task of the historian of culture and
the law. . . . the legal theorist must never incorporate the results of his own explicative considerations into his normative conceptual constructions.'

[46] Johann Friedrich Herbart, *Allgemeine Metaphysik*, pt. 1 (Königsberg: August Wilhelm
Unzer, 1828), § 120.

[47] 'RWNKW' 1181 (Kelsen's emphasis), repr. *WS I* 37.

[48] Annibale Pastore, 'Critica del fondamento logico della dottrina pura del diritto di
Kelsen', *RIFD*, 29 (1952), 198–212, at 205.

[49] See Adolf Julius Merkl, *Die Lehre von der Rechtskraft* (Vienna and Leipzig: Franz
Deuticke, 1923), at 194–228.

[50] See *ASL*, at § 36(a) (pp. 248–50).

[51] Reinhold Horneffer, *Die Entstehung des Staates. Eine staatstheoretische Untersuchung*
(Tübingen: J.C.B. Mohr, 1933), 68. See also Marck (n. 29 above), at 39–47.

of a norm means a link between *Sein* and *Sollen*, reality and value'.[52] Extreme positions often touch, and in fact Kelsen's neo-Kantian radical- ism—he was never willing to take the decisive step in the direction of a more coherent phenomenological position—is marked less, perhaps, by methodological purity (sustained by another neo-Kantian, Rudolf Stammler) than by a unified methodology, or by the 'preconceived opin- ion that the law is, for legal science, a pure *Sollen*'.[53]

The unifying character of Kelsen's methodology makes possible gen- uine transformations that would not otherwise be practicable, most fun- damentally that of law into power and, vice-versa, that of power into law. It is precisely the marked accentuation of logical deduction in the field of the law that renders the Pure Theory of Law a 'logic of *Sollen*',[54] even a sort of logico-formal natural law theory, lacking in specific content but at the same time a realistic doctrine of the political acts that serve to pro- duce norms, or a doctrine of the various diffuse political powers in the body of the legal system. The dynamic system is produced, not deduced, while the normative theory deduces, substantially on its own, that is, proceeding from the thought of the basic norm. (Logical) deduction and (factual) production meet, however, at a point that unifies everything, precisely at that fundamental, initial hypothesis that not only transforms power into law but at the same time transforms law into power, deduc- tion into production, and production into deduction. The existence of a (normative) legal system 'cannot be separated', as Norberto Bobbio has noted, 'from the carrying out of certain acts, and legal power consists in precisely these acts.'[55]

Once the (normative) legal system has been 'closed' by the basic norm (qua norm, not fact), this same system, reopened so to speak by that same initial hypothesis, is no longer seen as norm, as *Sollen*, but is seen as fact, as *Sein*.[56] Power produces knowledge, but at the same time knowledge produces power. At the top of the ladder, the apex of the sys- tem, 'law can no longer be separated from power, and, indeed, it becomes increasingly difficult to make out where one ends and the other begins'[57] in a continuous and homochronic transposition of '*lex facit*

---

[52] Julius Moór, 'Reine Rechtslehre, Naturrecht und Rechtspositivismus', in *Gesellschaft, Staat und Recht. Untersuchungen zur Reinen Rechtslehre*, ed. Alfred Verdross (Vienna: Springer, 1931), 58–105, at 68.   [53] Horneffer (n.51 above), 61.

[54] Ernst Bloch, *Naturrecht und menschliche Würde*, 2nd edn. (Frankfurt: Suhrkamp, 1980), 168, and see generally on Kelsen at 168–72.

[55] Bobbio, 'Kelsen and Legal Power' (n.10 above), § 6.

[56] To be sure, in the appendix to *RR 2*, at 444, Kelsen affirms that the fundamental norm 'does not change in any way into a fact, because a fact cannot be the basis for a normative system', that 'efficacy does not constitute the basis of validity of that system'. It is, however, no coincidence that we have here a polemical reply of Kelsen's, namely to A.P. d'Entrèves, *Natural Law* (London: Hutchinson, 1951), 2nd edn. (1970).

[57] Bobbio, 'Kelsen and Legal Power' (n.10 above), § 10.

regem' into '*rex facit legem'*. In this same way, between science and power, knowledge and dominion, there is a productive-normative intersection, corresponding to the historical period of the atomistic division of labour, of social roles that are at a loss to address the concrete individual (entrusted in a less than ingenuous *décalage* to the decomposition of the physical sciences, of biology, medicine, and psychology). Rather, it is the abstract normative entity[58] that is addressed, as well as a power that is known and exhaustively[59] self-generated in the fields of the *invariance* of purely formal and formalizing techniques (*normative-normalizing*), by means of which the images and abstract symbols are produced that are required in spreading and organizing networks of dominion over 'docile bodies'. These are objects of power only to the extent to which they are not extraneous to power (to the system) but are pure legal relations themselves—norms, figures, images from which every reference to the concretely 'irrational' has been removed and transferred. Except that, as Kelsen writes, this 'division of power originally concentrated at a single point', if it renders power 'subjectively more tolerable'[60] now by spreading it pluralistically, does not diminish in any way power's will to dominion.

From this perspective, 'democracy' and 'autocracy' can no longer be considered as alternative forms of the state; rather, both are legal systems, collections of norms. The distinction between democracy and autocracy makes sense for Kelsen only if these forms are considered as pure 'ideal types'. 'The problem of the form of the state', Kelsen writes in the *Allgemeine Staatslehre*, 'is a problem of the content of law,'[61] and the classification of the forms of the state is, therefore, 'possible only as a classification of law.'[62] The fundamental problem turns out to be the relationship between '*Konstitution*' in the logico-formal sense (the basic norm) and '*Verfassung*' in the juridico-positive sense (the constitution). The form of the state is, then, 'the possible method of creation of the state system.' If we are to be able to grasp the content of the law, it is perforce necessary to make room for a 'typifying conceptualization', and to distinguish clearly thereby between Plato's ideal type and the real type, which 'presupposes the ideal type.'

Democracy and autocracy can be distinguished only as ideal types, for the reality of positive law manifests a 'continuous series of passages from

---

[58] On the theme of the exclusion of the concrete individual from the world of law, in a comparison with Luhmann, see Horst Dreier, 'Hans Kelsen und Niklas Luhmann: Positivität des Rechts aus rechtswissenschaftlicher und systemtheoretischer Perspektive', *Rechtstheorie*, 14 (1983), 419–58, at 448–9.

[59] 'For legal cognition there is no other "power", no other "earthly force" than that of the legal system,' *PS* § 54 (p. 267).

[60] Kelsen (n.5 above), 57, repr. 1760.

[61] *ASL* § 44(b) (p. 321).   [62] *ASL* § 44(a) (p. 320).

one type to the other'.[63] There is no need to hypothesize as a condition for democracy that, in forming the will of the state, a majority of those who are subject to its norms really do participate. A democracy may very well exclude 'women and slaves' and nevertheless be a democracy (in Kelsenian parlance, a legal system): 'The number of those who form the will of the majority is, even in the most extreme democracies, hardly a third or a fourth of all norm-subjects.'[64]

For Kelsen, freedom, which has always determined the idea or the ideal of different forms of the state, is a *specific legality* opposed to another *specific legality*, that is, normative legality versus natural legality, society versus nature. In an initial, anthropological sense, freedom means only the antisocial '*Ur-Instinkt*' of the individual. This freedom, however, is not authentic freedom in the normative, spiritual sense, but only a pure naturality.

The step from the Germanic to the so-called classical formation (*Gestaltung*) of the problem of freedom is only the first stage of that inevitable process of trans-formation, that denaturing undergone by the original instinct (*Ur-Instinkt*) for freedom in the passage of human consciousness from the state of nature to that of the state coercive system.[65]

Freedom, understood as *Sollen*, as norm, is for Kelsen 'an objective principle of value'[66] and so the only authentic, possible freedom in a spir-itual, non-naturalistic sense. The process of freedom from the natural to the normative is precisely the objective process of *Weltgeist*, of the univer-sal reason of the world, which manifests itself in the juridicization of the world, in the formation—with science as the propulsive and productive force—of a world of norms, of a universal State, of a *civitas maxima* that is the possible realization of freedom as idea and as spirit.

Those who see the shadow of Hegel in all of this are not mistaken, for it is only as a 'concealed Hegelianism', whether or not Kelsen is aware of it, that his normativism acquires its complete sense, historical meaning, and density as a theoretical, ethical, and political project. It is not by chance that Kelsen separates the general theory of the state from politics as science, as a system of knowledge expressed in judgments, only to split politics at once into a part of ethics (as knowledge of morality) and a (causal) technique,[67] saving, perhaps, the most authentic, purely ideal meaning of politics for the (pure) science of law.

Notwithstanding opinions to the contrary, therefore, a heightened appreciation of the Kelsenian project is not possible without linking its author to the *fin de siècle* cultural environment in Central Europe, an

---

[63] *ASL* § 44(e) (p. 327).   [64] *ASL* § 45(a) (p. 328).
[65] *ASL* § 44(b) (p. 322).   [66] *ASL* § 7(b) (p. 29).
[67] *ASL* § 7(a) (p. 27).

environment dominated precisely by the schools of neo-Kantian critical idealism that were already moving toward a reappraisal of Fichte and Hegel, and—in a more subterranean but perhaps even more decisive way—by a certain 'nihilism' and the pessimistic philosophy of Schopenhauer. Again, it is only against this background that one can understand the distinction, received and radicalized by Kelsen, between object and method, reality and meaning.

'A plant', Kelsen writes, 'cannot say anything about itself to the botanist. It makes no attempt to explain itself in terms of the natural sciences,'[68] and it therefore does not 'impose on the scholar the necessity of substituting his objective knowledge for its subjective knowledge.'[69] This position is typical of the neo-Kantian approach as received by the Viennese theorist. Seeing what dominates the human sciences in this period dictates that social acts, unlike things and facts of nature, can very well carry with them qualifications of themselves: '[T]he act itself (if it expresses itself verbally) can say something about its meaning, can declare its own sense.'[70]

A social act is (almost) never necessitated in a naturalistic sense or according to a law of nature. It carries with it its own specific meaning, its own 'rationality'; it counts as a self-qualification. As such, a social act is never spontaneous or ingenuous, but looks toward something, an end that is to be realized. If this is true, however, then no social act— inasmuch as it is desired—is truly arbitrary or irrational (in the sense of alogical) as Kelsen claims. On the contrary, it is already to a certain extent the result of a valuation, a theoretical reflection, a pre-scientific conceptualization as Emil Lask defines it, echoing Heinrich Rickert.[71] This conceptualization imposes very precise limits on the 'constitutive' formation of the object, limits that Lask had the merit of underscoring but that Kelsen violated, thus opening himself to the criticism of Hermann Heller and others at the very level of epistemology.[72]

[68] *LT* § 3 (p. 9). For an analogous example, see 'Demokratie' (n.5 above), at 41, repr. at 1747.

[69] Ibid.

[70] *LT* § 3 (p. 9). In the words of Giovanni Tarello, 'the norm . . . does not have a meaning for the very good reason that it is (nothing other than) a meaning.' Tarello, *Diritto, enunciati, usi. Studi di teoria e metateoria del diritto* (Bologna: Il Mulino, 1974), 394.

[71] See Emil Lask, 'Legal Philosophy' (first published in 1905), in *The Legal Philosophies of Lask, Radbruch, and Dabin* (n.6 above), 1–42.

[72] Heller writes that Lask pointed out that the Copernican point of view, according to which reality has value as a product of syntheses of categories, has imposed 'very precise limits on all the sciences of culture, in particular, on legal science.' The 'problematic character of the latter', for Lask, 'lies precisely in the penetration of empirically and ideally juxtaposed research into meaning', and Lask would have underscored in advance the dangers of Kelsen's enterprise—the fact, specifically, that Kelsen's effort to apply Kant's 'Copernican turn' to the sciences of culture, in particular to legal science, turns on a confusion of methodology. Indeed, Heller continues, this goes so far that Kelsen 'tends to

Surely no human being ever does anything wholly independently of a 'theoretical' moment. The very conceptions of the world that Kelsen wanted to expunge from science as purely valuative, emotional, and atheoretical are in truth themselves contemplation, theory in action, speculative concretizations—a point that Lask underscored.[73] Both the observation of an object and the carrying out of an act presuppose a theoretical moment. Thus, just as we observe objects with eyes that are already impregnated with theory, so, analogously, we act while evaluating, comparing, reflecting on means and ends, presuppositions and circumstances—and, particularly in the field of the law, while assessing the value of the action.

The fundamental difference between the natural sciences and the normative sciences[74] consists, then, in the fact that in the first case the scientist (the observer) utters something, qualifies something on a given matter and there is in what he says no 'self-qualification', while, by contrast, the social scientist—the political scientist, historian, jurist—is never, in truth, neutral, but in qualifying something can always recognize himself therein.

The problem of the knowing subject's recognition of himself in the object and in his qualifications of the object raises delicate issues, all of them traceable to the problem of the ideology of the scientist—the presence, that is to say, of individual value judgments, the precise, prescientific choices of social, moral, religious, and political values made by the observer. We are dealing, that is, with the problem of distinguishing between judgments of fact and value judgments, with the lack of 'freedom from value' in science. Kelsen shares with Weber the constraint that the scientist is to limit himself to judgments of fact without confusing them with his own, personal judgments. (At the same time, Kelsen rejects Rickert's 'reference to value' vis-à-vis the judgments of the cultural sciences, which Weber endorses.) Kelsen's legal science is to be a non-ideological science, albeit a science having an object that is not neutral but is itself ideological; it is therefore a non-ideological science of a specific ideology, the law. With this affirmation Kelsen believes that he has set down the premises and starting points of his analysis. These are

---

deny those contents and facts that he cannot rationalize.' The significance of the Pure Theory of Law, for Heller, lies in its extreme tendency, in its unwitting *reductio ad absurdum* showing of the implications of what Heller termed 'juridico-logicistic positivism'. Hermann Heller, 'Die Krisis der Staatsrechtslehre', *Archiv für Sozialwissenschaft und Sozialpolitik*, 55 (1926), 289–316, at 304–6, repr. in Heller, *Gesammelte Schriften*, 2nd edn., ed. Christoph Müller, 3 vols. (Tübingen: J.C.B. Mohr, 1992), vol. II, 3–30, at 19–21.

[73] See Emil Lask, 'Zum System der Wissenschaften', in Lask, *Gesammelte Schriften*, 3 vols. (Tübingen: J.C.B. Mohr, 1923), vol. III, at 292.

[74] Or, in Kelsen's case, perhaps a single normative science, since he was ambivalent about the status of the related fields—theology, logic, grammar.

premises only in appearance, however, inasmuch as they are themselves the result of a valuation or, at least, of Kelsen's acceptance of
assessments that are shared by a specific, historically determined social
community. These are premises and options constituted substantially
by a specific ideology that makes a value of modern natural science,
specifically, a technologically productive value.

PART VI

Monism and Public International Law

28

Sovereignty*

HANS KELSEN

I. THE CONCEPT

Although the expression 'sovereignty' denotes one of the most significant fundamental concepts of both the traditional theory of state law and
that of international law, it is fraught with an ambiguity of dire consequence in the controversy over its meaning. The generally accepted
meaning found most frequently in the newer literature is all that is given
when sovereignty is characterized as that property according to which
the state is the supreme power or the supreme system of human behaviour, a meaning corresponding to the original sense of 'sovereignty' as
derived from the Latin '*superanus*'. Some authors who pronounce the
state to be essentially sovereign nevertheless qualify their position in that
they consider even the 'sovereign' state to be bound by the norms of
morality in general—or by a particular morality of religion, namely
Christianity—and therefore to be subject to this morality as to a higher
order. At the same time, they attempt to preserve the concept of state
sovereignty as a highest authority, understood simply as the highest
authority in the field of the law, that is, as a power or order not subject to
any higher legal order.

II. THE PROBLEM

This sovereignty of the state becomes problematic when international
law is brought into the picture as a legal system imposing obligations and
conferring rights on the state. That international law imposes obligations
and confers rights on the state to behave in a certain way does not mean,
as sometimes assumed, that international law imposes obligations and

* *Editors' note*: The German text of this paper first appeared in *Wörterbuch des
Völkerrechts*, 2nd edn., ed. Hans-Jürgen Schlochauer, 3 vols. (Berlin: de Gruyter, 1960–2),
vol. III (1962), 278–85. The translation is by the editors. An earlier English-language version
appeared under the title 'Sovereignty and International Law' (see n.5 below).

confers rights on a being that is not human but a kind of superman or superhuman organism. There is no such superman or superhuman organism in society, whose sole reality is the individual human being. What is characterized as a society or a community is either the actual coexistence of individual human beings or a normative system of their reciprocal behaviour. Only human beings can have obligations imposed and rights conferred on them to behave in a certain way; only the behaviour of human beings can be the content of legal obligations and rights. If international law imposes obligations and confers rights on the state to behave in a certain way, this means that it imposes obligations and confers rights on human beings, in their capacity as organs of the state, to behave in this way. That these human beings as organs of the state fulfil the obligations imposed and exercise the rights conferred by international law, and that their behaviour is seen as the behaviour of the state and is attributed to the state, means that international law applies to a personified legal system in which the human beings are specified who are to fulfil the obligations imposed and to exercise the rights conferred by international law. This is the legal system—in the familiar legal terminology that differentiates between the state and its law—that is characterized as the law 'of the state'. This law is a relatively centralized coercive system whose validity is limited to a certain territory. And this is the legal system, qua state legal system, that is distinguished from the relatively decentralized system of international law, whose territorial sphere of validity is unlimited. That international law imposes obligations and confers rights on the state to behave in a certain way means that international law leaves it to the state legal system to specify the human beings who are to behave in such a way as to fulfil these obligations and to exercise these rights; in other words, international law delegates powers to the state legal system to make this determination. The state qua system is what one calls 'one's own' law, a particular legal system; and the state qua person—that is, as a subject of international law—is the personification of this legal system. The notion of the state as superman or superhuman organism is the hypostatization of this personification. Sovereignty as a legal concept can only be the property of a legal system, and the problem of the sovereignty of the state is, therefore, the problem of the sovereignty of the state legal system in its relation to the system of international law.

Two theories about this relation are diametrically opposed: the dualistic theory—or, if one takes into account the multiplicity of states or state legal systems, the pluralistic theory—and the monistic theory. According to the dualistic theory, international law and state law (the individual state legal systems) are different systems of norms, systems that, in their validity, are independent of one another but at the same time equal.

Thus, according to the dualistic theory, particular human behaviour can be judged from the standpoint of international law and at the same time from the standpoint of state law, and not simply from one standpoint or the other. According to the monistic theory, international law and state law form a unity: Either international law is above state law, so that the basis of the validity of state law is to be found in international law (primacy of international law), or, conversely, state law is above international law, so that the basis of the validity of international law lies in state law (primacy of state law).

If one recognizes that the imposition of obligations and the conferral of rights on the state by international law simply means that international law delegates powers to the state legal systems to specify the human beings whose behaviour makes up the content of these obligations and rights, then the dualistic construction of the relation between international law and state law collapses. The dualistic construction would not be warranted unless there were, between the norms of international law and the norms of state law, conflicts that could only be described in contradictory statements by a legal science having legal systems of equal validity as its subject-matter. For then a unity of the two systems—which is simply an epistemic unity—would be out of the question. It can be shown, however, that it is possible for legal science to describe the relation between international law and state law without such contradictions, that, in other words, there are no conflicts between international law and state law that render a dualistic construction necessary. It can also be shown that, in the principle of effectiveness,[1] positive international law has a norm that determines the basis and sphere of the validity of the state legal system, so that there is no doubt about an epistemic unity of international law and state law.

III. MONISTIC THEORIES AND SOVEREIGNTY

For the solution to the problems of sovereignty, then, there is only the monistic construction of the relation between international law and state law, that is to say, either the primacy of international law or the primacy of state law. The difference between these two monistic constructions reaches only to the basis of the validity of international law and of state law, and not to the content of these legal systems. The content of international law is just the same in both cases. And from a juridico-

---

[1] [For Kelsen's understanding of the principle of effectiveness (*Effektivität*), see e.g. *LT* § 30(c)(d) (at pp. 61–3), § 50(g) (at pp. 120–1); Hans Kelsen, *Principles of International Law*, 1st edn. (New York: Rinehart, 1952), at 212–26, 288–91, 412–15; 2nd edn., ed. Robert W. Tucker (New York: Holt, Rinehart and Winston, 1967), at 312–17, 410–12, 560–2.]

theoretical standpoint, both constructions are equally possible. Their opposition to each other is simply the opposition of two different frames of reference.

If one's point of departure is state law as a normative system having the validity of *ought*, then the question arises of how, from this point of departure, the validity of international law can be established. This can be done solely by means of the assumption that international law is valid for a state only if it is recognized by that state as valid for that state, and, indeed, is recognized as valid in its actual form at the moment of recognition. Since this recognition can also be tacit, in that the state in question complies with and applies, in practice, the norms of international law, it is this theory of recognition, then, that also underlies the view of international law as valid for all states. Prevalent in Anglo-American law, this view is given expression in modern constitutions containing provisions that require law-applying organs to observe general international law as well as the particular international law created by the treaties of the state in question. Thus, international law is understood as a component of the state legal system, as 'external state law', and the basis of the validity of international law is shifted to the state legal system that serves as the point of departure for constructing the relation between the two systems. This construction represents the primacy of state law over international law, and it is this primacy of state law that is characterized, within the framework of a legal theory, as the sovereignty of the state.

Sovereignty in this sense does not represent a perceptible or otherwise objectively identifiable quality of a real object. Rather, it represents the presupposition of a normative system qua highest system, not derivable in its validity from any higher system. The question of whether the state is sovereign cannot be answered by enquiring into natural or social reality. The state sovereignty that is of interest from the standpoint of legal cognition is not a particular magnitude of real power. States that have no power comparable at all to that of the great nations are no less 'sovereign' than these. The question of whether a state is sovereign is the question of whether the state legal system is to be presupposed as the highest legal system. And this is the case where international law is considered to be valid for the state only if it is recognized by the state and its basis of validity is seen as the 'will' of the state.

If, however, one's point of departure is international law as a valid normative system, then the question arises of how, from this point of departure, the validity of the state legal system can be established. The basis of the validity of the state legal system must, in this case, be found in international law. And this is feasible, since the principle of effectiveness, a norm of positive international law, determines the basis as well as the sphere of the validity of the state legal system. This norm of international law, representing the basis of the validity of the state legal system, is expanded upon to the effect that, according to general international law, the government of a community existing within a certain clearly circumscribed territory, independent of other governments of similar communities and exercising effective control over the members of its community, is the legitimate government; and the community under this government is a state in terms of international law even if the effective control exercised by the government is based on a constitution first established by the government through revolution. This means that a norm of general international law empowers an individual or a group of individuals to establish and to apply, on the basis of an efficacious constitution, a normative coercive system, thereby legitimizing this coercive system as the valid legal system for the territorial and temporal sphere of its actual efficacy, and legitimizing the system's community as a state in terms of international law. If the efficacy of the state legal system is seen as a condition for the system's validity, and if this condition is set by a norm of international law, then the basis of the validity of the state legal system can be seen in this norm of international law. And international law, therefore, can be interpreted as a universal legal system above the state legal systems, encompassing them all as legal systems qua subsystems, and making possible their coexistence in space and succession in time.

This construction of the relation between international law and state law rules out the notion of state sovereignty in the original and proper sense of the expression. What is 'sovereign' qua highest system is international law, not the state legal system. If one speaks of 'sovereign' states in the context of this construction, the concept takes on a meaning that is altogether different from the original and proper sense. Here, it expresses simply the notion that the state legal system is subject to international law alone and to no other state legal system, and that therefore—in the personifying terminology of the law—the state is legally independent of other states. The so-called 'sovereignty' of the state, then, is nothing other than its immediate relation to international law. If one's point of departure is the primacy of international law, then the misleading expression 'state sovereignty' ought to be replaced by the expression of the state's immediate relation to international law. One may not speak of a 'relative' sovereignty of the states, for this expression amounts to a *contradictio in adjecto*.

Only by assuming the primacy of the state legal system can one speak of the sovereignty of the state in the original and proper sense of the expression. It seems more than questionable, however, that the authors who prefer this construction of the relation between international law and state law are willing to accept the consequences of their construction. For, according to this construction, only the sovereignty of a single state can be presupposed, which in turn precludes the sovereignty of all other states. But it is the sovereignty of all the states—so-called 'sovereign equality' qua equal sovereignty of all states, the notion that, in terms of their sovereignty, all states are equal—that is to be rescued by means of the construction representing the primacy of state law. The point of departure for this construction can indeed be any state whatever, but always just one single state. The relation of this state to the other states is established by international law, which is a component of the state legal system that serves as the point of departure for the construction. According to prevailing international law, a state considers another community to be a state, and the system constituting this community to be a valid legal system, only if the first state recognizes this community as a state in terms of international law, that is to say, only if, in the view of the authorized organs of the recognizing state, this community fulfils the conditions prescribed by international law.

If international law is a component of the legal system of the recognizing state, then for this state the basis of the legal existence of the other states—that is, the basis of the validity of the other legal systems—lies in the recognizing state's own legal system, or, figuratively speaking, in its own will. Thus, all other state legal systems must be seen as subordinate to the recognizing state's legal system with its component, international law; they cannot be presupposed as sovereign. As a component of the state legal system that is the basis for recognizing the other states, international law, too, has its basis of validity in this state legal system, in the 'will' of the recognizing state. Thus, this state alone—and so, only the state legal system that serves as the point of departure for the construction representing the primacy of state law—can be regarded as sovereign, as the highest legal system, for above it there is no higher legal system presupposed as valid.

If international law exists only as a component of a state legal system, however, then a distinction must be made between the state legal system in a narrower and a broader sense. The state legal system in the narrower sense comprises norms of the constitution and norms set in accordance with the constitution by means of acts of custom, legislation, adjudication, and administration. The state legal system in the broader sense includes, in addition, the state legal system in so far as it encompasses international law (recognized on the basis of the state legal system in the narrower sense), that is, in addition, norms that are created by means of the customs and treaties of the states. Taking into account the content of international law, the relation of the two components that make up the state legal system in the broader sense must be interpreted as a relation of superordination and subordination. This relation is figuratively expressed when one says that the state that recognizes international law as valid for itself is thereby subjecting itself to international law. The state legal system in the narrower sense, in its relation to international law (the other component of the state legal system in the broader sense), is just as subordinate as the legal systems of the other states and therefore no more sovereign than they, but simply enjoys a relation that is just as immediate as theirs to international law. This state legal system in the narrower sense, having recognized international law, has its basis of validity in international law just as all the other state legal systems do. International law is not, however, the ultimate basis of validity for the state legal system that renders international law valid as its component and that serves as the point of departure for the construction representing the primacy of state law. For international law itself has its basis of validity in the so-called 'will' of this state, that is, in the state legal system in the broader sense. The relation, between international law and state law, that is characterized as the primacy of the state legal system exists only between the state legal system in the broader sense and international law as its component. This legal system alone, not the state legal system in the narrower sense, is sovereign. And sovereignty here means simply that although international law is indeed assumed to be above the state legal system in the narrower sense, it is not assumed to be above the state legal system in the broader sense, whose component it is. Since what must be meant when one speaks of a sovereignty of the states is only (or at any rate primarily) the state legal system in the narrower sense or the community constituted by it, 'sovereignty' can only denote an immediate relation to international law. Only the state legal system in the broader sense, however, which renders international law, as its component, valid, could be characterized as 'sovereign' in the sole admissible meaning of the word. Thus, if this construction of the relation between international law and state law is chosen, it is well to speak of the primacy of state law rather than to use the misleading expression 'state sovereignty'.

The choice of one or the other of the two constructions of the relation between international law and state law, and, therefore, the presupposition or non-presupposition of the sovereignty of the state, has no influence on the content of international law. The content of state law, too, remains untouched by the construction of the relation and, therefore, by whether or not the state is presupposed as sovereign. It is a misuse, then, of either construction, or (what amounts to the same thing) a misuse of the concept of sovereignty, when decisions that can only be taken on the basis of the content of positive international or state law are drawn from the concept of sovereignty—which happens again and again. Thus, supporters of the primacy of international law claim that since the state is subject to international law and since international law is the higher legal system in relation to state law, it follows that in case of a conflict between international law and state law, international law has priority and so the conflicting [norm of] state law is null and void. A norm of state law can only be invalidatable,[2] however, not null and void. Moreover, it can only be invalidated, owing to its so-called 'contrariety to international law', if international law or state law provides for a procedure leading to its invalidation. General international law, however, does not provide for such a procedure, and the assumption that it is above the state cannot make up for the absence of such a procedure.[3] Positive international law merely attaches a sanction to the issuance of the questionable norm of state law, a sanction directed against the state whose law includes this norm. Thus, the norm of state law remains valid—indeed, valid from the standpoint of not only state law, but also international law; the state does, however, subject itself to a sanction imposed by international law. This circumstance can be described without any logical contradiction, for the law prescribes particular behaviour only in that it imposes an obligatory sanction in the event of the opposite behaviour. Two norms, one of which attaches a sanction to particular behaviour, and the other, a sanction to the opposite behaviour, can both be valid and applied. This remains true if one norm is a norm of international law, attaching to particular behaviour the specific sanction of international law (namely, war or retaliation), and the other is a norm of state law, attaching to the opposite behaviour the specific sanction of state law (punishment or a seizure of property). From the standpoint of legal policy, such a situation is undesirable, suggesting that a means be institutionalized either in international law or in state law for invalidating the state law norm that is 'contrary to international law'. Unless this is the case, both the norm of state law and the norm of international law are valid. There is a teleological conflict here, but not a logical contradiction, neither between international law and state law, nor between the statements that describe them. Neither the nullity nor the invalidatability of the norm that is 'contrary to international law' is necessary in order to maintain the epistemic unity of state law and international law in terms of the primacy of international law.

From the fact that international law is above the states, the conclusion is also drawn that the sovereignty of the state is fundamentally limited, making possible an efficacious organization of world law. In the political ideology of pacifism, the primacy of international law, excluding state sovereignty, plays a decisive role. The state sovereignty excluded by the primacy of international law, however, is altogether different from the

---

[2] [On 'invalidatable' ('*vernichtbar*'), see *LT* § 31(h) (at p. 73 n.56).]
[3] [Reading 'procedure' for the German '*Norm*'.]

state sovereignty limited by international law. The former means the highest legal authority, the latter means the state's freedom of action or the state legal system's unlimited authority. The authority of the state legal system is equally limited by international law understood either as a legal system above the states or as a component of a state legal system. An efficacious organization of world law is possible given the assumption of either construction of the relation between international law and state law.

Even more apt to be misused than the primacy of international law is the primacy of state legal systems, a primacy based on the assumption of the sovereignty of the state. To assume that international law is valid only on the strength of its recognition by the state and therefore only as a component of the state legal system is to assume that the state is sovereign. The conclusion drawn from this assumption is that the state is not necessarily bound by the international treaties it has entered into, that its nature is incompatible with its subjecting itself—even in a treaty entered into by the state—to an international court with obligatory jurisdiction or with its being bound by the majority decision of a collegial organ, even if this organ and its procedure have been created pursuant to a treaty entered into by the state. Just as the primacy of international law plays a decisive role in the ideology of pacifism, so the primacy of state law—the sovereignty of the state—plays a decisive role in the ideology of imperialism. Here as there, what is key is the ambiguity of the concept of sovereignty. If, however, international law has been recognized by the state and is therefore valid for this state, then it is valid just as if it were valid as a legal system above the states. Then the norm of international law to the effect that states are bound by the treaties they enter into is valid, regardless of the content given to the norms created by treaty. According to international law, no content of a norm created by treaty can be excluded on the ground that it is incompatible with the nature of a state entering into the treaty, in particular incompatible with the sovereignty of this state. The fact that no international law above the state limits the sovereignty of the state is altogether compatible with the fact that a state, on the strength of its sovereignty, recognizes international law and thereby turns international law into a component of the state legal system, that it limits its own sovereignty—and so its own freedom of action or its own authority—by assuming the obligations imposed by general international law and the treaties entered into by the state. The answer to the question of how far this sovereignty of the state is limitable by the international law recognized by the state can only be given on the basis of the content of international law, not derived from the concept of sovereignty. Positive international law, however, sets no bounds on limiting state sovereignty, that is, the freedom of action or the authority of the state. An international treaty can create an international organization so centralized that it has itself the character of a state, with the result that the states entering into the treaty and incorporated into the organization lose their character as states. How far a state government may or ought to limit by international treaty the freedom of action of the state is admittedly a question of politics. The answer cannot be drawn from either the primacy of international law or the primacy of state law.

The opposition of the two monistic constructions of the relation between international law and state law—that is, the two ways leading to the epistemic unity of all valid law—is strikingly parallel to the opposition that exists between a subjectivistic and an objectivistic *Weltanschauung*. The subjectivistic view, in order to comprehend the external world, takes as its point of departure one's own sovereign 'I', and can therefore comprehend this world only as an internal world, as the conception and will of the 'I', and not as an external world at all. So likewise, the construction characterized as the primacy of the state legal system, in order to comprehend the external world of the law, namely, international law and the other state legal systems, takes as its point of departure one's own sovereign state, and can therefore understand this external law only as internal law, as a component of one's own state legal system. A consequence of the primacy of one's own state legal system is that only one's own state can be comprehended as sovereign, for the sovereignty of that state excludes the sovereignty of all other states. In this sense, the primacy of one's own state legal system can be characterized as state subjectivism, indeed, as state solipsism. By contrast, the construction characterized as the primacy of the system of international law, in order to comprehend the legal existence of the individual states, takes as its point of departure the external world of the law—international law—qua valid legal system, but can, therefore, confer validity on these states only as legal systems qua subsystems incorporated into international law, and not as sovereign authorities. Scientific cognition of the world is completely untouched by the opposition between subjectivism and objectivism, and the world qua object of this cognition, as well as the natural laws that describe the world, remain the same, whether this world is thought of as the internal world of the 'I' or the 'I' is thought of as within the world. So likewise, the opposition between the two legal constructions has no influence on the content of either international law or state law, and the legal propositions that describe the content of the law remain the same, whether one thinks of international law as contained in state law or of state law as contained in international law.

The opposition between the two legal constructions can also be compared with the opposition that exists between the geocentric cosmic system of Ptolemy and the heliocentric cosmic system of Copernicus. Just as, according to the first of the legal constructions, one's own state is at the center of the legal world, so likewise, in the Ptolemaic conception, the earth is at the center of the universe, with the sun revolving around the earth. And just as, according to the other legal construction, international law is at the center of the legal world, so likewise, in the Copernican conception, the sun is at the center of the universe, with the earth revolving around the sun. But this opposition of two astronomical conceptions is simply an opposition of two different frames of reference. As Max Planck remarks:

If, for example, one accepts a frame of reference that is firmly tied to our earth, then one must say that the sun moves in the heavens; but if one shifts the frame of reference to a fixed star, then the sun is at rest. In the opposition of these two formulations, there is neither a contradiction nor a lack of clarity; there is simply the opposition of two different points of view. According to the theory of relativity, which can surely be counted among the established assets of physics at present, both frames of reference and the corresponding points of view are equally correct and equally warranted; it is fundamentally impossible, without being arbitrary, to choose between them on the basis of some kind of measurement or calculation.[4]

The same is true of the two legal constructions of the relation between international law and state law. Their opposition is based on the distinction between two different frames of reference. One frame of reference is firmly tied to one's own state legal system, the other to the system of international law. Both frames of reference are equally correct and equally warranted. It is impossible to choose between them on the basis of legal science. Legal science can only present them both, and establish that one or the other must be assumed if the relation between international law and state law is to be determined. The decision itself lies outside legal science. It can only be taken on the basis of nonscientific considerations, in particular political considerations. He who values the idea of the sovereignty of his own state because, in his heightened self-confidence, he identifies with his state will prefer the primacy of the state legal system over the primacy of the system of international law. He who finds the idea of an organization of world law more congenial will prefer the primacy of international law over the primacy of state law. This does not mean that the ideal of the organization of world law would be served less well by the theory of the primacy of the state legal system than by the theory of the primacy of the system of international law. The former does

---

[4] Max Planck, 'Vom Wesen der Willensfreiheit' [a lecture held under the auspices of the German Philosophical Society on 27 November 1936], in Planck, *Vorträge und Erinnerungen* (Stuttgart: S. Hirzel, 1949), 301–17, at 311. [*Vorträge und Erinnerungen* is the 5th edition of Planck's papers, prepared with the advice of Planck's widow, Marga von Hoeßlin Planck, and published posthumously; earlier editions had appeared under the title *Wege zur physikalischen Erkenntnis*.]

seem to justify, however, a politics that rejects any far-reaching limitation on the state's freedom of action. Such a justification is based on a
fallacy, involving in a disastrous way the ambiguity of the concept of sovereignty—meaning the highest legal authority and unlimited freedom of
action. This fallacy, however, is a permanent part of the political ideology
of imperialism, with its operative dogma of state sovereignty. The same
is true, *mutatis mutandis*, of the preference for the primacy of the system
of international law. It is no less propitious than the primacy of the individual state legal system for the ideal of the least possible limitation on
sovereignty in terms of the state's freedom of action. It does seem to justify, however, a far-reaching limitation on the state's freedom of action
more readily than the primacy of the state legal system does. This, too, is
a fallacy, but it plays a decisive role nevertheless within the political
ideology of pacifism.

In exposing these fallacies and stripping them of all pretence of logical
demonstration, which would be irrefutable, and in reducing them to
political arguments that can be met with political counterarguments,
legal science opens the way to one political development or the other
without postulating or justifying either. Legal science qua science
regards them both with complete indifference.[5]

---

⁵ [At the conclusion of Kelsen's essay, which first appeared in a reference work on international law, various titles are listed that the reader might consult on monism in inter-
national law and on sovereignty.] Charles Edward Merriam, *History of the Theory of
Sovereignty since Rousseau* (New York: Columbia UP, 1900); Wiktor Sukiennicki, *La
Souveraineté des états en droit international moderne* (Paris: A. Pedone, 1927); Luigi Raggi, *La
teoria della sovranità* (Genoa: A. Donath, 1908); Hugo Krabbe, *Die Lehre der
Rechtssouveränität* (Groningen: J.B. Wolters, 1906) [*Die moderne Staats-Idee* (The Hague:
Martinus Nijhoff, 1919) is, according to its preface, a closely related work; its English translation, by George H. Sabine and Walter J. Shepard, appeared under the title *The Modern Idea of
the State* (New York: Appleton, 1922)]; Leonard Nelson, *Die Rechtswissenschaft ohne Recht*
(Leipzig: Veit, 1917) [repr. in Nelson, *Gesammelte Schriften in neun Bänden*, ed. Paul Bernays
et al. (Hamburg: Fritz Meiner, 1970–2), vol. IX (1972), 123–324]; Alfred Verdross, *Die Einheit
des rechtlichen Weltbildes auf Grundlage der Völkerrechtsverfassung* (Tübingen: J.C.B. Mohr,
1923); Harold J. Laski, *Studies in the Problem of Sovereignty* (New Haven: Yale UP, 1917);
Kelsen, *PS*; Johannes Mattern, *Concepts of State, Sovereignty and International Law*
(Baltimore: Johns Hopkins Press, 1928); Dietrich W. Gunst, *Der Begriff der Souveränität im
modernen Völkerrecht. Eine wissenschaftliche Analyse* (Berlin: R. Oppermann, 1953); Ernst
Friedrich Sauer, *Souveränität und Solidarität. Ein Beitrag zur völkerrechtlichen Wertlehre*
(Göttingen: Musterschmidt Wissenschaftlicher Verlag, 1954); Maurice Bourquin, *L'État et
l'organisation internationale* (New York: Manhattan Publ. Co., 1959); Kelsen, *PTL*; Herbert
Krüger, 'Souveränität und Staatengemeinschaft', in *Zum Problem der Souveränität*,
Berichte der Deutschen Gesellschaft für Völkerrecht (Karlsruhe: C.F. Müller, 1957), vol. I, pp.
1–28; Georg Erler, 'Staatssouveränität und internationale Wirtschaftsverflechtung', ibid.
29–58; Hans Kelsen, 'Die Einheit von Völkerrecht und staatlichem Recht', *Zeitschrift für
ausländisches öffentliches Recht und Völkerrecht*, 19 (1958), 234–48 [repr. *WS II* 2213–29];
Kelsen, 'Sovereignty and International Law', *Georgetown Law Journal*, 48 (1959–60), 627–40
[an earlier English-language version of the essay translated here]; Gerhard Leibholz,
'Sovereignty and European Integration', in *Sciences humaines et integration européenne*,
preface by Robert Schuman (Leiden: A.W. Sijthoff, 1960), 156–76.

29

Monism and Dualism
in the Theory of International Law*

JOSEPH G. STARKE

A strictly theoretical treatment of the relation between international law and municipal law[1] is today of the utmost practical importance. While international law is developing at a pace without precedent in past centuries, there is some danger that the technique of its growth may be impaired by not giving a certain weight to theoretical considerations. The purpose of this article is to deal with the problem from an analytical, positivist point of view, and, to some extent therefore, it follows the principles of the Austrian school—Hans Kelsen, Josef Kunz, and Alfred Verdross.[2] This is not to say that the conclusions of that school are accepted without question; only their method is followed, and that method, it is submitted, represents their most decisive contribution to jurisprudence.

The Austrian school constantly employed the concept of the 'norm',[3] and it would be well to clarify its meaning as we shall be employing it throughout the article. A norm is in short a prescription enjoining a defined mode of action. A norm may be moral or it may be legal, but the legal norm differs from the moral by reason of its particular logical

* *Editors' note*: This paper first appeared in the *British Year Book of International Law*, 17 (1936), 66–81, and was reprinted in J.G. Starke, *Studies in International Law* (London: Butterworths, 1965), 1–19.

[1] The terms 'municipal law' and 'state law' are used interchangeably throughout the article to denote the internal law of a self-governing state, and are intended as a translation of the more exact French expression, '*droit interne*'.

The literature on the subject is formidable in quantity. See e.g. the bibliography in Dionisio Anzilotti, *Corso di diritto internazionale*, 3rd edn. (Rome: Athenaeum, 1928), at 19–38.

[2] For an account of these principles, see Hersch Lauterpacht, 'Kelsen's Pure Science of Law', in *Modern Theories of Law*, intro. by W. Ivor Jennings (London: Oxford UP, 1933), 105–38; Josef Kunz, 'The Theoretical Basis of the Law of Nations', *Transactions of the Grotius Society*, 10 (1924), 115–42; Kunz, 'Primauté du droit des gens', *Revue de Droit International et de Législation Comparée*, 6 (1925), 556–80, at 558–60.

[3] For a critical account, see Hans Morgenthau, *La réalité des normes, en particulier des normes du droit international* (Paris: F. Alcan, 1934).

structure and its power validly to direct the human will. It is obvious that such a general concept is essential for an analytical treatment of law, and indeed it helps to simplify and purify theoretical method. Municipal law thus becomes a normative order or particular system of norms having validity over certain persons within a certain defined territorial area, while international law is a normative order of wider validity and operation.

The problem of the relation between these two normative orders is by no means modern, but it has been brought to the fore in recent times by the growth of modern constitutions and their necessary modification in order to function in an international society.[4] The interrelation is capable of endless illustration, but it will suffice for our purposes to take Article 49(3) of the Danzig Constitution, which provides that constitutional alterations can only come into force after they have been submitted to the League of Nations and the League has not given voice to any objection. Obviously there is a certain connection between the norm created by this provision in the Constitution and the norms of international law that define the field of action of the League. Since the earliest times, theories explaining this relation have tended to answer certain specific questions. Are international law and municipal law concomitant aspects of the same juridical reality (monism), or are they quite distinct normative realities (dualism)? Which normative system stands higher in the legal hierarchy, international law or municipal law? Or are both of these questions meaningless, and is it more correct to say that international law is not law at all, so that the problem of its relation to municipal law does not arise?

With respect to these questions, there have consistently been three theories: (a) international law is not law; (b) dualism; (c) monism. These theories are not free from deep-seated philosophic influences, and their value is impossible to estimate without some knowledge of their history and background.[5]

I. ORIGINS OF THE THEORIES

There is a curious tendency in English books on jurisprudence to treat the history of the theory of sovereignty as a form of introduction to the Austinian doctrines. This is to lose sight, however, of the fact that the

---

[4] For detailed illustrations of this modern tendency of constitutions, see Boris Mirkine-Guetzévitch, *Droit constitutionnel international* (Paris: Recueil Sirey, 1933); Mirkine-Guetzévitch, 'Droit international et droit constitutionnel', *Recueil des cours*, 38 (1931), 307–465.

[5] See Kunz, 'Primauté du droit des gens' (n.2 above), at 568–77, for a detailed history of theory on the relation between international law and state law.

history of sovereignty has had less to do with state supremacy than with the relationship of state law to another normative order, whether natural law or international law. It is interesting to note that the early Catholic writers adopted a conception of state sovereignty which they were careful to reconcile with a monistic construction of law in general. For them, sovereignty represented a delegation from a superior legal order, a competence rather than an omnipotence.

Thus, it was Francisco Suárez who wrote: 'In universo humano genere potuerunt iura gentium moribus introduci.'

Even with Jean Bodin, in 1576, we find expressed that notion of a higher legal order from which state sovereignty is derived.

Sed legibus divinis aut naturalibus principes omnes ac populi aeque obligantur. ... Quod igitur summum in Republica imperium legibus solutum diximus, nihil ad divinas aut naturales leges pertinet.

Equally for the jurists of the natural law school, sovereignty represented no more than a competence given by international law, identified as part of the wider '*ius naturae*'.

In the middle of the eighteenth century, however, legal theory underwent a profound modification that may be attributed to the influence of Emmerich de Vattel and G.W.F. Hegel. Their conception of the position of the state in the international community reflected their political convictions rather than any objective scientific standpoint, and the result was that, when their doctrines spread, nothing did more to discourage the proper development of a scientific theory of international law. Thus, in 1758, Vattel wrote: 'Every sovereign state is free to determine for itself the obligations imposed upon it.'

Some time later Hegel had carried the position further by interpreting the state as a metaphysical reality with value and significance of its own, and by endowing it with the will to choose whether it should or should not respect law.

These teachings had lasting effects on the theory of international law. Even today, dualistic doctrine is deeply rooted in the Hegelian notion of the state-will, a notion whose persistence well illustrates the tenacity of unproved and irrational dogma. Georg Jellinek, who championed the theory of auto-limitation,[6] and Albert Zorn, who treated international law as external state law (*äußeres Staatsrecht*),[7] both reflected to some extent the spiritual inspiration of Hegel. Traces of that influence survived among those who held fast to the view that the initial hypothesis, the

---

[6] Georg Jellinek, *Allgemeine Staatslehre*, 1st edn. (Berlin: O. Häring, 1900).
[7] Albert Zorn, *Grundzüge des Völkerrechts*, 2nd edn., ed. Philipp Zorn (Leipzig: J.J. Weber, 1903).

Ursprungsnorm, at the basis of international law, is *pacta sunt servanda*.[8] In England, too, there was a noticeable transition from the Blackstonian theory of the binding effect on Parliament of the Law of Nations, to the nineteenth-century doctrine of Parliament's unlimited sovereignty.[9] Yet the logical structure of the Austinian theory was vitiated by its reliance on a political interpretation of the state, for the Hegelian thesis, whether transformed into the doctrine of absolute sovereignty or the doctrine of auto-limitation, always appeared to lack a juridical foundation.

State sovereignty reached its doctrinal plenitude in the nineteenth century, and began to decline when jurisprudence came under the influence of scientific positivism and empiricism. The penetrating analyses of Kelsen[10] and Léon Duguit[11] upset many time-worn notions, and the idea of sovereignty as omnipotence was one of the first to succumb. The Austrian school resolutely adopted monism as its creed, and the thesis was taken up by other thinkers in international law. The position today is that monism has obtained the widest theoretical acceptance, and the question appears to be a choice between state monism and international monism. On this question, contemporary jurists are about equally divided.

II. MONISM AND DUALISM

Above, we divided the theories into: (a) international law is not law; (b) dualism; (c) monism. The first theory lies outside the province of this article, and it will suffice to say that it is hardly taken seriously today. The fact that international law lacks those organs and that procedure which

---

[8] Anzilotti and Verdross both support this view, though Anzilotti upholds dualism and Verdross monism.

[9] See *Triquet* v. *Bath* (1764), 3 Burr. 1478; William Blackstone, *Commentaries on the Law of England*, 4 vols. (Oxford: Clarendon Press, 1769), vol. IV, at 66–7 (strd. pagination). The modern doctrine is stated by Cockburn C.J., in *R.* v. *Keyn* (1876), 2 Ex.D. 63. See also Cyril M. Picciotto, *The Relation of International Law to the Law of England and America* (New York: McBride, Nast, 1915), at 93–4, where the learned author accounts for the change in much the same way described above. He says that the case of *R.* v. *Keyn* 'clearly rests on a different conception of the basis of international law. Where the basis of this was mainly moral and *a priori* speculation founded on what were held to be the rules of absolute right, it was obvious that international law must be part of the common law since the common law was held to rest upon such rules of morality and right. But when international law came to be conceived as the sum of practice and its reasoning to be *a priori* then it became necessary for English judges to introduce the element of assent. And for them the assent required is of the strictest sort.'

[10] See Kelsen's *HP*, which to a certain extent represents the programme of the Austrian school.

[11] Léon Duguit, *Traité du droit constitutionnel*, 2nd edn., 5 vols. (Paris: E. de Boccard, 1921–5).

make state law so highly effective seems to be not an objection to its legal character, but a quality of its historical development.[12]

The other two theories call for more careful consideration.

(i) Heinrich Triepel and Dionisio Anzilotti are the leading exponents of the dualistic construction. Triepel[13] treats the systems of state law and international law as entirely distinct in nature. He contends first that they differ in the particular social relations they govern; state law deals with individuals, while international law regulates relations between states, which alone are subject to it. Secondly, he argues, their juridical origins are different; the source of municipal law is the will of the state itself, while the source of international law is the common will (*Gemeinwille*) of states.

Let us take the first point, that international law only binds states. Kelsen,[14] in a masterly discussion of the problem, has neatly quashed the notion that the state is some peculiar metaphysical reality. Scientific analysis shows that the state as a legal concept is merely a schema serving to embrace the totality of legal norms which apply over certain persons within a defined territorial area; the state and the law may indeed be described as synonymous terms. The concept of the state is used to express in normative language legal facts in which individuals alone are concerned. For example, if a functionary violates a duty of international law, that tortious wrong may be ascribed to the state by normative imputation[15] but the obligation itself rests with an individual. The responsibility of a state is nothing more than a normative expression denoting that the collectivity of individuals constrained by a defined totality of legal norms is bound to make good the breach of a wrong which has been imputed to the state. The affirmation that international law binds states merely signifies that the individual who has violated the legal duty is not directly envisaged by a norm of international law, but that international law leaves the determination of that individual to state law.[16]

Just as the execution or non-execution of these duties must take place through the action of individuals, so does the statement that international duties are the duties of the state simply amount to this, that it is an internal matter for the state alone to determine who are the individuals bound to fulfil these duties.[17]

---

[12] See Hersch Lauterpacht, *The Function of Law in the International Community* (Oxford: Clarendon Press, 1933), at 399–405; Hans Kelsen, 'Théorie générale du droit international public. Problèmes choisis', *Recueil des cours*, 42 (1932), 117–351, at 124–37.

[13] Heinrich Triepel, *Völkerrecht und Landesrecht* (Leipzig: C.L. Hirschfeld, 1899, repr. Aalen: Scientia, 1958). See also Triepel, 'Les rapports entre le droit interne et le droit international', *Recueil des cours*, 1 (1923), 73–121.

[14] See *PS*. See also Hans Kelsen, *Aperçu d'une théorie générale de l'état*, trans. Charles Eisenmann (Paris: M. Giard, 1927).

[15] For the theory of imputation, see Anzilotti (n.1 above).

[16] See Kelsen (n.12 above).   [17] Anzilotti (n.1 above).

In this respect, therefore, there is no real distinction between state law and international law. In the ultimate analysis, international law binds individuals, but only mediately, through the state.

An interesting technical recognition of this theory is contained in Article 4 of the Brussels Slavery Convention 1890.[18]

> The states exercising sovereign powers or protectorates in Africa may delegate to chartered companies all or part of the engagements that they assume in virtue of Article 3. *They remain nevertheless directly responsible* for the engagements that they contract by the present general act, and guarantee their execution.

The chartered companies thus have mediate obligations, but breaches of duty by their officers are *imputed* to the states, which are ultimately directly responsible.

Criticism of Triepel's first contention can be carried a stage further. International law is now gradually acquiring more and more immediate validity, and many of its norms not only directly determine the individuals bound by it, but also specifically prescribe the sanctions which those individuals incur. Of this direct operation of norms of international law, piracy and slavery are the best examples. The Brussels Slavery Convention 1890,[19] for instance, carefully defines the obligations and sanctions applying directly to those who take part in the slave trade. Section 3 of the unratified Convention on the use of Submarines and Poisonous Gas in time of War, concluded in Washington in 1922, also provides that an individual acting in breach of certain rules lays himself open to trial and punishment in any state in whose jurisdiction he may be, as if he had committed an act of piracy. On the strength of this provision, it may be objected that international law needs to be supplemented by the action of state organs, exercising their jurisdiction under the authority of norms of state law. This, however, does not prevent us from recognizing that the state organs function then as organs of international law, and that the position is exactly the same as if a statute had laid down a general principle and a subsequent regulation under the statute had prescribed the penalties or measures of execution.[20] The primary norms remain norms of international law, and individuals are none the less subject to them. Again, international law is more and more directly envisaging the individual as the object of its protection and conferring on

---

[18] *Recueil Martens*, 2nd ser., 17 (1892), 345.

[19] The Brussels Slavery Convention is now superseded by the Convention of St. Germain 1919, which abrogates the Brussels Convention as between the signatories, and by the Geneva Slavery Convention 1926, under which the signatories undertake to prevent and suppress the trade, and bring about progressively its entire suppression in all its forms. The Brussels Convention, nevertheless, remains a valuable technical illustration of the theory of international law.

[20] Kelsen (n.12 above).

him specific rights and remedies available on his own motion. Article 64 of the Brussels Convention provides that

any fugitive slave reaching the frontier of one of the states mentioned in Article 62 will be treated as free, and will have the right to claim a certificate of freedom from the competent authorities.

The individual thus becomes the subject of rights as well as obligations directly created by norms of international law.[21]

Triepel's second point, inspired as it is by the Hegelian thesis, naturally raises the question—what is meant by the will of the state? The truth is that the will of the state is a normative imputation to the state of a particular psychological quality implied from its acceptance of subjection to norms of international law. The will of the state is not an extra-juridical reality, but a technical expression for the fact that the state may become bound by international law. The concept draws its strength not from empirically justified theory, but from the political conviction that the state is an independent self-sufficient entity. Since it is always necessary to define the circumstances in which an act of the state legislature or other state organ will be treated as being a declaration of the will of the state, there must be some superior legal norm declaring when this act will bind the state as the expression of its will. Such an act—for example the ratification of a treaty—is only the condition on which the norm of international law becomes effective for the state. It is impossible for the will of the state to be the source of international law, since it presupposes a pre-existent rule defining when its expression subjects the state to international law.[22] The position is essentially the same with a collective declaration of state wills, which equally does not obviate the necessity for norms of superior validity. Triepel's *Gemeinwille* therefore does not reveal any true distinction between the norms of state law and the norms of international law.[23]

With Anzilotti the position is only slightly different. For him international law and state law equally constitute two distinct normative orders.

---

[21] For other examples of rights granted directly to individuals by international law, see § 297(e) and (h) of the Treaty of Versailles, 1919.

[22] Hugo Krabbe has dealt with this point in some detail in *Die Lehre von der Rechtssouveränität* (Groningen: J.B. Wolters, 1906), and in *The Modern Idea of the State*, trans. George H. Sabine and Walter J. Shepard (The Hague: M. Nijhoff, 1922).

[23] Lauterpacht (n.12 above), at 416, points out that though Triepel's doctrine is based on the will of the states as expressed in the *Vereinbarung* or collective declaration of wills, it recognizes the authority of the law over the will of the states. In a footnote he says that it is consequently impossible to accept Kelsen's view that Triepel's doctrine is merely a paraphrase of the auto-limitation theory.

Kelsen's criticism is, however, justified. Triepel's view is that the law created by the *Vereinbarung* thereby becomes superior to the will of states. But he fails to recognize that the source of these norms is not the *Gemeinwille*, but superior norms which give authority to the process of law-making by the *Vereinbarung*.

The former are binding by reason of the principle *pacta sunt servanda*, and cannot be repealed except as laid down by international law. The latter are binding by reason of the rule that enjoins obedience to the legislature's prescriptions, and can only be repealed in the manner provided by the public law of the particular domestic legal system in question.[24]

The two systems, being based on different initial hypotheses, must be quite separate from one another.[25] There are obvious difficulties in accepting this thesis. Is it always true that the norms of international law may be traced back to *pacta sunt servanda*? Without resorting to artificial constructions such as 'tacit consent' and the like, it is difficult to fit customary international law into this schema. A further objection is that it is common for legal norms to bind states without any form of consent expressed by or imputed to them. Thus, under the International Convention for Limiting the Manufacture and Regulating the Distribution of Narcotic Drugs 1931, the states' parties are under a general obligation not to exceed the estimates as furnished by them and finally determined by a body at Geneva, known as the Supervisory Body. The Supervisory Body also finally determines the estimates for non-parties, and, although the Convention does not explicitly impose on non-parties the obligation not to exceed their estimates, non-parties are none the less liable to embargo proceedings if they exceed the estimates fixed for them by the Supervisory Body. The juridical result is that states are bound by a norm to which they have not expressly or impliedly consented. *Pacta sunt servanda*, like the doctrine of state will, is not self-explanatory but a partial illustration of a much wider principle lying at the root of international law.[26]

The truth is that the whole dualistic position raises grave objections in principle. It seems to deny the juridical nature of international law by treating it as a kind of morality governing the relations between states and grounded only in their consent. Both Triepel and Anzilotti appear to reason much as if international law were natural law, as if its validity were independent of its legal nature. Logically, too, their thesis implies that the legal competence of the state is incapable of limitation save by the state itself. As Kelsen puts it, state egotism is substituted for legal pluralism. In light of the monistic construction, these objections stand out more clearly.

(ii) The leading adherent of monism is Kelsen.[27] For him, jurispru-

[24] Anzilotti (n.1 above), 51.
[25] In Anzilotti's view, there is such a complete separation between the two systems that one system cannot contain binding norms emanating from the other. There can, again, be no conflicts between them, but only *renvois* from the one to the other.
[26] On *pacta sunt servanda*, see Lauterpacht (n.12 above), at 420–3.
[27] See Hans Kelsen, 'Les rapports de système. Entre le droit interne et le droit international public', *Recueil des cours*, 14 (1926), 227–331, at 289–326.

dence is a science, and the object of a science is formed by cognition and its unity. Unity of cognition connotes unity of object, and this unity must be found in the relation between municipal law and international law. Dualism is inconsistent with the axiomatic unity of a science. Any construction other than monism is bound to constitute a denial of the legal character of international law. There is no half-way house between monism and the theory that international law is not law. Two normative systems with binding force in the same field must form part of the same order. Nor is it a valid objection that law and morals are examples of two normative systems applying in the same field yet nevertheless different. The science of law deals only with binding norms. It aims at unity of normative knowledge, which can only be expressed by the unity of a system of norms.

Having reached that conclusion, Kelsen turns to a structural analysis of the relation between state law and international law. It is here that his doctrine of 'a hierarchy of norms' becomes of importance. For Kelsen the legal fabric is built up in a different way from the natural sciences; legal norms are only explicable by other norms from which they derive their existence and their binding force; thus, the norm laid down in regulations is determined by a norm in a statute, and it in its turn by a norm in the constitution, and so on. Law

has the peculiarity of governing its own creation; a rule of law determines how another rule will be laid down; in this sense the latter depends on the former; it is this bond of dependence which links together the different elements of the legal order, which constitutes its principle of unity. The validity of a legal norm is based precisely on the norm which creates it; a norm is valid only if it conforms to the norm of superior force.[28]

From norm to norm, legal analysis eventually reaches one supreme, fundamental norm, which is the source and foundation of all law. This fundamental norm is a necessary scientific hypothesis, a postulate of the science of law.

The hypothesis itself is determined by the materials it must embrace, just as those materials are determined by the hypothesis. We have therefore the same correlation as between facts and hypothesis in the natural sciences.[29]

Further than that hypothesis the jurist cannot venture, for the ultimate origins of law are determined by *metajuridical* considerations.

The question now arises—what hypothesis will best express the relation between the positive norms of state law and the positive norms of international law as pertaining to one unitary system of law? Is that hypothesis to be found in the state order, or is it to be found in the international order?

[28] Kelsen, *Aperçu d'une théorie générale de l'état* (n.14 above), 26.
[29] *ASL* § 20(b) (p. 104).

III. THE QUESTION OF PRIMACY

Primacy of state law or primacy of international law. Kelsen, in contrast with his colleagues of the monistic school, treats the choice of one or the other as a matter of ethics or politics rather than of legal science. Provided that the logical consequences are strictly adhered to, he holds that the thesis of the superiority of state law is perfectly legitimate. The two theories being no more than hypotheses, the choice cannot rest with juridical science.

It cannot be asserted, as in the natural sciences, that the preferable hypothesis is the one which embraces the greatest number of given facts. For, here, we are not dealing with materials, with perceptible realities, but with rules of law—matter uncertain by its very nature; for in law, there is no objective necessity to envisage such and such element as a rule of law.[30]

It may be stated at once that Kelsen's idea of the possibility of a meta-juridical option has not escaped criticism. Georges Scelle[31] points out that Kelsen, having developed his thesis with meticulous logic, leaves us finally with an impression of insecurity. It is difficult to see how the choice of either system can avoid being based on strictly juridical con-siderations. Indeed, Kelsen himself admits that the choice depends in the last analysis on existing positive law. Kelsen's attitude seems to be, as Kunz says, rooted in his philosophy or scepticism and relativism. Kunz and Verdross, however, have refused to share his opinion, both taking the view that the only hypothesis scientifically possible is the primacy of international law.

Verdross raises one fundamental objection against the theoretical pos-sibility of either hypothesis. If international law derives its validity from constitutional norms, then it must necessarily cease to be in force once the constitution from which it draws its authority disappears. But nothing is more certain than that the validity of international law is not merely dependent on change or abolition of constitutions or on revolutions, but continues to operate despite alterations in the state normative order.

It is true that Kelsen inclines to the primacy of international law for objective (and therefore scientific) reasons. He says that the two hypotheses are closely linked with the philosophical theories of knowl-edge, the difference between them lying in the difference between the objective and subjective conceptions of knowledge.[32] A subjective con-ception necessarily results in a denial of the existence of law and conse-

---

[30] Kelsen (n.27 above), 313–14.

[31] Georges Scelle, *Précis du droit des gens* (Paris: Recueil Sirey, 1932–4), vol. I.

[32] See Kelsen (n.27 above), at 321–3.

quently of juridical science, for law exists only by reason of its objective validity. These statements are hard to reconcile with his notion of a metajuridical choice.

Yet no one has been more critical than Kelsen of the hypothesis of state primacy. In so far as it receives support today, that hypothesis bears testimony to the tenacious influence of the auto-limitation doctrine. We have a more violent form of that doctrine above, but its weakness is no less obvious here. Since it simply amounts to the statement that only municipal law can bind the subjects and functionaries of a state, auto-limitation fails to explain how international law, a system external to state law, can bind them. Even treaties which, because of the element of assent involved, seem to give support to the thesis of state primacy are really binding in virtue of those norms of international law which lay down that upon ratification treaty obligations become effective. Ratification is an act-condition authorized by an objective norm of international law, and the fact that it is also obligatory under the constitution of the state gives that provision force only as a declaratory statement of international law. Indeed, if the binding force of treaties rested solely on the constitution, it would follow that they cease to be obligatory if the constitution is changed. But treaties are regarded as binding no less after than before revolutions.[33]

Reduced to its lowest terms, the doctrine of state primacy is a denial of international law as law, and an affirmation of international anarchy. International law becomes merely that portion of the law of the state which governs its relations vis-à-vis other states. The juridical status of other countries in relation to a particular state is made to turn not on objective norms, but on a basic norm of that state order recognizing the existence of other states as normative systems. The thesis of state primacy thus raises fundamental inconsistencies of principle which in the last resort can only be reconciled by saying that international law as law does not exist.

The primacy of international law is the more scientific hypothesis because the more empirically justified. When we touch on such problems as the entry of new states into the international society, the disappearance of old states, and revolutions or transformations of legal

---

[33] See Declaration made at the London Conference of 1831, which decided that Belgium should be an independent and neutralized state and effected its separation from the Kingdom of the Netherlands. The relevant passage is contained in the Protocol of the Conference, dated 19 February, 1831, in *State Papers*, 17 (1830–1), 780:

The deliberations of the Ministers have led them to recognize the necessity . . . of recalling here the basic principle of public law, which is continually applied in the acts of the London Conference. According to this fundamental principle, treaties do not lose their force despite internal constitutional changes. (*D'après ce principe d'un ordre supérieur, les traités ne perdent pas leur puissance quels que soient les changements qui interviennent dans l'organisation intérieure des Peuples.*)

orders, we are at crucial theoretical points. The generally accepted principles seem to be these. International law binds new states without their consent, and if consent is expressed, it is only declaratory of a juridical situation already in existence. Once the new state steps into the international community, it becomes subject to the norms which bind other members of that society and accepts the obligations as well as the benefits of international organization. In the same way, once a revolution is successful, modification or transformation of the constitution proceeds within the ambit of norms of international law, for these alterations to the internal legal order are in the ultimate resort based on the norm of international law that a successful revolution gives a title to alter the constitution. In the interim, international law continues to bind individuals and to create obligations for the new state once its existence is established *de facto*. The sole scientific construction justified on a consideration of these principles is that state law is conditioned by international law.

How far is the so-called sovereignty and independence of states affected? Positive law in the form of Article 15(8) of the League Covenant seems to recognize a field quite outside the operation of international law:

> If the dispute between the parties is claimed by one of them, and is found by the Council to arise out of *a matter which by international law is solely within the domestic jurisdiction of that party*, the Council shall so report, and shall make no recommendation as to its settlement.

According to the opinions of some, this article envisages a field in which the state has absolute liberty of action, which is free from rules laid down by international law. The truth, however, is that the exclusive competence of a state extends only to those matters as to which international law empowers the state to exercise unfettered discretion. This is confirmed by the express language of Article 15(8) of the Covenant, which speaks of matters left by international law to the domestic jurisdiction of the state.[34] The exclusive jurisdiction is incapable of precise definition at any moment, but it naturally depends on the development of international organization whether a wide or narrow discretion is given to states within the limits of international law. Thus, although it is true that questions of nationality fall within the exclusive domain,[35] this does not preclude the validity of a norm of international law authorizing states to legislate only in accordance with fair and reasonable standards. We are

---

[34] On the question generally, see Nicolas-Socrate Politis, 'Le problème des limitations de la souveraineté et la théorie de l'abus des droits dans les rapports internationaux', *Recueil des cours*, 6 (1925), 1–121, at 43–6; J.L. Brierly, 'The Shortcomings of International Law', *British Year Book of International Law*, 5 (1924), 4–16, at 6–8.

[35] Permanent Court of International Justice, Series B, No. 4, p. 24.

led back again to the earlier conception of the sovereignty of states—the special competence which they possess by virtue of international law.

IV. THE THEORY OF FUNCTIONAL NORMS

At this stage it is desirable to summarize the results of our enquiry. We have rejected dualism and ascertained that the only construction justified is that of monism. Writers have been divided between monism of the state order and monism of the international order, and an examination of the issue has shown that the latter view is more scientifically correct. There is one question that we have not yet considered. When we speak of the primacy of international law, do we mean all international law, or are we referring only to a special group of its norms? Here is a matter that calls for some discussion, and it may be suggested at the outset that the truer view is that we mean only the primacy of a specific part of international law. We shall begin by considering the analogy between international law and the legal system of the federal state.

The analogy is safe. The federal state is a perfect example of 'normative hierarchy': from the fundamental norm that the constitution is to be obeyed radiate the federal and provincial norms that constitute the entire legal network. The federal legal order is monistic in character, and federal law conditions provincial law in the same way as international law conditions state law.

One necessary distinction in the federal system is that between federal constitutional law and federal law *simpliciter*. The connection between the two is one of dependence, constitutional law embodying *inter alia* the various powers and authorities that sanction the process of federal law-making whether legislative or judicial. Now provincial law is in the same dependent position with respect to constitutional law as federal law is. True, the constitution may provide that federal legislation in certain matters is to prevail over inconsistent provincial legislation,[36] but within these limits provincial law and federal law stand exactly in the same dependent relation to constitutional law. True, again, federal law has validity extending over a wider area, but with respect to dependence on the constitution, provincial law and federal law are on an equal footing. The federal legal order may therefore be described as a normative pyramid with constitutional law at the apex, and with federal law and provincial law at each end of the base-line.

It would only be natural to expect the same arrangement to be reflected in the international legal order. International law accordingly consists of two types of norms:

[36] For example, Constitution of Australia, sec. 109.

(a) functional or constitutional norms;
(b) norms dependent on these;

a dichotomy identical with that considered above.

Analogy with federal law helps us to determine what are, and what are not, functional norms. For instance, one quality which federal law and international law have in common is the 'mediacy' or indirect validity of their norms. Thus, it is a normal matter for federal legislation to vest in provincial courts federal jurisdiction with respect to its provisions, and these courts in exercising this jurisdiction act as federal organs. International law supplies fuller illustration of this mediate operation of legal norms, since to be effective it generally has to work through the organs of states empowered to act under its authority. Article 23(a) of the League Covenant is a notable example:

Subject to and in accordance with the provisions of international conventions existing or hereafter to be agreed upon, the members of the League:

(a) will endeavour to secure and maintain fair and humane conditions of labour
     for men, women, and children, both in their own countries and in all countries
     to which their commercial and industrial relations extend, and for that pur-
     pose will establish and maintain the necessary international organisations.

The states' members of the International Labour Organisation, the insti-tution set up to achieve this objective, exercise authority only as organs of international law.

The question now is, does this particular class of norms stand on the same footing as the functional norms of international law? The answer would appear to be in the negative. The true position is that there is a specific delegation of certain matters by virtue of a superior functional norm of international law. The same process is often reversed, state law itself delegating to international law authority in specific matters. As to the federal systems, the position is clearly illustrated by the Constitution of Australia. Section 51 gives the federal parliament power to legislate 'with respect to', *inter alia*,

matters referred to the Parliament of the Commonwealth by the Parliament or Parliaments of any State or States, but so that the law shall extend only to States by whose Parliaments the matter is referred, or which afterwards adopt the law.

And an illuminating example is provided by Article 23 of the League Covenant:

Subject to and in accordance with the provisions of international conventions existing or hereafter to be agreed upon, the members of the League:

(d) will entrust the League with the general supervision of the trade in arms and
     ammunition with the countries in which the control of the traffic is necessary
     in the common interest.

The ultimate conclusion we are led to is that primacy in the monistic legal order pertains solely to the functional norms of international law, and it is there alone that Kelsen's initial hypothesis, his '*Grundnorm*' is to be found. These functional norms are reached *inductively* from the structure of the international community and the shrinking legal competences of the state. The process is somewhat different from that in ordinary federal systems—the creation of a written constitution, which establishes the respective powers *inter se* of the federal state and the provinces. The international community is the result of a long historical growth, and it is natural for these functional norms to reflect that slow, empirical development. Something of this nature appears to be envisaged in the famous Judgment No. 10 of the Permanent Court of International Justice (the *Lotus* case), which seems to accept the principle that the competences of states do not derive from international law, but that international law confines itself to limiting them in certain directions. At page 18 the Court said:

International law governs relations between independent states. The rules of law binding upon states emanate from their own free will as expressed in conventions or by usages generally accepted as expressing principles of law and established in order to regulate the relations between these co-existing independent communities or with a view to the achievement of common aims. *Restriction upon the independence of states cannot therefore be presumed.*

At page 19 the Court also said:

All that can be required of a state is that it should not overstep the limits which international law places upon its jurisdiction; within these limits, its title to exercise jurisdiction rests in its sovereignty.

These principles are, however, statements of historical fact rather than analyses of an existing juridical situation. Similar historical statements are perfectly appropriate as to almost any legal system, but legal theory in the realistic sense that we understand it can only concern itself with synoptic descriptions of present fact.

Theory has shown that international law today forms part of a legal hierarchy embracing numbers of normative systems united by their ultimate dependence on those functional norms which may well be termed the international constitution. It is in this constitution that the initial hypothesis or *Ursprungsnorm* of both international law and municipal law is to be sought. Juridical monism alone is consistent with empirical realities as well as logical and theoretical requirements. Monism may be regarded as conditioned by the sociological fact of a world growing more and more interconnected, so that it becomes clear that the individual really is at the root of the unity of all law. Hersch Lauterpacht has well said:[37]

---

[37] Lauterpacht (n.12 above), 431.

It is true that international law is made for states, and not states for international law, but it is true only in the sense that the state is made for human beings and not human beings for the state.

This is a consideration which it is well to bear in mind, but it does not affect the thesis of this article—that international law and municipal law together constitute a normative order possessing an objective unity perceptible by methods of scientific analysis.

30

Kelsen's Doctrine of the Unity of Law*

H.L.A. HART

INTRODUCTION

In this essay I propose to examine one of the most striking doctrines expounded by Hans Kelsen in his *General Theory of Law and State* and his more recent *Pure Theory of Law*. Its central positive contention is that all valid laws necessarily form a single system,[1] and its central negative contention is that valid laws cannot conflict.[2] This is the strongest form of Kelsen's doctrine of the unity of law; but arguments are also to be found in Kelsen's books which support a weaker form of this doctrine, namely, that though it is not necessarily true that all valid laws form a single system and cannot conflict, it just is the case that they do form a single system and do not conflict. For Kelsen, this doctrine of the unity of law yields certain conclusions concerning the possible or actual relationships between international law and all systems of municipal

---

* *Editors' note*: Hart's essay first appeared in *Ethics and Social Justice*, ed. Howard E. Kiefer and Milton K. Munitz (Albany: New York State University Press, 1968), 171–99, and was reprinted in Hart, *Essays in Jurisprudence and Philosophy* (Oxford: Clarendon Press, 1983), 309–42.

Along with the English translation of the Second Edition of Hans Kelsen's *Reine Rechtslehre* (see the Table of Abbreviations, at *PTL*), Hart also used the French translation, *Théorie Pure de Droit*, trans. Charles Eisenmann (Paris: Dalloz, 1962), which he described as 'fuller and generally more accurate' than the English version. In the present printing of the essay, Hart's few French-language quotations have been traced back to the original German text, and translated anew into English.

[1] 'It is logically not possible to assume that simultaneously valid norms belong to different mutually independent systems', *GTLS* 363. See also *PTL* § 43(a) (at p. 328).

[2] Kelsen in *GTLS* and *PTL* regards conflicting norms as 'contradictory' (see § II below) and so expresses his doctrine that valid laws cannot conflict by saying, '[t]wo norms which by their significance contradict and hence logically exclude one another cannot be simultaneously assumed to be valid', *GTLS* 375, and see *PTL* § 16 (at p. 74). Note that from *PTL* § 4(e), at p. 18, end of second para., the translator has omitted the crucial passage appearing in the original German text, 'One can regard one norm or the other as valid, but not both at the same time.' *RR 2* § 4(e) (p. 18).

law.[3] On the strong version of his theory international law and systems of municipal law necessarily form one single system,[4] and there can be no conflicts between the laws of international law and municipal law.[5] On the weaker version it just is the case that all these laws form a single system and there are in fact no conflicts between them.[6] Kelsen develops similar, though not identical, views concerning the relationships between law and morals. He does not however contend that valid legal and moral norms either necessarily or in fact form a single system. Instead he argues that from one point of view there are only legal norms and from another point of view there are only moral norms; that these two points of view are exclusive of each other; and that they are exhaustive, so there is no third point of view from which there are both valid legal and valid moral norms.[7]

I believe, and shall attempt to show, that Kelsen's doctrine of the unity of all valid laws and his conclusions concerning the possible and actual relationships between international law and systems of municipal law are mistaken. But I think for a number of different reasons that much is to be learned from examining his doctrine. The effort of criticism of these difficult doctrines is, I think, rewarding because it brings to light at least two things. First, it shows that there is a good deal of unfinished business for analytical jurisprudence still to tackle, and this unfinished business includes a still much needed clarification of the meaning of the common assertion that laws belong to or constitute a *system* of laws, and an account of the criteria for determining the system to which given laws belong, and of what individuates one system from another. Secondly, the examination of certain features of Kelsen's doctrine takes us to the frontiers at least of the logic of norms and their interrelationships, and perhaps points beyond the frontiers to the need for something more comprehensive than the present familiar forms of deontic logic.

I shall discuss the main issues which I have mentioned in the following order. In section I, I shall consider Kelsen's theory of the unity of international law and municipal law, dealing first with the weaker version and then with the stronger version. In section II, I shall consider the 'no conflict' theory of international law and municipal law, dealing first with the strong version and then with the weaker version. In section III, I shall attempt to draw some morals from these criticisms of Kelsen's theories that may help in the construction of a more satisfactory analysis

---

[3] The unity of international law and municipal law in one system is called by Kelsen an 'epistemological postulate', *GTLS* 373, and to comprehend them as such is 'inevitable', *PTL* § 43(c) (p. 332), and see *PTL* § 43(a) (at p. 328).

[4] *PTL* § 43(a) (p. 329).   [5] *PTL* § 43(a) (p. 328).

[6] *PTL* § 43(b) (pp. 330–1). For the same doctrine in a different terminology, see *GTLS*, at 371–2.

[7] See *GTLS*, at 373–6, *PTL* § 43(a) (at p. 329).

of the notion of a legal system, and of the nature of the criteria determining its membership, and of the principles of individuation of legal systems.

I shall not, in this paper, discuss Kelsen's doctrine concerning the possibility of simultaneously valid legal and moral norms, and of their conflict. I omit this topic not only because I have discussed some aspects of it elsewhere,[8] but also because, though Kelsen repeats this doctrine in his latest book, he neither repeats his previous arguments for it nor adduces new ones.

I. THE UNITY OF INTERNATIONAL LAW AND MUNICIPAL LAW

A. Monistic and Pluralistic Theory.

Kelsen calls his own theory that international law and municipal law form one system a 'monistic' theory, and contrasts it with the traditional view that they are independent systems, which he terms a 'pluralistic' theory.[9] It is however a complication of Kelsen's doctrine that there are two possible forms of monistic theory:[10] 'two different ways of comprehending all legal phenomena as parts of a single system'.[11] For according to Kelsen it is possible to structure or arrange the components of the single system which comprehends both international law and all systems of municipal law in either of two ways. One of these ways ('primacy of international law') treats international law (or, more accurately, the basic norm of international law) as the foundation of a single unified system, and all the rest, including all systems of municipal law, as subordinate parts of the system ultimately deriving their validity from this foundation. The other way ('primacy of municipal law') treats one (any *one*) system of municipal law (or, more accurately, its basic norm) as the foundation of a single unified system, and all the rest, including international law and all other systems of municipal law, as subordinate parts of the single system deriving their validity from its foundation. The choice between these two alternative points of view (primacy of international law or primacy of municipal law) is, according to Kelsen, a matter of political ideology, not law, and is guided by ethical and political considerations.[12] However, the contents of both international law and municipal law are totally unaffected by this choice: the legal rights and obligations of states and individuals remain the same whichever of the

---

8 'Kelsen Visited' [in this volume, ch. 4].
9 *GTLS* 363–4; *PTL* § 43(a) (pp. 328–9).
10 *GTLS* 376–83; *PTL* §43(c)(d) (pp. 333–9).   11 *GTLS* 387.   12 *GTLS* 387–8.

two alternative systems is adopted.[13] I shall not in this essay question this complication of Kelsen's theory (though in fact I think it eminently questionable), for it is in fact not relevant to the main monistic doctrine of the necessary unity of all law, and Kelsen's arguments for the monistic theory of the relations of international law and municipal law are unaffected by his view that there is a choice between according primacy to international law or to a system of municipal law.

Kelsen claims that an analysis of the actual systems of international law and municipal law shows that they form a single system. But this claim rests on a special interpretation of the legal phenomena which seems to me, for the reasons I give below, profoundly mistaken. But before I examine this interpretation it may be helpful to characterize in general terms, with the aid of a simple example, the kind of error which in my view infects Kelsen's interpretation. Suppose the question arose whether I, Hart, wrote this paper in obedience to someone's order that I should write it. Let us assume that evidence is forthcoming that just before I sat down to write this paper the Vice-Chancellor of Oxford University dispatched to me a document purporting to order me to write a paper on Kelsen's Doctrine of the Unity of Law. It is plain that whether or not I wrote this paper in obedience to that order could not be settled by comparing the contents of the order ('Hart: write a paper on Kelsen's Doctrine of the Unity of Law') with a true description of my later conduct ('Hart wrote a paper on Kelsen's Doctrine of the Unity of Law'). This comparison would indeed show correspondence between the content of the order and the description of my conduct, in that the action-description contained in the order is applicable to my subsequent conduct. But though in order to establish that I did write this paper in obedience to this order it would be *necessary* to show this correspondence between the content of the order and the description of my conduct, plainly this would not be *sufficient*. It would also be necessary to establish certain facts that have to do not with the content of the order, but with the circumstances surrounding the issue and reception of the order, involving consideration of such questions as the following. Did Hart receive the Vice-Chancellor's missive? Did he recognize it as an order? Did he write the paper in order to comply with this order? Did anyone else give such an order? If so, whose order did Hart intend to obey? A 'pure theory' of imperatives that ignored such facts and circumstances surrounding the issue and reception of orders, and restricted itself to the characterization of the relationships between the contents of orders and the description of actions, would necessarily be incompetent to settle the question whether any person had obeyed a particular order. However,

---

[13] *GTLS* 387–8; *PTL* § 43(d) (pp. 340–2).

since the correspondence relationship between content and action-description is a necessary condition of obedience, the theory would be competent to identify cases where orders had not been obeyed; though it is important to remember that 'not obeyed' is not the same as 'disobeyed'.

I will try to show that in somewhat the same way, though not precisely the same way, the Pure Theory of Law suffers from the defects of my imaginary pure theory of imperatives, for it concentrates too exclusively on the content of laws and pays too little attention to circumstances that concern the making or origin of laws (rather than what laws say) and whether they are recognized as authoritative and by whom. When we have laws that explicitly or implicitly refer to other laws, or their existence or validity, we cannot determine from these relationships alone whether they belong to the same or different systems. This depends on facts concerning the making and recognition of laws. The Pure Theory of Law is too pure to attend to such facts; and, as I shall attempt to show, by treating what are at best necessary conditions as if they were sufficient conditions of laws belonging to the same system, the Pure Theory reaches false conclusions as to the unity of international and municipal law. With this general characterization of the type of error which I think is inherent in the content-obsessed Pure Theory of Law, let me turn to the examination of Kelsen's interpretation of the legal phenomena.

B. The Completion Relationship between Laws.

Kelsen attacks with some force a crude and misleading dichotomy between international law and municipal law. International law, it is sometimes said, imposes obligations and confers rights on states, whereas municipal law imposes obligations and confers rights on individuals. This distinction is often used to support the pluralistic theory. It is said that international law and municipal law are independent legal systems because they regulate different subject-matters: international law regulates the behaviour of states and municipal law regulates the behaviour of individuals. Kelsen criticizes this argument for pluralism in two ways.[14] He shows that there are rules of international law, no doubt exceptional, that apply directly to individuals in the same way as the rules of municipal law. Examples of these are the laws against piracy, and the rules of international law making punishable acts of illegitimate warfare, that is, hostile acts on the part of individuals not belonging to the armed forces of the country. But quite apart from these exceptional cases, Kelsen maintains that if we understand the logical structure of

[14] *GTLS* 342–8; *PTL* § 42(d) (pp. 324–8).

such expressions as 'the state' as a technique or method of referring indirectly to individuals identified by certain legal rules, and lay aside the misconception of a state as an entity over and above the individuals that compose it, it is apparent that laws which purport to apply directly to states in fact apply to individuals, though the manner of their application is indirect. Hence the description of the rules of international law as 'applying to states' should not be construed as contrasting with 'applying to individuals'; it is to be contrasted with applying *directly* to individuals, that is, without the aid of, or supplementation by, other rules identifying the individuals to whom the first rules are applicable.[15] The rules of international law, according to Kelsen, when they purport to apply to states are 'incomplete': they themselves specify only *what* is to be done or not to be done, but they leave or, as Kelsen says, 'delegate' the identification of the individuals who are or are not to do these things to the rules of municipal law,[16] and the latter rules, identifying the individuals, 'complete' the rules of international law.

Kelsen illustrates this completion of international law by the rules of municipal law with the following simple example.

There is a time-honoured rule of common international law to the effect that war must not be begun without a previous formal declaration of war. The Third Hague Convention of 1907 codified this rule in the stipulation (art. I) that hostilities 'must not commence without a previous and unequivocal warning, which shall take the form either of a declaration of war giving reasons, or of an ultimatum with a conditional declaration of war'.

This norm states only that a declaration of war has to be delivered, not by whom—that is to say, by which individual as organ of the State—it has to be done. Most constitutions empower the head of the State to declare war. The Constitution of the United States (art. I, sec. 8) says that 'the Congress shall have Power to declare War'. By thus determining the personal element, the American constitution completes the norm of international law just mentioned.

The characteristic of international law that it 'obligates States only' consists merely in the fact that its norms generally determine only the material element, leaving the determination of the personal element to national law.[17]

Let us call the relationship between a set of rules, one of which leaves to the other or others the identification of the individuals to whom the first applies, the 'completion relationship', and let us call the set of rules so related 'a completing set'. Kelsen's insistence that many rules of international law and municipal law are related by the completion relationship is in many ways illuminating, and I shall not quarrel with his use of this idea in attacking the crude and confused theory that international law and municipal law are independent or different systems because

---

[15] See *GTLS*, at 342, *PTL* § 42(d) (at pp. 325, 327).
[16] See *GTLS*, at 348–9, *PTL* § 42(d) (at p. 325).   [17] *GTLS* 343.

international law applies to states and municipal law to individuals. It is however very important to appreciate that the fact that the completion relationship holds between certain rules is not itself sufficient to show that the rules between which it holds belong to one and the same system: For unless it can be independently shown that the very idea of the existence of different systems of legal rules is illusory, and that there is only *one* system of rules, it seems quite clear that the completion relationship may hold either between the rules of the same system or between rules of different systems. It is necessary to stress this fact because it may be obscured by Kelsen's frequent (and, again, often illuminating) insistence on the similarity between the relationships holding on the one hand between the rules of international law and municipal law, and on the other hand between a statute of municipal law and the by-laws or regulations of a corporation.[18] This similarity, obscured by the personifying or reifying terminology of 'state' and 'corporation', resides in the following facts. When a rule of international law purports to impose some duty directly on a state it is in fact indirectly imposing those duties on the individuals identified by the state's municipal system, and those individuals' actions and obligations are imputed to the state. Similarly, when a statute of a municipal legal system imposes some duty on a corporation it indirectly imposes that duty on the individuals (officers or members of the corporation) identified by the internal by-laws or regulations of the corporation. Both cases thus exemplify the completion relationship.

The relation between the total legal order constituting the State, the so-called law of the State or national legal order, and the juristic person of a corporation is the relation between two legal orders, a total and a partial legal order, between the law of the State and the by-laws of the corporation. To be more specific, it is a case of delegation.[19]

In considering this interesting parallel between the relationships of municipal statutes to corporation by-laws on the one hand and international law to municipal law on the other, it is important not to lose sight of the fact that when a rule of municipal law, for example, an English statute, imposes obligations on a corporation incorporated under English law, the regulations or by-laws of the corporation which identify the individuals who, as officers or members of the corporation, are to execute this duty derive their validity from other English statutes determining the manner in which corporation regulations may be made and limiting their content. As Kelsen says, the by-laws constituting the corporation are created by a legal transaction determined by the national legal order. Hence, the statute imposing the obligation on the

---

[18] See *GTLS*, at 349, *PTL* § 42(d) (at p. 325); see also *PTL* § 33(e) (at p. 179).
[19] *GTLS* 100.

corporation, and the earlier statutes under which the company regulations were made, belong to the same legal system quite independently of the completion relationship holding between the statute imposing the obligation on the corporation and its regulations. These statutes and by-laws all belong to the same system because they satisfy the criteria recognized by English courts as identifying the laws which they are to enforce. Of course, an English statute might impose obligations on a foreign corporation, for example, a Swedish corporation. Here, too, the completion relationship would hold between the English statute and the regulations of the Swedish corporation, for the latter would identify those individuals who as officers or members of the corporation were bound to execute the duty. But the regulations of the Swedish corporation which would thus complete the English statute derive their validity from a statute of the Swedish legislature determining the manner in which Swedish corporation regulations are to be made. This Swedish statute exists as part not of English law but of Swedish law, and so existed before the enactment of the English statute imposing obligations on the Swedish corporation, whereas in the case where the English statute imposes obligations on the English corporation the regulations of the corporation existed as part of English law.

It is perhaps worth observing that completion relationships between laws of the same or different systems are not confined to cases where we speak of abstract juristic entities such as 'state' or 'corporation'. Thus an English statute might confer certain rights, for example, the right to vote, on individuals whom it might define only as persons liable to pay certain rates and taxes under some other English statute, or it might exempt from taxation certain foreigners if they are liable under the law of their own country to certain similar taxes. In the first case the completion relationship would hold between laws of the same system; in the second case it holds between laws of different systems.

C. The Relationship of Validating Purport.

In spite of some ambiguity of language,[20] Kelsen does not, I think, conceive of the completion relationship between laws as in itself sufficient to show that they belong to the same system, for he writes:

Since the international legal order not only requires the national legal orders as a necessary complementation, but also determines their spheres of validity in all respects, international and national law form one inseparable whole.[21]

The words which I have quoted introduce Kelsen's central argument for the monistic theory and, as I believe, his central mistake. The argument,

---

[20] Notably *GTLS*, at 349; and *PTL* § 42(d) (at p. 325).   [21] *GTLS* 351.

reduced to its essentials, is this. International law contains among its rules one that Kelsen terms the 'principle of effectiveness', which 'determines' or 'is the reason for' the validity of the national legal orders and their territorial and temporal spheres of validity. The contents of this principle of effectiveness are spelt out by Kelsen in his latest formulation of it, as follows:

A norm of general international law authorises an individual or a group of individuals, on the basis of an effective constitution, to create and apply as a legitimate government a normative coercive order. That norm thus legitimises this coercive order for the territory of its actual effectiveness as a valid legal order and the community constituted by this coercive order as a 'state' in the sense of international law.[22]

Because the principle of effectiveness thus legitimizes or validates the separate coercive orders effective in different territories, international law, to which the principle of effectiveness belongs, forms a single system together with the various systems of municipal law, which it legitimizes or validates. It forms with them, Kelsen says, 'one inseparable whole'.[23] In considering this argument it is important to understand precisely what in Kelsen's view is the relationship between the principle of effectiveness and the various municipal legal systems which it is said to legitimize, or the validity of which it is said to determine. The principle of effectiveness says that other rules of a certain description (that is, roughly, coercive rules effective in certain territories) are valid; and it is a fact that there are certain rules (the actual systems of municipal law) that satisfy this description. Let us call this relationship the relationship of validating purport. I shall argue that what was said above about the completion relationship applies also to the relationship of validating purport: it is not sufficient in order to establish that two rules form parts of a single system to show that one of them provides that rules of a certain description satisfied by the other are valid. I shall also argue that when such a relationship holds between two rules it is dangerously misleading to express this fact by stating, *without stressing a very important qualification*, that one rule 'determines the validity' of the other or is 'the reason for its validity'.

Kelsen's argument depends on the use he makes of the fact that the relationship of validating purport holds between the principle of effectiveness considered as a rule of international law and the rules of municipal legal systems. The inadequacy of this argument and also the character of the important qualification I have just mentioned can be seen from the following wild hypothetical example. Suppose the British Parliament (or *mutatis mutandis*, Congress) passes an Act (the Soviet Laws Validity Act,

[22] *PTL* § 34(h) (p. 215); see also *PTL* § 43(d) (at pp. 336–40), *GTLS*, at 121.
[23] *GTLS* 351.

1970) which purports to validate the law of the Soviet Union by providing that the laws currently effective in Soviet territory, including those relating to the competence of legislative and judicial authorities, shall be valid. The enactment of this Act by Parliament (or Congress) would not be a reason for saying that English (or American) law together with Soviet law formed one legal system, or for using *sans phrase* any of the Kelsenian expressions such as that Soviet law 'derives its validity' from English law or that English law was 'the reason for the validity' of Soviet law. The reason for refusing to assent to these propositions is surely clear and compelling: it is that the courts and other law-enforcing agencies in Soviet territory do not, save in certain special circumstances,[24] recognize the operations of the British (or American) legislature as criteria for identifying the laws that they are to enforce, and so they do not recognize the Soviet Laws Validity Act, though a valid English (or American) statute, as in any way determining or other-wise affecting the validity of Soviet law in Soviet territory. It is true indeed that the relationship of validating purport holds between the Act and the laws made by the Soviet legislature, which the Soviet courts do recognize; but the division of laws into distinct legal systems cuts across the relation-ship of validating purport, for that relationship, like the completion rela-tionship examined above, may hold either between laws of different systems or between laws of the same system.

The important qualification that should be made in drawing any con-clusion from the existence of the relationship of validating purport between rules is perhaps obvious. On the passing of the Soviet Laws Validity Act it would be right to say that *for the purposes* of English law, or according to English law, Soviet laws were validated by or derive their validity from an English statute, and the effect of this would be that English courts would apply Soviet law in adjudicating upon any transac-tion or conduct to which the Soviet authorities would apply Soviet law. The Soviet Laws Validity Act would make Soviet law part of English law for such purposes. But the two pairs of questions:

A1. Do English law and Soviet law form parts of a single system of law?
A2. Does Soviet law derive its validity from English law?

and:

B1. Does English law treat Soviet law as forming part of a single sys-tem with itself?
B2. Is Soviet law valid according to English law?

are questions of different kinds. The first pair are not questions that con-cern merely the content of laws and so are to be settled by considering

---

[24] On cases involving a 'foreign element', see § IV below, at numbered para. 3.

what laws say; whereas the second pair are questions concerning the content of laws and are settled in that way.

There is the same difference in kind between the pairs of questions:

C1. Do international law and municipal law form a single system?
C2. Does municipal law derive its validity from international law?

and:

D1. Does international law treat (for example, by its principle of effectiveness) municipal law as forming part of a single system with itself?
D2. Is municipal law valid according to international law (for example, through its principle of effectiveness)?

The Pure Theory blurs the distinctions between these very different types of question; it does so because it concentrates too much on what laws of validating purport *say* about other laws, and pays too little attention to matters that do not concern the content of laws but their mode of recognition. The Pure Theory, therefore, has a juristic Midas touch, which transmutes all questions about laws and their relationship into questions of the content of law or questions concerning what laws say; but the touch is perverse, for not all questions are of this kind.

I conclude that the arguments in support of the weaker version of Kelsen's version of the doctrine of the unity of international law and municipal law fail. This is not to say that arguments different from Kelsen's might not succeed in establishing the weaker version of his thesis—at least up to a point. For whether or not international law and the law of a state form one system depends on the manner in which and extent to which a given state recognizes international law. If in cases where international law conflicts with the law of the state the courts of the state treat the state law as invalid or overridden by international law, this would be a good reason for saying that international law and the law of that state form parts of a single system of law—or at any rate it would resemble the reason for saying that the law of a state of the United States and federal law form parts of a single system. But Kelsen's arguments fail because the fact that the relationship of validating purport exists between the principle of effectiveness, treated as a rule of international law, (or any other rules of international law purporting to determine the validity of municipal law) and the rules of municipal law does not show that the latter derive their validity from the former, and does not show that 'pluralists' are wrong in denying that international law and municipal law form a single system.[25]

[25] I consider later the possibility of *introducing* a meaning for 'legal system' such that the mere existence of the relationship of validating purport between laws is sufficient to

I now turn to the examination of the stronger form of Kelsen's thesis that international law and municipal law necessarily form one system.

D. The Necessary Unity of all Valid Law.

Very little by way of argument is to be found in support of Kelsen's stronger thesis that all valid law *necessarily* forms a single system, with its corollary that international law and municipal law necessarily constitute such a system. Kelsen asserts that this is a 'postulate of legal theory'.[26]

The unity of national law and international law is an epistemological postulate. A jurist who accepts both sets of valid norms must try to comprehend them as parts of one harmonious system.[27]

This postulate is frequently referred to in the terminology of logical necessity.

It is logically not possible to assume that simultaneously valid norms belong to different, mutually independent systems.[28]

For these assertions I have identified only two arguments. Neither need occupy us long. The first argument reduces to the contention that all that is law forms a single system because there is a form of knowledge ('jurisprudence'[29] or 'legal cognition'[30]) or a science of law which studies both international law and municipal law as falling under the single description 'valid laws' and thus represents 'its object' as a unity. Kelsen expresses this argument in the following words:

[The] 'pluralistic' construction . . . is untenable if both the norms of international law and those of the national legal orders are to be considered as simultaneously valid legal norms. This view implies already the epistemological postulate: to understand all law in one system . . . as one closed whole. Jurisprudence subsumes the norms regulating the relations between states, called international law, as well as the norms of the national legal orders under one and the same category of law. In so doing it tries to present its object as a unity.[31]

---

constitute the laws of a single system. This would not of course refute the conventional pluralist, for it is not in this sense of 'system' that he asserts that international law and municipal law are separate systems.

[26] *GTLS* 373.   [27] Ibid.   [28] *GTLS* 363.   [29] *PTL* § 43(a) (p. 328).

[30] *RR 2* § 43(a) (p. 329, para. 2, at line 12): 'legal cognition' ('*juristische Erkenntnis*') [not translated as such in *PTL*].

[31] *PTL* § 43(a) (p. 328). Professor J.L. Mackie has pointed out to me that Kelsen's claim that there can only be one system of valid laws resembles Kant's claim that there is only one space. 'For . . . we can represent to ourselves only one space; and if we speak of diverse spaces, we mean only parts of one and the same unique space' (Kant, *CPR* A25). I have the impression that underlying Kelsen's theory of law there is the *assumption* that there is a single 'normative space' which must be describable by a consistent set of 'rules in a descriptive sense'. See *PTL*, at § 43(a)–(d) (pp. 328–44).

Surely we might as well attempt to deduce from the existence of the history of warfare or the science of strategy that all wars are one or all armies are one.

The second argument really shows that Kelsen's argument for the necessary unity of valid law is dependent on his thesis that there can be no conflicts between valid laws, for he says:

If there should be two actually different systems of norms, mutually independent in their validity . . . both of which are related to the same object (in having the same sphere of validity), insoluble logical contradiction between them could not be excluded. The norm of one system may prescribe conduct *A* for a certain person, under a certain condition, at a certain time and place. The norm of the other system may prescribe, under the same conditions and for the same person, conduct non-*A*. This situation is impossible for the cognition of norms.[32]

Of course this does not deal with the possibility that there might be two legal systems simultaneously effective in different territories in which the possibility of conflicts is excluded because the constitution of each system secured that what Kelsen calls 'the sphere of validity' of the laws of each system should be different. The laws of the two systems might, for example, according to their constitutions apply to conduct in different territories. Kelsen asserts[33] that such a limitation would have to be imposed by a single superior law to which both systems with limited scope would be subordinate and with which they would form a single system. But he does not support this assertion with any arguments, and it is difficult to see why it should not just be the case that two communities chose independently to adopt constitutions limiting the scope of the laws in this way. However, the argument from the alleged impossibility of conflict, though it does not cover this case, remains Kelsen's only remaining argument for the necessary unity of all valid law.[34] I examine the thesis that conflict between valid laws is impossible in the next section.

II. THE 'NO CONFLICTS' THEORY[35]

Kelsen claims that in spite of appearances there really are no conflicts between international law and municipal law. He admits that if there

---

[32] *Phil. Fds.* § 13 (p. 408).　　　　[33] Ibid. § 13 (pp. 407–8).

[34] Quite apart from its failure to cover the case mentioned, this argument for the necessary unity of all valid law in one system is incomplete, even if conflict between valid laws is (contrary to the argument of the next section) admitted to be logically impossible. To complete the argument it would have to be shown that what Kelsen calls 'insoluble logical contradictions', which he thinks might arise in the case of two independent systems, could not arise in the case of one system.

[35] This section is concerned with Kelsen's views on conflicts as expounded in his books *GTLS* and *PTL*. In a later essay on 'Derogation' [see the Table of Abbreviations], Kelsen

were such conflicts the monistic theory that international law and municipal law form one system could not be sustained: indeed he says the absence of conflict is the 'negative criterion'[36] of the unity of international law and municipal law in a single system. If, however, there were such conflicts the result would be, according to Kelsen, not that international law and municipal law would constitute separate systems of valid laws, as the conventional 'pluralist' holds; instead we would have a choice between treating international law as valid while ignoring any conflicting rules of municipal law, or treating a system of municipal law as valid while ignoring any conflicting rules of international law. This is, according to Kelsen, actually the position with regard to laws and morality: when their norms conflict we have a choice between treating the legal rules as valid, ignoring conflicting moral norms, or treating moral norms as valid, ignoring any conflicting laws.[37]

Before we can evaluate these somewhat surprising doctrines it is plainly necessary to canvass some preliminary questions. What is it for laws or systems of laws to conflict? How is a conflict between laws related to logical inconsistency or contradiction? Unfortunately, Kelsen's own analysis in his books of the notion of conflicts between laws and norms consists only of a few scattered observations, though what he has to say touches upon some important and indeed controversial logical issues. This is not the place for full investigation of these issues, but in my statement and criticism of Kelsen's doctrines I will use, as undogmatically as I can, some relatively simple distinctions which have been drawn by writers on deontic logic and the logic of imperatives, who have concerned themselves with similar questions about conflicts.

A. Conflict as the Logical Impossibility of Joint Conformity.

Many writers favour the idea (which seems intuitively acceptable) that conflict between two rules requiring or prohibiting action is to be understood in terms of the logical possibility of joint obedience to them. Two such rules conflict if and only if obedience to them both ('joint obedience') is logically impossible. The crudest[38] case of such a conflict is rules

admits the logical possibility of conflicting valid norms. He does not however explain why he has abandoned his previous views or refer to the exposition of them in *GTLS* and *PTL*. Nor does he withdraw or modify the monistic theory of international law and municipal law expounded in these books. See, for an examination of this latest phase of Kelsen's thought, Amedeo G. Conte, 'In margine all'ultimo Kelsen', in *Studia ghisleriana*, ser. I, 4 (1967), 113–25 [translated in the present volume, ch. 18, as 'Hans Kelsen's Deontics'].

[36] *PTL* § 43(a) (p. 328).   [37] *GTLS* 410; *PTL* § 43(a) (p. 329).

[38] Crude, since most cases of conflict between two rules arise because some contingent fact makes it impossible only on a particular occasion to obey them both, and not because the rules by explicitly forbidding and requiring the same action are such that on no occasion could they both be obeyed.

which respectively require and forbid the same action on the part of the same person at the same time or times. The logical impossibility of joint obedience may be exhibited in the following way.[39] For any rule requiring or prohibiting action, we can form a statement (an 'obedience statement') asserting that the action required by the rule is done or the action prohibited by the rule is not done. Two such rules conflict if their respective obedience statements are logically inconsistent and so cannot both be true. Thus (to take one of Kelsen's examples), suppose one rule requires certain persons to kill certain other human beings, and another rule prohibits the same persons from killing the same other human beings, the obedience statements corresponding to those rules would be of the general form, 'killing is done', and 'killing is not done'. Of course, before we can determine whether two statements of this general form are logically inconsistent or not, they would have to be filled out with specifications of the agents and victims and times to which the rules, explicitly or implicitly, related. If the same agents are required by one rule to do, and by another rule to abstain from, the same action at the same time, this will be reflected in the corresponding obedience statements, which would be logically inconsistent. Joint obedience to the rules would be logically impossible.

It is to be observed that this definition of conflict between rules leaves entirely open the question whether or not it is logically possible for two conflicting rules to coexist as valid rules of either the same or different systems. To most people it would certainly seem possible for a law of one legal system made by one set of legislators to conflict with the law of another legal system made by another set of legislators; and it would perhaps seem equally obvious that one such law could conflict with some moral rule or principle. Joint obedience to these rules would be logically impossible, but their coexistence as valid rules would be logically possible. Further, though it would certainly be deplorable on every practical score if laws of a single legal system conflicted and the system provided no way of resolving such conflicts, it is still far from obvious that even this is a logical impossibility. So far as the nature and logical possibilities of conflict are concerned, there seems little difference between rules requiring and prohibiting action and simple second-person orders and commands addressed by one person to another. Two such orders ('kill' and 'do not kill') conflict if joint obedience to them is logically impossible, and this can be shown in the form of logically inconsistent obedience statements. But it is certainly logically possible for conflicting orders to

---

[39] See B.A.O. Williams, 'Consistency and Realism', *Proceedings of the Aristotelian Society, Supplementary Volume*, 40 (1966), 1–22, repr. (with additional note as appendix) in Williams, *Problems of the Self* (Cambridge: Cambridge UP, 1973), 187–206. I am much indebted to this lucid account of the logical issues involved.

be given by different persons to the same person, and though we might think a person who gave inconsistent orders at short intervals to the same person mad or split-minded or lacking a coherent will and perhaps in need of clinical attention, such situations do not seem logically impossible. In the end no doubt, if he insisted on producing streams of inconsistent orders and these could not be explained, for example, by lapse of memory, we should conclude that he did not understand what he was saying, and might well refuse to classify what he said as constituting orders at all.

In one important respect, however, which is relevant to Kelsen's theory, conflict between laws and other rules is more complicated than conflict between such simple orders. Laws and rules, as Kelsen acknowledges,[40] instead of requiring or forbidding action, may either expressly permit action or, by not forbidding action, tacitly permit it; and it is clear that there may be conflicts between laws that forbid and laws or legal systems that expressly or tacitly permit. To meet such cases, we should have to use not only the notion of obedience, which is appropriate to rules requiring or forbidding action, but the notion of acting on or availing oneself of a permission. We might adopt the generic term 'conformity' to comprehend both obedience to rules that require or prohibit and acting on or availing oneself of permission, and we could adopt the express 'conformity statements' to cover both kinds of corresponding statement. In fact, the conformity statement showing that a permissive rule (for example, permitting though not requiring killing) had been acted on will be of the same form as the obedience statement for a rule requiring the same action (killing is done). So if one rule prohibits and another rule permits the same action by the same person at the same time, joint conformity will be logically impossible and the two rules will conflict.[41]

B. Conflict and Logical Inconsistency.

Kelsen would I think accept such a definition of conflict between rules in terms of the logical impossibility of joint conformity. Certainly his few examples of conflicting rules and of what he sometimes terms 'opposite' or 'incompatible' behaviour are consistent with this, and he makes at least one passing though informal reference to what is in substance the joint-conformity test of conflict.[42] But Kelsen's account of the connec-

[40] *PTL* § 4(d) (p. 16). Kelsen describes such permissive rules (express or tacit) as 'negative regulation' of conduct, and distinguishes a positive sense of permission when rules prohibit interference with another's conduct.

[41] *PTL* § 4(e) (p. 18), but note text of *RR 2*, quoted at n.2 above; *PTL* § 5(a) (p. 25), § 34(e) (p. 205).

[42] The 'joint-conformity' test of conflict is applicable only to rules all or all but one of which require or prohibit action. Permissive rules cannot conflict, but joint conformity

tion between conflict between norms and logical inconsistencies is different and more controversial. For his doctrine as expounded in his books is that the statement that two valid norms conflict is or entails a contradiction; for Kelsen it is a logical impossibility that there should coexist valid but conflicting norms of either the same or different systems. And it is not merely the case for him that joint conformity to them is logically impossible.[43]

Kelsen's arguments for these conclusions depend on the use which he makes of a distinction (itself important and illuminating) between laws made or applied by legal authorities, for example, statutes of a legislature, which cannot be either true or false, and a class of statements describing the content of laws, which Kelsen called 'legal rules in a descriptive sense' and which can be either true or false. These rules in a descriptive sense are of the following general form: 'according to a certain positive legal order a certain consequence ought to take place,' or 'according to a certain legal norm something ought to be done or ought not to be done.' In such statements 'ought' according to Kelsen is used in a descriptive sense, and I shall refer to such statements as 'descriptive-ought statements'.[44]

A simple illustration of this doctrine is as follows. If there exists a legal order, for example, the English legal system, and among its duly enacted laws there is a statute requiring under certain penalties men on attaining the age of twenty-one to report for military service, these facts constitute part of the truth-grounds for the descriptive-ought statement 'according to English law the following persons . . . ought to report for military service . . .'. If there is such a law the descriptive-ought statement is true; if there is not, it is false. Three things however should be borne in mind when considering Kelsen's descriptive-ought statements.

1. 'Ought' is used by Kelsen in a special, wide sense, so that 'ought' statements include not only descriptions of laws that forbid or require

with two permissive rules may be logically impossible (for example, 'Opening the window is permitted', 'Shutting the window is permitted'). I am indebted to Professor J.L. Mackie for this point.

[43] *Phil. Fds.* § 14 (p. 409); *PTL* § 4(e) (p. 18), § 34(e) (pp. 205–8), § 43(a) (p. 329).

[44] *PTL* § 16 (p. 73), § 18 (p. 78). The corresponding term in the French translation of *RR 2*, namely *Théorie Pure de Droit*, trans. Charles Eisenmann (Paris: Dalloz, 1962), is '*proposition de droit*' as distinguished from '*norme juridique*', and in the original German is '*Rechtssatz*' as distinguished from '*Rechtsnorm*'. In a long footnote in *RR 2* § 16, at pp. 77–8 (omitted by the translator in *PTL*), Kelsen cites Christoph Sigwart in support of the notion of 'ought in a descriptive sense'; compare the similar views of von Wright on normative statements in *NA* 104–6 *et passim*; and see Hector-Neri Castañeda on 'deontic assertables' in 'Actions, Imperatives, and Obligations', *Proceedings of the Aristotelian Society*, 68 (1967–8), 25–48.

action, but also descriptions of laws or legal systems that expressly or tacitly permit action. 'Ought' in Kelsen's usage is a kind of deontic variable ranging over what he terms prescriptions (or commands), permissions, and authorizations.[45]

2. Descriptive-ought statements are not confined to the law. Similar statements, similarly capable of truth or falsity, may be made concerning non-legal, for example, moral norms:

Ethics describes the norms of a particular morality; it instructs us on how, according to this morality, we ought to behave, but, as a science, it does not prescribe how we ought to behave. The ethicist is not a moral authority who issues the norms that he describes in 'ought'-statements.[46]

3. The words which appear at the beginning of the formulation of descriptive-ought statements in the above quotation ('according to a certain positive legal order') and the words 'according to this [particular] morality' are important for the following reasons. Kelsen has sometimes been accused of holding a metaphysical belief that there is a realm of 'ought' (including the 'ought' of legal rules) which is not man-made but awaits man's cognition or discovery, and of believing that it is this realm of 'ought', over and above the world of facts, that true descriptive-ought statements describe. Against such critics, Kelsen insists that for him all norms are made and not merely discovered by human beings, and although, given the existence of positive legal orders or systems, true descriptive statements can be made about their content in the form of ought statements, the truth of such statements is not 'absolute' but relative[47] to the particular legal system or order concerned. Indeed it could be argued in support of Kelsen that so long as we bear in mind this essential relativity to a given system his account of descriptive-ought statements clarifies a certain kind of discourse frequent among lawyers. Lawyers often ask such questions as 'What is the legal position with regard to military service?' and tender in answer to such questions such statements as 'Men on attaining the age of twenty-one must report for military service', regarding these answers as true or false. There is frequent occasion for lawyers to describe what they might call the 'legal position' in relation to some subject without referring to the particular enactments or regulations or other sources of the relevant law, though of course it would be always understood that the 'legal position' thus described is that arising under the laws of a particular system, and a more accurate formulation would make this explicit by including such words as 'according to English law . . .'.

[45] See *PTL* § 4(b) (at p. 5).
[46] *RR 2* § 16 (p. 75n) (not translated in *PTL*).
[47] *PTL* § 4(e) (p. 18).

The immediate relevance of Kelsen's descriptive-ought statements to the question of conflicts between laws can be seen from the following quotation:

Since legal norms, being prescriptions (that is, commands, permissions, authorisations), can be neither true nor false, the question arises: How can logical principles, especially the principle of noncontradiction and the rules of inference, be applied to the relation between legal norms if, according to traditional views, these principles are applicable only to assertions that can be true or false? The answer is: Logical principles are applicable indirectly to legal norms to the extent that they are applicable to the rules of law that describe the legal norms and that can be true or false. Two legal norms are contradictory and can therefore not both be valid at the same time if the two rules of law that describe them are contradictory . . .[48]

Kelsen explains several times that descriptive-ought statements describing two legal rules requiring what he terms 'opposite' behaviour would be of the form '*A* ought to be' and '*A* ought not to be', and statements of this form referring to actions to be done by the same agents at the same time are said by Kelsen to ' "contradict" each other',[49] and their joint assertion is said to be meaningless: 'To say that *A* ought to be and at the same time ought not to be is just as meaningless as to say that *A* is and at the same time that it is not.'[50] Accordingly, it is a logical impossibility for two such rules to be valid: only one of them can be regarded as valid. Kelsen thus speaks throughout his books as if conflicts between laws were a form of logical inconsistency, so that it is logically impossible that conflicting rules should coexist, and not merely that joint conformity with them is logically impossible.

Kelsen's arguments raise a host of difficulties;[51] fortunately not all of them need detailed consideration here. We may waive for the moment (while noting for later use) the objection that, if '*A* ought to be' and '*A* ought not to be' are logically inconsistent, they are not contradictories, as Kelsen says, but contraries. The contradictory of '*A* ought not to be done' is 'it is not the case that *A* ought not to be done', and two ought-statements of this form would describe not two rules that required and prohibited the same action, but two rules, one of which prohibited and the other of which permitted the same action. But apart from this, it is not a self-evident truth of logic that '*A* ought to be done' and '*A* ought not to be done', even if they describe rules of the *same* system, are logically inconsistent at all. Certainly some argument is required to show that

---

[48] *PTL* § 16 (p. 74) [trans. altered].   [49] *PTL* § 34(e) (p. 206).   [50] Ibid.

[51] Among these difficulties, much in need of exploration, is the determination of the meaning for Kelsen of 'valid'. Sometimes he writes as if to say that a norm is 'valid' is to say that it is a final and uniquely correct standard of conduct and so excludes the validity of conflicting norms; see e.g. *Phil. Fds.* § 15 (at p. 410).

they are. No doubt, if we assume certain premises (namely, (1) 'ought' implies 'can', and (2) '*A* ought to be done and *A* ought not to be done' entails '*A* ought both to be done and not to be done'), it would then follow that '*A* ought to be done' and '*A* ought not to be done' cannot logically both be true.[52] It is also of course possible to define 'ought' in such a way that '*A* ought to be done' entails 'it is not the case that *A* ought not to be done'; but it is worth noting that logicians of repute in constructing systems of deontic logic have allowed for the possibility of conflicting obligations ('one ought to do *A*' and 'one ought not to do *A*'). There seems no formal inconsistency in such a notion, and a logical calculus which is out to catch the logical properties of actual human codes of behaviour should not rule out such possibilities of conflict in advance by taking it as an axiom that 'one ought to do *A*' entails that it is not the case that one ought not to do *A*.[53]

It is not necessary, however, in order to assess Kelsen's thesis that international law and municipal law cannot conflict, to press the point that conflict even between laws of the same system is not a logical impossibility. For Kelsen's arguments that there can be no such conflicts between international law and municipal law are intended by him to be independent of the thesis that they form one system.[54] Kelsen's arguments for the impossibility of conflicts turn entirely on his view of the logical relations between the descriptive-ought statements describing conflicting laws, and his arguments seem to be vitiated by a simple error. He disregards the important fact that, as he had previously himself observed, descriptive-ought statements when true are true only relative to the systems that they describe, and, accurately formulated, should be prefixed with such words as 'according to English law'.[55] Hence if we were to concede for the sake of argument that '*A* ought to be' and '*A* ought not to be' are, as Kelsen claims, logically inconsistent, or that laws of the same system could not conflict, it would not follow, nor is it the case, that descriptive-ought statements of the form 'according to international law *A* ought to be' and 'according to English law *A* ought not to be' are logically inconsistent. Indeed there seems no reason at all, once the relativity of descriptive-ought statements is borne in mind, for thinking that two statements of this form cannot both be true. Since Kelsen therefore has given no satisfactory reason for saying that international

---

[52] See Williams (n.39 above).

[53] For a clear discussion of this point, see E.J. Lemmon, 'Deontic Logic and the Logic of Imperatives', *Logique et Analyse*, 8 (1965), 39–71, at 45–51.

[54] His position is that if there were such conflicts we could not regard international law and municipal law as one system, and absence of conflict is the negative criterion of unity of system. See § II above, at 1st para.

[55] For example, *PTL* § 16 (p. 73), § 34(e) (p. 205).

law and municipal law form one system, there seems nothing to support the thesis that their rules cannot conflict.

C. The Weaker Version of the 'No Conflict' Theory.

With these rather top-heavy but necessary preliminaries we may turn to the evaluation of Kelsen's claim that there are in fact no conflicts between valid rules of international law and municipal law. His proof that there are no conflicts between international law and municipal law takes the following form.[56] According to a conventional 'pluralist' theory, a conflict between international law and municipal law arises if a state enacts a statute that is incompatible with a provision of a treaty to which it is a party and which is valid according to international law. He cites as an example the case of a treaty between two states, which I shall call *A* and *B*. The treaty provides that the members of a minority group in the population of state *B* should have the same political rights as the majority. If in state *B* a law is enacted depriving the minority of all political rights notwithstanding the treaty, conventional pluralist theory would claim that here the statute, valid according to the law of state *B*, and the treaty, valid according to international law, conflicted: it would be impossible to comply both with the treaty and with the statute, for this would be both to allow and not to allow the minority to exercise certain rights.

Kelsen argues that to regard such cases in this way is to misinterpret the rules of international law according to which such treaties are binding on states. Such rules make the enactment by a state of statutes that are incompatible with the terms of a valid treaty to which it is a party an offence or delict under international law, exposing the state to the sanctions of international law. But though the *enactment* of such a statute is forbidden by international law, once enacted it is none the less valid even according to international law (though illegally enacted), and does not conflict with the rules of international law relating to treaties; for their true force is exhausted in making the enactment by the state of such a statute illegal,[57] that is, a delict or offence against international law. In other words, the rule of international law does not seek to determine directly the content of state statutes, but only the legality or illegality of their enactment. There is therefore no conflict between the rule of international law, so interpreted, and the statute, though the latter's enactment violates the rule. Kelsen cites, as a parallel, one interpretation of constitutional provisions protecting fundamental rights in those systems of municipal law which contain no provision for judicial review or for the

---

[56] *PTL* § 43(b) (p. 330).   [57] *PTL* § 43(b) (p. 331), see also *PTL* § 35(j) (at p. 274).

nullification of statutes which are unconstitutional because they violate the fundamental rights which the constitution purports to protect. Instead of judicial review the constitution, in such cases, is interpreted as making officials or legislators liable to punishment for their part in the enactment of such unconstitutional statutes. In such cases the constitution does not directly determine the content of statutes, but only the legality of their enactment; and there is no conflict between the constitution so interpreted and the statute, which remains valid though its enactment constitutes a punishable offence under the constitution.

This argument is ingenious, but even if we concede the suggested interpretation of the rules of international law relating to treaties it does not, in fact, banish conflict between international and municipal law; it merely locates such conflict at a different point and shows it to be a conflict not between rules requiring and prohibiting the same action (the treaty and the statute) but between rules prohibiting and *permitting* the same action, that is, the enactment of the statute. It is a conflict of this latter form that arises when a state enacts a statute in violation of its treaty obligations, if its enactment is an offence according to international law but is not so according to municipal law. There are certainly many systems of municipal law, among them the English, according to which it is not an offence to enact or procure the enactment of any statute, and so this is permitted. It is logically impossible to conform (in the wider sense of this expression noted above) both to the permissive rule of municipal law permitting the enactment of any statute and to the rule of international law relating to treaties which (if we accept Kelsen's interpretation) prohibits such an enactment and makes it an offence or delict. This being the case, even if we accept Kelsen's interpretation of the rules of international law, this does not establish that they do not conflict with municipal law.[58]

---

[58] It is to be observed that throughout this section I have ignored, as Kelsen himself does, an argument in favour of the weaker form of the 'no conflict' theory which would be available if his own controversial interpretation of all laws as 'sanction-stipulating norms' addressed to organs or officials determining the condition under which sanctions 'ought' to be applied were taken seriously. According to this interpretation '[o]nly the coercive act, functioning as a sanction, ought to be', *PTL* § 28(b) (p. 119). That is, the only persons who 'ought' to do anything according to law are the 'organs' or officials, and what they 'ought' to do is to apply sanctions if the conditions stated in the law are fulfilled. Since in different states these organs or officials are different persons, no conflict would ever arise between the laws of different states: joint conformity to the laws would always be possible. Thus, even if laws of state *A* stipulated that sanctions ought to be applied by its officials to certain persons in the event of their doing certain specified actions, and the laws of state *B* forbade the application by its officials of sanctions under those same conditions, no conflict would arise since the officials of the two states would be different persons. Similarly, since the sanction-applying agencies in international law are (according to Kelsen) the representatives of the states against whom a delict or offence has been committed, whereas the sanction-applying agencies of a state are its own officials, no conflict could arise. There is

III. MEMBERSHIP OF A LEGAL SYSTEM

In this concluding section I shall try to distil from the above criticisms of Kelsen some more constructive points that may help our understanding of the concept of a legal system and of the criteria of the membership of different laws in a single system. I certainly am not able to advance a comprehensive analysis of these difficult notions. Such an analysis is, as I have said, part of the still unfinished business of analytical jurisprudence and I am not yet competent to finish it. Yet the general form or direction of such an analysis may perhaps be at least glimpsed from what follows.

A. Recognition and Validating Purport.

Let us reconsider that relationship between laws which I called the relationship of validating purport, and recall the Soviet Laws Validity Act, which I dreamed up in order to exhibit the absurdity of the view, which Kelsen seems to share, that this relationship is sufficient to make the laws between which it holds members of the same legal system. I argued that this view is absurd because the Soviet Laws Validity Act, though it purports to validate the lawmaking operations of Soviet legislators, would not be recognized by the Soviet law-identifying and law-enforcing agencies as having any bearing on the validity of Soviet law. Without such recognition, we can only say that the Soviet Laws Validity Act purports to validate the laws of the USSR, or that, according to English law or for the purposes of English law, Soviet law is a subordinate part of the English legal system; we cannot, unless there is such recognition, say that the validity of the laws of the USSR is derived from the Soviet Laws Validity Act, or that the law of the USSR and the UK form parts of a single system. Perhaps some qualification is needed of this last point. No doubt we could collect together all laws between which the relationship of validating purport holds, irrespective of the legal system from which they come, and call the group of laws so collected 'a single legal system'. This would be to introduce a new meaning for the expression 'legal system'; for a group of laws linked together solely by the relationship of validating purport would not correspond to the concept of a legal system that lawyers and political theorists or any serious thinkers about law and politics

nothing in Kelsen's accounts of what it is for laws to conflict which excludes this argument. I do not myself accept Kelsen's interpretation of law as sanction-stipulating norms and so would not regard this argument as sound. Kelsen might also have used as an argument in support of the 'no conflicts' theory his own (in my view erroneous) doctrine that the legal 'ought' must (to avoid a vicious regress) have the sense of 'permitted' or 'authorized' rather than 'commanded'. See *PTL* § 5(a) (at p. 25).

actually use. The new definition would have very little utility and would be retrograde if it displaced the existing sense of a legal system, and so barred us from saying that the laws of the UK and the USSR belong to different systems, notwithstanding the existence of the Soviet Laws Validity Act. 'Systems' of laws constructed solely out of the relationship of validating purport would ignore the dividing line introduced by the idea that recognition by the law-identifying and law-enforcing agencies effective in a given territory is of crucial importance in determining the system to which laws belong. It is surely obvious that these dividing lines could not be ignored by any fruitful legal or political theory. To deny their importance would be tantamount to denying the importance to lawyers and political theorists of the division between nation-states.

B. The Individuation of Laws.

When we turn our attention away from the relationship of validating purport to consider how the idea of recognition by courts or other identifying agencies effective in different territories is used to distinguish between legal systems and as a criterion of membership of laws in a single system, some important points thrust themselves upon us. For example, an important contrast now emerges between two different ways of individuating or distinguishing between different laws. On the one hand, we may individuate or distinguish a law simply by referring to its content (for example, as 'the law making the possession of LSD a criminal offence'). However, since the idea of two different laws with the same content is perfectly intelligible, we may and sometimes actually need to individuate or distinguish laws not only by their content (that is, by what the laws say or provide) but also by reference to their authors, mode of enactment, and date (for example, as 'the law making possession of LSD a criminal offence, enacted by the British Parliament on 30 December 1967').

The relevance of this to our present problem is as follows. The relationship of validating purport is a relationship between the content of those laws that purport to validate other laws or lawmaking operations and those other laws or operations. The most important examples of this relationship are laws that confer powers to legislate upon persons or bodies of persons. The simplest example of such power-conferring laws is a law conferring power upon an individual X (a monarch or a minister) to make laws or regulations. The law conferring such power in effect says 'the laws X enacts are to be obeyed'. In Kelsen's terminology, such a law conferring legislative power 'authorizes' X to create new laws, and X's enactment is 'a law-creating act or event', while the laws created by X are said to 'derive their validity' from the law conferring the legislative power which is 'the reason for their validity'. Clearly in such cases if a law conferring legislative power is to be a reason for the validity of other laws it is necessary that the description of those other laws (in this case 'enacted by X') should correspond to the description used in the law conferring the legislative power (for example, 'laws enacted by X are to be obeyed'). In order that the relationship of validating purport should hold between the law conferring the power and the enacted laws, this correspondence is not merely necessary but is sufficient. But, as I have argued above, though this is necessary, it is not sufficient to show that the laws made by X actually do derive their validity from the law purporting to confer upon X the power to make laws. What is needed in order that we may move from 'This law purports to validate laws enacted by X' to 'The laws enacted by X actually derive their validity from this law' is that the courts or law-identifying agencies of the territory concerned should recognize a particular law purporting to confer powers on X and treat it as a reason for recognizing also the laws it purports to validate. But in answering the question whether this law is so recognized, we must identify it not by its content alone as we did when we were concerned only with the relationship of validating purport, but by its authors or mode of creation or date or all of these. We must, in other words, shift our attention from content to these other individuating elements. That this shift in attention is necessary is evident from the following considerations. The actual constitution of the USSR and the Soviet Laws Validity Act may have precisely the same content, and both have the relationship of validating purport to the lawmaking operations of the Soviet legislature. But the Soviet courts would distinguish between them; and in recognizing not the Soviet Laws Validity Act but only the Soviet constitution as relevant to the validity of Soviet laws and belonging to the same system as those laws, they distinguish between them by such individuating factors as I have described above, notwithstanding the identity of content.

C. Derivations of Validity and Criterion of Membership.

These considerations show that in determining whether two laws belong to the same system or different systems we cannot use as our criterion of belonging to the same system the fact that one of them derives its validity from the other. This is so because until the question of membership is settled by the independent test of recognition we cannot discover whether one of the laws does derive its validity from the other. We can only know that one purports to validate the other. The criterion of membership of laws in a single system is therefore independent of and indeed presupposed when we apply the notion of one law deriving validity from another. Only when we know that the Soviet constitution is recognized by the Soviet courts as a reason for recognizing laws enacted in accordance with its provisions, and so belongs to the same system as those laws, are we in a position to state that the latter derive their validity from the former. Until we know that the constitution is so recognized all we can say is that this constitution, like the Soviet Laws Validity Act, purports to validate such laws.

D. The Basic Norm as a Criterion of Membership.

Readers of Kelsen will recall that in all the versions of his theory he adheres to the view that what unites different laws in a single system is the basic norm,[59] and it does so because all the positive laws of the system, according to him, derive their validity directly or indirectly from the basic norm. The basic norm, according to Kelsen, unlike all the other norms of a system, is not a positive or created norm:[60] Unlike all the other laws of a system (positive laws), it does not derive its validity from any other laws. It is a 'presupposed' norm that is 'the reason for the validity' of the constitution; it may be formulated as 'one ought to behave as the constitution prescribes',[61] and is presupposed by anyone who regards the constitution as a valid norm.[62]

Since the basic norm is the reason for the validity of the constitution that derives its validity directly from it, all the other laws of the system that derive their validity directly or indirectly from the constitution derive it indirectly and ultimately from the basic norm. Kelsen's view is that laws form one system because their validity is thus to be traced back and derived from one basic norm. If, however, as I have argued above, we can only trace back the validity of laws to other laws (as distinct from the relationship of validating purport), if we already know by the test of recognition to what system the laws belong, it cannot be traceability back to the basic norm that tells us to what system laws belong or accounts for their unity in a single system. Again, our hypothetical example makes this clear. The basic norm of the American constitution is (roughly) that the constitution is valid; but unless we have some independent criterion of what it is for laws to belong to one system we cannot trace the validity of laws back to the constitution and thence to its basic norm; we can only trace relationships of validating purport, and these, as we have seen, will cut across different legal systems. They will link together with the American consti-

---

[59] See *GTLS*, at 110, 367; *PTL* § 34(a) (at p. 195), § 34(d) (at p. 201).

[60] *PTL* § 34(c) (p. 199).

[61] *PTL* § 34(d) (p. 201): its formulation will be different if municipal law is regarded as a subordinate part of international law.

[62] *PTL* § 34(d) (p. 204 n.72).

tution not only the Soviet Laws Validity Act (supposing it to be enacted by Congress) but all the Soviet legislation that it purports to validate. If our sole criterion for membership of the system is the traceability of validating purport we cannot break off at the dividing line at which we would wish to break off. We cannot, as the Soviet courts do, stop at the Soviet constitution and ignore the Soviet Laws Validity Act as belonging to a different system, although it purports to validate Soviet law; we have to go on from the laws enacted by the Soviet legislator to the Soviet Laws Validity Act and thence to the American constitution, and thence to its basic norm, beyond which by definition no further relationship of validating purport is to be traced. But the journey is fruitless, because it shows neither that these laws derive their validity from the basic norm nor that they belong to a single legal system.

IV. PROBLEMS OF RECOGNITION

The previous section, as I have said, constitutes no more than a tentative account of the appropriate criterion for determining the membership of a legal system and for the individuation of different legal systems. It is plain that the notion of recognition that I have stressed will need refinement in different directions, and I shall end by explaining very briefly some of the considerations that have caused me to express myself thus tentatively.

1. I have spoken of recognition by the law-identifying and law-enforcing agencies effective in different territories. This obviously envisages arrangements of modern municipal legal systems where there are courts and special agencies for the enforcement of law. But we cannot leave out of sight more primitive arrangements: there may be no courts and no specialized enforcement agencies, and the application of sanctions for breach of the rules may be left to injured parties or their relatives, or to the community at large. International law, at least according to Kelsen, is itself such a decentralized system. Presumably, in such cases we shall have to use as our test of membership the notion of recognition by the society or the community, and certain problems in defining what constitutes sufficient recognition will have to be faced.

2. Even in the case of modern municipal legal systems the notion of recognition by a court is not without ambiguities. On a narrow interpretation, recognition by a court as a criterion of membership could mean that a rule could not be said to belong to a legal system until it had been actually applied by a court disposing of a case. This interpretation would come nearer to Gray's[63] theory and to the doctrine ascribed to some later

[63] See John Chipman Gray, *The Nature and Sources of the Law* (New York: Columbia UP, 1909).

American legal realists; but it is surely very unrealistic, for there seems little reason to deny that a statute enacted by the legislature of a normally functioning legal system is a law of the system even before it is applied by the courts in actual cases. However, the precise formulation of a wider interpretation of the idea of recognition which would include rules that courts would apply as well as those actually applied would not be uncontroversial.

3. All civilized legal systems contain special rules for dealing with cases containing a foreign element (for example, contracts or marriages made abroad). These special rules determine both when courts have jurisdiction to try cases with such foreign elements and which legal systems should guide the courts in the exercise of this jurisdiction. These are the rules known as private international law or conflicts of law, and if we are to take account of them the notion of recognition by courts will have to be refined in further, different directions. If a man and his wife whose marriage is valid according to the laws of the country where it was celebrated travel through many different countries, they can be confident that the courts of most of these countries will treat their marriage as valid, at least as far as the formalities of its celebration are concerned. This is only one very simple example of cases where courts of one country would be said to recognize and apply the laws of another country. Unless the notion of recognition advanced above as a criterion of membership is in some way qualified, we should have to draw the conclusion that laws of one country that are recognized and applied by the courts of another country belong to the legal system of the latter country as well as of the former. It is possible to object to the language I have used in describing such cases, since it may be said that when, for example, an English court treats a marriage solemnized in, say, the Soviet Union as valid because the formalities were those required by Soviet law though they differ from those of English law, it does not really apply Soviet law, but applies to the parties before it a rule similar in content to that which a Soviet court would apply to the parties if they appeared before it in a similar case but of purely domestic character.[64] This would avoid the awkwardness and the possibly misleading character of the assertion that one and the same rule was applied by courts of different systems; but it still leaves us without any satisfactory distinction between the kind of recognition that courts give to foreign laws in such cases involving foreign elements and the recognition that is to be used as a criterion of membership. We need such a distinction, for it seems plain that in some sense of recognition courts do *recognize* foreign laws in cases raising

---

[64] See Walter Wheeler Cook, *The Logical and Legal Bases of the Conflict of Laws* (Cambridge, Mass.: Harvard UP, 1942), at ch. 1.

questions of private international law even if, in deference to the argument cited above, we do not say they *apply* the foreign law, but apply a law of their own with a content similar to that of the foreign law that they recognize.

Perhaps this difficulty may be met by distinguishing two different sorts of recognition, which might be called 'original' and 'derivative' recognition. In an ordinary case where there is no foreign element, for example where an English court simply applies an English statute, the court does not base its recognition and application of the statute on the fact that courts of some other country have recognized or would recognize it; this is original recognition. But where, as in cases raising questions of private international law, part of the court's reason for recognizing a law is that it has been or would be originally recognized by the courts of another country, this is derivative recognition of the foreign law. Whether in such cases we should say that the court applies the law that is thus derivatively recognized or only that it applies a law with similar content does not, I think, affect this distinction, though I have no doubt it needs further elaboration.[65]

[65] For criticisms and comments, see Joseph Raz, 'The Identity of Legal Systems', in Raz, *AL* 78–102, and Raz, 'The Purity of the Pure Theory' [in this volume, ch. 12].

List of Contributors

Carlos E. Alchourrón (28 June 1931 – 13 January 1996). Professor Alchourrón taught in the Department of Philosophy and School of Law, University of Buenos Aires.

Deryck Beyleveld, Faculty of Law, University of Sheffield.

Norberto Bobbio, Faculty of Politics, University of Turin (retired).

Roger Brownsword, Faculty of Law, University of Sheffield.

Eugenio Bulygin, School of Law, University of Buenos Aires (retired).

Agostino Carrino, Faculty of Politics, University of Naples.

Bruno Celano, Department of Politics, Law, and Society, University of Palermo.

Amedeo G. Conte, Faculty of Law, University of Pavia.

Geert Edel is completing the *Habilitation* in the Department of Philosophy, University of Bonn.

Ernesto Garzón Valdés, Faculty of Politics, University of Mainz (retired).

Riccardo Guastini, Faculty of Law, University of Genoa.

Stefan Hammer, Faculty of Law, University of Vienna.

H.L.A. Hart (18 July 1907 – 19 December 1992). Hart was Professor of Jurisprudence at Oxford University until his retirement in 1968; thereafter he was Nuffield Fellow, University College, Oxford, and later Principal of Brasenose College, Oxford.

Tony Honoré, All Souls College, Oxford University (retired).

Hans Kelsen (11 October 1881 – 19 April 1973). Kelsen taught at the University of Vienna until 1930, and was during the 1920s also a Constitutional Court Justice; thereafter he held teaching positions in Cologne, Geneva, briefly in Prague, and at the University of California in Berkeley.

Gerhard Luf, Faculty of Law, University of Vienna.

Neil MacCormick, Faculty of Law, University of Edinburgh.

José Juan Moreso, Faculty of Law, University of Girona (Spain).

Pablo E. Navarro, National Council for Research in Science and Technology (CONICET), Buenos Aires.

Carlos Santiago Nino (3 November 1943 – 29 August 1993). Professor Nino taught in the School of Law, University of Buenos Aires.

Stanley L. Paulson, School of Law and Department of Philosophy, Washington University, St. Louis.

Joseph Raz, Balliol College, Oxford University.

Alf Ross (10 June 1899 – 17 August 1979). Professor Ross taught at the University of Copenhagen.

Dick W.P. Ruiter, Faculty of Public Administration and Public Policy, University of Twente, Enschede (The Netherlands).

Joseph G. Starke, Queen's Counsel, Sydney and Canberra (retired).

Ota Weinberger, Faculty of Law, University of Graz (retired).

Georg Henrik von Wright, Academy of Finland, Helsinki (retired).

Index of Kelsen's Writings

Full titles to which reference is made in this volume appear here, unless the work is listed in the Table of Abbreviations. (Where a listing in the Table of Abbreviations is not obvious, we refer the reader to the Table.) Where a title refers to a writing of Kelsen's that appears in this volume, the title is preceded by an asterisk.

Initial prepositions and articles are not counted in the alphabetization below.

Index of Names

All names in the text, notes, and introductory apparatus appear here, save for names of editors and translators.

Index of Subjects

The most significant entries, including in some instances subentries, are marked in bold type. Where the tilde (~) appears in the index, it always takes the place of the main entry. Thus, where main and subentries read—

basic norm
  as fiction
    rejection of ~ 303, 303 n.11

—the tilde stands for 'basic norm', and the combined entry reads: 'rejection of basic norm as fiction'.

602

Index of Subjects

Gerber's theory and significance (*cont.*):
two 'points of view' 39
'*Gesetz ist Gesetz*' ['a law is a law'] 147, 158
as species of quasi-positivism 58
not related to true positivism 148, 158
'Gorgon's naked power' 509, 509 n.7

Habilitation, Habilitationsschrift xxiv,
xxiv n.2
Hart's theory:
acceptance 484, 484 n.24
appeal to social facts xxxiv, xxxiv n.49
concept of social normativity 58
distinguished from reductive semantic
thesis 23 n.3
external statements 242–3, 242 n.11
finality vs. infallibility 288–9, 288 n.36
individuation 576–7
internal or legal statements (*see also*
legal proposition) 242–3, 242 n.11,
248–9
cp. Kelsen 243–4, 248–9
criticism of 248–9
non-cognitivist 243, 248
normative aspect 243
illocutionary force 243
socio-factual aspect 243
standard uses 243
truth-functional analysis 243
law and morality 248–9
law as complex social practice 243, 251
legal powers 448
criticism of Kelsen's view on 448, 448
n.32
legal validity 86, 86 n.43, 163, 163 n.39,
251–2
Hart vs. Kelsen on 252
membership, criteria of 575–9
problem of 575–81
nullity as a sanction 443–4
primary and secondary rules 506
recognition 575–81
problems of 579–81
'derivative' 581
'original' 581
rule of recognition 252, 274–5, 279–80,
279 n.18
as imposing duties 456
as providing alternative to adoption
274–5, 274 n.4, 275 n.6
as *terminus* of recursive definition 472
as unifying a complex of legal rules
498
structural similarity to Kelsen on 'middle
way' 144 n.77
Hegel's philosophy:
Kelsen on 172–3

significance of, for Kelsen's
normativism 519
Heidelberg Neo-Kantianism (*see also*
methodological dualism):
fact/value distinction in xxxi
Kelsen's 1916 study of 16, 16 n.41
Lask on 'Copernican turn' 520 n.72
Rickert's 'reference to value' 521
Simmel's interpretation of Kant 4
Windelband's interpretation of Kant 4
Heller's criticism of Kelsen 170 n.3
heteronymous norms 439
administrative order as example 439
hierarchical structure, doctrine of
(*Stufenbaulehre*) (*see also* legal
power(s), Merkl's contribution) xxvi,
xxvi n.11, xxviii, xxviii n.24, xxix,
13–14, 13 n.30, 516–17, 516
nn.49–50, 517 n.51
and law creation xxvi
metajuridical character of, in *HP* 12
as construction 507
comprehends law as 'regulating its own
creation' (*see also* 'law governs [*or*
regulates] . . .') 447, 447 n.27
derivative, non-derivative norms 250
empowering norms and xxv–xxvi, xxix,
xlvii–xlviii, 41–2
fed'l state as application of 549–50
gradation of norms in Kelsen vs.
'cascade of powers' in political
theory 437
identity of levels, and particular law-
making functions, historically
determined 511–12
Kelsen's adoption of xxv–xxvi, xxvi n.11,
xxviii–xxx, xxviii n.24, xxix nn.25–6,
13–14, 13 n.30, 41–2
legal power(s), *see* 'empowering norms',
this entry above
levels of concretization 13
norms linked by delegation relations 447
peripheral imputation and 41–2, 42 n.93
significance of, for relation between
int'l, state law 545
'tracing' or regressive process 437, 437
n.4
transforms law into an effective process
of acts of law production 516, 516
n.50
holism in the law, similarity of Kelsen,
Dworkin 109, 112
Holmes's theory xxxiv, xxxiv n.48
and Kelsen's hypothetical judgment
79–80
homo economicus 504–5
homo juridicus 504–5, 506